ABOUT THE AUTHOR

Tom Clynes is a freelance writer, brewer, and hack musician whose passions for music and travel have led him across North and South America, Europe, and Asia. Born and raised in the American Midwest, Clynes worked as a music columnist, copywriter, cook, and shell fisherman before writing *Wild Planet!* (Visible Ink Press), a critically acclaimed guide to the world's extraordinary festivals and celebrations. With *Music Festivals from Bach to Blues*, he turns his attention to the diverse music of his homeland. Clynes is based in Chicago, but continues to wander the world, trying to satisfy "a thirst for spectacle and a fascination for the planet's cultural nooks and crannies."

ALSO FROM VISIBLE INK PRESS:

HISTORIC FESTIVALS ✳ A TRAVELER'S GUIDE

Join travel writer George Cantor as he journeys coast to coast, celebrating America's history with visits to 300 community events, including Florida's Gasparilla Pirate Invasion, Iowa's Steamboat Days, and the Boston Tea Party Re-enactment in Massachusetts.

ISBN 0-7876-0824-6 * 6 x 9 * 392 pages * 100 photos

WILD PLANET! ✳ 1,001 EXTRAORDINARY EVENTS FOR THE INSPIRED TRAVELER

"An extensive and exhilarating guide to the world's festivals, celebrations, and other amazing moments." — *Outside Magazine*

"We love this guide! And so will you." — *New York Daily News*

Wanderlust leads Midwesterner Tom Clynes across the globe, searching for something different. This event-focused, travel guide details annual festivals of every kind on every continent — from Thailand's Surin Elephant Round-up to Scotland's Up-Helly-Aa to the Colombian National Beauty Contest for Burros.

ISBN 0-7876-0203-5 * 6 x 9 * 669 pages * 200 photos

Music Festivals

FROM BACH TO BLUES

MUSIC FESTIVALS

FROM BACH TO BLUES

A Traveler's Guide

TOM CLYNES

VISIBLE
INK
PRESS

DETROIT • NEW YORK • TORONTO

Music Festivals FROM BACH TO BLUES: A Traveler's Guide
by Tom Clynes

Copyright © 1996 Visible Ink Press™

Visible Ink Press is a trademark of Gale Research

Back cover photos: Aspen Music Festival, Alex Irvin/Aspen Music Festival; Fiesta Nevada Celebration, Reno News Bureau ; du Maurier Atlantic Jazz Festival, Tourism Nova Scotia; Cosby Dulcimer and Harp Festival, Tennessee Tourist Development.

Author photo: Walter Wasacz

Most Visible Ink Press™ books are available at special quantity discounts when purchased in bulk by corporations, organizations, or groups. Customized printings, special imprints, messages, and excerpts can be produced to meet your needs. For more information, contact Special Markets Manager, Gale Research Inc., 835 Penobscot Bldg., Detroit, MI 48226. Or call 1-800-776-6265.

Art Director: Pamela A. E. Galbreath

ISBN 0-7876-0823-8
Printed in the United States of America
All rights reserved
10 9 8 7 6 5 4 3 2

Library of Congress Cataloging-in-Publication Data

Clynes, Tom.
    Music festivals from Bach to blues : a traveler's guide /
by Tom Clynes.
            p.   cm.
    Includes indexes.
    ISBN 0-7876-0823-8
    1. Music festivals--United States--Guidebooks. 2. Music festivals--
Canada--Guidebooks.   I. Title.
ML35.C6 1996
780' .79'73--dc20   96-13930
                                                            CIP
                                                            MN

FOR MY SISTERS,
KAREN, JULIE, AND MELINDA

C O N T

ＪNTRODUCTION

If you've picked up this book, the odds are high that you've experienced a "great music moment." Maybe it came as you were reclining on a lawn at a classical music festival. Or sitting under a shady tree at a bluegrass hoedown. Or dancing barefoot in the mud at a reggae bash.

You don't just hear a great music moment, you feel it. It's a spell, a spontaneous groove where rhythm, melody, people, and place converge. Thoughts of past and future melt away in the heat of what's happening *right now*. Inhibitions vanish, big grins make friends of strangers, and people are drawn together in the realm of the revel.

Moments like these are the reason why music festivals are budding and blooming across North America. In a society where secularism, competition, and indifference have become the central facts of our daily lives, a live-music gathering brings back some measure of what the contemporary age has taken away—community.

We don't have the epic feasts and fiestas of Asia or Latin America to unite us under a single religion. We don't have the historical pageants of Europe to reaffirm our communal identity. In our mishmash of religions and cultures, it's *music* that transcends our differences and helps us communicate in a common language. "Music," said Concord Jazz Festival founder Carl Jefferson, "is the true Esperanto."

Coast to coast—in amphitheaters, auditoriums, and tents; on ski hills, riverbanks, and great lawns—music festivals pull us out of our insulated, workaday ruts, and throw us together in situations that bring out the best in people. As columnist Keith Owens put it, "A well-placed groove can knock down a barrier faster than any battering ram."

If this is so, then the resurgence of music festivals across the continent is cause for optimism. If people can still find the time to come together for a song, maybe everything isn't falling apart. Maybe, on some level, we're coming together.

*   *   *   *   *

Discovery—of great music, great places, and authentic culture—is the overriding theme of this book. In addition to each genre's classic festivals—the Jazz Fests, the Bean Blossoms, the Tanglewoods and Tellurides—you'll find lesser-known gems like an Acadian fiddle fest in Atlantic Canada, a blues meltdown on Washington's Olympic Peninsula, and chamber music gatherings from Newport's mansions to

California's Sierra. You'll also find tasty food, picturesque locations, and some of America's most precious and esoteric folk traditions.

When this project began, the research team was excited by the explosion of world-music festivals bringing sounds from all over the globe to North America. But we wondered if we would find as much interest in preserving homegrown, regional styles—the quirky sounds that are rarely played on commercial radio. Would we venture to the continent's nooks and crannies only to discover music as generic as the strip malls that are popping up everywhere? Would we find that distinct regional styles were being forgotten, homogenized, or demoted to the status of tourist soundtracks or beer-commercial clichés?

To find out, we set off for North America's musical and geographic extremes. We ventured to the eastern edge of the continent, to shake a leg with Newfoundland Celts as whales frolicked offshore. We chased the midnight sun north to Yellowknife, where Inuit throat singers shared the stage with Arctic punk rockers. In subtropical New Orleans we marched to the drums of Mardi Gras Indians, and in Lafayette we kicked up dust with zydeco old-timers.

We discovered some of the world's best chamber music in a psychedelic church on the remote Acadian Peninsula. We found worldbeat and alternative rock on a Colorado ski mountain, swam around floating stages in British Columbia, and swooned to symphonies under Wyoming stars. We loafed on a bluesy Chicago sidewalk, and got knocked around in a Los Angeles mosh pit.

If you're starting to get the feeling that we had a bit of fun, we heartily admit it. Along the way we discovered that diverse regional music is far from dead—it's alive and jumping for joy in festivals all over the continent. Organizers, volunteers, and entire towns and cities have discovered that festivals are a great way to preserve and celebrate local music, while reaffirming and strengthening the community.

We had a fantastic time at some of the big, well-known festivals. But we're more convinced than ever that the real action is on the outskirts of the American music scene. At a festival in Louisiana's St. Bernard Parish, for instance, the Isleno people still play the 10-stanza *decimas* their ancestors brought from the Canary Islands. In Alaska, Athabascan Indian fiddlers still venture in from the bush for a musical, prefreeze get-together. In the Mississippi Delta, old blues men still come back "down home" for authentic musical reunions.

In east Texas, sacred harp singers still worship with their tight six-part harmonies, as they've done since 1868. At Ozark Mountain festivals, traditional musicians are "as thick as fleas on a dog." And deep in the Appalachians, old-time string bands still keep to the tempo that much of the world forgot when bluegrass came along.

In the songs, we met the people and discovered their histories. We heard of triumphs and defeats, victories and disasters in the music of Texan yodelers, Cajun accordionists, Cape Breton fiddlers, Quebec balladeers, Hawaiian falsetto singers, and Native American drummers and dancers. And everywhere, we saw new musical forms developing as musicians mixed and mingled, incorporating new influences and innovations in a process that's older than any living language.

*   *   *   *   *

What makes a music festival great? Certainly more than excellent performers. Some festivals succeed because they have a keen ear for the cutting edge; others concentrate on safeguarding vanishing traditions. Some festivals attract crowds by booking big names; others draw more adventurous crowds by spotlighting unknown musicians who deserve recognition.

Place is a big consideration, especially for people who are planning vacations and other activities around a festival. A Chicago or New York skyline makes a choice backdrop, as does the French Quarter, or the Golden Gate Bridge. Equally stunning are the snowcapped peaks of the Rockies, the emerald hills of Prince Edward Island, or the vibrant rocks of Sonoma.

The festival venue should be intimate enough to allow everyone to get reasonably close to the performers. Thankfully, the days of the megastage are numbered, and even the big festivals have begun to realize that they can connect people more enjoyably to the music by providing more, smaller stages.

Many festivals are moving beyond simple entertainment, by offering interactive workshops where musicians become teachers and spectators become participants. Entertainers share their techniques and enthusiasm, often turning events into musical anthropology lessons or celebrations in human creativity.

The spirit of the community really comes through when organizers tap into the imagination and energy of local volunteers, or provide a forum for social and environmental causes. Interesting regional food adds to the fun (if it's reasonably priced), and so do local wines and microbrewed beer. But festivalgoers should have a choice in what they eat and drink, and organizers who bar BYO picnics and beverages run the risk of pricing many families out of the action.

Corporate sponsorship seems here to stay, but I'm disturbed by its growing obtrusiveness. Each year more advertising banners clutter the views, but the people who have to look at them aren't seeing any reductions in ticket prices. The commodification of the festival environment has brought few, if any, benefits to the festivalgoer.

Finally, some festival organizers seem to spend a lot of time and energy making rules to keep people in line. This emphasis on control quells the spirit of friendliness—and I've noticed that the best, most trouble-free festivals are the ones where the rules are unwritten, where promoters create an environment that encourages civility, respect, and fun.

Most of all, a music festival should be *festive*. A real festival is certainly more than a collection of concerts. It's a celebration that goes far beyond the sum of performers, location, sound quality, food, and drink. A great festival puts all these things together with a panache that cannot be duplicated. It's a part-organized, part-improvised collection of sound, movement, big grins, and uninhibited hearts—all reveling in great moments of music.

May this book lead you to many of those moments.

Tom Clynes
Chicago, Illinois
February 1996

⒜CKNOWLEDGMENTS

Music Festivals from Bach to Blues was created through the energies and imaginations of an outstanding research and editorial team. Special thanks goes to editorial assistant Cathy Mizgerd, who made an indelible imprint on this book through her creativity, perseverance, and good humor. Thanks also to writer/researchers Melinda Clynes and Maureen Mansfield for their fine reporting, and to student interns Erika Ehmsen and Jeremiah Van Hecke, whose work expressed a passion for music and travel. Elaine Glusac came through in many ways when the going got tough, and Jane Haldiman, Kevin Keyser, and Lisa Scott rounded out the editorial team.

Among the many people who helped us find our way to North America's best festivals, none stands out more than Bas Bouma, Tourism Program Manager with the Canadian Consulate General. Thanks as well to Air Canada and to Richard Griffith and Glynis Steadman of Griffith & Associates. We received a great deal of assistance from state and provincial tourist offices, convention and visitors bureaus, and individual music lovers. Although there's not room to acknowledge each personally, I'd like to thank the following people in the U.S. and Canada for going the extra mile (or kilometer) in arranging travel, gathering information, or helping in other ways: Steve Bachman, Marty Blackwell, Randy Brooks, Urban Carmichael, Karen Clynes, Pat and Bill Clynes, April Comeaux, Chuck Coon, Kay Coxworthy, Sharon Cruthers, Marla Daniels, Christiane Dickenson, Steffan Duerr, Charlie Fisher, Carol Horne, Valerie Kidney, Miles Harvey, Kelly Clement, George Hales, Joel Lava, Rachel Lenz, Percy Mallet, Elizabeth Martin, Stephanie McCracken, Rick Metcalf, Katie Mikesell, Theresa Mullen, Cathy Murphy, Tom Neer, Dean Olkowski, Heidi Olmack, Lori Pinard, Bill Rainaldi, Bill Rohde, Christine Ryan, Kelly Strenge, Charles Siler, Mia Schillace, Jenny Scoggin, Pamela Shelton, Barry Stoneman, Geoff Sturgeon, Brian Turner, Bev Winnicke.

I'd also like to acknowledge the people at Visible Ink Press, including Diane Dupuis, Becky Nelson, Pamela Galbreath, Jenny Sweetland, Lauri Taylor, Betsy Rovegno, and Ken Benson. Thanks also to Bob Griffin for his thorough copyedit and to Kathy Dauphinais.

Finally, I extend my appreciation and admiration to the people who organize and present North America's music festivals. Their efforts make a book like this possible; their festivals bring people together and make the world a richer and more musical place.

T.C.

HOW TO FIND FESTIVALS

Music Festivals from Bach to Blues is a genre-jumping guide to 1,001 of the most noteworthy music festivals in the United States and Canada. The book is arranged and indexed to help you discover festivals that fit your preferences for where you'd like to go, your vacation schedule, and your musical interests.

To find festivals in the area you'd like to visit (or where you live), consult the **Table of Contents**. Each state and province is covered within regional sections, and festivals are arranged chronologically within chapters, beginning with January. While you're browsing, keep your eyes open for alternatives and new discoveries. For instance, if the Santa Fe Chamber Music Festival is sold out, the surrounding pages will unearth a variety of interesting chamber events nearby. If you can't find a flight to New Orleans for the Jazz and Heritage Festival, a quick browse turns up the Festival International de Louisiane, a feast of world music that occurs at the same time in nearby Lafayette.

If you have a specific time frame in mind—say you have a vacation coming up in July, or you'll be in Chicago on business in August—consult the **Date Index** for festivals that fit your window of opportunity.

If you know the name of a festival, but you're not sure where it's located (or it seems to have moved), track it down via the **Festival Name Index**.

Finally, if you're interested in a particular type of music or a particular instrument—Celtic, ragtime, zydeco, or Hawaiian slack-key guitar—turn to the **Genre Index**.

A friendly word of caution is in order. The information in *Music Festivals from Bach to Blues* was painstakingly verified and confirmed, but there's always the possibility that a festival could be rescheduled or fall off the face of the earth in the time it takes to load paper onto the press. Be sure to take advantage of the contact information provided at the end of each entry, and call to confirm dates and locations before booking a flight or quitting your job. Telephone numbers and area codes change too, so if you don't reach the organizer via the **Tickets/Info** number, try calling the local tourist information sources listed under **Accommodations/Tourist Info.**

NEW ENGLAND

CONNECTICUT

ALTERNATIVE FEST
WOODBURY ✹ THIRD SUNDAY IN MAY

Resort owner Rod Taylor, himself a champion skier in the 1970s, hosts multiple music festivals throughout the Woodbury Ski Area's summer season, but none with more enthusiasm than Alternative Fest, affectionately known in past years as the "F— the Lollapalooza Tour" festival. The event showcases four bands and has included talents like Phish, Blues Traveler, the Spin Doctors, and Bad Brains. Audiences of up to 10,000 crowd the outdoor covered stage or sit on a grassy hill with blankets, coolers, and picnics, reveling in the excellent acoustics provided by the natural bowl. Concerts cost around $10 to $20, with lower prices for those who buy early. **LOCATION:** Woodbury Ski Area, four miles north of Woodbury on Route 47, 35 minutes from New Haven, 55 minutes from Hartford, and 90 minutes from New York City. From Waterbury head west on I-84 and take exit 17 to Route 64 west, to U.S. 6 north, to Route 47 in Woodbury. **TICKETS/INFO:** 203-263-2203 **ACCOMMODATIONS/TOURIST INFO:** 203-263-2203

MUSIC MOUNTAIN
FALLS VILLAGE ✹ JUNE THROUGH SEPTEMBER

Begun in 1930, Music Mountain is one of the oldest chamber music festivals in the United States. The 335-seat concert hall is located on a hilltop in the Litchfield Hills area, surrounded by woods. (It's hard to believe you're a mere 100 miles from New York City.) Over the course of the summer, Music Mountain presents 28 concerts by nationally known performers. The Appalachian Trail touches the outskirts of Falls Village in the northwestern corner of Connecticut. Tickets are around $15. **LOCATION:** Music Mountain in Falls Village, near the junction of U.S. 7 and Routes 63 and 126, in the northwestern corner of the state **TICKETS/INFO:** 860-824-7126 **ACCOMMODATIONS/TOURIST INFO:** 860-567-4506

STRAWBERRY PARK BLUEGRASS FESTIVAL
PRESTON ✹ FIRST WEEKEND IN JUNE, FRIDAY–SUNDAY

Strawberry Park Bluegrass Festival is a prime pick for family-oriented music and recreation. Traditional bluegrass is the focus, and some of the best is served up hot in the park's wooded amphitheater. Extensive recreational facilities are available, and the festival offers workshops, food, arts and crafts, and a children's area. Fees vary, but around $25 will get you in for the weekend, with camping included (RV hookups are available).   **LOCATION:** Strawberry Park in Preston, off Route 165 near the intersection with Route 164. The park is five miles east of Norwich and 38 miles southwest of Providence. **TICKETS/INFO:** 860-886-1944 **ACCOMMODATIONS/TOURIST INFO:** 800-863-6569, 860-444-2206

𝒫ILLAR POLKABRATION
PRESTON ✱ FIRST FULL WEEKEND IN JUNE

The great music and dance tradition of America's northern, blue-collar whites continues to flourish. At Strawberry Park Resort Campground, thousands of people come in from all over the country to sample dozens of meat-and-potato polka bands on two stages. Begun in 1965, this is the longest-running polka festival in America. Tickets are $8 to $14 each day, and camping is available.   **LOCATION:** Strawberry Park in Preston, off Route 165 near the intersection with Route 164. The park is five miles east of Norwich and 38 miles southwest of Providence. **TICKETS/INFO:** 860-848-8171 **AC-COMMODATIONS/TOURIST INFO:** 800-863-6569, 860-444-2206

𝒞AJUN, ZYDECO MUSIC & ART FESTIVAL
MOODUS ✱ SECOND WEEKEND IN JUNE

Music, dancing, art, and fun are on tap at this gig, which features a fairly mainstream sampling of bands on the Cajun and zydeco circuit. About five acts create the rhythms necessary to keep the crowd of about 1,000 dancing, and if you get tired you can always jump into the hot tub or swimming pool, which are available as part of the $20 entrance fee.   **LOCATION:** Sunrise Resort, off Route 151 in Moodus (around 35 miles southeast of Hartford). From Boston/Hartford follow the Massachusetts Pike to exit 9 (Hartford-New York) and go 42 miles on I-84 to exit 55. Take Route 2 east for 14 miles to exit 13. Turn right on Route 66 west and go four miles. Turn left on 196 south and go six miles. Turn left on Route 151 south and go one mile to the Sunrise Resort. **TICKETS/INFO:** 860-527-5044 **ACCOMMODATIONS/TOURIST INFO:** 800-486-3346, 860-347-0028

𝒮EA MUSIC FESTIVAL
MYSTIC ✱ SECOND WEEKEND IN JUNE, FRIDAY–SUNDAY

Dubbed the Sea Music Festival, this unusual event embraces and preserves music that developed on or near bodies of water of all kinds. But the bulk of the music here is actually *sea music,* which comes in two styles: shanties (also known as chanteys) and *fo'c'sle* songs (pronounced "foke-sull").

Dating back to English merchant ships of the 15th century, sea shanties were used to coordinate group work efforts; different jobs suggested different rhythms, yielding various subtypes of shanty, including the short-haul shanty, the halyard shanty, and the capstan shanty. A shantyman served as a "caller," and the sailors responded in unison. The shanty rhythm made the work flow smoothly by coordinating the men's efforts. Shanties are remarkable for their distinctive rhythms and their notable absence of narrative structure—allowing them to be tailored to the work at hand.

The fo'c'sle, on the other hand, traditionally tells a story, with major characters that may be inanimate (such as locks and canals) or human (such as river-exploring voyagers). The word *fo'c'sle* comes from *forecastle*, which generally refers to the section of a ship in front of the foremost mast, the area near the bow where the crew lives. In sea music, *fo'c'sle* refers to the sailors, songs of leisure—as opposed to the work-oriented shanties.

Generally, the festival preserves traditional songs, but occasionally it features new songs penned about aquatic and maritime concerns, such as the loss of fisheries. The Sea Music Museum, where this festival has been held every year since 1980, celebrates maritime life year-round, but draws its biggest crowds during the festival. Approximately 25 talents come from maritime regions worldwide, including Wales, England, Brittany, Atlantic Canada, Poland, Russia, and the United States. Yupik Eskimos have come to show their dance traditions, and U.S. performers have imparted song traditions hailing from the country's West Coast, Great Lakes, and riverbanks.

Friday night at the festival calls for an "all-hands" concert; as people arrive in Mystic from far-flung ports of call, they join a swelling mass of performers who stand up, each in his or her turn, to sing a song or two. Over the weekend, afternoon workshops and performances complement evening concerts showcasing well-known shantypeople and folksingers, such as Louis Killen, Cliff Haslam, and Laurie Holland. Plus, three scholars present papers on maritime music each year.

The settings are as interesting as the music. Under a large barn, 450 people sit in folding chairs and benches in front of the main outdoor stage. Workshop settings include an oyster shack, a New England-style meetinghouse, and a chapel. Adult admission costs from $30 to $40 for the entire weekend.   **LOCATION:** Mystic Seaport Museum, on Route 27 (Greenmanville Avenue) in Mystic **TICKETS/INFO:** 860-572-0711 **ACCOMMODATIONS/TOURIST INFO:** 860-444-2206, 800-863-6569

CONNECTICUT EARLY MUSIC FESTIVAL
NEW LONDON, NOANK, NIANTIC, AND WATERFORD ✷ LAST THREE WEEKENDS IN JUNE

The Connecticut Early Music Festival is one of the nation's best opportunities to experience baroque music at its most authentic. Performing styles are based on careful study of the actual practices used during the era from which the work came, and instruments are either antique originals or their exact replicas. Five picturesque southeastern Connecticut locations were selected for ambience and acoustic worthiness, and tickets (which sell out well in advance) are about $18 for reserved seating and $12 for general admission. Nearby attractions include Mystic Seaport, the Submarine Museum, and beaches.   **LOCATION:** Harkness Chapel and Lyman Allyn Art Museum, at Connecticut College in New London, one mile north of I-95 on Route 32; Noank Baptist Church, on Main Street two miles from Mystic Seaport in Noank; Children's Museum of Southeastern Connecticut, on Main Street in Niantic; Eugene O'Neill Theater Center, at 305 Great Neck Road in Waterford. **TICKETS/INFO:** 860-444-2419 **ACCOMMODATIONS/TOURIST INFO:** 800-863-6569, 860-444-2206

REGGAE FEST
WOODBURY ✷ THIRD SUNDAY IN JUNE

Summer weather converts a gorgeous winter ski resort into the perfect site for live reggae music. Each year, 500 to 5,000 fans say yes to bungee jumping, mountain biking, skateboarding, and Jamaican food at this festival whose raison d'être (amidst all these fabulous attractions) is nevertheless *music*, played in a natural outdoor amphitheater with excellent acoustics. Five featured acts usually include a mix of local, regional, and national names, such as the Wailers and Peter Tosh. Tickets are $10 to $20. **LOCATION:** Woodbury Ski Area, four miles north of Woodbury on Route 47, 35 minutes from New Haven, 55 minutes from Hartford, and 90 minutes from New York City. From Waterbury head west on I-84 and take exit 17 to Route 64 west, to Route 6 north, to Route 47 in Woodbury. From Danbury head east on I-84 and take exit 15 to Southbury, to U.S. 6 north, to Route 47 in Woodbury. **TICKETS/INFO:** 203-263-2203 **ACCOMMODATIONS/TOURIST INFO:** 203-263-2203

*N*ORFOLK CHAMBER MUSIC FESTIVAL
NORFOLK ✷ LATE JUNE THROUGH MID-AUGUST

In a historic music shed (built in 1906) where Sibelius, Caruso, and Rachmaninoff once performed, today's top chamber musicians gather for a summer of performances and training. Some 70 national and international performers form ad hoc ensembles and present dozens of concerts throughout the season, bringing about 15,000 listeners to this 70-acre estate with rolling hills and picturesque vistas. In addition, the program features workshops, demonstrations, meet-the-composer forums, preconcert lectures, and family events. Admission prices range from free to $35.   **LOCATION:** Norfolk, in the northwest corner of Connecticut near the junction of U.S. 44 and Route 272 **TICKETS/INFO:** 203-432-1966, 860-542-3000 **ACCOMMODATIONS/TOURIST INFO:** 860-567-4506

*B*OOM BOX PARADE
WILLIMANTIC ✷ JULY 4TH

More than a decade ago, the people of Willimantic had trouble getting a band for their local parade. In fact, they had so much trouble that they blew off the idea of a conventional marching-band parade and snubbed live music totally. Instead, participants march down the street blasting boom boxes that are all tuned in to a local radio station playing the best marching music it can find.

From pre-planned theme groups to freelance marchers, the town of Willimantic has embraced the Boom Box Parade with vigor. Organizers at WILI-AM 1400 ask only that people wear red, white, and blue . . . or a frog outfit. There's no registration and no cost, but be sure to say hello to grand marshall Wayne. God bless America . . . . **LOCATION:** Main Street in Willimantic. From Hartford take I-84 east to I-384 east, to U.S. 6 east, to Willimantic. **TICKETS/INFO:** 860-928-1228 **ACCOMMODATIONS/ TOURIST INFO:** 860-928-1228

*O*NE WORLD FESTIVAL
WOODBURY ✷ THIRD SUNDAY IN JULY

Since 1977, international worldbeat musicians have entertained hundreds (sometimes thousands) of visitors at the scenic Woodbury Ski Area during its summer racquet season, and a predictably upbeat audience enjoys it all. Taking advantage of the resort's natural amphitheater, recent festivals have featured prestigious talents like Senegal's Youssou N'Dour. When not plopped on a grassy hill beside the outdoor stage, sports enthusiasts engage in tennis, skateboarding, bungee jumping, and mountain biking.

Norfolk Chamber Music Festival: Young Artists Recitals by Yale Summer School of Music students complement concerts by internationally known chamber musicians. (See entry, page 5.) Courtesy of Enrico Ferorelli/Norfolk Chamber Music Festival

LOCATION: Woodbury Ski Area, four miles north of Woodbury on Route 47, 35 minutes from New Haven, 55 minutes from Hartford, and 90 minutes from New York City. From Waterbury head west on I-84 and take exit 17 to Route 64 west, to Route 6 north, to Route 47 in Woodbury. From Danbury head east on I-84 and take exit 15 to Southbury, to U.S. 6 north, to Route 47 in Woodbury. **TICKETS/INFO:** 203-263-2203 **ACCOMMODATIONS/TOURIST INFO:** 203-263-2203

G̶REAT CONNECTICUT TRADITIONAL JAZZ FESTIVAL

MOODUS ✶ FIRST FULL WEEKEND IN AUGUST, FRIDAY–SUNDAY

The Great Connecticut Traditional Jazz Festival presents jumping jazz music straight out of the past in dancehalls and under big-top tents. This summer jazz-o-rama draws 12,000 to 14,000 spectators over the weekend, making it one of the largest traditional jazz events on the East Coast.

More than 16 bands play the music of the twenties and thirties on the grounds of a 400-acre turn-of-the-century resort. Even though ragtime and Dixieland are American

Kookiness on parade: With flag and boom box in hand, radio personality Wayne Norman marshals in the Fourth of July during Willimantic's Boom Box Parade. (See entry, page 5.) Courtesy of WILI Radio

originals, bands come from as far away as Paris, Budapest, and England to jam with North American groups at this three-day extravaganza.

Prices vary from $20 for an evening of music to $62 for all three days. Camping is available on-site, and access to all resort facilities (including an Olympic-size pool, canoeing, basketball, and horseshoes) is included in the festival entrance fee. And, consistent with organizers' dedication to preserving and celebrating traditional jazz, admission is free with the donation of any usable instrument. Dancing, food, and workshops are on hand, and since Moodus isn't more than a short jaunt from anywhere in New England, this gem is perfect for a day trip or a weekend getaway. **LOCATION:** Sunrise Resort, off Route 151 in Moodus (around 35 miles southeast of Hartford). From Boston/Hartford follow the Massachusetts Pike to exit 9 (Hartford-New York) and go 42 miles on I-84 to exit 55. Take Route 2 east for 14 miles to exit 13. Turn right on Route 66 west and go four miles. Turn left on 196 south go six miles. Turn left on Route 151 south and go one mile to the Sunrise Resort. **TICKETS/INFO:** 860-483-9343 **ACCOMMODA-TIONS/TOURIST INFO:** 800-486-3346, 860-347-0028

ℭONNECTICUT RIVER VALLEY BLUEGRASS FESTIVAL

MOODUS ✳ SECOND WEEKEND IN AUGUST, FRIDAY–SUNDAY

This festival features 10 to 12 bands from the bluegrass touring circuit, plus lots of great campground jamming. Camping is available on-site, and access to all resort facilities (including an Olympic-size pool, canoeing, basketball, and horseshoes) is included in the festival entrance fee. **LOCATION:** Sunrise Resort, off Route 151 in Moodus (around 35 miles southeast of Hartford). From Boston/Hartford follow the Massachusetts Pike to exit 9 (Hartford-New York) and go 42 miles on I-84 to exit 55. Take Route 2 east for 14 miles to exit 13. Turn right on Route 66 west and go four miles. Turn left on 196 south go six miles. Turn left on Route 151 south and go one mile to the

*Classic crowd-pleaser: The Great Connecticut Traditional Jazz Festival pre-
sents three days and nights of traditional jazz. (See entry, page 6.)* Courtesy of Great
Connecticut Traditional Jazz Festival

Sunrise Resort. **TICKETS/INFO:** 860-347-5007 **ACCOMMODATIONS/TOURIST
INFO:** 800-486-3346, 860-347-0028

ℳ℘ORRIS BLUEGRASS FESTIVAL
MORRIS ✹ SECOND SUNDAY IN AUGUST

This contest-oriented festival features 10 categories, ranging from guitar finger-
picking to fiddling to best band. About 50 musicians compete for cash prizes in front of
some 2,500 people in a picturesque New England setting. The festival is known among
bluegrass aficionados for its great sound system, excellent contest judges, and tremendous musicianship. Admission is about $6.   **LOCATION:** At the junction of Route 61
and Route 109 in Morris, in the northwest part of the state about four miles south of
Litchfield **TICKETS/INFO:** 860-567-0270 **ACCOMMODATIONS/TOURIST INFO:**
860-482-6586

𝒞AJUN COUNTRY ZYDECO FESTIVAL
WOODBURY ✹ THIRD SUNDAY IN AUGUST

The scenic Woodbury ski resort specializes in bringing musical talents of all types
to its fine mountain venue to keep its summertime skateboarders, tennis players, bungee
jumpers, and mountain bikers entertained. This particular event features Cajun and

zydeco on an outdoor stage in a natural amphitheater whose bowl enclosure ensures excellent acoustics. Dancing fans press near the stage, while the more lethargic spread blankets on the grassy hill that overlooks the scene. Tickets run $10 to $20. **LOCATION:** Woodbury Ski Area, four miles north of Woodbury on Route 47, 35 minutes from New Haven, 55 minutes from Hartford, and 90 minutes from New York City. From Waterbury head west on I-84 and take exit 17 to Route 64 west, to Route 6 north, to Route 47 in Woodbury. From Danbury head east on I-84 and take exit 15 to Southbury, to U.S. 6 north, to Route 47 in Woodbury. **TICKETS/INFO:** 203-263-2203 **ACCOMMODATIONS/TOURIST INFO:** 203-263-2203; 203-597-9527

SCHEMITZUN FEAST OF GREEN CORN & DANCE
MASHANTUCKET ✸ SECOND WEEKEND AFTER LABOR DAY, THURSDAY–
SUNDAY (LABOR DAY IS THE FIRST MONDAY IN SEPTEMBER)

Started in 1991, the Schemitzun Feast of Green Corn & Dance has grown to become the largest festival of its kind in the country. Modeled after a traditional Native American ceremonial feast, the festival features powwow singing and a variety of other instrumental and vocal performances. Some 2,000 participants represent more than 150 tribes from all over the country.

The music has been passed down from generation to generation, and some predates Columbus's arrival in the Americas. All songs are in Native American languages and are committed to memory by the performers, many of whom have devoted their entire lives to keeping their cultural traditions alive. Drum contests and specialty dance contests award more than $750,000 in prizes.

Over 100,000 spectators typically flock to a tented arena in the center of a natural park, and each year some 20,000 tickets are doled out to lure students from Connecticut and Rhode Island schools. Traditional food and crafts are available at vendor stands, and experts demonstrate traditional cooking and dance. Alcoholic beverages are prohibited, as are pets, in the arena area. Daily admission is $5 for adults; a four-day pass is available for $10.   **LOCATION:** Mashantucket Pequot Tribal Reservation in Mashantucket, near the Rhode Island border, at the intersection of Route 214 and Route 2. From I-95 take exit 92 and go west on Route 2. **TICKETS/INFO:** 800-224-2676, 860-885-1441 **AC-COMMODATIONS/TOURIST INFO:** 800-863-6569, 860-444-2206

TAYLORMADE BLUES FEST
WOODBURY ✸ THIRD SUNDAY IN SEPTEMBER

Since 1973, resort owner Rod Taylor has put the Taylor into TaylorMade for this rockin' blues festival on the grounds of the Woodbury Ski Area. Well-known talents like B. B. King have been well received by the festival's audience of a few thousand, who revel in the venue's excellent acoustics, laid-back atmosphere, and recreational opportunities. Tickets cost from $10 to $20, but bring extra cash if you want to enjoy the recreational facilities.   **LOCATION:** Woodbury Ski Area, four miles north of Woodbury on Route 47, 35 minutes from New Haven, 55 minutes from Hartford, and 90 minutes from New York City. From Waterbury head west on I-84 and take exit 17 to Route 64 west, to Route 6 north, to Route 47 in Woodbury. From Danbury head east on I-84 and take exit 15 to Southbury, to U.S. 6 north, to Route 47 in Woodbury. **TICKETS/INFO:** 203-263-2203 **ACCOMMODATIONS/TOURIST INFO:** 203-263-2203; 203-597-9527

𝒩AVARATRI

MIDDLETOWN ✷ LATE SEPTEMBER, WEDNESDAY–SUNDAY

For more than 20 years, Wesleyan University's Music Department has brought the music of northern India to Middletown. About four evening concerts feature live music and dance, and some combine with an Indian dinner and Puja ceremonial blessing. **LOCATION:** World Music Hall at Wesleyan University in Middletown, just south of Hartford **TICKETS/INFO:** 860-685-3355 **ACCOMMODATIONS/TOURIST INFO:** 800-486-3346, 860-347-0028

REGGAE SKIBASH

CARRABASSETT VALLEY ✱ SECOND WEEKEND IN APRIL

Twenty-one hours of live reggae music and piles of early-spring snow attract a crowd of 5,000 to Sugarloaf, dubbed the Spring Skiing Capital of the East. Four regionally and nationally known reggae bands play on the ski lodge's outdoor deck in the Widowmaker Lounge and in the King Pine Room Friday and Saturday nights and Saturday and Sunday afternoons. Past talents have included Boston's I-tones and I-rations, the Maine-based Dani Tribesmen, and Jamaica native Winston Grennan. Visitors come from all over to enjoy live music and the East's only above-timberline, lift-serviced skiing, in a steep, wide-open bowl with a deep base. **LOCATION:** Sugarloaf/USA, on Highway 16/27 in Carrabassett Valley 10 miles north of Kingfield and 100 miles due north of Portland **TICKETS/INFO:** 207-237-2000; World Wide Web: http://www.sugarloaf.com **ACCOMMODATIONS/TOURIST INFO:** 800-843-2732

BOWDOIN SUMMER MUSIC FESTIVAL

BRUNSWICK ✱ LAST WEEK IN JUNE THROUGH THE FIRST WEEK IN AUGUST

Formed in 1964, this six-week event combines three festivals in one. The Friday night MusicFest features chamber, orchestral, and choral works by visiting students and prestigious national talents like Emanuel Ax and Michael Rabin. Wednesday night's UpBeat! series features chamber and contemporary music by composers such as Bartók, Handel, and Brahms and by composers-in-residence, who have included Bright Sheng, Sebastian Currier, and Elliott Schwartz. The three-day Gamper Festival of Contemporary Music features works by student composers and guest composers-in-residence.

Each summer has its own programmatic theme, and recent years have featured all-Schubert, all-Beethoven, all-Brahms, and all-Russian programs. The festival also includes a music school for 200 students, who come from all over the world for private lessons with visiting musicians from conservatories in New York City, Florida, and California. Traditionally, concert sites have included a church, an auditorium, and the school's quadrangles. **LOCATION:** First Parish Church, on Main Street at Bath Road across from Bowdoin College, and the Kresge Auditorium at Bowdoin College, in Brunswick **TICKETS/INFO:** 207-725-3895, 207-725-3322 **ACCOMMODATIONS/TOURIST INFO:** 207-725-8797

ᴰOWNEAST DULCIMER AND FOLK HARP FESTIVAL

BAR HARBOR ✳ FIRST OR SECOND WEEKEND IN JULY, FRIDAY–SUNDAY

This festival emphasizes traditional music played on hammered and mountain dulcimer, folk harp, bagpipes, and tin whistle. The festivities include two evening concerts at the Congregational Church, but what really makes this event unique is a strong emphasis on learning. At Agamont Park nationally known musicians offer free workshops to beginners and experts in several instruments, and areas are set aside for song sharing and handmade instrument sales. The workshop site at Agamont Park is of particular interest, with views of the Atlantic Ocean, islands, and Acadia National Park. **LOCATION:** Concerts are at the Congregational Church, on Mount Desert Street, and workshops are at Agamont Park (facing the town pier), in Bar Harbor. **TICKETS/INFO:** 207-288-5653 **ACCOMMODATIONS/TOURIST INFO:** 207-288-5103

ᴮAR HARBOR MUSIC FESTIVAL

BAR HARBOR ✳ FIRST SUNDAY IN JULY THROUGH THE SECOND SUNDAY IN AUGUST

This is a music festival with a mission: to help young artists who could very well become the great artists of tomorrow. Bar Harbor is one of the nation's proving grounds for gifted young artists, and the town's music festival is one of the few whose guiding purpose is to provide performance opportunities for outstanding up-and-coming talents. The festival highlights up to 40 individuals and ensembles playing a diverse program, including solo recitals, chamber music, pops, jazz, string orchestral works, and new compositions.

Depending on the venue, concerts may attract an intimate cluster of 100 or a bustling crowd of 1,000. Workshops, preconcert lectures, food, and arts and crafts engage listeners outside the concert performances, which take place in an acoustically excellent church, a shorefront family estate, a historic golf club, and an outdoor amphitheater set in spectacular Acadia National Park.

Bar Harbor is a recreational paradise with plenty of hiking, biking, sailing, swimming, fishing, golf, and tennis. Concert tickets cost around $15, or $10 for students and seniors.   **LOCATION:** Various locations, including the Bar Harbor Congregational Church, Breakwater 1904, Kebo Valley Golf Club, and Blackwoods Campground Amphitheater in Acadia National Park, all in Bar Harbor **TICKETS/INFO:** 207-288-5744, 212-222-1026 **ACCOMMODATIONS/TOURIST INFO:** 207-288-5103

ᴬRCADY MUSIC FESTIVAL

BAR HARBOR, BANGOR, DOVER-FOXCROFT ✳ THIRD WEEK IN JULY THROUGH THE END OF AUGUST, MONDAYS–WEDNESDAYS

Virtuosos from around the globe congregate in Maine each summer for this tasteful, energetic, and diverse music affair. Seven weeks of treats typically feature everything from Russian string quartets to American ragtime orchestras. Each group has a chance to perform in all three locations, visiting Bar Harbor on Monday, Bangor on Tuesday, and Dover-Foxcroft on Wednesday. In addition to the music, there are art exhibits and scenic treasures like the rustic beaches of Mount Desert Island and Sebec Lake, near Dover-Foxcroft. Accommodations are easy to find in these touristy sections of Maine, but keep in mind that summer is the busiest season. Admission is $15 per concert at the door, or

Music with a mission: Founder and artistic director Francis Fortier conducts the Bar Harbor Festival String Orchestra in an outdoor concert at Acadia National Park. Courtesy of Bob Noonan

$65 for the whole series.   **LOCATION:** College of the Atlantic, on Route 3 in Bar Harbor; Bangor Theological Society (exit at Union Street off I-95); and Dover-Foxcroft Congregational Church **TICKETS/INFO:** 207-288-3151, 207-288-2141; e-mail: mwilson@acadia.net **ACCOMMODATIONS/TOURIST INFO:** 207-288-5103, 207-947-0307, 207-564-7533

EAST BENTON FIDDLERS CONVENTION
EAST BENTON ✳ LAST SUNDAY IN JULY

The East Benton Fiddlers Convention is about the only thing that ever happens in this town—but that's okay, because organizers want to keep it small, short, and non-commercial. For more than 25 years, East Benton has hosted this gem of a gathering, which is held on a farm because "the field was just sitting there waiting for us to build a stage." Nowadays, thousands of people show up, but it still feels like a family reunion—with some of the oldest and greatest backfield fiddling talent this region has to offer. About 20 fiddlers play, many accompanied by piano and guitar, and bluegrass bands fill the in-between spots.   **LOCATION:** East Benton, about 20 miles east of Waterville. From I-95 take exit 35 and follow the signs. **TICKETS/INFO:** 207-453-2017 **ACCOMMODATIONS/TOURIST INFO:** 800-533-9595

MAINE FESTIVAL
BRUNSWICK ✶ FIRST WEEKEND IN AUGUST, THURSDAY–SUNDAY

A whopping nine stages host 1,000 performers for a rousing weekend of jazz, blues, rock, folk, ethnic, and classical music, as well as workshops, children's activities, dance performances, literary events, and art displays. Up to 20,000 guests pay the very reasonable admission fees of $6 to $9 for this multi-arts showcase of local, regional, and national talent. Recent performers include Jimmy Dale Gilmore, the subdudes, and Al Hawkes. It all happens on a grassy oceanside knoll with RV hookups and on-site camping. Food is available for purchase but alcohol, picnics, pets, and unregistered vendors are unwelcome.   **LOCATION:** Thomas Point Beach, just off Route 24, 10 minutes from downtown Brunswick. From Brunswick follow U.S. 24 about two miles to Cook's Corner, turn right, and follow the signs. **TICKETS/INFO:** 800-639-4212 **ACCOMMODATIONS/TOURIST INFO:** 800-533-9595

PORTLAND CHAMBER MUSIC FESTIVAL
PORTLAND ✶ LAST TWO WEEKS IN AUGUST, SATURDAY AND SUNDAY

Are you just a little more comfortable with the Beatles than with Brahms? If you want to experiment with classical music but have always been hesitant, the Portland Chamber Music Festival could be just the venue to take a nibble. As one local reporter put it, the festival's artistic directors "want to banish the notion that classical music is frumpy, formal and frozen in time."

Performances are designed to lessen the distance between performers and audience. Artists introduce the works they will present, and often play in small ensembles inside a modest auditorium where the audience is welcome to stay after shows and speak directly with musicians. Experienced chamber music buffs won't be bored either, since a dozen or more nationally recognized performers play everything from classics to modern pieces, and no composition is performed more than once in a season.

Admission is $10 for adults and $6 for students and seniors, and performers billet with local families in an effort to keep admission fees reasonable.   **LOCATION:** Ludcke Auditorium at Westbrook College, Stevens Avenue in Portland **TICKETS/INFO:** 800-320-0257; e-mail: jenelo@aol.com **ACCOMMODATIONS/TOURIST INFO:** 207-772-5800

THE RECORD FAMILY'S OXFORD COUNTY BLUEGRASS FESTIVAL
SOUTH PARIS ✶ THIRD WEEKEND IN AUGUST, FRIDAY–SUNDAY

Bluegrass greats like Mac Wiseman have graced the stage at the Record Family's Oxford County Bluegrass Festival, but the field pickin' is often just as intense as the stage action. Emcees Smokey Greene and Lester Wing team up to keep the lawn chair-toting crowd entertained while the bands swap places, and plenty of rough camping is available with a $25 (advance purchase) weekend ticket.   **LOCATION:** Rose-Beck Farm, on East Oxford Road off Route 119 in South Paris, about 10 miles west of Lewiston **TICKETS/ INFO:** 207-743-2905 **ACCOMMODATIONS/TOURIST INFO:** 800-533-9595

$ALTY DOG BLUEGRASS MUSIC FESTIVAL

CAMBRIDGE ✳ LAST WEEKEND IN AUGUST, FRIDAY–SUNDAY

This family-run bluegrass festival features regional talents over three days and lots of rules: no alcohol, no motorcycles, no fireworks, no dogs in the concert area, and no off-road vehicles. In addition to concerts Friday night and all day Saturday, Saturday morning features an all-instrument workshop and Sunday morning begins with a gospel service. Three-day tickets run $22 (in advance), including camping.   **LOCATION:** Festival grounds in Cambridge, at the junction of Routes 150 and 152, about 10 miles due west of Dexter and about 30 miles north of Waterville **TICKETS/INFO:** 207-277-5624 **ACCOMMODATIONS/TOURIST INFO:** 800-533-9595

THOMAS POINT BEACH BLUEGRASS FESTIVAL

BRUNSWICK ✳ LABOR DAY WEEKEND, FRIDAY–SUNDAY (LABOR DAY IS THE FIRST MONDAY IN SEPTEMBER)

When the Thomas Point Beach Bluegrass Festival began back in 1979, it was the first major gathering of national bluegrass talent in the Northeast. These days, the "high lonesome" sound is a bit more common, but Thomas Point Beach retains its position as one of the East Coast's most prestigious musical events.

This three-day gig is one of the best-managed and most family-oriented festivals on the circuit—and its location doesn't hurt. The festival is held on 64 acres of carefully groomed fields and pine groves overlooking the blue waters of Thomas Bay, adjacent to a tidewater beach. It looks and feels like the country, yet it's only minutes away from seafood houses, coastal harbors, and downtown Bath and Brunswick.

The musical lineup is dependably stellar; expect to see top dawgs of the bluegrass circuit like Bill Monroe, Ralph Stanley, J. D. Crowe, and the Cox Family. A "showcase preview" concert spotlights amateur bands, and Sunday morning gospel services round out the action. Three-day tickets are about $55, but many early-bird and one-day specials are available. Camping is also available.   **LOCATION:** Thomas Point Beach, just off Route 24, 10 minutes from downtown Brunswick. From Brunswick follow U.S. 24 about two miles to Cook's Corner, turn right, and follow the signs. **TICKETS/INFO:** 207-725-6009 **ACCOMMODATIONS/TOURIST INFO:** 207-725-8797

MASSACHUSETTS

NEW ENGLAND FOLK FESTIVAL

NATICK ✹ WEEKEND FOLLOWING THE THIRD MONDAY IN APRIL, FRIDAY–SUNDAY

It's difficult to imagine how a high school could be an inspiring site for a folk festival, but the New England Folk Festival generates enough shenanigans to fill Natick High School with musical magic. Each year, more than 5,000 folkies gather for this festival, which focuses on roots dance music from all over the Americas and from eastern and western Europe.

In an effort to get everyone to participate, organizers offer instrument workshops in piano, guitar, hammered dulcimer, and fiddle. If you want to play in an ensemble dedicated to a particular type of traditional music, you can join a band workshop or drop in on one of the many jam sessions that spontaneously erupt in hallways and on the lawn, weather permitting.

Workshops and demonstrations in dance are usually accompanied by live musicians. They cover everything from Bulgarian line dancing to square dancing, contra dancing, and traditional English sword dancing. Craft and folk bazaars, ethnic-food booths, and loads of costumed volunteers add to the ambience, and children's activities are built into each day's schedule. **LOCATION:** Natick High School, on West Street just off Oakland Street in Natick, about 25 miles west of Boston **TICKETS/INFO:** 617-354-1340 **ACCOMMODATIONS/TOURIST INFO:** 800-888-5515, 617-536-4100

BLACKSMITH HOUSE DULCIMER FESTIVAL

CAMBRIDGE ✹ LAST WEEKEND IN APRIL OR FIRST WEEKEND IN MAY, FRIDAY–SUNDAY

Within the walls that housed the village blacksmith in the 1700s, today's master dulcimer players perform and teach their time-honored skills. The festival features concerts for both children and adults and workshops focusing on the mountain and hammered dulcimer. There's plenty of informal jamming within the cozy confines of this historic Cambridge landmark. **LOCATION:** Blacksmith House, 56 Brattle Street, Cambridge. Leave your car at home; easiest access is via the MTA Red Line—disembark at Harvard Square. **TICKETS/INFO:** 617-547-6789 **ACCOMMODATIONS/TOURIST INFO:** 800-888-5515, 617-536-4100

$\mathcal{B}$RANDEIS SUMMER MUSIC FESTIVAL
WALTHAM ✴ FIRST THREE WEEKS IN JUNE

Although chamber concerts by the esteemed Lydian String Quartet are the highlight of this festival, its three weeks are filled with a variety of lectures, demonstrations, master classes, sight-reading sessions, and student concerts. Young professional musicians in the Brandeis summer program concertize in the 225-seat Slosberg Recital Hall, presenting a broad sampling of the chamber music repertoire from the 18th through the 20th centuries. **LOCATION:** Slosberg Recital Hall at Brandeis University in Waltham, which is 10 miles west of Boston. From downtown take I-90 west to exit 15 to Route 30, then turn left onto South Street and continue for two miles. **TICKETS/INFO:** 617-736-3424; e-mail: summerschool@logos.cc.brandeis.edu; World Wide Web: http://www.brandeis.edu/sumsch/rabb.htm **ACCOMMODATIONS/TOURIST INFO:** 800-888-5515, 617-536-4100

$\mathcal{B}$OSTON FESTIVAL OF BANDS
BOSTON ✴ FIRST SATURDAY IN JUNE

Seven of New England's finest community bands and one military band gather in Faneuil Hall's Great Hall for a full day of classical and pops music. Air-conditioned comfort, free admission, and a resting place for weary feet make the Boston Festival of the Bands a welcome break from the Freedom Trail and other tourist activities. **LOCATION:** The Great Hall at Faneuil Hall in downtown Boston **TICKETS/INFO:** 617-983-1370 **ACCOMMODATIONS/TOURIST INFO:** 800-888-5515, 617-536-4100

$\mathcal{R}$OCKPORT CHAMBER MUSIC FESTIVAL
ROCKPORT ✴ EARLY JUNE THROUGH THE FIRST WEEK IN JULY, THURSDAYS—SUNDAYS

With artistic director and pianist David Deveau leading a wholehearted celebration of chamber music's past, present, and future, this five-week extravaganza presents lectures, concerts, and conversations in an idyllic seaside town well known for its decades-old artists' colony. Each concert draws between 125 and 250 people—an ideal size to preserve the intimacy of the chamber music.

About 30 performers share the festival's limelight, and past talents have included the Lark and Ying String Quartets, the Figaro Trio, the Apple Hill Chamber Players, and the Boston Artists Ensemble. Typically, the festival receives six to eight ensembles in residence plus numerous guest artists, all of whom arrange themselves into varying collaborations for performance.

By balancing standard works by well-known composers with little-known works and world premieres by contemporary composers, organizers have won a reputation for innovative programming. Lectures, workshops, and discussions team audiences with performers for frank and lively exchanges exploring, for example, the strained relationship between audiences and composers, or why modern audiences typically resist hearing contemporary works. In hosting these candid discussions, the festival goes where few others dare.

The Rockport Art Association was formed in the 1920s to give Rockport's artists both a place to present their works and a forum for mutual support. Since 1982, the association has housed the chamber music festival, and the art gallery adjacent to the acoustically fine Main Gallery displays work by local artists. The Cape Ann town of Rockport, replete with opportunities for fishing, sailing, whale-watching, and beach-combing, has inspired painters like Winslow Homer, Harrison Cady, and Childe Hassam and writers like Ralph Waldo Emerson and Katherine Anne Porter. Concert tickets are about $17, with discounts for subscribers, seniors, and students.   **LOCATION:** Main Gallery of the Rockport Art Association, 12 Main Street in Rockport **TICKETS/INFO:** 508-546-7391 **ACCOMMODATIONS/TOURIST INFO:** 508-546-6575

♪OSTON EARLY MUSIC FESTIVAL

BOSTON ✷ SECOND WEEK IN JUNE, IN ODD-NUMBERED YEARS ONLY

For lovers of early music, the only problem with the Boston Early Music Festival is the grueling two-year wait between its uncompromising banquets of music. But time after time, the festival proves itself worth the wait as more than 100 concerts, operas, and special events celebrate medieval, Renaissance, baroque, and early classical music.

As the largest festival of its kind in the United States, the event draws some 10,000 people to Boston's historic halls from all over the world. Many events (such as certain symposia and trade forums) appeal to specialists only; others attract even those with no knowledge of early music or classical music in general.

Churches, theaters, halls, and pubs throughout Boston and Cambridge host theater pieces, concerts, workshops, and demonstrations, all of which feature period instruments and reconstructions. A festive mood unites disparate cosmopolitan forces; over the course of the week recorder builders from New Zealand rub elbows with soprano singers from Germany, harpsichordists from Holland and musical/comedy ensembles like "Five Babes Go for Baroque." Schmoozers can mingle with publishers, dealers, collectors, artisans, and manufacturers. Concert tickets range from $15 to $55. **LOCATION:** Boston Park Plaza Castle and Hotel Conference Center and many other venues in Boston and Cambridge **TICKETS/INFO:** 617-661-1812 **ACCOMMODA-TIONS/TOURIST INFO:** 800-888-5515, 617-536-4100

☼RISH FESTIVAL

NORTH EASTON ✷ SECOND WEEKEND IN JUNE, FRIDAY–SUNDAY

One of the largest and liveliest Irish festivals on the East Coast draws 30,000 spectators and more than 300 musicians, many of whom are internationally known. Music and dance workshops, children's amusements, trade exhibits, dog shows, and pony shows complement the musical fare on the festival's five stages.   **LOCATION:** Stonehill College in North Easton, about 25 miles south of Boston just off Route 138 **TICKETS/INFO:** 617-323-3399 **ACCOMMODATIONS/TOURIST INFO:** 800-288-6263, 508-997-1250

♪OSTON GLOBE JAZZ FESTIVAL

BOSTON, CAMBRIDGE ✷ ONE WEEK IN MID- OR LATE JUNE

The *Boston Globe* presents dozens of locally and nationally known jazz artists in this weeklong series of free and ticketed concert events. Previous years have featured such entertainers as Ray Charles, Lou Rawls, and Al Jarreau, performing at the Hatch Memorial Shell and at various Boston clubs and hotels. Up to 45,000 people attend. **LOCATION:** Various venues in Boston **TICKETS/INFO:** 617-929-2649 **ACCOMMO-DATIONS/TOURIST INFO:** 800-888-5515, 617-536-4100

Boston Globe Jazz Festival: Members of the Marcus Roberts Group play at the Hatch Shell. Tracy Aiguier/The Picture Cube

ANGLEWOOD

LENOX ✷ LAST WEEKEND IN JUNE THROUGH FIRST WEEKEND IN SEPTEMBER

Founded in 1934, the nation's oldest classical music festival is also one of the world's most esteemed. The Boston Symphony Orchestra performs in the center of a 210-acre estate near a beautiful New England town in the Berkshire Mountains. It's easy to see why novelists Nathaniel Hawthorne and Edith Wharton were so inspired by Tanglewood, and why more than 350,000 people flock here during the summer months to enjoy the best in classical music in one of America's greenest concert venues.

The Boston Symphony Orchestra was the first American orchestra to combine a music festival with a school. In major American symphony orchestras today, more than 20 percent of the musicians (and 30 percent of the first chairs) have attended Tanglewood Music Center.

During the summer's almost-nightly concerts, guest conductors and soloists abound. In addition to symphonic productions, each summer's billing includes chamber music, musical theater, choral music, jazz, and a Festival of Contemporary Music. Concerts are performed in the Music Shed, which dates back to 1938 and accommodates 5,000 under cover (plus more on the lawn), and in the new Seiji Ozawa Hall. Tickets range from $12 on the lawn to $65 for the best seats, and Saturday rehearsals are free and open to the public.   **LOCATION:** Tanglewood Music Center, on West Street in Lenox, about two-and-a-half hours west of Boston and two hours north of New York City. From the Massachusetts Turnpike take exit 2 and follow the signs north to Lenox and

Seiji Ozawa conducts the Boston Symphony at Tanglewood, the nation's oldest classical music festival. (See entry, page 19.) Alan Solomon/Boston Symphony Orchestra

Tanglewood. **TICKETS/INFO:** 413-637-5165, 617-226-1492 **ACCOMMODATIONS/ TOURIST INFO:** 800-237-5747

CITY OF PRESIDENTS BLUES FESTIVAL
QUINCY ✷ LAST SUNDAY IN JUNE

Gather 'round, boys and girls—it's time for a family-oriented blues session. That's right, this Sunday celebration features seven to ten regional blues acts in an enclosed, alcohol-free environment. A local club owner throws the big shindig, hoping to promote exposure of New England blues musicians. International food and nonspiked beverages abound, so leave the coolers at home (but bring the blankets). The $10 adult and $2 children's tickets aren't a bad deal, and proceeds augment funding for community projects.   **LOCATION:** Veterans Memorial Stadium, on Hancock Street in Quincy **TICKETS/INFO:** 617-472-9383 **ACCOMMODATIONS/TOURIST INFO:** 617-479-1111

MUSICORDA SUMMER FESTIVAL
SOUTH HADLEY ✷ EARLY JULY THROUGH MID-AUGUST, FRIDAYS AND SUNDAYS

In conjunction with Musicorda's professional training program for gifted students of the violin, viola, and cello, Musicorda Summer Festival presents an outstanding roster of international soloists and chamber ensembles. The Friday night festival series has hosted such luminaries as the St. Petersburg String Quartet, the Turtle Island Quartet, and the Anderson Quartet. In addition, a Sunday night series highlights young artists. Programs run the gamut of the chamber music repertoire but emphasize pieces for the piano and strings.   **LOCATION:** Chapin Auditorium at Mount Holyoke College in South Hadley, north of Springfield on Route 116, between Holyoke and Amherst **TICKETS/INFO:** 413-538-2590 **ACCOMMODATIONS/TOURIST INFO:** 413-584-1900

*A*STON MAGNA FESTIVAL

GREAT BARRINGTON ✷ MID-JULY THROUGH FIRST WEEK IN AUGUST

Started in 1972 by Lee Elman and harpsichordist Albert Fuller, the Aston Magna Foundation for Music brings together musicians, scholars, and instrument makers to play and promote the music of the 17th and 18th centuries. Aston Magna brings its music to Great Barrington five Saturdays each summer for early-music concerts using period instruments and authentic musical techniques. (See also: Aston Magna Festival, Annandale-on-Hudson, New York.)   **LOCATION:** St. James Church, at the corner of Route 7 and Taconic Avenue in Great Barrington **TICKETS/INFO:** 413-528-3595, 914-758-7425 **ACCOMMODATIONS/TOURIST INFO:** 413-528-1510

*B*ERKSHIRE CHORAL FESTIVAL

SHEFFIELD ✷ MID-JULY THROUGH MID-AUGUST, SATURDAYS

The Berkshire Choral Festival is the only extended festival in the United States devoted to choral music, and its chorus unites singers from all across the nation and world. Soloists and a symphony orchestra join about 200 choristers, and the entire musical unit spends a full week preparing for each Saturday night concert so that listeners will experience the highest-quality performances.

Berkshire's repertoire spans the range of classical choral music, including major oratorios and operatic choruses. Concerts are presented in a 1,000-seat open-sided shed, with the Berkshire hills in the background. Strategically minded concertgoers arrange their trips to the Berkshires so that they can combine a Berkshire Choral Festival concert with a symphonic or chamber concert at nearby Tanglewood.   **LOCATION:** The Concert Shed on the campus of the Berkshire School, on Route 41 in Sheffield, just north of the Connecticut border in western Massachusetts **TICKETS/INFO:** 413-229-3522 **ACCOMMODATIONS/TOURIST INFO:** 413-258-1510

*M*ARBLEHEAD SUMMER MUSIC FESTIVAL

MARBLEHEAD ✷ MID-JULY THROUGH MID-AUGUST, SATURDAYS

With its yacht-choked harbor and string of Victorian mansions, Marblehead offers an elixir of recreational pleasures for which the Marblehead Summer Music Festival can be considered a cultural nightcap. For six Saturday evenings, the festival features performances by the respected Cambridge Chamber Players, who are joined by a who's who of international classical musicians and composers.

The festival got its start in 1971 on the Greek island of Paros, where musicians Chester Brezniak (clarinet), Richard Sher (cello), and Robert Stallman (flute) played for five years. In 1977, they moved to Marblehead and renamed the growing group. Programming aims for popularity, with mostly mainstream chamber music punctuated by occasional contemporary compositions, many specifically written for the Cambridge Players.

Musicians emphasize audience connection and often introduce each work personally. Thus, the audience might learn the meaning of a French song before it is sung, or that Debussy composed a piece while battling cancer. Reviewing a concert, the *New York Times* once said that "each piece was performed as though the musicians really liked it and wanted to share their enthusiasm with the audience." Concerts take place in the intimate and acoustically excellent Old North Church. Individual tickets cost $16; senior and student discounts apply.   **LOCATION:** Old North Church, 41 Washington Street in Marblehead, about 40 miles north of Boston. Follow Route 1A to Route 129 in Marblehead and turn right at Washington Street. **TICKETS/INFO:** 617-631-8110 **ACCOMMODATIONS/TOURIST INFO:** 617-631-2868

☙AMHERST EARLY MUSIC FESTIVAL
AMHERST ✹ TWO WEEKS FROM LATE JULY THROUGH EARLY AUGUST

Fifteen concerts entertain the local academic community and its visitors with music from the baroque, medieval, and Renaissance eras. Vocalists and instrumentalists perform both sacred and secular pieces and are often accompanied by historical dancers. Concurrent weeklong workshops in early music attract about 150 amateur and preprofessional players and singers. Buckley Recital Hall is located on the peaceful, tree-lined Amherst College campus, and a $10 donation is suggested for each concert. **LOCATION:** Buckley Recital Hall in the Music Building at Amherst College in Amherst, 20 miles north of Springfield on Route 9 **TICKETS/INFO:** 413-542-3072, 212-222-3351 **ACCOMMODATIONS/TOURIST INFO:** 800-723-1548, 413-787-1548

☙LOWELL FOLK FESTIVAL
LOWELL ✹ LAST FULL WEEKEND IN JULY, THURSDAY–SUNDAY

The Lowell Folk Festival shakes up the quiet community of Lowell when zydeco kings, Cape Breton fiddle queens, and mariachi aces hit the streets with parades, concerts, and dance parties. For three days, five stages in parks and courtyards offer a breathless lineup of more than two dozen musical groups that run the gamut of worldwide folk traditions.

Since 1987, promoters of this well-organized, free event have worked to preserve traditions through the celebration of local and ethnic music, dance, crafts, and food. The well-chosen music represents a breadth of traditions that rivals many of America's larger and more famous world music events.

Recent years have featured such performers as Yup ik Eskimo singer and dancer Chuna McIntyre, Cape Verdean dance group the Ice Band, Piedmont bluesman Warner Williams, and the classical Vietnamese group known as the Perfume River Ensemble.

Nearly 200,000 spectators converge on Lowell, a city restored to recall its heyday during the Industrial Revolution. There's plenty else to do if you tire of the Puerto Rican gourd-carving demonstrations or German polka bands. National Park exhibits, museums, Atlantic beaches, historical sites, and recreational areas are all within easy reach. **LOCATION:** Downtown Lowell, 24 miles northwest of Boston at U.S. 3 and I-495. By car take the Lowell Connector from either Route 495 (exit 36) or Route 3 (exit 30N); follow the signs for Lowell National Historical Park and Lowell Folk Festival. Commuter rail service leaves from Boston's North Station. **TICKETS/INFO:** 508-970-5000 **AC-COMMODATIONS/TOURIST INFO:** 508-459-6150

ℭAPE AND ISLANDS CHAMBER MUSIC FESTIVAL

CAPE COD, MARTHA'S VINEYARD, AND NANTUCKET ✴ FIRST THREE WEEKS IN AUGUST

Each August, historic New England churches from one end of Cape Cod to the other resound with chamber music. Established artists from Boston and New York team up with emerging local musicians to perform in various combinations, including a string quartet. Concerts regularly feature chamber music and occasionally feature jazz; educational programs and open rehearsals are also available. Tickets average $20, but children 16 years and under are admitted free.   **LOCATION:** Churches and clubs in Wellfleet, Woods Hole, Centerville, and other locations on Cape Cod, Nantucket, and Martha's Vineyard **TICKETS/INFO:** 508-255-9509 **ACCOMMODATIONS/TOURIST INFO:** 508-362-3225

ℰISTEDDFOD FESTIVAL OF TRADITIONAL MUSIC AND CRAFTS

NORTH DARTMOUTH ✴ THIRD WEEKEND IN SEPTEMBER

Like the hundreds of *eisteddfodau* that dot the Welsh countryside each summer, this event brings people together for a weekend of song and dance. A wide-ranging, high-quality program includes the music of the British Isles plus Appalachian, Cajun, and other forms of American music. One main stage and six workshop sites draw a total of 2,000 people over the course of the weekend, making this an intimate and manageable way to experience and really *celebrate* traditional music and dance. The college campus site is a bit antiseptic, but there's nothing staid about this event's approach to music and folklore. North Dartmouth is just minutes from the historic whaling town of New Bedford, and less than an hour from Cape Cod.   **LOCATION:** The University of Massachusetts Dartmouth Campus in North Dartmouth, just west of New Bedford. From I-195 use the North Dartmouth exit and go south, following the signs to the campus. **TICKETS/INFO:** 508-999-8515; e-mail: tbullard@umassd.edu **ACCOMMODATIONS/TOURIST INFO:** 508-997-1250

ℬLACKSMITH HOUSE ANNUAL FOLK FESTIVAL

CAMBRIDGE ✴ SECOND WEEKEND IN NOVEMBER, FRIDAY–SUNDAY

Within the walls that housed the village blacksmith in the 1700s, today's master folk crafters perform and teach their time-honored skills. This small venue draws the attention of Cambridge folk enthusiasts with its concerts, open jam sessions, and songwriting workshops (led by headlining artists). Over the weekend, three major acts appear, and a low-priced Sunday family concert rounds out the action at this Harvard Square folk-out.   **LOCATION:** Blacksmith House, 56 Brattle Street, Cambridge. Leave your car at home; easiest access is via the MTA Red Line—disembark at Harvard Square. **TICKETS/INFO:** 617-547-6789 **ACCOMMODATIONS/TOURIST INFO:** 800-888-5515, 617-536-4100

NEW HAMPSHIRE

FESTIVAL OF NEW MUSIC
HANOVER ✷ ONE OR TWO EVENINGS IN APRIL OR MAY

Groundbreaking talents in avant-garde music typically distinguish themselves less as virtuosic instrumentalists than as innovative composers. This event's strength lies in its provision of a forum for composers already conversant in new-music trends. The programming is particularly strong in electroacoustical and computer music, both of which are current interests of the Dartmouth faculty. (Electroacoustics deals with the interaction or interconversion of electric and acoustic phenomena. For example, it might use electric resources to simulate acoustic sounds.)

The festival's evening programs feature two or three international guest performers and six or eight Dartmouth-based performers. For the occasion, 400 to 500 listeners gather in a stone chapel that is distinctive not only for its extraordinary non-electroacoustics but also for its disarming appeal as a structure over 100 years old. **LOCATION:** Rollins Chapel at Dartmouth College, two hours north of Boston and easily accessible from I-89 and I-91 **TICKETS/INFO:** 603-646-3493 **ACCOMMODATIONS/TOURIST INFO:** 603-643-3115

PORTSMOUTH JAZZ FESTIVAL
PORTSMOUTH ✷ LAST WEEKEND IN JUNE

New Hampshire's oldest jazz festival hosts national talents and emerging artists in the intimate setting of a historic port community and for a devoted northeastern audience. Kids of all ages sample traditional jazz during practice sessions, demonstrations, and screenings of videotaped children's performances. The idyllic setting inspires daylong listening, picnicking, and lounging. **LOCATION:** Music Hall, at 28 Chestnut Street, and Alumni Fields, alongside South Mill Pond, both in Portsmouth **TICKETS/INFO:** 603-436-7678 **ACCOMMODATIONS/TOURIST INFO:** 603-436-1118

OLD-TIME FIDDLERS CONTEST
LINCOLN ✷ LAST SATURDAY IN JUNE

Two to three dozen fiddlers compete for the title of best fiddler—though in reality there are several bests. Contests are stratified into "bambino" (under age 11), junior,

24

advanced, senior, and "tricks and fancy." The runoffs take place on a flatbed truck in front of the rail station. Proceeds from the event (admission is $5) go to local Lions Club charities.   **LOCATION:** Hobo Junction Railroad Station, on Hobo Railroad in Lincoln. From Plymouth take I-93 north to exit 32, then go east on Route 112. **TICKETS/INFO:** 603-745-3563 **ACCOMMODATIONS/TOURIST INFO:** 603-745-6621

STARK FIDDLERS' CONTEST
STARK ✱ LAST SUNDAY IN JUNE

Fiddling, food, and dancing on the grassy knoll add up to a smacking good Sunday in Stark, located just 50 miles from the Canadian border. Fiddlers aged four to 85 compete from the back of a flatbed truck decorated with geraniums and plenty of red, white, and blue bunting. The contest features six different divisions: championship, senior, open, trick and fancy, junior, and junior-junior (the youngsters).

Since the first fiddler's contest over 20 years ago, Stark seems to have changed very little. The covered bridge and the church, built in 1853, are still around, as is the Ammonoosuc River, which threads its way along the valley floor through the narrow pass between Mill Mountain and Devil's Slide Mountain. Admission is $6, and B&B inns and camping are nearby.   **LOCATION:** Whitcomb Field in Stark. From I-93 take U.S. 3 north, then Route 110 east to Stark, and follow the signs to Whitcomb Field. **TICKETS/INFO:** 603-636-1325 **ACCOMMODATIONS/TOURIST INFO:** 603-636-2118, 603-636-1325

NEW HAMPSHIRE MUSIC FESTIVAL
PLYMOUTH ✱ SIX WEEKS BEGINNING THE SECOND WEEK IN JULY, ON TUESDAYS, THURSDAYS, AND FRIDAYS

Begun in 1952, this event features prestigious national and international talents, including an orchestra, numerous chamber music ensembles, and several guest artists who perform well-known and well-loved classical, symphonic, and chamber music pieces. In past years, organizers have wooed and won new listeners with promises of musical programs created "just for them"—and, to the festival's credit, they delivered on that promise.

The festival excels at crowd-pleasing programming that (figuratively speaking) favors the major key over the minor, Beethoven's even-numbered symphonies to his odd, and the time-tested and euphonic to the groundbreaking and dissonant. Appreciative audiences reward organizers for their fine talent-scouting and popular programming (and dependable air-conditioning) by buying up all the seats for most concerts. Concerts are reasonably priced (especially the chamber music), with discounts for children, students, and subscribers.   **LOCATION:** Hanaway Theater and Smith Recital Hall at the Silver Cultural Arts Center, on Main Street at Plymouth State College in Plymouth (from I-93 take exit 25 and turn right on Holderness Road, then left on Main Street); Gilford Middle High School, off Route 11A on Alyah Wilson Boulevard in Gilford. **TICKETS/INFO:** 603-524-1000 **ACCOMMODATIONS/TOURIST INFO:** 603-524-5531

Stark Fiddlers' Contest: Fiddling, food, and dancing on a grassy knoll in the White Mountains. (See entry, page 25.) Courtesy of Joe Dennehy/State of NH Tourism

ℳONADNOCK MUSIC

VARIOUS TOWNS IN THE MONADNOCK REGION ✱ MID-JULY THROUGH LATE AUGUST

Monadnock is an Indian word meaning "mountain which stands alone," perhaps reflecting this festival's maverick status and its penchant for 20th-century compositions in addition to traditional classics. With its high quality and strong commitment to new music, Monadnock Music's programming keeps a sense of discovery brewing among its 35 musicians, most of whom come from institutions that favor a more predictable repertoire.

The festival was founded in 1966 by composer and conductor Peter Bolle, who has earned a reputation for championing interesting works by unknown composers and digging up obscure compositions by great masters. Monadnock's budget is small, especially in comparison to giants like Tanglewood, but its musical programs rival those of any American festival. Plus, Monadnock's prices (tickets range from free to $28) are only a fraction of those of other New England giants.

Monadnock's concerts are presented at various sites in or near small towns in the Monadnock region. Events range from piano recitals and chamber music to full orchestra and concert opera performances. Artists are typically a mix of rising stars (e.g., cellist Pieter Wispelwey and pianist Haesun Paik) and established names (e.g., Russell Sherman and Lois Shapiro).   **LOCATION:** Peterborough Town House at 1 Grove Street in Peterborough; Pine Hill Auditorium at the Pine Hill Waldorf School in Wilton;

and churches and meeting houses in 15 towns throughout the Monadnock region. **TICKETS/INFO:** 603-924-7610 **ACCOMMODATIONS/TOURIST INFO:** 603-924-7234

MUSIC IN THE WHITE MOUNTAINS WITH THE NORTH COUNTRY CHAMBER PLAYERS

SUGAR HILL AND LINCOLN ✴ MID-JULY THROUGH MID-AUGUST, FRIDAYS AND SATURDAYS

The breathtaking beauty of the White Mountains and the collective talent of 12 professional musicians create an atmosphere unique to this North Country celebration. The ensemble's musicians present a broad range of chamber music, from classical masterworks to 20th-century compositions, in two charming New England settings. General admission is $12 for adults, and a variety of lodging and dinner packages at cozy inns are available. The area's camping, hiking, golfing, and boating opportunities are all superb.   **LOCATION:** Friday nights in Sugar Hill at the Meeting House (exit 38 off I-93 to Route 117); Saturday nights in Lincoln (call for location) **TICKETS/INFO:** 603-869-3154 **ACCOMMODATIONS/TOURIST INFO:** 800-227-4191, 603-745-6621

PEMI VALLEY BLUEGRASS FESTIVAL

CAMPTON ✴ FIRST WEEKEND IN AUGUST, FRIDAY–SUNDAY

Nestled among mountain vistas and open meadows at the border of the White Mountain National Forest, the Pemi Valley Bluegrass Festival offers two stages of traditional bluegrass and country music. Over the three-day weekend, about 10 groups pick, holler, and hoot their way through bluegrass standards, and around campfires spontaneous jams last until the wee hours of the morning.

Friday night features a competition for amateur bluegrass players, most of whom arrive with instruments in hand. Many novices take advantage of workshops taught by the professionals, and there are loads of learning and recreational activities for children. Musical instrument vendors, down-home barbecues, country dancing, church breakfasts, and Sunday morning gospel add to the occasion. Tickets run just under $30 for a three-day adult pass, and camping (both trailer and tent sites) is free for ticket holders. **LOCATION:** Branch Brook Campground, on Route 49 in Campton, about one-half mile from I-93's exit 28 **TICKETS/INFO:** 603-726-3471 **ACCOMMODATIONS/TOURIST INFO:** 603-726-3804

PORTSMOUTH BLUES FESTIVAL

PORTSMOUTH ✴ LABOR DAY WEEKEND, SATURDAY AND SUNDAY (LABOR DAY IS THE FIRST MONDAY IN SEPTEMBER)

With no blues style to call its own, New England embraces opportunities like the Portsmouth Blues Festival, when the Portsmouth Blues Bank Collective presents everything from Delta blues to Chicago blues to Memphis jug-band blues. Led by musician and human rights activist T. J. Wheeler, the festival spotlights "artists who deserve more attention than they get." Recent years have featured acts like octogenarian pianist Pinetop Perkins, blues/jazz saxophonist Benny Waters, and blues banjoist Jimmy Mazzy.

One of New England's most thoughtful, intimate, and enjoyable blues festivals typically draws 1,000 to 2,000 people to downtown Portsmouth's Harbour Place, a multilevel complex of courtyards and a dock. Each year features a different sociopolitical theme, and extras include club gigs and an all-you-can-eat blueberry pancake breakfast and gospel jubilee on Sunday morning at the Unitarian Universalist Church. Admission is about $15 per day at the gate, or $25 for the entire weekend.   **LOCATION:** Harbour Place, at the waterfront in downtown Portsmouth, and several other venues **TICKETS/ INFO:** 603-929-0654, 603-436-8596; e-mail: Bluesbank@aol.com **ACCOMMODA-TIONS/TOURIST INFO:** 603-436-1118

RHODE iSLaND

BIG EASY BASH
ESCOHEAG ✱ LAST WEEKEND IN JUNE

This late-June celebration features the music, dance, and food of Louisiana and its neighbors. Over two days, expect to hear a well-chosen sampling of Cajun, zydeco, blues, and R&B music on two stages. Previous years have featured R&B piano wizard Marcia Ball, zydeco sizzler Beau Jocque, and Cajun traditionalists Steve Riley and the Mamou Playboys. Even the dance workshops feature live music. Tickets are about $20 at the gate (although there are several multiday and early-bird specials). **LOCATION:** Stepping Stone Ranch in Escoheag, about 30 miles south of Providence. From I-95 take exit 5A to Route 3 south, continuing about one-half mile, then take Route 165 west and go about seven miles to Escoheag Hill Road and watch for the signs. **TICKETS/INFO:** 401-351-6312, 800-738-9808 **ACCOMMODATIONS/TOURIST INFO:** 401-789-4422

SUMMER CHAMBER MUSIC FESTIVAL AT URI
WEST KINGSTON ✱ LATE JUNE AND EARLY JULY

This festival plumbs the heart of the 19th-century chamber music repertoire, with occasional forays into earlier and later periods. With a program that at times rivals Newport's—but at a fraction of the price—the University of Rhode Island's Summer Chamber Music Festival attracts internationally acclaimed musicians. **LOCATION:** University of Rhode Island's Fine Arts Recital Hall, on Upper College Road in West Kingston **TICKETS/INFO:** 401-789-0665, 401-294-6823, 401-364-7535 **ACCOMMO-DATIONS/TOURIST INFO:** 800-326-6030, 401-847-1600

NEWPORT MUSIC FESTIVAL
NEWPORT ✱ TWO WEEKS IN MID-JULY

Starting in mid-July, the Newport Music Festival presents a unique feast for lovers of classical music. Concerts are played in the ballrooms and on the lawns of the neoclassical and baroque summer mansions of millionaires. In these summer "cottages," the festival presents some 55 concerts by more than 60 artists from around the world. The event takes place over two weeks, during which there are up to five concerts a day. One of the most spectacular venues is the Great Hallway of the Breakers, a lavish mansion resembling a 16th-century Italian palace that was built in 1895 by Cornelius Vanderbilt.

The musical selection is diverse but focuses on chamber music, since it was written to make rooms in palaces like Newport's come alive. General director Mark P. Malkovich III researches and selects works from the 19th-century chamber and vocal repertoire, as well as romantic-era piano literature. Each year, a series of 15 afternoon concerts presents a popular retrospective of a particular composer, such as Schubert, Brahms, or Tchaikovsky.

Since the festival began in 1969, it has presented more than 70 artists and ensembles in their American debuts. Tickets are $25 to $30.   **LOCATION:** Various Newport mansions **TICKETS/INFO:** 401-849-0700, 401-846-1133; e-mail: nmfestival@aol.com **ACCOMMODATIONS/TOURIST INFO:** 800-326-6030, 401-847-1600

NEW ENGLAND REGGAE FESTIVAL
ESCOHEAG ✶ LAST WEEKEND IN JULY, SATURDAY AND SUNDAY

This reggae campout weekend features about a dozen internationally and regionally known bands on a stage in the midst of a large natural amphitheater. Since the crowd typically hovers around 2,000, southern New England's only major reggae festival is an intimate opportunity to hear stars like Sister Carol, Eek-A-Mouse, and Arrow—all of whom have played here at one time or another.

The music is mostly classic roots reggae, with elements of dancehall, ska, and other world music thrown in. Jamaican and health foods, crafts, clothing, drum circles, and several sideshows round out the event, and the ranch itself features horseback riding and swimming. Camping is available at two campsites across the street.   **LOCATION:** Stepping Stone Ranch, at Escoheag Hill Road in Escoheag, about 30 miles south of Providence. From I-95 take exit 5A to Route 3 south for one-half mile, then take Route 165 west about seven miles to Escoheag Road and watch for the signs. **TICKETS/INFO:** 401-331-7910 **ACCOMMODATIONS/TOURIST INFO:** 401-789-4422

NEWPORT RHYTHM AND BLUES FESTIVAL
NEWPORT ✶ LAST WEEKEND IN JULY, SATURDAY AND SUNDAY

The first of three festival weekends at Newport's beautiful and historic bayside state park is actually a benefit whose proceeds go to the Rhythm & Blues Foundation, dedicated to "Preserving America's Soul." Ben & Jerry's Newport Folk Festival and the JVC Jazz Festival appear on the same stage on the two summer weekends subsequent to this festival.

About 15 local, regional, and national talents perform each day for a crowd of around 10,000. Expect to see and hear stars like Bonnie Raitt and Don Henley as well as classic R&B acts like Clarence Fountain & the Blind Boys of Alabama, Ruth Brown, vocalist Pops Staples of The Staple Singers, and Allen Toussaint & His Orchestra. Admission costs about $35.   **LOCATION:** Fort Adams State Park, off Ocean Drive in Newport. From New York and Connecticut take I-95 north to exit 3A/Highway 138 east and follow the signs to Newport. From Boston take I-93 south to Highway 24. After entering Newport, follow the signs to Fort Adams State Park. **TICKETS/INFO:** 401-847-3700 **ACCOMMODATIONS/TOURIST INFO:** 401-849-8098, 800-326-6030

Newport Music Festival: Russian pianist Mikhail Pletnev performs at the Breakers mansion in his North American debut. (See entry, page 29.) Courtesy of
John Hopf/Newport Music Festival

𝓑EN & JERRY'S NEWPORT FOLK FESTIVAL

NEWPORT ✸ FIRST OR SECOND WEEKEND IN AUGUST, SATURDAY AND SUNDAY

One of the most pop-oriented of the U.S. folk festivals features a lineup of high-profile acts like the Indigo Girls, Joan Baez, John Hiatt, and Victoria Williams. The focus is on performance rather than workshops and other participatory events, and the festival draws a crowd of about 20,000 to the laid-back surroundings of Fort Adams State Park, which overlooks Narragansett Bay and Newport Harbor. **LOCATION:** Fort Adams State Park, off Ocean Drive in Newport. From New York and Connecticut take I-95 north to exit 3A/Highway 138 east and follow the signs to Newport. From Boston take I-93 south to Highway 24, and after entering Newport, follow the signs to Fort Adams State Park. **TICKETS/INFO:** 401-847-3700, 212-496-9000 **ACCOMMODATIONS/TOURIST INFO:** 800-326-6030, 401-847-1600

*Stanley Jordan
brings his unique
and spirited gui-
tar style to the
JVC Jazz Festival
Newport.* William K.

Daby/AP/Wide World Photos

♫VC JAZZ FESTIVAL—NEWPORT

NEWPORT ✹ EARLY TO MID-AUGUST, FRIDAY–SUNDAY

One of the world's premier jazz festivals, this 1954-born event was also the first outdoor jazz festival to exist in the United States and is credited with launching luminaries like Count Basie and Duke Ellington into the big time. These days, an array of outstanding jazz talents—including vocal and instrumental soloists, big bands, and combos—take the stage, which overlooks Narragansett Bay and Newport Harbor in the historic seaside resort town of Newport. They play to a total of 20,000 fans, who, over the festival's three days, claim the state park's grassy promontory as their own.

The festival welcomes the well-loved jazz legend and the young, rising star alike. Recent rosters have dazzled listeners with stellar lineups including such diverse talents as Ray Charles, Roy Hargrove, and Tito Puente and his Latin Jazz Ensemble. The Newport Casino hosts the festival's Opening Night Gala for $25 to $60, and tickets for the state park concerts cost about $30 per day.   **LOCATION:** Fort Adams State Park, off Ocean Drive in Newport. From New York and Connecticut take I-95 north to exit 3A/Highway 138 east and follow the signs to Newport. From Boston take I-93 south to Highway 24, and after entering Newport, follow the signs to Fort Adams State Park. The Tennis Hall of Fame's Newport Casino, 194 Bellevue Avenue, Newport. **TICKETS/INFO:** 401-847-3700 **ACCOMMODATIONS/TOURIST INFO:** 401-849-8098, 800-326-6030

℃AJUN & BLUEGRASS MUSIC-DANCE-FOOD FESTIVAL

ESCOHEAG ✻ LABOR DAY WEEKEND, FRIDAY–SUNDAY (LABOR DAY IS THE FIRST MONDAY IN SEPTEMBER)

When this festival began back in 1980, a lot of folks thought it was a dumb idea. Bluegrass aficionados eyed the dance floor and predicted that the Cajun music would draw nothing but yahoos. And Cajun and zydeco lovers weren't so sure they wanted to hang out with a bunch of gray-haired bluegrassers.

Luckily, the "try it, you'll like it" mentality prevailed, and these days about 12,000 East Coasters get hillbilly harmonies and Cajun joie de vivre all in one event. There's also a bit of zydeco and some old-time country thrown in, just to keep things interesting. In addition to music on two stages, the festival features children's activities, spicy foods, and workshops in dance, music, and culture. The audience is invited to pitch a tent and stay for a family-friendly weekend. Tickets are about $20 each day. **LOCATION:** Stepping Stone Ranch in Escoheag, about 30 miles south of Providence. From I-95 take exit 5A to Route 3 south, continuing about one-half mile, then take Route 165 west and go about seven miles to Escoheag Hill Road, and watch for the signs. **TICKETS/INFO:** 401-351-6312, 800-738-9808 **ACCOMMODATIONS/TOURIST INFO:** 401-789-4422

Cajun chords and hillbilly harmonies mix easily at Escoheag's Cajun &
Bluegrass Music-Dance-Food Festival. Kindra Clineff/The Picture Cube, Inc.

🎵 BLUEGRASS MUSIC SHOW
WESTON ✹ THIRD SATURDAY IN FEBRUARY

This musical review features strictly traditional bluegrass and old-time country music. The Weston Playhouse Theatre, where Lloyd Bridges got his start, has housed the Bluegrass Music Show for 15 years. The old theater has great acoustics and draws 500 to 600 people for the shows. Tickets are $8 when purchased in advance, and similar shows are held in late April and early November. **LOCATION:** Weston Playhouse Theatre, on Main Street in Weston, 40 miles northeast of Bennington on Highway 100. From Bennington take U.S. 7 north to Route 11 east; take Route 11 to Route 100 north for five miles into Weston. **TICKETS/INFO:** 802-824-6674 **ACCOMMODATIONS/TOURIST INFO:** 800-837-6668

🎵 BLUEGRASS MUSIC SHOW
WESTON ✹ LAST SATURDAY IN APRIL

Similar to the late-February Bluegrass Music Show, this review features traditional bluegrass and old-time country music. (See above for more details.) A Bluegrass Music Show is also held in early November. **LOCATION:** Weston Playhouse Theatre, on Main Street in Weston, 40 miles northeast of Bennington on Highway 100. From Bennington take U.S. 7 north to Route 11 east; take Route 11 to Route 100 north for five miles into Weston. **TICKETS/INFO:** 802-824-6674 **ACCOMMODATIONS/TOURIST INFO:** 800-837-6668

🎵 DISCOVER JAZZ FESTIVAL
BURLINGTON ✹ SECOND WEEK IN JUNE, TUESDAY–SUNDAY

Acid-jazz freaks and bebop lovers alike are turned on during Burlington's six-day extravaganza of jazz. You'll find all sorts of jazz all over town, in traditional venues like parks, theaters, concert halls, and clubs, and in less conventional places like street corners, rooftops, churches, buses, and ferries. In fact, you can hear about 150 acts at as many as 50 sites around town—which would seem overwhelming if it weren't for this city's mellow, intimate vibe.

The Rebirth Brass Band romps on Main Street during Burlington's Discover Jazz Festival. (See entry, page 35.) Courtesy of Jeff Clarke/Discover Jazz Festival

Burlington is a relatively small city, and its Discover Jazz Festival has been cited as a model for community-based festivals around the country. The majestic shoreline of Lake Champlain and the horizon of the Green Mountains provide great backdrops for this musical celebration, which mixes locally and nationally famous acts.

Workshops, clinics, live TV and radio broadcasts, food, and beverages accompany the performances during the week. Most of the events are free, but where tickets are needed, plan to spend anywhere from $1 to $26.   **LOCATION:** Fifty sites in and around Burlington **TICKETS/INFO:** 800-639-1916, 802-863-7992 **ACCOMMODA-TIONS/TOURIST INFO:** 802-863-3489, 800-837-6668

ꬰEN & JERRY'S ONE WORLD ONE HEART FESTIVAL
WARREN ✳ FOURTH WEEKEND IN JUNE

Amid giant postcard campaigns to Congress, voter registration drives, recycling, and plenty of other social and environmental causes, you'll find a cool mix of folk, blues, and other music on Ben & Jerry's two stages. What's more, the festival is free, aside from a $5 parking fee (to encourage carpooling, of course). Held on hilly terrain at the base of a ski resort in the Green Mountains, the fest brings together six to seven acts, with a mix of regional and national talent. There's plenty of food and ice cream to buy. But alcohol, glass, and pets are not allowed.   **LOCATION:** Sugarbush Resort in Warren, 50 miles southeast of Burlington off Route 100 **TICKETS/INFO:** 800-253-3787, 802-244-6959;

World Wide Web: http://www.benjerry.com **ACCOMMODATIONS/TOURIST INFO:**
800-537-8427, 800-837-6668

$\mathcal{K}$ ILLINGTON MUSIC FESTIVAL

KILLINGTON ✷ SUNDAYS IN LATE JUNE THROUGH MID-AUGUST

A distinguished group of musicians delivers chamber music of the 17th, 18th, and 19th centuries to small audiences at this mountaintop location. Performances feature the works of Bach, Mozart, Schubert, Brahms, Haydn, Beethoven, and more, and in addition to the Killington Music Festival's visiting faculty, guest artists are often part of the program. The annual chamber orchestra concert is usually presented the last Sunday in July.   **LOCATION:** Killington Music Festival, on Killington Road just off U.S. 4 **TICKETS/INFO:** 802-773-4003 **ACCOMMODATIONS/TOURIST INFO:** 802-773-4181, 800-837-6668

$\mathcal{Y}$ ELLOW BARN MUSIC FESTIVAL

PUTNEY ✷ EARLY JULY THROUGH MID-AUGUST

The Yellow Barn is a 27-year-old institution nestled in the small town of Putney. The festival offers four or five chamber concerts each week over a five-week period, showcasing world-class artists and serious students from the barn's summer training institute. The charming, refurbished concert barn seats only about 150; if you can get in, you'll experience a rare feeling of informality and intimacy between listeners and performers. Children's concerts, garden tours, and community-based suppers add to the small-town friendliness.   **LOCATION:** Village Center in Putney, just off I-95 north of Brattleboro **TICKETS/INFO:** 800-639-3819; 802-387-6637 **ACCOMMODATIONS/TOURIST INFO:** 802-254-4565, 800-837-6668

$\mathcal{M}$ ANCHESTER MUSIC FESTIVAL

MANCHESTER ✷ THURSDAYS AND SATURDAYS IN JULY AND AUGUST

The Manchester Music Festival draws music lovers interested in hearing great classical masterpieces in intimate settings amid the mountains of southeastern Vermont. Festival concerts coincide with a six-week summer program of instruction for young professional musicians from the United States and abroad; tickets are $7 to $25. **LOCATION:** Arkell Pavilion at the Southern Vermont Art Center, on West Road, just north of Manchester, near the intersection of West Road and Ways Lane; also at other halls in Manchester, which is 24 miles north of Bennington and 30 miles south of Rutland.   **TICKETS/INFO:** 800-639-5868, 802-362-1956 **ACCOMMODATIONS/TOURIST INFO:** 802-362-2100, 800-837-6668

$\mathcal{S}$ UMMER FESTIVAL ON THE GREEN

MIDDLEBURY ✷ WEEK AFTER JULY 4, SUNDAY–SATURDAY

Everyone from the least adventurous listener to the most heroic musical experimenter will find something to savor during the Summer Festival on the Green. In fact, even the gnarly old gnomes from the surrounding forest are said to come into town for the festivities. In a natural amphitheater on Middlebury's town green, one stage provides a mix of eclectic music, including folk, blues, worldbeat, bluegrass, and jazz. All events are accessible and free, drawing about 1,000 onlookers each night. The rain location is

Ben & Jerry's One World One Heart Festival mixes folk, blues, and other music with the hippy creamery's favorite causes. (See entry, page 36.) Couretsy of Charlie Brown/VT Dept. of Travel and Tourism

the Town Hall.   **LOCATION:** The town green in Middlebury, in the middle of the state between Burlington and Rutland, just off U.S. 7 **TICKETS/INFO:** 802-388-0216 **ACCOMMODATIONS/TOURIST INFO:** 802-388-7951, 800-837-6668

VERMONT REGGAE FESTIVAL
BURLINGTON AREA ✸ SECOND OR THIRD SATURDAY IN JULY

The location changes every year or two, but you can count on the free Vermont Reggae Festival to draw one heck of a crowd. In past years, 20,000 to 30,000 reggae fans have managed to track down the Burlington-area site and have gathered enthusiastically and peacefully to promote unity, peace, understanding, and the one-drop rhythm.

This one-day event is one of the biggest and best reggae events in New England, with eight to 10 bands swapping the spotlight in an impressive and super-sonically quick fashion. Regional and North American favorites take the stage early in the day, and international headliners are saved for the end. Organizers typically choose wilderness locations near Burlington, which makes for a scenic gig. The volunteers who run the free festival do it solely to expose people to reggae music and politics (and to get a free T-shirt).

Regulations are quite tight, with no glass, styrofoam, alcohol, or pets allowed. In addition, spectators (many of whom are teenagers) are responsible for their own garbage and do a surprisingly good job on self-inflicted trash patrol. Although festival admission is free, fees apply for parking and camping.   **LOCATION:** A Burlington-area location

Peace, unity, and the one-drop beat: Bobby Hackney of Lambsbread performs at the Vermont Reggae festival. Sallie Chafer

that changes from year to year **TICKETS/INFO:** 802-862-3092 **ACCOMMODATIONS/ TOURIST INFO:** 802-863-3489, 800-837-6668

WAREBROOK CONTEMPORARY MUSIC FESTIVAL
IRASBURG ✷ SECOND WEEKEND IN JULY, FRIDAY–SUNDAY

Bringing together well-known masterworks and world premiere performances, the Warebrook Contemporary Music Festival presents an adventurous program in an unusual locale—a tiny town in northernmost Vermont. This gem, begun in the late 1980s, was created by a woman frustrated by her hometown's lack of musical opportunities. The program encompasses 20th-century vocal and chamber works, electronic music, one-act operas, and dance. Lectures and workshops in numerous venues around town are also part of the weekend.   **LOCATION:** Various locations in Irasburg, in northeastern Vermont. From I-91 use exit 26. **TICKETS/INFO:** 802-754-6631; e-mail: warebrook@aol.com **ACCOMMODATIONS/TOURIST INFO:** 802-334-7782, 800-837-6668

VERMONT MOZART FESTIVAL

CHAMPLAIN VALLEY ✳ SECOND SUNDAY IN JULY THROUGH FIRST SUNDAY IN AUGUST

This midsummer classical festival brings the music of Mozart and his contemporaries to the Vermont wilderness. Showcasing regional talent, the festival occupies three weeks in various indoor and outdoor venues around the Lake Champlain resort area and other communities. Mansions, lodges, ferry boats, churches, and theaters host concerts almost every evening. **LOCATION:** Eleven locations around Burlington and Champlain Valley **TICKETS/INFO:** 800-639-9097 **ACCOMMODATIONS/TOURIST INFO:** 802-863-3489, 800-837-6668

MARLBORO MUSIC FESTIVAL

MARLBORO ✳ MID-JULY THROUGH MID-AUGUST

"Caution: Musicians at Play" warns the sign at the entrance to the Marlboro Music Festival. It's a telling description of the spirited endeavors of the 75 eminent musicians who gather in this small community each year for one of the most prestigious chamber music events in the country.

Many musical giants have been "students" at Marlboro, including Aaron Copland, Lukas Foss, Pablo Casals, and James Levine. The musicians typically study up to 100 works each week and select seven to 10 for weekend presentations. Because selections are chosen during each week's course of study, no advance schedule is provided, but listeners have come to expect a wide variety of chamber works from all periods, including pieces that involve unusual combinations of instruments. The large repertoire combines brass, strings, voice, woodwind, and piano in combinations ranging from duos to large chamber ensembles.

Tickets range from $5 to $20, and most concerts sell out well in advance. Call far ahead to reserve your seat in the 650-seat Southern/CountryAuditorium, a unique structure resembling a Norse banquet hall. Marlboro is located in the foothills of the Green Mountains, where there is plenty of hiking, biking, and other mountain recreational opportunities. **LOCATION:** Persons Auditorium on the Marlboro Campus. From Brattleboro, take Route 9 about 10 miles west and follow signs to the college. **TICKETS/INFO:** 215-569-4690, 802-254-2394 **ACCOMMODATIONS/TOURIST INFO:** 802-254-4565, 800-837-6668

CRACKER BARREL FIDDLERS CONTEST

NEWBURY ✳ FRIDAY OF THE LAST FULL WEEKEND IN JULY

In the spirit of old-time Vermont music making, about 1,000 people gather with chairs and blankets for one heck of a night of fiddling. On a seven-acre common typical of New England, a covered bandstand welcomes 40 fiddlers for junior, senior, and open showdowns. At $5 for adults, this festival is well worth the price. **LOCATION:** Newbury's Village Common. The town is located on U.S. 5 near Vermont's border with New Hampshire, about 40 miles southeast of Montpelier. **TICKETS/INFO:** 802-866-5518 **ACCOMMODATIONS/TOURIST INFO:** 802-866-5521, 800-837-6668

☉LD-TIME FIDDLER'S CONTEST
HARDWICK ✹ LAST SATURDAY IN JULY

The competition is heated at the Old-Time Fiddler's Contest, where more than 60 contestants from around North America and Ireland vie for trophies and recognition. With the Green Mountains as a backdrop, Hardwick provides a picturesque setting for one of the largest fiddling events in the Northeast. Bluegrass fiddling, old-time Appalachian fiddling, and French Canadian fiddling are spotlighted. Admission is $6 for adults, but children get in free. **LOCATION:** Shepard's Field, on Bridgeman Hill Road in Hardwick, 25 miles north of Montpelier **TICKETS/INFO:** 802-472-6425; 802-472-5501 **ACCOMMODATIONS/TOURIST INFO:** 800-837-6668

𝕳ARMONY RIDGE BRASS CENTER SUMMER FESTIVAL
POULTNEY ✹ FIRST WEEK IN AUGUST

This wide-ranging week of music showcases musicians and composers who specialize in trumpets, horns, trombones, tubas, and other brass instruments. More than 100 soloists and ensembles from around the world gather in Poultney to present pieces in repertoire sessions and public concerts that demonstrate the variety and complexity of brass musical literature. New works by some of today's leading composers—some commissioned by Harmony Ridge—are premiered each year. Most performances are presented in Ackley Hall, and a Finale Concert is staged in Withey Hall on the final evening of the festival. Green Mountain College is a small private college set in a pastoral valley in central Vermont. Admission starts at about $10. **LOCATION:** Green Mountain College is in Poultney, southeast of Rutland. From Rutland take U.S. 4 west to Route 30 south and go about eight miles. **TICKETS/INFO:** 802-287-2462; e-mail: stephen.langley@valley.net **ACCOMMODATIONS/TOURIST INFO:** 802-287-2462, 800-837-6668

ℭHAMPLAIN VALLEY SUMMER FOLK FESTIVAL
BURLINGTON ✹ FIRST WEEKEND IN AUGUST, FRIDAY–SUNDAY

A diverse, enticing assortment of musical acts makes the Champlain Valley Summer Folk Festival one of the foremost folk festivals in the United States. The festival highlights traditional music, with particular attention to the "local" region covering Vermont, southern Québec, and the Adirondacks of New York.

Five stages, 30 performers, and nearly nonstop dancing are complemented by food, arts and crafts, and a children's area. The stages and demonstration areas (all covered by tents) are nestled in an ancient pine grove on a college campus in northern Vermont's Champlain Valley. About 2,000 spectators each year pay an admission fee of about $15 a day. **LOCATION:** Redstone Campus of the University of Vermont in Burlington **TICKETS/INFO:** 802-899-1111; e-mail: byellin@together.net **ACCOMMODATIONS/TOURIST INFO:** 802-863-3489, 800-837-6668

VERMONT'S GREEN MOUNTAIN IRISH MUSIC FESTIVAL

DOVER ✴ FIRST WEEKEND IN AUGUST, SATURDAY AND SUNDAY

Bagpipe bands, cabbage dinners, and a beer garden with Guiness on tap await music fans at this Irish hootenanny, which was launched in 1995. Three stages with international talent draw thousands for two days of Irish music and dance. Because it's held outdoors in a lovely mountain valley, you're encouraged to bring blankets and lawn chairs (but no coolers or pets). Tickets average $12 each day for adults, and children enter free.   **LOCATION:** Mount Snow Ski Resort in southwestern Vermont. Mount Snow is located just off Route 100 between Brattleboro and Bennington. **TICKETS/ INFO:** 800-245-7669 **ACCOMMODATIONS/TOURIST INFO:** 800-245-7669, 800-837-6668

CENTRAL VERMONT CHAMBER MUSIC FESTIVAL

RANDOLPH ✴ LAST TWO WEEKENDS IN AUGUST

Just 40 minutes south of Montpelier, the capital of Vermont, Chandler Music Hall hosts the Central Vermont Chamber Music Festival each August. The repertoire, presented in a restored, acoustically superb hall, is heavy on the standards but always includes something out of the ordinary. Anywhere from two to five musicians make up each performing ensemble, drawing about 300 listeners per concert. Individual tickets are $10 for adults and $5 for students. Rehearsals are open to the public, and a children's concert is presented each season.   **LOCATION:** Chandler Music Hall, 71-73 Main Street, in Randolph. From I-89 take exit 4, then Route 66 to Randolph's Main Street. **TICKETS/INFO:** 802-728-7133, 212-932-1226 **ACCOMMODATIONS/TOURIST INFO:** 800-837-6668, 802-223-3443

LABOR DAY WEEKEND CLASSICAL MUSIC FESTIVAL

GUILFORD ✴ SATURDAY NIGHT AND SUNDAY AFTERNOON OF LABOR DAY WEEKEND (LABOR DAY IS THE FIRST MONDAY IN SEPTEMBER)

The discovery of a mid-19th-century pipe organ in a barn instigated this classical music festival, held every Labor Day weekend in the tiny southeastern Vermont town of Guilford. You'll find this uncrowded jewel at the end of a dirt road in a very rural part of the country. A variety of classical concerts are performed, and the pipe organ is used during the Saturday night concert, still held on the old farmstead. Admission is free, but donations are always welcome.   **LOCATION:** Guilford Organ Barn in Guilford, near Brattleboro. From I-91 take exit 1 and follow Route 5 south 1.5 miles to Guilford; look for the signs that say Guilford Organ Barn. Take a right turn onto Guilford Center Road and follow it for two miles to Weatherhead Hollow Road, where you'll take a left. Follow it for five miles, then take a right on Packer Corners Road and follow that road for three miles. **TICKETS/INFO:** 802-257-1961 **ACCOMMODATIONS/TOURIST INFO:** 800-837-6668

New World Festival: Celtic and French-Canadian music liven up a historic 1800s village. Courtesy of Robert Eddy

NEW WORLD FESTIVAL
RANDOLPH ✳ SUNDAY OF LABOR DAY WEEKEND

Working to expose the relationship between French Canadian and Celtic music, the New World Festival enlists 10 local bands to help preserve this region's musical heritage. The festival is held in the center of a historic 1800s village, and festivalgoers experience an unusual mix of two separate, but related, musical traditions.

French Canadian and Celtic music is performed under tents, in churches, at Chandler Music Hall, and in art galleries. Randolph is beautifully rural, with fishing, hunting, hiking, and mountain biking offering fine accompaniment to a day of music and song. Adult tickets are $12; children's tickets are $3.   **LOCATION:** Downtown Randolph is just off exit 4 on I-99. **TICKETS/INFO:** 802-728-9878 **ACCOMMODATIONS/TOURIST INFO:** 802-728-9027, 800-837-6668

NATIONAL TRADITIONAL OLD-TIME FIDDLERS & STEPDANCERS CONTEST
BARRE ✳ THIRD OR FOURTH WEEKEND IN SEPTEMBER, FRIDAY–SATURDAY

The strains of old-time fiddle music ring out across the valley from the top of Barre's Seminary Hill as participants from across North America compete in one of the continent's oldest and best old-time fiddle contests. Held in a civic auditorium, the contest attracts up to 50 fiddlers, who are judged by remote control (allowing judges to evaluate each contestant on sound alone, without visual distraction).

The competition is fierce, but the crowd is friendly, and some of the most enjoyable music is made in the informal jam sessions that spring up on the building's lower level. The junior-junior category is always a crowd pleaser, as is the step-dancing competition. One formal concert is held Saturday night, and throughout the event vendors sell books on fiddle music, fiddle records, musical instruments, and food. Tickets range from $8 to $15.   **LOCATION:** Municipal Auditorium, on Seminary Hill in Barre, which is in central Vermont just southeast of Montpelier **TICKETS/INFO:** 802-879-1536, 802-862-6708 **ACCOMMODATIONS/TOURIST INFO:** 802-223-3443, 802-229-0154, 800-837-6668

NEW ENGLAND BACH FESTIVAL
MARLBORO, BRATTLEBORO, AND NEARBY TOWNS ✷ FIRST THREE WEEKS IN OCTOBER

Bach worshippers unite! Here's your chance to hear the finest instrumental and vocal soloists as the Blanche Moyse Chorale and the Bach Festival Orchestra present music by J. S. Bach. The festival's conductor and artistic director, Blanche Moyse, has devoted her career to interpreting Bach, and the festival receives rave reviews from around New England and beyond. Tickets are priced from $10 to $40. Plus, the festival's timing is perfect for catching Vermont's brilliant autumn colors.   **LOCATION:** Persons Auditorium at Marlboro College in Marlboro (just off Route 9, 10 miles west of Brattleboro), and other locations around the Brattleboro area **TICKETS/INFO:** 802-257-4523 **ACCOMMODATIONS/TOURIST INFO:** 802-254-4565, 800-837-6668

BLUEGRASS MUSIC SHOW
WESTON ✷ FIRST SATURDAY IN NOVEMBER, THIRD SATURDAY IN FEBRUARY, AND LAST SATURDAY IN APRIL

Similar shows are held in late February and late April. See page 35 for all the details on Weston's bluegrass scene.   **LOCATION:** Weston Playhouse Theatre, on Main Street in Weston, 40 miles northeast of Bennington on Highway 100. From Bennington take U.S. 7 north to Route 11 east; take Route 11 to Route 100 north for five miles into Weston. **TICKETS/INFO:** 802-824-6674 **ACCOMMODATIONS/TOURIST INFO:** 800-837-6668

MiD-aTLaNTiC

GOSPELFEST

DOVER ✷ SECOND SUNDAY IN FEBRUARY

Since 1971, African American gospel choirs have traveled through rain, snow, and sometimes even blue skies to perform at this benefit event. Beginning at 3 P.M., count on seeing from six to eight choirs, each of which performs two or three songs (which often stretch up to 20 minutes apiece). Gospelfest raises money for scholarships, so the 1,500 spectators, who pay about $6, and the choirs, which perform free of charge, all come in the spirit of giving. **LOCATION:** Humanities Auditorium, Delaware State University, Dover **TICKETS/INFO:** 302-736-0101 **ACCOMMODATIONS/TOURIST INFO:** 800-233-5368, 302-734-1736

NEW MUSIC DELAWARE

NEWARK ✷ A MONDAY AND TUESDAY IN MARCH OR EARLY APRIL

This two-day festival features outstanding new music by composers from the mid-Atlantic region who compete for cash prizes. Compositions are written for and performed by soloists and ensembles affiliated with the University of Delaware. An informal, informative atmosphere prevails at the contests/concerts and at the event's panel discussions and composer round tables. **LOCATION:** Loudis Recital Hall, Amy DuPont Music Building, at the University of Delaware in Newark **TICKETS/INFO:** 302-831-2577; e-mail:mzinn@udel.edu **ACCOMMODATIONS/TOURIST INFO:** 800-422-1181, 302-652-4088

EASTERN SHORE BLUEGRASS ASSOCIATION FESTIVAL

HARRINGTON ✷ THIRD WEEKEND IN JUNE

Since 1980, the Eastern Shore Bluegrass Association has brought about a dozen bands to its festival from all over the mid-Atlantic. Recent-year headliners have included the Lonesome River Band and Jerry McCoury, and a band contest brings local talent out of the woodwork. Two to three thousand bluegrass lovers venture to the Delaware State Fairgrounds, which has plenty of RV hookups and level-ground camping. **LOCATION:** Delaware State Fairgrounds in Harrington. From Dover go south on U.S.

13 to Harrington; the fairgrounds are just off the main highway. **TICKETS/INFO:** 302-492-1048 **ACCOMMODATIONS/TOURIST INFO:** 800-233-5368, 302-734-1736

﹖UNE JAM
HARRINGTON ✹ FOURTH SATURDAY IN JUNE

Delaware's biggest outdoor concert festival is a rocking, well-organized event that brings about a dozen bands onto three stages. Since 1979, the music in this beautiful park has ranged from southern blues/rock and classic '70s rock to alternative rock, blues, and even some folk; recent headliners have included Blackfoot, James Cotton, Molly Hatchet, and Kansas. Rain or shine, the music begins at noon with local bands and peaks with two headliners that play until 10 P.M. Other activities include tugs-of-war, relay races, children's games, and raffles to raise money for charity. Tickets range from $15 to $25, depending on when you buy, but no tickets are available the day of the show. **LOCATION:** McCauley's Pond, on Route 15 about five miles east of Harrington, which is 20 miles south of Dover **TICKETS/INFO:** 302-284-5863 **ACCOMMODATIONS/TOURIST INFO:** 800-233-5368, 302-734-1736

ᴸAMB JAM
MILTON ✹ WEDNESDAY–SATURDAY IMMEDIATELY AFTER JULY 4 (INDEPENDENCE DAY)

One of the mid-Atlantic's largest Christian music festivals draws some 15,000 people over four days. On two stages, more than a dozen bands supply a mix of rock 'n' roll and folk-oriented contemporary Christian music geared toward young people ages 12–21. Admission price is about $10 per day (including camping), and the site is just minutes from Rehoboth Beach.   **LOCATION:** Milton, at the corner of Route 1 and Route 16 **TICKETS/INFO:** 302-424-4300 **ACCOMMODATIONS/TOURIST INFO:** 800-357-1818, 302-856-1818

ᴿEHOBOTH BEACH JAZZ FESTIVAL
REHOBOTH BEACH ✹ THIRD WEEKEND IN OCTOBER, THURSDAY–SUNDAY

The Rehoboth Beach Jazz Festival brings four days of contemporary and classic jazz to one of the East Coast's most beautiful and historic beaches. The event features several national and international names, but mainly focuses on up-and-coming local and regional musicians. Jazz soloists and ensembles entertain crowds at free outdoor concerts on the boardwalk, as well as at ticketed concerts and meet-the-artist programs at the convention center and downtown restaurants. Proceeds go toward educational programs and scholarships for young musicians.   **LOCATION:** Various locations in downtown Rehoboth Beach **TICKETS/INFO:** 302-226-3844, 800-296-8742 **ACCOMMODATIONS/TOURIST INFO:** 800-441-1329, 302-227-2233

MaRYLaND

EAST COAST JAZZ FESTIVAL

GAITHERSBURG ✳ PRESIDENTS' DAY WEEKEND, THURSDAY–SUNDAY
(PRESIDENTS' DAY IS THE THIRD MONDAY IN FEBRUARY)

"More jazz party than jazz festival" is how one reviewer described the East Coast Jazz Festival. This shindig features 40 hours of music, mingling high and low forms of the art with its inclusion of everything from national touring groups to high school jazz combos. Organized by husband and wife musicians Ron Elliston and Ronnie Wells, the event supports the Fish Middleton Jazz Scholarship Fund, named after a D.C. jazz radio programmer. The biggest acts on the bill play Saturday night, when the grand ballroom of a suburban D.C. hotel hosts a concert that doesn't quit until 4 A.M. Admission is about $30, but other programs are free, including workshops on topics like "How to Accompany a Vocalist" and "The Business of Music." **LOCATION:** Gaithersburg Marriott Washingtonian Center, just off I-270 and Sam Eig Highway in Gaithersburg. From Washington, D.C., take I-495 to I-270, then take exit 9B for Sam Eig Highway west. **TICKETS/INFO:** 301-933-1822 **ACCOMMODATIONS/TOURIST INFO:** 301-588-8687, 800-925-0880, 301-428-9702

WINTERSONG

FREDERICK ✳ LAST SATURDAY IN FEBRUARY

This midwinter event brings dozens of folk masters into the Adult Recreation Center for a day of concerts and do-it-yourself music making. A main stage features five or six acts throughout the day, and workshops spring up in all corners of the building. At 8 P.M., an evening dance helps folks shake off the midwinter chills and cabin fever. Daytime events and the dance are $6 each. **LOCATION:** The Adult Recreation Center, at the corner of Second and Bentz Streets in downtown Frederick **TICKETS/INFO:** 301-663-8687, 800-999-3613 **ACCOMMODATIONS/TOURIST INFO:** 301-663-8687, 800-999-3613

EARTH DAY FOLK FESTIVAL

FROSTBURG ✳ A SATURDAY IN LATE APRIL

Although this celebration doesn't always occur precisely on Earth Day, it does bring some earthy folk bands to this university town just 10 miles from Cumberland. The concerts are held outdoors in the campus's main quadrangle, and music is typically singer-songwriter folk, with the occasional Celtic or reggae band thrown into the mix. The vibe is mellow, with crafts, food, and plenty of Frostburg State University students milling around and playing Frisbee.   **LOCATION:** Frostburg State University's main quadrangle, in Frostburg, 10 miles from Cumberland. From I-68 use exit 33. **TICKETS/ INFO:** 301-687-4151 **ACCOMMODATIONS/TOURIST INFO:** 800-508-4748, 301-777-5905

♭ALTIMORE/WASHINGTON JAZZFEST AT COLUMBIA, MARYLAND

COLUMBIA ✻ THIRD WEEKEND IN MAY, THURSDAY–SUNDAY

Columbia's main thoroughfare races with jazz in late May, with some 20 acts from around the region and around the country. Venues include hotels, clubs, restaurants, and the African Art Museum of Maryland, which holds special exhibitions of jazz memorabilia. Tickets range from $20 to $135, depending on the package. **LOCATION:** Various venues along Route 175 in Columbia **TICKETS/INFO:** 410-730-7105 **ACCOMMODATIONS/TOURIST INFO:** 410-313-1900, 800-288-8747

♭ATERSIDE MUSIC FESTIVAL

SOLOMONS ✻ SATURDAY OF MEMORIAL DAY WEEKEND (MEMORIAL DAY IS THE LAST MONDAY IN MAY)

Hosted by the museum that promotes southern Maryland's marine and maritime heritage, the Waterside Music Festival began in 1982 as a showcase for bluegrass, folk, and sea songs. Recently, though, the festival's program has taken a turn toward the mainstream, and visitors to this stunning seaside setting can now expect nationally known rock, blues, and jazz acts as well as straight-ahead folk. The music is complemented by an acoustically perfect outdoor amphitheater, nestled near the water with a view of a century-old lighthouse. Admission ranges from $15 to $30, and vendors sell a variety of local seafood specialties.   **LOCATION:** Calvert Marine Museum, on Route 2/4 in the Calvert County town of Solomons, near the point where the mouth of the Patuxent River meets Chesapeake Bay. From Washington, D.C., take the Beltway (I-495) to Route 4 south and continue south for 58 miles. **TICKETS/INFO:** 410-326-2042 **ACCOMMODATIONS/TOURIST INFO:** 410-535-4583, 800-331-9771, 301-855-1880 (D.C.)

♭NNAPOLIS JAZZFEST

ANNAPOLIS ✻ FIRST SUNDAY IN JUNE

Alongside a peaceful creek that trickles through the historic lower campus of St. John's College (founded in 1696), a large stage supports five local bands, some of whom have national reputations. Guitarist Charlie Byrd serves as music adviser and often appears on the program. The event raises funds for the Annapolis Symphony and features tape and CD sales, food booths, and a boathouse brunch for sponsors. Admission is about $15.   **LOCATION:** College Creek, on the lower campus of St. John's College in Annapolis. From Washington, D.C., take the Beltway (I-495) to Highway 301/ 50 east and go about 20 miles to Highway 70 (Roscoe C. Rowe Highway), then follow the signs. **TICKETS/INFO:** 410-849-3623 **ACCOMMODATIONS/TOURIST INFO:** 410-280-0445, 410-837-1636, 800-282-6632

ℬAY COUNTRY MUSIC FESTIVAL

CENTREVILLE ✷ SECOND SATURDAY IN JUNE

This Lions Club fund-raiser brings the area's best country and country-rock bands to Centreville for one of the Eastern Shore's biggest outdoor music events. **LOCATION:** Downtown Centreville, at the junction of Route 213 and Route 304, just west of U.S. 301 **TICKETS/INFO:** 410-827-4810, 410-626-2208 **ACCOMMODATIONS/TOURIST INFO:** 410-827-4810

𝒟EER CREEK FIDDLERS' CONVENTION

WESTMINSTER ✷ SECOND SUNDAY IN JUNE

Calling all fiddlers! When Deer Creek puts out the word, Baltimore-area fiddlers (and folks who like the sound of old-time and bluegrass fiddling) hit the road for Westminster. About 35 musicians and 4,000 listeners typically make the scene. **LOCATION:** 500 South Center Street in Westminster, northwest of Baltimore. From I-795 take exit 19. **TICKETS/INFO:** 410-848-7775, 800-654-4645 **ACCOMMODATIONS/TOURIST INFO:** 410-848-1388, 410-857-2983, 800-272-1933

𝒯ANGIER SOUND COUNTRY MUSIC FESTIVAL

CRISFIELD ✷ FOURTH SATURDAY IN JUNE

With a full day of boot-scootin' music and other countrified shenanigans, Tangier Sound draws folks from the lower Eastern Shore and all over the Mid-Atlantic. Bookings typically include Nashville's hottest stars, and previous years have drawn the likes of Brooks and Dunn, Ricky Van Shelton, Mary Chapin Carpenter, and Pam Tillis. Aside from the music, much of the event's appeal is the waterside setting at Hammock Pointe, where the crowd of more than 15,000 can relax and take in the sights, bask in the Eastern Shore sun, or cool off with a shower in the "rain tent." A shuttle bus brings festivalgoers to nearby Crisfield, with its dock, restaurants, and shops.   **LOCATION:** Hammock Pointe in Crisfield, on the lower Eastern Shore in Somerset County. From Salisbury take U.S. 13 south to Route 413 south into Crisfield. **TICKETS/INFO:** 800-521-9189, 410-651-2968 **ACCOMMODATIONS/TOURIST INFO:** 800-521-9189, 410-651-2968

𝒻RIENDSVILLE FIDDLE AND BANJO CONTEST

FRIENDSVILLE ✷ THIRD SATURDAY IN JULY

Since 1964, Friendsville has hosted fiddlers and banjoists from all around this rural area for a Saturday full of pickin' and sawin'. Soloists, accompanied musicians, and full bands play music in the old-time and bluegrass traditions, and a few hundred locals pay about $5 for the privilege of gathering around to watch the musical sparks fly. The park is located on the bank of Bear Creek in Friendsville, in the far western corner of Maryland.   **LOCATION:** The Town Park in Friendsville, in the far northwest corner of Maryland just off U.S. 48 **TICKETS/INFO:** 301-746-8194 **ACCOMMODATIONS/TOURIST INFO:** 301-334-1948

REGGAE WINE FESTIVAL
MOUNT AIRY ✱ THIRD WEEKEND IN JULY, SATURDAY AND SUNDAY

The reggae beat tempers the July heat for two days on a hilly, wooded 230-acre plantation near Mount Airy. Word's still out on that truckload of Red Stripe, but as luck would have it the festival is held at the Linganore Winecellars and is catered by a D.C.-area Caribbean restaurant. In addition to reggae, expect to hear Caribbean and worldbeat rhythms played by three to four locally, regionally, and (in some cases) internationally known bands. Festivalgoers are encouraged to bring beach chairs or blankets, and to stretch out and let the one-drop bass line sooth the tired soul. The $5 admission fee includes wine samples and cellar tours. And with picnic tables, shade trees, and spacious lawns, the grounds are perfect for picnics, hikes, volleyball, and kites.   **LOCATION:** Linganore Winecellars, 13601 Glissans Mill Road, four miles north of New Market (junction of I-70 and Highway 27) and four miles east of Highway 75. From Washington, D.C., take I-270 west to exit 22, then drive 14 miles to Glissans Mill Road, and then four miles east to the winery. **TICKETS/INFO:** 800-514-8735, 301-831-5889 **ACCOMMODATIONS/TOURIST INFO:** 800-999-3613, 301-663-8687, 800-570-2836

DRUMFEST
CUMBERLAND ✱ LAST SATURDAY IN JULY

One of the few drum-and-bugle competitions in the summer months, Cumberland's Drumfest draws the top echelon of corps from throughout the United States and Canada. The Marine Corps often shows up, dropping jaws with its awe-inspiring precision. Tickets are about $15.   **LOCATION:** Greenway Avenue Stadium in downtown Cumberland **TICKETS/INFO:** 301-777-8325 **ACCOMMODATIONS/TOURIST INFO:** 301-777-5905, 800-508-4748

ROCKY GAP MUSIC FESTIVAL
CUMBERLAND ✱ FIRST WEEKEND IN AUGUST, FRIDAY–SUNDAY

If you've been looking for the midsummer spot where Ricky, Dolly, Billy Ray, and Garth are going to touch down, set your sights high in the mountains of western Maryland. Each summer, the mid-Atlantic region's highest concentration of hot new country stars can be found on the shores of Habeeb Lake, in the beautiful confines of Rocky Gap State Park.

Friday evening through Sunday afternoon, the park teems with big-stage events, as well as participatory workshops, sing-alongs, and craft demonstrations. Line dancers shuffle and stomp (instruction is available for those who need it), and in addition to new-country acts a variety of traditional country, bluegrass, gospel, folk, and dance is featured at smaller stages.

Though the action at times gets rowdy in a country and western sort of way, the scene is decidedly family-oriented, and to keep it that way organizers set up an impressive array of children's activities. No alcohol is sold in the parks, but attendees can bring beverages of their choice in cans or plastic containers. Swimming, boating, and picnicking are popular activities in the 3,200-acre park and throughout Allegany County, which is Maryland's most mountainous. Some 15,000 to 20,000 spectators pay about $30 (adult) each day at the gate, but a variety of early-bird specials are available. **LOCATION:** Rocky Gap State Park, just west of Cumberland **TICKETS/INFO:** 800-424-

2511, 310-724-2511 **ACCOMMODATIONS/TOURIST INFO:** 301-777-5905, 800-508-4748

LITTLE MARGARET'S BLUEGRASS AND OLD-TIME COUNTRY MUSIC FESTIVAL

LEONARDTOWN ✱ SECOND WEEKEND IN AUGUST, FRIDAY–SUNDAY

Even if you're not a member of Joseph Goddard's family, you may walk away from this bluegrass and old-time country event feeling like you've just spent the weekend at your own clan's family reunion. Named after Goddard's daughter (who died in an automobile accident), the family-style event features about a dozen bands, with no shortage of old-timey licks. Holders of three-day tickets ($35 at the gate) who arrive early are treated to a barbecue dinner and potluck at 6 P.M. Thursday. Goddard roasts two pigs ("so you don't have to cook as soon as you get here"), and everyone brings a side dish to pass.   **LOCATION:** Two miles south of Leonardtown, just off Route 5. Leonardtown is 50 miles south of Washington, D.C., via Route 5. **TICKETS/INFO:** 301-475-8191 **ACCOMMODATIONS/TOURIST INFO:** 301-475-4626, 301-472-4105 (TDD), 800-327-9023

BAYOU RAZZ-JAZZ WINE FESTIVAL

MOUNT AIRY ✱ THIRD WEEKEND IN AUGUST, SATURDAY AND SUNDAY

This midsummer feast for the senses includes music, food, and wine at Mount Airy's Linganore Winecellars. The musical fare is diverse ("bayou to bop," say the organizers), which means that in a given year you might hear zydeco, New Orleans jazz, blues, and R&B. Visitors spread blankets and set up lawn chairs on a hilltop to catch the music as it drifts toward the woods and farmlands of this 230-acre plantation. Barbecued food and wine from the onsite cellars are available. Admission costs $5 for adults. **LOCATION:** Linganore Winecellars, 13601 Glissans Mill Road, four miles north of New Market (junction of I-70 and Highway 27) and four miles east of Highway 75. From Washington, D.C., take I-270 west to exit 22, then drive 14 miles to Glissans Mill Road, and then four miles east to the winery. **TICKETS/INFO:** 800-514-8735, 301-831-5889 **ACCOMMODATIONS/TOURIST INFO:** 800-999-3613, 301-663-8687, 800-570-2836

POLKAMOTION BY THE OCEAN

OCEAN CITY ✱ SECOND WEEKEND AFTER LABOR DAY, WEDNESDAY–SUNDAY (LABOR DAY IS THE FIRST MONDAY IN SEPTEMBER)

Imagine 1,500 couples (that's 6,000 feet) whirling in a single ballroom to the sounds of the country's very best polka bands and you'll get the idea that this polka frenzy is all about *fun* in a big way. This famous polka weekend (now nearing its 20th birthday) features about 20 of the nation's hottest bands over its five-day run, along with food and drink and the accompanying camaraderie. A Wednesday night pre-Polkamotion jam session gets everyone in the proverbial mood.   **LOCATION:** Ocean City Convention Center, on Coastal Highway and 41st Street in Ocean City **TICKETS/INFO:** 410-388-1998, 410-787-8675, 302-436-4854 **ACCOMMODATIONS/TOURIST INFO:** 410-289-8181, 410-289-2800

⟶RCADIA BLUEGRASS FESTIVAL

UPPERCO, ARCADIA ✴ LAST WEEKEND IN SEPTEMBER

Upperco's family-oriented bluegrass festival benefits the local fire department. Sixteen bands over the weekend draw about 1,500 people each day. Hundreds camp, and there's plenty of parking-lot picking. Cost is about $32 for four days. **LOCATION:** Fire Company Carnival Grounds, 5415 Arcadia Avenue in Upperco. Upperco is 20 miles south of the Pennsylvania border and 30 miles northwest of Baltimore on Route 30. **TICKETS/INFO:** 410-374-2895 **ACCOMMODATIONS/TOURIST INFO:** 410-583-7313, 800-570-2836

⟶INTAGE JAZZ WINE FESTIVAL

MOUNT AIRY ✴ THIRD WEEKEND IN OCTOBER, SATURDAY AND SUNDAY

Food from the Louisiana Delta and wine from the Linganore Winecellars complement some diverse musical fare as four jazz bands play new tunes and old standards from noon till six for two days. Typically, the talents include two bands known in the D.C. metropolitan area and two known nationwide. The roster ranges from bop-inclined ensembles to 10-piece Latin jazz bands to saxophone quintets. The $5 admission fee includes wine tasting and a tour of the cellars. The 230-acre plantation features a children's recreational area, picnic tables, 25 arts and crafts vendors, farmlands, and hikeable woods.   **LOCATION:** Linganore Winecellars, 13601 Glissans Mill Road, four miles north of New Market (junction of I-70 and Highway 27) and four miles east of Highway 75. From Washington, D.C., take I-270 west to exit 22, drive 14 miles to Glissans Mill Road, then four miles east to the winery. **TICKETS/INFO:** 800-514-8735, 301-831-5889 **ACCOMMODATIONS/TOURIST INFO:** 800-999-3613, 301-663-8687, 800-570-2836

CAPE MAY JAZZ FESTIVAL

CAPE MAY ✳ WEEKEND FOLLOWING EASTER, FRIDAY–SUNDAY

Since 1994, jazz fans have been planning their Cape May holidays for April to coincide with one of the few major jazz happenings in south Jersey. The festival aims to honor and preserve traditional New Orleans-style jazz by offering master classes, jam sessions, and concerts featuring East Coast talents. Three days of music entertain some 2,000 fans in hotel and nightclub venues in beautiful Cape May, with programs and lineups that have included mainstream jazz by talents like trumpeter Marlon Jordan, pianist Lenore Raphael, and Philadelphia-based siren Rosella Clemmons Washington. Single events cost around $10, but multievent bargain passes are available. If you miss this one, another jazz festival is held here in November.   **LOCATION:** Marquis de Lafayette Hotel, 501 Beach Drive, and Carney's, 401 Beach Drive, in Cape May. From Atlantic City take the Atlantic City Expressway west to the Garden State Parkway and go south all the way to New Jersey's southern, coastal tip. **TICKETS/INFO:** 609-884-7277 **ACCOMMODATIONS/TOURIST INFO:** 609-884-5508, 609-465-7181

CAPE MAY MUSIC FESTIVAL

CAPE MAY ✳ MID-MAY THROUGH THE END OF JUNE

The quaint and charming seaside resort town of Cape May comes alive with the sounds of chamber, orchestra, jazz, folk, and choral music during 20 or more late-spring concerts. Joined by guest ensembles and soloists, internationally renowned groups like the New York Chamber Ensemble take up residence for four weeks. The concert hall seats 250, and most performances draw an intimate group of around 185. Daytime activities include daily open rehearsals, walking and trolley tours, craft and antique shows, cruises, and shoreline hikes. Cape May is a 2-hour drive from Philadelphia and a 2.5-hour drive from New York City.   **LOCATION:** Congress Hall Hotel on Beach Drive in Cape May. From Atlantic City take the Atlantic City Expressway west to the Garden State Parkway and go south all the way to New Jersey's southern, coastal tip. **TICKETS/ INFO:** 800-275-4278, 609-884-5404; World Wide Web: http:// www.beachcomber.com/capemay/mac.html **ACCOMMODATIONS/TOURIST INFO:** 609-884-5508, 609-465-7181

New Orleans jazz in New Jersey: U.S. Coast Guard Band trumpeter Clifford Buggs takes a solo at the 1995 Cape May Jazz Festival.

Jennifer Kopp, courtesy Cape May

Star and Wave

⊙CEAN GROVE IRISH & SCOTTISH MUSIC FEST & FAIR

OCEAN GROVE ✷ LAST SATURDAY IN MAY

Same ocean, different side. . . . The Jersey shore resounds to the music of Ireland and Scotland in Victorian Ocean Grove during this outdoor/indoor festival. An afternoon of traditional dances, games, and sing-alongs is topped by an old-country headliner in a nearby auditorium. **LOCATION:** The mall at Ocean Beach and the Ocean Grove Auditorium, both in Ocean Grove, just south of Asbury Park. From the Garden State Parkway, exit at Route 33 and go east about five miles. **TICKETS/INFO:** 610-825-7268 **ACCOMMODATIONS/TOURIST INFO:** 908-775-0035

ⒶPPEL FARM ARTS AND MUSIC FESTIVAL

ELMER ✷ FIRST SATURDAY IN JUNE

Devoted to contemporary performing songwriters, the Appel Farm Festival is a rural kickback for fans of acoustic folk and blues. Roughly 7,000 show up for the one-day event featuring a mix of 12 local and national acts. This is an especially kid-friendly festival, with a children's village, crafts, and an alcohol ban.   **LOCATION:** Appel Farm Arts & Music Center, 457 Shirley Road in Elmer, about 45 minutes southeast of Philadelphia **TICKETS/INFO:** 1-800-394-1211; e-mail: appelarts@aol.com; World Wide Web: http://www.rowan.edu/-appel **ACCOMMODATIONS/TOURIST INFO:** 609-935-1415

ⒿERSEY JAZZFEST AT WATERLOO

STANHOPE ✷ FIRST OR SECOND WEEKEND IN JUNE, FRIDAY–SUNDAY

Held in a restored 18th- and 19th-century village on 360 acres of New Jersey state park, this outdoor jazz festival boasts a rare setting. With a brook the kids can play in and more than 20 renovated historical sites, the parklands are ideal for families who want to mix picnicking or camping with the tristate area's finest jazz. Three performance sites feature continuous music Friday evening, all day Saturday, and all day Sunday. Each venue is unique and provides an intimate setting for jazz: the largest is an open-ended outdoor tent that seats 3,500 people; the second is a gazebo with surrounding grass for the audience; the third is a magnificent building that seats up to 300.

Musicians include mainstream and traditional jazz artists like Kenny Davern, Johnny Varro, Dan Barrett, Derek Smith, and Bucky Pizzarelli. During the festival many of the musicians mix it up and jam with each other, making things exciting for the more than 4,000 jazz fans who attend each year. Daily admission price varies, but the entire festival is usually $75 for all three days.   **LOCATION:** Waterloo Village, 525 Waterloo Road in Stanhope, in Allamuchy Mountain State Park, one hour west of New York City. From Route 80 use exit 25. **TICKETS/INFO:** 201-543-4496, 201-347-0900 **ACCOMMODATIONS/TOURIST INFO:** 201-347-0900

ⒷRIDGETON FOLK FESTIVAL

BRIDGETON ✷ SECOND OR THIRD SATURDAY IN JUNE

Rootsy-grass and folk-rock tunes play continuously from noon until 8 P.M. for several thousand people at the large and lovely outdoor amphitheater in Bridgeton's lakeside park. The roster is heavy on English folk and progressive bluegrass, and performers come in from around the region, the country, and the world. Past talents have included guitarist Kristina Olsen, English electric folk pioneer Richard Thompson, Toronto's Moxy Früvous, and New Jersey's own Snake Brothers. Many of the performers sell original recordings at the event (for later rekindling of memories of the day's live music). The site also has picnic areas, food, arts and crafts vendors, and a life-guarded swimming area. Admission (for adults) costs around $10 in advance or $12 at the gate. **LOCATION:** Donald Rainear Amphitheater at Sunset Lake, on Park Drive in Bridgeton, 50 miles west of Atlantic City. From Atlantic City take the Atlantic City Expressway west to U.S. 40 west, to Highway 552 west, to Highway 49 west. **TICKETS/INFO:** 609-451-9208 **ACCOMMODATIONS/TOURIST INFO:** 609-691-7400

OPERA FESTIVAL OF NEW JERSEY

LAWRENCEVILLE ✸ MID-JUNE THROUGH MID-JULY

Romantically situated in an intimate theater on the grounds of a prestigious boarding school, this festival interprets and presents a mixture of traditional and 20th-century opera works. More than 5,000 fans pay $20 to $50 to enjoy critically acclaimed performances featuring national solo vocal talents, a regional orchestra, and local choral talents. Many also partake of the festival's symposia, lectures, children's learning sessions, and family days. While on campus, visitors enjoy picnicking on lush grounds just five minutes from the historic university town of Princeton.   **LOCATION:** Kirby Arts Center at the Lawrenceville School in Lawrenceville, about five miles south of Princeton via U.S. 206 **TICKETS/INFO:** 609-936-1500 **ACCOMMODATIONS/TOURIST INFO:** 609-683-1760

POLKA SPREE BY THE SEA

WILDWOOD ✸ LAST WEEKEND IN JUNE, THURSDAY–SUNDAY

Twelve hours of nonstop dancing each day has been the hallmark of this festival since its inception in the early 1970s. Thousands of people flock to the beachside boardwalk site to hear 16 bands send out the polka beat from one big stage. Because a wide selection of hotels and restaurants is just a short walk away, you can park your car and forget about it for the entire weekend.   **LOCATION:** Civic Center, on the boardwalk in Wildwood. From Atlantic City head west on the Atlantic City Expressway, then south on the Garden State Parkway, all the way to the southeastern tip of New Jersey's Atlantic Ocean shore; then use Highway 147 to Wildwood. **TICKETS/INFO:** 800-237-6436, 908-359-5520 **ACCOMMODATIONS/TOURIST INFO:** 609-729-9000

MONTCLAIR BLUES & JAZZ FESTIVAL

MONTCLAIR ✸ WEEKEND CLOSEST TO JULY 4 (INDEPENDENCE DAY)

Mixing local and regional talent, this free festival (established in 1985) features about 15 bands over the Fourth of July weekend. Concerts are presented at two outdoor stages, and the scene heats up with a bluesy pub crawl involving a half-dozen local bars and restaurants.   **LOCATION:** Various venues in Montclair, 12 miles west of New York City and four miles west of the Garden State Parkway, via Route 506 **TICKETS/INFO:** 201-509-4910; e-mail: kshane@intac.com; World Wide Web: http://www.intac.com/mbjf **ACCOMMODATIONS/TOURIST INFO:** 201-242-6237

HARBOR MUSICFEST

ATLANTIC CITY ✸ FIRST WEEKEND IN AUGUST, SATURDAY AND SUNDAY

Set in a historic waterfront park at the northeast tip of Atlantic City, this family-friendly festival features popular rock, blues, jazz, and folk artists. Four well-known bands, some dating from the 1950s, perform each day on one main stage, while two local acts stomp around on a side stage. Admission to Harbor MusicFest is about $10 for adults, and the waterfront setting features a maritime museum, a marina, and seafood restaurants.   **LOCATION:** Gardner's Basin, 800 North New Hampshire Avenue, on the northeast tip of Atlantic City **TICKETS/INFO:** 609-347-5427 **ACCOMMODATIONS/TOURIST INFO:** 609-348-7001

BLUEGRASS FESTIVAL AT ROUND VALLEY
LEBANON ✭ SECOND WEEKEND IN AUGUST, FRIDAY–SUNDAY

The campsites open Thursday morning, but the music starts on Friday evening at this three-day fest of traditional bluegrass music, featuring well-known talents like Ralph Stanley, Charlie Waller, the Del McCoury Band, and the Charlie Sizemore Band. Charismatic emcees, plenty of friendly jamming, and the breathtaking beauty of the Round Valley Lake area make this a sure stop on the bluegrass route to happiness. **LOCATION:** Round Valley Youth Center in Lebanon, which is 20 miles west of Bridgewater at the junction of U.S. 22 and Highway 512 **TICKETS/INFO:** 908-638-8400 **ACCOMMODATIONS/TOURIST INFO:** 908-735-5955

FESTIVAL OF THE ANDES
STANHOPE ✭ THIRD WEEKEND IN AUGUST, SATURDAY AND SUNDAY

Charangos, quenas, wangaras, and other traditional instruments of the mountains of South America can be heard at this wide-ranging festival of Andean culture. On five stages, eight to 10 bands play the highland music of Ecuador, Peru, and Bolivia. Plus, you can learn how to play some of the dozens of common instruments from this region at workshops throughout the day. A special evening concert rounds out the festivities; admission is $8 for adults.   **LOCATION:** Waterloo Village, 525 Waterloo Road in Stanhope, in Allamuchy Mountain State Park, one hour west of New York City. From Route 80 use exit 25. **TICKETS/INFO:** 201-543-4496, 201-347-0900 **ACCOMMODA-TIONS/TOURIST INFO:** 201-347-0900

DELAWARE VALLEY BLUEGRASS FESTIVAL
WOODSTOWN ✭ LABOR DAY WEEKEND, FRIDAY–SUNDAY (LABOR DAY IS THE FIRST MONDAY IN SEPTEMBER)

The Brandywine Friends of Old-Time Music present this Labor Day weekend bash, which brings around 15 bands to the Salem County Fairgrounds. Traditional favorites alternate with hot new bands on the covered stage, and the crowd of 2,500 or so gets revved up during spirited campground jam sessions.   **LOCATION:** Salem County Fairgrounds, on U.S. 40 between the Delaware Memorial Bridge and Woodstown **TICKETS/INFO:** 302-475-3454; World Wide Web: http://www.sas.upenn.edu/~jlupton/bfotm.html **ACCOMMODATIONS/TOURIST INFO:** 609-935-1415

SCANDINAVIAN FEST
STANHOPE ✭ SUNDAY OF LABOR DAY WEEKEND

The music of Scandinavia often gets lost in the shuffle of the worldwide folk revival, but Scandinavians (many of whom lived in relative isolation until recently) have a rich and well-preserved variety of folk music traditions. Stanhope's Scandinavian Fest showcases the music and cultures of Norway, Iceland, Denmark, Finland, and Sweden. About 18 Scandinavian music and dance groups from all over North America converge on this National Historic Site for a day of music making on three stages, plus musical workshops, crafts, imported gifts, and kids activities.   **LOCATION:** Waterloo Village, 525 Waterloo Road in Stanhope, in Allamuchy Mountain State Park, one hour west of New York City. From Route 80 use exit 25. **TICKETS/INFO:** 201-543-4496, 201-347-0900 **ACCOMMODATIONS/TOURIST INFO:** 201-347-0900

$\mathbb{C}$APE MAY JAZZ FESTIVAL

CAPE MAY ✳ WEEKEND CLOSEST TO VETERANS DAY (NOVEMBER 11),
FRIDAY–SUNDAY

This is a semiannual event, happening the weekend after Easter and the weekend closest to Veterans Day. See page 54 for details.   **LOCATION:** Marquis de Lafayette Hotel, 501 Beach Drive, and Carney's, 401 Beach Drive, in Cape May. From Atlantic City take the Atlantic City Expressway west to the Garden State Parkway and go south all the way to New Jersey's southern, coastal tip. **TICKETS/INFO:** 609-884-7277 **ACCOMMO-DATIONS/TOURIST INFO:** 609-884-5508, 609-465-7181

PINES HOTEL IRISH TRADITIONAL MUSIC WEEKEND

SOUTH FALLSBURG ✷ THIRD WEEKEND IN FEBRUARY

This new winter festival features six stages of traditional Irish music within the snug confines of a 500-room hotel nestled in the mountains. In addition to the more than 100 performers who make up 12 traditional acts, attractions include Irish food, beverages, and excellent accommodations. Plus, there's plenty of great alpine skiing within 10 minutes of the hotel. **LOCATION:** Pines Hotel in South Fallsburg. From Middletown, take Highway 17 about 30 miles to Highway 42, then go north about eight miles and follow signs to the resort. **TICKETS/INFO:** 800-367-4637, 518-943-3736 **ACCOMMO-DATIONS/TOURIST INFO:** 800-367-4637, 800-882-2287

BLUEGRASS WITH CLASS

SOUTH FALLSBURG ✷ THIRD WEEKEND IN MARCH, THURSDAY–SUNDAY

Anyone snobby enough to detect an oxymoron in this festival's title probably wouldn't be interested in seeing the top names in bluegrass music in the posh ambience of a five-star resort hotel. Each year, 18 acts (which have included Jim & Jesse, the Del McCoury Band, and Southern Rail) converge on the Pines Hotel for a four-day weekend of music in the 1,600-seat ballroom. Nearly the entire audience stays at the hotel, taking advantage of concert/meal/room packages that start at about $290 per person. **LOCATION:** Pines Hotel in South Fallsburg. From Middletown take Highway 17 about 30 miles to Highway 42, then go north about eight miles and follow the signs to the resort. **TICKETS/INFO:** 607-363-2211, 914-434-6000 **ACCOMMODATIONS/TOUR-IST INFO:** 914-434-6000, 800-882-2287

INDEPENDENT MUSIC FEST

NEW YORK CITY ✷ LAST WEEKEND IN MARCH

Run by students on New York University's Program Board, the Independent Music Fest was the first music conference designed to highlight only independent labels and unsigned bands. Industry panels, exhibitions, and record fairs provide daytime diversion, while showcases give unknown bands from across the continent a chance to be heard and critiqued by indie-label representatives and you. Venues include the university's student center and 15 clubs in downtown New York. Admission is $35 for a three-day pass, $15 for students.   **LOCATION:** New York University's Loeb Student Center in Greenwich Village and other nearby locations **TICKETS/INFO:** 212-998-4987; e-mail: programboard@nyu.edu **ACCOMMODATIONS/TOURIST INFO:** 212-484-1250

*L*ONG ISLAND MOZART FESTIVAL
OYSTER BAY ✷ MEMORIAL DAY WEEKEND AND THE FOLLOWING WEEKEND (MEMORIAL DAY IS THE LAST MONDAY IN MAY)

In its quest to preserve the Viennese classical tradition, the Long Island Mozart Festival's repertory usually stretches well beyond the familiar strains of Mozart to interesting and unusual works by his contemporaries. Each year, 10 outdoor concerts balance classical "hits" with works that are interesting but rarely performed.

Distinguished artists play in the historic Hay Barn courtyard, in the middle of a 400-acre arboretum ranking among the East's finest. This decidedly populist festival encourages casual attire and includes features like readings, lectures, and films, plus a café, wine tent, and arts and crafts fair. Tickets start at $18.   **LOCATION:** Planting Fields Arboretum State Historic Park, Oyster Bay, on Long Island's northern shore **TICKETS/INFO:** 516-671-6263 **ACCOMMODATIONS/TOURIST INFO:** 516-794-4222, 516-951-3440

*B*ANG ON A CAN FESTIVAL
NEW YORK CITY ✷ ONE WEEK IN LATE MAY OR EARLY JUNE

At this gathering of the world's preeminent new-music composers and performers, consciousness-altering music is the name of the game. Postminimalist extravagance rules as performers stomp about on stage with their eyes closed or play anything from two pianos to a dozen boom boxes. You may hear a stunning string quartet, a soprano imitation of an airheaded disc jockey, or long stretches of silence.

The Bang on a Can Festival is by far the nation's most extravagant large-scale celebration of new music and probably the best place on the continent to get a sampling of the true cutting edge. It was founded in Lower Manhattan in 1987 by three Yale-educated composers who wanted to bring adventurous new music from around the world to New York. They invited young, innovative composers from nearby as well as from places as far-flung as Holland, Japan, and Russia. Their antics began attracting attention (and crowds) immediately, although the festival moved all around Manhattan before finding a permanent (for now) home at Lincoln Center.

The venue's imposing confines have done nothing to dull the spirit of Bang on a Can. Among the performers, you'll find a strong sense of classical music history, as well as a strong desire to break free of its conventions. Over six days—which always conclude with an eight-hour marathon of some 20 composers and 100 performers—it's impossible to say what will happen. In fact, any expectations at all are typically wiped away in a blur of potent, provocative music.   **LOCATION:** Main concerts in Lincoln Center's Alice Tully Hall in Manhattan; other events in various downtown galleries and clubs **TICKETS/INFO:** 212-777-8442; e-mail: BangCan@aol.com **ACCOMMODATIONS/TOURIST INFO:** 212-484-1250

The Bang on a Can All-Stars bring potent, provocative sounds to the nation's most extravagant celebration of experimental music. (See entry, page 61.)

Courtesy of Peter Serling/Bang on a Can

SYRACUSE JAZZ FEST
SYRACUSE ✸ FIRST WEEKEND IN JUNE, FRIDAY–SUNDAY

Young lions meet the legends of jazz at the largest free jazz festival in the northeastern United States. About two dozen groups—most of whom are national and international talents—play on three stages among the trees and fountains of Syracuse's downtown park area. Over three days, expect to hear jazz of all types, from vocal to instrumental, bop to big band, Dixieland to avant-garde. Organizers present legendary jazz masters to demonstrate where the art form of jazz has come, and innovative up-and-comers to demonstrate where it's going. About 50,000 people attend the Syracuse Jazz Fest's free concerts, and many take advantage of free workshops, clinics, jam sessions, and noon performances over the three days.   **LOCATION:** Clinton Square in downtown Syracuse **TICKETS/INFO:** 315-437-5627 **ACCOMMODATIONS/TOURIST INFO:** 315-470-1900, 800-234-4797

THOUSAND ISLANDS BLUEGRASS FESTIVAL
CLAYTON ✸ FIRST WEEKEND IN JUNE, FRIDAY–SUNDAY

Just south of the Canadian border, the rolling hills along the shore of the St. Lawrence River resound with bluegrass in early June. Several bands of local, regional, and national renown present concerts and workshops to about a thousand bluegrass lovers, and campground picking lasts late into the night. Admission is $10 to $15, and RV hookups are available.   **LOCATION:** Capt. Clayton's Campgrounds, on Route 12 three miles east of Clayton and five miles west of I-81 **TICKETS/INFO:** 315-686-5385 **ACCOMMODATIONS/TOURIST INFO:** 800-252-9806, 315-686-3771

ROCHESTER IRISH FESTIVAL

GATES/ROCHESTER ✷ SECOND WEEKEND IN JUNE, SATURDAY AND SUNDAY

The sounds of the harp, fiddle, tin whistle, accordion, flute, and bodhrán emanate nonstop from this festival's main stage, but for those who would like to become more involved, workshops are scheduled for hands-on instruction in Irish instruments, dance, and language. Look for traditional dance performances, cultural organizations, food, and a children's area complete with crafts, storytellers, and magicians (so kids don't get bored while their parents listen to the great music). One corner of the site is reserved for impromptu jam sessions by traditional musicians, most of whom stick around until each day's end for a musicians' ensemble and dance. The entrance fee is $5 for adults and $3 for children, with a family maximum of $15. **LOCATION:** Festival grounds adjacent to Gates Memorial Park in Gates, just outside Rochester. From I-90 take exit 46 and go north on Route 390, then west on Lyell Road for one-half mile. **TICKETS/INFO:** 716-234-3746, 716-482-2843; e-mail: jrosenbe@ix.netcom.com **ACCOMMODATIONS/ TOURIST INFO:** 716-454-2220, 800-677-7282

CLEARWATER'S GREAT HUDSON RIVER REVIVAL

VALHALLA ✷ FATHER'S DAY WEEKEND, SATURDAY AND SUNDAY (FATHER'S DAY IS THE THIRD SUNDAY IN JUNE)

This event is the brainchild of rebel-with-a-cause Pete Seeger, who, nearly 30 years ago, wanted to find a way to educate people about the serious pollution problems facing the Hudson River. Together with some friends, the folksinger and songwriter organized an afternoon of music that raised money for educational projects, including the construction of a 106-foot replica of the Hudson River sloop *Clearwater.*

The *Clearwater*'s voyages raised awareness of the plight of the Hudson, which is now much cleaner. And the modest afternoon of music has grown into a two-day event with more than 60 musicians performing on seven stages. As you might expect, there's plenty of nostalgic singer-songwriter folk here, but the festival also branches out into new folk and traditional American music like gospel, bluegrass, blues, and Native American songs. Environmental groups sponsor exhibits, and other features include children's areas, food, juried crafts, and roving entertainers. In addition, this is one of the few outdoor events that goes the extra mile for people with disabilities, with fully accessible performance areas, braille maps, and a sign language interpreter on every stage. Tickets are about $29 for the weekend (at the gate), and advance-purchase and other deals are available. **LOCATION:** Westchester Community College in Valhalla, just northeast of White Plains, off I-64 **TICKETS/INFO:** 914-454-7673, 914-677-5667 **ACCOMMODATIONS/TOURIST INFO:** 914-948-0047, 800-833-9282

WHAT IS JAZZ? FESTIVAL

NEW YORK CITY ✷ LAST TWO WEEKS IN JUNE

What Is Jazz? was created by the Knitting Factory's Michael Dorf in 1987 as a "supplement" to the JVC Jazz Festival, which runs almost concurrently and has long been regarded as the venerable king of the New York jazz summer. But these days, What Is Jazz? is beginning to look more like a contender for JVC's throne.

The contrasts between JVC and What is Jazz? could hardly be more dramatic. JVC's shows at old-guard venues like Lincoln Center and Carnegie Hall draw a mostly older audience and cost up to $60 per concert, even though they are sponsored by major jazz labels. What Is Jazz? is headquartered at Dorf's Knitting Factory, a vibrant, community-based outlet for new music located in the heart of Manhattan's Tribeca neighborhood. The club has three stages, and for one affordable ticket ($15-$22) you can glimpse nine different performances each evening, moving from room to intimate room while rubbing elbows with a young audience eager to check out new sounds in jazz and related music.

What Is Jazz? presents a sprawling roster of more than 100 acts, many of which push the limits of the art form and offer new answers to the question posed by the festival's name. Performers come from New York and all over the world, and the schedule is rich with European improvisers, Latin American percussionists, and talent drawn from the Russian mainstream and the Japanese cutting edge. A relationship with Holland's sprawling North Sea Jazz Festival and other worldwide events ensures a healthy talent pool in which well-known headliners are mixed and matched with underexposed talent.

With music in all corners of the club, the relaxed atmosphere encourages experimentation and adaptation, which often move along interesting tangents. Expect to experience poetry and other spoken-word forms, visual arts, and movement—sometimes all in one show. The Knitting Factory's nine shows each night are augmented by additional shows—many of them free—at City Hall Park, Washington Square Park, Central Park, Battery Park, and other locations.   **LOCATION:** The Knitting Factory, at 74 Leonard Street (four blocks south of Canal Street between Church Street and Broadway) in Manhattan's Tribeca neighborhood, and other locations around New York City **TICKETS/INFO:** 212-219-3006; e-mail: kf@knittingfactory.com; World Wide Web: http://www.knittingfactory.com/ **ACCOMMODATIONS/TOURIST INFO:** 212-484-1250

*M*OHONK'S MUSIC WEEK
NEW PALTZ ✷ LAST WEEK IN JUNE

Mohonk's Music Week presents a range of musical styles that leans heavily toward classical but includes just about everything except rock 'n' roll. The week includes concerts, open rehearsals, and lectures, all at the Victorian, castlelike Mohonk Mountain House, on a hill overlooking Lake Mohonk. Recent guests have included Peter Schickele, David Amram, the Leontovych String Quartet, and the Woodstock Chamber Orchestra. **LOCATION:** Mohonk Mountain House, on Lake Mohonk in New Paltz. From New York State Thruway (I-87) take exit 18, turn left at the stoplight onto Route 299 west and follow it two miles until you cross a small green bridge. Turn right after the bridge onto Mountain Rest Road and follow the signs. **TICKETS/INFO:** 800-772-6646 **ACCOMMODATIONS/TOURIST INFO:** 800-772-6646, 914-452-4910

*N*EWPORT JAZZ FESTIVAL AT SARATOGA
SARATOGA SPRINGS ✷ LAST WEEKEND IN JUNE, SATURDAY AND SUNDAY

Saratoga's Newport Jazz Festival brings regional and national stars to the Saratoga Performing Arts Center for two noon-to-midnight shows. About 30 mainstream jazz and pop/jazz acts appear over the two days, drawing family-oriented crowds of about 15,000 each day. Tickets are about $40 for reserved seats and $26 for lawn seating, and an arts and crafts fair runs concurrently.   **LOCATION:** Saratoga Performing Arts Center, in Saratoga Springs **TICKETS/INFO:** 518-587-8330 **ACCOMMODATIONS/TOURIST INFO:** 518-584-3255

⚙LD SONGS FESTIVAL OF TRADITIONAL MUSIC AND DANCE

ALTAMONT ✸ LAST FULL WEEKEND IN JUNE, FRIDAY–SUNDAY

If traditional music from North America and Europe is your cup of coffee, you'll be hard-pressed to find any eastern event that offers more variety and spirit than Old Songs. The festival isn't huge—a good year draws 6,000 or so—but it is immaculately produced and endowed with an atmosphere of celebration and discovery.

More than 20 individual and group acts from New York, New England, eastern Canada, and farther afield perform over three days. Expect to hear anything from Irish reels to old Appalachian harmonies to French Canadian fiddle tunes. In addition to Friday and Saturday evening headliner concerts, miniconcerts, dances, and workshops are held in eight different areas with titles like "Regional Traditions," "Potpourri at the Dutch Barn," and "Learn How!" In fact, participatory activities are the glue that holds Old Songs together, and promoters urge everyone to bring their voices and instruments.

. . .Or their dancing shoes, since an area titled "Participatory Dancing" features performance and instruction in styles that, depending on the year, might include contra, flamenco, or Cajun.

For families and kids, a family performance area features storytelling, hands-on crafts, and even lullabies in the evening. Juried crafts, food, and camping are available, and admission ranges from $15 to $25.   **LOCATION:** Altamont Fairgrounds, about 20 miles west of Albany. From the New York Thruway take exit 24 to U.S. 20 west, then Route 146 south to Altamont. **TICKETS/INFO:** 518-765-2815; e-mail: fennig@aol.com **ACCOMMODATIONS/TOURIST INFO:** 800-258-3582, 518-434-1217 ext. 301, 518-372-5656

♩VC JAZZ FESTIVAL—NEW YORK

NEW YORK CITY ✸ TEN DAYS IN LATE JUNE AND EARLY JULY

For as long as many New Yorkers can remember, late June and early July have meant that wherever you turn in New York City, there's jazz. The JVC (formerly Kool, formerly Newport) Jazz Festival pumps New York full of more jazz than one person could possibly consume, with some 40 concerts over 10 days.

Over the years and through its various incarnations, this festival has provoked ambivalent feelings—controversy, boredom, ecstasy—but recent years have seen it move toward big-name bookings and prestigious venues like Carnegie Hall and Lincoln Center. The problem is that few of today's living jazz stars can sell out such venues, so organizers increasingly have turned to performers like Ray Charles and Celia Cruz (who are undeniably great, but not really jazz).

Under pressure from the younger, scrappier What Is Jazz? festival, which runs almost concurrently, JVC has recently taken steps to alternate its old-guard acts with more adventurous up-and-comers. In addition, JVC spices its venue menu with concerts in citywide clubs and the well-maintained Bryant Park. Admission ranges from free to $65.   **LOCATION:** Carnegie Hall, Avery Fisher Hall, Bryant Park, and various clubs throughout New York City **TICKETS/INFO:** 212-510-1390, 212-878-2020; e-mail: CMPRNews@aol.com **ACCOMMODATIONS/TOURIST INFO:** 212-397-8200, 212-484-1250

JVC Jazz Festival: Jazz giants like Milt Hinton shake up the New York City summer. (See entry, page 65.)

Malcolm Clarke/AP/Wide World

℃ARAMOOR MUSIC FESTIVAL

KATONAH ✸ LATE JUNE THROUGH MID-AUGUST, THURSDAY–SUNDAY EVENINGS

For more then 20 years, New Yorkers looking for a romantic summertime breakaway have made the drive out to Caramoor, winding along a beautiful country road and arriving at the Mediterranean-style estate of the late Walter and Lucie Rosen. There, under the direction of André Previn, some of the best musicians of our time perform the compositions of ageless masters and modern-day innovators.

An open-air theater seats 1,500 and has a large stage that can accommodate the Symphony Orchestra of St. Luke's, or a grand opera. The theater sits at the front end of a sunken, formal garden and is built around marble Greek and Roman columns salvaged from a 15th-century villa in Italy. The estate's Spanish Courtyard, a romantic, open-air space for 550 that's surrounded by Caramoor House, hosts solo recitals and concerts by the St. Luke's Chamber Ensemble.

Metro New York's largest and most aristocratic outdoor music festival is just an hour north of Midtown Manhattan, in the northeast corner of Westchester County.

LOCATION: Caramoor Center for Music and the Arts, in Katonah, in the northeast corner of Westchester County just off I-684 TICKETS/INFO: 914-232-1252; e-mail: CMPRNews@aol.com ACCOMMODATIONS/TOURIST INFO: 914-232-2668, 212-397-8200

⌐ⒶDIRONDACK FESTIVAL OF AMERICAN MUSIC

SARANAC LAKE ✱ THROUGHOUT JULY

A lakeside town in the heart of the Adirondack Mountains makes the hills come alive each July with the sounds of American classical and choral music. Since 1973, the Adirondack Festival has presented only American works in concerts and workshops at seven area churches and theaters. The festival's performing ensembles include the 21-member Adirondack Chamber Orchestra, the Gregg Smith Singers, and 60 choristers. Additional guest performers present cabaret acts and chamber music.   LOCATION: Various stages in Saranac Lake, 150 miles north of Albany off I-87 TICKETS/INFO: 212-874-2990, 518-891-1057 ACCOMMODATIONS/TOURIST INFO: 800-347-1992

ⒼLIMMERGLASS OPERA

COOPERSTOWN ✱ THROUGHOUT JULY AND AUGUST

In a pastoral setting on the shores of Otsego Lake, Glimmerglass Opera brings a sense of discovery and excitement to both familiar and rarely performed works. Riding a crest of critical and popular acclaim, the opera recently extended its season to eight weeks, with four productions each year. Recent productions have ranged from Cavalli's 17th-century masterpiece La Calisto to Jack Beeson's neglected 20th-century work Lizzie Borden.

Built in 1987, the Alice Busch Opera Theater stands in harmony with the setting's nearby trees and lakeshore. No seat is more than 70 feet from the stage, and the side walls slide back to reveal the natural beauty of the surroundings and to let fresh air circulate before the show and during intermissions.

It was in the first half of the 19th century that James Fenimore Cooper, inspired by Otsego Lake, dubbed it "Glimmerglass" in his fictional Leatherstocking Tales. Since Glimmerglass Opera's opening in 1975, its sense of history has gone hand in hand with its fully up-to-date quest for artistic excellence. Time magazine has hailed Glimmerglass for presenting "opera on a level of taste, imagination, and musicality that would do any of the world's most celebrated opera houses proud."   LOCATION: On Route 80, eight miles north of Cooperstown, on the shores of Otsego Lake TICKETS/INFO: 607-547-2255 ACCOMMODATIONS/TOURIST INFO: 607-547-9983, 607-432-4500, 800-843-3394

ⒽONEST BROOK CHAMBER MUSIC FESTIVAL

MEREDITH ✱ JULY AND AUGUST, SATURDAY AND SUNDAY EVENINGS

Honest Brook's unique classical series is held in a (thoroughly) cleaned and preserved dairy barn in upstate New York. Nationally and internationally known musicians play a repertoire that ranges from chamber and choral concerts to vocal and instrumental recitals. Recent performers have included soprano Camellia Johnson and pianists Veda Zuponsic and Michael Cannon.   LOCATION: Honest Brook Road, off Route 28 between Delhi and Mendale, in Delaware County TICKETS/INFO: 607-746-3770 ACCOMMODATIONS/TOURIST INFO: 607-746-2281, 800-642-4443

Taste, imagination, and musicality: Glimmerglass Opera features classic works like Monteverdi's L'Incoronazione di Poppea *(Dana Hanchard, David Daniels, and Marguerite Krull are shown in a 1994 production). (See entry, page 67.)* Courtesy of Rose Mackiewicz/Glimmerglass Opera

◌̈INTERNATIONAL AFRICAN ARTS FESTIVAL

BROOKLYN ✸ FIVE DAYS SURROUNDING AND INCLUDING JULY 4 (INDEPENDENCE DAY)

Brooklyn bubbles over with traditional African, jazz, blues, R&B, reggae, Caribbean, Brazilian, and other music of the African diaspora during the tristate region's largest festival of African culture. Over five days, some 100,000 people turn out to hear stars like Sugar Minot, the Last Poets, Charles Earland, and the Great Divas of Gospel, who perform on three stages set up on a crowded athletic field. Various corners of the site resemble villages in different African countries—complete with authentic music, food, crafts, and living-history exhibits. There's also theater, dance, and lots of stuff for kids. Admission is about $7 for adults.   **LOCATION:** Boys and Girls High School, 1700 Fulton Street (between Utica and Schenectady Avenues), Brooklyn **TICKETS/ INFO:** 718-638-6700; e-mail: CMPRNews@aol.com **ACCOMMODATIONS/TOURIST INFO:** 212-397-8200, 212-484-1250

⚙️LD IRELAND TRADITIONAL MUSIC FESTIVAL
LEEDS ✸ WEEKEND CLOSEST TO JULY 4

In parts of the Catskill Mountains, you'd be forgiven for imagining you were on the Emerald Isle—especially if you were to wander into Leeds during the town's Old Ireland Traditional Music Festival. Set up to resemble an Irish *fleadh ceoil* (party overflowing with traditional music), this weekend celebration brings in six to eight well-known musical acts—some of whom travel all the way from Ireland—and dozens of lesser-known musicians for an orgy of music, merrymaking, and hands-on music workshops. **LOCATION:** Main Street in Leeds, just west of exit 21 on the New York Thruway (I-87), about 35 miles south of Albany **TICKETS/INFO:** 518-943-3736 **ACCOMMODATIONS/ TOURIST INFO:** 518-943-3223, 800-542-2414

🎻EL-SE-NANGO FIDDLE & BLUEGRASS FESTIVAL
MCDONOUGH ✸ FIRST SUNDAY FOLLOWING JULY 4

McDonough is a tiny town with a general store, one large colonial home, a few smaller homes, and chickens running across the road. Its Del-Se-Nango Fiddle & Bluegrass Festival features live old-time music and bluegrass and encourages families to participate in and learn about traditional music and different styles of traditional dancing. Children and adults can learn square dancing and Appalachian clogging (a fast-foot shuffle done to fiddle music) on a nice hardwood floor with about 250 local music lovers. The town itself is worth a visit, with its explicitly rural flavor and its general store, which is truly "general," with everything from food to plumbing supplies. Admission to the festival is about $5.   **LOCATION:** Del-Se-Nango Music Haven, in McDonough, about 30 miles from Binghamton. From Route 12 in Oxford take Route 220 west for 10 miles. **TICKETS/INFO:** 607-847-8501 **ACCOMMODATIONS/TOURIST INFO:** 800-836-6740, 607-772-8860, 607-334-1401

🎵STON MAGNA FESTIVAL
ANNANDALE-ON-HUDSON ✸ MID-JULY THROUGH FIRST WEEK IN AUGUST, FRIDAYS

Started in 1972 by Lee Elman and harpsichordist Albert Fuller, the Aston Magna Foundation for Music gathers musicians, scholars, and instrument makers to play and promote the music of the 17th and 18th centuries. Aston Magna brings its music to Bard College five Fridays each summer for early-music concerts using period instruments and authentic musical techniques. (See also: Aston Magna Festival, Great Barrington, Massachusetts.)   **LOCATION:** Bard College, in Annandale-on-Hudson. From the Taconic State Parkway take the Red Hook/Route 199 exit, drive west on Route 199 through the village of Red Hook to Route 9G, turn right onto Route 9G, and drive north 1.6 miles. **TICKETS/INFO:** 914-758-7425, 413-528-3595 **ACCOMMODATIONS/TOURIST INFO:** 914-463-4000, 914-876-4778

🎼AROQUE FESTIVAL
GREENFIELD CENTER AND SARATOGA SPRINGS ✸ MID-JULY THROUGH EARLY AUGUST

Baroque music lovers will find plenty to like in the concerts and collateral events at this wide-ranging festival of baroque music and dance—the first of its kind in the United

States when it was established in 1959. In an ultra-intimate 110-seat hall just outside Saratoga Springs, musicians play period instruments like the violin, flute, lute, harpsichord, and viola da gamba. In addition to baroque-era compositions, the program often includes newly composed music for baroque instruments. Also featured are baroque dancers, workshops in early brass, and a Leipzig Coffee House, modeled on the celebrated café where Bach regularly performed his chamber music.   **LOCATION:** Baroque Festival Studio, 165 Wilton Road, in Greenfield Center, about six miles outside Saratoga Springs. One concert is held at Skidmore College in Saratoga Springs. **TICKETS/INFO:** 518-893-7527 **ACCOMMODATIONS/TOURIST INFO:** 518-584-3255

MOSTLY MOZART FESTIVAL
NEW YORK CITY ★ MID-JULY THROUGH LATE AUGUST

New York's trend-setting Mostly Mozart Festival began in 1966 and has grown to become one of the city's biggest and best summer musical events. The Lincoln Center stage hosts a stellar roster of artists, with recent appearances by violinist Itzhak Perlman, pianist André Watts, and soprano June Anderson, each performing with the festival orchestra. The festival also has featured extraordinary ensembles like Canadian Brass, the Tokyo Quartet, and France's baroque vocal/instrumental ensemble Les Arts Florissants.

In addition to bringing scores of deserving new artists to the front rank of the musical world, Mostly Mozart has been a leader in the large-scale use of period instruments and has pioneered presentations of early Mozart operas in concert form. Concerts are held in Lincoln Center's Avery Fisher Hall, and many evenings feature preconcert recitals by the evening's soloists.   **LOCATION:** Avery Fisher Hall at Lincoln Center in Manhattan **TICKETS/INFO:** 212-721-6500 **ACCOMMODATIONS/TOURIST INFO:** 212-484-1250

MACINTOSH NEW YORK MUSIC FESTIVAL
NEW YORK CITY AND CYBERSPACE ★ THIRD WEEK IN JULY

In the vacuum left by the sloppy demise of the New Music Seminar, the owners of the Knitting Factory and Irving Place banded together with 13 other New York City clubs in 1995 to create a new festival to fill the mid-summer void. The MacIntosh New York Music Festival continues the seminar's goal of putting deserving new bands in front of a talent-hungry music industry. Its more expansive goal, though, is to explore the impact of technology on live entertainment by creating an interactive union between music and computers.

Gone are the New Music Seminar's cumbersome industry panels; gone are its unpaid bands and employees. In their place are electronic kiosks, a massive Internet presence, and very conspicuous support from Apple Computer. More than 350 untested (and mostly low-tech) bands are joined by big-name trailblazers of the interactive music scene, like Todd Rundgren, Laurie Anderson, the Residents, and Jaron Lanier. Some of these performers use computers and video screens in their sets, some demonstrate CD-ROMs they've developed, others integrate live music with computer technology.

Each of the participating clubs—the Knitting Factory, Irving Place, CBGB, S.O.B.'s, the Mercury Lounge, the Fez, and many more—has MacIntosh interactive kiosks on-site, which are linked to the festival's World Wide Web server. Although the execution often doesn't live up to expectations, the idea is that festivalgoers can manipulate the kiosks to find out what's going on at other festival sites, thus getting the information needed to decide whether to stay or go.

Quick-time camera operators send video images and digital snapshots that capture the performers and club ambience, and every 15 minutes in-club "reporters" upload fresh text (which can range from dramatic performance descriptions to messages like "I am VERY DRUNK"). Plus, web browsers worldwide can get much the same thing by clicking to the festival's various web pages. Organizers claim a half-million such "hits" per night of the festival and want to expand it to include clubs in different cities (e.g., Tokyo, London), all connected via modem and presenting music around the clock.

In the festival's first year (1995), these ambitious technical endeavors were not without their glitches. Cynics took note of the sponsor's omnipresent marketing materials and wondered why anyone would want to go out to the clubs if they could experience the music "virtually." And the music itself? Well, future festivals promise more than the first year's hastily thrown together roster of mostly local alternative rock bands augmented by the occasional big-name act and a few truly buzz-worthy newcomers.

Most telling of all is that, amid all the high-tech hopes and dreams, the vast majority of the festival's performers still use nothing more than guitar, drum, and voice—rock 'n' roll's essential tools since the 1950s. And most fans still want to actually *be there* when their favorite rocker dives into the crowd. Now *that's* interactive.   **LOCATION:** Fifteen clubs in New York City **TICKETS/INFO:** 212-777-6800; World Wide Web: http://www.sonicnet.com/festival/ **ACCOMMODATIONS/TOURIST INFO:** 212-484-1250

*F*INGER LAKES GRASSROOTS FESTIVAL OF MUSIC AND DANCE

TRUMANSBURG ✷ THIRD WEEKEND IN JULY, THURSDAY–SUNDAY

With four days and nights of the best African, Cajun, zydeco, old-time Appalachian, alternative rock, and more, the Finger Lakes Grassroots Festival is a stroke of genius that seems tailor-made to make new-breed eclectics think they've died and gone to heaven. The event was conceived and established by, and is produced and hosted by, the Ithaca-based band Donna the Buffalo, and it's managed to maintain a volunteer-based, grassroots feel while pulling in the top rank of musicians from several genres.

Performances are held on four stages and have included the South African reggae of Lucky Dube, the honest country of Jimmy Dale Gilmore, the Zimbabwean struggle-pop of Thomas Mapfumo, and the up-tempo marches of the Rebirth Brass Band. The laid-back, "dance-til-dawn" mentality typically draws thousands, who pay about $45 at the gate (less in advance) for the weekend of music.   **LOCATION:** Trumansburg Fairgrounds, on Route 96, 10 miles north of Ithaca on the west side of Cayuga Lake **TICKETS/INFO:** 607-387-5098 **ACCOMMODATIONS/TOURIST INFO:** 800-264-8422, 607-535-4300, 315-539-5655

*L*AKE GEORGE OPERA FESTIVAL

QUEENSBURY ✷ THIRD WEEKEND IN JULY THROUGH SECOND WEEKEND IN AUGUST

If you like the idea of opera but can't quite get around that language barrier, take note: these operas are performed in English. The Lake George Opera Festival has been known as a training ground for budding young American singers, helping them gain the performance skills necessary to move on to bigger stages. Expect dependably good, and at times outstanding, performances from singers as well as from the 37-member orchestra. Festival organizers take pride in presenting neglected masterpieces that are rarely seen on American stages, and recent years have featured the likes of Menotti's *The Old Maid and the Thief*, Puccini's *Gianni Schicchi*, and Massenet's *Cinderella*. The main venue is the 875-seat Queensbury High School Auditorium, but an accompanying chamber music program makes use of local churches and museums.   **LOCATION:** Queensbury High School Auditorium. From the Adirondack Northway (I-87) take exit 19 and go west one-quarter mile. **TICKETS/INFO:** 518-793-3859 **ACCOMMODA-TIONS/TOURIST INFO:** 518-761-6366, 800-365-1050

PEACEFUL VALLEY BLUEGRASS FESTIVAL
SHINHOPPLE ✹ THIRD WEEKEND IN JULY, THURSDAY–SUNDAY

In the midst of Peaceful Valley's world-class trout fishing, traditional bluegrass and southern gospel music permeate the Catskill mountain air. The 20-band lineup tends toward the spiritual and down-homey rather than the cutting edge (with the Lewis Family among the recent musical guests), and some 10,000 people turn out to enjoy the music in an alcohol-free environment. Delaware River fishing, canoeing, and hiking opportunities are nearby.   **LOCATION:** Peaceful Valley Campsite. From Middletown take Highway 17 to Highway 30/206 and go north eight miles along the river; follow the signs to the campsite. **TICKETS/INFO:** 607-363-2211 **ACCOMMODATIONS/TOUR-IST INFO:** 607-363-2211, 914-294-5151 ext. 1647, 800-762-8687

WINTERHAWK BLUEGRASS FESTIVAL
ANCRAMDALE ✹ THIRD WEEKEND IN JULY, THURSDAY–SUNDAY

Among the Northeast's many bluegrass festivals, Winterhawk is legendary. This four-day gathering features amazing music, deft organization, a spectacular location, and great children's programs. If you love bluegrass, Winterhawk is a sure bet any year.

Just two and one-half hours from either Boston or New York, the event attracts lots of city folks with hillbilly hearts. One reason is the lineup. On any given year, Winter-hawk skims the best acts off the top of both the traditional and contemporary bluegrass heaps and serves them up, one after another, for its audience of about 6,000. Imagine seeing Doc Watson, Alison Krauss, Ralph Stanley, Del McCoury, the Cox Family, and the Nashville Bluegrass Band, all in one year. It's happened here.

The festival is set on the Rothvoss farm in the Berkshire foothills. Views are magnificent, and you can actually camp on a hill in sight of the stage. (Note that many people bring two sets of lawn chairs—one for the campsite and one to save a place in front of the stage.) Food, water, hot showers, and ice are available on-site.

Although pets aren't welcome (that's the only restriction), kids certainly are. In fact, Winterhawk prides itself as "the Bluegrass Family Festival," and organizers go all out to make the festival family-friendly. A children's tent features a full schedule of special concerts and creative activities, and teen programs attempt to keep adolescent angst in check. Other features include band contests, music workshops, square dances, and a scholarship program. Admission is $75 for four days (including camping), and a variety of one-day and early-bird prices are available.   **LOCATION:** Rothvoss farm, off Route 22 between Hillsdale and Millerton, just east of Ancramdale, near the New York/Massachusetts/Connecticut border **TICKETS/INFO:** 518-390-6211; e-mail: mgdoub@aol.com **ACCOMMODATIONS/TOURIST INFO:** 518-828-3375, 800-724-1846

Winterhawk Bluegrass Festival: Big-name bands and late-night jams. Courtesy of
Brad Glass/Winterhawk Bluegrass Festival

ᴊ̈RISH TRADITIONAL MUSIC FESTIVAL
EAST DURHAM ✷ THIRD SATURDAY IN JULY

Supported by the National Endowment for the Arts, the Irish Traditional Music Festival features the folk songs, dance, and historic narratives of the Emerald Isle. This is one of North America's best opportunities to experience outstanding talent like Altan, Trian, and Joe Derrane. In addition to dozens of performers from Ireland and Northern Ireland, expect to see many Irish-American acts who admirably carry on old-world traditions.

Four tented stage areas include the main stage, dance stage, acoustic stage, and children's stage. The festival is preceded by the Catskills Irish Arts Week, a week of music and dance workshops and pub sessions with master artists from Ireland and the United States. Admission is about $12 at the door. **LOCATION:** Irish Cultural Centre Festival Grounds, on Route 145 in East Durham. From New York City take I-87 to exit 21 (Catskill) and follow the signs to Durham. **TICKETS/INFO:** 800-434-3378 **ACCOM-MODATIONS/TOURIST INFO:** 800-355-2287

⚙LD-TIME MUSIC FESTIVAL
ORLEANS ✷ THIRD SUNDAY IN JULY

Held at a centuries-old farm that now houses the Agricultural Museum in rural Orleans, this festival is a great place to experience old-time country, traditional, and folk music. About 60 musicians come from rural corners of the surrounding three counties, forming 15 to 20 bands. The festival serves as a fund-raiser for the Agricultural Museum, which houses historical agricultural tools, clothing, and other objects used during the early settler years of America. Several historical buildings include a cheese factory and an original one-room schoolhouse. Attendance averages around 400, and admission is about $2 per person.   **LOCATION:** The Agricultural Museum in Orleans, near Watertown. From Syracuse take I-81north to Watertown, then Route 12 north about 10 miles to Gunn Corners and turn right toward the Agricultural Museum (about two miles up the road). **TICKETS/INFO:** 315-788-2882 **ACCOMMODATIONS/TOURIST INFO:** 315-349-8322, 800-248-4386

ℱALCON RIDGE FOLK FESTIVAL
HILLSDALE ✸ FOURTH WEEKEND IN JULY, FRIDAY–SUNDAY

More community than concert event, Falcon Ridge brings folk-circuit favorites, newcomers, and nonstop dancing to the rolling fields and wooded hills at the foot of the Berkshires. Headliners run the gamut of singer-songwriters like Ani DiFranco, Patty Larkin, and John Gorka, while Afro-Brazilian percussion ensembles and other acts join the party from the far corners of the globe.

The event gets going Friday night with the New Artists Showcase, featuring 10-minute sets by 28 acts (selected from more than 250 entrants). The main stage is complemented by a workshop stage featuring programs like "The Songwriting Process," "Traditional Stringed Instruments," and "Folkies on the Internet." At the dance stage, you can learn Cajun, contra, swing, and African dances, then practice your new moves during all-day-and-into-the-night dances.

A family stage features storytelling and crafts for the kids, and in keeping with the family-friendly mood, no "open containers" are allowed on the grounds. For an outdoor festival, Falcon Ridge has made phenomenal strides in making the grounds fully accessible to people with disabilities, and many events are interpreted in sign language. Weekend tickets are $45 to $55.   **LOCATION:** Long Hill Farm in Hillsdale, on Route 23 just west of Route 22, about six miles east of the Taconic State Parkway near the tristate corner of New York, Massachusetts, and Connecticut **TICKETS/INFO:** 860-364-0366; e-mail: FalcRidge@aol.com **ACCOMMODATIONS/TOURIST INFO:** 860-364-0366

𝒮ARATOGA CHAMBER MUSIC FESTIVAL
SARATOGA SPRINGS ✸ LAST WEEK IN JULY THROUGH SECOND WEEK IN AUGUST

Tucked midway into the Saratoga Performing Arts Center's comprehensive summer schedule of ballet, opera, jazz, and orchestral and pop music, the Saratoga Chamber Music Festival brings six chamber performances to the town once known as "America's Greatest Spa." Recent years have featured provocative programming like "Music Banned by the Third Reich," which featured a commissioned work by Berthold Goldschmidt, and performances of Hindemith's sprawling *Kammermusik* by Yo Yo Ma and others. The Chamber Music Festival is usually held during the Philadelphia Orchestra's residence at Saratoga, so visiting music lovers can catch symphonic performances on nights when the chamber program is idle.   **LOCATION:** Most performances take place in the Spa Little Theater in Saratoga Springs. **TICKETS/INFO:** 518-587-3330, 518-584-9330 **ACCOM-MODATIONS/TOURIST INFO:** 518-584-3255

WORLD FOLK MUSIC FESTIVAL

CORNING ✹ LAST WEEKEND IN JULY, THURSDAY–SUNDAY

Authentic traditional musicians from around the world ascend the small stage in Corning's public square for four nights of music in late July. Organizers are careful to select primary music sources, rather than interpreters, and have brought in acts ranging from Cuban salseros to full traditional klezmer bands. An arts and crafts festival runs concurrently on Saturday and Sunday. **LOCATION:** Centerway Square, on Market Street in central Corning. The town is about 15 miles west of Elmira and 15 miles north of the Pennsylvania state line. **TICKETS/INFO:** 607-936-4647 **ACCOMMODATIONS/ TOURIST INFO:** 607-936-4686, 607-974-2066

LONG ISLAND JAZZ FESTIVAL

OYSTER BAY ✹ LAST WEEKEND IN JULY OR FIRST WEEKEND IN AUGUST, FRIDAY–SUNDAY

Long Island's "Gold Coast" hosts a glimmering roster of jazz artists over a three-day weekend in late July. Recent musical guests have included Marian McPartland, Dave Brubeck, and David Benoit. The performers swing and sing for a picnicking crowd on the lawn of a gorgeous 400-acre estate. Tickets range from $15 to $40; children under 12 are admitted free. **LOCATION:** Planting Fields Arboretum State Historic Park, Oyster Bay, on Long Island's northern shore **TICKETS/INFO:** 516-922-0061; e-mail: ArtsFriend@aol.com **ACCOMMODATIONS/TOURIST INFO:** 516-951-3440, 516-794-4222

FOX FAMILY BLUEGRASS FESTIVAL

OLD FORGE ✹ WEEKEND FOLLOWING THE FIRST SUNDAY IN AUGUST, FRIDAY–SUNDAY

This two-stage bluegrass festival, held at a ski center and game refuge, features 12 to 14 bands over a three-day weekend. In addition to headliners running the full spectrum from traditional to progressive, this family-oriented festival features a wide variety of workshops and children's music and activities. About 1,500 bluegrass lovers pay about $30 for the weekend (children under 12 get in free), and rough camping is available. **LOCATION:** McCauley Mountain Ski Area, just south of Old Forge. From Utica or the New York Thruway take exit 31 and head north on Route 12 to Alder Creek, then follow Route 28 north to Old Forge and follow the signs to McCauley Mountain. **TICKETS/ INFO:** 315-369-6983 **ACCOMMODATIONS/TOURIST INFO:** 518-648-5239, 800-724-0242

SKANEATELES FESTIVAL

SKANEATELES ✹ SECOND WEEKEND IN AUGUST THROUGH FIRST WEEKEND IN SEPTEMBER

Offering an alluring combination of great setting, repertoire, talent, and hospitality, this classical music festival attracts listeners of all ages and backgrounds. The local musicians and music lovers who began this festival named it Skaneateles (pronounced "Skan-e-atlas" and derived from the Iroquois word for "long lake")—a name that, in English, does little justice to this beautiful body of water.

Skaneateles Festival: Talent, hospitality, and a beautiful lakeside setting attract music lovers to the village of Skaneateles. Courtesy of Skaneateles Festival

Musicians come from across the United States and overseas and have recently included Andres Cardenes, Ian Hobson, and Ruth Laredo. Indoor chamber concerts draw people off the streets of this New England-style village to a century-old church that holds about 450 people. Outdoor concerts on the grass tempt listeners to take off their shoes, spread blankets on the lush lawn, and enjoy wine and picnic dinners while listening to orchestral music and watching the stars come out.

Musicians and listeners alike praise the Skaneateles Festival's "family feeling" and intimate atmosphere in which musicians and audiences mingle enthusiastically. Since much of the audience already knows the musicians before they put bows to strings, informal talks before concerts often take on a lively, humorous tone. Each week sees about 10 different guest musicians in rehearsal and on stage, and performers are mixed and matched in chamber ensembles and chamber orchestras, playing an adventuresome repertoire that ranges from new composers to old favorites.

In an attempt to help parents introduce their children to classical music, a preopening Children's Fair is presented the first Saturday in August. On the veranda of a grand Victorian home, musicians bring to life a children's selection—such as "Babar," or "The Pied Piper Story"—and on the lawn children play old-fashioned games. The Children's Fair costs about $3 per person, and concert tickets range from $8 to $20. **LOCATION:** Brook Farm in Skaneateles, off U.S. 20 about 40 minutes southwest of Syracuse at the northern end of Skaneateles Lake **TICKETS/INFO:** 315-685-7418 **ACCOMMODATIONS/TOURIST INFO:** 315-684-0552, 315-470-1800, 800-234-4797

$\mathcal{C}$ORINTH BLUEGRASS FESTIVAL

CORINTH ✹ SECOND FULL WEEKEND IN AUGUST, THURSDAY–SUNDAY

With a strong focus on traditional bluegrass, Corinth's festival brings in 10 bands from all over the United States. The stage sits in a gorgeous bowl at the bottom of a hill, and the music wafts up the slope to the 2,000 to 3,000 spectators surrounding the stage. Other highlights include free camping, good food, a flea market, and the illustrious host and emcee, who is, and (according to organizers) always will be, Smokey Green. Tickets are about $35 at the gate for the weekend.   **LOCATION:** A large natural amphitheater in Corinth, just off U.S. 9N between Lake George and Saratoga. Look for the signs to the Bluegrass Festival. **TICKETS/INFO:** 518-654-9424 **ACCOMMODATIONS/TOURIST INFO:** 518-696-3500, 518-584-3255

$\mathcal{B}$RIDGEHAMPTON CHAMBER MUSIC FESTIVAL

BRIDGEHAMPTON ✹ TWO WEEKS IN MID-AUGUST

With an intimate venue and an emphasis on American composers as well as great masters of the classical period, the Bridgehampton Chamber Music Festival is the longest-lived and most popular of Long Island's East End festivals. Many festival performers return year after year for a total of seven to nine concerts in a 19th-century white church, covering a repertoire that ranges from baroque to classical and romantic. And although there's no air conditioner, players and listeners faithfully and enthusiastically sweat their way through some of the chamber repertoire's most challenging and powerful music (perhaps succumbing to occasional thoughts of the nearby beach). The festival also features a children's concert. Tickets are $15 to $20.   **LOCATION:** Bridgehampton Presbyterian Church, on Route 27 in Bridgehampton, on Long Island's South Fork **TICKETS/INFO:** 516-537-3507 **ACCOMMODATIONS/TOURIST INFO:** 800-441-4601

$\mathcal{N}$EW YORK REGGAE MUSIC FESTIVAL

BROOKLYN ✹ A WEEKEND IN MID-AUGUST

The founder of the New York Reggae Music Festival allegedly picked this Coney Island beach setting because the surf, sand, and sun reminded him of Jamaica. The seedy amusement park and boardwalk notwithstanding, the illusion is real enough to induce more than 10,000 to the shore, where dancehall posses "big up" before classic reggae stars like Third World and Steel Pulse take over.

New York City has a huge Caribbean population, and this festival is one of the fastest-growing reggae events in the United States. Organizers boast that it's also the safest and encourage families to attend. You can't bring alcohol along, but you can easily buy a Red Stripe—as well as Caribbean goodies like jerk chicken and beaded jewelry. **LOCATION:** Steeple Chase Park, Coney Island, Brooklyn **TICKETS/INFO:** 718-941-4629 **ACCOMMODATIONS/TOURIST INFO:** 212-484-1250

$\mathcal{B}$ARD MUSIC FESTIVAL

ANNANDALE-ON-HUDSON ✹ TWO WEEKENDS IN MID-AUGUST

Begun in 1990, the Bard Music Festival is so purely conceived and intended—and so flawlessly executed—that it has quickly become an essential gem of the American musical summer. The critically acclaimed festival focuses two August weekends around

The Bard Music Festival: An essential gem of the American musical summer.

Courtesy of Steve Sherman/Bard Music Festival

an in-depth and intimate celebration of a single composer. In 11 concerts and other events, the program offers a variety of recital, chamber, and orchestral music, with an international roster of guest musicians joining the American Symphony Orchestra in its summer residence.

The Bard Music Festival spent its first few years presenting musical feasts by romantic composers, including Strauss and Dvorák. That done, it turned its attention to 20th-century innovators like Béla Bartók and Charles Ives—and despite naysayers' warnings that "no one will come," the concerts regularly sell out.

Each of the 11 programs focuses on a different aspect of the festival's central figure. Illuminating preconcert talks and panel discussions by renowned musicians, speakers, and musicologists allow listeners to enter into the world in which the music was composed and first performed. A festival book, published each year by Princeton University Press, brings together original essays by leading scholars and first-time translations of contemporary source materials for further enlightenment on the subject.

Over two consecutive weekends, Bard College takes on a casual, summer festival atmosphere. Orchestra concerts are presented in a 900-seat acoustical tent on the campus grounds, while chamber music and recitals are performed in the intimate, 370-seat F. W. Olin Auditorium. The wooded Bard College campus borders the Hudson River and is ideal for walks, hikes, and picnics. Tickets are $15 to $20 per concert. **LOCATION:** Bard College, in Annandale-on-Hudson. From the Taconic State Parkway take the Red Hook/Route 199 exit, drive west on Route 199 through the village of Red Hook to Route 9G, turn right onto Route 9G, and drive north 1.6 miles. **TICKETS/**

INFO: 914-758-7410; e-mail: ezer@bard.edu; World Wide Web: http://www.bard.edu/
ACCOMMODATIONS/TOURIST INFO: 914-463-4000, 914-876-4778

BLUEGRASS FESTIVAL

LONG LAKE ✴ THIRD SATURDAY IN AUGUST

Established in 1980, this low-key festival brings in three regionally known bluegrass bands for all-day music and dancing. The setting is a natural hillside amphitheater near a lake.   **LOCATION:** Mount Sabattis Recreation Park, near the junction of Route 28N and Route 30 (Deerland Road), about 50 miles southwest of Saranac Lake **TICKETS/INFO:** 518-624-3077 **ACCOMMODATIONS/TOURIST INFO:** 518-624-3077, 518-648-5239

MUSIC FESTIVAL IN THE ADIRONDACKS

PAUL SMITHS ✴ THIRD SATURDAY IN AUGUST

Nestled deep in the Adirondacks, the lakeside campus of Paul Smith's College is a beautiful setting for this wide-ranging music festival. The program is anchored by acoustic, singer-songwriter folk but often cuts swaths into bluegrass, Celtic, jazz, and even funk and ska. Four performance sites include a main stage, an alternative stage, a workshop-instruction stage, and a children's stage. Theater and dance and arts and crafts can also be found among the woods and open meadows at the shores of Lower St. Regis Lake.   **LOCATION:** Paul Smith's College, 17 miles northwest of Saranac Lake at the junction of Routes 86 and 30 **TICKETS/INFO:** 518-962-8778 **ACCOMMODATIONS/TOURIST INFO:** 800-347-1992, 518-483-6788

PANASONIC VILLAGE JAZZ FESTIVAL

NEW YORK CITY ✴ ONE WEEK IN LATE AUGUST

With intimate venues, a hot roster, and an abundance of sidelights, this community-based festival brings a late-summer surge of excitement to one of the world's most productive breeding grounds for great jazz. The festival began in 1982 as a means to encourage jazz fans to visit Greenwich Village's jazz clubs. Nowadays, bigger and better acts—the likes of Roy Hargrove, Ellis Marsalis, and Betty Carter—present dozens of nighttime club concerts and a free afternoon concert at Washington Square Park. Other offerings include a very comprehensive Jazz Film Series and walking tours featuring 1920s and 1930s hot spots like Café Borgia, Le Figaro, and Café Reggio. **LOCATION:** Greenwich Village in New York City **TICKETS/INFO:** 212-929-5149; e-mail: CMPRNews@aol.com **ACCOMMODATIONS/TOURIST INFO:** 212-397-8200, 212-484-1250

KINGDOM BOUND FESTIVAL

DARIEN LAKE ✴ FOURTH WEEK IN AUGUST, WEDNESDAY–SATURDAY

Got an ear for grunge with gospel lyrics? Rap with a righteous roll? A little J.C. in your C&W? All modes of pop music meet their makers at Kingdom Bound, a four-day festival of contemporary Christian music and worship.

But music is only one form of praise. Kingdom Bound also sets up a worship tent, a sports clinic with demonstrations by Christian pro athletes, a singles fellowship, children's activities, and a teen ministry—all with the goal of drawing an all-ages audience, which at last count numbered more than 50,000. The *Christian Herald* called Kingdom Bound "a taste of what Heaven will be like." If so, the hereafter may be a crowded place; all 2,000 campsites available at the theme park sell out by April.   **LOCATION:** Darien Lake Theme Park, located between Rochester and Buffalo. From I-90 exit 48A and travel five miles south on Route 77. **TICKETS/INFO:** 800-937-7977 **ACCOMMODATIONS/TOURIST INFO:** 716-633-1117

CHARLIE PARKER JAZZ FESTIVAL
NEW YORK CITY ✹ LAST SUNDAY IN AUGUST

Even if Charlie "Bird" Parker hadn't lived the last four years of his life in a house facing Tompkins Square Park, its old trees and asymmetrical configurations would make it the perfect location for a free festival celebrating the life and work of the most influential saxophonist in modern jazz. Five acts feature musicians (such as Butch Morris and Arthur Blythe) who either played with Bird or were influenced by him. Sounds range from bebop to hard bop, with occasional diversions into swing and other styles. Since 1993, the festival has drawn more than 5,000 jazz lovers each year, many of whom steal a glance in the direction of 151 Avenue B. A film series and composers' workshop are featured earlier in the week.   **LOCATION:** Tompkins Square Park, downtown Manhattan, New York City **TICKETS/INFO:** 212-449-9609 **ACCOMMODATIONS/TOURIST INFO:** 212-484-1250

CMJ MUSIC MARATHON & MUSIC FESTIVAL
NEW YORK CITY ✹ A WEEKEND IN SEPTEMBER OR OCTOBER

Despite an often-disastrous (and sometimes hilarious) flair for disorganization, CMJ continues to feed New York's appetite for alternative rock. Over three days and four nights, some 400 bands from all over the world perform showcase concerts at various clubs, creating a fertile spawning ground for unsigned bands and a talent-starved music industry. Presented by *College Music Journal*, the festival favors unsigned bands, but plenty of bigger names always seem to make it onto the bill.   **LOCATION:** Various clubs and other venues in New York City **TICKETS/INFO:** 516-466-6000, 800-265-9997 **ACCOMMODATIONS/TOURIST INFO:** 212-484-1250

WEST INDIAN/AMERICAN DAY CARNIVAL
BROOKLYN ✹ LABOR DAY WEEKEND, THURSDAY–MONDAY (LABOR DAY IS THE FIRST MONDAY IN SEPTEMBER)

Nothing in the world compares to Carnival in Trinidad. But if you can't make it there, or if you were there and need a late-summer injection of "jump-up," this event is the next best thing. In terms of magnitude, the West Indian/American Day Carnival is on a par with London's Notting Hill Carnival and Toronto's Caribana. About two million people show up over the long weekend, augmenting the half-million or so West Indians who live in Brooklyn. Short of taking an extended tour through the Caribbean, attending this event is probably the best way to sample the diversity of West Indian culture.

One of New York's most musical and artistic street festivals, this carnival is known for its amazing bouts of street dancing and for some of the most incredible costumes north of the Caribbean. Many of the mas (masquerade) groups begin making costumes and practicing in their "mas camps" several months in advance. On Labor Day, as soca and steel drum bands rage, people dressed as sailors, dragons, and long-beaked birds

*Bebop in bird-
land: Saxophonist
Charles McPher-
son salutes his
greatest influence
at Tompkins
Square's Charlie
Parker Jazz Fes-
tival.* Courtesy of Michael

Hanulak/Charlie Parker Jazz

Festival

dance through the streets, and stilt dancers high-step confidently amidst the flamboyant finery.

Although you can hear some reggae, dancehall, and sounds of the Spanish Carib-bean, the majority of the music is based on Trinidadian traditions of calypso, soca, and steel drums. The steel drum, or pan, was pounded out of steel oil drums after World War II in Trinidad (it's one of the few new musical instruments this century). Unlike most drums, the steel drum is more an instrument of melody than percussion. Each drum is painstakingly tuned to deliver its notes in one of four ranges, which are called ping-pong, guitar-pan, cello-pan, and bass.

Like Trinidad's carnival, Brooklyn's free event demands *participation*. You'll feel welcome as you jump into the sweaty crowd and succumb to the gigantic power of the calypso beat. Dancers fuel themselves with rum, beer, and spicy-sweet foods like hot *roti* (barbecued goat), and neighborhood parties keep the action going late into the night. **LOCATION:** Franklin Avenue in Brooklyn **TICKETS/INFO:** 718-834-4544, 718-774-8807, 718-773-4052 **ACCOMMODATIONS/TOURIST INFO:** 212-484-1250

BRASILIAN STREET FESTIVAL

NEW YORK CITY ✷ SUNDAY OF LABOR DAY WEEKEND

Mostly because Brazil has some of the most exciting music in the Americas, the Brasilian Street Festival is one of the most exciting street festivals in the New York summer. Since the early 1980s, live bands have presented authentic Brazilian music, causing crowds—which last year numbered 500,000—to break out in daylong frenzies of samba ecstasy. Drum groups roam the streets, and food vendors sell foods from the different regions of Brazil.   **LOCATION:** 46th Street between Madison and Broadway, in the heart of Manhattan **TICKETS/INFO:** 212-382-1630 **ACCOMMODATIONS/ TOURIST INFO:** 212-484-1250

LONG ISLAND FIDDLE AND FOLK MUSIC FESTIVAL

STONY BROOK ✷ SECOND SUNDAY IN SEPTEMBER

With two featured performers and informal jams throughout the day, the Long Island Fiddle and Folk Music Festival has become a convention of sorts for amateur and professional folk musicians from all over the area. Headliners have included Celtic American duo Farther Shore, and hard-driving bluegrassers Buddy Merriam and Back Roads. Musicians who wish to participate in solo, group, or open sessions can preregister to secure a place on the program schedule. The grounds open for informal jamming at 10 A.M. Admission is about $5 for adults.   **LOCATION:** The Museum at Stony Brook. From the Long Island Expressway (Route 495) take exit 62 and go north on County Road 97 to its end. Turn left onto Route 25A for one and one-half miles, then turn left on Main Street in Stony Brook; the museum is on the right. Trains run to Stony Brook from Pennsylvania Station in Manhattan. **TICKETS/INFO:** 516-751-0066, ext. 212 **ACCOM-MODATIONS/TOURIST INFO:** 800-441-4601

PeNNSYLVaNia

GREATER PHILADELPHIA MID-WINTER SCOTTISH & IRISH MUSIC FESTIVAL & FAIR

KING OF PRUSSIA ✻ SECOND WEEKEND IN FEBRUARY, SATURDAY AND SUNDAY

A neighborly stew characterizes the bill of fare at the Greater Philadelphia Mid-Winter Scottish & Irish Music Festival & Fair. Scottish and Irish musicians from the homelands, as well as Canada and the United States, present two full days of music punctuated by storytelling, singing, dancing, and comic acts. To complete the cultural immersion, the festival features Scottish and Irish gifts, a Celtic art show, tartan displays, foods like fish and chips and meat pies, and the ever popular whiskey tasting—which, along with the beer garden, gets this event humming. **LOCATION:** Valley Forge Convention Center, at Route 363 (Gulf Road) and First Avenue in King of Prussia **TICKETS/INFO:** 610-825-7268 **ACCOMMODATIONS/TOURIST INFO:** 215-636-1666, 800-537-7676

PECO ENERGY JAZZ FESTIVAL

PHILADELPHIA ✻ A WEEKEND IN MID-FEBRUARY, FRIDAY–SUNDAY

Philadelphia's largest jazz festival makes for a hot weekend in the middle of a cold month. Five major concerts over three days have included the likes of Herbie Mann, the Count Basie Orchestra, and Nancy Wilson, performing in hotel ballrooms and downtown convention centers. In addition, more than 100 musical sideshows include midnight sessions, a Latin Jazz Dance Party, a Jazz Marketplace, and the Jazz 'til Sunrise all-night music marathon. Prices range from free to $25. **LOCATION:** Several concert venues in downtown Philadelphia **TICKETS/INFO:** 215-636-1666 **ACCOMMODATIONS/TOURIST INFO:** 215-636-1666

MUMMERS STRING BAND SHOW OF SHOWS

PHILADELPHIA ✻ TWO WEEKENDS IN LATE MARCH OR EARLY APRIL

The European tradition of mummery, or costumed merrymaking, began in the Philadelphia area in the 1600s and continues to this day in the city's extensive New Year's parade. The 16 Philadelphia-area mummers string bands that provide the parade's essential sound track gather one other time each year—for this fabulous spring musical fête. Over two consecutive weekends, you can catch toe-tapping songs like "Alabama Jubilee" and "Oh, Them Golden Slippers" and take part in a long-standing tradition that's unique to the Philadelphia area.   **LOCATION:** Civic Center, at 34th and Spruce Streets in Philadelphia **TICKETS/INFO:** 215-336-3050 **ACCOMMODATIONS/TOURIST INFO:** 215-636-1666, 800-321-9563

♪ JAZZ FEST AT CHERRY BLOSSOM TIME
WILKES-BARRE ✱ FIRST WEEKEND IN MAY, FRIDAY–SUNDAY

They call it a jazz fest but it's an anything-goes event when the cherry trees blossom, signalling spring's arrival to the outdoors-eager. Up to 10,000 per day take in 22 acts on two alternating stages; not only jazz, but rock 'n' roll oldies, country, blues, and zydeco are part of the program. In addition to the concerts, this free event features carnival rides and a food midway filled with funnel cakes, french fries, and Philly cheese steaks. **LOCATION:** Kirby Park, on Market Street in Wilkes-Barre **TICKETS/INFO:** 717-823-3165, 717-457-1320 **ACCOMMODATIONS/TOURIST INFO:** 800-245-7711, 717-457-1320

GETTYSBURG BLUEGRASS CAMPOREE
GETTYSBURG ✱ FIRST FULL WEEKEND IN MAY

Gettysburg kicks off the bluegrass season in these parts with four full days of music on two stages and plenty of workshops for the do-it-yourself bluegrasser. In addition to the mix of national and local talent, this festival's use of a luxury campground means that there's plenty here for the youngsters. The park features a water slide, a pool, boating and fishing lakes, a restaurant, and a game room. Note that a couple of unusual restrictions apply: no motorcycles and no dogs over 20 pounds.   **LOCATION:** Granite Hill Campground, 3340 Fairfield Road, six miles west of Gettysburg on Route 116 **TICKETS/INFO:** 717-642-8749 **ACCOMMODATIONS/TOURIST INFO:** 717-642-8749

BETHLEHEM BACH FESTIVAL
BETHLEHEM ✱ SECOND AND THIRD WEEKENDS IN MAY, FRIDAYS AND SATURDAYS

Since 1900, a brass choir has heralded the opening of the Bethlehem Bach Festival from the belfry of Bethlehem's Moravian Church. Thus begin two weekends of music by composer Johann Sebastian Bach, sung by the oldest Bach-dedicated choir in the United States.

Each year, the festival attracts classical and religious music lovers eager to experience some of the greatest choral music ever written. The choir itself consists of 110 passionate volunteers (more than Bach might have used, but amazingly sensitive and powerful). Accompanied by a professional orchestra and often by guest soloists, the choir sings through the range of Bach's works—from the short, spiritual cantatas to the large-scale reverence of Bach's Mass in B Minor, the annual capstone performance of the choir concert.

Bach's instrumental works are performed in chamber music concerts by members of the professional Bach Festival Orchestra. A festival Highlights program features a sampling of the longer concerts, including some well-known choruses from the Mass in B Minor. Concerts are held in the Packer Memorial Church on the hilly campus of

Lehigh University, and tickets start at $15.   **LOCATION:** Packer Memorial Church at Lehigh University, Bethlehem. From Route 22 exit at Route 378 to Hill Bridge and bear left to Third Street. Turn right at Brodhead Avenue, and left at Packer Avenue; the church is on the right. **TICKETS/INFO:** 610-866-4382 **ACCOMMODATIONS/TOURIST INFO:** 610-868-1513

ℳUSIC AT GRETNA
MOUNT GRETNA ✷ WEEKENDS IN MID-MAY THROUGH EARLY SEPTEMBER

Music at Gretna brings world-class chamber music and jazz to the covered, open-air Mount Gretna Chautauqua Playhouse, nestled in a Victorian lakeside resort village. Over the summer, about 30 acts—which have included Ruth Laredo, Herbie Mann, and the Shanghai Quartet—perform in the playhouse, as well as in an acoustically superb 1,000-seat hall resembling a European opera house. Both venues overlook a quiet, picture-book setting on the wooded campus of Elizabethtown College and tiny Lake Placida. **LOCATION:** Leffler Chapel and Performance Center at Elizabethtown College, on College Avenue off Route 230 in Elizabethtown **TICKETS/INFO:** 717-964-3836, 717-361-1508 **ACCOMMODATIONS/TOURIST INFO:** 717-272-8555

ℰPRING GULCH FOLK FESTIVAL
NEW HOLLAND ✷ WEEKEND BEFORE MEMORIAL DAY WEEKEND, FRIDAY–SUNDAY (MEMORIAL DAY IS THE LAST MONDAY IN MAY)

Smack-dab in the middle of Amish country, Spring Gulch Resort presents nationally known folk, country, bluegrass, and blues musicians at its three-day May festival. About 15 bands draw some 4,000 listeners, many of whom stay at the campground/resort and take advantage of its pools and other facilities. Admission ranges from $10 to $75, depending on the package purchased.   **LOCATION:** Spring Gulch Resort Campground, 475 Lynch Road in New Holland, just off Route 23 about 20 miles east of Lancaster **TICKETS/INFO:** 800-255-5744 **ACCOMODATIONS/TOURIST INFO:** 717-299-8901

ℙITTSBURGH FOLK FESTIVAL
PITTSBURGH ✷ MEMORIAL DAY WEEKEND, FRIDAY–SUNDAY

The Pittsburgh Folk Festival celebrates the music and heritage of the many ethnic groups that immigrated to western Pennsylvania. Founded in 1956, this is one of America's oldest folk festivals and one of its largest, drawing 25,000 annually. Music and dance troupes, with more than 3,500 performers, include people from 30 nations of Europe, Africa, Asia, and Latin America—and some cultures without a country, such as Carpatho-Rusyn. A Walk Around the World program helps introduce children to diversity; other features include cooking demonstrations, dance lessons, and craft workshops. Daily admission is $5.   **LOCATION:** David L. Lawrence Convention Center in downtown Pittsburgh **TICKETS/INFO:** 412-281-4882 **ACCOMMODATIONS/TOURIST INFO:** 800-359-0758, 412-281-7711, 800-366-0093

Jambalaya Jam: Louisiana's finest get the good times rolling at Penn's Landing in Philadelphia. Courtesy of Butler Photo/USAir Jambalaya Jam

USAIR JAMBALAYA JAM

PHILADELPHIA ✷ MEMORIAL DAY WEEKEND, SATURDAY–MONDAY

What may be the largest celebration of New Orleans food and music outside Louisiana draws thousands of good-time seekers to Penn's Landing. For more than a decade, performers like Rockin' Dopsie, Beausoleil, the Neville Brothers, and the Preservation Hall Jazz Band have used the site's five stages to carpet the area with authentic jazz, Cajun, zydeco, and R&B sounds. Thousands of local music lovers shimmy 'n' shake, then chow down on gumbo, alligator po'boys, and red beans and rice, while Louisiana craftspeople sell jewelry, musical instruments, and voodoo dolls. The children's Junior Jam features a Mardi Gras parade, special concerts, musical workshops, and crafts like mask making and jewelry making. Adult admission is about $12. **LOCATION:** Great Plaza at Penn's Landing, on Chestnut Street at Columbus Boulevard in downtown Philadelphia **TICKETS/INFO:** 215-636-1666 **ACCOMMODATIONS/ TOURIST INFO:** 215-636-1666

$\mathcal{M}$ELLON JAZZ FESTIVAL
PITTSBURGH ✹ TEN DAYS IN MID-JUNE

Over 10 days, Pittsburgh's esteemed Mellon Jazz Festival presents an eclectic lineup of more than 25 acts performing in about 30 venues. In addition to big names like Wynton Marsalis and Tony Bennett, who play in prestigious venues like Heinz Hall, the festival takes a turn toward stylistic diversity with bits of fusion, free-form, bebop, gospel, and even Latin jazz. Most of the more adventurous acts play in thoughtfully chosen, nontraditional spaces like Temple Rodef Shalom and the Regent Theatre. Although tickets for some events cost up to $35, many concerts are free.   **LOCATION:** Various locations throughout the Pittsburgh area, including Point State Park, Heinz Hall, Hartwood Acres, and Manchester Craftsmen's Guild **TICKETS/INFO:** 412-281-3881, 215-893-1930, 212-496-9000 **ACCOMMODATIONS/TOURIST INFO:** 800-359-0758, 412-281-7711, 800-366-0093

$\mathcal{M}$ELLON PSFS JAZZ FESTIVAL
PHILADELPHIA ✹ SECOND AND THIRD WEEKS IN JUNE FOR 10 DAYS

Philadelphia's largest jazz blowout features 10 days of concerts with a focus on local, emerging, and unsung artists. Lately, the festival has moved from presenting big names that often had only a tangential relationship to jazz to presenting mavericks whose names are known and respected by true jazz aficionados. Recent years have brought in alto saxophonist Lou Donaldson, trumpeter Jon Faddis, and pianist Mulgrew Miller. In addition to concerts at various halls and Philly night clubs, the festival honors one veteran local jazz talent each year with feature concerts, record signings, and other events.   **LOCATION:** Various venues throughout the Philadelphia metropolitan area **TICKETS/INFO:** 610-667-3559, 212-496-9000 **ACCOMMODATIONS/TOURIST INFO:** 215-636-1666, 800-537-7676

$\mathcal{C}$LEARFIELD COUNTY GOSPEL SING
CLEARFIELD ✹ THIRD WEEKEND IN JUNE, FRIDAY–SUNDAY

Sponsored by the local gospel singing group called the Testimonials, this festival brings in gospel talents from Pennsylvania, Ohio, West Virginia, and Kentucky. The weekend of fellowship is anchored by performances in which new groups swap the stage every 20 minutes (soloists get two songs apiece). About two dozen groups are invited, but anyone is welcome to sing—as long as they sing gospel. Admission is by freewill donation.   **LOCATION:** Clearfield County Fairgrounds. From I-80, use exit 19. **TICKETS/INFO:** 814-339-7316 **ACCOMMODATIONS/TOURIST INFO:** 800-348-9393, 814-849-5197

$\mathcal{P}$OCONOS COUNTRY MUSIC FESTIVAL
LAKE HARMONY ✹ THIRD OR FOURTH WEEKEND IN JUNE

This country music festival features regional bands, plus dance instruction and plenty of food, in a stunning Poconos setting near Big Boulder Lake.   **LOCATION:** Big Boulder Ski Area, near Lake Harmony in the Pocono Mountains of northeastern

Pennsylvania. From I-80 take exit 43 and follow the signs. **TICKETS/INFO:** 717-722-0100 **ACCOMMODATIONS/TOURIST INFO:** 800-762-6667, 800-468-2442, 717-424-6050

CREATION FESTIVAL
MOUNT UNION ✺ LAST FULL WEEK IN JUNE, WEDNESDAY–SATURDAY

The nation's largest outdoor Christian festival brings more than 50,000 people to Agape Farm for four days of music, camping, and fellowship. Most of the top names in contemporary Christian music (rock and pop, alternative, country, folk, metal, and blues) can be found on the main stage, and plenty of gospel and other talents are featured on five smaller stages. In addition to the music (presented in a natural amphitheater at the foot of a mountain), the 350-acre mountainside site offers inspirational speakers, Christian life seminars, food and crafts vendors, a late-night coffee house, children's areas, a big yellow children's tent, and a music store.

Veterans say that to experience the full impact of this gathering, you should bring along camping gear and become a part of the minimetropolis of tents and RVs that springs up overnight. Admission is about $20 a day, and many packages and multiday specials are available.   **LOCATION:** Agape Farm in Mount Union. From the Pennsylvania Turnpike take exit 13 and follow Route 522 north until just outside the town of Shirleysburg, then turn left on Keystone Road and continue three miles to the festival entrance. **TICKETS/INFO:** 800-327-6921, 609-654-8440; World Wide Web: http://www.creationfest.com **ACCOMMODATIONS/TOURIST INFO:** 814-643-6308

POLKA FIREWORKS
CHAMPION ✺ FIRST WEEKEND IN JULY

For more than 20 years, folks have been kicking up their heels and swirling their skirts at the Polka Fireworks—an annual showcase for the nation's top polka bands. The festival is held at Seven Springs Ski Resort, a mountain setting that's a perfect backdrop for such polkagreats as Toledo Polkamotion, Happy Louie, and festival coorganizer Eddie Blazonczyk and his Versatones. The festival aims to preserve the traditional sounds of polka, but also encourages new and innovative twists. Around 25 bands are featured over five days. There are two formal stages, but more casual polka parties spring up around the pool and elsewhere, so keep your eyes and ears open. The site has three restaurants, RV hookups, and hotel accommodations. Other activities include bowling, swimming, and hiking. Admission is $11 to $13 per night.   **LOCATION:** Seven Springs Resort in Champion, 30 miles south of Pittsburgh's eastern city limits, via I-70/76 (the Pennsylvania Turnpike). Take exit 9 (Donegal) and follow signs to the resort. **TICKETS/INFO:** 708-594-5182 **ACCOMMODATIONS/TOURIST INFO:** 800-925-7669, 412-238-5661

CANYON COUNTRY BLUEGRASS FESTIVAL
WELLSBORO ✺ SECOND WEEKEND IN JULY, FRIDAY–SUNDAY

Traditional and progressive bluegrassers gather for three days each July near Pennsylvania's Grand Canyon. The nine or 10 featured bands include local, regional, and national acts, and about 1,000 people show up for this low-key, family-style event. Camping is available, and the surrounding area is rich with opportunities for hiking, biking, rafting, and fishing. Tickets are about $28 for the weekend.   **LOCATION:**

Creation Festival: The nation's largest outdoor Christian festival brings the top names in contemporary Christian music to its main stage. Courtesy of NOBLE & NOBLE, Muncy, PA

Stony Fort Creek Campground in Wellsboro, just off U.S. 6 in north-central Pennsylvania **TICKETS/INFO:** 800-724-7277 **ACCOMMODATIONS/TOURIST INFO:** 717-724-1926

𝕿URK'S HEAD MUSIC FESTIVAL
WEST CHESTER ✸ THIRD SUNDAY IN JULY

This festival's two stages feature about 10 acts that cover a variety of musical genres. About 10,000 locals turn out to catch musicians from West Chester and throughout the Philadelphia metro area, and the park sports the usual crafts and food vendors. Admission is free.   **LOCATION:** Everhart Park, at Miner and Bradford Avenues in West Chester. From Philadelphia take Route 3 west just past U.S. 202. **TICKETS/INFO:** 610-436-9010 **ACCOMMODATIONS/TOURIST INFO:** 800-228-9933, 610-344-6365

𝕻OCONO BLUES FESTIVAL
LAKE HARMONY ✸ FOURTH WEEKEND IN JULY

This relatively young festival has quickly made a name for itself by booking interesting and nonmainstream blues artists from across the country. Set in a wooded ski area in northeastern Pennsylvania's Pocono Mountains, Pocono Blues has featured the likes of Jerry McCain, Little Milton, Smokey Wilson, and Juanita Williams. Many of the musical guests lead workshops in addition to performing on the main stage. **LOCATION:** Big Boulder Ski Area, near Lake Harmony in the Pocono Mountains of northeastern Pennsylvania. From I-80 take exit 43 and follow the signs. **TICKETS/INFO:** 717-722-0100 **ACCOMMODATIONS/TOURIST INFO:** 800-762-6667, 800-468-2442, 717-424-6050

CHESTER COUNTY OLD FIDDLERS' PICNIC

WAGONTOWN ✷ SECOND SATURDAY IN AUGUST

With fiddles, banjos, guitars, dulcimers, and accordions in tow, festivalgoers come to play at the Old Fiddlers' Picnic, a reunion for fiddlers and their sidekicks from Pennsylvania, Maryland, Delaware, and New Jersey. Each year more than 6,000 old-time music lovers show up at this picnic, which began in the late 1920s and changed locations several times before settling at the 800-acre Hibernia County Park.

Musicians begin signing up for stage time at 9 A.M., and slots are usually filled by 11 A.M. Solo acts are allotted 10 minutes on stage, and groups get 20 minutes. But the real action takes place in the woodlot beside the stage, where impromptu groups assemble, disassemble, and reassemble under the shade trees, creating rare and spontaneous music.

A covered picnic pavilion is cleared of tables for four hours of square dancing, followed by another two hours of country and western line dancing. Visitors bring lawn chairs, blankets, picnic baskets, and pets (on six-foot leads)—but not alcohol. Hayrides are available, as are food and crafts. The picnic is free, but parking costs $5. **LOCATION:** Hibernia County Park, in Wagontown four miles north of Coatesville, off the Route 82 exit of the Route 30 Bypass in Chester County **TICKETS/INFO:** 610-344-6415 or 610-384-0290; e-mail: c-snowberger@mail.co.chester.pa.us **ACCOMMODA-TIONS/TOURIST INFO:** 610-344-6365

LANCASTERFEST: CELEBRATION OF CULTURES

LANCASTER ✷ SECOND SATURDAY IN AUGUST

Each August, Lancaster celebrates its diverse ethnic mix by throwing a musical street party featuring some 24 acts on three stages. The festival depends on local talent, which means festivalgoers can count on hearing German, Celtic, Polynesian, Latin American, African, and eastern European music. Multicultural crafts and children's activities are also available at this free downtown shindig.   **LOCATION:** Queen Street between Penn Square and Lancaster Square in downtown Lancaster **TICKETS/INFO:** 717-399-7977 **ACCOMMODATIONS/TOURIST INFO:** 717-299-8901, 800-723-8824

MUSIKFEST

BETHLEHEM ✷ NINE DAYS BEGINNING THE SECOND SATURDAY IN AUGUST

Each August, Pennsylvania's Bethlehem comes alive with music from around the world. Thousands of people gather to experience more than 650 free performances at indoor and outdoor "platzes," each with its own unique flavor. The Americaplatz features blues, jazz, rock, swing/big band, and R&B; the Festplatz features polka, country, and other dances; the Familienplazt has acoustic music; and the Liederplatz has folk, cabaret, and bluegrass.

Germanic themes prevail, but Musikfest is actually one of America's most cosmopolitan and comprehensive eclectic music festivals. Traditional and cutting-edge music from all corners of the continent—zydeco, Latin American, reggae, and much more—can be heard over nine days in this town, which was settled in the 1700s by Moravians. In addition to the music, the festival features art, crafts, flower displays, and more than 60 ethnic-food vendors. Some events are ticketed, but the vast majority are free. **LOCATION:** Various locations in Bethlehem, which is just north of the Philadelphia area

Musikfest gathers traditional and cutting-edge musicians from all corners of the continent. Terry Wild Studios

via Route 309 **TICKETS/INFO:** 610-861-0678, 800-360-3378 **ACCOMMODATIONS/ TOURIST INFO:** 610-882-9200

℘ENNSYLVANIA STATE GOSPEL SINGING CONVENTION

MARTINSBURG ✷ SECOND FULL WEEKEND IN AUGUST, THURSDAY–SUNDAY

With performances by up to 40 gospel talents each day, this free festival is one of the North's best opportunities to hear mass quantities of gospel music. Many of the 10,000 attendees plan their annual vacations around this event, coming in from all over the country and creating a scene that's a lot like a family reunion. Morrison Cove Memorial Park, where the festival has been held since the 1960s, has one main stage and two covered stages in case of rain, plus plenty of recreational facilities. **LOCATION:** Morrison Cove Memorial Park, Martinsburg. From Altoona take Route 36 south. **TICKETS/INFO:** 814-695-9356 **ACCOMMODATIONS/TOURIST INFO:** 800-842-5866, 814-943-4183

GETTYSBURG BLUEGRASS CAMPOREE

GETTYSBURG ✹ FOURTH WEEKEND IN AUGUST

This is a semiannual event, happening the first full weekend in May and the fourth weekend in August. See page 84 for details.   **LOCATION:** Granite Hill Campground, 3340 Fairfield Road, six miles west of Gettysburg on Route 116 **TICKETS/INFO:** 717-642-8749 **ACCOMMODATIONS/TOURIST INFO:** 717-642-8749

PHILADELPHIA FOLK FESTIVAL

SCHWENKSVILLE ✹ LAST WEEKEND IN AUGUST

With folk music on four stages, camping, and lots of drumming and dancing, the Philadelphia Folk Festival has become an annual East Coast revival of the spirit of Woodstock (the first Woodstock, that is). A legendary hillside location and a laid-back (if a bit conservative) vibe draw about 6,000 folkies—including many who have come almost yearly since the event began in 1963.

These days, they unload the kids from minivans and set up camp on Thursday, a day before the event officially begins. Old Pool Farm is nestled in rolling, wooded hills northwest of Philadelphia, and campsites go fast, so if you want a good spot, a Thursday arrival is de rigueur.

The music revolves around the singer-songwriter folk tradition, with acts ranging from a few big folk names to lots of good but lesser-known performers from around the East Coast and points farther afield. Main performances are held in the afternoons and evenings, and in addition to concerts there are workshops, dances, crafts, storytelling, and plenty of children's activities. Plus, the informal tentside jamming is so fantastic that it's said some folks never make it off the campground—even for the concerts. **LOCATION:** Old Pool Farm in Schwenksville, northwest of the Philadelphia metropolitan area, near the junction of Routes 29 and 73 **TICKETS/INFO:** 215-242-0150; World Wide Web: http://www.voicenet.com/1/voicenet/homepages/brucep/index.html **ACCOMMODATIONS/TOURIST INFO:** 215-636-1666, 800-321-9563

BLUE MOUNTAIN GOSPEL FESTIVAL

KEMPTON ✹ LAST SATURDAY IN AUGUST THROUGH THE FIRST SUNDAY IN SEPTEMBER

Forty performers over nine days draw 10,000 of the spiritual to this bluegrass and southern-style gospelfest, one of the largest in the East. A sheltered pavilion guarantees all-weather performances by 40 acts of regional and national repute, and the hillside, open-air setting invites campers to stick around.   **LOCATION:** Kempton Community Grounds in Kempton, west of Allentown. From I-78/U.S. 22 exit at Krumsville (exit 12) and take Route 737 north to Kempton. **TICKETS/INFO:** 717-872-5615 **ACCOMMODATIONS/TOURIST INFO:** 800-443-6610, 610-375-4085

CHADDS FORD WINERY JAZZ FESTIVAL

CHADDS FORD ✹ LABOR DAY WEEKEND, SATURDAY–MONDAY (LABOR DAY IS THE FIRST MONDAY IN SEPTEMBER)

Jazz is the soundtrack for this intimate festival's wine-tasting activities. An estate winery in Brandywine Valley, Chadds Ford Winery opens its winemaking and barrel-aging cellars to a maximum audience of 1,500 for sips of the local juice and sounds from local jazz groups. Outdoor tent seating and picnic tables are conducive to snacking on sophisticated concessions like snapper soup, portabello mushrooms with crab, and, *bien sur*, pâté.   **LOCATION:** Chadds Ford Winery, at 632 Baltimore Pike in Chadds Ford, 30 miles southwest of Philadelphia and 15 miles north of Wilmington, Delaware, on U.S. Route 1 five miles south of Route 202 **TICKETS/INFO:** 610-388-6221; e-mail: leem@locke.CCIL.org **ACCOMMODATIONS/TOURIST INFO:** 610-344-6365

♩AZZ AT SEVEN SPRINGS
CHAMPION ✻ LABOR DAY WEEKEND

Set in the pristine beauty of Pennsylvania's Laurel Highlands, Seven Springs Mountain Resort tempts city folk with a jazz-filled weekend getaway. Ray Brown, Kenny Burrell, and Chuck Mangione have been recent headliners, presenting a range of indoor and outdoor concerts and workshops. After a day of music, golf, swimming, and other recreational pursuits, guests unwind with jazz dinners and late-night music in the Alpine Room.   **LOCATION:** Seven Springs Mountain Resort in Champion, in the Laurel Highlands region. From the Pennsylvania Turnpike take exit 9 (Donegal) and turn left on Route 31 east; drive one mile and turn right on Route 711 south and follow the signs. **TICKETS/INFO:** 800-297-6160, 814-443-2433 **ACCOMMODATIONS/TOURIST INFO:** 800-452-2223, 814-445-6431

♩OHNSTOWN FOLKFEST
JOHNSTOWN ✻ LABOR DAY WEEKEND, FRIDAY–SUNDAY

In the late 1800s, thousands of Poles, Slovaks, Ukrainians, and other European ethnics migrated to Johnstown to work the city's famous steel mills. Many made their homes in what is now the historic, tree-filled neighborhood of Cambria City, which hosts the Johnstown FolkFest each September. On three stages placed throughout this neighborhood, America's musical traditions come alive through performances by masters of gospel, zydeco, polka, salsa, klezmer, and the blues.

Recent festivals have featured such artists as blues guitarist Johnny Clyde Copeland, polka master Lenny Gomulka, and zydeco great Rockin' Dopsie. The lively, working-class neighborhood and the Labor Day date seem just right for a festival celebrating the ethnic traditions that created so much great American music, and more than 100,000 people typically turn out over the weekend. In addition to three days of concerts, the festival features children's performers and crafts, 50 or more ethnic-food vendors, and walking tours of Cambria City's historic churches.   **LOCATION:** Ten blocks of Chestnut Street in Johnstown's historic Cambria City neighborhood **TICKETS/INFO:** 514-539-1889 **ACCOMMODATIONS/TOURIST INFO:** 514-539-3838

♩O! PHILADELPHIA FESTIVAL
PHILADELPHIA ✻ LABOR DAY WEEKEND, SUNDAY AND MONDAY

This nostalgic celebration features the music that Philadelphia danced to in days past, from big band and jazz to rock 'n' roll, soul, and gospel. Recent acts have included Dion, Solomon Burke, Harold Melvin and the Blue Notes, and the Doc Givvs African American Gospel Choir. In addition to the classics, the Yo! Rising Stars Stage presents an eclectic selection of the city's hot new bands. Children's activities, art, and sports are included in this celebration, which costs about $6 for adults.   **LOCATION:** Great Plaza at Penn's Landing, on Chestnut Street at Columbus Boulevard in downtown Philadelphia **TICKETS/INFO:** 215-636-1666 **ACCOMMODATIONS/TOURIST INFO:** 215-636-1666

🦪HAWNEE MOUNTAIN SCOTTISH & IRISH FESTIVAL
SHAWNEE-ON-DELAWARE ✳ THIRD WEEKEND IN SEPTEMBER, SATURDAY AND SUNDAY

A ski resort in the Poconos Mountains creates a picturesque autumnal backdrop for this Scottish/Irish fest. Thistle meets shamrock in an all-day lineup of bagpipes, fiddlers, and step dancers. Since it's billed as a family event, there's plenty here for the kids, including a sheep dog show and children's games. For adults there's whiskey tasting and beer drinking, along with the centuries-popular caber toss (in which grunting lads compete to see who can toss a tree trunk the farthest and the most stylishly). **LOCATION:** Shawnee Mountain Ski Area in Shawnee-on-Delaware, just northeast of East Stroudsburg. From Route I-80 take exit 52 to Route 209 north. **TICKETS/INFO:** 610-825-7268 **ACCOMMODATIONS/TOURIST INFO:** 717-421-7231, 800-762-6667, 717-424-6050

🐚CTUBAFEST
CARLISLE ✳ SECOND OR THIRD SATURDAY IN OCTOBER

Brassy bass notes run rampant through the streets of Carlisle in mid-October as tuba players and ensembles converge from all over the country. Running concurrently with the town's wide-ranging Arts Festival, Octubafest has recently featured the U.S. Navy Tuba Quartet, the Hot House Trio, and Euphuba. Octubafest began in the mid-1980s and was held outside with the Arts Festival for the first few years. When Hurricane Hugo threatened, the event was moved indoors to the Weiss Center of Dickinson College, and everyone liked the venue so much that organizers decided to keep Octubafest inside. In addition to concerts, the festival closes with a grand finale featuring both amateur and professional talent. **LOCATION:** Weiss Center of Dickinson College, in the center of Carlisle, just west of Harrisburg and just off I-81 and the Pennsylvania Turnpike **TICKETS/INFO:** 717-245-2648 **ACCOMMODATIONS/TOURIST INFO:** 800-995-0969, 717-232-1377

ViR✦GiNia

BAY BEACH MUSIC FESTIVAL

VIRGINIA BEACH ✺ THIRD WEEKEND IN MAY

Live beach music inspires the uniquely Southern dance tradition of "shagging" at Virginia Beach's nostalgic, weekend-long dance party. Shagging was the dance of choice for '50s and '60s kids who frequented southern beach towns to catch regional and national R&B acts like Chuck Berry, Joe Turner, and the Drifters. The Drifters themselves have appeared at recent Bay Beach Music Festivals, as have the Embers, Maurice Williams and the Zodiacs, and other old favorites of beach music devotees. **LOCATION:** Thirtieth Street on the ocean and other venues in Virginia Beach **TICKETS/INFO:** 800-446-8038, 804-427-3580 **ACCOMMODATIONS/TOURIST INFO:** 804-437-4700, 800-822-3224

WASHINGTON IRISH FOLK FESTIVAL

WOLF TRAP FARM/VIENNA ✺ SUNDAY OF MEMORIAL DAY WEEKEND
(MEMORIAL DAY IS THE LAST MONDAY IN MAY)

Fans and performers of Irish music consistently rank the Washington Irish Folk Festival as one of the best—if not *the* best—of the Irish music festivals in the United States. Established in 1976, it's certainly one of the oldest, and year after year its collection of musicians and musical styles admirably represents the great range of music in the Irish genre, with performers from both North America and the Emerald Isle itself.

The Greater Washington Ceili Club organizes the festival, which is held at idyllic Wolf Trap Farm, America's only national park dedicated to the performing arts. Five stages present the very top echelon of Irish and related music; recent years have featured Cape Breton fiddle master Buddy MacMaster, classic Irish singer-songwriter Andy Irvine, and folk/rock hybrid Wolfstone. Add to this more than 150 musicians, singers, and dancers and you have a day of more great music than any one person has the right to hope for. The weather seldom cooperates during this late-May jaunt, but the event's volunteer organization, impeccable sound, and solid booking of both traditional and cutting-edge Irish music make this one of the genre's most prestigious and enjoyable festivals. **LOCATION:** Wolf Trap, 20 minutes outside Washington, D.C. From the Capital Beltway take exit 12 to Route 267 west (Dulles Toll Road), take the Wolf Trap exit, and follow the signs. **TICKETS/INFO:** 703-218-6500, 703-255-1860; World Wide

Web: http://www.wolf.trap.org/ **ACCOMMODATIONS/TOURIST INFO:** 703-790-3329

NORTHERN NECK BLUEGRASS FESTIVAL
WARSAW ✹ MEMORIAL DAY WEEKEND, SATURDAY AND SUNDAY

You'd be hard-pressed to find a more perfect setting for a festival of traditional and gospel-oriented bluegrass. Heritage Park Resort is a former plantation overlooking the Rappahannock River, and the campground is set on a former Indian encampment. Wild turkeys hide in the shade trees, and eagles often fly overhead. About eight bands play each year, with talent ranging from regional favorites to local up-and-comers and an occasional national act. Admission is about $20 for two days, and about 1,000 bluegrass lovers typically show up to listen to the down-home harmonies echoing through the pines. The resort also features a pool, tennis courts, and a boat ramp. **LOCATION:** Heritage Park Resort in Warsaw, on Route 624 about 2.5 miles north of U.S. 360 **TICKETS/INFO:** 804-333-4038 **ACCOMMODATIONS/TOURIST INFO:** 804-333-4038

MEMORIAL DAY JAZZ FESTIVAL
ALEXANDRIA ✹ MEMORIAL DAY

Nostalgic jazz, big band, and swing keep things jumping on the outdoor stage at Jones Point Park. About 5,000 picnickers take over the lawn from noon until 8 P.M., enjoying a seven-band roster of local talent that often includes the U. S. Navy Commodores Big Band. **LOCATION:** Jones Point Park, entered via the south end of Royal Street **TICKETS/INFO:** 703-883-4686 **ACCOMMODATIONS/TOURIST INFO:** 703-838-4200, 800-388-9119

GRAVES' MOUNTAIN FESTIVAL OF MUSIC
SYRIA ✹ WEEKEND AFTER MEMORIAL DAY, THURSDAY–SATURDAY

America's bluegrass region rolls straight east from Kentucky into Virginia's Blue Ridge Mountains, where the Graves' Mountain Festival camps out for three days of dueling banjos of national repute. The lineup is dependably stellar, and the scenery is awesome. The Graves family have been innkeepers for more than 130 years in the Blue Ridge Mountains, and their lodge and working farm are famous for their hearty southern cooking and hospitality. RVs are welcome, but motorcycles and dogs are not. **LOCATION:** Graves' Mountain Lodge, near the end of Route 670 in Syria, about an hour from Charlottesville and two hours from Washington, D.C. From Charlottesville take Route 29 north to Madison, go through Madison on Business Route 29, then turn left on Route 231 north and go seven miles to Banco; turn left onto Route 670 and follow it four miles to the lodge. **TICKETS/INFO:** 540-923-4231 **ACCOMMODATIONS/TOURIST INFO:** 540-923-4231

CAPITAL JAZZ FEST
FAIRFAX ✹ WEEKEND AFTER MEMORIAL DAY, SATURDAY AND SUNDAY

"A weekend of hot fun and cool jazz" is the rallying cry of the Capital Jazz Fest in the D.C. commuter community of Fairfax, Virginia. The contemporary jazz lineup consists of 12 to 14 national acts, plus "surprise" opening acts. Tickets range from $20 to $100. **LOCATION:** Bull Run Regional Park in Fairfax. From I-66, take exit 52 (Route 29) at Centreville, drive 2 miles south, turn left on Bull Run Post Office Road, and follow signs to the park entrance. **TICKETS/INFO:** 703-913-2948; e-mail: capitaljaz@aol.com **AC-COMMODATIONS/TOURIST INFO:** 703-790-3329

VIVA ELVIS FESTIVAL
VIRGINIA BEACH ✹ FIRST WEEKEND IN JUNE

Elvis, if you're out there, you probably don't need the money, but if you ever do, there's a cool million waiting for you if you join in the festivities at Virginia Beach's Viva Elvis Festival. Just elbow your way through four days of impersonators (who have included both the Black Elvis and Mexico's El Vez). Or hop a ride up Atlantic Avenue during Saturday's Elvis Parade (which features a high school marching Elvis band). Be careful to dodge "the Flock of Elvi" (skydiving Elvises) descending to the beach and the masses lining up to watch your movies or imitate you in the karaoke contest. If you manage to show up, the $1 million reward is guaranteed by Lloyd's of London; fingerprints will be required.   **LOCATION:** Virginia Beach stages at 17th and 24th Streets and various other oceanfront locations **TICKETS/INFO:** 804-437-4700, 800-822-3224 **ACCOMMODATIONS/TOURIST INFO:** 804-437-4700, 800-822-3224

LOUISIANA SWAMP ROMP
WOLF TRAP FARM/VIENNA ✹ SUNDAY OF THE FIRST WEEKEND IN JUNE

This romping gig transports the lively music, food, and culture of Louisiana to the Virginia countryside for one day in early June. On Wolf Trap Farm's Filene Center Stage, old favorites like the Hackberry Ramblers, Beausoleil, and Allen Toussaint trade licks with new-generation stars like the Iguanas, the subdudes, and Nathan and the Zydeco Cha-Chas. Each year features about half a dozen acts ranging from Cajun and zydeco to New Orleans funk-jazz and Latin R&B—plus Cajun food and arts and crafts.

Wolf Trap Farm was named for the traps, set for wolves, that made walking in the region dangerous in the 1700s. Wolf Trap is the United States' only national park for the performing arts and is set among the rolling foothills of the Blue Ridge Mountains. Its centerpiece is Filene Center, an open-sided amphitheater with a gracefully sloping roof that blends harmoniously with surrounding woods.   **LOCATION:** Wolf Trap, 20 minutes outside Washington, D.C. From the Capital Beltway take exit 12 to Route 267 west (Dulles Toll Road), take the Wolf Trap exit, and follow the signs. **TICKETS/INFO:** 703-218-6500, 703-255-1860; World Wide Web: http://www.wolf.trap.org/ **ACCOM-MODATIONS/TOURIST INFO:** 703-790-3329

SEAWALL FESTIVAL
PORTSMOUTH ✹ FIRST FULL WEEKEND IN JUNE, FRIDAY–SUNDAY

If you've ever tuned in to a classic-rock radio station and wondered how that teen heartthrob has held up over the years, there's a good chance you can find out at the Portsmouth Seawall Festival (though certain things are best left to the imagination). Three stages along the Elizabeth River feature beach music and golden oldies played by old salts of the rock 'n' roll and beach music eras. The festival is held in conjunction with the town's annual Harborfest, and along with more than 25 bands, the three days feature plenty of seafood, barbecue, arts and crafts, and boating.   **LOCATION:** The Olde

Towne waterfront area in downtown Portsmouth, which is just west of Norfolk **TICK-ETS/INFO:** 800-296-9933; e-mail: portsva@aol.com **ACCOMMODATIONS/TOURIST INFO:** 800-767-8782, 804-393-5327

JUNE JUBILEE
RICHMOND ✭ SECOND WEEKEND AFTER MEMORIAL DAY

This wide-ranging event celebrates Richmond's artistic talent in all art forms, but the big draw is the music. On five stages, more than 50 local bands produce sounds ranging from rock and pop to country, blues, alternative, and classical. In addition, the free event features children's activities, visual arts demonstrations, clowns, and jugglers—all in downtown Richmond.   **LOCATION:** Downtown Richmond **TICKETS/INFO:** 804-643-2826 **ACCOMMODATIONS/TOURIST INFO:** 804-782-2777

BIG STONE GAP GOSPEL SINGING CONVENTION
BIG STONE GAP ✭ SECOND SUNDAY IN JUNE

Trios, quartets, and full bluegrass bands sing gospel at this long-standing classic. The event began in 1920, and today listeners still feel the surge of that old-time religion as about 10 groups let loose their enchanting, soul-lifting harmonies. The event is free, and a playground is on hand to keep the kids busy.   **LOCATION:** Bullitt Park on First Avenue east of U.S. 58A in Big Stone Gap. The town is located in the far west corner of the state; from I-81 take exit 1 to U.S. 58/421 west to U.S. 23 north to U.S. 58A. **TICKETS/INFO:** 540-523-2060 **ACCOMMODATIONS/TOURIST INFO:** 540-523-2060, 540-468-2550, 804-288-3065

BAYOU BOOGALOO AND CAJUN FOOD FESTIVAL
NORFOLK ✭ A WEEKEND IN MID-JUNE, FRIDAY–SUNDAY

The Hampton Roads area raises a holler over the Bayou Boogaloo's combination of red-hot Louisiana rhythms and spicy Cajun and Creole cooking. About 50,000 people pack Town Point Park over three days to hear six to eight of the top touring bands on the Cajun/zydeco/R&B circuit. Previous years have featured Dr. John, the Neville Brothers, and Nathan and the Zydeco Cha-Chas. Admission is free at this heavily sponsored event. **LOCATION:** Town Point Park in downtown Norfolk. From I-64 take I-264 toward downtown and exit left onto Waterside Drive. **TICKETS/INFO:** 804-441-2345 **ACCOMMODATIONS/TOURIST INFO:** 804-441-5266, 800-368-3097

CELTIC FESTIVAL AT OATLANDS PLANTATION
LEESBURG ✭ A WEEKEND IN MID-JUNE

Although this pan-Celtic affair features headliners like Northern Ireland's Armagh Rhymers and Scotland's MacTalla, its major goals are to showcase local Celtic performers and societies and to encourage beginners. Three amplified stages, an acoustic stage, a harper's tent, and a workshop area ensure that there's plenty of music at Oatlands Plantation, a historic mansion with spacious grounds.

This festival's musical offerings go well beyond the now familiar Irish and Scottish music, offering a rare glimpse of the colorful cultures of Celtic people from Cornwall, Wales, the Isle of Man, Prince Edward Island (Canada), Galicia (Spain), and Brittany (France). In addition to the music, the festival offers Highland athletics, living-history

The Ash Lawn-Highland Summer Festival celebrates America's artistic heritage with opera, classical music, jazz, blues, and more. Courtesy of Ash Lawn-Highland Summer Festival

groups, storytellers, and a pub tent. Admission is about $8.   **LOCATION:** Oatlands Plantation, six miles south of Leesburg, Virginia, on Route 15 **TICKETS/INFO:** 703-777-3174 **ACCOMMODATIONS/TOURIST INFO:** 703-777-0518

SHENANDOAH VALLEY BACH FESTIVAL
HARRISONBURG ✷ ONE WEEK IN MID-JUNE

Since the revival of *St. Matthew Passion* in 1829, Bach's music has received nearly universal appreciation. This thoughtfully presented festival features a week of music by Bach and others, superbly performed by soloists and ensembles. In addition to straightforward concerts, the program includes lunch, dinner, and dessert performances. Participatory children's events often include costumed evenings of singing, instrumental music, and dancing. Plus, a youth symphony orchestra program brings in young musicians from around the mid-Atlantic region for instruction by festival musicians. **LOCATION:** Lehman Auditorium and Campus Center Greeting Hall, at Eastern Mennonite University in Harrisonburg. From I-81, take exit 251 and follow the signs. **TICKETS/INFO:** 540-432-4367, 540-432-4250, 540-432-4225; e-mail: nafzigeh@emu.edu **ACCOMMODATIONS/TOURIST INFO:** 540-434-2319

ASH LAWN-HIGHLAND SUMMER FESTIVAL
CHARLOTTESVILLE ✷ MID-JUNE THROUGH MID-AUGUST

Opera and education are the twin themes of the Ash Lawn-Highland Summer Festival. The former home of President James Monroe, Ash Lawn-Highland is now a museum run by the College of William and Mary. Since 1978, its colonial boxwood gardens have hosted this well-regarded celebration of America's artistic heritage, making good on Thomas Jefferson's request that Monroe buy the estate adjacent to his own Monticello to form "a society to our taste."

Today that taste runs from opera classics like *The Barber of Seville* to symphonic and chamber music, jazz, blues, and more. The festival typically presents about 28 performances of three operas, with productions that are typically focused and spirited—and lots of fun even for a non-operagoer. A pre-opera lecture series accompanies many weekend performances, and the audience often indulges in gourmet picnics on the premises. Non-opera Music at Twilight performances make use of a variety of local venues, and a Summer Saturdays series features family entertainment.   **LOCATION:** From I-64 take exit 121 to Route 20 south, then turn left onto Route 53 east. Pass Monticello and continue 2.5 miles to Route 795. Turn right and proceed one mile to Ash Lawn-Highland.   **TICKETS/INFO:** 804-293-4500, 804-979-0122 **ACCOMMODATIONS/TOURIST INFO:** 804-293-6789

WOLF TRAP'S JAZZ AND BLUES FESTIVAL
WOLF TRAP FARM/VIENNA ✹ A WEEKEND IN LATE JUNE, FRIDAY–SUNDAY

In the Virginia countryside just outside Washington, D.C., Wolf Trap's three-day program makes every effort to include all forms of the jazz and blues genres. Friday night might feature Sarah Vaughan and the Duke Ellington Orchestra, while Saturday night might host blues guitarist Buddy Guy and Brazilian jazz stylist Marisa Monte. Sunday, the whole park opens up as 10 acts—jazz, blues, R&B, and more—perform on two stages. Admission ranges from $14 to $20, depending on the day.

Wolf Trap Farm was named for the traps, set for wolves, that made walking in the region dangerous in the 1700s. Wolf Trap is the United States' only national park for the performing arts and is set among the rolling foothills of the Blue Ridge Mountains. Its centerpiece is Filene Center, an open-sided amphitheater with a gracefully sloping roof that blends harmoniously with surrounding woods.   **LOCATION:** Wolf Trap, 20 minutes outside Washington, D.C. From the Capital Beltway take exit 12 to Route 267 west (Dulles Toll Road), take the Wolf Trap exit, and follow the signs. **TICKETS/INFO:** 703-218-6500, 703-255-1860; World Wide Web: http://www.wolf.trap.org/ **ACCOMMODATIONS/TOURIST INFO:** 703-790-3329

HAMPTON JAZZ FESTIVAL
HAMPTON ✹ THIRD WEEKEND IN JUNE, THURSDAY–SUNDAY

First staged in 1968 to celebrate Hampton University's 100th anniversary, the Hampton Jazz Festival focuses on mainstream jazz and often crosses the line into pop, with performers like Anita Baker, Gladys Knight, George Benson, and Ray Charles. The venue, the Hampton Coliseum, has received a major facelift, and because of the festival's growing popularity, organizers recently added a fourth day to the festival. **LOCATION:** Hampton Coliseum in Hampton **TICKETS/INFO:** 804-838-4203, 804-827-5665 **ACCOMMODATIONS/TOURIST INFO:** 800-487-8778, 804-722-1222

AFRIKAN AMERICAN FESTIVAL
HAMPTON ✹ THIRD SATURDAY IN JUNE

Held in conjunction with the Hampton Jazz Festival, this family-oriented event celebrates the diversity of African American heritage. Mill Point Park's waterfront stage comes to life with live reggae, gospel, jazz, and special children's performances. The festival also features African arts and crafts, ethnic foods, and a children's carnival area. The nonalcoholic event is free, and proceeds from vendor sales benefit the Peninsula

Wolf Trap's Jazz and Blues Festival: Kenny Burrell performs in the nation's only national park for the performing arts. Courtesy of Paula Jones/Wolf Trap Foundation for the Performing Arts

Association for Sickle Cell Anemia.   **LOCATION:** Mill Point Park, at the corner of Eaton Street and Settlers Landing Road, on downtown Hampton's waterfront **TICKETS/ INFO:** 804-838-4721, 804-838-8043 **ACCOMMODATIONS/TOURIST INFO:** 800-487-8778, 804-722-1222

THE BIG GIG
RICHMOND ✴ TWO WEEKS IN MID-JULY

Richmond's sprawling and eclectic summer music festival brings two weeks of music to more than a dozen stages throughout the city. You can line-dance in the heart of downtown with a rising country star, or merengue the afternoon away to live Caribbean rhythms. Blues artists make hearts ache, and classical concerts enhance the mood for lazy summer afternoons in the park.

In addition to local talent in parks and neighborhoods, expect to see international stars at free concerts in Festival Park. The World Music Weekend showcases the high-energy talent of the Caribbean and Latin America, with dance-crazed acts like Trinidad's Mighty Sparrow and Puerto Rico's Descarga Boricua. A Centenary Classics program brings choral and instrumental music to the Centenary United Methodist Church and other venues, and JAZZ! Weekend traditionally brings the Big Gig to a close. **LOCATION:** Several different venues in Richmond **TICKETS/INFO:** 804-643-2826 **ACCOMMODATIONS/TOURIST INFO:** 804-782-2777

The Hampton Jazz Festival brings jazz, blues, and even pop music to Hampton. (See entry, page 100.) Courtesy of Hampton Conventions and Tourism

ℳINERAL BLUEGRASS FESTIVAL
MINERAL ✷ THIRD WEEKEND IN JULY, THURSDAY–SATURDAY

In a beautifully shaded park, some of the top names in bluegrass music gather each year in mid-July for three days of hillbilly pickin'. Bill Monroe, Jim and Jesse, Ralph Stanley—they've all been here, and chances are they'll be back again. The atmosphere is family-style, with strictly enforced restrictions on alcohol and plenty of free camping. Admission at the gate costs about $20 each day, but plenty of bargain tickets are available through advance-purchase and multiday options.   **LOCATION:** Walton Park in Mineral, just off U.S. 522, about 20 miles north of I-64. Turn off U.S. 522 at Millers Market and follow the signs. **TICKETS/INFO:** 706-864-7203 **ACCOMMODATIONS/TOURIST INFO:** 804-782-2777

ℙENDLETON BLUEGRASS FESTIVAL
CAMP PENDLETON/VIRGINIA BEACH ✷ THIRD WEEKEND IN JULY,
FRIDAY–SUNDAY

This weekend concert series showcases music with a Kentucky flair and benefits SHARE Mid-Atlantic, a program of the Food Bank of Southeastern Virginia. Over three days, seven or eight headliners and many more local bands perform at Camp Pendleton, with Sunday's sets emphasizing gospel-oriented bluegrass (no alcohol is allowed this day). Daily tickets are about $10, and camping is available both on the premises and nearby.   **LOCATION:** Camp Pendleton, Virginia Beach **TICKETS/INFO:** 800-253-7842, 804-853-1608 **ACCOMMODATIONS/TOURIST INFO:** 804-437-4700, 800-822-3224

SHENANDOAH VALLEY MUSIC FESTIVAL
ORKNEY SPRINGS ✱ LAST TWO WEEKENDS IN JULY AND SECOND WEEKEND IN AUGUST

Before there was Wolf Trap, before there was Bluemont, music lovers in the mid-Atlantic region came to the Shenandoah Valley to hear classical and pops music on the lawn of the historic Orkney Springs Hotel. Since 1963, well-known performers have converged on this very quaint town to play music from a rustic, open-air pavilion among turn-of-the-century white frame houses in view of the Massanutten Mountains.

The multicultural music program focuses on music not typically heard in rural settings, and recent years have featured American folk singers, big bands, and a Brazilian song-and-dance group. But more often than not, symphonic music is played by the festival's orchestra in residence, the Fairfax Symphony Orchestra. An arts and crafts show runs concurrently, and tickets range from $9 to $15. Orkney Springs also hosts a music festival over Labor Day weekend.   **LOCATION:** The grounds of the Orkney Springs Hotel, about a two-hour drive from the Washington suburbs. From Jackson, Virginia, take Route 263 west about 15 miles into Orkney Springs. **TICKETS/INFO:** 800-459-3396 **ACCOMMODATIONS/TOURIST INFO:** 540-477-3115

GOSPELRAMA
PORTSMOUTH ✱ FIRST WEEKEND IN AUGUST, SATURDAY AND SUNDAY

This annual gospel music explosion promotes unity through music. Expect to see more than 30 acts—quartets, soloists, choirs, and even rappers—from throughout the region, performing on a single stage overlooking the Elizabeth River and Norfolk Harbor.   **LOCATION:** The Olde Towne waterfront area in Portsmouth, which is just west of Norfolk **TICKETS/INFO:** 800-767-8782; e-mail: portsva@aol.com **ACCOMMO-DATIONS/TOURIST INFO:** 800-767-8782, 804-393-5327

OLD FIDDLERS' CONVENTION
GALAX ✱ SECOND WEEKEND IN AUGUST, WEDNESDAY–SATURDAY

Back in the spring of 1935, Galax's new Moose Lodge was looking for a way to raise funds and attract a little publicity. Someone suggested a fiddlers' convention to keep alive "the memories and sentiments of days gone by and make it possible for people of today to hear and enjoy the tunes of yesterday." Word got out and the first Old Fiddlers' Convention drew some 1,300 people—most of whom arrived on foot or in horse-drawn buggies.

Within two years the number of spectators and contestants had increased so much that organizers moved the convention to Felts Park, where it's been ever since. These days, more than 30,000 people attend over three days, including some 2,000 competitors from all over North America and points farther afield (in fact, a Japanese musician recently won the mandolin competition).

This is one of the country's best opportunities to catch acoustic performances by masters of everything from the autoharp to the bull fiddle—plus hoards of cloggers and

Hoedown hoard: Master musicians from across the country bring the old songs back to life at the Old Fiddlers' Convention. Courtesy of Old Fiddlers' Convention

flatfoot dancers. The rules allow only public domain songs—the ones passed down from generation to generation and "owned" by all of us. Musicians compete for cash prizes, trophies, and ribbons in vocal and instrumental performances on guitar, dulcimer, banjo, and more, in styles ranging from old-time to bluegrass.

Despite the cosmopolitan crowd, the event still has the atmosphere of a small-town festival in the Blue Ridge Mountains. A covered grandstand seats 5,000, and many more sit on blankets under the sky, reveling in the formal concerts at 7 P.M. each night and at noon on Saturday. The music and dancing goes on pretty much nonstop in the streets and in the parking lot/campground. Here the musicians get in tune and work out arrangements before heading onto the stage, and roving minstrels put on impromptu shows that many swear are better than those on stage. Tickets are $5 to $20, and no dogs or public displays of alcohol are allowed.   **LOCATION:** Felts Park in Galax, near the North Carolina border. From I-77 take U.S. 58/221 south into Galax and follow the signs. **TICKETS/INFO:** 540-236-8541, 540-236-6355 **ACCOMMODATIONS/TOUR-IST INFO:** 540-236-2184

TOWN POINT JAZZ & BLUES FESTIVAL
NORFOLK ✳ FOURTH WEEKEND IN AUGUST, FRIDAY–SUNDAY

Each August, some of the East Coast's hottest jazz sounds can be found in Town Point Park, a green seven-acre oasis in Norfolk's waterfront area. Friday through Sunday nights bring more than 60,000 people downtown to revel in the sounds of mainstream jazz acts like Spyro Gyra, Wynton Marsalis, and Earl Klugh. It's hot here in August, but the park offers plenty of trees to shade listeners while they enjoy the largest free jazz festival in the mid-Atlantic region.   **LOCATION:** Town Point Park in downtown Norfolk. From I-64 take I-264 toward downtown and exit left onto Waterside Drive. **TICKETS/INFO:** 804-441-2345 **ACCOMMODATIONS/TOURIST INFO:** 804-441-5266, 800-368-3097

AMERICAN MUSIC FESTIVAL
VIRGINIA BEACH ✳ LABOR DAY WEEKEND, WEDNESDAY–MONDAY (LABOR DAY IS THE FIRST MONDAY IN SEPTEMBER)

Virginia Beach hosts one of the East Coast's biggest celebrations of rock 'n' roll oldies, with six days of performances on or near the resort area's beach. Expect to see some of the biggest stars of America's rock 'n' roll era, such as the Beach Boys, Wilson Pickett, Three Dog Night, and Junior Walker. Collectively, featured bands boast more than 50 number one hits and 400 albums. Tickets are about $10 in advance plus service charges, and hotel packages keep you right in the middle of the fun.   **LOCATION:** Various beachfront stages in Virginia Beach **TICKETS/INFO:** 800-446-8038, 804-491-7866 **ACCOMMODATIONS/TOURIST INFO:** 804-437-4700, 800-822-3224

SHENANDOAH VALLEY MUSIC FESTIVAL
ORKNEY SPRINGS ✳ LABOR DAY WEEKEND, SATURDAY AND SUNDAY

Orkney Springs hosts this music festival twice a year—in late July/early August and again over Labor Day weekend. See page 103 for details.   **LOCATION:** The grounds of the Orkney Springs Hotel, about a two-hour drive from the Washington suburbs. From Jackson, Virginia, take Route 263 west about 15 miles into Orkney Springs. **TICKETS/ INFO:** 800-459-3396 **ACCOMMODATIONS/TOURIST INFO:** 540-477-3115

ROCKBRIDGE MOUNTAIN MUSIC & DANCE CONVENTION
BUENA VISTA ✳ SECOND WEEKEND AFTER LABOR DAY, FRIDAY AND SATURDAY

Country memories, genial spirits, and lots of dancing make this a can't-miss event for lovers of old-time mountain music and dance. Set in a park at the foot of the Blue Ridge Mountains just east of Lexington, the festival features about three headlining mountain bands plus plenty of opportunities for amateur jam sessions. Dance is a big part of the festivities, and on-site experts can teach you how to do it square or round— or, if you only brought along your cement shoes, just sit back and enjoy the music and atmosphere from your campsite. The Rockbridge Friends of Mountain Music & Dance have put on this event for a decade, and they make sure plenty of food (vegetarian and otherwise) is available. Admission is about $10 for the weekend.   **LOCATION:** Glen Maury Park, one-half mile south of downtown Buena Vista. From Lexington take Route 60 east to Buena Vista, then take Route 501 south to parking on 10th Street. **TICKETS/ INFO:** 540-463-3777, 540-463-4010, 540-377-2231 **ACCOMMODATIONS/TOURIST INFO:** 540-261-2880, 540-463-3777

ᵁMOJA FESTIVAL
PORTSMOUTH ✷ THIRD WEEKEND IN SEPTEMBER

This free African American cultural celebration features R&B, jazz, reggae, African music, and educational activities for children. One of the highlights is a procession of African drummers, who lead dancers and other revelers to the Portsmouth waterfront. Sunday features mainly gospel music, and throughout the event there's plenty of cultural cuisine, African American crafts, and more.   **LOCATION:** Downtown Portsmouth, which is just west of Norfolk **TICKETS/INFO:** 800-767-8782, 804-393-8481; e-mail: portsva@aol.com **ACCOMMODATIONS/TOURIST INFO:** 800-767-8782, 804-393-5327

ᴵNTERNATIONAL CHILDREN'S FESTIVAL
WOLF TRAP FARM/VIENNA ✷ A WEEKEND IN LATE SEPTEMBER

The International Children's Festival was created to help children understand and appreciate music and culture from around the world and to promote children's interest in the arts. An international cast of musicians—some children, and some adults whose acts are geared toward children—perform on several stages around the beautiful grounds of Wolf Trap, while puppeteers and clowns move through the crowd. Student artists from as far away as Latvia and Taiwan join American children to stage musical and theatrical productions, while a wide variety of hands-on workshops ensures that these two days contain nary a dull moment.

Wolf Trap Farm was named for the traps, set for wolves, that made walking in the region dangerous in the 1700s. Wolf Trap is the United States' only national park for the performing arts and is set among the rolling foothills of the Blue Ridge Mountains. Its centerpiece is Filene Center, an open-sided amphitheater with a gracefully sloping roof that blends harmoniously with surrounding woods. Admission is $10 to $15. **LOCATION:** Wolf Trap, 20 minutes outside Washington, D.C. From the Capital Beltway take exit 12 to Route 267 west (Dulles Toll Road), take the Wolf Trap exit, and follow the signs. **TICKETS/INFO:** 703-218-6500, 703-255-1860; World Wide Web: http://www.wolf.trap.org/ **ACCOMMODATIONS/TOURIST INFO:** 703-790-3329

ᴮLUES AT THE BEACH FESTIVAL
VIRGINIA BEACH ✷ SECOND WEEKEND IN OCTOBER

Virginia Beach's 24th Street Park is filled with the sounds of the blues during the second weekend in October. Sponsored by the Natchel Blues Network, the festival features guitar-oriented blues on Saturday afternoon and big-band blues on Sunday afternoon. Local, regional, and national blues artists are presented.   **LOCATION:** Twenty-Fourth Street Park, at 24th and the oceanfront **TICKETS/INFO:** 804-456-1675 **ACCOMMODATIONS/TOURIST INFO:** 804-437-4700, 800-822-3224

✶MITHFIELD FOLK FESTIVAL

SMITHFIELD ✶ THIRD WEEKEND IN OCTOBER, FRIDAY AND SATURDAY

Smithfield's folk festival is held on the grounds of Windsor Castle, on the banks of the Pagan River. An opening folk concert Friday evening is followed by Saturday's schedule of workshops, craft demonstrations, and an evening concert.   **LOCATION:** Windsor Castle in Smithfield, on Virginia's Isle of Wight **TICKETS/INFO:** 804-357-3288, 800-365-9339 **ACCOMMODATIONS/TOURIST INFO:** 804-357-5182, 800-365-9339

WASHINGTON, D.C.

DUKE ELLINGTON BIRTHDAY CELEBRATION

WASHINGTON, D.C. ✱ A SATURDAY IN LATE APRIL

This musical blast celebrates Duke Ellington's legacy and features nothing but the Duke's compositions all day. Some of the best jazz musicians in the capital area form half a dozen groups, bringing their own stylings to Ellington's music. The festival also features one internationally renowned headliner. Admission is free, and about 5,000 people typically make the scene. **LOCATION:** Freedom Plaza, at 14th Street and Pennsylvania Avenue NW, in Washington, D.C. **TICKETS/INFO:** 202-331-9404 **AC-COMMODATIONS/TOURIST INFO:** 202-789-7000

HFSTIVAL

WASHINGTON, D.C. ✱ FIRST OR SECOND SATURDAY IN JUNE

Inaugurated in 1990, HFStival may be the granddaddy of all the alterna-fests made popular by the younger Lollapalooza tour and sideshow (which recently attracted only half the crowd). About $17 buys 10 value-packed hours of alternative rock by the likes of Soul Asylum, Courtney Love, P. J. Harvey, and a dozen more national headliners and local openers. When attention strays from music and moshing, check out the parking lot cluttered with a second stage, carnival attractions, ecological and political action booths, and food and trinkets. Sponsored by alternative radio station WHFS-FM, the festival is one of the largest radio events in the country, drawing about 60,000 fans annually to RFK Stadium. **LOCATION:** RFK Stadium in Washington, D.C. **TICKETS/INFO:** 800-321-9437; e-mail: whfs@aol.com **ACCOMMODATIONS/TOURIST INFO:** 202-789-7000

HOT SALSA FESTIVAL

WASHINGTON, D.C. ✱ A SATURDAY IN LATE JUNE

Here's a chance to catch three or four of the hottest salsa and Latin jazz orchestras in the capital area, all in one day. Freedom Plaza is filled with Afro-Caribbean sounds, and about 5,000 listeners and dancers typically make the scene. Admission is free. **LOCATION:** Freedom Plaza, at 14th Street and Pennsylvania Avenue NW, in Washington, D.C. **TICKETS/INFO:** 202-331-9404 **ACCOMMODATIONS/TOURIST INFO:** 202-789-7000

*F*ESTIVAL OF AMERICAN FOLKLIFE

WASHINGTON, D.C. ✴ TEN DAYS IN THE LAST WEEK IN JUNE AND FIRST
WEEK IN JULY (INCLUDING JULY 4)

This popular annual festival celebrates America's cultural richness and diversity. Each year, five programs focus on the music, dance, crafts, and other traditions of ethnic groups living in the United States. The music is rich and varied, with yearly themes that have included such treats as "Native American Women Singers," "Czech Folk Culture," and "the Cape Verdean Connection." The festival is painstakingly researched and presented and features only the most authentic practitioners of living musical traditions. **LOCATION:** The National Mall in Washington, D.C. **TICKETS/INFO:** 202-287-3424 **ACCOMMODATIONS/TOURIST INFO:** 202-789-7000

D.C. CARIBBEAN CARNIVAL

WASHINGTON, D.C. ✴ LAST SATURDAY IN JUNE

The 35,000 West Indians living in the Washington area are joined by thousands of other Caribbean-music lovers in this romping parade and concert. The dancing begins along Georgia Avenue Northwest, where, after weeks of costume making and rehearsal, some 25 "mas camps" (masquerade groups) dance and parade in their extravagant costumes to live soca and pan (steel drum) music. The parade ends at Banneker Park, where a free concert presents four bands from the United States and the Caribbean. Previous years have featured Trinidad's soca great Superblue and other soca, calypso, steel drum, reggae, and Haitian acts. Don't forget your dancing shoes, *mon!* **LOCATION:** The parade begins at Emory Park (Georgia and Missouri Avenues) and concludes at Banneker Recreation Park (Georgia Avenue and Barry Place), where the concert is held. **TICKETS/INFO:** 202-726-2204 **ACCOMMODATIONS/TOURIST INFO:** 202-789-7000

*F*REEDOM JAZZ

WASHINGTON, D.C. ✴ JULY 4

On Independence Day, Freedom Plaza in downtown Washington rings with the sounds of jazz. This landmark celebration draws thousands to the district's heart to hear progressive and improvisational jazz performers. Recent-year headliners have included the David Murray Quartet, the Willem Breuker Kollektif, and Andrew White. Freedom Jazz is part of the Jazz Arts festival season of international music and art, which begins in late May and wraps up in mid-September. **LOCATION:** Freedom Plaza, at 14th Street and Pennsylvania Avenue NW, in Washington, D.C. **TICKETS/INFO:** 202-783-0360 **ACCOMMODATIONS/TOURIST INFO:** 202-789-7000

*J*AMFEST

WASHINGTON, D.C. ✴ SECOND OR THIRD WEEKEND IN JULY, SATURDAY
AND SUNDAY

Nearly a neighbor to the White House, Jamfest is spiritually immersed in the Caribbean. The event dishes up Jamaican music, food, crafts, and art in a two-day celebration of island culture. At least six bands play reggae, calypso, and other Caribbean music, drawing crowds of more than 50,000. Admission is free. **LOCATION:** Free-

D.C. Blues Festival: Deitra Farr and James Wheeler of Mississippi Heat celebrate the blues with a few thousand friends.

Courtesy of Elin Peltz/D.C. Blues Festival

dom Plaza, 14th Street and Pennsylvania Avenue NW **TICKETS/INFO:** 202-452-0660 **ACCOMMODATIONS/TOURIST INFO:** 202-789-7000

℗.℃. BLUES FESTIVAL

WASHINGTON, D.C. ✶ SATURDAY AFTER LABOR DAY (LABOR DAY IS THE FIRST MONDAY IN SEPTEMBER)

D.C. Blues Society members, their friends, and a few thousand other Washingtonians have gathered annually since 1989 to celebrate the blues and have a great time. A typical lineup might feature a couple of nationally known electric acts plus acoustic performers who emphasize the Piedmont and mid-Atlantic regions' country blues traditions. Held in an outdoor amphitheater in the middle of a park, this family-oriented event features workshops in guitar, harmonica, dance, vocals, and children's percussion. **LOCATION:** Carter Barron Amphitheatre, 16th Street and Colorado Avenue NW in Rock Creek Park, Washington, D.C. **TICKETS/INFO:** 202-828-3028; e-mail: gray@mrcwdc.com; World Wide Web: http://intelus.com/dcblues/ **ACCOMMODATIONS/TOURIST INFO:** 202-789-7000

WEST VIRGINIA

APPALACHIAN WEEKEND
PIPESTEM ✹ SECOND WEEKEND IN MARCH, FRIDAY–SUNDAY

With bluegrass, gospel, and rustic fiddle- and banjo-based Appalachian music, the Appalachian weekend showcases mountain culture for guests who come from around the world to the Pipestem Resort State Park. Each night, four or five acts play to crowds of about 250, many of whom also take advantage of late-season ski packages. **LOCATION:** Pipestem Resort State Park, on Route 20 about 15 miles northeast of I-77, near the Virginia/West Virginia state line **TICKETS/INFO:** 800-225-5982 **ACCOMMODATIONS/TOURIST INFO:** 304-466-5420

SPRING DULCIMER WEEK AND FESTIVAL
ELKINS ✹ A WEEK IN LATE APRIL

There's probably no better way to hear, learn, and enjoy the mountain and hammered dulcimers than the annual Spring Dulcimer Week. Days are filled with intensive classes, and evenings are filled with song swaps and jam sessions. Thursday night features a public concert by guest artists and the teaching staff, and Friday night wraps things up with a very musical farewell party.   **LOCATION:** Augusta Heritage Center at Davis and Elkins College, near the junction of U.S. 33 and U.S. 219. From I-79 take exit 99 and go east on U.S. 33. **TICKETS/INFO:** 304-637-1209, 304-636-1903; e-mail: augusta@dne.wvnet.edu **ACCOMMODATIONS/TOURIST INFO:** 800-422-3304, 304-636-2717

SPRING MOUNTAIN FESTIVAL
PETERSBURG ✹ LAST WEEKEND IN APRIL, SATURDAY AND SUNDAY

Mountain music, rock 'n' roll oldies, bluegrass, country, and gospel are all on tap at this springtime festival, which tries to satisfy the wide-ranging tastes of the music lovers in this Potomac Highlands town. Along the Potomac River, the music runs nonstop all day Saturday and Sunday with 10 bands, which have included the U.S. Navy Band and other regional favorites.   **LOCATION:** City Park in Petersburg in the Potomac Highlands. From Washington D.C. take I-66 west to Route 55 west. **TICKETS/INFO:** 304-257-2722 **ACCOMMODATIONS/TOURIST INFO:** 304-257-2722

Old masters converge on Fairmont for the Traditional Music Weekend.

Courtesy of Steve Shaluta, Jr./West

Virginia Division of Tourism

ᴙRADITIONAL MUSIC WEEKEND
FAIRMONT ✹ SECOND WEEKEND IN MAY

Held in the lush springtime at Pricketts Fort State Park, this festival is an exceptional opportunity to experience some of West Virginia's best performers of traditional Appalachian music. Expect to hear both bluegrass and pre-bluegrass country songs rendered by old masters and young performers, all united to preserve the state's outstanding musical heritage and have some fun in the process. With a whopping roster of more than 50 banjo pickers, fiddle players, and ballad singers, this festival's $5 entrance fee is one of the best bargains in traditional American music.   **LOCATION:** Pricketts Fort State Park near Fairmont. From I-79 take exit 139 and follow the signs. **TICKETS/INFO:** 800-225-5982, 304-363-3030 **ACCOMMODATIONS/TOURIST INFO:** 304-363-7037

ᗷLUEGRASS! AT THE SAGEBRUSH ROUND-UP

FAIRMONT/BUNNER RIDGE ✶ THIRD WEEKEND IN MAY, FRIDAY
AND SATURDAY

This little festival is a bluegrass jewel—seven regional bands are featured over two days, and spectators are invited to be participants, mingling with performers and joining in the many jam sessions that crop up throughout the weekend. Traditional bluegrass is featured, and tapes and CDs by performers are available along with food and local arts and crafts. Admission is $6 to $10 per day.   **LOCATION:** The Music Complex at Bunner Ridge. From I-79 take exit 139 and follow the signs to Bunner Ridge. **TICKETS/ INFO:** 304-387-1103 **ACCOMMODATIONS/TOURIST INFO:** 800-225-5982

ᒍACKSON COUNTY GOSPEL SING

COTTAGEVILLE ✶ THIRD WEEKEND IN MAY

Soulful harmonies echo through the Jackson County Fairgrounds as 20 of the region's top gospel quartets and other performers sing out to benefit the Special Olympics. Admission is free, but donations are accepted. Other free gospel events are held at the Jackson County Fairgrounds the last weekend in June, the third weekend in July, and the last weekend in August.   **LOCATION:** Jackson County Fairgrounds, just off Route 33 near Cottageville, which is about 45 miles north of Charleston via I-77. From the I-77 take exit 138 and head west about seven miles. **TICKETS/INFO:** 304-273-4407, 304-273-5224 **ACCOMMODATIONS/TOURIST INFO:** 800-225-5982

ᘟEMORIAL DAY MUSIC FESTIVAL

NEW MANCHESTER ✶ MEMORIAL DAY WEEKEND (MEMORIAL DAY IS THE LAST
MONDAY IN MAY)

This free outdoor festival features four traditional country and folk bands each day. The mostly local talent draws about 700 spectators to Tomlinson Run State Park, which features camping, RV hookups, a playground, and food vendors.   **LOCATION:** Tomlinson Run State Park, 19 miles north of Weirton, West Virginia, and 38 miles west of Pittsburgh, Pennsylvania. From Pittsburgh take U.S. 22 west to Highway 2 north, then Highway 8 north; the park is five miles on the left. **TICKETS/INFO:** 304-564-3651 **ACCOMMODATIONS/TOURIST INFO:** 800-225-5982

ᐯANDALIA GATHERING

CHARLESTON ✶ MEMORIAL DAY WEEKEND

As diverse a celebration as the cultures that created West Virginia's heritage, the Vandalia Gathering takes the ingredients of America's melting pot and simmers them over music, dancing, crafts, and traditional arts. For more than 20 years, Vandalia has celebrated West Virginia folklife, providing a beautiful venue for traditional musicians and music lovers over the Memorial Day weekend—the traditional homecoming time for mountain people.

While quality crafts are plentiful and the modes of entertainment diverse, the music is what really stands out at this event. Competitions in fiddle, banjo, dulcimer, and dancing bring traditional musicians from all over the state, and a special bus travels to outlying hollows to fetch octogenarian banjo players and others who wouldn't otherwise be able to make it.

Vandalia Gathering: Old-fashioned mountain music finds plenty of friends under the shade trees. (See entry, page 113.) Courtesy of Michael Keller/West Virginia Division of Culture and History

Although there are several stages, much of the music finds its finest venue under the overhanging branches of old trees. Generation-spanning jam sessions pass on musical traditions, and the organizers do everything they can to encourage 'em. Plus, workshops in gospel music and other forms take place throughout the mellow, shady grounds.

Surrounding the fountain in the Capitol Circle, some of West Virginia's finest craftspeople demonstrate their skills in basketry, quilting, pottery, and furniture making. A liar's contest brings in the big talkers, and a juried quilt exhibition draws some of the best quilters in the country.   **LOCATION:** The Cultural Center and Capitol Complex Grounds, at 1900 Kanawha Boulevard East in Charleston. From I-64/77 take exit 99/ Greenbrier Street. **TICKETS/INFO:** 304-558-0220 **ACCOMMODATIONS/TOURIST INFO:** 800-733-5469, 304-344-5075

SAGEBRUSH ROUNDUP COUNTRY MUSIC FESTIVAL
FAIRMONT/BUNNER RIDGE ✷ THIRD WEEKEND IN JUNE, FRIDAY AND SATURDAY

Sponsored by the Country Music Association of West Virginia, this event mixes old and new country with bluegrass and gospel. It began in the late 1980s with jam sessions in local homes, but when hundreds of people started showing up, it gained the status of full-fledged festival. Nowadays, anywhere from 2,000 to 4,000 people come to hear about a dozen country bands that range from top-notch locals to national names. Primitive camping is available, and if you miss this early summer event, another is held the second weekend in September.   **LOCATION:** The Music Complex at Bunner Ridge. From I-79 take exit 139 and follow the signs to Bunner Ridge. **TICKETS/INFO:** 304-363-6366, 304-363-4864 **ACCOMMODATIONS/TOURIST INFO:** 800-225-5982

ℳUSIC IN THE MOUNTAINS
SUMMERSVILLE ✷ LAST FULL WEEKEND IN JUNE, THURSDAY–SUNDAY

Bluegrass, country music, and gospel are on the agenda at this rootsy festival, which serves as a homecoming for Nashville musicians and many others. In all, about 35 groups perform over four days, and thousands of people show up early to enjoy the jamming that fills the campground all week.

This is one of the country's largest rural bluegrass gatherings and the biggest event of the year in the sleepy, "almost-heaven" hills and hollows that are a day's drive from Washington, Richmond, Columbus, or Pittsburgh. Lovers of hillbilly music come from across the country and as far away as Europe or Australia, many rolling in with RVs that are bigger than most houses around here.

Hundreds of the rigs stand fender-to-fender in the hayfields, creating a mini-city, and on makeshift patios and beneath shady oaks, circles of strangers meet to resurrect mountain melodies with banjos, fiddles, mandolins, and voices in four-part harmony. Organizers stress that this is a family event and strictly enforce their prohibition on alcohol and drugs. Day tickets run $25 to $30.   **LOCATION:** Summersville Music Park, 45 miles north of Beckley and 75 miles east of Charleston. From Charleston take I-79 north to exit 57, then Route 19 south for 28 miles. At the traffic light in Summersville go left on Route 41 for 1.5 miles and take a left onto the grounds. **TICKETS/INFO:** 304-872-3145 **ACCOMMODATIONS/TOURIST INFO:** 304-872-1588

𝒮INGING IN THE MOUNTAINS
SUMMERSVILLE ✷ FIRST OR SECOND WEEKEND IN JULY

This four-day Southern gospel sing brings about 35 professional groups to the Summersville Music Park. Many musicians and listeners treat the event as a homecoming, returning every year and staying for all four days of music from morning to midnight. Organizers stress that this is a family event and strictly enforce a prohibition on alcohol. Day tickets are about $17.   **LOCATION:** Summersville Music Park, 45 miles north of Beckley and 75 miles east of Charleston. From Charleston take I-79 north to exit 57, then Route 19 south for 28 miles. At the traffic light in Summersville go left on Route 41 for 1.5 miles and take a left onto the grounds. **TICKETS/INFO:** 304-872-3145 **ACCOMMODATIONS/TOURIST INFO:** 304-872-1588

𝒟OO-WOP SATURDAY NIGHT
CLIFFTOP ✷ THIRD SATURDAY IN JULY

This concert features national doo-wop and R&B artists of the fifties and sixties under the stars at Camp Washington-Carver's beautiful mountaintop facility. The festival's repertoire branches well beyond the doo-wop genre, with such recent-year performers as the Coasters, the Dixie Cups, Chubby Checker, and the Marvellettes.

You won't find any cement for miles around Camp Washington-Carver, which was built by the Civilian Conservation Corps in 1939 and named to honor African American leaders Booker T. Washington and George Washington Carver. Hiking, fishing, horse-shoes, volleyball, and a playground and day care are available for children. **LOCATION:** Camp Washington-Carver in Clifftop, on Route 41 two miles south of U.S. 60. From Charleston take U.S. 60 east to Route 41 south. **TICKETS/INFO:** 304-558-0220, 304-438-6429 **ACCOMMODATIONS/TOURIST INFO:** 800-225-5982

WEST VIRGINIA BLUEGRASS FESTIVAL
WALKER ✭ THIRD WEEKEND IN JULY, FRIDAY AND SATURDAY

Set on 35 acres that host wooded camping areas and a permanent stage with pavilion seating, the West Virginia Bluegrass Festival provides two days of traditional bluegrass and bluegrass gospel music. Eight bands from the area and across the country perform for a crowd of about 600 to 1,000. Camping is free with a weekend pass, and throughout the grounds jam sessions go on long into the night. Admission ranges from $6 to $10 per day; food and arts and crafts vendors are on-site.   **LOCATION:** Cox's Field, nine miles east of Parkersburg at Route 47 and Walker Road, seven miles east of I-77 (Staunton Avenue exit) **TICKETS/INFO:** 304-387-1103 **ACCOMMODATIONS/TOURIST INFO:** 800-225-5982

APPALACHIAN STRING BAND MUSIC FESTIVAL
CLIFFTOP ✭ FIRST WEEKEND IN AUGUST

If you're looking for truly "alternative" music, check out the Appalachian String Band Music Festival. In a mountainside camp, string musicians from around the world gather for a weekend of concerts, contests, and jam sessions, playing the traditional Appalachian music that went out of fashion with the advent of bluegrass.

In the "traditional" category, look for dueling banjos, fiddles, guitars, and upright basses. The "non-traditional" category urges participants to apply old-fashioned string-band instruments to alternative tunes, techniques, and influences. You might see string bands playing with tubas, or string bands playing while lying flat on their backs with horns blaring above them. The weekend also includes CD recording sessions in a makeshift studio, concerts by featured performers, and contests for full bands, soloists, and dancers. Home-cooked meals—including vegetarian fare—are served in the dining hall of the Great Chestnut Lodge, one of the largest log structures in the world.

You won't find any cement for miles around Camp Washington-Carver, which was built by the Civilian Conservation Corps in 1939 and named to honor African American leaders Booker T. Washington and George Washington Carver. Hiking, fishing, horse-shoes, volleyball, and a playground and day care are available for children. **LOCATION:** Camp Washington-Carver in Clifftop, on Route 41 two miles south of U.S. 60. From Charleston take U.S. 60 east to Route 41 south. **TICKETS/INFO:** 304-558-0220, 304-438-6429 **ACCOMMODATIONS/TOURIST INFO:** 800-225-5982

AUGUSTA HERITAGE FESTIVAL
ELKINS ✭ SECOND WEEKEND IN AUGUST

The Augusta Heritage Festival caps off six weeks of Augusta Heritage workshops at Davis and Elkins College. Concerts showcase traditional music and dance, while craft exhibits and other folk paraphernalia complement the music. Each year features a couple of different themes, such as Appalachian old-time music, African American music, or music from the British Isles.

Appalachian String Band Music Festival: When it comes to jamming, any spot's a good one in Clifftop. Courtesy of Michael Keller/West Virginia Division of Culture and History

At the main stage and workshop stage, you can sample the depth and breadth of musical traditions from America and the world. The festival typically starts Friday with a concert and an old-time dance, and the music continues Saturday with concerts, participatory instrument and dance workshops, storytelling, and juried crafts. A kids' tent has mask making, music storytelling, mime, and more. The festival wraps up Sunday morning with a nondenominational gospel sing.

For those who believe folk music is really all about doing it yourself, the festival is a great introduction to the comprehensive workshop programs at this pioneering folk music school. Concerts feature many of the prestigious teaching staff from the summer's weeklong programs in blues, Cajun, Celtic, and much more. (See the Music Workshops chapter, page 497, for more information.)   **LOCATION:** Elkins City Park and Augusta Heritage Center at Davis and Elkins College, near the junction of U.S. 33 and U.S. 219. From I-79 take exit 99 and go east on U.S. 33. **TICKETS/INFO:** 304-637-1209, 304-636-1903; e-mail: augusta@dne.wvnet.edu **ACCOMMODATIONS/TOURIST INFO:** 800-422-3304, 304-636-2717

OLD-TIME DAY AND GOSPEL CELEBRATION

CLIFFTOP ✷ THIRD SATURDAY IN AUGUST

After a day of Appalachian games (like watermelon seed-spitting contests, greased-pig chases, and cow-chip bingo), visitors to this mountaintop center unwind with an evening of gospel music. This event brings in national talents in both the white and black gospel traditions; previous years have featured stars like Ethel Caffie-Austin, the Perrys, and the Christ Inspiration Delegation. Old-Time Day activities are free; the Gospel Celebration costs $10 for adults.   **LOCATION:** Camp Washington-Carver in Clifftop, on Route 41 two miles south of U.S. 60. From Charleston take U.S. 60 east to Route 41 south. **TICKETS/INFO:** 304-558-0220, 304-438-6429 **ACCOMMODATIONS/TOURIST INFO:** 800-225-5982

♪ACKSON COUNTY GOSPEL SING
COTTAGEVILLE ✳ LAST WEEKEND IN AUGUST

With more than 50 performers and 5,000 spectators, this sprawling event proves that the Southern gospel tradition is alive and well in West Virginia. Regionally known quartets and other performers send their soulful harmonies echoing through the hilly campground, and admission is free for the sing. Other free gospel events are held at the Jackson County Fairgrounds the third weekend in May, the last weekend in June, and the third weekend in July. The campground is outfitted with water and electric facilities; no alcohol is allowed.   **LOCATION:** Jackson County Fairgrounds, just off Route 33 near Cottageville, which is about 45 miles north of Charleston via I-77. From I-77 take exit 138 and head west about seven miles. **TICKETS/INFO:** 304-4273-4407, 304-273-5224 **ACCOMMODATIONS/TOURIST INFO:** 800-225-5982

♫AGEBRUSH ROUNDUP COUNTRY MUSIC FESTIVAL
FAIRMONT/BUNNER RIDGE ✳ SECOND WEEKEND IN SEPTEMBER, FRIDAY AND SATURDAY

This is a semiannual event, happening the third weekend in June and the second weekend in September. See page 114 for details.   **LOCATION:** The Music Complex at Bunner Ridge. From I-79 take exit 139 and follow the signs to Bunner Ridge. **TICKETS/INFO:** 304-363-6366, 304-363-4864 **ACCOMMODATIONS/TOURIST INFO:** 800-225-5982

♪UGUSTA OLD-TIME WEEK AND FIDDLERS' REUNION
ELKINS ✳ A WEEK IN MID- OR LATE OCTOBER

This unique and heartwarming event gathers West Virginia's foremost fiddlers and other old-time musicians for a week of jam sessions, concerts, dancing, and renewal of friendships. The event is sponsored by the Augusta Heritage Center.   **LOCATION:** Augusta Heritage Center at Davis and Elkins College in Elkins, near the junction of U.S. 33 and U.S. 219. From I-79 take exit 99 and go east on U.S. 33. **TICKETS/INFO:** 304-637-1209, 304-636-1903; e-mail: augusta@dne.wvnet.edu **ACCOMMODATIONS/TOURIST INFO:** 800-422-3304, 304-636-2717

SOUTHEAST

MOBILE JAZZ FESTIVAL
MOBILE ✱ LAST WEEKEND IN MARCH

About 5,000 jazz fans show up each year to see eight college bands in competition, plus one nationally known headliner and two or three guest artists. Fans can also usually count on good weather during this time of year in Alabama. Tickets are free, and high school and college student clinics are held in conjunction with the festival. **LOCATION:** Saenger Theatre and Bienville Square in downtown Mobile **TICKETS/ INFO:** 334-479-5555 **ACCOMMODATIONS/TOURIST INFO:** 334-415-2000

BLUEGRASS SUPERJAM
CULLMAN ✱ FIRST WEEKEND IN APRIL, FRIDAY AND SATURDAY

This semiannual event features stars from the Grand Ole Opry, plus other nationally, regionally and locally known bluegrassers. The indoor concert is held in a rodeo-like arena with bleacher seating, but organizers encourage everyone to bring a lawn chair and get down in the dirt in front of the stage for more comfort and better sight and sound. Some 2,000 to 3,000 people show up for this event, paying $11 to $13 at the gate. A nearly identical bluegrass festival is held at the same place the first weekend in November.   **LOCATION:** Cullman Agricultural Trade Center, on Highway 31 north in Cullman **TICKETS/INFO:** 205-747-1650, 205-734-0454 **ACCOMMODATIONS/ TOURIST INFO:** 205-734-0454

BRIERFIELD MUSIC FESTIVAL
BRIERFIELD ✱ FIRST WEEKEND IN MAY, FRIDAY AND SATURDAY

The Brierfield Music Festival offers a spicy blend of music, including bluegrass, country, folk, and Cajun. The annual festival attracts 3,500 music lovers and up to a dozen performers each year and is held at historic Brierfield Ironworks Park, which is full of wooded, shady areas where you can sit a spell and hear fiddle tunes fill the air. Other festival activities include the annual Brierfield Chili Championship, a large variety of children's activities, arts and crafts, and great food from the Plaza Cafe. Tickets are $10 for Friday and Saturday nights, $4 for Saturday during the day, and weekend passes for all three shows cost $20 in advance.   **LOCATION:** Brierfield Ironworks State Park in Brierfield, about seven miles south of Montevallo and 14 miles southwest of Centreville on Alabama Highway 25 **TICKETS/INFO:** 205-665-1856 **ACCOMMODATIONS/ TOURIST INFO:** 205-458-8000

JUBILEE CITY FEST

MONTGOMERY ✦ MEMORIAL DAY WEEKEND, FRIDAY–SUNDAY (MEMORIAL DAY IS THE LAST MONDAY IN MAY)

Since the late 1970s, the Jubilee City Fest has welcomed visitors to the banks of the Alabama River with a variety of music. Four music stages offer country, rock, bluegrass, jazz, blues, gospel, zydeco, and more, and some 50 acts attract nearly 80,000 spectators each year. Performances for children, arts and crafts, and fireworks make this a great family event for the extended weekend. Admission is about $10 per day, and picnicking, pets, and coolers are prohibited, but food is sold at the festival.   **LOCATION:** Four stages located throughout downtown Montgomery **TICKETS/INFO:** 334-834-7220 **AC-COMMODATIONS/TOURIST INFO:** 334-240-9455

SALUTE TO HANK WILLIAMS SR. DAY

GEORGIANA ✦ FIRST WEEKEND IN JUNE, FRIDAY–SUNDAY

Georgiana is the boyhood home of Hank Williams Sr., country music's greatest songwriter and natural talent. Hank died before he could celebrate his 30th birthday, but in six short years he recorded dozens of hits ("Your Cheatin' Heart," "I'm So Lonesome I Could Cry") and left an indelible impression on every country performer that would follow him.

This salute to Hank Williams pays homage to his low-key genius and brings traditionalists out of the woodwork for three days of concerts by 20 to 30 bands. Although no one will ever match Hank's haunting, harrowing vocals and simple, honest guitar work, you'll hear plenty of excellent and well-intended covers of his songs and those of his contemporaries. The festival's two stages are set in a shady area adjacent to his boyhood home, which has been converted to a museum in his honor. Each year, 5,000 to 10,000 people show up. Admission is about $15.   **LOCATION:** Hank Williams Museum, at 127 Rose Street in Georgiana. From I-65 take exit 114, then go two miles east into downtown Georgiana. **TICKETS/INFO:** 334-376-2396 **ACCOMMODA-TIONS/TOURIST INFO:** 334-376-2555

ALABAMA JUNE JAM

FORT PAYNE ✦ FIRST OR SECOND SATURDAY IN JUNE

With their four-part harmonies and songs of patriotism and small-town values, the band Alabama has sold more records than any other group in country music history. But each year in early June, just as Nashville's Country Music Fan Fair is wrapping up, the boys from Fort Payne come home.

Held in a 47-acre hay field that's transformed into a mini-city, the Alabama June Jam is a huge event that draws between 30,000 and 60,000 people. The band members typically invite a dozen of their favorite country artists (which have included Pam Tillis and Billy Ray Cyrus), and if past years are any indication, you can bet on seeing the local heroes on stage for a few numbers. Various homecoming events take place all week, and the concert is Saturday. The event includes children's areas, corporate and VIP areas, food, and RV parking. Tickets are about $30 in advance, and all profits go to charity. **LOCATION:** Fort Payne High School, at 45th Street and Old Valley Head Highway in

Fort Payne. From I-59 use exit 222. **TICKETS/INFO:** 205-845-9300 **ACCOMMODATIONS/TOURIST INFO:** 205-845-2741

ITY STAGES

BIRMINGHAM ✸ FATHER'S DAY WEEKEND, FRIDAY–SUNDAY (FATHER'S DAY IS THE THIRD SUNDAY IN JUNE)

In the tradition of the New Orleans Jazz and Heritage Festival, Birmingham's City Stages is an incredibly comprehensive festival that features nearly every form of American music—plus lots of African and worldbeat performers. This is as musically diverse a festival as you could hope to find anywhere in the world. It promises and actually delivers on the cliché "something for everyone" by offering 12 simultaneously operating stages and performance venues.

The 18-square-block site centers around Linn Park and Kelly Ingram Park (the site of historic events in the civil rights movement), and as you walk through the uniquely constructed gateways you get the impression that you're leaving the rest of the city behind. The festival both preserves traditions and aims for the cutting edge. For example, the Alabama Sampler area features music that has been handed down through generations in Alabama, such as country, blues, gospel, bluegrass, and sacred harp singing. On another stage, college and alternative bands hold forth. The Afrikan Village stage books international performers like King Sunny Adé, Kanda Bongo Man, and Arrow. In between, there's everything from a Classical Music Oasis to a Music Café featuring the world's finest folk singer-songwriters. Also expect to see huge quantities of jazz, blues, country, bluegrass, Cajun, and zydeco.

Over three days, some 265,000 people attend, paying around $20 for an advance weekend pass, or $15 for a day pass. Other events include a Jazz Camp, a parade, Alabama arts and crafts, charity events, and Unity Glow, a program for high school students that seeks to break down racial barriers and discourage stereotyping. Restrictions are enforced on pets, BYO alcohol, coolers, video and audio equipment, skates and skateboards. Alcoholic beverages are sold on-site.   **LOCATION:** Birmingham City Center, bounded by Eighth Avenue North, 21st Street, Fifth Avenue North, and 18th Street **TICKETS/INFO:** 800-277-1700, 205-715-6000; World Wide Web: http:/// www.citystages.org/1996 **ACCOMMODATIONS/TOURIST INFO:** 800-458-8085, 205-458-8000

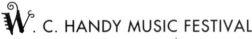 C. HANDY MUSIC FESTIVAL

FLORENCE AND NEARBY TOWNS ✸ FIRST SUNDAY IN AUGUST THROUGH THE FOLLOWING SATURDAY

Born in 1873 of two generations of preachers, William Christopher Handy was raised in a log cabin in Florence and nourished by sacred hymns and traditional black spirituals. As a young boy he would sneak down to the Tennessee River to hear black laborers sing as they worked, and as a teenager he bought a cornet and ran away from home, embarking on a musical odyssey that took him to Memphis, St. Louis, Chicago, and New York. While leading a vaudeville orchestra, he said he came across a ragged black man playing "the weirdest music I have ever heard" and turned his attention toward nurturing that raw, heartfelt sound that he would simply call "the blues."

In this weeklong celebration of Handy's legacy, parties and musical activities pop up all over Florence and nearby Sheffield, Tuscumbia, and Muscle Shoals. Venues for the nearly 200 events include churches, restaurants, the street, the riverside, or anywhere

Something for everyone: At Birmingham's City Stages, 12 performance areas feature music from the Americas and beyond.

Courtesy of BCHF/Rowland Scher-

man/Alabama Bureau of Tourism

& Travel

else a musician can pull up a seat and pull out a guitar. Unlike many large-scale music events, the W. C. Handy Music Festival is refreshingly homespun and features a huge variety of musicians with roots in the Shoals area. A Saturday night headliner concert features blues, jazz, classical, big band, and more. More than 90 percent of the events are free.   **LOCATION:** Florence and the neighboring towns of Sheffield, Tuscumbia, and Muscle Shoals (about 70 miles west of Huntsville in the northwest corner of the state) **TICKETS/INFO:** 800-472-5837, 205-766-7642 **ACCOMMODATIONS/TOURIST INFO:** 205-764-4661

ANNUAL STATE FIDDLING AND BLUEGRASS CONVENTION

HUNTSVILLE ✴ THIRD WEEKEND IN SEPTEMBER, FRIDAY AND SATURDAY

This festival has become popular with bluegrass and country musicians throughout the United States. Held on 90 rustic acres at the Cahaba Shriners Temple in Huntsville, the festival, begun in the mid-1980s, draws anywhere from 3,000 to 5,000 spectators each year and features musicians from all over the country. The musical mix is heavy on acoustic fiddling and bluegrass, with some country music thrown in later in the evenings.

The festival centers around a variety of highly entertaining competitions that include buck dancing (a form of clogging), bluegrass banjo, bluegrass band, junior fiddle (to age 49), senior fiddle, and a climactic fiddling playoff in which junior and senior fiddling champs square off against "the Fiddling King." Each competition features cash awards, and paid bands entertain after the competitions. Organizers take pride in the relaxed, friendly atmosphere that prevails, and note that if it rains all the festivities can move inside the Cahaba Shriners Temple. Numerous campsites are available among cedar and pine trees, and tickets cost about $6 a day.   **LOCATION:** Cahaba Shriners Temple, on Winchester Street in Huntsville **TICKETS/INFO:** 205-859-4471, 205-883-4576 **ACCOMMODATIONS/TOURIST INFO:** 800-772-2336, 205-553-5723

*M*OUNTAIN DULCIMER FESTIVAL
HUNTSVILLE ✶ THIRD SUNDAY IN SEPTEMBER

The word *dulcimer* comes from the Latin for "sweet sound," and lots of sweet sounds can be heard at this festival as musicians make their way through crowds and sit under shady trees coaxing delicate tones from their instruments. This festival attracts mountain dulcimer makers and players from several surrounding states, providing a blend of informal jam sessions, performances, demonstrations, and displays. The Burritt Museum grounds are set on Round Top Mountain and overlook the Tennessee Valley and the city of Henderson. The park includes a collection of 19th-century farmsteads from the years 1850 to 1900. It also contains nature trails, an 1860s coal mine, and the museum itself, which is a restored 1930s house in the shape of an *X*. A $2 donation is suggested for adults.   **LOCATION:** Burritt Museum and Park, 3101 Burritt Drive, in Huntsville **TICKETS/INFO:** 205-536-2882 **ACCOMMODATIONS/TOURIST INFO:** 205-533-5723

*B*AYFEST
MOBILE ✶ FIRST WEEKEND IN OCTOBER, FRIDAY–SUNDAY

With a population representing ethnic groups from more than 50 countries, Mobile locals naturally have eclectic musical tastes. This growing festival caters to those tastes in a big way, with pure, unadulterated music in the streets. Local radio stations sponsor four stages, competing to book the best of the rock/pop, roots, reggae, jazz, blues, country, R&B, and zydeco genres.

Oldies-but-goodies like Three Dog Night and the Temptations offer predictability for those who want it, while trendsetters like Sonny Landreth, Cake, and Bela Fleck keep progressives interested. In all, more than 65 acts—many of them regional favorites—perform over the three days, and the action is rounded out by food and art vendors, two children's areas, and workshops. The event takes place just one block from historic Dauphin Street, Mobile's booming restaurant and entertainment area.   **LOCATION:** St. Joseph Street and the surrounding area in downtown Mobile. From I-65 take exit 9 to Water Street; from I-10 take exit 26B to Water Street. **TICKETS/INFO:** 334-470-7730, 334-434-7970 **ACCOMMODATIONS/TOURIST INFO:** 334-415-2000

TENNESSEE VALLEY OLD-TIME FIDDLERS CONVENTION

ATHENS ✷ FIRST FULL WEEKEND IN OCTOBER

The Tennessee Valley Old-Time Fiddlers Convention is actually a competition, with approximately 200 contestants competing each year in 14 categories. Nearly 15,000 spectators show up to watch local, regional, and even national talents as they compete for cash prizes in competitions including harmonica, mandolin, guitar, bluegrass banjo, dulcimer, old-time singing, and several categories of fiddle.

This festival began in country kitchens in the early 1950s, with just a few musicians meeting every now and then to jam. These pioneers decided it was time to bring fiddling out of the kitchens and onto the stage, and in the summer of 1957 the Tennessee Valley Old-Time Fiddlers Association was formed. Since then, the festival has helped to revive old-time music traditions. Craftsmen from around the area display their arts and crafts in conjunction with the musical competition. Tickets are $3 on Friday, $4 on Saturday, or $6 for both days.   **LOCATION:** On the campus of Athens State College, 300 North Beaty Street, in Athens, which is about 15 miles south of the Alabama-Tennessee border, midway between Nashville and Birmingham. **TICKETS/INFO:** 205-233-8100 **ACCOMMODATIONS/TOURIST INFO:** 205-233-8205

BIRMINGHAM JAM

BIRMINGHAM ✷ COLUMBUS DAY WEEKEND, FRIDAY–SUNDAY (COLUMBUS DAY IS OBSERVED ON THE SECOND MONDAY IN OCTOBER)

The Birmingham Jam showcases the best of the southern musical heritage, with four stages of jazz, blues, and gospel. Featuring towering talents like the Five Blind Boys from Alabama, the Count Basie Orchestra, the Fabulous Thunderbirds, and Dr. John, the festival draws up to 30,000 music lovers to the unique grounds of the Sloss Furnaces, a preserved iron foundry. A comprehensive Kids' Karnival provides hands-on activities and performances for the younger members of the family. Food and merchandise booths are handpicked to demonstrate the very best the South has to offer. Tickets are about $10 per day or $15 for the entire weekend.   **LOCATION:** Sloss Furnaces National Historic Landmark, at 20 32nd Street North, in Birmingham. From I-20/59 use the exit for 31st Street and follow the signs to Sloss Furnaces. **TICKETS/INFO:** 205-323-0569; World Wide Web: http://www.bhm.tis.net/bhmjam/ **ACCOMMODATIONS/TOURIST INFO:** 205-458-8000

FRANK BROWN INTERNATIONAL SONGWRITERS FESTIVAL

FAIRHOPE, GULF SHORES, ORANGE BEACH ✷ FIRST THURSDAY–SECOND SUNDAY IN NOVEMBER

Here's a chance to visit the whitest beaches in the world and discover new and veteran songwriting talents in several genres, including country, blues, and gospel. At 15 intimate bars, churches, and eateries in six cities around the Florida-Alabama border, more than 150 songwriters showcase their songs. Like the huge Kerrville Folk Festival in Texas, this event is one of the few to focus on songwriters and to feature only original music. In addition to entertaining an audience of thousands, the festival provides an atmosphere for songwriters to interact freely with their peers and to develop as artists and professionals. Admission fees vary depending on venue.   **LOCATION:** Various venues in Fairhope, Gulf Shores, and Orange Beach in Alabama, and in Perdido Key, Pensacola, and Pensacola Beach in Florida. Call for locations. **TICKETS/INFO:** 334-981-5678, 904-492-7664; e-mail: songfest@amaranth.com; World Wide Web: http:// www.amaranth.com/~ken/fbrown.html **ACCOMMODATIONS/TOURIST INFO:** 334-968-6901, 904-492-4660, 904-438-4081

𝒟EEP SOUTH DULCIMER FESTIVAL
MOBILE ✷ FIRST WEEKEND IN NOVEMBER, FRIDAY–SUNDAY

The Deep South Dulcimer Festival exclusively features lap dulcimer players. This is truly a musician's festival, with about 30 dulcimer players entertaining a mere 150 spectators (in fact, nearly everyone who attends is a lap dulcimer player or the spouse of one). The festival is set in Chickasabougue Park, a gorgeous, wooded area with great campsites—which is important since tradition mandates that everyone stay up through the night jamming. The festival tends to be very social, with old friends meeting new friends around big cookouts and barbecues. Dulcimer players in their late sixties or early seventies hold informal teach-ins for younger players who are carrying on the lap dulcimer tradition. Larger jam sessions develop in a waterside pavilion with a giant fireplace. "We more or less take the park over and jam all week" is how longtime festival organizer Nell Hoyt put it. The ticket price is $8, including a workshop taught by a lap dulcimer pro, or $5 without the lesson.   **LOCATION:** Chickasabougue Park, near Mobile. From I-65 take exit 13 and look for signs to the park. **TICKETS/INFO:** 334-633-7739 **ACCOMMODATIONS/TOURIST INFO:** 334-415-2000

𝓑LUEGRASS SUPERJAM
CULLMAN ✷ FIRST WEEKEND IN NOVEMBER, FRIDAY AND SATURDAY

This is a semiannual event, happening the first weekends in April and November. See page 120 for details.   **LOCATION:** Cullman Agricultural Trade Center, on Highway 31 north in Cullman **TICKETS/INFO:** 205-747-1650, 205-734-0454 **ACCOMMODATIONS/TOURIST INFO:** 205-734-0454

ARKANSAS

ARKANSAS FOLK FESTIVAL
MOUNTAIN VIEW ✳ THIRD WEEKEND IN APRIL

In certain circles, Mountain View is considered the "Folk Music Capital of the World." This Ozark Mountain town of 2,500—where haircuts still cost $5 and life still moves at a slow, simple pace—is musical beyond belief. For as long as anyone can remember, folks have brought their guitars and fiddles down to the porches and bonfires near Courthouse Square to play and sing in any of the several jam sessions that carry on just about every night when the weather's good.

Locals became so accustomed to seeing one another cradling instruments on Courthouse Square that they decided to go ahead and establish themselves a festival. So, in 1961, people gathered on the square for the first annual Arkansas Folk Festival. More than three decades later, the festival is still on, and in addition to the eight or 10 talents playing on the main stage, roving musicians still crowd the Courthouse Square until they're "as thick as fleas on a dog," as one local put it.

Guitars, banjos, upright basses, and acoustic instruments twang with Ozark folk and gospel music. An estimated 35,000 people visit the square over the weekend, vastly outnumbering the town's population of 2,500. Folk emissaries ("people from off," as locals dub out-of-towners) come from all over the country and the world, many carrying instruments with them. Saturday features a parade, often with an educational theme, and the whole brouhaha's free. Bring an instrument—or be prepared to clap, stomp, or sing along to old ballads and tunes like "Greenback Dollar" and "Losing You."

The Ozark Folk Center, just a couple of minutes from Courthouse Square, has evening performances and special events during the festival.   **LOCATION:** Stone County Courthouse Square, on Main Street between Howard and Peabody in Mountain View, about 100 miles north of Little Rock. From U.S. 65 take Highway 16 east to Highway 9 north. **TICKETS/INFO:** 501-269-3851, 501-269-8068 **ACCOMMODA-TIONS/TOURIST INFO:** 501-269-8068, 800-264-3655

OZARK SCOTTISH FESTIVAL
BATESVILLE ✳ FOURTH WEEKEND IN APRIL

The Ozark Scottish Festival blends the spirit and traditions of the old Scottish Highland gatherings with the music and crafts of the Ozark Mountains. This is a fitting

Arkansas Folk Festival: Acoustic musicians are "as thick as fleas on a dog."
(See entry, page 127.) Courtesy of A.C. Haralson/Arkansas Department of Parks and Tourism

combination, since the contemporary culture of the Ozarks is rooted in that of the Scottish and Irish settlers who came to this area in the 1800s. In addition to Scottish and local folk singers, the event features competitions in Highland dancing and bagpiping, a Scottish Country Dance Ball, sheep dog demonstrations, a parade of tartans, and more. Tickets are $5 to $7 for adults.   **LOCATION:** Lyon College, on College Street just east of U.S. 167 in Batesville, 95 miles north of Little Rock **TICKETS/INFO:** 501-698-4241 **ACCOMMODATIONS/TOURIST INFO:** 501-793-2378

TRIBUTE TO MERLE TRAVIS & NATIONAL THUMBPICKING GUITAR CHAMPIONSHIP
MOUNTAIN VIEW ✷ FOURTH WEEKEND IN MAY

One of the most influential guitarists and songwriters in country music, the late Merle Travis was first to transfer the banjo roll to the guitar, using his thumb to play the bottom notes and two fingers to play the melody. This festival brings guitar hotshots and guitar buffs to the Ozark Folk Center for workshops and contests in "Travis picking," as the style is sometimes called. Local and national thumb-style masters often make appearances.   **LOCATION:** Ozark Folk Center and other locations in Mountain View, about 100 miles north of Little Rock. From U.S. 65 take Highway 16 east to Highway 9 north. **TICKETS/INFO:** 501-269-3851, 501-269-8068 **ACCOMMODATIONS/TOURIST INFO:** 501-269-8068

Piper's paradise: The Ozark Scottish Festival blends Scottish Highland tradi-
tions with the spirit of the Ozark Mountains. (See entry, page 127.) Courtesy of
Lyon College Ozark Scottish Festival

✿UREKA SPRINGS BLUES FESTIVAL
EUREKA SPRINGS ✸ WEEKEND AFTER MEMORIAL DAY, THURSDAY–SUNDAY
(MEMORIAL DAY IS THE LAST MONDAY IN MAY)

The beautifully restored Victorian resort town of Eureka Springs comes alive with
the sounds of traditional acoustic and cutting-edge electric blues. Listeners receive a
Blues Ticket (at about $100 for four days) and travel between 15 different venues via
foot, bus, and trolley as more than 20 bands play in 15 different clubs, theaters, and
ballrooms in town.

Eureka Springs has welcomed tourists since they first arrived in the late 1800s to
"take the waters." It's a historic jumble of little cottages, imposing mansions, rock
formations, and museums. The town is filled with music halls and more than 60
restaurants and is located close to the Buffalo National River, an untamable, snaky
ribbon of hairpin turns, chutes, and waterfalls.   **LOCATION:** Eureka Springs, in the
northwest corner of Arkansas about 180 miles northwest of Little Rock via U.S. 65
TICKETS/INFO: 501-253-5366 **ACCOMMODATIONS/TOURIST INFO:** 501-253-
8737

PORT FEST

JACKSONPORT ✷ LAST FULL WEEKEND IN JUNE

The bustling steamboat port of Jacksonport was so loyal to its river that it refused to grant a right-of-way for a railroad being built in the mid-1870s. The railroad moved a few miles to the south and Jacksonport gradually lost its importance—which meant that its historic courthouse and other buildings were never the victim of urban renewal. This festival celebrates the good, slow life on the grassy, shaded banks of the White River, one of America's most beautiful. A main stage features country stars like Pam Tillis and Tanya Tucker on Friday, and classical music on Saturday. A blues stage runs Saturday afternoon and night and features the likes of Clarence "Gatemouth" Brown and Bobby "Blue" Bland. Other hot spots include a children's stage and a Catfish Stage, where a state-sanctioned catfish-cooking contest is held. Admission is about $10. **LOCATION:** Jacksonport State Park, on the banks of the White River at Highway 69 three miles northwest of Newport and U.S. 67 **TICKETS/INFO:** 501-523-3618 **ACCOMMODATIONS/TOURIST INFO:** 501-523-3618

OPERA IN THE OZARKS

EUREKA SPRINGS ✷ LATE JUNE THROUGH JULY

Opera in the Ozarks presents three fully staged and costumed operas with orchestral accompaniment in a covered, open-sided theater seating 300. With the festival's rotating repertoire and performances nearly every day, opera lovers who stay in town for a few days can catch all three of the company's summer offerings. Tickets are $10-$13, and advance reservations are requested.

Opera in the Ozarks was founded in 1950, but Eureka Springs has welcomed tourists since they first arrived in the late 1800s to "take the waters." It's a historic jumble of little cottages, imposing mansions, rock formations, and museums. The town is filled with music halls and more than 60 restaurants and is located close to the Buffalo National River, an untamable, snaky ribbon of hairpin turns, chutes, and waterfalls. **LOCATION:** Inspiration Point Fine Arts Colony, seven miles west of Eureka Springs off Highway 62, in the northwest corner of Arkansas about 180 miles northwest of Little Rock via U.S. 65 **TICKETS/INFO:** 501-253-8595 **ACCOMMODATIONS/TOURIST INFO:** 501-253-8737

OLD-TIME GATHERING ON THE SQUARE AND JULY FOURTH CELEBRATION

MOUNTAIN VIEW ✷ JULY 4 (INDEPENDENCE DAY)

Although there's no shortage of fine locally made music in Mountain View any day of the year, this free gathering brings even more musicians out of the woodwork. In the spirit of civil service, one local band volunteers its talent to headline during the festivities—and in the spirit of Mountain View, dozens of others make impromptu music on the square. Musicians play the ballads and folk tunes they've known (it seems) since birth, and a street dance marks the noontime hour. Heels kick and sparks fly as contests get underway in the jig, two-step, and waltz, and music resounds from nearby music spots like Jimmy Driftwood's Barn and the Ozark Folk Center. **LOCATION:** Stone County Courthouse Square, on Main Street between Howard and Peabody in Mountain View, about 100 miles north of Little Rock. From U.S. 65 take Highway 16 east to

Highway 9 north. **TICKETS/INFO:** 501-269-8068 **ACCOMMODATIONS/TOURIST INFO:** 501-269-8068

⚡LBERT E. BRUMLEY MEMORIAL SUNDOWN TO SUNUP GOSPEL SING

SPRINGDALE ✴ FIRST FULL WEEKEND IN AUGUST, THURSDAY–SATURDAY

Up to 30,000 gospel music lovers gather under the stars to listen to some 20 quartets and other gospel acts at the "grandaddy of outdoor gospel fests." Four-part harmonies fill the early-morning hours as families sit on lawn chairs and bleachers and try to make it through the night without dozing. This event grew from the dream of one of gospel music's greatest songwriters, Albert E. Brumley. Brumley composed more than 800 gospel and religious songs, including the classics "I'll Fly Away" and "Turn Your Radio On." Tickets are $11 for adults and $2 for children.   **LOCATION:** Parsons Rodeo Arena, in Springdale, just north of Fayetteville **TICKETS/INFO:** 417-435-2225 **ACCOMMODATIONS/TOURIST INFO:** 501-751-4694

⚡UTOHARP JAMBOREE

MOUNTAIN VIEW ✴ SECOND WEEKEND IN AUGUST

Autoharp enthusiasts aren't exactly a dime a dozen, but at the Autoharp Jamboree you'll find at least a passel. This festival, begun in 1982, features concerts and workshops focusing on the traditional autoharp. The daytime is filled with miniconcerts and workshops in which special guest instructors teach classes at all levels, from beginning to advanced. Evening concerts (about $7) feature guest performers.   **LOCATION:** Ozark Folk Center and other locations in Mountain View, about 100 miles north of Little Rock. From U.S. 65 take Highway 16 east to Highway 9 north. **TICKETS/INFO:** 501-269-3851 **ACCOMMODATIONS/TOURIST INFO:** 501-268-8068, 800-264-3655

⚡OGAN COUNTY GOSPEL SINGING CONVENTION

BOONEVILLE ✴ THURSDAY AND FRIDAY BEFORE THE FOURTH SUNDAY IN AUGUST

This small gathering brings together shape-note singers from all over the South for two days of singing and congregational sight-reading. The event begins Thursday evening in Booneville's First United Methodist Church and continues all day Friday, with a pause for a potluck lunch and supper. (For more on shape-note singing, see the East Texas Sacred Harp Singing Convention, Henderson, Texas.)   **LOCATION:** First United Methodist Church, on Broadway in Booneville, southeast of Fort Smith at the junction of Highway 23 and Highway 10 **TICKETS/INFO:** 501-675-3613 **ACCOMMODATIONS/TOURIST INFO:** 501-675-2666

⚡RIBUTE TO JIMMIE RODGERS

MOUNTAIN VIEW ✴ LAST WEEKEND IN AUGUST

Jimmie Rodgers, known variously as "the Blue Yodeler" and "the Singing Brakeman," is referred to in the Country Music Hall of Fame as simply "the man who started it all." Though he died in 1933, his legend endures, and at this event guest performers and

Ozark Folk Center musicians pay tribute to him with evening concerts, afternoon miniconcerts, seminars, video presentations, and other special activities. Admission is $7.   **LOCATION:** Ozark Folk Center and other locations in Mountain View, about 100 miles north of Little Rock. From U.S. 65 take Highway 16 east to Highway 9 north. **TICKETS/INFO:** 501-269-3851 **ACCOMMODATIONS/TOURIST INFO:** 501-268-8068, 800-264-3655

ꟻORT SMITH RIVERFRONT BLUES FESTIVAL
FORT SMITH ✷ A WEEKEND IN EARLY SEPTEMBER, THURSDAY–SATURDAY

Also known as "the best little blues festival in America," the Fort Smith Riverfront Blues Festival is a great place to see national blues talents without having to cope with large crowds. On the banks of the slowly rolling Arkansas River, traditional and legendary artists appear alongside newer blues sensations. Away from the electrified main stage are music workshops, acoustic stages, and southern-style food to satisfy your belly when it howls louder than the bluesmen on stage. Tickets range from $5 to $10. **LOCATION:** Downtown Fort Smith at the riverfront **TICKETS/INFO:** 501-783-6353 **ACCOMMODATIONS/TOURIST INFO:** 800-637-1477

ꞔUREKA SPRINGS JAZZ FESTIVAL
EUREKA SPRINGS ✷ THIRD WEEK IN SEPTEMBER

Sponsored by the Eureka Springs Jazz Society, this festival has run annually since 1985. Jazz musicians play at the Performing Arts Center and various other locations around town; soloists as well as ensembles perform traditional jazz, swing, and contemporary jazz.

Eureka Springs has welcomed tourists since they first arrived in the late 1800s to "take the waters." It's a historic jumble of little cottages, imposing mansions, rock formations, and museums. The town is filled with music halls and more than 60 restaurants and is located close to the Buffalo National River, an untamable, snaky ribbon of hairpin turns, chutes, and waterfalls.   **LOCATION:** Downtown Eureka Springs, in the northwest corner of Arkansas about 180 miles northwest of Little Rock via U.S. 65 **TICKETS/INFO:** 501-253-6258, 501-253-8737 **ACCOMMODATIONS/TOURIST INFO:** 501-253-8737

ᴀRKANSAS OLD-TIME FIDDLE CHAMPIONSHIPS
MOUNTAIN VIEW ✷ THIRD WEEKEND IN SEPTEMBER

Autumn brings the old-time fiddlers to the Ozark Folk Center. Arkansas residents compete in old-style, pre-bluegrass fiddling for the state title in junior, senior, and open categories. Admission is about $7.   **LOCATION:** Ozark Folk Center and other locations in Mountain View, about 100 miles north of Little Rock. From U.S. 65 take Highway 16 east to Highway 9 north. **TICKETS/INFO:** 501-269-3851 **ACCOMMODATIONS/TOURIST INFO:** 501-268-8068, 800-264-3655

ꞞRIGINAL OZARK FOLK FESTIVAL
EUREKA SPRINGS ✷ LAST WEEKEND IN SEPTEMBER

This very traditional folk festival began in 1953 and has run continuously since then, featuring music, clog dancing, and comedy. The festival strongly favors the local and traditional but in recent years has made some concessions to the contemporary by featuring the likes of Leo Kottke, Tom Paxton, and Maura O'Connell among its 14 acts. Admission varies between $8 and $14, depending on the show.

Eureka Springs has welcomed tourists since they first arrived in the late 1800s to "take the waters." It's a historic jumble of little cottages, imposing mansions, rock formations, and museums. The town is filled with music halls and more than 60 restaurants and is located close to the Buffalo National River, an untamable, snaky ribbon of hairpin turns, chutes, and waterfalls.   **LOCATION:** City Auditorium, 44 South Main Street in Eureka Springs, in the northwest corner of Arkansas about 180 miles northwest of Little Rock via U.S. 65 **TICKETS/INFO:** 501-253-8737 **ACCOMMO-DATIONS/TOURIST INFO:** 501-253-8737

FIDDLE AND DANCE JAMBOREE
MOUNTAIN VIEW ✱ SECOND WEEKEND IN OCTOBER

Begun in 1974, the Ozark Folk Center's Fiddle and Dance Jamboree features exhibition fiddling and traditional dances throughout the day, plus evening concerts by visiting dance groups and fiddlers from across the Ozarks region. Admission is about $7. **LOCATION:** Ozark Folk Center and other locations in Mountain View, about 100 miles north of Little Rock. From U.S. 65 take Highway 16 east to Highway 9 north. **TICKETS/INFO:** 501-269-3851 **ACCOMMODATIONS/TOURIST INFO:** 501-268-8068, 800-264-3655

KING BISCUIT BLUES FESTIVAL
HELENA ✱ SECOND WEEKEND IN OCTOBER, FRIDAY–SUNDAY

This here's the real thing—three days of the best in Delta blues, according to the many blues greats who got their start in Helena on the old King Biscuit Time radio show. In this Mississippi River town halfway between Memphis, Tennessee, and Greenville, Mississippi, four stages host a whopping 75 acts. Plenty of nationally known names play, but in this neck of the woods, the smart money's on the locals, who work hard at preserving one of America's most cherished art forms. Special features include gospel blues performances, a children's blues stage, and free admission. The festival sits in a natural amphitheater created by the Mississippi levee, and spectators typically bring blankets, lawn chairs, and picnics.   **LOCATION:** The downtown historic district along Cherry Street in Helena, on the Mississippi River about halfway between Memphis, Tennessee, and Greenville, Mississippi **TICKETS/INFO:** 501-338-9798 **ACCOMMODA-TIONS/TOURIST INFO:** 501-338-9798

BEAN FEST
MOUNTAIN VIEW ✱ LAST WEEKEND IN OCTOBER

It all started in 1981 when someone convinced town locals to build and decorate their very own traditional outhouses, put them on wheels, and push them around the courthouse square in pursuit of prizes for the speediest and prettiest creations. And since the people of Mountain View ("Folk Music Capital of the World") seem to tow their musical instruments along whenever they visit the courthouse square, this event blossomed into a large-scale jam session, featuring plenty of impromptu folk, gospel, and country music, both on and off an outdoor stage set up amid all the shenanigans.

King Biscuit Blues Festival: The smart money's on the locals. (See entry, page 133.)

Courtesy of A.C. Haralson/Ar-

kansas Dept. of Parks and Tourism

Local musicians fuel a street dance with music, and 50 to 60 craftspeople market their wares.

The event's name comes from a simultaneous bean contest. The town sets 30 cooking pots on the square, and contestants arrive early to fix their own country-style spiced pinto beans, with plenty of corn bread on the side. At noon, everybody eats. The festival is free (although contestants pay an entry fee), and while the musicians go unpaid, the prettiest and speediest outhouses win cash prizes for their creators, as do the most scrumptious beans.   **LOCATION:** Stone County Courthouse Square, on Main Street between Howard and Peabody in Mountain View, about 100 miles north of Little Rock. From U.S. 65 take Highway 16 east to Highway 9 north. **TICKETS/INFO:** 501-269-8068 **ACCOMMODATIONS/TOURIST INFO:** 501-269-8068

ZARK CHRISTMAS

MOUNTAIN VIEW ✹ FIRST WEEKEND IN DECEMBER

Here's a great opportunity to enjoy the traditional Christmas music of the Ozark Mountains. Mountain View's many fine local musicians perform folk songs on acoustic instruments, and fourth-graders in the Mountain View Band sing carols. A community sing is capped by an appearance by the fat guy in red. Tickets are about $7, and there's always impromptu folk jamming in Mountain View's Courthouse Square. **LOCATION:** Ozark Folk Center and other locations in Mountain View, about 100 miles north of Little Rock. From U.S. 65 take Highway 16 east to Highway 9 north. **TICKETS/ INFO:** 501-269-3851 **ACCOMMODATIONS/TOURIST INFO:** 501-268-8068, 800-264-3655

FLoRiDa

SOUTH FLORIDA FOLK FESTIVAL
OAKLAND PARK ✳ SATURDAY AND SUNDAY IMMEDIATELY PRECEDING THE
THIRD MONDAY IN JANUARY (MARTIN LUTHER KING, JR., DAY)

There's a performer for every 20 of the approximately 1,000 spectators at the intimate South Florida Folk Festival. Sponsored by the Broward Folk Club, the gathering draws a hands-on crowd that enjoys music on five stages. Days include a national songwriters' competition, and at night song swaps are held around campfires. Anything except glass containers goes at this friendly gathering just 30 minutes from Miami Beach. **LOCATION:** Easterlin Park, 1000 Northwest 38th Street in Oakland Park, near Fort Lauderdale **TICKETS/INFO:** 954-832-0386, 954-430-7004; e-mail: A029377T@BCFreenet.seflin.lib.fl.us **ACCOMMODATIONS/TOURIST INFO:** 954-761-5000

INTERNATIONAL CARILLON FESTIVAL
LAKE WALES ✳ NINE DAYS IN FEBRUARY, USUALLY STARTING THE
SECOND SATURDAY

Bok Gardens was named a National Historic Landmark in 1994, and its annual carillon festival celebrates beauty in many incarnations. Carillon bells demonstrate the magnificence of sound; the 205-foot tower that houses the bells stands as a monument to architectural grandeur, and a 128-acre sanctuary surrounding the tower celebrates peacefulness in the midst of nature's thriving.

Carillon players from around the world gather at the gardens in temperate mid-February to take turns eliciting musical beauty from the 57-bell carillon, whose bells span five octaves and range from 17 pounds to nearly 12 tons. Musical selections vary from show tunes by Leonard Bernstein to duets by Debussy and opera arias by Mozart. Plus, international players bring the carillon repertoires of home countries such as Spain and Belgium.

A nine-day garland of afternoon concerts has as its crowning jewel a moonlight recital that organizers usually schedule to coincide with a full moon. Audiences sit amid moonlit flowers on lush grounds as carillon bells resound melodically; afterward, listeners meet musicians at a champagne and dessert reception.

Other festival attractions include children's activities such as hands-on puppet making, guided walking tours of the grounds, and meet-the-artist events. Energetic visitors can hike through the Pine Ridge Nature Preserve, which butts against the northern and eastern edges of the Fred Olmsted-designed grounds. Hikers might run across a placard with a quote culled from a letter written to the gardens' founder, Edward Bok. The quote reads: "I come here to find myself. It is so easy to get lost in the world." If you should get lost in the world on the way to the carillon festival, just stop and listen, for a cavalcade of bells will beckon you back to the middle of it all.   **LOCATION:** Bok Tower Gardens on County Road 17A (Burns Avenue), three miles north of Lake Wales, which is at the junction of Alternate U.S. 27 and State Road 60. From Orlando drive south on I-4 to U.S. 27 and continue south to Alternate U.S. 27, then go east and south to County Road 17A. **TICKETS/INFO:** 941-676-1408 **ACCOMMODATIONS/TOURIST INFO:** 941-676-3445

ℬACH FESTIVAL OF WINTER PARK
WINTER PARK ✴ LAST WEEKEND IN FEBRUARY

The Bach Festival Society of Winter Park (which recently celebrated its 60th anniversary) presents one of the oldest continuously running Bach festivals in the United States. In a Spanish Gothic chapel, auditioned volunteers comprise the orchestra and choir, and international soloists join them in presenting the works of J. S. Bach and other choral masterpieces from the baroque, classical, and romantic periods. The internationally known artists also offer lectures and recitals. Concerts cost $18 each, and past festivals have drawn crowds of more than 2,400. Note that organizers enforce a dress code, and that performances are for adults only.   **LOCATION:** Knowles Memorial Chapel on the Rollins College campus in Winter Park **TICKETS/INFO:** 407-646-2182 **ACCOMMODATIONS/TOURIST INFO:** 407-644-8281, 407-425-1234

𝒞ARNAVAL MIAMI
MIAMI ✴ FIRST TWO WEEKENDS IN MARCH

Little Havana's Calle Ocho (Eighth Street) goes wild during one of the largest street festivals in the country. The music is exceptional, with 100 bands from the Spanish Caribbean fueling nonstop dancing to salsa, merengue, mambo, and cumbia rhythms. A giant parade features floats, cars, and people in full regalia, and the event includes folkloric sites, soccer matches, dog and bike races, cooking contests, a battle of the bands, and an eight-kilometer run.   **LOCATION:** The Little Havana neighborhood of Miami, especially up and down Calle Ocho (Eighth Street) **TICKETS/INFO:** 305-644-8888 **ACCOMMODATIONS/TOURIST INFO:** 305-539-3000

𝒞ARL ALLEN'S ANNUAL STATE CHAMPIONSHIP BLUEGRASS FESTIVAL
AUBURNDALE ✴ THIRD WEEKEND IN MARCH, FRIDAY–SUNDAY

Florida's largest bluegrass festival is absolutely free, and it includes a hot-air balloon race as part of the festivities. Two stages support about 50 traditional bluegrass bands, and the grounds are chock-full of side shows like clogging and banjo contests, beauty

Bach Festival of Winter Park: International soloists join the Festival Choir in a Spanish Gothic chapel. (See entry, page 137.)

Courtesy of Bach Festival Choir of

Winter Park

pageants, arts and crafts exhibitions, and children's activities. The music and merriment draw about 100,000 people.   **LOCATION:** International Market World, at 1052 Highway 92 west in Auburndale, which is about halfway between Tampa and Orlando, just northwest of Winter Haven **TICKETS/INFO:** 941-967-4307, 941-299-9489, 941-665-0062 **ACCOMMODATIONS/TOURIST INFO:** 800-828-7655

JAZZ & BLUES FESTIVAL
TALLAHASSEE ✻ THIRD WEEKEND IN MARCH

This is a great opportunity to see Florida's best jazz and blues artists in a setting that offers both natural beauty and historic surroundings. Nearly 1,300 music fans come out each year to see six of Florida's most talented blues acts burn up the stage. The festival is held at the Tallahassee Museum, which features a hands-on science center and historic buildings. Festival tickets are $6 for adults and $4 for children.   **LOCATION:** Tallahassee Museum, 3945 Museum Drive, in Tallahassee **TICKETS/INFO:** 904-575-8684 **ACCOMMODATIONS/TOURIST INFO:** 800-628-2866

Child of the Sun Jazz Festival: Trombonist Bill Watrous and his band perform under palm trees and springtime stars. Courtesy of Child of the Sun Jazz Festival

CHILD OF THE SUN JAZZ FESTIVAL
LAKELAND ✴ LAST WEEKEND IN MARCH, FRIDAY AND SATURDAY

Set on the Frank Lloyd Wright-designed campus of Florida Southern College, this growing festival presents about 10 performers over two days. The festival leans toward traditional mainstream and bebop, and it has premiered several new works by performers such as Lakeland cornetist Nat Adderley.   **LOCATION:** Florida Southern College, at 111 Lake Hollingsworth Drive in Lakeland **TICKETS/INFO:** 941-680-4217, 941-680-4136 **ACCOMMODATIONS/TOURIST INFO:** 941-687-8910

SARASOTA JAZZ FESTIVAL
SARASOTA ✴ A WEEKEND IN LATE MARCH OR EARLY APRIL

Seeking to preserve and perpetuate jazz in the Sarasota area, this festival features about 60 internationally known jazz musicians during its weekend run. To beat the heat, which is already starting to well up outside, organizers bring all the music indoors to the Van Wezel Performing Arts Hall, where assigned seating is available. About 6,000 spectators show up to hear the multiday lineup of mainstream jazz.   **LOCATION:** Van Wezel Performing Arts Hall, 777 North Tamiami Trail, in Sarasota **TICKETS/INFO:** 941-366-1552; e-mail: sarajazzel@aol.com **ACCOMMODATIONS/TOURIST INFO:** 941-957-1877, 800-522-9799

SUNFEST
WEST PALM BEACH ✴ FIRST WEEKEND IN MAY

One of the largest annual music festivals in Florida, SunFest attracts more than 250,000 music fans annually—and with its fantastically eclectic lineup and great side events, it is easy to see why. Recent performers at SunFest have represented a wide range of music, with blues, jazz, alternative, reggae, and pop all visible at some point during the festival. The 1995 lineup, with more than 50 bands in five days, included blues favorites B. B. King and Koko Taylor, hippy-rockers Widespread Panic, dawg-grasser David Grisman, jazz-grass banjoist Bela Fleck, soul/R&B favorites the subdudes, pop icons Fleetwood Mac, and local favorites like the electric folksters the Shack Daddys and funky Cajun rockers Inhouse.

With this much going on, the festival needs every one of its four stages, which are set up along the palm-lined Intracoastal Waterway. This interesting area of West Palm Beach also features a number of good pubs and clubs for anyone who starts to get a bit too much sun. Other features include music clinics, food, a juried art show, a crafts marketplace, water events, and a youth park.

Prices range from $8 per day in advance to $25 for all five days. This averages out to 50¢ a band—a pretty good deal for this much music.   **LOCATION:** Downtown West Palm Beach, on Flagler Drive between Banyan Boulevard and Lakeview Avenue **TICK-ETS/INFO:** 407-659-5980; World Wide Web: http://www.emi.net/sunfest/ **ACCOMMODATIONS/TOURIST INFO:** 407-471-3995

͗SARASOTA MUSIC FESTIVAL
SARASOTA ✶ FIRST THREE WEEKS IN JUNE

Over its three-week run, Sarasota's famed classical music festival brings more than 10,000 to the Van Wezel Performing Arts Hall to experience more than 40 performances by national and international talents. Sarasota's own Festival Orchestra is joined by guest artists who demonstrate their talents in voice, piano, and string and wind instruments.

The Sarasota Music Festival offers a look at some of tomorrow's stars as they collaborate to perform works by such greats as Vivaldi, Brahms, Mendelssohn, and Rossini. Master classes in instrumental techniques and coaching in chamber music are offered daily, as are seminars, miniclasses, and lectures. Tickets are free for student concerts and $30 for professional concerts. Performances are held Thursday afternoons in Holley Hall and Friday and Saturday evenings in the Van Wezel Performing Arts Hall. **LOCATION:** Van Wezel Performing Arts Hall, 777 North Tamiami Trail, in Sarasota **TICKETS/INFO:** 941-953-4252 **ACCOMMODATIONS/TOURIST INFO:** 941-957-1877, 800-522-9799

͗SUWANNEE RIVER GOSPEL JUBILEE
LIVE OAK ✶ THIRD WEEKEND IN JUNE

This festival, which aims to preserve the traditions of southern gospel music, is held along the shores of the Suwannee River. Nearly 3,000 gospel music fans attend each year, enjoying regional and national gospel talent in a tree-shaded natural amphitheater. Workshops, food, arts and crafts, and a children's area round out the festival's attractions.

The Spirit of the Suwannee Park is a 580-acre music park and campground with a northern boundary along two miles of the Suwannee River. In the park and in the surrounding woodlands and game sanctuary, recreational opportunities include fishing, swimming, boating, camping, hiking, and touring an old-time farm museum. Another Suwannee River Gospel Jubilee is held the first weekend in October.   **LOCATION:** Spirit of the Suwannee Park, in Live Oak. From I-75 take exit 85 to Highway 129, then proceed south 4.5 miles. **TICKETS/INFO:** 904-364-1683 **ACCOMMODATIONS/TOURIST INFO:** 904-364-1683

❊WAMP STOMP

TALLAHASSEE ✳ A SATURDAY IN MID-JULY

The Tallahassee Museum's annual Swamp Stomp brings in six bands that play a mixture of old and new folk, bluegrass, and traditional music. The event attracts about 1,000 people each year, with tickets priced at about $6 for adults and $4 for children. The museum also offers historical buildings, a hands-on science center, and Florida's indigenous animals for kids and curious adults.   **LOCATION:** Tallahassee Museum, at 3945 Museum Drive in Tallahassee **TICKETS/INFO:** 904-575-8684 **ACCOMMODA-TIONS/TOURIST INFO:** 800-628-2866

❡UNDERWATER MUSIC FESTIVAL

BIG PINE KEY ✳ SECOND SATURDAY IN JULY

Held entirely underwater at Looe Key National Marine Sanctuary, this may well be the only music festival of its type in North America. The festival, which traditionally attracts more than 500 divers and snorkelers (and possibly a dolphin or two with an ear for music), features reggae and New Age compositions interspersed with reef-awareness messages, played for four uninterrupted hours by a local radio station. The broadcasts reach divers via special speakers dangling beneath boats strategically positioned around the reef.

Festival coordinator Bill Becker, who created the event almost 10 years ago, says the rhythmic reggae and ethereal New Age music achieve remarkably good fidelity underwater. He views the festival as a rare opportunity for diving audiophiles to relish some good tunes while checking out beautiful coral reefs and learning how to preserve them.

Divers and snorkelers who wish to participate in the Underwater Music Festival can charter boats from a number of local dive operators in the Lower Keys, and visitors and residents with their own boats can launch from public ramps throughout the area. To cap the day of music, the Lower Keys Chamber of Commerce serves a seafood dinner featuring specialties like conch fritters and conch chowder.   **LOCATION:** Looe Key National Marine Sanctuary, six miles south of Big Pine Key **TICKETS/INFO:** 800-872-3722 **ACCOMMODATIONS/TOURIST INFO:** 800-872-3722, 305-872-2411

❡MIAMI REGGAE FESTIVAL

MIAMI ✳ FIRST SUNDAY IN AUGUST

This festival celebrates Jamaica's traditions in a Jamaica-like tropical environment. As one of the largest reggae festivals in the United States, it attracts 20,000 to 50,000 spectators and features local, national, and international bands. Admission is $10 for this festival, which has been exposing new talent for more than a decade. Also featured are island food, arts and crafts, and recreational areas for children. No pets are allowed. **LOCATION:** Bayfront Park, in the heart of Miami at 301 North Biscayne Boulevard **TICKETS/INFO:** 305-891-2944, 305-891-1242 **ACCOMMODATIONS/TOURIST INFO:** 305-539-3000

Underwater Music Festival: Scuba divers, snorkelers, and reef fish relish some bubbly tunes while cavorting among the coral. (See entry, page 141.)

Courtesy of Florida Keys and Key West

𝒥ESTIVAL MIAMI
CORAL GABLES ✴ MID-SEPTEMBER THROUGH MID-OCTOBER

Festival Miami is one of the biggest classical music festivals presented by a university school of music in the United States. Founded in 1983, the festival features a wide range of guest artists from all over the world, who appear in concert with the award-winning student performing ensembles and faculty artists of the University of Miami's School of Music.

The monthlong series of performances are presented at the University of Miami campus in Coral Gables. Larger ensembles play in the acoustically superb, 600-seat Maurice Gusman Concert Hall, and chamber musicians perform in the 147-seat Clarke Recital Hall. Tickets top out at $18, although many concerts are free.   **LOCATION:** Maurice Gusman Concert Hall and Clarke Recital Hall, on the University of Miami Campus in Coral Gables. From Miami take I-95 to U.S. 1 south to Southwest 57th

Avenue; then turn right on Miller Drive, left at the first traffic light, and right at the first university entrance. **TICKETS/INFO:** 305-284-4940 **ACCOMMODATIONS/TOURIST INFO:** 800-283-2707, 305-539-3063

SARASOTA/BRADENTON BLUES FESTIVAL
SARASOTA ✹ A WEEKEND IN LATE SEPTEMBER OR EARLY OCTOBER

Sweet home Sarasota! Set against a backdrop of breathtaking beaches, this festival brings the blues down to Florida's Gulf Coast. Between 8,500 and 10,000 spectators gather at an outdoor venue to soak up the blues produced by seven national, regional, and local acts. Vendors serve a variety of foods, and younger festivalgoers can take advantage of a special children's area. Other area attractions include golf, shopping, dog racing, and beachcombing. Admission is $12 for the day.   **LOCATION:** Sarasota Fairgrounds, 3000 Ringling Boulevard, in Sarasota. From I-75 take exit 39 and head west on Fruitville Road for two miles. **TICKETS/INFO:** 941-377-3279 **ACCOMMODA-TIONS/TOURIST INFO:** 941-957-1877

SUWANNEE RIVER GOSPEL JUBILEE
LIVE OAK ✹ FIRST WEEKEND IN OCTOBER

This is a semiannual event, happening the third weekend in June and the first weekend in October. See page 140 for details.   **LOCATION:** Spirit of the Suwannee Park, in Live Oak. From I-75 take exit 85 to Highway 129, then proceed south 4.5 miles. **TICKETS/INFO:** 904-364-1683 **ACCOMMODATIONS/TOURIST INFO:** 904-364-1683

JACKSONVILLE JAZZ FESTIVAL
JACKSONVILLE ✹ SECOND WEEK IN OCTOBER

Held on the banks of the St. John's River in a beautiful performing-arts park, this weeklong festival features 28 performers from across the nation and is perhaps best known for its Great American Jazz Piano Competition. Since 1980, the event has provided "the best entertainment possible" for jazz lovers. Past performances by top jazz names like Miles Davis, Dave Brubeck, Grover Washington Jr., Diane Schurr, and David Sanborn have wowed crowds of 35,000 to 50,000 people. A food court, kids' tent, and arts and crafts are available, but restrictions apply on picnicking, pets, recording equipment, flash cameras, bicycles, and umbrellas. Admission ranges from free to about $9.   **LOCATION:** Metropolitan Park in downtown Jacksonville, directly across from Jacksonville Municipal Stadium **TICKETS/INFO:** 904-353-7770 **ACCOMMODA-TIONS/TOURIST INFO:** 904-978-9148

SUWANNEE RIVER COUNTRY MUSIC JAM
LIVE OAK ✹ SECOND WEEKEND IN OCTOBER

Up to 30,000 country music fans show up at a tree-shaded natural amphitheater along the Suwannee River for music by headliners like Willie Nelson, Merle Haggard, Billy Ray Cyrus, Patty Loveless, and Waylon Jennings. Suwannee River's 15 to 20 acts include a balanced mix of traditional and new country, and festivalgoers sit on the grassy banks of the Suwannee River.

Acoustic Alchemy play at a recent Jacksonville Jazz Festival. (See entry, page 143.) © Herb Snitzer

The Spirit of the Suwannee Park is a 580-acre music park and campground with a northern boundary along two miles of the Suwannee River. In the park and in the surrounding woodlands, recreational opportunities include fishing, swimming, boating, camping, hiking, and touring an old-time farm museum. Tickets range from $30 to $60, and special VIP tickets are available for about $150.   **LOCATION:** Spirit of the Suwannee Park, in Live Oak. From I-75 take exit 85 to Highway 129, then proceed south 4.5 miles. **TICKETS/INFO:** 904-364-1683 **ACCOMMODATIONS/TOURIST INFO:** 904-364-1683

𝓕RANK BROWN INTERNATIONAL SONGWRITERS FESTIVAL

PERDIDO KEY, PENSACOLA, PENSACOLA BEACH ✻ FIRST THURSDAY THROUGH SECOND SUNDAY IN NOVEMBER

Here's a chance to visit some of the whitest beaches in the world and discover new songwriting talents in several genres, including country, blues, folk, and gospel. At 15 different bars, churches, and eateries in six cities around the Florida-Alabama border, more than 150 songwriters showcase their songs. Like the huge Kerrville Folk Festival in Texas, this event is one of the few to focus on songwriters and to feature only original music. In addition to entertaining an audience of thousands, the festival provides an atmosphere for songwriters to interact freely with their peers and to develop as artists and professionals. Admission fees vary depending on venues.   **LOCATION:** Various venues in Fairhope, Gulf Shores, and Orange Beach in Alabama, and in Perdido Key, Pensacola, and Pensacola Beach in Florida. Call for locations. **TICKETS/INFO:** 334-981-5678, 904-492-7664; e-mail: songfest@amaranth.com; World Wide Web: http://www.amaranth.com/~ken/fbrown.html **ACCOMMODATIONS/TOURIST INFO:** 334-968-6901, 904-492-4660, 904-438-4081

CARIBE CARNIVAL

JACKSONVILLE ✹ FIRST WEEKEND IN NOVEMBER

This pan-Caribbean frenzy brings more than 50 performers to Jacksonville's River Walk for three days of music making, dancing, pageantry, and partying. Perhaps no other event in North America offers this diverse a sampling of Caribbean music. Expect to hear reggae and dancehall from Jamaica; salsa and son from Cuba; compas and rara from Haiti; cumbia and vallenato from Colombia; jazz and R&B from New Orleans; and soca, calypso, and steel drums from Trinidad.

Afro-Caribbean polyrhythms pulse from two stages, and like Carnaval Miami and Key West's Fantasy Fest, Caribe Carnival brings lots of people onto the streets in costume. A two-mile parade snakes through downtown, and stilt walkers wow the crowds of more than 30,000. Ethnic foods, arts and crafts, and folklore demonstrations round out the action—but mostly it's music and dancing in the park! **LOCATION:** North Bank River Walk Park, just off Water Street near the Civic Auditorium **TICKETS/ INFO:** 904-260-3843, 904-260-3843 **ACCOMMODATIONS/TOURIST INFO:** 904-978-9148

NEW YEAR'S BLUEGRASS FESTIVAL
JEKYLL ISLAND ✹ NEW YEAR'S WEEKEND, THURSDAY–SATURDAY

This festival puts a heaping helping of bluegrass into the New Year's festivities, offering top-notch performers like Mac Wiseman, Ralph Stanley, and the Sand Mountain Boys. All concerts are indoors, and camping is allowed in the convention center parking lot. Don't plan on getting too crazy, though—the event is family style and no alcohol is allowed in the concert area.   **LOCATION:** Jekyll Island Convention Center at 1 Beach View Drive on Jekyll Island, near Georgia's southern border and 10 miles east of Brunswick. From I-95 take exit 6 and head east; once on the island, follow the signs to the convention center. **TICKETS/INFO:** 706-864-7203 **ACCOMMODATIONS/TOURIST INFO:** 800-841-6586

FREAK NIK
ATLANTA ✹ A WEEKEND IN APRIL

This citywide hip-hop blowout turns Atlanta on its head as college students take over the town with boom boxes and subwoofers on wheels. The spring break event isn't technically sponsored by anyone (in fact, the local officialdom hates it), but those who are into rap and hip-hop will be in the know.   **LOCATION:** Throughout downtown Atlanta **ACCOMMODATIONS/TOURIST INFO:** 404-521-6600

FOLK LIFE FESTIVAL & FIDDLERS' JAMBOREE
TIFTON ✹ FOURTH SATURDAY IN APRIL

The Georgia Agrirama Living History Museum presents award-winning fiddlers from Georgia, Alabama, and Florida who jam and cavort amidst an extensive folklife exhibit. About 20 fiddler/accompanist acts play on a single stage during the day, on the grounds of a restored turn-of-the-century farmhouse and town. The site features traditional crafts and demonstrations in sheepshearing, soap making, butter churning, logrolling, and more. Admission is about $8 for adults.   **LOCATION:** Georgia Agrirama Living History Museum, on Eighth Street in Tifton. From I-75 take exit 20 to Tifton. **TICKETS/INFO:** 912-386-3344 **ACCOMMODATIONS/TOURIST INFO:** 912-386-0216

LEWIS FAMILY HOMECOMING AND BLUEGRASS FESTIVAL

LINCOLNTON ✦ FIRST WEEKEND IN MAY, THURSDAY–SATURDAY

The Lewis Family invites you and yours to come home to the sweet sounds of bluegrass. This toe-tapping family-style event draws top-rated performers to the backwoods of Georgia—or at least 447 acres of it in the Elijah Clark State Park. The event is hosted by "America's first family of bluegrass gospel music," and it often includes such notables as Mac Wiseman, the Osborne Brothers, and Jimmie Davis (a former governor of Louisiana and a member of both the Country Music and Gospel Music Halls of Fame). Plenty of RV hookups and campsites are available, along with a few lakefront cottages. The festival also features hot food and arts and crafts, but note that alcohol is not permitted and there is no stationary seating (so BYO lawn chairs and blankets). Admission is $49 for a weekend pass.   **LOCATION:** Elijah Clark State Park, on U.S. 378 in Lincolnton. From Athens use U.S. 78 to U.S. 378. **TICKETS/INFO:** 706-864-7203 **ACCOMMODATIONS/TOURIST INFO:** 706-359-4729, 706-359-7970

MUSIC MIDTOWN

ATLANTA ✦ FIRST WEEKEND IN MAY

Started in 1994, this multistage festival has quickly drawn immense, expectant crowds to midtown Atlanta. Six stages feature top national musical talents, while one hosts local up-and-comers. The lineup provides audiences of over 100,000 with samples of diverse musical genres. The festival also offers food, a children's stage and activity area, and arts markets selling works by local and regional artisans.   **LOCATION:** Midtown Atlanta, at 10th and Peach streets **TICKETS/INFO:** 404-872-1115 **ACCOMMODATIONS/TOURIST INFO:** 404-521-6600

SPRING MUSIC FESTIVAL

HIAWASSEE ✦ THIRD WEEKEND IN MAY, FRIDAY AND SATURDAY

The Georgia Mountain Fair presents three shows of top regional country musicians in this spring festival of traditional music. Each night, and Saturday afternoon too, visiting country acts swap the stage with the house band, playing to a music-hall crowd of about 3,000. Each show also features local clogging teams.   **LOCATION:** Georgia Mountain Fair, one mile west of Hiawassee on U.S. 76 **TICKETS/INFO:** 706-896-4191 **ACCOMMODATIONS/TOURIST INFO:** 706-896-4191

ATLANTA JAZZ FESTIVAL

ATLANTA ✦ MEMORIAL DAY WEEKEND, SATURDAY–MONDAY (MEMORIAL DAY IS THE LAST MONDAY IN MAY)

As one of the largest free jazz festivals held in the southern United States, the Atlanta Jazz Festival is a magnet for up to 100,000 jazz lovers a year. With a good mix of local, regional, and national talent appearing on one stage, the festival never fails to entertain and sometimes even challenges the large crowd that gathers in beautiful Grant Park. Festival organizers seek to preserve jazz traditions while presenting new and up-and-coming artists along with the stars of today's jazz world. Other attractions include food, arts and crafts, workshops, lectures, jam sessions, films, and all that Atlanta has to offer.

Springtime whoop-up: Down-home country music's on the agenda at the Georgia Mountain Fair's Spring Music Festival. (See entry, page 147.) Courtesy of Georgia Mountain Fair

LOCATION: Grant Park, in southeast Atlanta near the junction of I-20 and Boulevard Road. **TICKETS/INFO:** 404-817-6815 **ACCOMMODATIONS/TOURIST INFO:** 404-521-6600.

ℯ𝒜TLANTA PEACH CARIBBEAN CARNIVAL
ATLANTA ✷ LAST WEEKEND IN MAY

The best of the Caribbean comes to Atlanta during this explosion of island culture and merrymaking. In addition to visual arts, drama, books, and dance, the event features live calypso, soca, reggae, steel drum, zouk, and other Caribbean music—much of it from English-speaking islands. Previous years have featured such greats as Trinidad's David Rudder, Trinidad's Black Stalin, and Barbados's Ras Iley.   **LOCATION:** A changing venue in downtown Atlanta; call for details. **TICKETS/INFO:** 404-753-3497 **ACCOMMODATIONS/TOURIST INFO:** 404-521-6600

ℯ𝒜NNUAL COUNTRY BY THE SEA MUSIC FESTIVAL
JEKYLL ISLAND ✷ FIRST SATURDAY IN JUNE

Country music's hottest groups trade the stage with up-and-coming bands at this unique festival that takes place right on the beach. A stage is set up on a deck overlooking the shoreline, and fans frolic in the sand or sit in the "back rows," actually in the water. On the night before the festival, the Country Under the Stars Band Competition and

Dance fills the Convention Center's Caldwell Hall. Bands try to win the hearts and boots of the dance-floor crowd; it decides which band will appear as Saturday's opening act. Tickets are $15 for Saturday's show and $5 for Friday's.   **LOCATION:** Beach Deck, next to the Jekyll Island Convention Center at 1 Beach View Drive on Jekyll Island, near Georgia's southern border and 10 miles east of Brunswick. From I-95 take exit 6 and head east; once on the island, follow the signs to the convention center. **TICKETS/INFO:** 800-841-6586, 912-635-3636 **ACCOMMODATIONS/TOURIST INFO:** 800-841-6586, 912-635-3636

$\mathcal{D}$AHLONEGA BLUEGRASS FESTIVAL
DAHLONEGA ✱ THIRD WEEKEND IN JUNE, THURSDAY–SATURDAY

Three days of banjo pickin' by the likes of Bill Monroe, Doc Watson, and Jimmy Martin set things twangin' at this big northern Georgia festival. Bluegrass fans and families pitch camp for the duration, as they have since 1974. Kids can swim in the pool, but the pooch and the hooch have to stay home. Tickets are $25 per day or $70 for the weekend.   **LOCATION:** Blackburn Park and Campground, seven miles south of Dahlonega on U.S. 19 (Old Highway 9E). From the south take U.S. 19 to Burnt Stand Road, then go 3.3 miles. Dahlonega is about 50 miles north of Atlanta. **TICKETS/INFO:** 706-864-7203 **ACCOMMODATIONS/TOURIST INFO:** 706-864-7203

$\mathcal{T}$HOMAS DORSEY GOSPEL FESTIVAL
VILLA RICA ✱ SATURDAY BEFORE JULY 4

One of America's best-loved gospel songwriters was born in Villa Rica, Georgia, and went on to write many of the most beautiful songs in the Christian repertoire, including gems like "Peace in the Valley" and "Precious Lord Take My Hand." Each year, Thomas A. Dorsey's boyhood church presents this festival honoring its favorite son and his numerous blues and gospel compositions.

This event has a reputation for friendliness and attracts national and regional performers and music-savvy audiences. Dorsey's innovative career mixed and matched traditional blues with gospel and shape-note singing, and the festival is dedicated to preserving the traditions of—and connections between—sacred music and secular forms like blues and jazz.

A free gospel concert featuring the Thomas Dorsey Birthplace Choir starts the festival off Saturday afternoon. The choir, made up of singers from numerous western Georgia churches, was inducted in October 1995 into the National Convention of Gospel Choirs and Choruses, which Dorsey founded in 1932. After the gospel concert, the festival moves to Gold Dust Park, where nationally known blues and gospel acts perform the works of Dorsey's early years, amid picnicking and a fireworks display. **LOCATION:** Afternoon: Mount Prospect Baptist Church, 133 Sunset Drive. Evening: Gold Dust Park, 646 Industrial Boulevard. Villa Rica is 32 miles from downtown Atlanta. From I-20 use exit 5. **TICKETS/INFO:** 770-459-7019 **ACCOMMODATIONS/TOURIST INFO:** 770-832-2446, 770-942-5022

$\mathcal{D}$EKALB INTERNATIONAL CHORAL FESTIVAL
ATLANTA ✱ SECOND WEEKEND IN JULY

Festival organizers claim that this is the largest annual community choral event of its kind in the world, attracting approximately 80,000 people a year to hear more than

The DeKalb International Choral Festival draws more than 600 world-class voices. *Courtesy of DeKalb International Choral Festival*

600 international singers. Performances are held in churches, concert halls, universities, and pubic performance spaces all over Atlanta. Saturday night's grand finale is held on the main stage at Underground Atlanta, and each year a festival CD is recorded, featuring all the groups participating in the festival. The event benefits The Children's Wish Foundation International, an Atlanta-based organization that grants the wishes of terminally ill children.   **LOCATION:** Various concert halls in Atlanta **TICKETS/INFO:** 404-378-2525 **ACCOMMODATIONS/TOURIST INFO:** 404-521-6600

MONTREUX ATLANTA INTERNATIONAL MUSIC FESTIVAL
ATLANTA ✷ ONE WEEK ENDING THE FIRST MONDAY IN SEPTEMBER (LABOR DAY)

This is the place to be if you want to see a big, diverse blend of music the week before Labor Day and on the end-of-summer holiday. With jazz, reggae, Latin, blues, gospel, rock, country, African, and zydeco music all fairly represented, you can be sure nearly everyone will be inspired to shake a leg. Up to 125,000 music lovers show up each year to catch 30 or 40 bands on three stages in scenic Piedmont Park. Lectures, jam sessions, workshops, food, and arts and crafts round out the festival action. Admission is free.   **LOCATION:** Piedmont Park, on 10th Street between Piedmont and Monroe in Atlanta **TICKETS/INFO:** 404-817-6815 **ACCOMMODATIONS/TOURIST INFO:** 404-521-6600

$\stackrel{\varepsilon^\nu}{\mathcal{S}}$AVANNAH FOLK MUSIC FESTIVAL

SAVANNAH ✳ THIRD WEEKEND IN SEPTEMBER, FRIDAY–SUNDAY

This three-day festival celebrates the diversity of folk music and dance with local, regional, and international talents in gospel, old-time, bluegrass, Celtic, and blues traditions. A Saturday dance is followed by Sunday's main event, in which all groups play twice in beautiful Daffin Park under a canopy of ancient moss-covered oak trees. Past festivals have drawn about 1,000 spectators, who hear musicians like John Jackson and Etta Baker. Except for the Saturday dance, the festival is free.   **LOCATION:** Sunday's main event is held at Daffin Park; other events are held at City Market and Oatland Island Educational Center, all in Savannah. **TICKETS/INFO:** 912-927-1376 **ACCOMMODATIONS/TOURIST INFO:** 912-944-0456

$\mathcal{N}$ORTH GEORGIA FOLK FESTIVAL

ATHENS ✳ FIRST WEEKEND IN OCTOBER, FRIDAY AND SATURDAY

This thoroughly interesting festival celebrates the roots of Georgia music by digging deep into the history of what has become today's folk music. The festival, which attracts 2,500 spectators each year, features a wide range of styles, including bluegrass, hillbilly, Cajun, blues, and old-time string and gospel music. In two days some 15 bands, all made up of residents or former residents of Georgia, perform on two stages. In addition, a musicians' picking tent is set up for informal jamming.

Sandy Creek Park is a beautiful, wooded park just outside Athens, and during the festival folklife demonstrations highlight traditional crafts and living skills—throwing pottery, blacksmithing, chair caning, and more—that were once a part of everyday life in Georgia. The festival also features a storytelling competition, traditional and vegetarian foods, children's activities, and dance performances. Tickets are $6 for adults, and tent and RV camping are available at the park.   **LOCATION:** Sandy Creek Park, five minutes north of Athens on Holman Road, off U.S. 441 20 miles south of I-85 **TICKETS/ INFO:** 706-613-3620 **ACCOMMODATIONS/TOURIST INFO:** 706-613-3631, 706-546-1805

$\stackrel{\varepsilon^\nu}{\mathcal{S}}$UGAR CREEK BLUEGRASS FESTIVAL

BLUE RIDGE ✳ SECOND WEEKEND IN OCTOBER

Local, regional, and national performers gather in this park set in the mountains of northern Georgia not far from Atlanta. About a dozen bands play to crowds of around 2,000 at the main pavilion stage, and food booths and arts and crafts fill out the festival offerings. RV hookups are available.   **LOCATION:** Sugar Creek Music Park, 1220 Cox Road, in Blue Ridge, just off U.S. 76 **TICKETS/INFO:** 706-632-2560 **ACCOMMODA-TIONS/TOURIST INFO:** 706-632-5680

$\mathcal{G}$EORGIA'S OFFICIAL STATE FIDDLERS CONVENTION

HIAWASSEE ✳ TEN DAYS IN MID-OCTOBER

This festival, held during the peak of the fall leaf season in the beautiful northern Georgia mountains, is an ideal opportunity to hear bluegrass and "ole-timey music." The best of the Hill Country's pickers and singers play alongside national talent in front of nearly 10,000 spectators on the shore of Chatuge Lake. While most of the music is outdoors, some acts perform in the enclosed 3,000-seat Anderson Music Hall. A crafts area features wood carving, leatherwork, applehead dolls, and corn-shuck dolls. Food includes smoked rainbow trout, barbecue meats, and hot funnel cakes. Organizers put out an open invitation for anyone to play, so bring your fiddle. Tickets are about $6, and the Georgia Mountain Fairground has 188 campsites at Chatuge Lake.   **LOCATION:** One mile west of Hiawassee, on U.S. 76 near Georgia's border with North Carolina **TICKETS/INFO:** 706-896-4191 **ACCOMMODATIONS/TOURIST INFO:** 706-896-4191

KENTUCKY

HILLBILLY DAYS
PIKEVILLE ✺ THIRD WEEKEND IN APRIL, THURSDAY–SATURDAY

As April crocuses and jonquils bloom and the colors of spring buds dot the rolling landscape, hillbilly folks from nearly every state and several countries descend upon the former stompin' grounds of the Hatfields and the McCoys for Hillbilly Days. Over three days nearly 130,000 festivalgoers celebrate the clear mountain air and warm spring days with mountain music, clogging, and square dancing—while listening to 40 local and regional bluegrass and country bands.

In addition to the music, the festival features "stump speaking," in which "candidates" boisterously tout their qualifications and opinions; mountain arts and crafts; a parade; lots of good food; and a walking tour. The festival is free, and proceeds from the sale of food go to Shriners Hospitals for Crippled Children. **LOCATION:** Downtown Pikeville, just off U.S. 23 in eastern Kentucky **TICKETS/INFO:** 800-844-7453 **ACCOMMODATIONS/TOURIST INFO:** 800-844-7453

RED MILE BLUEGRASS FESTIVAL
LEXINGTON ✺ THIRD WEEKEND IN MAY

Top-name bluegrass performers team up with harness racers to entertain the May crowds at Lexington's Red Mile Harness Track. About 20 bands play over the three days, drawing about 4,000 people. Food and concession booths are available; no dogs or coolers are allowed in the concert area. **LOCATION:** Red Mile Harness Track, on Red Mile Road in Lexington **TICKETS/INFO:** 606-266-1991 **ACCOMMODATIONS/TOURIST INFO:** 606-233-1221

SOUTHERN HARMONY SINGING
BENTON ✺ FOURTH SUNDAY IN MAY

Not a festival per se, this annual gathering focuses on the preservation and presentation of traditional sacred harp or "shape note" singing. This form of Christian folk music dates back to the early 1800s, when people learned to sight-read music by associating each note of the scale with a shape (triangle, circle, square, or diamond) and a syllable (fa, sol, la, mi).

Singing takes place in one morning and one afternoon session, which are both free of charge. To preserve this musical tradition, the organizers not only sponsor this event but also produce records and books of musical scores.   **LOCATION:** Marshall County Court House, on Main Street in Benton, just off I-24 near Kentucky Dam **TICKETS/ INFO:** 502-527-8616 **ACCOMMODATIONS/TOURIST INFO:** 502-527-7665

⌖TTER CREEK PARK BLUEGRASS FESTIVAL
LOUISVILLE ✷ MEMORIAL DAY WEEKEND (MEMORIAL DAY IS THE LAST MONDAY IN MAY)

Three days of camping, lots of bluegrass music, and workshops are offered at this festival on the Ohio River. A mix of national, local, and regional performers covers the bluegrass bases, from old-timey to contemporary and nontraditional, with the occasional novelty act thrown in for good measure. As a family-oriented event, the festival offers children's activities to match the adult concerts and workshops. The festival also features storytelling, songwriting, dancing, hayrides, arts and crafts, and round-the-clock jamming in the camping area.

The campground offers full, handicapped-accessible camping and RV facilities, as well as a range of outdoor sports activities. Alcohol is allowed as long as it's not displayed openly.   **LOCATION:** Otter Creek Park, 30 miles south of Louisville and 10 miles north of Fort Knox **TICKETS/INFO:** 502-583-3577 **ACCOMMODATIONS/TOURIST INFO:** 502-583-3577

⌖ESTIVAL OF THE BLUEGRASS
LEXINGTON ✷ SECOND FULL WEEKEND IN JUNE

The genre's big, big names play at this festival, which takes place in the bluegrass state itself, in the heart of America's "Fertile Crescent" of bluegrass. For over 20 years this festival has celebrated bluegrass, mixing traditional and contemporary performers but emphasizing the genre's musical heritage. In addition to concerts, the festival features sing-alongs, square dancing and clogging, musical activities for children, and instrumental lessons. Round-the-clock jamming brings mountain folk and city folk together to trade their best licks, and a Memories Tent gets everyone to swapping stories and discussing historic moments in bluegrass.   **LOCATION:** Kentucky Horse Park Campground, 4089 Iron Works Pike in Lexington. From I-75 take exit 120 and follow signs for one-half mile to the park entrance. **TICKETS/INFO:** 904-364-1683, 606-846-4995 **ACCOMMODATIONS/TOURIST INFO:** 606-233-1221

⌖. C. HANDY BLUES & BARBECUE FESTIVAL
HENDERSON ✷ ONE FULL WEEK STARTING THE SECOND SUNDAY IN JUNE

Held in Henderson on the banks of the Ohio River, this festival features about 25 local and nationally known acts that gather every year to pay tribute to "the Father of the Blues," W. C. Handy. Handy lived in Henderson for about 10 years, and this close-knit community presents a mixture of blues, Dixieland jazz, and gospel music in his honor. When it comes to food, barbecue takes center stage as several vendors vie for the title of "best barbecue in Henderson." Admission to most events is free.   **LOCATION:** Henderson Fine Arts Center, Central Park, John F. Kennedy Center, and Henderson

Riverfront, all in Henderson, which is just across the river from Evansville, Indiana **TICKETS/INFO:** 502-826-3128 **ACCOMMODATIONS/TOURIST INFO:** 800-648-3128

MUSIC AT MAPLE MOUNT
MAPLE MOUNT ✷ SECOND AND THIRD WEEKS IN JUNE

Maple Mount is where musical dreams debut as hundreds of young people (ages 11-19) perform in chamber ensembles, orchestras, and a 125-member chorus. Eleven performances are open to the public. (See also: Music at Maple Mount Chamber Music Week, New Harmony, Indiana.)   **LOCATION:** Several venues in Maple Mount, just southwest of Owensboro on Highway 56 **TICKETS/INFO:** 502-686-4229 **ACCOMMODATIONS/TOURIST INFO:** 800-489-1131

OLD JOE CLARK BLUEGRASS FESTIVAL
RENFRO VALLEY ✷ FIRST WEEKEND IN JULY

Old Joe Clark has established a reputation as a bluegrass performer and humorist, but this three-day event tests his talents as a party host. Mindful of Old Joe's pledge that "it's got to be fun for everybody, or else I'm not going to do it," bluegrass greats like the Osborne Brothers, Lonesome River Band, IIIrd Tyme Out, and the Stevens Family look forward to the festival nearly as much as the fans.

The weekend takes on the atmosphere of a congenial family reunion as Old Joe and his son Terry open each day's entertainment by hosting an open stage, encouraging old-timers and newcomers to take turns at the microphones. The festival is located in a complex with two restaurants, a motel, cabins, a campground, two show-barn theaters, and a crafts village.   **LOCATION:** Renfro Valley Festival Field in Renfro Valley, about halfway between Lexington, Kentucky, and Knoxville, Tennessee. From I-75 take exit 62. **TICKETS/INFO:** 800-765-7464 **ACCOMMODATIONS/TOURIST INFO:** 606-256-9814

SUMMER MOTION
ASHLAND ✷ JULY 4 AND THE NEAREST WEEKEND

Since 1977, the first days of July have brought the sounds of Motown, classic rock, and country music to Ashland. Free concerts draw up to 40,000 over the weekend, which also includes sports events, a food fair, and, of course, fireworks. Weekday evening concerts are presented at Ashland Boat Ramp, and weekend performances, exhibits, and activities take place at Central Park. Both venues are free.   **LOCATION:** Ashland Boat Ramp and Ashland Central Park in Ashland, on Kentucky's western border, accessible via I-64, U.S. 60, U.S. 23, and U.S. 52 **TICKETS/INFO:** 800-416-3222, 304-552-8141 **ACCOMMODATIONS/TOURIST INFO:** 606-329-1007

OFFICIAL KY STATE CHAMPIONSHIP OLD-TIME FIDDLERS CONTEST
FALLS OF ROUGH ✷ THIRD FULL WEEKEND IN JULY, FRIDAY–SUNDAY

More than 150 musicians gather for this authentic old-time event featuring competitions in four categories of fiddle, plus guitar, mandolin, banjo, harmonica, bluegrass band, and string band. Local hotels and accommodations often fill up months in advance, and on a sunny day the festival has been known to gather up to 5,000 spectators. Food booths and arts and crafts booths are also set up, but since the festival is held in a state park, no alcohol is allowed. **LOCATION:** Rough River Dam State Resort Park is on the western shore of the Rough River Lake and on the northern end of Falls of Rough, 40 miles north of Bowling Green via Highway 185. **TICKETS/INFO:** 502-259-0450 **ACCOMMODATIONS/TOURIST INFO:** 502-259-3578

OSBORNE BROTHERS HOMECOMING

HYDEN ✷ FIRST WEEKEND IN AUGUST

This fairly new festival features the Osborne Brothers and other top bluegrass names. Fifteen bands play to about 3,500 spectators, who each pay from $8 to $12 per day. As a bonus, advance-ticket holders are treated to a free pig roast on Friday. **LOCATION:** Nixon Center, on Highway 421 in Hyden, about 22 miles southwest of Hazard **TICKETS/INFO:** 606-266-1991 **ACCOMMODATIONS/TOURIST INFO:** 606-233-1221

INTERNATIONAL STRANGE MUSIC WEEKEND

OLIVE HILL ✷ LAST FULL WEEKEND IN AUGUST

If you agree with the motto "Everybody Needs a Little Strange," there's a place for you once a year at the Carter Caves State Park in Kentucky. At great peril to their reputations, an ensemble of six otherwise-professional musicians courageously coaxes musical numbers from every imaginable contraption that can be made to honk, shriek, ring, whir, blat, gurgle, or twang.

The ensemble presents familiar tunes played on unfamiliar instruments—including "real" instruments, such as Renaissance music-makers that were once mainstream, and contrived instruments, such as the "six-handed PVC trombolo." Invented by a gentle singer-songwriter who doubles as the ensemble's music director, this contraption of plastic pipes combines brass and woodwind instrumental principles, and requires four people to play—with one standing on the shoulders of the other three.

Everything from vaccuum cleaners to human hands can be made to evoke parts of the musical range; one musician's hand-farts have a two-octave musical range adept at capturing a wide repertoire, which includes "Somewhere My Love," "76 Trombones," and a host of Christmas carols. Another ensemble member, a folk musician and raconteur, invented the "L.A. pennywhistle," which comes with its own gas mask (for smog-stuck musicians). And the ensemble's premier "snout flautist" (that's a musician who plays a flute with his nose) can produce unusually stirring renditions of songs such as "You Light Up My Life" and "You are So Beautiful" on his snoot flute.

A mere 200 people show up on the lush campgrounds most years, although the low census may improve with the recent departure of a state park superintendent who expressed his essential disfavor for the event by refusing to assign it anything but a floating date each year, leaving everybody guessing as to when it would be held. Whether the floating date will continue remains to be seen, and only the park can confirm annual dates. **LOCATION:** Carter Caves State Resort Park, about 30 miles northeast of Morehead. From I-64 take exit 161 (United States. 60) and look for the signs. **TICKETS/INFO:** 800-755-0076 **ACCOMMODATIONS/TOURIST INFO:** 800-225-8747

Oddity-o-rama: Blake Barker's "L.A. Penny-whistle" is one of many musical inventions typically encountered at the International Strange Music Weekend. Courtesy of

International Strange Music

Weekend

ɀENLAKE'S HOT AUGUST BLUES FESTIVAL

KENLAKE STATE RESORT PARK ✹ WEEKEND PRIOR TO LABOR DAY WEEKEND, FRIDAY–SUNDAY (LABOR DAY IS THE FIRST MONDAY IN SEPTEMBER)

Devoted to the many traditions of the blues, this festival offers Texas, Chicago, and Mississippi blues and much more. Friday and Saturday concerts feature local musicians, and Sunday concerts spotlight nationally known acts. Art exhibits and sales of antique clothing and other unusual items run concurrently. Prices range from free to $15. **LOCATION:** On the shoreline of Kentucky Lake in Kenlake State Resort Park, near the junction of Highways 80 and 94 **TICKETS/INFO:** 800-325-0143 **ACCOMMODATIONS/TOURIST INFO:** 800-467-7145

ɀVERLY BROTHERS HOMECOMING

CENTRAL CITY ✹ SATURDAY OF LABOR DAY WEEKEND

The Everly Brothers Homecoming brings favorite sons Don and Phil back to Central City for a benefit concert to raise money for scholarships. Aside from their soaring two-

Ko Ko Taylor and Her Blues Machine pitch a Wang Dang Doodle at Kenlake's Hot August Blues Festival. (See entry, page 157.) Courtesy of Kentucky Department of Parks

country, rock, and pop genres. The outdoor festival is run completely by volunteers and draws up to 20,000 annually. Tickets will put you back a mere $12.   **LOCATION:** Central City Elementary School gymnasium, on U.S. 431 north in Central City **TICKETS/INFO:** 502-754-9603, 502-754-2360 **ACCOMMODATIONS/TOURIST INFO:** 800-225-8747

MASTER MUSICIANS FESTIVAL
SOMERSET ✷ FIRST WEEK AFTER LABOR DAY

Consistent with its name, the Master Musicians Festival celebrates accomplished musicians of all ages, but gives special emphasis to the "masters," or those who have reached age 50. This extraordinary gathering brings nearly 30 musicians from all over the world to Somerset for four days of concerts on three stages.

Few venues in North America offer this diverse a selection at one place and one time. The area's traditional Appalachian music is just part of the musical pastiche that moves from somber classical notes one moment to foot-stompin' bluegrass the next. Recent musicians who have played at the festival include 95-year-old blues piano legend "Pigmeat" Jarret, gospel/bluegrass favorites the Cox Family, Celtic tin whistle and flute player Seamus Egan, Appalachian guitar-picking wizard Ben Mattingley, and the International Children's Chorus.

The majority of the festival is held in Pulaski County Park, a large, wide-open milieu on the shores of Lake Cumberland. The wide array of music is complemented by artists' workshops, arts and crafts exhibits, camping, boating, hiking, swimming, volleyball, Frisbee golf, and sheltered pavilions for eating. Tickets are $10 for adults and $3 for children.   **LOCATION:** Downtown Somerset and Pulaski County Park **TICKETS/ INFO:** 606-678-2225 **ACCOMMODATIONS/TOURIST INFO:** 800-642-6287, 606-679-6394

CARTER CAVES GATHERING
CARTER CAVES STATE RESORT PARK/OLIVE HILL ✴ WEEKEND AFTER LABOR DAY, THURSDAY–SUNDAY

The Carter Caves Gathering is the reincarnation of the Fraley Family Festival, which Annadeene Fraley organized for 25 years before she took ill. In the tradition that brought the Fraley Family Festival so near and dear to so many hearts, the festival is now organized by John Tierney at Carter Caves.

There's very little bluegrass here; instead the festival features old-time country, mountain fiddling, and folk music (or "whatever anybody grew up with," as Annadeene put it). Musicians who don't have paying gigs that weekend just seem to drop in, and recent years have attracted the likes of John Hartford and Mike Seeger. The event's charm lies in the totally informal atmosphere, the great jamming, and its rarity as a Kentucky musical event not overrun by bluegrassers. Also, the festival has always drawn a lot of female singers. Only a few hundred people can fit into the grounds, and the campground always fills up the Tuesday before the festival starts, so plan ahead. Tickets range from $8 to $12 each day.   **LOCATION:** Carter Caves State Resort Park, about 30 miles northeast of Morehead. From I-64 take exit 161 (U.S. 60) and look for the signs. **TICKETS/INFO:** 606-286-4411 **ACCOMMODATIONS/TOURIST INFO:** 800-225-8747

BLUES TO THE POINT—TWO RIVERS BLUES FESTIVAL
CARROLLTON ✴ FRIDAY AND SATURDAY AFTER LABOR DAY

About 10 blues bands play at the confluence of the Kentucky and Ohio Rivers during this two-day festival featuring lots of local talent in addition to a couple of regionally and nationally known blues artists. Between 2,000 and 3,000 people show up to enjoy the music and partake of options like food, volleyball, and tent camping. Tickets run about $10 a day, and alcohol is prohibited at the festival.   **LOCATION:** Point Park Pavilion, at Second and Main Streets in Carrollton, about 50 miles southwest of Cincinnati, Ohio. From I-71 exit at Highway 227 (exit 44) and head northwest. **TICK-ETS/INFO:** 800-325-4290 **ACCOMMODATIONS/TOURIST INFO:** 800-325-4290

NATIONAL QUARTET CONVENTION
LOUISVILLE ✴ THIRD WEEK OF SEPTEMBER

Since 1957, Southern gospel music's biggest annual event has showcased the nation's top quartets. About 80 acts serenade crowds of 60,000 from three stages, while motivational speakers and music-merchandise vendors hawk their spiritual and material wares. Entrance into this world of music costs about $16.   **LOCATION:** Kentucky Fair & Expo Center, at 937 Phillips Lane in Louisville **TICKETS/INFO:** 800-846-8499 **ACCOMMODATIONS/TOURIST INFO:** 502-584-2121

GREAT AMERICAN DULCIMER CONVENTION

PINEVILLE ✹ FOURTH WEEKEND IN SEPTEMBER

Dating back to 1978, the Great American Dulcimer Convention ranks among the largest gatherings of dulcimer musicians in the country. In a picturesque mountain setting, 300 to 400 dulcimer enthusiasts gather to watch and listen to one band, two duos, and four solo artists displaying both traditional and contemporary techniques of dulcimer virtuosity. Hammered and lap dulcimer players all thrive here. Square dancing, fine southern dining, music sales, arts and crafts, and handcrafted instruments are some of the crowd-pleasing features of this festival, in addition to its outstanding musical savvy. Tickets are $10 for the weekend.   **LOCATION:** Pine Mountain State Resort Park, 1050 State Park Road in Pineville, about 12 miles north of Middlesboro in the southeast part of the state **TICKETS/INFO:** 606-337-3066 **ACCOMMODATIONS/ TOURIST INFO:** 606-337-3066

IBMA BLUEGRASS FAN FEST

OWENSBORO ✹ LAST FULL WEEKEND IN SEPTEMBER, FRIDAY–SUNDAY

Festival organizers say that Owensboro, Kentucky, is known as the "Barbecue Capital of the World," and while many towns across the South might get hickory-smokin' mad about that statement, the music in Owensboro during the Bluegrass Fan Fest sure is finger-lickin' good. Many of the top names in bluegrass show up to play for up to 20,000 spectators and to take part in the International Bluegrass Music Awards. Since it's a fanfest, there are plenty of autographing and meet-the-musician events in beautiful, shady English Park, located on the shores of the Ohio River. The Bluegrass Fan Fest is also home to a bluegrass event known as the World's Greatest all-Female Jam.

Lots of informal jam sessions take place here, too, so even if you don't plan on getting up on stage to play in front of 20,000 people, you might still want to lug your favorite instrument. Since Owensboro is only a couple of hours from Nashville, you never know who might show up to hop on stage and dazzle the crowd. Other goings-on include master workshops, an Ohio River cruise, and a children's stage. Camping is available.   **LOCATION:** English Park, at 25 Hanning Lane (on the banks of the Ohio River) in Owensboro **TICKETS/INFO:** 502-684-9025 **ACCOMMODATIONS/TOURIST INFO:** 502-926-1100

GARVIN GATE BLUES FESTIVAL

LOUISVILLE ✹ SECOND FULL WEEKEND IN OCTOBER, FRIDAY–SUNDAY

One of Louisville's most culturally diverse music festivals brings about a dozen regionally and nationally known blues talents to one outdoor street stage. An eclectic audience mills around in Old Louisville, listening to the free music, eating food, and browsing for crafts.   **LOCATION:** The 1200 block of Garvin Place in the heart of Old Louisville, less than a mile from the business district **TICKETS/INFO:** 502-495-9089 **ACCOMMODATIONS/TOURIST INFO:** 800-626-5646

CELEBRATION OF TRADITIONAL MUSIC

BEREA ✹ LAST FULL WEEKEND IN OCTOBER

Older and lesser heard performers get their day in the spotlight at this gathering. On a single indoor stage, about ten acts play the old-time music that was king in Kentucky in

*Finger-lickin' good bluegrass: IIIrd Tyme Out bring the house down with an
a capella number at IBMA's 1995 Bluegrass Fan Fest.* Courtesy of MaryE Yeomans/IBMA

the days before bluegrass made its celebrated debut. About 800 spectators show up for
this day of concerts, instrumental workshops, and dancing, paying about $6 each.
LOCATION: Berea College Campus in Berea, just off I-75 about 30 miles south of
Lexington **TICKETS/INFO:** 606-986-9341, ext. 5140 **ACCOMMODATIONS/TOURIST
INFO:** 606-986-9760

ᘻᕊERLE TRAVIS FESTIVAL
CENTRAL CITY ✱ SATURDAY FOLLOWING THANKSGIVING DAY (THE FOURTH
THURSDAY IN NOVEMBER)

This may be the only festival in which you can enjoy the fine art of thumb-pick
guitar, then celebrate the late Merle Travis's birthday by eating his favorite meal: beef
stew, corn bread, and a dessert of peach cobbler. You'll also get a chance to see recent
thumb-picking national champions like Bob Saxton, Paul Mosely, John Matsel, Pat
Kirtley, and Steve Rector. Tickets cost $6 for adults and $3 for children. Proceeds from
the festival go the Everly Brothers Foundation Scholarship Fund.   **LOCATION:**
Central City Elementary School gymnasium, on Highway 431 (Sate Road) in Central
City **TICKETS/INFO:** 502-754-9603, 502-754-2360, 502-754-2881 **ACCOMMODA-
TIONS/TOURIST INFO:** 800-225-8747

ℳARTIN LUTHER KING ZYDECO EXTRAVAGANZA
LAKE CHARLES ✳ SUNDAY BEFORE THE THIRD MONDAY IN JANUARY (MARTIN LUTHER KING DAY)

This single-day event usually draws three or four top zydeco bands—and in these parts that means an accompanying mob of dancers and fans. The Zydeco Extravaganza comes in the middle of 11 days of events honoring Martin Luther King Jr. and is usually backed up by a rodeo and plenty of food. This is a great chance to catch authentic zydeco music in the midst of the culture in which it was born.   **LOCATION:** Lake Charles location changes from year to year. **TICKETS/INFO:** 318-491-9955 **ACCOMMODATIONS/TOURIST INFO:** 800-456-7952, 318-436-9588

ℒOUISIANA STATE UNIVERSITY FESTIVAL OF CONTEMPORARY MUSIC
BATON ROUGE ✳ ONE WEEK AT THE END OF FEBRUARY OR BEGINNING OF MARCH

The region's only festival focusing on contemporary classical music is one of the nation's oldest, having run continuously since its inception in 1944. Focusing on 20th-century music, the festival brings in a major composer to work with students (one year John Cage taught). Typically, several world premieres are featured, and students and faculty from all areas of performance—opera, choruses, orchestras, dance ensembles, and chamber ensembles—contribute.   **LOCATION:** The School of Music on the LSU campus, in south Baton Rouge. From I-10, take the Dalrumple Road exit and follow signs to the campus. **TICKETS/INFO:** 504-388-3261 **ACCOMMODATIONS/TOURIST INFO:** 800-527-6843, 504-383-1825

ℱUPER SUNDAY
NEW ORLEANS ✳ SUNDAY CLOSEST TO MARCH 19 (ST. JOSEPH'S DAY), WEATHER PERMITTING

A couple of weeks after Fat Tuesday, the fantastic street music of the Mardi Gras Indians turns Crescent City neighborhoods into a romping, musical pageant. African American "tribes" march through the streets in outlandish outfits and feathered head-

Back-street boogie: On Super Sunday, the Mardi Gras Indians turn New Orleans neighborhoods into a romping, musical pageant. Richard Pasley/Viesti Associates

dresses reminiscent of American Indians, drumming and chanting in the tradition that inspired the music of the Wild Magnolias, Wild Tchoupitoulas, and Neville Brothers.

One of America's most precious and picturesque folk traditions evolved from the days of slavery, and, like much in New Orleans, synthesizes the traditions of Africans, Europeans, and Native Americans. This backstreet answer to the elaborate Mardi Gras parades of the uptown krewes began when local Indians made friends with newly arrived African slaves (and possibly helped to shelter runaways).

Originally, the Africans dressed up as Indians to honor their friends, but the costumes soon became part of the plantation carnival celebrations. After abolition, many African Americans moved to New Orleans, but they were shut out of European-American carnival krewes. (The big Mardi Gras parades now invite the Indian gangs to participate, but most prefer to celebrate independently.)

On Super Sunday, gangs drum and chant their way through the streets, often meeting other groups and staging mock confrontations filled with esoteric ritual. Once-violent clashes are now visual and verbal duels in which each gang claims to have the "prettiest chief." As the chief dances in his fabulous suit of feathers and beads, flag boys whirl and carry the gang's flag, while spy boys scout ahead and secretly signal the group to change direction or musical tempo. You'll also see Indian queens, romping children in feathered outfits, consular chiefs, and trail chiefs watching the rear. The shamanlike, horned "wild man" clears the way for the chief, and bystanders are warned not to get anywhere near him.

Uptown gangs—including the very musical Wild Magnolias and Golden Eagles, and the spectacularly costumed Golden Star Hunters—typically start around Shakespeare Park and end up in Armstrong Park, singing as they cross the stage. Downtown gangs—including the Yellow Pocahontas and the Monogram Hunters—start around Bayou St. John and work their way toward Hunter's Field at St. Bernard and Claiborne Avenues. In both locations, you'll notice outfits ranging from ragtag to the sophisticated stylings of the Creole Osceola, with their Haitian-looking flags and sequins, and the Spirit of the Fi-Yi-Yi (formerly the Mandingo Warriors) with their very African-looking suits and animistic masks.

Through it all, the "second line" beats on drums, tambourines, and pickle barrels. The variations of beat are subtle but distinct, and rhythms such as the *bamboula* and *changa* beats can be traced to their origins in Africa and the Caribbean. As the gangs move in unstructured parades through the streets and parks, they stop at the homes of elderly and shut-in neighbors, performing routines on front porches. Brass bands and second-line social clubs also jump into the fray.

As with most true folk traditions, the best word is word of mouth. When the Indians are to begin assembling, announcements move by flyer and public radio. When you hear the news, hit the streets and get ready for a spectacle of funky sights and sounds that's unique in North America—and on this planet!   **LOCATION:** Uptown gangs usually parade from Shakespeare Part to Louis Armstrong Park (bounded by Basin, Villere, Saint Phillip, and Rampart Streets). Downtown gangs usually parade from Bayou St. John to Hunter's Field (at St. Bernard and Clairborne Avenues). **TICKETS/INFO:** 504-568-1239 (WWOZ) and word of mouth **ACCOMMODATIONS/TOURIST INFO:** 504-566-5011, 504-566-5031

*L*OS ISLENOS HERITAGE AND CULTURAL FESTIVAL
ST. BERNARD ✴ LAST WEEKEND IN MARCH, SATURDAY AND SUNDAY

Descended from Canary Islanders who arrived at the same time as the Acadians, the Spanish-speaking Islenos of St. Bernard Parish create some of Louisiana's most obscure and interesting music. At this festival you'll hear the traditional ten-stanza *decima*, a complex story song that tells stories of everything from cruel knights in the Middle Ages to lazy fishermen in modern-day Delacroix. The isolated Islenos were able to maintain much of their cultural independence until recent times, and the fiesta brings about 7,000 people to the grounds of a restored home built in the 1850s and now functioning as a museum. Also featured are ethnic foods (be sure to try the delicious *caldo*) and demonstrations of traditional Isleno arts like shrimp-net making, duck-decoy carving, and lace making.   **LOCATION:** Islenos Museum, 1357 Bayou Road, St. Bernard (about 20 miles southeast of New Orleans on Highway 46) **TICKETS/INFO:** 504-682-0862 **ACCOMMODATIONS/TOURIST INFO:** 504-278-4200

*A*CADIANA MUSIC FESTIVAL
EUNICE ✴ SECOND SUNDAY AFTER EASTER

Bring your dancin' shoes to this authentic musical romp, hosted by the local chapter of the Cajun French Music Association (CFMA) since 1991. In addition to four local Cajun bands, there's plenty of home-cooked food, a raffle, and door prizes. And if you're interested in learning Cajun accordion, fiddle, guitar, or dance, the CFMA holds a series of workshops during the summer in Eunice (see the Music Workshops chapter, page 497).   **LOCATION:** Northwest Community Center Pavilion, 501 Samuel Drive,

French Quarter Festival: America's coolest quarter hosts 12 stages of sounds from Louisiana, the Caribbean, and beyond. Courtesy of Louisiana Office of Tourism

Eunice, on Highway 13 just south of U.S. 190 **TICKETS/INFO:** 318-457-3014 **ACCOMMODATIONS/TOURIST INFO:** 800-346-1958 (U.S.), 800-543-5340 (Canada), 318-232-3737

ℱRENCH QUARTER FESTIVAL
NEW ORLEANS ✹ SECOND FULL WEEKEND IN APRIL, FRIDAY–SUNDAY

The French Quarter is home to some of America's legendary sights, but its *sounds* steal the show at this free festival. A whopping 12 music stages keep locals and visitors dancing nonstop; expect to hear homespun jazz, Cajun, zydeco, and music from the Caribbean, Latin America, and Africa. With plenty of other events—including fireworks and the world's largest jazz brunch—this fest is a great way to experience the Quarter while avoiding the heat of summer or the crowds of Mardi Gras or Jazzfest. **LOCATION:** Throughout the French Quarter and in Woldenberg Riverfront Park, on the southeast periphery of the French Quarter, north of the Aquarium of the Americas, on the Mississippi River bank. **TICKETS/INFO:** 504-522-5730 **ACCOMMODATIONS/TOURIST INFO:** 504-566-5011 or 504-566-5031

Diversity in the air: the Master Drummers of Burundi perform at a recent Festival International de Louisiane.

Courtesy of Festival International

de Louisiane/Philip Gould

ℱESTIVAL INTERNATIONAL DE LOUISIANE
LAFAYETTE ✹ LAST WEEK IN APRIL, TUESDAY–SUNDAY

The festival is smaller and the town isn't as cool, but many world-music buffs rank this musical feast more highly than the Jazz and Heritage Festival of New Orleans. Downtown Lafayette is overwhelmed with Francophile rhythms and culture as bands representing some 35 different nationalities around the French-speaking world— Europe, West Africa, Madagascar, Canada, and the Caribbean—converge in Cajun and zydeco country to perform with the best of the locals.

Southwest Louisiana was culturally isolated from much of the United States until the last few decades, but Acadian settlers kept tenuous ties with France and its former colonies. The festival serves to highlight and strengthen these ties through a series of performances covering not just music, but film, theater, art, and even beer. Some performers fly in early to get together with local artists, and the shows that result from this international networking give the event much of its unique spirit. You might see a traditional band from Madagascar jamming with a fiddle-accordion duo from Opelousas, or a master Cajun fiddler sitting in with a *zouk* combo from the French West

Indies. Local people take a great deal of pride in the festival, and at any of the five stages you'll find lots of dancing and zero indifference.

The Festival International de Louisiane coincides with the first weekend of the New Orleans Jazz and Heritage Festival, but here the similarities stop. Unlike Jazzfest, this multistage event is free, and the music here lasts late into the evenings. Alternative offerings include everything from a gourmet beerfest (great beer; boring speakers) to plays, dance exhibitions, and street musicians. There are also forums, lectures, and films.

Lafayette doesn't have the beauty, bars, or nonstop excitement of New Orleans, but the surrounding countryside is a cultural treasure chest. The food is great, the prices are lower, and in roadhouses and juke joints local bands lay down searing boogie sessions as neighbors dance on springy floorboards.   **LOCATION:** Downtown Lafayette, 54 miles west of Baton Rouge along I-90 **TICKETS/INFO:** 318-232-8086; World Wide Web: URLhttp://www.usl.edu/Regional/Festival/   **ACCOMMODATIONS/TOURIST INFO:** 800-346-1958 (U.S.), 800-543-5340 (Canada), 318-323-3737

NEW ORLEANS JAZZ AND HERITAGE FESTIVAL

NEW ORLEANS ✷ LAST WEEKEND IN APRIL (FRIDAY–SUNDAY) AND FIRST WEEKEND IN MAY (THURSDAY–SUNDAY)

"Jazzfest" is the American music lovers' rendezvous, a two-weekend event in the city where the spring comes early and the dancing comes easy. It's been called everything from a low-key version of Mardi Gras to a victim of its own success, but the most diverse music festival on the continent continues to bring in bigger crowds every year. With simultaneous music on six stages, tons of great food, and New Orleans's all-night bar and club scene, the festival draws visitors from all over North America, Europe, and East Asia.

The diversity of music draws all types: garden variety rock 'n' rollers, gospel devotees, jazz disciples, enigmatic world-beatniks, and plenty of new-breed eclectics from both coasts. Jazzfest is big—attendance is now pushing half a million—and it keeps getting bigger and more crowded, mostly because nearly everyone who attends once comes back the next year with friends in tow.

A daily entrance fee of about $12 buys a lot more than jazz. At the Fais Do Do Stage, there's Cajun (the traditional music of rural, white Louisiana) and zydeco (the traditional music of black, Creole Louisiana). The Ray Ban/WWL and Polaroid/WVUE stages feature bigger names like Bonnie Raitt or the Neville Brothers. At the WWOZ tent it's pure jazz; at Congo Square there's African, Caribbean and R&B. And at the Rhodes/WYLD Gospel Tent you'll hear the soul-raising stuff of salvation. With so much happening at once, decisions are tough, and even during a great performance it's often impossible to resist the urge to sprint over to the next stage and "discover" a Creole fiddler, a singing cowboy, or a *soukous* combo from Zaire.

Crafts, workshops, parades, and demonstrations provide plenty of nonmusical diversion, but much of the festival's draw is New Orleans itself and all that comes with it. The mood in this subtropical port is more Caribbean than North American, with unique music, food, architecture—and that rarest of American rarities, the drive-through daiquiri shop. New Orleans loves to party, loves to make visitors feel at home, and loves to tell you that if you can't have fun here, it's your own damned fault!

At the festival, the beer selection is tragically limited to mainstream canned products, but food pavilions reflect the diversity of Louisiana culture. You can sample alligator po'boys, red beans and rice, crawfish Monica, muffaletta, gumbo, and

New Orleans Jazz and Heritage Festival: The spring comes early and the dancing comes easy. Courtesy of Louisiana Office of Tourism

jambalaya. It's all great, but it doesn't come cheap or in large portions. For deals, stick around until police start clearing the grounds and vendors try to unload surplus food rather than cart it home.

Official Jazzfest nighttime events take place in arena settings that are neither intimate nor cheap, and the unofficial offerings of the city's bars and clubs are much better. For many people, the daytime events are just a menu of appetizers, a prelude to the main course of music at night. Live music is everywhere, from bowling alleys to record stores to the bars of the Marigny District (Café Brazil, Café Istanbul, the Saturn Bar) or uptown (Jimmy's, the Maple Leaf, Benny's, Tipatina's). In these humid barrooms there's no closing time—the bands cut loose, the people get giddy, and the possibilities get bigger in the swampy bottom of the American night.   **LOCATION:** Daytime events take place at the New Orleans Fair Grounds Race Track, 1751 Gentilly Boulevard in New Orleans; nighttime events take place at various venues in New Orleans. **TICKETS/INFO:** 504-522-4786 **ACCOMMODATIONS/TOURIST INFO:** 504-525-9326

ℬREAUX BRIDGE CRAWFISH FESTIVAL AND CREOLE CRAWFISH FESTIVAL
BREAUX BRIDGE ✷ FIRST WEEKEND IN MAY, FRIDAY–SUNDAY

What started as a local *fais do do* in 1959 became a riot of 100,000 people by the 1980s, overwhelming this town of 7,000. The Crawfish Festival had to be reeled in, but tens of thousands of locals and visitors still make it a major party with plenty for the music lover. Now, two simultaneous festivals are contained in two separate locations. The Crawfish Festival, in Park Hardy, features 25-30 Cajun bands on two stages, plus Cajun music workshops, crafts, and contests for peeling, racing, and eating the illustrious swamp bug. The Creole Crawfish Festival is smaller, but some of the best zydeco music in the country blisters almost continuously from a single stage on the National Guard Armory grounds. Admission to each festival is $5.   **LOCATION:** Park Hardy and National Guard Armory in Breaux Bridge, one mile south of I-10 on Highway 31 (10 miles east of Lafayette). **TICKETS/INFO:** 318-332-6655 (Crawfish Festival); 318-332-2537 (Creole Crawfish Festival) **ACCOMMODATIONS/TOURIST INFO:** 800-346-1958 (U.S.), 800-543-5340 (Canada), 318-232-3737

NORTH SHORE JAZZ FESTIVAL
COVINGTON ✳ A SATURDAY IN MID-MAY

Both traditional and progressive jazz is offered at this indoor/outdoor event on the banks of the Bogue Falaya River. This festival, one of the few on Lake Pontchartrain's north shore, usually draws about a dozen performers from around Covington (many of whom have moved to north shore from New Orleans) and a handful from the Crescent City itself. Outdoor events are held on top of the scenic Columbia Street Landing, while indoor events are next door at Masonic Hall. Admission is $3.   **LOCATION:** Columbia Street Landing and Masonic Hall, Covington **TICKETS/INFO:** 504-892-8650 **ACCOMMODATIONS/TOURIST INFO:** 800-634-9443, 504-892-0520

FIESTA AMERICANA
NEW ORLEANS ✳ SATURDAY AND SUNDAY OF MEMORIAL DAY WEEKEND
(MEMORIAL DAY IS THE LAST MONDAY IN MAY)

New Orleans's sizable Hispanic population displays its musical and economic vitality at this two-day, two-stage event. You'll hear local bands supplying dancers with salsa, merengue, and crossover sounds, as well as guest artists from Central America and the Caribbean. Organizers of this free event say that as the local Haitian community continues to expand, visitors can expect to hear more *rara* and other Haitian rhythms. **LOCATION:** Louis Armstrong Park, near the French Quarter and bounded by Basin, Villere, Saint Phillip, and Rampart Streets **TICKETS/INFO:** 504-581-9986 **ACCOMMODATIONS/TOURIST INFO:** 504-566-5011, 504-566-5031

BLUEGRASS FESTIVAL
ATHENS ✳ FIRST WEEKEND IN JUNE

Since 1985, this down-homey campground fest has featured both traditional and modern bluegrass, plus the sweet harmonies of gospel bluegrass. In addition to paid performers, many in the crowd of about 1,000 pick and sing the night away informally at campsites. June is hot in these parts, but the site offers plenty of shade under hardwood trees, plus ponds for swimming and fishing, hiking trails, and 200 RV hookups. **LOCATION:** Home Place Acres, about seven miles southwest of Athens on Highway 108, just north of I-20, midway between Shreveport and Monroe **TICKETS/INFO:** 318-258-4943 **ACCOMMODATIONS/TOURIST INFO:** 318-258-5863

MAMOU CAJUN MUSIC FESTIVAL
MAMOU ✳ FIRST FULL WEEKEND IN JUNE, FRIDAY AND SATURDAY

Downtown Mamou, in the heart of Cajun country, boils over in early June with plenty of traditional Cajun music. A single stage supports a nonstop array of local musicians, while locals participate in contests that include guinea chasing, egg throwing, arm wrestling (often women versus men), nail driving, greased-pole climbing, and boudin eating. And don't forget to stop into America's coolest tourist trap, Fred's Lounge, for some fine dancing and drinking.   **LOCATION:** Downtown Mamou, 10 miles north of Eunice on Highway 13 and Highway 95 **TICKETS/INFO:** 800-346-1958 (U.S.), 800-543-5340 (Canada), 318-323-3737 **ACCOMMODATIONS/TOURIST INFO:** 800-346-1958 (U.S.), 800-543-5340 (Canada), 318-323-3737 (international)

℞EGGAE RIDDUMS INTERNATIONAL ARTS FESTIVAL
NEW ORLEANS ✳ SECOND WEEKEND IN JUNE, FRIDAY–SUNDAY

Set in a mellow park in North America's most Caribbean city, this festival features three days of reggae, calypso, worldbeat, and New Orleans music. About 25 bands make their way from the islands as well as from Africa, Europe, and the United States, producing a mellow vibe for 30,000 people who show up over three days. There's also great food from the Caribbean and plenty of red, green, and gold shopping. Admission is about $15 each day.   **LOCATION:** Marconi Meadows in City Park, bounded by Orleans Avenue, Wisner Drive, and Lake Pontchartrain **TICKETS/INFO:** 504-367-1313 **ACCOMMODATIONS/TOURIST INFO:** 504-566-5011, 504-566-5031

♪LUESBERRY FESTIVAL
COVINGTON ✳ A SATURDAY IN MID-JUNE

The Bluesberry Festival offers a chance to savor the sounds of the great many blues musicians on the north shore of Lake Pontchartrain as well as the tastes of freshly harvested blueberries. From noon until 7 P.M., about 10 groups provide continuous music both outside on a wharf at the Bogue Falaya River, and inside at the Masonic Hall. Much of the food (ice cream, jam, etc.) is made from local blueberries. Admission is $3, and a few hundred people usually make the scene.   **LOCATION:** Columbia Street Landing and Masonic Hall, Covington **TICKETS/INFO:** 504-892-8650 **ACCOMMODA-TIONS/TOURIST INFO:** 800-634-9443, 504-892-0520

ℭFMA CAJUN MUSIC AND FOOD FESTIVAL
LAKE CHARLES ✳ THIRD WEEKEND IN JULY, SATURDAY AND SUNDAY

Deep in the sweltering days of July, Lake Charles's Cajun traditions swing inside the air-conditioned Burton Coliseum. Over two days, 10-15 bands fuel frenzied waltzes, while volunteers cook cauldrons of étouffée and judge contests in dancing, accordion playing, and cooking. All songs are sung in French, and Sunday begins with a Cajun French mass. The festival also features the Cajun French Music Association (CFMA) "Le Cajun" music awards competition, honoring outstanding southwest Louisiana musicians.   **LOCATION:** Burton Coliseum, Gulf Highway, Lake Charles **TICKETS/INFO:** 800-456-7952, 318-436-9588 **ACCOMMODATIONS/TOURIST INFO:** 800-456-7952, 318-436-9588

ℭFMA LE CAJUN FESTIVAL & AWARDS SHOW
LAFAYETTE ✳ THIRD WEEKEND IN AUGUST

Saturday and Sunday afternoon bring Cajun music and dancing—lots of dancing—to Lafayette. More than 3,000 people pack the huge dance floor, where they whirl away to at least 10 bands and salute Cajun Country's best and brightest musical stars. Since outdoor events are out of the question in the stifling August heat, this one's in the air-conditioned Blackham Coliseum, and the town's best restaurants are invited in to serve up spicy Cajun cuisine. On Saturday the music and dancing run from 10 A.M. to 11 P.M.; Sunday from 10 A.M. to 1 P.M. with an awards ceremony at 2 P.M. The event is sponsored by the Cajun French Music Association (CFMA).   **LOCATION:** Blackham Coliseum, Johnston Street, Lafayette. Lafayette is 54 miles west of Baton Rouge along I-90. **TICKETS/INFO:** 800-346-1958 (U.S.), 800-543-5340 (Canada), 318-323-3737 **ACCOMMODATIONS/TOURIST INFO:** 800-346-1958 (U.S.), 800-543-5340 (Canada), 318-323-3737

CUTTING EDGE MUSIC BUSINESS CONFERENCE
NEW ORLEANS ✹ THURSDAY–SUNDAY PRECEDING LABOR DAY (THE FIRST MONDAY IN SEPTEMBER)

The bars, clubs, parks, and even churches of the Crescent City are the perfect setting to hear more than 100 newly emerging performers in several genres. Although the festival is designed as another of the quickly proliferating "music business conferences" (business workshops and schmoozefests), the huge variety of showcase performances is most interesting. The lineup is weighted toward alternative/college rock, but there's also plenty in the way of country, singer-songwriter folk, reggae, hip-hop, metal, and even gospel and brass bands. The stage at riverfront Woldenberg Park is free, and each night a $5 pass gets you into about a dozen club venues where performances are scheduled every half hour.   **LOCATION:** Various venues in New Orleans, including Woldenberg Riverfront Park, on the southeast periphery of the French Quarter, north of the Aquarium of the Americas, on the Mississippi River bank. **TICKETS/INFO:** 504-827-5700; e-mail: 74777.754@compuserve.com **ACCOMMODATIONS/TOURIST INFO:** 504-566-5011, 504-566-5031

SOUTHWEST LOUISIANA ZYDECO MUSIC FESTIVAL
PLAISANCE ✹ SATURDAY BEFORE LABOR DAY

The blues-based, accordion-laced music of black Creole Louisiana is featured in this steamy one-day gig, which is Louisiana's (and the world's) oldest zydeco festival. What started in 1982 with three bands, a large farmer's field, and a stage made of sweet-potato pallets has grown into an extravaganza of 11 bands and more than 20,000 dancing zydeco lovers from all over North America.

The crowd, once a few dozen old-timers, is now younger—as are the performers. Expect to see high-energy newcomers like Keith Frank and the Soileau Zydeco Band, Beau Jocque and the Zydeco Hi-Rollers, or Rosey Ledet and the Zydeco Playboys—as well as amazingly nimble veterans like Boozoo Chavis and the Magic Sounds.

No one makes fiddles out of cigar boxes and screen doors anymore, but the rhythmic sounds of the accordion, washboard, and guitar fill the air from 11 A.M. until around midnight. Cajuns and Creoles mix with visitors from everywhere to dance away the afternoon and night. The biggest problem is the heat—in fact, this may be the physically hottest festival in America. Luckily, ice chests are welcome at the festival, as are tents and campers. You'll also find plenty of regional cuisine and African American arts and crafts.

The festival is the major fund-raising event for the Southern Development Foundation, a nonprofit group concerned with improving economic and social conditions for low-income minorities in the rural South. Admission is $10 for adults, $2 for children. **LOCATION:** Southern Development Foundation Farm in Plaisance, on Highway 167,

Southwest Louisiana Zydeco Music Festival: Louisiana's favorite Creole sons converge at this spirited blow-out near Opelousas. (See entry, page 171.) Doug

Bryant/D. Donne Bryant Stock Photography Agency

six miles northwest of I-49, near Opelousas **TICKETS/INFO:** 318-942-2392 **ACCOM-MODATIONS/TOURIST INFO:** 800-424-5442, 318-948-6263

𝄞LUEGRASS FESTIVAL

ATHENS ✴ SECOND WEEKEND IN SEPTEMBER

This is a semiannual event, happening the first weekend in June and the second weekend in September. See page 169 for all the details. (It's still hot here in September, but the site does offer plenty of shade under hardwood trees, plus ponds for swimming and fishing, hiking trails, and 200 RV hookups.) **LOCATION:** Home Place Acres, about seven miles southwest of Athens on Highway 108, just north of I-20, midway between Shreveport and Monroe **TICKETS/INFO:** 318-258-4943 **ACCOMMODA-TIONS/TOURIST INFO:** 318-258-5863

LOUISIANA FOLKLIFE FESTIVAL
MONROE ✳ SECOND FULL WEEKEND IN SEPTEMBER, SATURDAY AND SUNDAY

In Louisiana, folklife refers to the living present, rather than a past that's long gone. At the Folklife Festival, you can see, smell, taste, and feel a broad sampling of Louisiana traditions, but the festival centers around music—the rhythmic heart of Louisiana life for centuries. In fact, nowhere else can you see and hear so many of the state's musical traditions.

Much of the Folklife Festival is a tribute to Louisiana's ongoing musical vitality. Set in sleepy Monroe (in northeast Louisiana), the festival explores diverse and contrasting voices from all over the state—and often takes visitors on fascinating tours into the unfamiliar. Three stages offer everything from the brass bands, funk, jazz, funeral dirges, and rap of New Orleans to the zydeco and Cajun of the bayou country. And for the fanatic of rare styles, there's an ear-popping selection: South Louisiana swamp pop, 10-stanza *decimas* from Spanish-speaking Islenos, shape-note gospel singing, country string ballads, even the traditional flute music of the Koasati Indian tribe.

The festival's mission is to preserve and promote the state's folk culture, and if you spend a little time here, you'll be convinced of just how different Louisiana is from the rest of the country. Nonmusic activities include traditional crafts, cooking demonstrations, a narrative stage, rodeo and ranch events, and processions. There's little in the way of tourist-oriented flash, but plenty of high-quality crafts and storytelling by traveling bards and Choctaw Indian elders. Everything is creatively researched and astoundingly authentic, a tribute to the organizers' ability to track down the state's living treasures.

The event begins on Friday night, and continues all day Saturday and Sunday, drawing comfortable crowds of about 6,000.   **LOCATION:** Downtown Monroe on the Ouachita Riverfront **TICKETS/INFO:** 318-329-2375 **ACCOMMODATIONS/TOURIST INFO:** 318-387-5691

FESTIVALS ACADIENS
LAFAYETTE ✳ THIRD WEEKEND IN SEPTEMBER

Celebrating the rhythms of Cajun and Creole life, the Festivals Acadiens is actually a three-day blur of festivals that includes the Festival de Musique Acadienne, Downtown Alive, Bayou Food Festival, Louisiana Native Crafts Festival, and Kids Alive.

In terms of music, organization, and local spirit, few festivals come close. The music begins on Friday afternoon and evening in downtown Lafayette, with big-name Cajun and zydeco acts like Beausoleil or Nathan and the Zydeco Cha Chas. Traditional-music lovers will want to spend most of Saturday and Sunday in Girard Park, the site of the Festival de Musique Acadienne. For more than 20 years, this festival has highlighted Cajun and Creole musical traditions, serving as catalyst for the revival of these once-dying, now-thriving styles.

The main Festival de Musique Acadienne stage features an authentic and lively mix of Cajun, zydeco, and swamp pop, while the Heritage Pavilion serves as an informal workshop and performance stage. The workshops generate some of the most interesting action; attractions have included a master fiddle workshop with Michael Doucet and Mitchell Reed, as well as accordion workshops, Cajun dance workshops, and even "Kids Who Play Cajun Music."

Best of the bayou: The Festivals Acadiens celebrates Cajun and Creole life with music and more. Courtesy of Louisiana Office of Tourism

Between musical events, you can participate in street dances or watch someone make a fiddle, a fish trap, or a nutria stew. One popular spot is the "How Men Cook" pavilion, with its massive and delectable output of food and humor. The festival is mostly free, and the climate in late September is usually agreeable.   **LOCATION:** Girard Park and downtown Lafayette **TICKETS/INFO:** 800-346-1958(U.S.), 800-543-5340 (Canada), 318-323-3737 **ACCOMMODATIONS/TOURIST INFO:** 800-346-1958 (U.S.), 800-543-5340 (Canada), 318-323-3737

RED RIVER REVEL ARTS FESTIVAL
SHREVEPORT ✷ LAST SATURDAY IN SEPTEMBER THROUGH THE FIRST SATURDAY IN OCTOBER

Music plays a big part in the largest outdoor festival in northern Louisiana, which attracts about 240,000 people from a five-state region. Over eight days, four performance stages present eclectic, nonstop music (mostly local performers with a few nationally known headliners), with an emphasis on Appalachian, zydeco, classical, and country and western. Children's activities are designed to introduce young people to the visual and performing arts: kids can learn how to play a reggae rhythm (on wood blocks and plastic bottles) or appreciate a kazoo band during the weekdays. Festival events are free until 4 P.M.; there's a nominal admission fee at night.   **LOCATION:** Shreveport's downtown riverfront **TICKETS/INFO:** 318-424-4000 **ACCOMMODATIONS/TOURIST INFO:** 800-551-8682, 318-222-9391

𝓣ANGIPAHOA BLACK HERITAGE FESTIVAL
HAMMOND ✷ FIRST SUNDAY IN OCTOBER

The musical focus is on soul-lifting gospel at this one-day event that features the likes of the Mississippi Mass Choir, the Fantastic Violinars, and other nationally recognized African American choirs. Voices are supplemented by lots of food booths and visual artists from all over the world. Cost is $12 at the gate.   **LOCATION:** Zemurray Park in downtown Hammond, just northeast of the intersection of I-12 and I-55 **TICKETS/INFO:** 504-345-9134 **ACCOMMODATIONS/TOURIST INFO:** 504-542-7521

𝓑ATON ROUGE BLUES FESTIVAL
BATON ROUGE ✷ A SATURDAY AND SUNDAY IN EARLY OR MID-OCTOBER

With four stages of big-name blues over two days, the Baton Rouge Blues Festival is one of the largest blues gatherings in the South. The Mississippi levee in downtown Baton Rouge resounds with headliners like Charles Brown, John Mayall, and Johnny Adams, as well as classic blues artists like Guitar Gable, Harmonica Fats, and Bo Bo Melvin. As a bonus, the festival runs simultaneously with Blues Week, a seven-day frenzy of club performances all over Baton Rouge. Creole cuisine is featured at food booths, and admission is a very reasonable $5 per day.   **LOCATION:** Downtown Baton Rouge at the Mississippi River levee **TICKETS/INFO:** 800-527-6843, 504-383-1825 **ACCOMMODATIONS/TOURIST INFO:** 800-527-6843, 504-383-1825

𝓒ARNAVAL LATINO
NEW ORLEANS ✷ SECOND WEEKEND IN OCTOBER

Latin jazz and traditional Latin American music are highlighted at this three-day festival in Armstrong Park, near the French Quarter. The scene is fairly commercialized, with a large midway and lots of banners and beer company inflatables, but big-name headliners and a bustling crowd of about 40,000 make this free event quite palatable. **LOCATION:** Louis Armstrong Park, near the French Quarter and bounded by Basin, Villere, Saint Phillip, and Rampart Streets **TICKETS/INFO:** 504-879-3561 **ACCOMMODATIONS/TOURIST INFO:** 504-566-5011 or 504-566-5031

𝓐BITA SPRINGS WATER FESTIVAL
ABITA SPRINGS ✷ A SATURDAY IN MID- OR LATE OCTOBER

Although the musical events are only one part of this large and very traditional town festival, they are many and vigorous. Several bands come down from the town's famous Piney Woods Opry to play the old-time, pre-bluegrass country music for which the Florida parishes are famous. In between the flying fiddles, you can catch old-time Anglo-American gospel, as well as music workshops, instrument-building demonstrations, and interviews with performers. About 300 people can fit into the main seating area, and monitors are set up outside for the overflow.   **LOCATION:** Abita Springs Tourist Park. From New Orleans take the Pontchartrain Causeway, then go east on I-12, and north on Highway 59. **TICKETS/INFO:** 504-892-0711 **ACCOMMODATIONS/TOURIST INFO:** 504-892-0520

CELTIC NATIONS FESTIVAL

NEW ORLEANS ✱ A SATURDAY AND SUNDAY IN MID- OR LATE OCTOBER

Performers from Wales, Ireland, Scotland, Brittany, the United States, and Canada are featured at this two-day event among the oak trees and lagoons of New Orleans's beautiful City Park. Founded in the late 1980s by O'Flaherty's Pub owner Danny O'Flaherty, the event features nonstop music on two stages from 10 A.M. to 5 P.M. There's also a dance stage, Highland games, Celtic dogs, artisans, furniture making, a children's pavilion, and plenty of Irish beer.   **LOCATION:** Marconi Meadows in City Park, bounded by Orleans Avenue, Wisner Drive, and Lake Pontchartrain **TICKETS/INFO:** 504-891-5484 **ACCOMMODATIONS/TOURIST INFO:** 504-566-5011, 504-566-5031

LOUISIANA STATE GOSPEL SINGING CONVENTION

BERNICE ✱ FIRST SUNDAY IN NOVEMBER AND THE PRECEDING FRIDAY AND SATURDAY

Since the 1930s, singers from Louisiana, Arkansas, Texas, and Mississippi have gathered here to sing gospel in the traditional "shape-note" or "do-so-me-do" style. Nowadays, the reunion attracts a mostly older crowd of about 150 singers and an audience of about 300. Some songs are done a capella, while others are accompanied by organ, piano, or even three pianos played simultaneously. The concerts are Friday, 6 P.M. to 8 P.M.; Saturday, 1 P.M. to 3:45 P.M. and 6 P.M. to 8 P.M.; and Sunday morning 9 A.M. to noon (a church service).   **LOCATION:** Bernice High School, on Highway 2 near U.S. 167 in northern Louisiana **TICKETS/INFO:** 318-778-4407 **ACCOMMODATIONS/ TOURIST INFO:** 318-285-9333

Mississippi

THE NATCHEZ OPERA FESTIVAL
NATCHEZ ✷ WEEKENDS IN MAY, THURSDAYS–SUNDAYS

In an all-out effort to become "the Santa Fe of the South," this scrappy, all-volunteer company produces three operas and a host of collateral events over its four-week run. Each year the program moves from English-language light opera to heavier programming; for instance, a typical season might begin with Gilbert and Sullivan's *Pirates of Penzance,* and end with Puccini's *Tosca,* sung in the original Italian. Organizers bring in artists from all over the world for festival events, including the Thursday night Plantation Recitals in huge, historic antebellum homes outside the city. The festival also features three concert series with string, wind, and symphonic music, creating weekends full of high-brow sights and sounds in this history-soaked area.   **LOCATION:** Natchez City Auditorium, on Jefferson Street in Natchez, which is about 115 miles southwest of Jackson on the banks of the Mississippi River **TICKETS/INFO:** 601-442-7464 **ACCOMMODATIONS/TOURIST INFO:** 800-647-6724, 601-446-6345

JIMMIE RODGERS FESTIVAL
MERIDIAN ✷ LAST WEEK IN MAY, ALWAYS INCLUDING MAY 26

The Country Music Hall of Fame refers to Meridian's favorite son as simply "the man who started it all." This annual tribute to "the Singing Brakeman" is held on his death anniversary and features daytime talent contests and nighttime concerts in the town's historic Temple Theater. Recent entertainers have included some of the top names in country music, including Willie Nelson, Tammy Wynette, Hank Williams Jr., and Merle Haggard. The festival draws nearly 50,000 people from throughout North America and from as far away as Europe and Japan. Admission fees range from free to $15.   **LOCATION:** Temple Theatre, at 2320 8th Street in Meridian. From I-20/59 take the downtown Meridian exit and follow the signs. **TICKETS/INFO:** 800-396-5882, 601-693-5353, 601-483-5763 **ACCOMMODATIONS/TOURIST INFO:** 800-748-9970, 601-693-1306

ℬ. B. KING HOMECOMING AND INDIAN BAYOU FESTIVAL

INDIANOLA ✷ LAST WEEKEND IN MAY OR FIRST WEEKEND IN JUNE

This three-day weekend brings blues legend B. B. King home for an outdoor concert that also includes other local blues artists. The concert is scheduled for Friday night, and the festival continues throughout the weekend with more music, arts and crafts, carnival rides, and concessions. Admission is about $5 for this event, which is usually held the same weekend as the Pops Staples Blues and Gospel Heritage Festival in nearby Drew. **LOCATION:** Fletcher Park in Indianola, about 28 miles east of Greenville on U.S. 82 **TICKETS/INFO:** 601-887-4454 **ACCOMMODATIONS/TOURIST INFO:** 601-887-4454

ℙOPS STAPLES BLUES AND GOSPEL HERITAGE FESTIVAL

DREW ✷ FIRST SATURDAY IN JUNE

Roebuck "Pops" Staples was born in Winona, Mississippi, in 1915 and grew up in Drew. Before he moved to Chicago and recorded a string of gospel and soul hits with his family, he played solo blues guitar at dances all around the Delta. This festival welcomes him home to the heart of the Delta (he's getting up in age, but has made it most years) with gospel and blues music from about a half-dozen acts. The free event is usually held the same weekend as the B. B. King Homecoming in nearby Indianola, so savvy travelers can hit both on a single road trip.   **LOCATION:** Downtown Drew, about 30 miles north of Indianola on U.S. 49W **TICKETS/INFO:** 601-745-6576 **ACCOMMODA-TIONS/TOURIST INFO:** 601-887-4454

𝓜AIN STREET SALUTES THE BLUES

MERIDIAN ✷ THIRD WEEKEND IN JULY, FRIDAY AND SATURDAY

Meridian is the town where country legend Jimmie Rodgers was born, but in late July this town's many visitors have blues music on their minds. Moving between a downtown park (Friday night) and a nearby lakeside park (Saturday), this festival draws spectators from all over the South and performers from all over Mississippi. The sense of camaraderie is so thick that even some of the locals bring their campers, just to schmooze with out-of-towners. Performances usually begin with traditional Delta blues (which especially appeals to the older audiences and young folks in the know) and wind up with hard-hitting crossover blues by the end of the night. Friday night performances are free, while Saturday admission costs $15-$20. Friday also features a band contest in which the best of the little-known bands wins $500 and an opportunity to play as part of the bigger-name lineup on Saturday's larger Bonita Lakes stage.   **LOCATION:** Friday in downtown Meridian (from I-20 take the 22nd Avenue exit and follow signs); Saturday at Bonita Lakes (from I-20 take the Bonita exit) **TICKETS/INFO:** 601-485-1996 **ACCOM-MODATIONS/TOURIST INFO:** 800-748-9970, 601-693-1306

OO BLUES

HATTIESBURG ✷ LAST SATURDAY IN AUGUST

Since 1994, blues artists like Little Milton have sung the blues at the Hattiesburg Zoo—so the animals won't have to. This fund-raising event brings about a half-dozen regionally and nationally known acts to the zoo for a day of (mostly acoustic) blues. Some 6,000 music lovers show up, paying about $10 at the gate. **LOCATION:** Hattiesburg Zoo, 107 South 17th Avenue. From the intersection of Highway 49 and Hardy go east two blocks to 17th Avenue. Hattiesburg is about 90 miles southeast of Jackson. **TICKETS/INFO:** 601-545-4576; e-mail: hattzoo@aol.com **ACCOMMODATIONS/TOURIST INFO:** 601-268-3220

ℰLMORE JAMES HICKORY STREET FESTIVAL

CANTON ✷ FIRST SATURDAY IN SEPTEMBER

Elmore James's singing and slide-guitar genius helped define Chicago-style blues, but his music has solid roots in the Mississippi Delta where he grew up. This festival goes well beyond the blues, featuring R&B, gospel, jazz, and even reggae—in addition to acoustic and electric blues. About a dozen Mississippi bands send their notes flying over historic Hickory Street, and the festival (sponsored by the county Department of Human Resources) provides an information booth to educate audiences about Canton community services. **LOCATION:** Hickory Street in Canton, about 15 miles north of Jackson along U.S. 51 **TICKETS/INFO:** 601-859-5703 **ACCOMMODATIONS/TOURIST INFO:** 601-859-1307

ℳISSISSIPPI DELTA BLUES FESTIVAL

GREENVILLE ✷ THIRD WEEKEND IN SEPTEMBER

Although this event wasn't embraced by locals until recently, the many travelers who come to Greenville to pay homage to the blues can count on a great day in the foot-stomping land once haunted by Robert Johnson, Charley Patton, and Sonny Boy Williamson. Fantastic music, good food, and warm welcomes are in high supply, and performers emphasize acoustic, Delta-style blues played on traditional instruments.

Greenville, in the heart of the Delta from which the blues sprang, is in many ways the perfect place for one of the nation's most authentic blues festivals. The land here is steeped in memories—many joyful, many sobering. Slaves weren't allowed to talk while working, but they could sing, and the blues eventually developed out of their melodic, African-inspired work songs. The festival spotlights their old instruments—jugs, har-monicas, and primitive slide guitars—and although several high-powered, electrified performers are always in evidence, "un-plugged" sets are most common. In addition to the music, a delectable spread of red beans and rice, catfish, and locally made arts and crafts provide tangible tastes of the Mississippi Delta's culture and cuisine. **LOCATION:** Highway 1 south at Route 454, just outside Greenville **TICKETS/INFO:** 601-335-3523, 800-467-3582 **ACCOMMODATIONS/TOURIST INFO:** 800-467-3582

ℱARISH STREET HERITAGE FESTIVAL

JACKSON ✷ FOURTH WEEKEND IN SEPTEMBER, FRIDAY AND SATURDAY

The Farish Street Historic District was built by former slaves whose great-great-grandchildren still live and work in the neighborhood. In celebration of this history, the neighborhood is decked out with colorful banners, tents, and three stages that feature blues, jazz, gospel, R&B, and reggae. About 30,000 spectators attend the event, which also features African American performers in dance, theater, and visual arts. **LOCATION:** Farish Street Historic District in downtown Jackson **TICKETS/INFO:** 601-960-2383, 601-960-1891 **ACCOMMODATIONS/TOURIST INFO:** 601-960-1891

NORTH CAROLINA

♪AZZ'N JANUARY
PINEHURST ✳ LAST WEEKEND IN JANUARY, FRIDAY AND SATURDAY

Traditional jazz is on the agenda each January at the Pinehurst Resort and Country Club. Look for four or five nationally known bands and plenty of dancing in the grand ballroom. About 1,000 jazz lovers are attracted to this mid-South golf resort over the weekend; admission is $35 to $40.   **LOCATION:** Pinehurst Resort and Country Club, Carolina Vista Drive and Highway 2, Pinehurst **TICKETS/INFO:** 910-692-4356, 910-295-8415 **ACCOMMODATIONS/TOURIST INFO:** 910-692-3330, 800-346-5362

⌀NNUAL BIG BAND DANCE WEEKEND
ASHEVILLE ✳ FIRST WEEKEND IN FEBRUARY, FRIDAY AND SATURDAY

Now that a new generation of Americans is crowding big band dance floors from coast to coast, the Grove Park Inn extends an invitation to lace up those dancing shoes and grab your partner. This big band extravaganza brings in two nationally known orchestras and a show band, and includes dance instruction and cocktail receptions—all within the confines of a historic resort inn. Dance party tickets start at $18, and weekend accommodation packages are available.   **LOCATION:** Grove Park Inn Resort in Asheville. From I-240 take exit 5B and go north one-half mile on Charlotte Street, then turn right on Macon Avenue and travel four-fifths mile to the Grove Park Inn entrance on the left. **TICKETS/INFO:** 704-252-2711 **ACCOMMODATIONS/TOURIST INFO:** 704-258-6111, 800-257-1300

♪C JAZZ FESTIVAL
WILMINGTON ✳ FIRST WEEKEND IN FEBRUARY, FRIDAY AND SATURDAY

This two-day jazz festival starts off with a Friday night concert, then moves into a Saturday brunch for patrons, followed by a big Saturday night concert. Regionally and nationally known musicians are featured.   **LOCATION:** Hilton Hotel, 301 North Water Street, downtown Wilmington **TICKETS/INFO:** 910-763-8585, 910-763-5900 **ACCOMMODATIONS/TOURIST INFO:** 800-222-4757, 910-341-4030

☯LD TIME FIDDLERS AND BLUEGRASS CONVENTION

STATESVILLE ✷ FIRST SATURDAY NIGHT IN MARCH

Twenty to 30 local fiddlers and accompanists raise a ruckus at Statesville High School each March, drawing about 1,000 spectators. Cash prizes are awarded for the best fiddler, best bluegrass band, best old-time band, and best instrumentalists on half a dozen string instruments. Admission is $7 at the door, and plenty of barbecue is available.   **LOCATION:** Senior High School Auditorium on North Center Street in downtown Statesville, which is 40 miles due north of Charlotte, near the junction of I-40 and I-77 **TICKETS/INFO:** 704-872-6776, 704-628-9704 **ACCOMMODATIONS/TOURIST INFO:** 704-521-3666

ℬEAUFORT MUSIC FESTIVAL

BEAUFORT ✷ LAST FULL WEEKEND IN APRIL, FRIDAY–SUNDAY

This entirely free festival offers five performance sites and a variety of music, from classical to country. Each year, more than 30 bands present Cajun, folk, jazz, rock, country, bluegrass, classical, and show tunes. Two stages sit right on the waterfront, where festivalgoers recline on blankets or lawn chairs. Regional food and a special children's area round out the festival offerings, and the historic town of Beaufort has beautiful stretches of beach and many restored pre-Civil War homes.   **LOCATION:** On and along Front Street, on Beaufort's historic waterfront. Beaufort is just east of Morehead City, in coastal Carteret County. **TICKETS/INFO:** 919-728-6894 **ACCOMMODATIONS/TOURIST INFO:** 800-786-6962, 919-726-8148

ℳERLE WATSON FESTIVAL

WILKESBORO ✷ LAST FULL WEEKEND IN APRIL

You wanna see some pickin'? This is the place to be for anyone who loves traditional American music of all kinds. Founded by Arthel "Doc" Watson to honor the memory of his son, Merle, the festival features a whopping eight stages of hard-charging music, laid down by more than 100 acts.

Doc Watson is, quite simply, an American treasure. He was born in Deep Gap, North Carolina, and became known for his beautiful voice and his extraordinary talents on the flat-pick guitar. Throughout the sixties and seventies he was probably the most influential acoustic guitarist in America, and he performed for more than 15 years with his son, Merle, an outstanding talent in his own right. Merle died in a tractor accident on the family farm in 1985, and Doc began this festival to keep his memory alive.

The Merle Watson Festival is one of the few places on the continent where the music lover can experience the breadth and depth of American music as interpreted by its most authentic and masterful tradition keepers. The festival brings more than 40,000 people to the campus of Wilkes Community College for a musical feast that includes country, bluegrass, gospel, blues, jazz, and folk. Recent acts have included Alison Krauss, Cephas and Wiggins, Emmylou Harris, Mark O'Connor, and Claire Lynch, with most bringing their crack bands with them up onto the stage.

In addition to the concerts, the festival offers workshops in just about any acoustic instrument or folk performance style. A "little pickers" area encourages youngsters in

You wanna see some pickin'? For traditional American music of all kinds, check out the Merle Watson Festival. Courtesy of William Russ/NC Travel and Tourism

their musical endeavors, and contests in banjo, songwriting, and several styles of guitar reward the talented. Heritage craft demonstration tents and vendors of musical instruments are also featured. And the festival's peak moment comes when Doc Watson steps on stage and proceeds to blow the audience away with his encyclopedic knowledge and sparkling delivery of America's traditional songs.   **LOCATION:** Doc and Merle Watson Theatre, Wilkes Community College Gardens, in Wilkesboro. Wilkesboro is in the northwest part of the state, about 50 miles west of Winston-Salem via U.S. 421. **TICKETS/INFO:** 800-343-7857, 800-666-1920, 910-838-6291 **ACCOMMODATIONS/TOURIST INFO:** 800-849-5093, 704-322-1335

☆PRING JAZZ AND ART FESTIVAL

RALEIGH ✸ WEEKEND BEFORE MEMORIAL DAY WEEKEND (MEMORIAL DAY IS THE LAST MONDAY IN MAY)

Raleigh's gentle urban environment surges with jazz and blues on two outdoor stages and several smaller indoor performance areas. About 25 acts play each year, and recent stars have included Eddie Palmieri, Joshua Redman, and Arturo Sandoval, playing for crowds of about 80,000 over the weekend. The music is free; other attractions include a juried art show, children's activities, and food vendors.   **LOCATION:** Moore Square Art District and Fayetteville Street Mall in downtown Raleigh **TICKETS/INFO:** 919-832-8699 **ACCOMMODATIONS/TOURIST INFO:** 919-834-5900, 800-849-8499

Brushy Mountain breakdown: Union Grove's Ole Time Fiddler's and Bluegrass Festival. Courtesy of Clay Nolen/NC Travel and Tourism

🌀LE TIME FIDDLER'S AND BLUEGRASS FESTIVAL
UNION GROVE ✳ MEMORIAL DAY WEEKEND, FRIDAY–SUNDAY

One of the most prestigious and authentic fiddling events in the United States has been around for nearly three-quarters of a century. Today, as always, the focus is on traditional American music, and the festival draws a crowd with a serious interest in "the purest mountain music this side of the Mississippi."

Located in a wooded area in the foothills of the Brushy Mountains, this festival is limited to the first 5,000 people who buy tickets, since the organizer, Harper Van Hoy, doesn't want it to get too crowded to be enjoyable. It's also a very low-key, family-oriented event, as evidenced by his proclamation that "we don't cater to people who like to party."

Performers occupy two stages and include 36 old-time traditional bands and 25 bluegrass bands. Competition categories include fiddle, twin-fiddle, autoharp, banjo, mandolin, harmonica, and bluegrass band. One of the most anticipated is the old-time fiddle category for performers over 55 years of age. In this competition, stiff fingers get a workout as the old mountain tunes are resurrected with vigor. Weekend tickets are $40 for adults and $20 for children 8 to 15, and camping is available.   **LOCATION:** Fiddler's Grove Family Campground in Union Grove, about 40 miles west of Winston-Salem. From I-77 take exit 65 and go west on Memorial Highway (Highway 901) for 1.5 miles. **TICKETS/INFO:** 704-539-4417 **ACCOMMODATIONS/TOURIST INFO:** 704-873-2892, 704-521-3666

𝓜ORAVIAN MUSIC FESTIVAL AND SEMINAR
WINSTON-SALEM ✳ THIRD WEEK IN JUNE

This festival is one of the few places where you can hear modern Moravian Americans performing works written by their 18th- and 19th-century ancestors. As many as 20 compositions preserved from Moravian settlements in Salem, Nazareth,

Lititz, and Bethlehem are presented to the 800 or so festivalgoers. In addition, the festival includes children's choirs, a large chorus, concert bands, vocal soloists, and Christmas anthems. Salem College also presents seminars and workshops for classical music lovers. Admission is free for the concerts; a nominal registration fee applies for seminars and workshops.   **LOCATION:** The Fine Arts Center at 500 East Salem Avenue, on the Salem College campus, and at the Stevens Center at 405 West Fourth Street in downtown Winston-Salem **TICKETS/INFO:** 910-725-1107 **ACCOMMODATIONS/ TOURIST INFO:** 910-725-2361, 800-331-7018

$\mathscr{S}$INGING ON THE MOUNTAIN
GRANDFATHER MOUNTAIN/LINVILLE ✹ FOURTH SUNDAY IN JUNE

Started by Joseph L. Hartley as a family reunion in 1924, this annual gathering is the longest-running gospel music convention in the southern Appalachians. Hartley died in 1966, but his family still comes, and two sons emcee the event. The extended Hartley family now includes some 10,000 gospel devotees who annually flock to a meadow at the foot of the highest of the Blue Ridge Mountains to sing for the glory of God. Half of the roster's dozen bands are nationally acclaimed acts, and the remainder are prominent regional and local talents.

To augment the occasion, visiting preachers deliver sermons; and it's impossible not to feel wonder and awe at the sound of human voices drifting through the palpable mist of the Appalachian mountain range. The event costs nothing, and worldly goods such as food and crafts are available. Camping is welcome in this rugged and lovely terrain, but alcohol most certainly is not.   **LOCATION:** Grandfather Mountain, on U.S.-221, two miles north of Linville and one mile south of the Blue Ridge Parkway **TICKETS/INFO:** 704-733-4337 **ACCOMMODATIONS/TOURIST INFO:** 800-438-7500

$\mathscr{B}$REVARD MUSIC FESTIVAL
BREVARD ✹ LATE JUNE THROUGH MID-AUGUST

Brevard's ambitious and adventurous music program presents some 55 concert events over seven weeks. Each summer, more than 70,000 people come to this town in the foothills of the Blue Ridge Mountains to hear symphonic, chamber, opera, and Broadway music. Begun in 1936, Brevard is North Carolina's premier music-teaching center, with educational programs that include electronic music workshops and conductors' workshops. Prices range from $16 to $22.   **LOCATION:** Brevard Music Center, on the outskirts of Brevard. From Asheville take I-26 to U.S. 280; once in downtown Brevard, follow Probart Street to the music center entrance. **TICKETS/INFO:** 704-884-2019 **ACCOMMODATIONS/TOURIST INFO:** 800-648-4523, 704-883-3700

$\mathscr{A}$N APPALACHIAN SUMMER FESTIVAL
BOONE ✹ THROUGHOUT JULY

This fine-arts festival places heavy emphasis on classical music but also includes jazz, folk, bluegrass, and world music. The North Carolina Symphony and Broyhill Chamber Ensemble are frequent performers; others have included the Newport Jazz Festival All-Stars, the Louisville Orchestra, Doc Watson, and Chet Atkins.

Singing on the Mountain: Voices of praise rise through the southern Appalachian mist. (See entry, page 185.) Courtesy of Hugh Morton/Grandfather Mountain

With 15 to 20 bands each year, this unique festival attempts to educate and inspire while it entertains, with lectures and workshops exploring unique aspects of the fine arts. Three stages include a 1,700-seat auditorium, a 400-seat recital hall, and a 300-seat theater.

Appalachian State University is nestled in some of the most pristine, spectacular mountain country in the eastern United States. Nearby are such national treasures as Great Smoky Mountains National Park, Linville Falls, and Grandfather Mountain—so if you get an aesthetic overload at the festival, you can divert yourself with camping, biking, and white-water rafting. Most music, theater, and dance performances are $15 for adults and $8 for students, although several events are offered free of charge. **LOCATION:** On and around the campus of Appalachian State University in Boone, off U.S. 321 in the heart of North Carolina's Blue Ridge Mountain region, in the northwest corner of the state **TICKETS/INFO:** 800-841-2787 **ACCOMMODATIONS/TOURIST INFO:** 800-852-9506, 704-262-3516

DOYLE LAWSON & QUICKSILVER'S BLUEGRASS FESTIVAL

DENTON ✸ WEEKEND AFTER JULY 4, THURSDAY–SUNDAY

Calling itself "America's foremost family-style bluegrass festival," this North Carolina gathering has been serving up bluegrass in its many varieties—middle of the road, traditional, contemporary, and gospel—since 1981. The event is organized by bluegrass/gospel great Doyle Lawson, who picks the best of the old-timers and up-and-comers.

Doyle's puristic programming doesn't allow any folk or jazz licks to rear up and tamper with the tempo. Along with top traditional acts like Bill Monroe (the father of bluegrass music), Doyle and the boys of Quicksilver itself can be counted upon to do a few sets. Also, the festival's Thursday afternoon International Bluegrass Showdown features emerging bluegrass talents, who duke it out for the title. True to its down-home roots, the festival takes place on 135 rural acres, updated with RV hookups, of course. Daily entrance fees run about $25.   **LOCATION:** Denton Farm Park, near the intersection of Route 49 and Route 109 in Denton. The town is 12 miles west of Asheboro and 30 miles south of Greensboro. **TICKETS/INFO:** 704-252-1233 **ACCOMMODATIONS/TOURIST INFO:** 910-388-9830

NORTH CAROLINA INTERNATIONAL FOLK FESTIVAL

WAYNESVILLE ✸ ELEVEN DAYS ENDING THE LAST SUNDAY IN JULY

In the years since its founding in 1984, this large international folk festival has hosted more than 120 musical groups from 69 countries. In any given year, the festival typically treats some 75,000 folk and world music fans to the sounds of about 400 musicians, including soloists and ensembles of all sizes from at least 10 countries. The festival also includes traditional and stylized dancers wearing authentic and reproduced costumes. A crafts festival and a children's program add yet another dimension to this lively festival. Admission ranges from $8 to $16.   **LOCATION:** 236 Haywood Street in Waynesville, about 35 miles west of Asheville in the far western corner of the state, on U.S. 19/74 just off I-40 **TICKETS/INFO:** 704-452-2997 **ACCOMMODATIONS/TOURIST INFO:** 704-256-3021

CAPE FEAR BLUES FESTIVAL

WILMINGTON ✸ LAST WEEKEND IN JULY, WEDNESDAY–SUNDAY

The Cape Fear Blues Festival is a relaxed, no-hype festival that dedicates itself to the advancement of America's indigenous musical expressions. Each night, seven local bars and clubs in downtown Wilmington present local and regional blues performers who let audience members participate in small-group jam sessions.

Festival organizers say the festival is like hangin' out on your neighbor's front porch (except you pay for the beer and someone else empties the ashtrays), since you don't just "see" the musicians but also meet them and maybe even jam with them. These jam sessions cover several styles, ranging from ragtime to acoustic blues, electric blues, and Texas rhythm and blues.

Two cruises on the riverboat Henrietta feature concerts, with tickets costing about $20 per person, including hors d'oeuvres. Formal workshops educate anyone interested in learning more about songwriting, blues harmonica, blues history, or slack-key guitar.

The Cape Fear Blues Amateur Talent Contest welcomes all interested contenders to compete at the Icehouse on Saturday night. Throughout the festival, the clubs don't charge cover, but they hope you'll have a drink and maybe some of the area's great seafood as you enjoy 20 or 30 of the region's finest blues men and women. Other local attractions include the beach, golf, and historic plantations.   **LOCATION:** Concerts are at various clubs throughout downtown Wilmington. Workshops are at Finkelstein's Music Center, at Front and Market Streets, and the Community Arts Center, at Second and Orange Streets. The amateur contest is at the Icehouse, 115 South Water Street. **TICKETS/INFO:** 910-313-2612 **ACCOMMODATIONS/TOURIST INFO:** 800-222-4757, 910-341-4030

ℐAZZ AT BREVARD
BREVARD ✷ SECOND OR THIRD SATURDAY IN AUGUST

Created in 1991 by a few retired musicians who just wanted to get together and have some fun, Jazz at Brevard has become the premier jazz event in western North Carolina. Held in a peaceful, beautiful mountain setting, the festival presents a cross section of jazz ranging from big band to Dixieland to contemporary, and draws fans from all over the Southeast. The festival features big names like the Count Basie Orchestra, Herbie Mann, and Tuck and Patti but also provides a venue for area artists. Most events are held in a 1,600-seat, covered outdoor amphitheater, and tickets cost $15 to $20 for each concert. The dates of the jazz concerts fall during a six-week classical music program held every year at Brevard, so plenty of visitors take advantage of the chance to take in a bit of classical music while in town for the live-jazz extravaganza. Others take time to hike among Transylvania County's many waterfalls.   **LOCATION:** Brevard Music Center, on the outskirts of Brevard. From Asheville take I-26 to U.S. 280; once in downtown Brevard, follow Probart Street to the music center entrance. **TICKETS/INFO:** 704-884-2787 **ACCOMMODATIONS/TOURIST INFO:** 800-648-4523, 704-883-3700

𝒞HEROKEE BLUEGRASS FESTIVAL
CHEROKEE ✷ FOURTH WEEKEND IN AUGUST, THURSDAY–SATURDAY

Like most other festivals produced by bluegrass devotees Norman Adams and Tony Anderson, this one brings in the biggest names in the biz. It's not unusual for one year's roster to feature all bluegrass's favored sons (and even its occasional daughters), like Bill Monroe and the Bluegrass Boys, the Lewis Family, the Del McCoury Band, the Country Gentlemen, and Ralph Stanley and the Clinch Mountain Boys.

In three days of nonstop music totaling 36 hours there's plenty of time for all these stars (and more) to appear on the festival's one outdoor stage, set near Cherokee in a breathtaking region of mountains and national forests. You can park your RV right on-site, and if you come early enough, you can park your lawn chair near the stage. Plenty of food and arts and crafts are available, and tickets cost around $22 for adults (or less for a three-day pass). To preserve the family atmosphere, the festival prohibits alcohol. **LOCATION:** Happy Holiday Campground, four miles east of Cherokee on U.S. 19N **TICKETS/INFO:** 706-864-7203 **ACCOMMODATIONS/TOURIST INFO:** 704-497-7250

Major-league blues: The view from backstage at the Bull Durham Blues Festival. Courtesy of Durham Convention & Visitors Bureau

𝕭ULL DURHAM BLUES FESTIVAL
DURHAM ✸ FIRST WEEKEND IN SEPTEMBER, FRIDAY AND SATURDAY

You won't need a baseball mitt, but bring along your dancing shoes for this major league blues event. The Durham Athletic Park—built in 1938 and the former home of the Durham Bulls—hosts about 9,000 spectators who arrive from across the country to hear local North Carolina blues as well as regional and national acts.

Five bands perform nightly, showcasing traditional, acoustic, and zydeco-style blues. Recent heavy hitters have included Dr. John, Junior Walker, The Fabulous Thunderbirds, and Chubby Carrier & the Bayou Swamp Band. You can sit in the grandstand or bring blankets and lawn chairs for close-up infield seating. Other festival highlights include the Marketplace, featuring local art and mouth-watering Carolina specialty foods. Admission costs $15 per night, and free parking is available. Outside food and beverages are not permitted inside the park.   **LOCATION:** Durham Athletic Park, 428 Morris Street. From I-85 exit Gregson Street, go one mile to Trinity Avenue, then left two blocks to Washington Street. Turn right and go one block to the park. **TICKETS/INFO:** 919-683-1709 **ACCOMMODATIONS/TOURIST INFO:** 800-446-8604

𝒫INEY WOODS FESTIVAL
WILMINGTON ✱ LABOR DAY WEEKEND, SATURDAY AND SUNDAY (LABOR DAY IS THE FIRST MONDAY IN SEPTEMBER)

This 20-year-old festival varies from year to year, sometimes taking an international focus (Latino, Caribbean, Korean) and sometimes emphasizing American folk, jazz, and blues. About 20 regional and local acts take turns performing on two stages—one in the center of a baseball field, the another in a picnic shelter—for weekend crowds of up to 12,000. Along with the barrage of music, more than 80 food booths offer culinary delights from around the world. There are also crafts, face painting, livestock, and a juried art exhibit. The festival is sponsored by the Arts Council, which accepts donations at the gate.   **LOCATION:** Hugh McRae Park, at South College and Oleander Streets in Wilmington **TICKETS/INFO:** 910-762-4223 **ACCOMMODATIONS/TOURIST INFO:** 800-222-4757, 910-341-4030

𝒮MOKY MOUNTAIN FOLK FESTIVAL
LAKE JUNALUSKA ✱ LABOR DAY WEEKEND

This festival features Appalachian music that calls up the memory of the Scottish and Irish immigrants who settled this area. Evening performances at the main stage feature 20 to 30 acts playing traditional and original folk, ballads, and bluegrass. Circus tents around the main stage make way for informal jamming, and two smaller stages provide space for square dancing and children's activities like storytelling and riddle-songs. Founded in the early 1970s, the festival draws around 1,000 visitors each day. No alcohol is allowed on the grounds, and pets must be kept on a leash.   **LOCATION:** Stuart Auditorium in Lake Junaluska, 20 miles due west of Asheville on Highway 20 just north of I-40 **TICKETS/INFO:** 704-452-1688 **ACCOMMODATIONS/TOURIST INFO:** 704-456-3021

𝓕ALL JAMBOREE
SALISBURY ✱ WEEKEND AFTER LABOR DAY

Local string bands, old-time country and gospel singers, and other musicians come together at this festival of traditional country music. About 75 groups play all day Saturday and half of Sunday (which is devoted to gospel music), entertaining a crowd of several thousand visitors. Since the jamboree is held in a state park, alcohol and pets are not allowed.   **LOCATION:** Sloan Park, on Highway 150 just west of Salisbury in Rowan County **TICKETS/INFO:** 704-636-7170 **ACCOMMODATIONS/TOURIST INFO:** 704-638-3100

𝓜USIC IN THE MOUNTAINS FOLK FESTIVAL
BURNSVILLE/CELO ✱ THIRD SATURDAY IN SEPTEMBER

Featuring performers from the music-rich hills of western North Carolina, this modest folk festival is a great opportunity to experience traditional mountain music, bluegrass, ballads, and storytelling. A single stage supports about 20 performers within a rustic, open-air log pavilion (so the show goes on, rain or shine), and workshops cover guitar, banjo, sacred harp, singing, clogging, and fiddling. The site is next to the beautiful South Toe River, and the nearby Black Mountains hold countless opportunities for hiking and fishing. Admission is $7 for the day.   **LOCATION:** Toe River

Campground, 10 miles from Burnsville, in Yancey County. From Asheville take U.S. 19 north to Highway 80 south to Blue Rock Road and follow the signs. **TICKETS/INFO:** 704-682-7215 **ACCOMMODATIONS/TOURIST INFO:** 704-682-7413

OCKTOBERFEST

CHARLOTTE ✷ FIRST WEEKEND IN OCTOBER

Charlotte's bars and clubs erupt with rock 'n' roll during the first week in October, when some 20 bands come to town. National top-40, hard-rock, and alterna-rock bands play at five stages (three inside and two outside), and about 30,000 people pay about $5 each to get in on the action.   **LOCATION:** College Street between 5th and 6th Streets in uptown Charlotte **TICKETS/INFO:** 704-333-2263 **ACCOMMODATIONS/TOURIST INFO:** 800-231-4636, 704-334-2282

CITY STAGE CELEBRATION

GREENSBORO ✷ FIRST FULL WEEKEND IN OCTOBER

Forty local and regional bands and three national headliners attract up to 150,000 people to the City Stage Celebration in downtown Greensboro, making it one of the largest fall festivals in the region. With a variety of activities at the festival—all celebrating the arts in one way or another—it's nearly impossible to sit still, and nearly impossible not to have a good time.

City streets, three beer gardens (which limit their wares to the generic products of a single major brewery), a cultural arts center, and a governmental plaza all transform into six different stage areas that host big-name retro performers like the Supremes and the Guess Who. A block party ushers in the weekend on Friday night with three local and regional bands and a small admission fee of about $5. Throughout the weekend, the diverse musical attractions include bluegrass, pop, rock, country, reggae, gospel, jazz, folk, blues, classical, and choral.

More than 50 international food booths feed the crowds, and exhibitors all over the grounds demonstrate crafts and lifestyles from different cultures. A Folk Life area at the Greensboro Historical Museum exhibits colonial and folk crafts, and artists and crafts-people sell their original designs and creations throughout the festival area. An official Fun & Games area features high-tech interactive hands-on art activities for people of all ages. Except for the block party, admission is free for all concerts.   **LOCATION:** The streets of downtown Greensboro **TICKETS/INFO:** 910-333-7440 **ACCOMMODA-TIONS/TOURIST INFO:** 800-344-2282

SOUTH CAROLINA

SOUTHERN GOSPEL CONCERT

COLUMBIA ✹ THIRD OR FOURTH SATURDAY IN MARCH

This festival draws local and regional talent plus some of the top gospel artists in the nation. Recent guests have included the King's Men Quartet and the Gold City Quartet. Nearly 2,000 people show up to hear four groups who sing some of the most inspiring religious music this side of Jericho. Tickets are $12.   **LOCATION:** Jamil Shrine Temple, 216 Jamil Road in Columbia **TICKETS/INFO:** 803-772-9380 **ACCOMMODATIONS/TOURIST INFO:** 800-264-4884

LOWCOUNTRY CAJUN FESTIVAL

CHARLESTON ✹ THIRD OR FOURTH SATURDAY IN APRIL

Going well beyond the Cajun music alluded to in its name, the Lowcountry Cajun Festival also features the zydeco and R&B music of Louisiana's Creole people. In a park about 10 minutes from historic Charleston, three bands take turns playing on a single stage; special features include a kid's corner, crawfish-eating and crawfish-racing contests, and lots of spicy food. Tickets cost about $6, and park amenities include campsites, RV hookups, and cottages.   **LOCATION:** James Island County Park, on Riverland Drive in Charleston. From Highway 17 take Highway 171 (Folly Road) to Highway 700 (Maybank Highway); turn left onto Riverland Drive and go about two miles; the park is on the right. **TICKETS/INFO:** 803-762-2172 **ACCOMMODATIONS/TOURIST INFO:** 803-853-8000, 800-868-8118

SPOLETO FESTIVAL USA

CHARLESTON ✹ LAST WEEK IN MAY AND FIRST WEEK IN JUNE

Spoleto Festival USA is the American version of a comprehensive arts festival that originated in Spoleto, Italy. Like its sisters in Europe, and now Australia, Charleston's Spoleto features master and apprentice artists performing in operas, chamber music and symphonic concerts, plays, and dances in various venues around the city.

Gian Carlo Menotti, who founded Italy's Spoleto in 1958, searched until 1977 before he selected Charleston as the American counterpart to his "Festival of Two Worlds." He chose Charleston for its beauty and charm, and for its fertile arts commu-

Swampy Saturday: Roy Carrier and the Night Rockers perform at a recent Lowcountry Cajun Festival. Courtesy of Charleston County Park & Recreation Commission

nity. The most immaculately preserved of North America's 18th-century cities, Charleston is filled with historic homes, gardens, plantations, and churches.

Charleston also has a rich musical heritage, and during the festival, if you want to, you can easily immerse yourself totally in music. Top young musicians from conservatories and universities all over the country comprise the festival orchestra, which is joined by spectacular soloists and led by the world's leading conductors. Chamber music concerts have featured the likes of Chee Yun, Anne-Marie McDermott, and Richard Goode. And as for opera, Spoleto has earned a reputation for staging especially difficult and relatively unknown works.

The city's historic district is home to one of Spoleto's finest old venues, the Dock Street Theatre, a 1930s re-creation of a 1730s Charleston theater. Charleston's auditoriums, churches, courtyards, parks, plantations, and gardens resonate with music every day of the festival.

In casual contrast to Spoleto Festival USA, Piccolo Spoleto is a city-sponsored fringe festival that runs concurrently and showcases southern and local performers and artists in informal settings. Piccolo's attractions have included the Appalachian Ballet Company, the Clemson University Players, and the Northwest Florida Ballet. Each year, fireworks and a major symphonic performance celebrate the end of the two-week festival in a grand finale staged at a plantation just outside of town.   **LOCATION:** Various venues throughout Charleston's historic district **TICKETS/INFO:** 800-255-4659, 803-722-2764 **ACCOMMODATIONS/TOURIST INFO:** 800-868-8118

Among its many musical treats, Spoleto Festival USA presents world-class chamber music in Charleston's historic Dock Street Theatre. (See entry, page 192.) Courtesy of William Struhs/Spoleto Festival USA

HILLBILLY DAY
MOUNTAIN REST ✷ JULY 4 (INDEPENDENCE DAY)

Now approaching its 40th year, the Hillbilly Day Fourth of July celebration is a must-hear event—especially if you have a hankerin' to let out the Jed Clampett that's in you (and in us all). Bluegrass is the music of choice, and the Carolina Mountain Boys can usually be counted on to throw some sizzling licks into the hickory smoke that fills everyone's nose on the eve of the Fourth of July.

The stage is surrounded by old wooden cabins in a rustic wooded area, and bluegrass fans sit on old stumps to enjoy the music of five bands, all of whom donate their time. By the morning of the Fourth, about 10,000 people have shown up, and even those among them who are not banjo or fiddle fans have a lot to see and do. Activities include clogging and square dancing, and the greased-pole climb, in which eager participants shimmy up a 25-foot greased pole to claim a $10 bill at the top. If climbing isn't for you but you still want to get some grease all over you, try your luck at the greased-pig chase. The winner gets to keep the pig, but more often than not the lucky swine get away. Other events include a tug-of-war, a log toss, and a shoe-kick for women, which originated in the old days when a woman would land a good kick to her husband's rear after he came home from boozing at the whiskey still.

Speaking of stills, the state allows the festival to use an old-time still to distill some of its own white-lightning moonshine during the event. If you weren't a hillbilly before you arrived, a few sips of it will have you howling at the moon. For the less adventurous, an animal farm houses possums, raccoons, and other rodents. Several booths with local mountain crafts are scattered throughout the area, and there is food aplenty. The festival and parking are free, since the barbecue and home-distilled liquor fund the fun and games. Nearby camping, hotels, and motels are available.   **LOCATION:** Mountain Rest, on Route 28. From I-85 take U.S. 76 west through Clemson and Seneca, then take a right on Route 28 and follow it 10 miles to Walhalla and another 12 to Mountain Rest. **TICKETS/INFO:** 803-638-6871 **ACCOMMODATIONS/TOURIST INFO:** 800-849-4766

SOUTH CAROLINA STATE BLUEGRASS FESTIVAL
MYRTLE BEACH ✷ FOURTH THURSDAY IN NOVEMBER (THANKSGIVING DAY) THROUGH SATURDAY

The extended bluegrass family gathers for Thanksgiving weekend and welcomes home its wandering muses—talents like Mac Wiseman, Ralph Stanley, the Country Gentlemen, and about a dozen more well-known performers. The indoor stage has plenty of reserved and general-admission seating, and a large area is set aside for off-stage jamming. The show costs about $25 per day, with free parking but no on-site RV hookups.   **LOCATION:** Myrtle Beach Convention Center, on Oak Street at 21st Avenue **TICKETS/INFO:** 706-864-7203 **ACCOMMODATIONS/TOURIST INFO:** 803-626-7444

♪ BEALE STREET MUSIC FESTIVAL
MEMPHIS ✷ FIRST WEEKEND IN MAY

As part of the wide-ranging Memphis in May festivities, the Beale Street Music Festival brings lots of blues, rock, and R&B to one of the world's most famous musical streets. Several stages are set up along Beale Street and on the banks of the Mississippi River, and the lively Beale Street bar scene rocks out late with live music. Admission fees vary.   **LOCATION:** Various venues including Tom Lee Park, at the foot of Beale Street at Riverside Drive and the banks of the Mississippi River **TICKETS/INFO:** 901-525-4611 **ACCOMMODATIONS/TOURIST INFO:** 901-543-5333

♪ TRIANGLE JAZZ PARTY
KINGSPORT ✷ FIRST WEEKEND IN MAY, FRIDAY AND SATURDAY

Hailed as one of the "best small jazz parties in America," this event strives to re-create the intimate feel of jazz clubs in the twenties, thirties, and forties with cabaret-style seating in a local ballroom. The room seats about 300 jazz enthusiasts at each of three five-hour sessions and features 22 jazz greats from around the country over the two days. Past lineups have included masters of improvisational jazz, like Harry "Sweets" Edison, Milt Hinton, and Butch Miles. Admission is $25 per stage session and $125 for a weekend patron's package, and proceeds benefit health-care organizations and jazz education programs in schools.   **LOCATION:** Ramada Inn in Kingsport, in the north-east corner of Tennessee near the Virginia border and just off I-181 **TICKETS/INFO:** 423-288-2519; e-mail: HEARTsdb@aol.com **ACCOMMODATIONS/TOURIST INFO:** 800-743-5282

♪ SUMMER LIGHTS IN MUSIC CITY
NASHVILLE ✷ WEEKEND AFTER MEMORIAL DAY, THURSDAY–SUNDAY
(MEMORIAL DAY IS THE LAST MONDAY IN MAY)

Family-oriented Summer Lights turns on the twang beneath the Nashville skyline, showcasing music-city talent on several downtown city blocks. Nashville hosts six outdoor and two indoor stages, with musical styles including country, jazz, alternative, gospel, bluegrass, and classical. Nearly 300 acts perform for more than 135,000 visitors during the weekend, and food, children's activities, arts and crafts, and street performers

Summer Lights in Music City: Nashville's eclectic street party features more than 300 acts on eight stages. Courtesy of Tennessee Tourist Development

add to the entertainment. Admission is about $7 per day; picnicking and pets are not allowed.   **LOCATION:** Downtown, in the area bounded by Second and Seventh Avenues North, and by Union and Charlotte Avenues **TICKETS/INFO:** 615-259-3956 **ACCOMMODATIONS/TOURIST INFO:** 615-259-4755, 615-259-4730

COSBY DULCIMER AND HARP FESTIVAL
COSBY ✷ SECOND FRIDAY IN JUNE

The Cosby Dulcimer and Harp Festival focuses on the music and instruments of America's early European immigrants. A few hundred people gather for performances and workshops at an open gazebo where musicians play the harp and dulcimer, as well as old-time instruments like the saw and bones. Children's activities and storytelling round out the daytime events, and about 25 musicians perform in the evening. Electrical instruments, open alcohol, and pets are not allowed.   **LOCATION:** Folklife Center of the Smokies, at 267 South Highway 32 in Cosby, between Newport and Gatlinburg just off I-40 **TICKETS/INFO:** 423-487-5543 **ACCOMMODATIONS/TOURIST INFO:** 423-623-7201

RIVERBEND FESTIVAL AND BESSIE SMITH STRUT
CHATTANOOGA ✷ NINE DAYS ENDING THE LAST SATURDAY IN JUNE

Considering the diversity of the music heard on each of Riverbend's five stages, each stage could be considered a music festival in itself. One location features rock 'n' roll from the fifties through the eighties, another presents country music legends, another showcases jazz and world music, and still another brings in mellow singer-songwriters. More than 500,000 people come down for the festivities, paying about $25 at the gate for an unlimited nine-day pass. Monday evening's Bessie Smith Strut, named after the legendary blues singer, is one of the largest blues block parties in the world, with five stages of blues entertainment and some of the best barbecue in the South. **LOCATION:** Ross's Landing Park and downtown Chattanooga **TICKETS/INFO:** 423-756-2212 **ACCOMMODATIONS/TOURIST INFO:** 423-756-8687

SEWANEE SUMMER MUSIC CENTER & FESTIVAL
SEWANEE ✷ LAST WEEK IN JUNE THROUGH LAST WEEK IN JULY

For more than 40 years, students have come to this small university town to study and gain stage experience with the Sewanee Summer Music Center's international faculty. The public is invited to many of the concerts performed by Sewanee's three symphony orchestras. Concerts take place in Guerry Hall, and sometimes in the courtyard outside. Tickets range from free to $6.   **LOCATION:** Guerry Hall, 735 University Avenue in Sewanee, five miles from I-24, between Nashville and Chattanooga **TICKETS/INFO:** 615-598-1225; e-mail: mmccrory@seraph1.sewanee.edu **ACCOMMODATIONS/TOURIST INFO:** 615-598-1225

SMITHVILLE FIDDLERS' JAMBOREE
SMITHVILLE ✷ WEEKEND CLOSEST TO JULY 4, FRIDAY AND SATURDAY

If you don't happen to like old-time, toe-tapping music, then give this fiddle convention a wide berth. Roughly 640 amateur contestants—ranging from 10-year-old musical prodigies to 60-something orchestra-jumpers—make the scene and concentrate

Sweet and mellow: The Cosby Dulcimer and Harp Festival brings old-time instruments and songs to the heart of the Smoky Mountains. Courtesy of Tennessee Tourist Development

on the old-time Appalachian way of playing music, with no electricity. In about 28 competition categories, expect to see all kinds of old-timey instruments, including harmonicas, dobros, banjos, guitars, spoons, bones, and more.

You may hear a bit of bluegrass here, but the repertoire more typically focuses on pre-1900 dance music with certifiable roots in traditional European or American folk music. In the main event, fiddle-wielders compete by playing a waltz, a hoedown, and a tune of their own choosing, within strict time limits. Old-time fiddlers are showmen at heart, and in the trick-fiddling category, you'll see flashy, crowd-pleasing stunts with every odd draw of the bow.

In addition to the contestants, some 75,000 people gravitate toward this cool mountain town to take in the music, and many haul their own instruments along for the impromptu jams that pop up everywhere. The event also features a juried crafts fair, dancing contests, and appearances by dance groups like the Choo-Choo Cloggers from Chattanooga.   **LOCATION:** Smithville's courthouse square. From Nashville take I-40 east to exit 273, turn south on Highway 56, and drive 11 miles to Smithville. **TICKETS/ INFO:** 615-464-6444, 615-597-4163 **ACCOMMODATIONS/TOURIST INFO:** 615-464-6444, 615-597-4163

Dancers' delight: All-ages action at the Smithville Fiddlers' Jamboree. (See entry, page 198.) Joe Viesti/Viesti Associates

ℳEMPHIS MUSIC & HERITAGE FESTIVAL
MEMPHIS ✹ SECOND WEEKEND IN JULY

The Mid-South's biggest comprehensive music and heritage festival brings more than 1,000 musicians, craftspeople, and other performers to Memphis for a three-day weekend. This free event features four stages of spirited Memphis music, including blues, gospel, country, bluegrass, rockabilly, soul, and jazz. In addition, the festival brings in a sampling of musicians from other corners of the country, ranging from Mexican American mariachi and conjunto bands to Cajun and zydeco rabble-rousers from Louisiana.

Presented by Beale Street's Center for Southern Folklore, the festival is held in downtown Memphis, with stages set up in parks, parking lots, and along closed-off streets. In addition to performers like Ann Peebles, Charlie Musselwhite, and Billy Lee Riley, you can catch acoustic acts at a special nighttime stage, check out food and craft demonstrations, and engage yourself or your kids in children's activities. **LOCATION:** Main Street Mall, in the Court Square area of downtown Memphis **TICKETS/INFO:** 901-525-3945 **ACCOMMODATIONS/TOURIST INFO:** 901-543-5333

Soul on a roll: Rufus Thomas performs at the 1995 Memphis Music and Heritage Festival. © 1996, Center for Southern Folklore

UNCLE DAVE MACON DAYS

MURFREESBORO ✷ SECOND WEEKEND IN JULY, FRIDAY–SUNDAY

This nostalgic festival seeks to preserve and perpetuate the country music that was popular in the rural South in the early days of the Grand Ole Opry, prior to the commercial explosion of country music. Held in a historic Southern village, the program features more than 100 dancers and musicians, many of whom compete in the National Championships in old-time banjo, buckdancing, and clogging. Generally, the first two days feature country music and Sunday features a gospel showcase and bicycle race.

Throughout the weekend, arts and craft vendors line the streets, and a motorless parade on Saturday afternoon draws more than 30,000. The event also includes a presentation of Uncle Dave Macon's Heritage Award; past winners have included Roy Acuff, Grandpa Jones, Bashful Brother Oswald, and Bill Monroe. Alcohol is prohibited, but pets on leashes and picnicking are both fine. Admission is free and open to all. **LOCATION:** Cannonsburgh Pioneer Village in Murfreesboro, about 25 miles southeast of Nashville **TICKETS/INFO:** 615-848-0055 **ACCOMMODATIONS/TOURIST INFO:** 800-716-7560

FRANKLIN JAZZ FESTIVAL

FRANKLIN ✷ FIRST WEEKEND IN AUGUST, FRIDAY–SUNDAY

Wide-ranging jazz sounds get the right-of-way as Franklin's historic Town Square and the surrounding streets are closed to traffic. The three-day event features about a dozen bands on the outdoor stage; admission is free.   **LOCATION:** Town Square, at Main Street and Third Avenue in downtown Franklin, which is 15 miles south of Nashville. From I-65 take exit 65 (Franklin), then Highway 96 straight into the park. **TICKETS/INFO:** 615-794-1225, 615-791-9924 **ACCOMMODATIONS/TOURIST INFO:** 615-794-1225

𝓜EMPHIS BLUES FESTIVAL

MEMPHIS ✻ A WEEKEND IN AUGUST

At the foot of Beale Street on the Mississippi River banks, Memphis has revved up its own blues festival every year since 1990. A single stage features about seven acts, most of whom are nationally known. Expect to hear both acoustic and electric blues, and to pay about $15 in advance.   **LOCATION:** Tom Lee Park, at the foot of Beale Street at Riverside Drive and the banks of the Mississippi River **TICKETS/INFO:** 901-525-1515, 901-398-6655, 800-332-1991 **ACCOMMODATIONS/TOURIST INFO:** 901-543-5300

𝓙NTERNATIONAL ELVIS TRIBUTE WEEK

MEMPHIS ✻ NINE DAYS IN MID-AUGUST

Just mention the King of Rock 'n' Roll and it becomes clear that the word "fan" is short for fanatic. Elvis may or may not be dead, but his memory will definitely not be laid to rest any time soon. In the nine days surrounding the anniversary of his (supposed) death on August 16, 1977, more than 50,000 fans from around the globe flock to his house to relive the golden years of rock 'n' roll.

In addition to a rock, country, and gospel tribute concert uniting performers who worked with Elvis, Graceland hosts performances, Elvis art contests, laser light shows, dances, and banquets. Sporting contests in tribute to Elvis include a 5K run and a karate tournament, and in between the special events you can take the standard tour of Graceland—not exactly a mansion, but more of a time-frozen tribute to 1970s kitsch. Choice spots on the tour are the Jungle Den, with its carpeted ceiling, and the TV Room, equipped with three screens to allow Elvis to watch three football games at once. The "dumpster of doom" is conspicuously off-limits, but be sure to check out the Elvis Automobile Museum in Graceland Plaza, with a great reconstruction of a drive-in movie theater and a fantastic Harley Davidson golf cart.

In Memphis, local nightclubs host the inevitable Elvis Impersonation contests, so don't be surprised if you're among the many who sight the King. A candlelight vigil on August 15 is the crowning requiem in honor of a man whose popularity continues to hold millions captive.   **LOCATION:** Graceland Mansion, at 3734 Elvis Presley Boulevard in Memphis **TICKETS/INFO:** 800-238-2000; World Wide Web: http://www.elvis-presley.com/~king **ACCOMMODATIONS/TOURIST INFO:** 901-543-5300

𝓜ID-SOUTH JAMMIN' JAMBOREE

EASTVIEW ✻ LABOR DAY WEEKEND (LABOR DAY IS THE FIRST MONDAY IN SEPTEMBER)

This festival is dedicated to the preservation of old-time country and bluegrass music and features traditional acoustic performers from the surrounding region. Musicians compete and jam on guitar, dulcimer, mandolin, and banjo (no electrical instruments or drums are allowed). Tickets are sold at the gate to crowds that range from 1,500 to 2,000 people. Food is served, but no alcohol is allowed in the city park. **LOCATION:** City Park in Eastview, near the Tennessee-Mississippi state line. From U.S. 45 exit to Tennessee Highway 57. **TICKETS/INFO:** 901-645-3797 **ACCOMMODA-TIONS/TOURIST INFO:** 901-645-6360

ℳEMPHIS DULCIMER FESTIVAL

MEMPHIS ✱ LAST WEEKEND IN SEPTEMBER, FRIDAY AND SATURDAY

Despite its name, this festival's loyalty to the dulcimer is not exclusive, and it offers concerts and instructional workshops on almost every kind of stringed instrument. A daytime workshop and storytelling stage draws up to 400 participants, and an evening concert stage draws 25 to 30 performers and nearly 1,000 spectators. A weekend package includes five concerts and two full days of workshops for $75; individual concerts are $15.   **LOCATION:** Idlewild Presbyterian Church, at 1750 Union Avenue in Memphis **TICKETS/INFO:** 901-725-6976 **ACCOMMODATIONS/TOURIST INFO:** 901-543-5300, 901-543-5333

ℛENO REVIVAL

NASHVILLE ✱ FIRST OR SECOND WEEKEND IN OCTOBER

This tribute to legendary banjoist Don Reno is a banjo enthusiast's dream, with four days of workshops, demonstrations, and performances. Organized by Reno's son Don Wayne Reno, the festival features appearances by Don's two brothers, Ronnie and Dale, and by many master banjo players. There's also an opportunity to play "Nellie," Don Reno's legendary banjo, which he got from Earl Scruggs in a trade.   **LOCATION:** Hermitage Landing Park and other Nashville locations **TICKETS/INFO:** 615-889-4197 **ACCOMMODATIONS/TOURIST INFO:** 615-259-4755, 615-259-4730

GReaT LaKeS

ᏳᎡᎡᎪᎢ PLAINS FOLK FESTIVAL

PALOS HILLS ✷ LAST WEEKEND IN APRIL, FRIDAY–SUNDAY

If your interest in folk extends to playing it, this suburban Chicago festival is a hands-on chance to learn from the experts. Organized to pass on folk music traditions, the festival features beginner and master workshops on instruments ranging from the autoharp to the zither—all of which are on sale at the festival. In the spirit of "something for everyone," dancers can take part in clogging, contra, and step workshops, and the vocally inclined can learn how to yodel!

The festival, a continuation of the now defunct Great Black Swamp Folk Festival at Ohio State University, kicks off with a Friday night barn dance and continues with main-stage performances Saturday evening and Sunday afternoon. Performers demonstrate traditional acoustic styles ranging from folk to bluegrass, blues, and Celtic. Day ($20) and weekend ($40) passes are available, as is vegetarian food.   **LOCATION:** Moraine Valley Community College, 10900 South 88th Avenue, in Palos Hills, a southwestern-Chicago suburb accessible via I-294 **TICKETS/INFO:** 708-251-6618, 708-974-5745, 708-974-5500 **ACCOMMODATIONS/TOURIST INFO:** 312-744-2400, 312-567-8500

ᎷᎪYFEST AND ARMADILLO DAY

EVANSTON ✷ MEMORIAL DAY WEEKEND, FRIDAY AND SATURDAY

It's the day after finals at Northwestern University, and the kids just want to play Frisbee. That's how Mayfest got its start more than a decade ago, and its feel-good philosophy comes in many musical forms. Three stages feature everything from alterna-tive rock to funk to reggae, while vendors sell arts, crafts, and Guatemalan goods.

The two students from Texas who founded this party dubbed Saturday "Armadillo Day" after their favorite armor-plated mammal. You can't swim from the grassy Lake Michigan frontage, but hacky-sack and Frisbee are encouraged, and for a fee you can hurl yourself at a wall of Velcro, David Letterman-style. The music is free. **LOCATION:** Northwestern University's Lake Michigan waterfront, on North Sheridan Road. From Chicago take Lakeshore Drive north to Sheridan Road. **TICKETS/INFO:** 708-467-1381; e-mail: LCY992@lulu.acns.nwu.edu **ACCOMMODATIONS/TOURIST INFO:** 312-744-2400, 312-567-8500

WORLD CHAMPIONSHIP OLD-TIME PIANO PLAYING CONTEST

DECATUR ✷ MEMORIAL DAY WEEKEND, FRIDAY–SUNDAY (MEMORIAL DAY IS THE LAST MONDAY IN MAY)

Dedicated to preserving piano-playing styles of 1880 to 1929, the ragtime, honky tonk, and Tin Pan Alley specialists who come to Decatur dress in costume and get down to serious fun while competing for the World Champion Old-Time Piano Playing title.

The event crowned its first champ in 1975 after he played an antique piano on the back of a caboose to a crowd of about 40 at the Monticello Railway Museum. Today, the weekend brings a much expanded crowd of about 2,000 to a downstate Illinois hotel for a spirited contest that measures flair as well as talent. To win takes equal measures of skill in technique, style, interpretation, showmanship, and costume. Even spectators often "turn back the clock" in their clothing.

The contest begins Friday night with informal piano Tune-Ups by contestants and spectators alike. Title challengers begin competing Saturday, and by Sunday afternoon 10 semifinalists are battling it out on the ivories, with judges narrowing the roster down to a final five before selecting a winner. In addition to the competitions, the main stage launches a giant Saturday Night Sing-Along. Two piano-equipped party rooms host piano workshops and a Sunday night afterglow party that caps the nostalgic festivities. **LOCATION:** Holiday Inn Conference Resort, at U.S. 36 west and Wycles Road in Decatur **TICKETS/INFO:** 217-428-2403 **ACCOMMODATIONS/TOURIST INFO:** 217-423-7000

ILLINOIS GOSPEL SING

DECATUR ✷ FIRST WEEKEND AFTER MEMORIAL DAY, FRIDAY–SUNDAY

One of the Midwest's largest indoor southern gospel festivals brings about a dozen nationally touring bands to the warm confines of the Decatur Holidome. The music stays pretty much under the southern/country gospel flag, with styles ranging from the ultratraditional harmonies of the Speer Family to the contemporary pop-gospel stylings of Bill and Gloria Gaither. In addition, occasional African American quartets are featured.

Major-artist concerts are intermingled with participatory features like songwriting seminars, vocal workshops, and contests for amateurs. And with lots of children's activities, three restaurants, and a swimming pool, there's plenty here to create an enjoyable weekend getaway for the family.   **LOCATION:** Holiday Inn Select Hotel, in Decatur. From I-72 take exit 133A. **TICKETS/INFO:** 217-243-3159 **ACCOMMODA-TIONS/TOURIST INFO:** 217-422-8800

CHICAGO BLUES FESTIVAL

CHICAGO ✷ FIRST WEEKEND IN JUNE

Chicago didn't create the blues, it just took the acoustic music of the rural South and made it into a northern, urban, electrified thing. Nevertheless, when Chicago gets the blues nowadays, it's an international event. For three days, lakefront Grant Park is packed with dozens of bands and thousands of listeners celebrating the blues in the city that made them famous. Over the years, the extravagant roster has featured the likes of Junior Wells, David "Honeyboy" Edwards, Willie Dixon, Muddy Waters, Memphis Slim, Brownie McGhee and Robert Jr. Lockwood.

Never mind the main stage! Local bluesman Todd Rushing scorches the side-walks at the Chicago Blues Festival. © 1996 Basil Fairbanks Studio

The festival draws some 600,000 listeners, but if you were to hit only the main-stage events you'd be tempted to say the whole thing is just silly. Only a few spectators manage to get good seats near the Petrillo Music Shell, and tens of thousands have to watch the big-name performers from half a mile away—through a chain-link fence!

Luckily, there's a lot more to this festival than the main stage. The Front Porch Stage is downright intimate, and its roster bridges the gap between classic and Chicago blues by showcasing both local styles and those typical of other regions. Along Grant Park's sidewalks, musicians set up makeshift performance grounds and belt out both acoustic and electric sets. Fuzzy amps twist and torment notes, and spectators dance or pick up instruments and jam along. You never know what you'll come across—a big-name blues man or woman might stop by to do a song with a no-name friend, or a 10-year-old guitar sensation might leave an audience of 100 whooping in butt-kicked disbelief. Street performers peddle their itinerant howls, and drumbeaters transform bridges and tunnels into rhythm passages.

At night the performances continue in Chicago's many blues bars, but again the spirit of the blues isn't in obvious places. Famous northside clubs are packed with well-heeled crowds who revel in the lazy, bent-note clichés of the big names, while in grittier neighborhood dives you'll find up-and-coming or down-and-out bluesmen who care enough to actually try. Like the daytime festival, the best of the night isn't planned; it's found in random, spontaneous moments—just like the blues.   **LOCATION:** Grant Park, along the Chicago lakefront between Columbus Drive and Jackson Boulevard, and various Chicago blues clubs **TICKETS/INFO:** 312-744-3370, 312-744-3315; World Wide Web: http://www.ci.chi.il.us **ACCOMMODATIONS/TOURIST INFO:** 312-744-2400, 312-567-8500

ᴊ̈NTERNATIONAL CARILLON FESTIVAL
SPRINGFIELD ✴ SECOND FULL WEEK IN JUNE, SUNDAY–SUNDAY

Possibly the world's premier carillon festival, this event draws the top players worldwide to Springfield's Thomas Rees Memorial Carillon, one of the largest carillons in the United States. Carillons—sets of 23 or more large, tuned bells sounded by keyboard-driven hammers—are capable of playing intricate trills, arpeggios, runs, and full harmonies.

The festival was founded in 1962 and now attracts crowds of 15,000 to a picnic-conducive park. Participants include a number of musicians from Europe—especially Belgium, France, and Germany—where the music was popularized in the Middle Ages. With centuries of repertoire available, the festival emphasizes classical scores while also showcasing new compositions.   **LOCATION:** Thomas Rees Memorial Carillon in Washington Park, at Fayette and Chatham Roads in Springfield **TICKETS/INFO:** 217-753-6219 **ACCOMMODATIONS/TOURIST INFO:** 217-789-2360

ℭHICAGO GOSPEL FESTIVAL
CHICAGO ✴ SECOND WEEKEND IN JUNE

Two glorious days of gospel music fill Chicago's lakefront Grant Park with emotion and inspiration as 24 of the genre's hottest acts serenade a crowd of more than 200,000. Begun in 1983, the festival has featured such big pop names as Tremayne Hawkins and Stephanie Mills, and traditional groups like the giant Mississippi Mass Choir.

The world's largest free outdoor gospel festival is a soul-stirring, heartwarming, toe-tapping gospel party. As choirs like Lonnie Hunter and Voices of St. Mark sing songs like "Jesus Can Work It Out," participants in the crowd—for there are few mere observers here—rise to their feet, clap their hands, and sing out enthusiastically. The roster includes mainly African American choirs, but the festival also hosts choirs like the Pentecostals of Chicago, composed of blacks, whites, and Latinos.

The two dozen acts on two stages are broken up by "interludes," featuring up-and-coming performers who sing while the stage is changed over. Other aspects of the festival include the Voices of Tomorrow Youth Gospel Choir Competition, children's activity areas, and a signer for the hearing impaired.   **LOCATION:** Grant Park, along the Chicago lakefront between Columbus Drive and Jackson Boulevard **TICKETS/INFO:** 312-744-3370, 312-744-3315; World Wide Web: http://www.ci.chi.il.us **ACCOMMO-DATIONS/TOURIST INFO:** 312-744-2400, 312-567-8500

Country in the big city: Ricky Skaggs jams with members of Bill Monroe's Bluegrass Boys at the 1995 Chicago Country Music Festival. Courtesy of Mayor's Office of Special Events

CHICAGO COUNTRY MUSIC FESTIVAL
CHICAGO ✱ WEEKEND IN LATE JUNE

Country comes to the big city for three days during the Taste of Chicago, an annual showcase of Chicago area restaurants. While suburbanites graze on the tiny, pricey portions of nouvelle cuisine, citified hillbillies can be found over at the stage devouring tons of beef and beer while listening to the likes of Dwight Yoakam, Ricky Skaggs, and Suzy Bogguss.

The music flows from two outdoor stages on Chicago's lakefront and features a variety of country music, including new country, bluegrass, western swing, and Cajun. Six big-name bands perform on the main stage, while about 15 rising stars keep the second stage humming. About 250,000 spectators gather for the music and for high jinks like country karaoke (at the children's stage). Arts and crafts and chef's demonstrations attract creative types, and others find amusement in the wine garden, on the ferris wheel, or in the virtual-reality simulator. And over at the Taste of Chicago, a plethora of area restaurants provide everything from "elephant ears" to Japanese tempura dinners. Concerts are free, and alcohol is available for purchase. **LOCATION:** Grant Park, along the Chicago lakefront between Columbus Drive and Jackson Boulevard **TICKETS/INFO:** 312-744-3370, 312-744-3315; World Wide Web: http://www.ci.chi.il.us **ACCOMMODATIONS/TOURIST INFO:** 312-744-2400, 312-567-8500

JUNE JAM
GRAND DETOUR ✱ LAST SUNDAY IN JUNE

Each June, music lovers head out to historic Dixon to see a mix of bluegrass, country, gospel, and folk music. With one stage, small crowds, and 10 or more local and regional bands, this family-style festival features plenty of music in an intimate setting. The concert is set at the John Deere Historic Site, where John Deere made history with his many inventions, literally changing the way the world sows its oats. John Deere's home and blacksmith shop, dating back to 1837, are open for tours, and the music can be experienced for a $3 admission fee.   **LOCATION:** John Deere Historic Site, in Grand Detour, 5.5 miles north of Dixon on Illinois Route 2 **TICKETS/INFO:** 815-652-4551 **ACCOMMODATIONS/TOURIST INFO:** 800-678-2108, 800-248-6482

RAVINIA FESTIVAL
HIGHLAND PARK ✴ LATE JUNE THROUGH LABOR DAY WEEKEND

More accessible than Tanglewood and nearly as well known, the Ravinia Festival brings music to a park in northwest suburban Chicago for about 80 consecutive nights each summer. One night you might catch the Chicago Symphony Orchestra interpreting Mahler. The next night it's Los Lobos interpreting their Latin roots. Classical giants like Yo Yo Ma and Pinchas Zukerman have played Ravinia, along with crossover country star Mary Chapin Carpenter and jazzman Oscar Peterson.

Although the lion's share of Ravinia's programming is dedicated to classical music (the Chicago Symphony Orchestra makes its summer home at Ravinia), Ravinia can also rock 'n' roll—but it won't mosh. The music is dedicated primarily to baby-boomer tastes, with "high culture and popular entertainment . . . as much a part of the program mix as candelabra and lawn chairs," as the *Chicago Tribune* put it.

Picnicking is the pastime of choice at Ravinia, where elaborate lawn spreads find polite listeners whispering requests to "pass the caviar" during performances. The lawn adjoins the acoustic-shelled Pavilion and sound is broadcast around the grounds on state-of-the-art speakers. The three stages on the 36-acre woodland property include the Pavilion (3,300 seats), Martin Theatre (850 seats) and Bennett Hall (450 seats). The smaller indoor venues are used for solo recitals and chamber music.

Since 1936, nonprofit Ravinia's organizers have nobly aimed to "present great music to the public for a ticket price well below the cost of production" and have commendably succeeded. The approximately $7 cost of lawn seats is now below the average price of a movie in the Chicago area.   **LOCATION:** Ravinia is located in Highland Park, a northern suburb of Chicago, at Lake Cook and Green Bay Roads. From I-94 follow the Ravinia exits at either Route 41 or I-294. **TICKETS/INFO:** 312-728-4642; e-mail: RavFest@aol.com **ACCOMMODATIONS/TOURIST INFO:** 312-744-2400, 312-567-8500

AMERICAN MUSIC FESTIVAL
BERWYN ✴ WEEKEND CLOSEST TO JULY 4, THURSDAY–SUNDAY

Located in Chicago's traditionally Irish suburb of Berwyn, Fitzgerald's is known for its ongoing showcases of regional talent that's not necessarily from the Chicago region. During the four-day American Music Festival, the club uses the same recipe but with bigger portions, presenting dozens of "real thang" performers from the nation's musical hot spots.

A combination club/yard-party atmosphere is achieved by removing the furniture from the club, Texas roadhouse-style, and throwing up another stage under tents in the parking lot. The booking showcases the breadth and depth of American roots and rock styles and in recent years has presented the dynamite talents of Caribbean rhythm-and-bluesmen like the Iguanas, country-swing yodelers like Don Walser, and traditional Cajun countrymen like the Hackberry Ramblers.

It's ironic that Chicago's most eclectic and interesting popular music event is in the suburbs, but with its amazing lineup, diverse crowd, and plenty of Cajun and barbecued food, Fitzgerald's puts some real fireworks into an all-American weekend. **LOCATION:** Fitzgerald's, 6615 West Roosevelt Road, in Berwyn. From Chicago take I-290 west to the Austin exit; go one-half mile south on Austin Avenue and turn right onto Roosevelt Road. **TICKETS/INFO:** 708-788-2118; e-mail: FitzMail@aol.com **ACCOMMODATIONS/TOURIST INFO:** 312-744-2400, 312-567-8500

CORNERSTONE FESTIVAL
BUSHNELL ✸ FIRST WEEKEND IN JULY, THURSDAY–SUNDAY

On the first weekend in July, the faithful flock to "heaven-on-earth," as the Cornerstone Festival has been christened by its devoted. Set on 579 acres of lush recreational land, this four-day festival features fun and relaxation, along with plenty of Christian groups who span the musical spectrum. Genres like Christian industrial, Christian rap, and Christian heavy metal share the spotlight with more traditional folk, blues, and alterna-rock styles. Recent acts have included the Crucified, Cauzin' Efekt, Sixpence None the Richer, and many other holy rollers.

About 12,000 festivalgoers come from all over the country to enjoy more than 100 national and international bands on 12 stages. The festival strives to achieve a sense of community through music, arts, and Christianity and presents a variety of seminars and workshops focusing on Christian views of such topics as racial reconciliation and psychology and the church. Art, poetry, and film workshops are also featured, along with many outdoor activities, such as camping, volleyball, basketball, swimming, canoeing, hiking, fishing, and biking. Special events are organized for children and adolescents throughout this family-style weekend. Admission costs from $50 to $65. **LOCATION:** Cornerstone Farm, on Highway 41, about three miles south of Bushnell, which is 50 miles west of Peoria **TICKETS/INFO:** 312-989-2087 **ACCOMMODATIONS/TOURIST INFO:** 312-989-2087

MID-MISSISSIPPI MUDDY WATER BLUES BASH
QUINCY ✸ SECOND WEEKEND IN JULY, FRIDAY–SUNDAY

Although the singular "Water" in this festival's name refers to the river rather than the legendary bluesman, he surely would approve of this celebration. National acts from Chicago, St. Louis, and farther afield spend three days baptizing the crowd with a hail of frenzied electric guitar notes, as well as traditional acoustic sounds. Some 16 to 20 acts draw about 7,000 people to the single main stage and several instrumental workshops. Admission is $8 per day, or $15 for three days; camping is nearby. **LOCATION:** Washington Park in downtown Quincy, on the Mississippi River about 20 miles north of Hannibal, Missouri **TICKETS/INFO:** 314-393-2011 **ACCOMMODATIONS/TOURIST INFO:** 217-223-1000, 800-978-4748

RIVERSIDE BLUES FEST
MURPHYSBORO ✸ THIRD SATURDAY IN JULY

This one-day festival favors down-home, deep-and-dirty blues from the Deep South, along with electric acts from Chicago, St. Louis, and Memphis. Typically, three or four local bands warm up the stage for a couple of nationally known headliners, playing to a laid-back crowd of about 3,000 (including children and pets, both of which are welcome). The festival is set in an interesting, one-of-a-kind outdoor amphitheater built during the Depression by the WPA. Tickets, which are sold only at the gate, cost $10 for adults and $5 for children and seniors. Murphysboro barbecue teams compete (and win) often in regional contests, so the food is dependably awesome.   **LOCATION:** Riverside Park, in Murphysboro, near the junction of Routes 127 and 13, just west of Carbondale in southern Illinois **TICKETS/INFO:** 618-684-3333 **ACCOMMODATIONS/TOURIST INFO:** 618-684-6421

WOODSTOCK MOZART FESTIVAL
WOODSTOCK ✳ LAST WEEKEND IN JULY AND FIRST TWO WEEKENDS IN AUGUST

Although its restored 1880s European-style Opera House is reason enough to make the trek to Woodstock, Illinois, this festival has absolutely no shortage of extraordinary music. Begun in 1987, the Woodstock Mozart Festival soon attracted national attention with airings on National Public Radio's *Performance Today* series. In 1993, organizers adopted a guest-conductor format, allowing audiences to enjoy Mozart's music in a different performance style each weekend. Conductors and soloists rotate weekly, teaming up with a superb chamber orchestra of freelance players to present music that's a fitting complement to the intimate venue and warm summer evenings. Tickets range from $18 to $35.   **LOCATION:** Woodstock Opera House, 121 Van Buren Street, in Woodstock. From Chicago take I-94 west to U.S. 14 northwest to Highway 47 north. Once in Woodstock, turn left on Lake Street and right on Dean Street and continue for two blocks to Van Buren Street. **TICKETS/INFO:** 815-338-5300 **ACCOMMODATIONS/ TOURIST INFO:** 815-338-2436

DECATUR CELEBRATION
DECATUR ✳ A WEEKEND IN EARLY AUGUST

One of the Midwest's biggest family-oriented festivals brings more than 40 musical acts to 15 stages in downtown Decatur. In addition to a standard lineup of oldies acts, the festival creates an international splash with additions like South African artist Hugh Masakela, and the Tokorozawa Folk Dancers of Japan.   **LOCATION:** Downtown Decatur, at the intersection of U.S. 51 and U.S. 36, in the center of the state **TICKETS/ INFO:** 217-423-4222 **ACCOMMODATIONS/TOURIST INFO:** 217-423-7000

¡VIVA! CHICAGO LATIN MUSIC FESTIVAL
CHICAGO ✳ LAST WEEKEND IN AUGUST OR FIRST WEEKEND IN SEPTEMBER, SATURDAY AND SUNDAY

Since 1989, this hot-blooded festival has provided two days of free entertainment featuring the best of Latin music, including salsa, cumbia, merengue, mariachi, banda, bolero, mambo, ranchera, punta, and many more styles from all over the Americas. Local, regional, national, and international talents entertain a crowd of 150,000 in the open-air setting at Chicago's lakefront. Food, arts and crafts, and a children's area are available. (1996 dates are moved to May 25–26 because of the Democratic Convention.) **LOCATION:** Grant Park, along the Chicago lakefront between Columbus Drive and Jackson Boulevard **TICKETS/INFO:** 312-744-3370, 312-744-3315; World Wide Web: http://www.ci.chi.il.us **ACCOMMODATIONS/TOURIST INFO:** 312-744-2400, 312-567-8500

CHICAGO JAZZ FESTIVAL

CHICAGO ✳ LABOR DAY WEEKEND, FRIDAY–SATURDAY (LABOR DAY IS THE FIRST MONDAY IN SEPTEMBER)

For nearly 20 years, the Windy City summer has closed with the nation's largest free jazz festival. This series of major lakefront concerts and smaller club shows is *big*, with 27 acts and up to 300,000 spectators over its three-day run. Yet despite its size, this sprawling jazz party is known for breaking up the mainstream with satisfying doses of the cutting edge.

The event's preamble begins Wednesday as buses take visitors around to various Chicago jazz clubs. Thursday night is typically reserved for a ticketed indoor show, but by this time the city's nightspots are bursting at the doors with live jazz. By Friday evening, the event has kicked into high gear, with jazz on two outdoor stages at Grant Park on Chicago's lakefront. Recent guests have included Cassandra Wilson, Stanley Turrentine, Eddie Palmieri, and Bobby Hutcherson. Plus, the event is known for putting together once-in-a-lifetime ensembles like 1995's explosive combination of Muhal Richard Abrams, Roscoe Mitchell, Anthony Braxton, Joseph Jarman, Henry Threadgill, Leroy Jenkins, and George Lewis.

In terms of overall impact, the Grant Park site is dazzling, sandwiched between Lake Michigan and the Chicago skyline, but the overall quality of sound can be spotty. The Jazz on Jackson stage provides the best listening experience, whereas the Petrillo Music Shell's grounds provide quality sight and sound only for the fortunate few who are up front. All city-sponsored concerts and events are free, but cover charges apply at club events.   **LOCATION:** Grant Park, along the Chicago lakefront between Columbus Drive and Jackson Boulevard, and various Chicago jazzclubs **TICKETS/INFO:** 312-744-3370, 312-744-3315; World Wide Web: http://www.ci.chi.il.us **ACCOMMODATIONS/ TOURIST INFO:** 312-744-2400, 312-567-8500

QUEERCORE

CHICAGO ✳ LABOR DAY WEEKEND, SATURDAY AND SUNDAY

Queercore puts the queer into hard-core punk with a weekend of music, politics, and slam dancing. Chicago's radical gay punk community comes out in force, as do performers and audiences from all over the country.

Over two nights, a single stage features 10 bands that produce everything from art-noise to straight-ahead pop punk to modern alternative, no-wave, Latino punk, and riot grrrl sounds. Recent headliners have included Team Dresch, Los Crudos, Tride 8, Pedro Muriel & Esther featuring Vaginal Creme Davis, Vitapup, Third Sex, and Pansy Division.

Homocore Chicago, which organizes the festival, says, "Queercore is about fags and dykes together." Organizers look for ways to break down the walls between gay men and lesbians, and at the festival you'll see women not only in the audience but in the bands or at the mixing board. Performers may even call "Girls Up Front" for an all-grrrl mosh pit.

Though the mosh area gets a lot of action, organizers encourage gay people who aren't into punk to come for the politics and also say that supportive straight people are welcome too. Off to the side of the stage, tables are set up for people selling zines, records, T-shirts, artwork, anarchist politics, and lots of do-it-yourself stuff from queer-core culture. The event is held at an all-ages Chicago club or gallery, and the venue changes from year to year. Prices range from $5 to $10 per show.   **LOCATION:** All-ages venues in Chicago that change every year. Call or e-mail for information. **TICKETS/**

INFO: 312-384-6437; e-mail: mfreitas@lante.com **ACCOMMODATIONS/TOURIST INFO:** 312-744-2400, 312-567-8500

ℱESTIVAL OF LATIN MUSIC
CHICAGO ✴ FIRST OR SECOND WEEKEND IN OCTOBER, USUALLY A SATURDAY

Since 1983, the Festival of Latin Music has hosted the U.S. debuts of authentic Latin American groups that no other commercial promoter had deemed viable. The depth and range of the music is astounding; past bills have included pipe-driven music from the Peruvian Andes, Colombian *llanero* cowboy tunes, and upbeat *son jarocho* folk from Veracruz, Mexico. Local Latin acts often open the show, which typically showcases three to four international bands in a club setting for less than $20. The festival is sponsored by the Old Town School of Folk Music, a premier Chicago institution for preserving traditional folk and world music.   **LOCATION:** A music club (changes from year to year) within the city of Chicago **TICKETS/INFO:** 312-744-3370, 312-744-3315; World Wide Web: http://www.ci.chi.il.us **ACCOMMODATIONS/TOURIST INFO:** 312-744-2400, 312-567-8500

𝒢REATER DOWNSTATE INDOOR BLUEGRASS MUSIC FESTIVAL
DECATUR ✴ SECOND WEEKEND IN NOVEMBER, FRIDAY–SUNDAY

Here's a midwinter chance to enjoy top bluegrass bands, pick the banjo all night without getting frostbitten fingers, sleep late, and lounge around the pool. The Midwest's largest indoor bluegrass festival brings about a dozen nationally touring bands to the warm confines of the Decatur Holidome. Since its inauguration in 1988, this multifaceted, family-oriented gig has booked the gamut of traditional and contemporary bluegrass names—Jim & Jesse, the Osborne Brothers, the Cox Family, Claire Lynch—and provided a venue for around-the-clock "parking lot picking" under a big roof. The auditorium seats 1,500 for big concerts, and with workshops, children's activities, and three restaurants, you can always find something happening in this domed area that's about the size of a football field.   **LOCATION:** Holiday Inn Select Hotel in Decatur. From I-72 take exit 133A. **TICKETS/INFO:** 217-243-3159 **ACCOMMODATIONS/ TOURIST INFO:** 217-422-8800

i**N**🎵**Dia**N**a

🎵IREFLY FESTIVAL FOR THE PERFORMING ARTS
SOUTH BEND ✺ WEEKENDS FROM MID-JUNE THROUGH JULY

Every summer since 1981, this award-winning Michiana-area event has entertained thousands of families and friends under the stars. Bring along chairs or blankets and seat yourself in the park beside the St. Joseph River, where a proscenium stage supports a diverse spectrum of music played by local, national, and international performers. Pops, jazz, blues, Cajun, world music, gospel, and Broadway musicals are typically on the bill. Recent acts have included the South Bend Symphony Pops, Lionel Hampton, Koko Taylor, Beausoleil, and Ray Charles. Other entertainment includes theater, dance, hands-on crafts, and workshops for kids. Admission runs from $8 to $18 for adults. **LOCATION:** St. Patrick's County Park, at 50651 Laurel Road. From I-80/90 go north on Route 31/33, then west on Auten Road, and north on Laurel. **TICKETS/INFO:** 219-288-3472 **ACCOMMODATIONS/TOURIST INFO:** 219-234-0051

🎵NDIANA UNIVERSITY SCHOOL OF MUSIC SUMMER FESTIVAL
BLOOMINGTON ✺ MID-JUNE THROUGH EARLY AUGUST

At the Summer Music Festival, students enrolled in the Indiana University School of Music team up with nationally known guest artists to present concerts on five stages around campus. All venues are intimate spaces, and all feature excellent acoustics. The Summer Festival also presents two operas. Prices vary from free to $20.   **LOCATION:** The Indiana University School of Music Complex, in Bloomington at the southeast corner of the IU campus **TICKETS/INFO:** 812-855-7433; World Wide Web: http://www.music.indiana.edu/som/publicity/ **ACCOMMODATIONS/TOURIST INFO:** 812-334-8900

🎵EAN BLOSSOM BLUEGRASS FESTIVAL
BEAN BLOSSOM ✺ THIRD WEEKEND IN JUNE, THURSDAY–SUNDAY

You wouldn't expect Mozart to show up at a Mozart festival or W. C. Handy to come sauntering into a blues festival. Yet each year at the Bean Blossom Bluegrass Festival, music lovers are treated to an appearance by the father and almighty creator of bluegrass music, Bill Monroe. Always attracting the top talents in modern bluegrass music, the event is held for five days each spring at Monroe's 100-acre park. Here, pickers and grinners as well as plain old bluegrass lovers from around the country stake their claims to five days in the Jerusalem of the genre.

Although the hillbilly music tradition extends back several centuries, it was Monroe, a high-mountain tenor and mandolin player extraordinaire, who made bluegrass into a unique musical form. Named after Monroe's band, the Blue Grass Boys, who began playing in 1938, bluegrass music has evolved to encompass a wide variety of styles that take their lead from Monroe himself. Small groups of virtuoso musicians—usually playing guitar, banjo, fiddle, mandolin, and bass—weave intricate, quick-tempo instrumental and vocal harmonies around traditional melodies.

Bill Monroe founded this festival in 1965 as a way of bringing his friends together to play that "high lonesome" sound he pioneered, and today Bean Blossom is the longest-running bluegrass festival in the United States. Expect the very best in the way of bluegrass and country-roots musicians like Emmylou Harris, but also note that bluegrass is a music that attracts participants as well as listeners, so it's not unusual to find as much entertainment in the campground as up on stage. Workshops are also featured, as well as competitions among musicians.

The festival takes a spiritual approach, with a promotional brochure that bids, "Oh come, let us sing unto the Lord." As for earthly matters, the festival grounds offer a tour, of sorts, of Bill Monroe's roots. Monroe spent his teenage years in Uncle Pen's Cabin (named for Monroe's Uncle Pendelton Vandiver), which is now restored and open to visitors. A Walkway of Stars paves the entry to a museum with Hollywood-style bronze stars for bluegrass greats. The 5,000-square-foot museum tells the story of bluegrass beginnings with memorabilia and houses the Bluegrass Hall of Fame, which includes innovators like Lester Flatt and Earl Scruggs.

Bean Blossom is a spring event, but another three-day stomp in the fall celebrates Monroe's birthday. Monroe was born in 1911 and is in declining health, so it would behoove the fans who wish to see him to waste no time. The nearby town of Nashville, Indiana, is a haven of bed and breakfasts and gift shops authentic enough to charm even the most cynical tourist-trap avoider into staying long enough to have a meal. **LOCATION:** Bean Blossom is five miles north of Nashville, Indiana, on Route 135, about halfway between Bloomington and Columbus. From I-65 exit at Route 46 and head west to Nashville, then north on Route 135. **TICKETS/INFO:** 615-868-3333, 812-988-6422 **ACCOMMODATIONS/TOURIST INFO:** 800-753-3255, 812-988-7303

𝓜USIC AT MAPLE MOUNT CHAMBER MUSIC WEEK
NEW HARMONY ✳ FOURTH WEEK IN JUNE

Kentucky's Maple Mount summer music school moves across the state line to the aptly named New Harmony, Indiana, for this week of student chamber concerts. The week of music features chamber ensembles, a chamber chorus, and solo recitals, all by students aged 11 to 19. All events are free. (See also: Music at Maple Mount, Maple Mount, Kentucky.)   **LOCATION:** Several settings in New Harmony, on Highway 66 in the southwest corner of Indiana. From I-64 take exit 4 and head south five miles. **TICKETS/INFO:** 502-686-4229 **ACCOMMODATIONS/TOURIST INFO:** 800-433-3025, 812-425-5402

MIDSUMMER FESTIVAL

INDIANAPOLIS ✸ FIRST SATURDAY FOLLOWING THE SUMMER SOLSTICE
(JUNE 21 OR 22)

Begun in 1975, this event has grown into the largest one-day festival of contemporary music in Indiana, with bands on four stages belting out a continuous thunder of
rock, jazz, country, and alternative music all day long. The lineup consists mostly of up-
and-coming, local, and regional bands, and the festival attracts up to 25,000 spectators.
Tickets are about $5 in advance or $7 at the door.   **LOCATION:** Monument Circle, at
the intersection of Meridian and Market Streets in downtown Indianapolis **TICKETS/
INFO:** 317-637-4574 **ACCOMMODATIONS/TOURIST INFO:** 800-323-4639, 317-
639-4282

INDIANA FIDDLERS' GATHERING

BATTLE GROUND ✸ LAST FULL WEEKEND IN JUNE, FRIDAY–SUNDAY

This festival, held under the wise old oak trees at Tippecanoe Memorial Battlefield,
feels historic straight from the get-go. Despite its name, this is no typical country fiddle
gathering. Instead, it embraces fiddle traditions from all over the world. Recent years
have featured the likes of legendary jazz violinist Johnny Frigo, Basque fiddler Aurkene
Alzua, and bluegrass legend Alison Krauss. Up to 10,000 people attend the festival,
which also includes a gospel show, a dance workshop, a quilt show, and the sights and
sounds of the Tippecanoe Museum.   **LOCATION:** Tippecanoe Memorial Battlefield, at
Battle Ground, just north of Lafayette. From I-65 take exit 178 and follow the signs to
Tippecanoe Memorial Battlefield. **TICKETS/INFO:** 317-742-1419; e-mail: khallman
@dcwi.com **ACCOMMODATIONS/TOURIST INFO:** 317-447-9999

BLUEGRASS FESTIVAL

CONVERSE ✸ FIRST WEEKEND IN JULY, THURSDAY–SUNDAY

A handful of regional bands team up with at least one big name to present the
musical fare at this small, early July ramble. Bands play on a single outdoor stage and
move under tents in case of bad weather. Plus, there are plenty of places set aside for
people who want to jam (but BYO lawn chair). Organizers invite everyone to come to
town early for the free ham-and-beans dinner the night before the festival. The event also
includes the crowning of the Hoosier Bluegrass Personality of the Year. Tickets are about
$22 for the weekend.   **LOCATION:** Converse Fairgrounds, on Jefferson Street in
Converse, just off Highway 18 about 17 miles west of I-69 **TICKETS/INFO:** 317-674-
5117 **ACCOMMODATIONS/TOURIST INFO:** 317-668-5435

EAGLE CREEK FOLK MUSIC FESTIVAL

EAGLE CREEK ✸ LAST WEEKEND IN JULY

For more than 20 years, the Eagle Creek Folk Music Festival has presented
traditional acoustic folk in an amphitheater near the outlet of the Eagle Creek Reservoir.
This small, informal event usually features about half a dozen soloists and groups and
brings out a comfortable, picnicking crowd of about 300 people. There's lots of contact
between performers and spectators, and a "no vendors" policy ensures that the scene
won't be cluttered by arts and crafts.   **LOCATION:** Eagle Creek Park Amphitheater,

just west of Indianapolis. From I-465 exit at 71st Street and head west. **TICKETS/INFO:** 317-462-9681 **ACCOMMODATIONS/TOURIST INFO:** 800-323-4639, 317-639-4282

*G*OSPEL MUSIC FESTIVAL FOR M.D.A.
SOUTH WHITLEY ❋ LAST SUNDAY IN AUGUST

With a wholesome family atmosphere and lots of old-fashioned fun, this festival has the noble goal of raising money for the Muscular Dystrophy Association. As many as 500 people come out each year to hear a mix of southern, country, and contemporary gospel in a peaceful country setting with a three-acre pond and plenty of woods for hiking. Aside from the music, there's an Amish bake sale, an auction, and a dunk tank, plus great food, clowns, and games. Suggested donations are $3 for adults.   **LOCATION:** River City Ministry and Campground, on River Road in South Whitley, 1.5 miles off State Road 5, about 28 miles west of I-69 **TICKETS/INFO:** 219-723-4444 **ACCOMMODA-TIONS/TOURIST INFO:** 219-723-4444

*♪*LUEGRASS FESTIVAL
CONVERSE ❋ WEEKEND FOLLOWING LABOR DAY, FRIDAY–SUNDAY (LABOR DAY IS THE FIRST MONDAY IN SEPTEMBER)

This is a semiannual event, happening the first weekend in July (when the Hoosier Bluegrass Personality of the Year is crowned) and the weekend following Labor Day. Tickets are about $18 for this end-of-summer weekend. See page 218 for all the details. **LOCATION:** Converse Fairgrounds, on Jefferson Street in Converse, just off Highway 18, about 17 miles west of I-69 **TICKETS/INFO:** 317-674-5117 **ACCOMMODATIONS/ TOURIST INFO:** 317-668-5435

*L*OTUS WORLD MUSIC & ARTS FESTIVAL
BLOOMINGTON ❋ FIRST OR SECOND WEEKEND IN OCTOBER, THURSDAY–SUNDAY

This worldbeat weekend features many of the same artists as its Chicago friend, the Old Town School of Folk Music, and provides some of the finest opportunities in the Midwest to hear a mixed roster of international artists. The weekend includes three dozen nationally and internationally recognized world music acts, plus several regional and local talents.

Artists play to small crowds in packed and intimate nightclubs, art centers, convention centers, and theaters. A $13 nightly admission fee lets you bop from club to club, and you'll as likely hear the African *kora* as the zydeco rub-board, blues guitar, or bluegrass banjo. Moving freely between venues spaced a stone's throw from one another, you could hear a Greek wedding band, a Latin American salsa band, a South African duo, and a Native American flute player.

An international bazaar features ethnic food and display areas, plus information on local and statewide ethnic groups and the artists who play in their traditions. The event caps an 18-day celebration of art, film, theater, and spirituality.   **LOCATION:** Multiple venues on Fourth Street between Walnut and College in downtown Bloomington **TICKETS/INFO:** 812-336-6599 **ACCOMMODATIONS/TOURIST INFO:** 800-800-0037, 812-334-8400

Cats gone crazy: The Frantic Flattops rip up the 1995 Rockabilly Rebel Weekend. © 1996 Basil Fairbanks Studio

ℛOCKABILLY REBEL WEEKEND AND TRIBUTE TO JAMES DEAN

INDIANAPOLIS ✻ A WEEKEND IN NOVEMBER, FRIDAY AND SATURDAY

This reunion brings a crazed band of fifties fanatics from all over the planet to a restored theater in downtown Indianapolis for a weekend of rockabilly insanity. Twang-crazy legends like Ronnie Dawson join about a dozen crackling-hot new bands playing fifties-style rockabilly—some of whom come all the way from Europe.

Out on the dance floor, boards creak under the weight of cats gone mad, as guys use one hand to twirl the gals and the other to cradle long-necks, creating a sea of pompadours, poodle skirts, leather biker jackets, and incredible tattoos. The action continues for two nights in the 1920s-era theater, which has an attached 1950s diner, billiard hall, and bowling alley.

The Rockabilly Rebel Weekend began in Fairmount, the Indiana town that produced the rebel without a cause, James Dean. Although the event quickly outgrew the town's biggest venue, it's still organized by Fairmount's James Dean Gallery. Many visitors make the one-hour drive to the gallery, which houses nostalgic posters, monuments, news clippings, and a screening room with footage of screen tests and other rare James Dean moments.   **LOCATION:** Fountain Square Theater, 1105 East Prospect Street, downtown Indianapolis **TICKETS/INFO:** 317-948-3326 **ACCOMMODATIONS/ TOURIST INFO:** 800-323-4639, 317-670-4282

MiCHiGaN

ANN ARBOR FOLK FESTIVAL
ANN ARBOR ✦ FOURTH SATURDAY IN JANUARY

Ann Arbor's old folkies come out of the winter woodwork for this marathon fund-raising event at a 4,100-seat university auditorium. Each year typically brings singer-songwriters, a storyteller, and a musical act from overseas. On the positive side, an eclectic, star-studded lineup includes a broad range of acoustic and folk music (where else would you find Doc Watson and Ani DiFranco on the same bill?). On the negative side, the crowd is a bit stiff for rousing, danceable acts like Mahlathini and the Mahotella Queens, and the six-hour program is far too long for the hands-on-your-lap auditorium setting.

The Ann Arbor Folk Festival is a fund-raising event for the Ark, a coffeehouse and longtime fixture of the Ann Arbor folk scene. Admission fees for the music marathon event run between $25 and $30. **LOCATION:** Hill Auditorium, at 825 North University, on the Ann Arbor campus of the University of Michigan **TICKETS/INFO:** 313-763-8587; e-mail: lsiglin@umich.edu; World Wide Web: http://www.umich.edu/~mevents **ACCOMMODATIONS/TOURIST INFO:** 313-995-7281

WESTERN INVITATIONAL JAZZ FESTIVAL
KALAMAZOO ✦ FIRST OR SECOND SATURDAY IN MARCH

This festival and teach-in brings high school jazz musicians together for a day and evening of clinics and concerts. Young musicians come from all over the Midwest and spend the day learning and practicing in big bands and small ensembles. Organizers select outstanding students, along with a renowned guest artist, to present evening concerts in the 500-seat venue. **LOCATION:** Dalton Center at Western Michigan University's School of Music in Kalamazoo **TICKETS/INFO:** 616-387-4693 **ACCOMMODATIONS/TOURIST INFO:** 616-381-4003

ANNUAL FIDDLERS JAMBOREE
GRAND RAPIDS ✦ LAST WEEKEND IN APRIL

Expect to hear plenty of fiddling and other string-play during this day and evening of music. The spirit is noncompetitive as fiddlers, guitarists, and banjoists take the stage

Acoustic eclectics: The marathon Ann Arbor Folk Festival concludes with an all-star jam featuring (in 1995) LaRon Williams, BETTY, Jack Lawrence, Doc Watson, Alison Krauss & Union Station, Victoria Williams, Leo Kottke, the Dixie Power Trio, and others. (See entry, page 221.) Randy Austin-Cardona/The Ark

to sing and play, and organizers make sure there's no "stage hogging." At night a three-hour dance features round and square dances. The jamboree is free, but donations are requested.   **LOCATION:** Highland Middle School, 4645 Chandy NE in Grand Rapids **TICKETS/INFO:** 616-361-3444 **ACCOMMODATIONS/TOURIST INFO:** 616-459-8287

♫ANJO-RAMA
DAVISON ✻ FIRST SATURDAY IN MAY

About 50 banjo players gather to concertize, promote banjo music, and raise money for music scholarships. The festival draws performers from the Flint area and across North America. Food, beer, and wine are served. Admission is around $12; in past years the event has raised up to $30,000 dollars.   **LOCATION:** 404 North Dayton Street in Davison, which is five miles east of of Flint **TICKETS/INFO:** 810-687-1573 **ACCOMMODATIONS/TOURIST INFO:** 810-232-8900

MICHIGAN MOSH FESTIVAL

HASTINGS ✱ THIRD OR FOURTH WEEKEND IN MAY

Christian hardcore is on the agenda at this "mosh mellow" event with a main stage and another for lower-key entertainment. About 28 bands show up to play for about 2,000 people in exhibition buildings at the Barry County Fairgrounds. Collateral events include seminars and church services; camping is available and the event is free. **LOCATION:** Barry County Fairgrounds, 5778 Middleville Road in Hastings, which is 15 miles southeast of Grand Rapids **TICKETS/INFO:** 810-773-3361 **ACCOMMODATIONS/TOURIST INFO:** 616-456-8557

PINE MOUNTAIN MUSIC FESTIVAL

VARIOUS UPPER PENINSULA TOWNS ✱ THROUGHOUT JUNE

This roving festival brings opera, symphony, chamber music, and jazz to small theaters, churches, and turn-of-the-century opera houses in towns throughout Michigan's Upper Peninsula. The festival began in 1990 and was the brainchild of Laura Deming, a cellist in the orchestra of the Lyric Opera of Chicago. Deming realized that only through a multicommunity collaboration could the festival afford to bring top talent to this area, which is economically depressed and far from major transportation hubs. About two dozen performances comprise the monthlong festival, whose program is typically ambitious and artistically excellent. Tickets range from $8 to $24. **LOCATION:** Various venues in Iron Mountain, Kingsford, Houghton/Hancock, Calumet, Marquette, and Escanaba **TICKETS/INFO:** 906-487-2093 **ACCOMMODATIONS/TOURIST INFO:** 800-338-7982, 906-226-6591, 800-437-7496

CHILDREN'S MUSIC FESTIVAL

DETROIT ✱ FIRST SATURDAY IN JUNE

This unique and extraordinary festival is designed to introduce children to the wonders of music. Masters in many genres—blues, jazz, classical, soul, and more—lead workshops to help children discover music and nurture their hidden talents. Programs have included such provocative topics as "the jazz roots of Motown" and have featured the likes of bluesman Robert Jones and blues/folk revivalist Josh White Jr., as well as musicians from the Detroit Symphony Orchestra. In addition to the music, the festival features storytelling and face painting. Admission is $5.   **LOCATION:** Friends School, at Lafayette and St. Aubin Streets on Detroit's near East Side **TICKETS/INFO:** 810-746-4030, 313-832-0455, 810-469-2968 **ACCOMMODATIONS/TOURIST INFO:** 800-338-7648, 313-259-4333

K&q COUNTRY MUSIC FEST

SAGINAW ✱ MID-JUNE

This free gathering brings major new-country artists from Nashville to Saginaw's Ojibway Island. Each year, about four national talents play at this family-oriented event; past bookings have included Trisha Yearwood, Pam Tillis, Diamond Rio, and Collin Raye.   **LOCATION:** Ojibway Island in Saginaw, just off Business Route M-13 one block from the Waterworks in Celebration Square **TICKETS/INFO:** 517-752-8161 **ACCOMMODATIONS/TOURIST INFO:** 517-752-7164

ÎNTERLOCHEN CENTER FOR THE ARTS FESTIVAL
INTERLOCHEN ✷ MID-JUNE THROUGH LATE AUGUST

Although country and pop artists occasionally make it onto Interlochen's summer roster of stars, this esteemed music and arts school keeps its focus mainly on classical music. Over the 10-week summer session, students and faculty present nearly 400 concerts, and internationally known guest artists present 35 more. A covered, open-sided amphitheater seats up to 4,000 for orchestral concerts, while Carson Auditorium seats up to 1,000 for chamber concerts and dance recitals.   **LOCATION:** Interlochen Center for the Arts in Interlochen, which is about 10 miles southwest of Traverse City and two miles south of U.S. 31 **TICKETS/INFO:** 616-276-6230, 616-276-7200 **ACCOMMODATIONS/TOURIST INFO:** 800-872-8377, 616-947-1120

ŠPIRIT OF THE WOODS FOLK FESTIVAL
BRETHREN ✷ THIRD SATURDAY IN JUNE

Traditional, old-timey folk and bluegrass music is on the agenda at this festival, which features five or six acts over the course of a Saturday. The music runs from noon until midnight, drawing up to 1,000 people to a township park with a lake that's perfect for an invigorating swim.   **LOCATION:** Dixon Township Park in Brethren, about 15 miles east of Manistee. From Manistee take M-55 east about 15 miles, then go north on County Road 669 (High Bridge Road) about four miles and look for the signs. **TICKETS/INFO:** 616-477-5381 **ACCOMMODATIONS/TOURIST INFO:** 800-225-2537, 616-775-9776

ᏢOLKAFEST AMERICANA
ST. IGNACE ✷ THIRD OR FOURTH WEEKEND IN JUNE, FRIDAY–SUNDAY

This binational event draws about 1,000 Michiganders and Canadians for nine hours of nonstop polka music. Four or five bands play both inside and outside the hall, and the event presents a variety of polka styles that often go well beyond the typical Polish to include Slovenian, Czechoslovakian, German, and even the Spike Jones-style polka of Bob Brock and the B-Tones.   **LOCATION:** Knights of Columbus Hall, at 49 Spring Street just off Main Street in St. Ignace, which is just north of the Mackinac Bridge in Michigan's Upper Peninsula **TICKETS/INFO:** 800-338-6660, 906-643-8717, 906-643-7558 **ACCOMMODATIONS/TOURIST INFO:** 800-338-6660, 906-643-8717

₣ROG ISLAND FESTIVAL
YPSILANTI ✷ FOURTH WEEKEND IN JUNE, FRIDAY–SUNDAY

Set in Ypsilanti's historic Depot Town area, Frog Island brings people together from southeastern Michigan's many diverse communities for a day of dancing to blues, zydeco, gospel, Latin, Caribbean, and more. This picniclike event always has plenty of interesting music from New Orleans and farther afield and has in recent years featured the likes of Marcia Ball, Los Lobos, Tabu Ley Rochereau, and Mahlathini and the Mahotella Queens. In addition, expect to hear such savvy favorites from the Detroit and Ann Arbor areas as blues/jazz pianist Mr. B and Afro/Caribe party poppers the Sun Sounds Orchestra.

About 16 acts play over the weekend on the tent's main stage; seats are available under the tent, and there's plenty of room outside for blankets on the lawn. Cajun and

Rockin' roots party: Al Rapone & Zydeco Express tear up the 1995 Frog Island Festival. Randy Austin-Cardona/The Ark

Creole foods are in large supply, as are beer, wine, and music merchandise. Advance ticket prices are about $15-$18 per day, or $35-$40 for the weekend. **LOCATION:** Frog Island in Depot Town, near downtown Ypsilanti. From I-94 take exit 183, go north on Huron Street, turn right on Cross Street, and look for the festival site on the left. **TICKETS/INFO:** 313-487-2229 **ACCOMMODATIONS/TOURIST INFO:** 313-483-4444

HISPERING WINDS
NIRVANA ✴ JULY 4 WEEKEND

Gospel, bluegrass, and the occasional comedian or new-country act are on tap at this longtime family favorite. A single stage features about five acts, which have included Continental Divide, Charlie Sizemore, and R & L Bluegrass. The price varies for individual days but is $26 for the weekend. Alcohol is prohibited. Another Whispering Winds festival is held the first weekend in October. **LOCATION:** King's Highway, 1.5 miles north of U.S. 10 in Nirvana, about 30 miles south of Cadillac and 15 miles north of Big Rapids **TICKETS/INFO:** 810-546-7424 **ACCOMMODATIONS/TOURIST INFO:** 800-225-2537, 616-775-9776

KALAMAZOO BLUES FESTIVAL
KALAMAZOO ✴ A WEEKEND IN MID-JULY, THURSDAY–SUNDAY

This two-day festival spotlights local, regional, and even some national blues and R&B performers in the original hometown of Gibson Guitars. Along with more than a dozen performers and the usual food and crafts vendors, this event also features musical instrument vendors and a blues education booth. Cost is $5 per day, and about 6,000 people usually show up. **LOCATION:** Arcadia Creek Festival Site, in downtown Kalamazoo **TICKETS/INFO:** 616-381-6514 **ACCOMMODATIONS/TOURIST INFO:** 616-381-4003

BLISSFEST

BLISS/CROSS VILLAGE ✷ SECOND WEEKEND IN JULY, FRIDAY–SUNDAY

The VW microbuses begin arriving on Thursday, rolling onto an old farmstead in a beautiful rural area two miles from Lake Michigan. Once the kids, conga drums, and hurdy gurdies are unloaded, the featured musicians begin to make the scene. These typically include folk singers from Québec, blues traditionalists from Louisiana, bluegrassers from Appalachia, and plenty of local northern Michigan hippy bands.

The magic of Blissfest goes well beyond the sum of the 20 musical groups who play on its three stages. Since 1981, this festival has drawn up to 4,000 people for three very mellow days of camping, fun, and music. All the elements are here: a low price ($35 for the weekend, including camping), no restrictions on food and alcohol, unlimited reentries, and a stellar vibe brought on by lots of diverse and well-chosen music. **LOCATION:** Festival Farm is at 3695 Division Road, between Bliss and Harbor Springs in the Lower Peninsula's far northwest corner. **TICKETS/INFO:** 616-348-2815; e-mail: jgill@sunny.ncmc.cc.mi **ACCOMMODATIONS/TOURIST INFO:** 800-845-2828

GREAT LAKES FOLK & BLUEGRASS FESTIVAL

PORTAGE ✷ SECOND SATURDAY IN JULY

This increasingly popular one-day festival offers a slice of America's musical heritage. The six folk and bluegrass acts generally include local and regional talents like Sweetcorn and Carrie Newcomer, as well as nationally known groups like the Red Clay Ramblers, and J. D. Crowe and the New South. Workshops, food, and recordings of the bands are available, and a Barn Dance is held in the Hayloft Theatre at festival's end. Alcohol may be brought in, but pets and overnight camping are prohibited. Admission is about $8 for adults.   **LOCATION:** Celery Flats Historical Area, at 7335 Garden Lane in the center of Portage. From I-94 use exit 76A for South Westnedge; go two miles south on Westnedge to Garden Lane, then east one-half mile and follow the signs. **TICKETS/ INFO:** 616-329-4522 **ACCOMMODATIONS/TOURIST INFO:** 616-381-4003

DULCIMER FESTIVAL

EVART ✷ THIRD WEEKEND IN JULY, THURSDAY–SUNDAY

Begun more than 25 years ago to preserve and perpetuate the music of the hammered dulcimer, this festival features dulcimers with acoustic guitar accompaniments. Thousands of people—the majority of whom are campers—attend each year to jam in the campground and hear performers from all over the United States. Recent years have brought in the likes of Lucille Riley, David Moran, Jim Hudson, and Russell Cook, and many of the performers teach workshops for adults and children. Organizers set up a large stage and bleachers, as well as a vending area with music-related items.

Tickets are only $2, including workshops. Alcohol is prohibited.   **LOCATION:** Osceola fairgrounds in Evart, between Clare and Reed City on U.S. 10. From Big Rapids take U.S. 131 north to U.S. 10 east. **TICKETS/INFO:** 616-459-6716 **ACCOMMODA- TIONS/TOURIST INFO:** 800-225-2537, 616-775-9776

*A*LL AMERICAN MUSIC FEST

PRUDENVILLE ✷ THIRD WEEKEND IN JULY, FRIDAY AND SATURDAY

Three Polish bands provide the dance rhythms for this festival devoted to preserving Polish heritage and polka traditions. On one of the largest inland lakes in Michigan, the resort town of Prudenville brings in performers from the local area and from as far away as Chicago. Between 5,000 and 10,000 dancers and spectators show up, paying about $6 per day to dance either inside the hall or outside under a huge tent. **LOCATION:** Knights of Columbus Hall and grounds, on the southeastern shore of Houghton Lake, on M-55 in Prudenville **TICKETS/INFO:** 517-422-4695 **ACCOMMODATIONS/TOURIST INFO:** 517-422-3931

*F*ONTANA MUSIC FESTIVAL

SHELBYVILLE ✷ LAST TWO WEEKS IN JULY AND THROUGHOUT AUGUST

The Fontana Music Festival brings art to the heartland with this six-week concert series in the former general store of rural Shelbyville. Now called the Art Emporium, the store has been renovated into an art gallery and 200-seat concert hall housing the classical-and-beyond Fontana program. The schedule features chamber music on Wednesdays and Sundays and nonclassical programs—such as ragtime piano—on Saturdays. Musicians are a mix of local, regional, and national, and postshow receptions encourage interaction with the artists in this intimate setting. Two art exhibitions share the six-week run.   **LOCATION:** The Art Emporium, at 952 124th Avenue in Shelbyville, which is one mile east of U.S. 131 via exit 59, midway between Kalamazoo and Grand Rapids **TICKETS/INFO:** 616-382-0826 **ACCOMMODATIONS/TOURIST INFO:** 616-381-4003, 616-345-0748, 616-672-7822

*C*OUNTRY-CAJUN-POLISH MUSIC FESTIVAL

PORT AUSTIN ✷ LAST WEEKEND IN JULY

A mix of country, cajun, and polka rhythms graces the Port Austin-area community in late July. The festival offers live music on Saturday night and Sunday afternoon at a big baseball diamond, with nearby RV hookups and cabins available to rent. About 500 people attend this family-oriented event each night; tickets are $6 for adults and free for children.   **LOCATION:** Port Austin KOA Campgrounds, at 8195 North Van Dyke in Port Austin, near the tip of Michigan's Thumb **TICKETS/INFO:** 517-738-2267 **ACCOMMODATIONS/TOURIST INFO:** 517-738-7600

*T*HE MICHIGAN FESTIVAL

EAST LANSING ✷ FIRST FRIDAY THROUGH THE SECOND SUNDAY IN AUGUST

This festival showcases the diversity of Michigan performing arts, with nine mainstage concerts and additional music on several smaller stages. The festival is dedicated to providing a venue to Michigan musicians and to making world-class music and cultural events accessible to as many people as possible.

Musically, expect a retro-oriented blend of country, pop, rock, jazz, classical, and folk, with artists running the gamut from classic soulsters Earth, Wind and Fire to contemporary Christian singer Amy Grant. Seven stages include the main stage, a Michigan music stage, and a children's stage featuring hands-on activities and shows. Folklife stages offer hands-on exhibitions of Michigan's diverse cultures and communities, with crafts, music, and food. More than 300,000 spectators usually attend the fair; adult admission is less than $20 in advance for all 10 days.   **LOCATION:** Various sites on the campus of Michigan State University in East Lansing. The main stage is on the field south of Munn Ice Arena, which is bordered by Birch and Chestnut Roads and Shaw Lane. **TICKETS/INFO:** 800-935-3378; e-mail: SMyers3745@aol.com **ACCOMMODA-TIONS/TOURIST INFO:** 800-968-8474

༜UMMER MUSIC FEST
FRANKENMUTH ✳ NINE DAYS BEGINNING THE SECOND FRIDAY IN AUGUST

Bavarian look-alike Frankenmuth is one of the state's biggest tourist towns. Its Summer Music Fest draws 25,000 revelers over nine days and does what Frankenmuth does best: it feeds its visitors rollicking polka and big band music, along with hearty German food, then sets them spinning over 10,000 square feet of dance floor. **LOCATION:** Heritage Park, on the banks of the Cass River in Frankenmuth, roughly 90 miles north of Detroit. From I-75, take exit 136. **TICKETS/INFO:** 517-652-3378 **AC-COMMODATIONS/TOURIST INFO:** 800-386-8696

༜ORD MONTREUX DETROIT JAZZ FESTIVAL
DETROIT ✳ LABOR DAY WEEKEND, FRIDAY–MONDAY (LABOR DAY IS THE FIRST MONDAY IN SEPTEMBER)

Since 1980, this festival has run the gamut of jazz and blues styles, ranging from Dixieland to fusion, from Latin to bebop, and more. Striving to define itself as a community event in the best sense, the festival devotes plenty of stage time to the many traditions of Detroit jazz. On Sunday, the festival gives the entire day to cutting-edge music, and other days feature comprehensive showcases of international R&B, jazz, and blues stars.

In all, more than 75 acts play over the festival's four days. Four stages come in sizes ranging from large to medium to a small stage for workshops, jamming, and children's activities. The festival also features high school performers, who meet and jam with stars. The event is entirely free, the crowds are friendly, and a wide range of food offerings keeps stomachs satisfied.   **LOCATION:** Hart Plaza, on Jefferson Avenue at the foot of Woodward Avenue in downtown Detroit, on the banks of the Detroit River **TICKETS/INFO:** 313-963-7622 **ACCOMMODATIONS/TOURIST INFO:** 313-259-4333

༜NN ARBOR BLUES & JAZZ FESTIVAL
ANN ARBOR ✳ SECOND WEEKEND IN SEPTEMBER, FRIDAY–SUNDAY

More soulful and bluesy than jazzy, this indoor/outdoor event brings music to two locations in Ann Arbor. Expect to see legends like Al Green, Bonnie Raitt, James Cotton, and Booker T. and the MG's, performing both outdoors at Gallup Park (10-15 acts) and indoors at the Michigan Theater (about 20 acts). This event is the latest incarnation of a tradition of Ann Arbor jazz and blues festivals dating back to the sixties.   **LOCATION:** Daytime on Saturday and Sunday: Gallup Park, on Fuller Road at Huron Parkway in Ann Arbor. Nighttime on Friday and Saturday: Michigan Theater, 603 East Liberty, just west of State Street. **TICKETS/INFO:** 313-747-9955 **ACCOMMODATIONS/TOURIST INFO:** 313-995-7281

Motor City jazz-out: The Ford Montreux Detroit Jazz Festival brings an international roster of jazz stars to downtown Detroit. Courtesy of Montreux Detroit Jazz Festival

🄳ALLY IN THE ALLEY

DETROIT ✶ SECOND OR THIRD SATURDAY IN SEPTEMBER

Detroit's foremost gathering of freaks and other folks commandeers a complex of alleys in the historic, rundown Cass Corridor, home to Detroit's artistic cutting edge since the sixties. What's basically an intimate street fair and gathering includes local bands on two stages, arts and crafts, food, beer, and old friends. This safe, lively event is Detroit at its Bohemian best.   **LOCATION:** A complex of alleys between Second, Third, and Forest Avenues, just south of the campus of Wayne State University **TICKETS/INFO:** 810-469-2968 **ACCOMMODATIONS/TOURIST INFO:** 800-338-7648, 313-259-4333

🅆HISPERING WINDS

NIRVANA ✶ FIRST WEEKEND IN OCTOBER

This is a semiannual event happening the July 4 weekend and the first weekend in October. See page 225 for details.   **LOCATION:** King's Highway, 1.5 miles north of U.S. 10 in Nirvana, about 30 miles south of Cadillac and 15 miles north of Big Rapids **TICKETS/INFO:** 810-546-7424 **ACCOMMODATIONS/TOURIST INFO:** 800-225-2537, 616-775-9776

ℭHEBOYGAN FIDDLER'S JAMBOREE

CHEBOYGAN ✶ SECOND SATURDAY IN OCTOBER

Each fall, northern Michigan fiddlers gather in a hall near the top of Michigan's Lower Peninsula. The music ranges from old-time country to bluegrass.   **LOCATION:** Cheboygan Knights of Columbus Hall, two miles south of Cheboygan **TICKETS/INFO:** 616-627-5811 **ACCOMMODATIONS/TOURIST INFO:** 616-627-7183

ℳINNESOTA FESTIVAL OF MUSIC
NEW ULM ✷ FIRST OR SECOND WEEKEND IN APRIL, SATURDAY AND SUNDAY

Sponsored by the Minnesota Music Hall of Fame, this festival showcases Minnesota's musicians, whether they play country, jazz, bluegrass, folk, or old-time music. Musicians perform on the festival's one indoor stage, and about 2,000 visitors cheer them on. The event also offers food, folk art workshops, and a large wooden dance floor. And if you're into Minnesota music, be sure to visit the Minnesota Music Hall Museum, located at Randall's Old Tyme Cafe, 1615 North State Street in New Ulm. **LOCATION:** Vogel Arena, at 122 South Garden in New Ulm, which is about 85 miles southwest of Minneapolis **TICKETS/INFO:** 507-354-7305 **ACCOMMODATIONS/ TOURIST INFO:** 507-354-4217

ℐWAYED PINES FOLK FESTIVAL
COLLEGEVILLE ✷ LAST SATURDAY IN APRIL

Since 1973, this family-oriented festival has offered traditional music and international food in its celebration of cultural diversity. Fiddle competitions and jam sessions account for much of the event's musical fare, and traditional folk concerts round out the rest. There is a charge for evening concerts (with two or three headliners), but the craft fair and fiddle contest are free. More than 10,000 people attend annually. **LOCATION:** St. John's University in Collegeville. From I-94 take exit 156, about 70 miles northwest of the Twin Cities. **TICKETS/INFO:** 612-363-3231; e-mail: dpikkaraine@csbsju.edu; World Wide Web: http://www.csbsju.edu **ACCOMMODA-TIONS/TOURIST INFO:** 612-251-2940

ℐTATE MUSIC AND POLKA FESTIVAL
MOUNDS VIEW ✷ A WEEKEND IN MID-JUNE

For more than 25 years, this festival has brought 20 bands into a large ballroom filled with more than 4,000 dancers. A lively and happy-go-lucky atmosphere fuels spirited bouts of polka, waltz, and fox-trot dancing. Outside are more concerts, accordion jam sessions, camping, a biergarten, and the ever popular Sunday polka mass. Ticket prices are between $7 and $19, depending on the headlining band. **LOCATION:** Bel-Rae Ballroom, at 5394 Edgewood Drive in Mounds View, a northern suburb of the Twin Cities **TICKETS/INFO:** 612-786-4630 **ACCOMMODATIONS/ TOURIST INFO:** 800-445-7412, 612-661-4700

$\overset{\text{\textcircled{}}}{\textbf{E}}$DDIE COCHRAN FESTIVAL
ALBERT LEA ✸ THIRD WEEKEND IN JUNE

If you get to thinking there ain't no cure for the summertime blues, you might consider a road trip to Albert Lea, the birthplace and longtime home of Eddie Cochran. Cochran wrote edgy teen anthems like "Summertime Blues" and "C'mon Everybody," paving the way for the rebellious turn that rock 'n' roll would take in the sixties. He carved an indelible niche in the history of rockabilly music before he was killed in a car crash in 1960 while in England, on his way to catch a flight back home to his family in Albert Lea.

Although his memory has been kept alive overseas more intensely than in the United States, the folks of Albert Lea are hoping to change that. This festival features displays, picnics, car cruises, dances, and concerts by rockabilly revivalists and special guests such as Cochran's backing band, the Kelly Four. Admission fees are minimal. **LOCATION:** The fairgrounds at 1029 Bridge Street in Albert Lea, which is 10 miles north of the Iowa border near the junction of I-90 and I-35 **TICKETS/INFO:** 800-345-8414 **ACCOMMODATIONS/TOURIST INFO:** 800-345-8414

$\overset{\text{\textcircled{}}}{\textbf{J}}$UDY GARLAND FESTIVAL
GRAND RAPIDS ✸ FOURTH WEEKEND IN JUNE

Each June, Judy Garland fans follow the yellow brick road to Grand Rapids, the birthplace of the prolific singer and actress who is perhaps best known for her role as Dorothy in *The Wizard of Oz*. Some of the original munchkins are on hand to welcome visitors to the Judy Garland Festival, and a host of musicians and singers (including Judy's daughter, Lorna Luft) perform songs from Garland's prolific recording career (more than 24 albums and nearly 100 singles).

This festival is rife with family-oriented activities, such as a parade, hands-on arts and crafts for kids, and Wizard of Oz karaoke. For dedicated Oz revivalists and other curious spectators, the festival features a Garland/Wizard of Oz collectors' exchange, a tour of Judy's childhood home, a gala dinner reception with the munchkins, and several big-screen showings of the original movie classic. Admission varies; many events are free.   **LOCATION:** Judy Garland Birthplace Historic House and Museum grounds, 2727 U.S. 169 south in Grand Rapids, about 175 miles north of Minneapolis **TICKETS/ INFO:** 800-664-5839 **ACCOMMODATIONS/TOURIST INFO:** 800-472-6366

$\overset{\text{\textcircled{}}}{\textbf{S}}$UMMERFOLK
BLOOMINGTON ✸ FOURTH SUNDAY IN JUNE

Started as a promotional event for Red House Records, Summerfolk has grown into a major live survey of contemporary folk, blues, bluegrass, and more. The roster leans heavily toward singer-songwriters and has featured the likes of Townes Van Zandt, Tom Paxton, Ferron, and Ani DiFranco.

Summerfolk has become one of the most eagerly anticipated events on the Twin-Cities folk calendar and draws a diverse audience of about 5,000. In addition to music on two stages, the festival features a huge array of activities for children, including giant sandboxes, a water slide running down the side of the park's ski hill, and hands-on educational activities. Tickets are about $18 at the gate, and alcohol and pets are prohibited. **LOCATION:** Highland Hills Ski Area in Bloomington, on the southern outskirts of Minneapolis about one mile south of I-494 **TICKETS/INFO:** 800-695-4687, 612-379-1089; e-mail: rhrpub@aol.com **ACCOMMODATIONS/TOURIST INFO:** 612-296-5029, 800-657-3700

ᵁPTOWN STREET JAM
MINNEAPOLIS ✱ FOURTH SUNDAY IN JUNE

This midsummer Minneapolis gathering brings a crowd of about 15,000 to Uptown's Hennepin Avenue for an afternoon and evening of local music. Formerly called the Uptown Jazz Festival, the event has expanded its musical offerings to include gospel (in the early afternoon), rock, and pop. This free festival runs between noon and 7 P.M., and features plenty of on-site food vendors. **LOCATION:** Hennepin Avenue in Uptown, Minneapolis **TICKETS/INFO:** 612-823-4581 **ACCOMMODATIONS/TOURIST INFO:** 612-296-5029, 800-657-3700

ᴵNTERNATIONAL POLKAFEST
CHISHOLM ✱ LAST WEEKEND IN JUNE, WEDNESDAY–SUNDAY

One of the country's biggest and best polka festivals draws about 30 top-name groups and a foot-stomping hoard of polka fanatics. The festival has an atmosphere of authenticity, since it's held in a mining region where many eastern European immigrants settled. In addition to the common Polish polkas, expect to hear German, Slovenian, and other styles. The center also offers an educational exhibition of musical instruments, food, drink, and extras like a polka mass. Up to 15,000 people come to hear and dance to music on three stages. The festival is held at Iron World Discovery Center, a history center and theme park in northeastern Minnesota. **LOCATION:** Iron World Discovery Center, on Highway 169 in Chisholm **TICKETS/INFO:** 218-254-3321, 800-372-6437 **ACCOMMODATIONS/TOURIST INFO:** 218-254-3600

ᴴERITAGEFEST
NEW ULM ✱ SECOND AND THIRD WEEKENDS IN JULY

This old-world celebration features authentic German music played by four European groups, New Ulm's famous Concord Singers, and many more local and regional performers. Hundreds of tubas blast away at the Tuba Mania concert, and with four stages there's always something going on. Ethnic food complements the music, along with parades and footraces for adults and kids. Admission costs $8 for adults and $3 for children ages 7-12. **LOCATION:** Brown County Fairgrounds in New Ulm, about 85 miles southwest of Minneapolis **TICKETS/INFO:** 507-354-8850 **ACCOMMODATIONS/TOURIST INFO:** 507-354-4217

ᶠOLK FESTIVAL
TWO HARBORS ✱ THIRD WEEKEND IN JULY

Located in a scenic park along the Lake Superior shoreline, this festival presents regionally and nationally known folk acts on a single large stage surrounded by picnickers and campers. Friday night features dancing while Saturday offers folk music

International Polkafest: Thirty big-name bands and a foot-stomping hoard of polka fanatics. (See entry, page 233.) © Minnesota Office of

Tourism

workshops and a family tent. Attendance has reached 1,000—a good many of whom are summer visitors. Admission is $20 for the weekend.   **LOCATION:** Two Harbors, about 25 miles northeast of Duluth along Highway 61 **TICKETS/INFO:** 218-834-4898 **ACCOMMODATIONS/TOURIST INFO:** 800-554-2116, 800-777-7384

FEST

DETROIT LAKES ✶ FIRST FULL WEEKEND IN AUGUST

Hot dawg! This festival, begun in 1985, has grown to become one of the most popular and anticipated annual country music festivals in the nation. Country-politan headliners like Vince Gill, Reba McEntire, and Shelby Lynne light up the stage for upward of 120,000 country music fans each year. In all, 16 national acts and a handful of local acts appear over the festival's three days. The crowd gets so big that a Jumbotron video screen is needed to help folks in the back see what's happening onstage.

Soo Pass Ranch is located in the heart of Minnesota's beautiful Lakes Region, so you can hardly dance a square without falling into one of the 412 lakes located within 20

The old world in New Ulm: Heritagefest features a "Tuba Mania" concert and plenty of authentic German music on four stages. (See entry, page 233.) Courtesy of Heritagefest

miles of the concert site. The ranch's eight campgrounds have ample space for more than 7,000 camping units. People camp in everything from pup tents to giant recreational vehicles, and many have favorite campsites they revisit each year with family and friends.

Tickets range from $45, in advance, for all three days, to $400 for VIP seats, which include a three-day pass, parking, priority seating, and two meals a day. Camping ranges from $60 to $150, and all campers must buy a three-day pass to the festival. The money-spending options are never-ending, with souvenir and gift shops featuring everything from cowboy hats to handcrafted silver jewelry to woven rugs. The range of food is incredible, too: from egg rolls and stir fry to barbecued turkey legs and pork chops. In the unlikely event that you still need even more action, the Shooting Star Casino is located 45 miles north of the ranch.   **LOCATION:** Soo Pass Ranch, in Detroit Lakes, about 185 miles northwest of the Twin Cities and 45 miles east of Moorhead. Follow the signs from U.S. 10 or U.S. 59. **TICKETS/INFO:** 218-847-1340; World Wide Web: http://www.tnnet.com **ACCOMMODATIONS/TOURIST INFO:** 218-847-9202

₽OLKAFEST IN THE PARK

LAKE CITY ✹ SECOND SUNDAY IN AUGUST

This free polka fest is held outside, under the sky at Patton Park—just like in the old days. Each year a regional band goes onstage in the center of town and plays for a crowd of around 300. Other attractions include scenic boat rides and an ice cream social. Picnicking is prohibited.   **LOCATION:** Patton Park, one block west of Main Street (U.S. 61) in downtown Lake City, which is on the western bank of Lake Pepin, about 50 miles southeast of the Twin Cities **TICKETS/INFO:** 800-369-4123 **ACCOMMODA-TIONS/TOURIST INFO:** 800-369-4123

₿AYFRONT BLUES FESTIVAL

DULUTH ✹ SECOND OR THIRD WEEKEND IN AUGUST

In terms of both attendance and caliber of artists, this North Country gig ranks among the top blues festivals in America. At a site overlooking Duluth's harbor, blues lovers can hear some of the genre's top purveyors of styles ranging from Chicago blues to Mississippi blues—with a little R&B and zydeco thrown in for good measure. The rapidly expanding festival now presents more than 20 acts on two stages over three days. Other events include Moonlight Blues Cruises, which are live performances held on the water Friday and Saturday, and late-night concerts, both at Connors Pointe Festival Park in Superior and in clubs and bars around Duluth.   **LOCATION:** Bayfront Festival Park, near I-35 and 5th Avenue West in downtown Duluth **TICKETS/INFO:** 715-394-6831 **ACCOMMODATIONS/TOURIST INFO:** 800-438-5884

$\mathcal{J}$RI-C JAZZFEST
CLEVELAND ✻ THROUGHOUT APRIL

Cuyahoga Community College not only puts the three C's in "Tri-C" but also puts the "Jazz" in JazzFest. This humongous educational festival caps off a year-round program of performances, workshops, field trips, and community outreach—all designed to preserve and perpetuate the grand art of jazz—with a concentrated series of concerts, clinics, master classes, and jam sessions. This is a great place for jazz enthusiasts of any age or expertise to learn Latin percussion, experiment with vocal techniques, or jam under the leadership of a talented jazz pianist. A good 10,000 fans attend festival events, which include concerts by more than 100 local, regional, and world-class musicians. Mel Torme, Paquito D'Rivera, and Ramsey Lewis have all been here, as has the Cleveland Jazz Orchestra. Admission fees for concerts vary. **LOCATION:** Concert halls and classrooms on the campus of the Cuyahoga Community College, at 2900 Community College Avenue in Cleveland **TICKETS/INFO:** 216-987-4400 **ACCOMMODATIONS/TOURIST INFO:** 800-321-1004, 800-321-1001, 216-621-5967

$\mathcal{R}$OSCOE VILLAGE DULCIMER DAYS FESTIVAL AND COMPETITION
COSHOCTON ✻ FIRST FULL WEEKEND IN MAY, SATURDAY AND SUNDAY

This all-out celebration of the sweet-sounding dulcimer features impromptu concerts and several categories of competition, but its centerpiece is the Mid-Eastern Regional Dulcimer Championship. The contest awards handmade dulcimers to its winners—and invites them to the national competition in Winfield, Kansas. Talented traditional instrumentalists offer free workshops and a Saturday night concert. Roscoe Village is an 1830s restored canal town, and the beautiful festival park is perfect for swimming, biking, golfing, fishing, and horse-drawn canal-boat riding. Campers are welcome, and RV hookups are available. Prices range from free to $5 per day. **LOCATION:** Coshocton Lake Park Pavilion in Coshocton's Roscoe Village, on Route 16/83 near its junction with U.S. 36 in east-central Ohio **TICKETS/INFO:** 614-622-9310, 800-877-1830 **ACCOMMODATIONS/TOURIST INFO:** 614-622-9315

Cleveland's TRI-C JazzFest thrives on educational programs like ¡Percussion Latina!, which introduces children to Latin rhythms. (See entry, page 237.)

Courtesy of TRI-C JazzFest

ℙEPSI JAMMIN' ON MAIN

CINCINNATI ✱ SECOND WEEKEND IN MAY, FRIDAY AND SATURDAY NIGHTS

Despite its unfortunate moniker, this two-night festival doesn't seem a sellout to the roughly 30 local bands who play at three outdoor stages and a dozen nearby clubs. Expect to hear anything from rock and blues to jazz, reggae, and even zydeco. Located in Cinci's once German, now gentrifying downtown entertainment district known as Over the Rhine, Jammin' on Main is produced by the Cincinnati Arts Festival and typically draws about 20,000 fans each year.   **LOCATION:** Over the Rhine district, on Main Street in downtown Cincinnati, easily accessible from I-71 and I-75 **TICKETS/INFO:** 513-744-8820 **ACCOMMODATIONS/TOURIST INFO:** 800-246-2987

𝒮ING CINCINNATI!

CINCINNATI ✱ THIRD WEEK IN MAY, THURSDAY AND FRIDAY

If it uses the voice as the main musical instrument, it's here. Sing Cincinnati! celebrates this city's choral music heritage by showcasing its numerous vocal styles, including gospel, barbershop quartets, musical theater, children's choirs, university glee clubs, and more. A national headliner joins the mostly local and regional talents, who add up to more than 3,000 vocalists. Several downtown venues provide the festival's 11 stages and host crowds of about 14,000 people. The fee of around $5 for adults also covers admission to the visual arts component of the festival.   **LOCATION:** Several downtown Cincinnati locations, including Music Hall, Memorial Hall, Aronoff Center, and Plum Stree Temple **TICKETS/INFO:** 513-744-9491 **ACCOMMODATIONS/TOUR-IST INFO:** 800-246-2987, 800-344-3445

CINCINNATI MAY FESTIVAL

CINCINNATI ✶ LAST TWO WEEKENDS IN MAY

Internationally renowned soloists join the Cincinnati Symphony Orchestra and the May Festival Chorus in the country's oldest festival dedicated to preserving choral masterworks. Music director James Conlon presides over the chorus and internationally known soloists in the historic Music Hall, built in 1878. The nationally registered landmark seats 3,300, and the two weekends of performances draw between 12,000 and 13,000 listeners. Ticket prices range from $10 to $45.   **LOCATION:** Music Hall, 1241 Elm Street in Cincinnati, and the Cathedral Basilica of the Assumption, 1140 Madison Avenue in Covington, Kentucky. Both locations can be accessed readily from I-76. **TICKETS/INFO:** 513-381-3300 **ACCOMMODATIONS/TOURIST INFO:** 800-543-2613

BIG BEAR RHYTHM & FOOD FESTIVAL: A TASTE OF COLUMBUS

COLUMBUS ✶ MEMORIAL DAY WEEKEND, FRIDAY–SUNDAY (MEMORIAL DAY IS THE LAST MONDAY IN MAY)

Nearly 175,000 people flood into a downtown riverfront park in Columbus for a weekend orgy of food and music. Offerings reflect the rich variety of musical and culinary styles of faraway Louisiana; blues and zydeco figure prominently, but the approximately 17 local and national talents represent a variety of musical genres. Big-name stars such as Dr. John, Buckwheat Zydeco, and Koko Taylor have graced the rosters, and nearby, celebrants can sample gourmet Louisiana fare like crab cakes, shrimp étoufée, and crème brulée. Both the main stage and the children's stage offer free music; gardens and fountains adorn casual lawn seating.   **LOCATION:** Bicentennial Park, along the banks of the Scioto River in downtown Columbus. From I-70 use the downtown exit. **TICKETS/INFO:** 614-645-7995 **ACCOMMODATIONS/TOURIST INFO:** 614-221-2489

TOLEDO ROCK, RHYTHM AND BLUES FESTIVAL

TOLEDO ✶ MEMORIAL DAY WEEKEND, FRIDAY–SUNDAY.

Toledo goes all-outdoors for this riverfront festival of rock, blues, R&B, zydeco, and anything else that's loosely related. More than 100,000 show up annually for this free urban party, which features a range of talent—including many national names—on two amphitheater stages over three days. The rules don't allow booze or pets, but kids are welcome—they even get their own "junior jamboree."   **LOCATION:** Promenade Park, at Summit and Water Streets in downtown Toledo **TICKETS/INFO:** 419-243-8024 **ACCOMMODATIONS/TOURIST INFO:** 800-243-4667

CINCINNATI OPERA SUMMER FESTIVAL

CINCINNATI ✶ THIRD WEEKEND IN JUNE THROUGH SECOND WEEKEND IN JULY, THURSDAYS AND SATURDAYS

A national and international cast joins the Cincinnati Symphony Orchestra and Chorus to perform in the country's second-oldest opera festival (begun in 1920). The festival's venue changed dramatically when it moved from the zoo (where calls of the

Opera in the heartland: Donnie Ray Albert and Frances Ginsberg in the Cincinnati Opera Summer Festival's 1995 production of Aida. *Courtesy of Philip J. Groshong/*

Cincinnati Opera

wild occasionally accompanied the oratorios of famous opera stars) to Cincinnati's Music Hall—an elegant, century-old National Historic Landmark. The festival's dedication to high-caliber opera remains the same, and a traditional operatic repertoire draws consistently enthusiastic audiences. Admission costs run from $8 to $43, and pre-performance dinners are available with advance registration.   **LOCATION:** Music Hall, at 1241 Elm Street in Cincinnati. From I-75 take the Ezzard-Charles exit east, turn right on Central Parkway, then left on Elm Street. **TICKETS/INFO:** 513-241-2742 **ACCOMMODATIONS/TOURIST INFO:** 800-246-2987, 800-344-3445

COLUMBIANA COUNTY BLUEGRASS FESTIVAL
LISBON ✷ THIRD WEEKEND IN JUNE, FRIDAY AND SATURDAY

Seven regional talents play nonstop traditional bluegrass and bluegrass gospel music on an outdoor stage near Ohio's western border. Near the stage are plenty of flat, tree-studded grounds, ideal for (free) rough camping, and a historic covered bridge, which adventurous types are sure to find. Vendors tempt the audience with food, arts and crafts, cassette tapes, and compact discs. Tickets cost $6-$10 per day for adults and children over 12.   **LOCATION:** Scenic Vista Park, on Wayne Bridge Road just off U.S. 30 near Lisbon, in western Ohio near the Pennsylvania-West Virginia border **TICKETS/ INFO:** 304-387-1103 **ACCOMMODATIONS/TOURIST INFO:** 216-424-9078

JAMBOREE IN THE HILLS
ST. CLAIRSVILLE ✷ THIRD FULL WEEKEND IN JULY, THURSDAY–SUNDAY

If you're looking for a bigger and better new-country festival than Jamboree in the Hills, good luck. The "Superbowl of Country Music," as it's called, features up to two dozen of today's hottest new-country stars, and a few traditionalists, too. Begun in 1977, this sprawling four-day event has grown into one of the country's most respected showcases of country talent. Just about everyone who's anyone in country music has played here, including Garth, Reba, Loretta, Tammy, and George, just to name a few.

During breaks in the onstage action, the redneck rowdiness and country flirtations continue nonstop. Squirt gun battles erupt as guys chase girls around (and vice versa) in what has become a Jamboree in the Hills tradition. The irresistible temptation of giving someone a soaking (or getting one; it's hot here in July!) sells out every toy store within a 30-mile radius of the festival.

Set in the Ohio River countryside near the West Virginia border, the festival has become a traditional annual get-together for thousands of fans. If you walk around the campground area during the four days, you'll see family reunions, family vacations, weddings, and engagements. Many stay in the campground the full four days and nights, and organizers provide plenty of diversions to keep everyone occupied, including children's activities, an arts and crafts festival, and a Country Showdown contest for regional performers with eyes on the big time.   **LOCATION:** St. Clairsville, near the West Virginia border. From I-70 take exit 208 or 213 and follow the signs to the entrance off Route 40/National Road. **TICKETS/INFO:** 800-624-5456 **ACCOMMODATIONS/TOURIST INFO:** 304-234-0050, 304-233-2575

Country-music Superbowl: Ricky Van Shelton leads an all-star lineup at a recent Jamboree in the Hills. (See entry, page 241.) Coutesy of Larry Belcher/West Virginia Division of Tourism

COLUMBUS JAZZ & RIB FEST
COLUMBUS ✷ LAST FULL WEEKEND IN JULY, FRIDAY–SUNDAY

Nationally known jazz artists with diverse styles perform free concerts on two stages in a downtown park near the Scioto River. One stage actually floats on the river, while the other sits in the park among fountains and gardens. Along with local talent, big-name acts are common among the more than 30 performances, and past artists have included Ahmad Jamal, Bela Fleck, Tito Puente, and Spyro Gyra. Guests digest a mélange of jazz sounds, from mainstream traditional to Latin, fusion, experimental, and avant-garde. Visitors can sample some 30 different kinds of ribs prepared by restaurants from around the country. Bring a lawn chair or blanket.   **LOCATION:** Bicentennial Park, along the banks of the Scioto River in downtown Columbus. From I-70 use the downtown exit. **TICKETS/INFO:** 614-645-7995 **ACCOMMODATIONS/TOURIST INFO:** 614-221-2489

LITTLE MOUNTAIN FOLK FESTIVAL
KIRTLAND HILLS ✷ LAST FULL WEEKEND IN JULY

With no main stage, this all-acoustic festival avoids headliners and presents a mixed repertoire of folk music of various origins, played on seven stages spread across the 15-acre grounds. Roaming from stage to stage, visitors would certainly hear the traditional country and folk sounds of the dulcimer, fiddle, and banjo, but might also get a smattering of anything from Spanish-style folk to klezmer bands. Trees shade the area, which also offers food, crafts, and a children's area (featuring magic shows and puppet shows). Tickets range from free to $5.   **LOCATION:** Lake County Historical Society, at 8610 King Memorial Road in Kirtland Hills, which is about 20 miles east of Cleveland **TICKETS/INFO:** 216-255-8979 **ACCOMMODATIONS/TOURIST INFO:** 800-321-1004, 800-321-1001, 216-621-4110

CLEVELAND HARDCORE FESTIVAL
CLEVELAND ✻ SECOND WEEKEND IN AUGUST, FRIDAY–SUNDAY

Leaving a pile of deaf and ecstatic ears in its smoldering path, the Cleveland Hardcore Festival lines up about 35 bands whose music ranges from hardcore to classic punk, emo, straight edge, and high-energy ska. This is the year's biggest chance for Cleveland-area punks to test their mettle in the mosh pit; the roster has featured the likes of Los Crudos, California's Fifteen, and Less than Jake.

Since proceeds go to a Cleveland-area charity, this underground-music weekend could be called hardcore with a heart. And in addition to the music, the festival serves as an outlet for political expression and features record, book, T-shirt, and food sales. About 1,000 punks and weekend punks can be counted upon to show up at the festival, which costs around $20 for the whole weekend.   **LOCATION:** A Cleveland-area venue that changes from year to year **TICKETS/INFO:** 216-321-4071, 216-984-3213, 216-749-5745; e-mail: rht3@po.cwru.edu **ACCOMMODATIONS/TOURIST INFO:** 800-321-1004, 800-321-1001, 216-621-4110

BUCKEYE INVITATIONAL BARBERSHOP MUSIC FESTIVAL
COLUMBUS ✻ THIRD WEEKEND IN AUGUST, THURSDAY–SUNDAY

While most of the world's top barbershop conventions travel from city to city, the Buckeye Invitational stays put in Columbus and manages to attract choruses and quartets from as far as Sweden, Holland, Great Britain, and New Zealand. Whether you're an enthusiast or a newcomer, this is a great chance to experience the barbershop style, which is basically a capella vocal music sung in four-part harmony.

Columbus is the only place in America where men's quartets and choruses compete with women's quartets and choruses, and the Ladies Association of British Barbershop Singers annually sends its reigning champion quartet to the Buckeye Invitational. A free outdoor concert hosts the international champion quartets, as well as a comedy quartet competition, and quartets from around the world perform with the Singing Buckeyes, who sponsor the event. The many informal, family-style events include concerts, cookouts, breakfasts, a riverboat cruise, and "pickup singing," where individual singers meet and spontaneously combine in harmony.   **LOCATION:** A variety of venues in downtown Columbus, including the renovated Palace Theatre at the corner of Broad and High, diagonal to the State Capitol. Take either I-70 or I-71 to downtown Columbus. **TICKETS/INFO:** 614-221-4480; e-mail: mrenner@ag.oh.gov **ACCOMMODATIONS/ TOURIST INFO:** 614-221-4480, 614-221-2283

Barbershop 'til you drop: Harmony and comaraderie unite at the world-renowned Buckeye Invitational. (See entry, page 243.) Courtesy of Clark Hanmer

GRANDIN FESTIVAL

CINCINNATI ✷ LAST TWO WEEKS IN AUGUST

One of the few festivals to feature a repertoire of chamber music written for vocal/instrumental combinations, the Grandin Festival features masterworks of the 18th, 19th, and 20th centuries. Concerts are held in several venues, and the more than 70 musicians include advanced students, young professionals, guest artists, and faculty members of the Cincinnati College Conservatory of Music. **LOCATION:** Cincinnati College Conservatory of Music, University of Cincinnati **TICKETS/INFO:** 513-556-9198 **ACCOMMODATIONS/TOURIST INFO:** 513-352-3750

EMERALD CITY FOLK FESTIVAL

CLEVELAND ✷ LAST SUNDAY IN AUGUST

Everybody gets involved when the historic village of Frostville hosts this free, interactive, and family-oriented festival to preserve and perpetuate the various sounds of traditional American music, including country, folk, blues, and gospel. About 6,000 people show up to hear a nationally known headliner and eight regional talents performing on a main stage and in a dance tent, family tent, and Song Swap and Jam area.

The weekend's continuous entertainment includes humorous singers; workshops, dances, and performances in square and contra dancing; instrument-building demonstrations; a silk-screening area; and a folk arts and crafts area. Guests bring picnics, lawn chairs, and blankets, and pay nothing to attend. **LOCATION:** The Rocky River Reservation grounds of the Frostville Museum, on Cedar Point Road in North Olmsted, between Valley Parkway and Columbia Royal Road/Route 252 **TICKETS/INFO:** 216-351-6300 **ACCOMMODATIONS/TOURIST INFO:** 216-621-4110

ℳOHICAN BLUEGRASS FESTIVAL

GLENMONT ✴ SECOND WEEKEND AFTER LABOR DAY (LABOR DAY IS THE FIRST MONDAY IN SEPTEMBER)

This growing bluegrass festival impresses performers and audiences alike with its classy venue and its national talents. A dozen big-name bands play the festival's sizable main stage, and spectators set up jam sessions on the campgrounds, which lope across two miles of hills along the banks of the Mohican River. The camp offers "first-class camping," with 250 sites, RV hookups, and plenty of opportunities for swimming, canoeing, and horseback riding. Weekend passes cost around $40, and daily fees cost $12-$22. Pets and alcohol are fine on the campsite but should be kept from the stage area.   **LOCATION:** 22462 Wally Road in Glenmont,which is on Highway 520 about five miles southwest of Millersburg and 60 miles south of Cleveland **TICKETS/INFO:** 614-599-6741 **ACCOMMODATIONS/TOURIST INFO:** 800-345-4386, 614-222-6262

WINTERFEST

MILWAUKEE ✸ THROUGHOUT JANUARY

Winterfest warms up downtown Milwaukee's Olympic-size refrigerated ice rink by presenting an array of popular musical styles. About 75 local, regional, and national acts perform rock, zydeco, Cajun, alternative, and pop music, while festivalgoers enjoy figure- and hockey-skating exhibitions, ice sculpting, strolling bands, and other sidelights. About 40,000 skaters are included in the crowd of 200,000 who visit the festival during its six weeks, which begin in mid-December. Admission costs $2 for adults and $1 for children and includes music and skating. **LOCATION:** Cathedral Square Park, at North Jackson and East Wells Streets in Milwaukee **TICKETS/INFO:** 414-273-3378 **ACCOMMODATIONS/TOURIST INFO:** 800-554-1448

WISCONSIN POLKAFEST

CONCORD ✸ THIRD WEEKEND IN MAY

Since the late 1970s, about nine oompah bands have come to Concord to fuel two wooden dance floors full of polka fanatics. The star-studded roster features eclectic polka styles—from standard Polish to Czech, Slovenian, German, and country and western—and has included top names like Barbara and the Carousels, Becky and the Ivanhoe Dutchmen, Don Peachy, Roger Bright, and the Take Five Band. Admission costs $5-$9 daily or $19 for a three-day pass. Sandwiches, chili, and donuts provide physical nourishment, and Sunday's ecumenical mass offers spiritual replenishment. **LOCATION:** Concord House in Jefferson County, about 40 miles from Milwaukee. From I-94 take exit 275 at Sullivan and follow the signs. **TICKETS/INFO:** 414-387-5443 **ACCOMMODATIONS/TOURIST INFO:** 414-674-7295

RIVER JAM

KAUKAUNA ✸ FIRST WEEKEND IN JUNE, FRIDAY–SUNDAY

Kaukauna's Fox River shore hosts this annual three-day festival of rock and country music. Two big-name talents headline Friday and Saturday nights, and local acts round out the roster. Food and trinkets also compete for visitors' attention. Admission is about $12 daily, except for Sunday, which is free. **LOCATION:** Central Park (behind the town library), on Highway 55 in Kaukauna, about 20 miles east of Appleton **TICKETS/ INFO:** 414-766-6300 **ACCOMMODATIONS/TOURIST INFO:** 414-734-3358

AYFEST

GREEN BAY ✳ SECOND FULL WEEKEND IN JUNE, FRIDAY–SUNDAY

Nestled among the rolling hills of the University of Wisconsin's Green Bay Campus on the shore of Green Bay, this festival showcases locally and regionally known musicians, foods from around the world, and a full range of carnival attractions. Around 40 performers offer a range of musical styles, including jazz, fusion, rock, reggae, and country. The "costar" of this festival is food: 25 booths serve international and domestic cuisines. In addition, the festival features carnival rides and Friday night fireworks. **LOCATION:** University of Wisconsin's Green Bay campus, on Nicolet Drive in northeast Green Bay and easily accessible from I-43 and Highway 57 **TICKETS/INFO:** 414-465-2145 **ACCOMMODATIONS/TOURIST INFO:** 800-236-3976, 414-494-9507

PORTERFIELD COUNTRY MUSIC FESTIVAL

MARINETTE ✳ FOURTH WEEKEND IN JUNE, FRIDAY–SUNDAY

Big-time country stars sometimes show up in unlikely places—like the modest family campground called Green Acres. For more than 10 years, top Nashville performers like Waylon Jennings, Don Williams, and Trisha Yearwood have come to Green Acres to serenade some 7,000 people over three days. About 13 national acts and even more regional favorites play new and sometimes traditional country and bluegrass tunes on one main stage and on a small after-hours stage. Many fans have been coming every year since the event started, and the early birds start driving to the campground a week in advance in anticipation of "fond memories and sweet country music." Camping, eating, and paradeside shenanigans complement the musical feast.   **LOCATION:** Green Acres Campground, on Highway 64 six miles west of Marinette and 12 miles east of U.S. 141 **TICKETS/INFO:** 715-789-2130 **ACCOMMODATIONS/TOURIST INFO:** 715-735-6681

SUMMERFEST

MILWAUKEE ✳ ELEVEN DAYS BEGINNING THE LAST THURSDAY IN JUNE

Set on the Lake Michigan shoreline of one of the Midwest's most underrated cities, Summmerfest is an 11-day musical explosion of country, pop, alternative rock, jazz, folk, zydeco, bluegrass, world music, and more, played by national and local acts. Music sounds continuously from 12 stages (including the 24,000-seat Marcus Amphitheater), and audience members can dance or eat at the many food courts that dot the sprawling 90-acre site.

Promoters claim that Summerfest is both "the world's greatest music festival" and "the world's largest music festival." A less controversial boast would be "the world's most conspicuously sponsored music festival." Beer and soft drink company banners are everywhere, creating an in-your-face commerciality that's probably the only thing detracting from the success of this very comprehensive sampling of American and world music styles. In addition to hundreds of musical acts, the festival features a comedy cabaret, a circus, sporting events, amusement rides, a children's theater, arts and crafts, and other exhibitions. Some 900,000 people attend over 11 days. Admission costs $8-

This note's for you: Summerfest brings a massive, mid-summer explosion of music to Milwaukee's lake front. Courtesy of Wisconsin Department of Tourism

$9, less if you buy in advance.   **LOCATION:** Along the shore of Lake Michigan, centering around 200 North Harbor Drive **TICKETS/INFO:** 800-273-3378, 414-273-3378 **ACCOMMODATIONS/TOURIST INFO:** 800-554-1448

C̸HIPPEWA VALLEY COUNTRY FEST
CADOTT ✷ LAST WEEKEND IN JUNE, THURSDAY–SUNDAY

Camping and crooning are the specialties of Country Fest, a huge, four-day fête of country music with roughly 16 national and eight local bands in a Jumbotron-equipped concert area. Immediately surrounding the area are 320 acres with 7,000 campsites, plus food and novelty vendors. This is a big, big festival, drawing more than 30,000 people daily.   **LOCATION:** Just outside Cadott, about 30 minutes northeast of Eau Claire via Highway 29 **TICKETS/INFO:** 800-326-3378, 715-289-4401 **ACCOMMODATIONS/ TOURIST INFO:** 800-344-3866, 715-831-2345

R̸OCKIN' ON THE RIVER
PRESCOTT ✷ A WEEKEND IN EARLY JULY

The small Wisconsin town of Prescott makes a dance floor out of its downtown thoroughfare near the St. Croix riverfront. Local talent plays crowd-pleasing rock and country music, and a Taste of Prescott food festival keeps everyone chewing. **LOCATION:** First Street between the two bridges in downtown Prescott. The town is located on the St. Croix River, about 25 minutes southeast of St. Paul, Minnesota, via U.S. 61 and U.S. 10. **TICKETS/INFO:** 715-262-3512, 715-262-3284, 715-262-3950 **ACCOMMODATIONS/TOURIST INFO:** 715-262-3284

*B*ELOIT RIVERFEST

BELOIT ✷ FIRST OR SECOND WEEKEND IN JULY, THURSDAY–SUNDAY

Wisconsin's second-largest music festival (next to Milwaukee's Summerfest) celebrates diversity with a wide-ranging selection of music. Rock, reggae, blues, rap, jazz, pop, big band, country, bluegrass—it's all here, in a huge park on the banks of a river and lagoon. On four stages, more than 40 bands, including four nationally known headliners, play for up to 100,000 people over four days. In addition to the music, there are novelty acts, strolling entertainers, arts and crafts, boat races, water-ski shows, a volleyball tournament, carnival rides, and an excellent children's area.   **LOCATION:** Riverside Park, on Riverside Drive at the junction of Highways 81 and 51. Beloit is at the Illinois-Wisconsin border, about 47 miles south of Madison and 18 miles north of Rockford, Illinois. **TICKETS/INFO:** 800-423-5648 **ACCOMMODATIONS/TOURIST INFO:** 800-423-5648

*C*OUNTRY JAM USA

EAU CLAIRE ✷ THIRD WEEKEND IN JULY, THURSDAY–SUNDAY

Each July, more than 100,000 country fans from across the Midwest drive, bus, or hitchhike their way to this sprawling camp-and-country event on the banks of the Chippewa River. Stars like Clint Black, Tricia Yearwood, and Alabama dish up 36 hours of entertainment over four days. In addition to the new-country acts, organizers sprinkle a little traditional country and old-time rock 'n' roll onto the event's three stages. Ticket prices range from $50 for a one-day pass to $100 for a four-day pass; early-bird discounts are available.   **LOCATION:** Summer Festival Grounds in Eau Claire. From I-94 take exit 65 and go east on Clairmont Avenue, then left on Menomonie to Ferry Street and follow the signs. **TICKETS/INFO:** 800-780-0526 **ACCOMMODATIONS/ TOURIST INFO:** 800-344-3866, 715-831-2345

*R*OCKFEST

CADOTT ✷ THIRD WEEKEND IN JULY, THURSDAY–SUNDAY

Up to 35,000 spectators make their way to RockFest, many of them camping on the site's 320 acres, which have been developed into 7,000 campsites. One main stage and four side stages keep the entertainment steady from two dozen national and local acts. The roster includes a variety of rock 'n' roll flavors, but leans toward classic rock. **LOCATION:** Just outside Cadott, about 30 minutes northeast of Eau Claire via Highway 29 **TICKETS/INFO:** 800-326-3378, 715-289-4401 **ACCOMMODATIONS/TOURIST INFO:** 800-344-3866, 715-831-2345

*M*IDSUMMER IN THE NORTHWOODS BLUEGRASS FESTIVAL

MANITOWISH WATERS ✷ LAST WEEKEND IN JULY, THURSDAY–SUNDAY

This intimate, folksy event presents a top-notch lineup of Bluegrass Hall of Fame honorees like Bill Monroe, the Osborne Brothers, and Ralph Stanley. Organizers don't try to compete with the plugged-in and decked-out country shows that draw hundreds of thousands; instead they outfit the Cozy Cove Restaurant and World Loppet Lodge with four simple stages—including one on the back porch. The acoustic music sounds great under the maples, oaks, and Norwegian pines, and the northern Wisconsin friendliness complements a country-simple menu of bratwurst and corn on the cob.

Organizers are emphatic that "bluegrass is not just a spectator sport" and encourage dancing and jamming. They even throw in the occasional folk or Cajun band just to keep things interesting. In addition, this is one of the few bluegrass events with children's activities and performances. Bands perform each day from noon until midnight, and special features include a Friday fish fry and a Sunday stir-fry. Nearby lakeside parks offer camping facilities. Tickets for the morning-'til-midnight marathons cost $12 per day; festival passes are $48.   **LOCATION:** Cozy Cove Restaurant, on Highway 51 in Manitowish Waters, about 100 miles north of Wausau in northern Wisconsin, just south of the Michigan border **TICKETS/INFO:** 715-543-2166 **ACCOMMODATIONS/TOURIST INFO:** 715-543-8488

PENINSULA MUSIC FESTIVAL
FISH CREEK ✳ FIRST THREE WEEKS IN AUGUST

Although beautiful Door County is known as "the Cape Cod of the Midwest," this festival's many Chicago-area performers and audience members make it feel like "the Windy City in exile." Chamber and symphonic music makes up a 10-concert series that hosts the likes of Marilyn Horne and John Browning. A commitment to up-and-coming young artists and 20th-century repertoires is unusual in this area, and the resident Festival Orchestra includes some of America's finest talent. Recent programs have featured works by Webern and Bartók, as well as Renaissance, baroque, and French chamber music. Concerts are held in the intimate Door Community Auditorium. **LOCATION:** Door Community Auditorium in Fish Creek, on the Door Peninsula **TICKETS/INFO:** 414-854-4060 **ACCOMMODATIONS/TOURIST INFO:** 800-527-3529, 414-743-4456

GREAT RIVER JAZZ FESTIVAL
LA CROSSE ✳ FIRST OR SECOND WEEKEND IN AUGUST, THURSDAY–SUNDAY

Jazz bounces across the hills and valleys along the Mississippi River during August's Great River Jazz Festival. Of the festival's four stages, two are located outside on a paved, permanent festival site, while two other stages are indoors in downtown restaurants or hotels. About a dozen national and international acts cover a wide spectrum of traditional and contemporary jazz. To help develop budding jazz men and women, Great River offers workshops and scholarships to college-bound musicians. A weekend pass costs $60; dailies are $12.   **LOCATION:** La Crosse Festgrounds and two indoor venues in downtown La Crosse, just off I- 90 **TICKETS/INFO:** 608-791-1190 **ACCOMMODATIONS/TOURIST INFO:** 800-477-2920

ALLENTON CONCERTINA JAMBOREE FESTIVAL
ALLENTON ✳ LABOR DAY WEEKEND, FRIDAY–SUNDAY (LABOR DAY IS THE FIRST MONDAY IN SEPTEMBER)

Rule No. 1 at the Allenton Concertina Jamboree Festival is "Do not confuse a concertina with an accordion." Should you violate Rule No. 1, you'll likely get an explanation that concertinas differ from accordions in that each button on a concertina produces two notes: one when the box is pulled apart, and another when it's squeezed

Peninsula Music Festival: Up-and-coming artists and a 20th-century reper-toire. Courtesy of J. Shimon & J. Lindemann/Peninsula Music Festival

together. Accordion keys produce only one note. Therefore, a concertina is much harder to play—according to concertina players.

The songs conjured by the instrument at this gathering typically include forties show tunes, die-hard polka rhythms, and crowd-rousing sing-alongs. But what you'll hear actually depends on what the self-selecting artists feel like playing during the 20 minutes of stage time allotted to each. About 100 concertina artists from the Great Lakes region (and occasionally from farther afield) strut their stuff throughout the jamboree, which lasts for 12 hours on Saturday and asks only a $1 donation from spectators. Many of the musicians are retirees, while others use the occasion to promote their bands in hopes of roping a gig. Occasionally, a soloist might be joined by a saxophonist or a brass instrumentalist, but the unwritten Rule No. 1 is that the concertina always takes the lead. **LOCATION:** Addison Town Hall in Allenton, 30 miles north of Milwaukee on Highway 41 at Highway 33 **TICKETS/INFO:** 414-255-3454, 414-629-5232 **ACCOMMODA-TIONS/TOURIST INFO:** 800-231-0903, 414-273-7222

PRECHERFEST

GLENDALE ✷ LABOR DAY WEEKEND, FRIDAY AND SATURDAY

This midsize rock- and blues-fest feels more like a big house party than a corporate-sponsored extravaganza. Presented by the Sprecher microbrewery, the two-day, two-stage gig brings in about 10 acts, a couple of which are nationally known. Expect to hear zydeco from Louisiana, or college-rock favorites like the Freddie Jones Band. Entry is cheap ($4), and so is the beer—in fact, with several Sprecher varieties on tap, beer tasting is a big part of the festivities. Each year, 10,000 or more people attend. **LOCATION:** Old Heidelberg Park, at 700 West Lexington Boulevard in Glendale, a suburb of Milwaukee. From downtown Milwaukee take I-43 north. **TICKETS/INFO:** 414-964-2739 **ACCOMMODATIONS/TOURIST INFO:** 414-964-2739

WINTERFEST

MILWAUKEE ✷ MID-DECEMBER THROUGH LATE JANUARY

See description on page 246 for all the details.   **LOCATION:** Cathedral Square Park, at North Jackson and East Wells Streets in Milwaukee **TICKETS/INFO:** 414-273-3378 **ACCOMMODATIONS/TOURIST INFO:** 800-554-1448

GREAT PLAINS

CORNELL COLLEGE SPRING MUSIC FESTIVAL
MOUNT VERNON ✹ FIRST WEEKEND IN MAY, FRIDAY–SUNDAY

Founded in 1898 as a showcase for classical music only, this spring festival expanded in the 1970s to include one evening of jazz greats like Sonny Rollins. The real star, though, is the college's King Chapel, a yellow-limestone American Gothic church built in 1875. The chapel houses a 65-rank Moeller pipe organ with 86 English and Flemish carillon bells, and each year its fine acoustics welcome regionally and nationally known guest artists and ensembles. Admission is free, and everyone's invited to the reception following each concert to mingle with performers and old friends in this outstanding venue. **LOCATION:** Cornell College's King Chapel in Mount Vernon, about 12 miles east of Cedar Rapids just north of U.S. 30 and west of Highway 1 **TICKETS/INFO:** 319-895-4000 **ACCOMMODATIONS/TOURIST INFO:** 319-895-8214, 319-472-5135

GLENN MILLER FESTIVAL
CLARINDA ✹ SECOND WEEKEND IN JUNE, THURSDAY–SUNDAY

With gracious hospitality, Glenn Miller's birthplace welcomes a few thousand far-flung visitors into the fold of the Miller musical family to celebrate the big band era's most enduring legend. For four days in Clarinda, big bands are everywhere. National, international, civilian, and military bands (including the Glenn Miller Orchestra) take turns on the three stages, belting out dance hits like "In the Mood," "Chattanooga Choo Choo," and "Tuxedo Junction." Much of the crowd just listens, but dance floors are never far away, and many fans consider the Big Band Dance on Saturday night to be the highlight of the festival.

Between listening and dancing, you can check out the small green frame house where Alton Glenn Miller was born on March 1, 1904. The house has been restored to its 1904 condition by the Glenn Miller Birthplace Society, which organizes the festival.

The Glenn Miller Society hosted the first festival in 1976, 33 years after Miller disappeared over the English Channel while on a flight to promote the morale of World War II forces. The society recently gained a chapter in Japan, and because of this connection Japanese big band talents often perform at the festival, through a program called "Bridging the Pacific." Other attractions include picnics, museum visits, lectures, and panel discussions. High school musicians compete for a big band scholarship, and their parents host a luncheon during the festival.   **LOCATION:** Clarinda Community High School and downtown Clarinda, 95 miles southwest of Des Moines near the junction of U.S. 71 and Highway 2 **TICKETS/INFO:** 712-542-2461 **ACCOMMODA-TIONS/TOURIST INFO:** 712-542-2461, 712-623-4232

🎵DES MOINES METRO SUMMER FESTIVAL OF OPERA
INDIANOLA ✹ MID-JUNE THROUGH MID-JULY

Grand-scale opera meets a small midwestern college town, culling performers from around the country to sing the scores of American and classical operatic history. Each year three operas are performed in English, fulfilling the promise of opera's charm and pageantry yet sparing the linguistically challenged opera lover the distraction of reading the libretto in translation. This format wins many new friends for Des Moines-area opera, and the 500-seat theater is usually sold out well in advance. Individual performances are priced at $24 to $49, and season tickets are a bargain at $56 to $142. The season also features several chamber music concerts.   **LOCATION:** Simpson College's Blank Performing Arts Center is at the corner of North D Street and West Detroit Avenue in Indianola, about 15 miles south of Des Moines at the junction of U.S. 69 and Highway 92. **TICKETS/INFO:** 515-961-6221 **ACCOMMODATIONS/TOURIST INFO:** 515-286-4960, 800-285-5842, 515-832-4808

🎵AMERICAN MUSIC FESTIVAL (BURLINGTON STEAMBOAT DAYS)
BURLINGTON ✹ SIX DAYS ENDING THE THIRD SUNDAY IN JUNE (FATHER'S DAY)

More than 100,000 people are drawn to Burlington's Mississippi riverfront to celebrate American popular music and to dance in "the world's longest conga line." Each night highlights an American musical era or style; over six days, you might hear fifties and sixties rock 'n' roll, R&B, and country. The main stage features one headliner each night—the likes of the Shirelles, Randy Travis, or Willie Nelson—and the south stage lights up with a high-energy local band. More than 20 concessionaires vend to the crowds, and many visitors camp nearby. A one-time outlay of $16 gets you unlimited entries for six days.   **LOCATION:** Burlington's riverfront, in the parking lot of Memorial Auditorium immediately south of the Great River Bridge. Burlington is on the Mississippi River in the southeast corner of Iowa. **TICKETS/INFO:** 800-827-4837, 319-754-4334 **ACCOMMODATIONS/TOURIST INFO:** 800-827-4837, 319-472-5135, 800-891-3482

🎵IOWA CITY JAZZ FESTIVAL
IOWA CITY ✹ JULY 3 AND 4

Perhaps because Iowa tends to export its best crop of musicians, you don't typically associate the state with jazz. But when you consider the long list of jazz superstars who have come from Iowa—Glenn Miller, Bix Beiderbecke, and Art Farmer, to name a few— the Iowa City Jazz Festival makes perfect sense. Conceived by an inspired music professor and backed by a music-loving businessman, this blossoming young festival (it began in 1991) aims to acquaint and reacquaint Iowans with jazz's diverse roots. Legendary masters team up with new talent, playing a range of jazz and its tangents, including blues, swing, and even salsa, and drawing the blankets and lawn chairs of some 18,000 people around the single stage. Despite an official ending time of 9:30 P.M., the free festival typically rambles on until midnight. Two days of clinics are geared to high school and college jazz musicians, but are open to the public.   **LOCATION:** At the junction of Washington and Dubuque Streets in downtown Iowa City, 25 miles south of Cedar Rapids **TICKETS/INFO:** 319-351-1700 **ACCOMMODATIONS/TOURIST INFO:** 319-351-1700, 319-337-6592, 319-337-9637

ℳℐSSISSIPPI VALLEY BLUES FESTIVAL
DAVENPORT ✱ FIRST FULL WEEKEND IN JULY

Sponsored by the Mississippi Valley Blues Society, this festival's slogan is "Keepin' the Blues Alive," but its sounds also include zydeco, country, gospel, and rock 'n' roll. Some 30,000 people show up ready to receive the blues, and the music delivers until midnight. Two outdoor stages host local talent early in the day and end with major headliners. Each year's festival honors a particular blues musician and offers free workshops (such as Honeyboy Edwards discussing "the octogenarian bluesman"). Organizations like the Chicago Blues Museum often visit, bringing additional blues-related films and activities.   **LOCATION:** Le Claire Park, in downtown Davenport, along the Mississippi River **TICKETS/INFO:** 319-322-5837 **ACCOMMODATIONS/TOURIST INFO:** 319-788-7800, 800-747-7800

ℬLUEGRASS AND OLD-TIME COUNTRY MUSIC
STRATFORD ✱ SECOND WEEKEND IN JULY, FRIDAY EVENING THROUGH SUNDAY

You'll hear no electric instruments whatsoever at this straightlaced, old-time festival featuring talents both local and professional. Old favorites like Possum Trot have returned to perform every year since the festival began in 1984, but five or six more bands typically come in from Iowa, Missouri, Oklahoma, and Kansas. The sounds of the banjo, fiddle, dobro, bass, and guitar emanate from the one outdoor stage as well as from nearby camping sites, where everyone jams informally. Sunday shows are all gospel and gospel-bluegrass, and although you should BYO lawn chairs and blankets, organizers request that you leave the alcohol at home. A weekend pass is $12.   **LOCATION:** Stratford City Park in Stratford, 50 miles north of Des Moines on Highway 175, seven miles west of Highway 17 **TICKETS/INFO:** 515-838-2311 **ACCOMMODATIONS/TOURIST INFO:** 515-242-4705, 515-832-4808, 800-285-5842

𝒜LL-DAY COUNTRY GOSPEL SING
PELLA ✱ THIRD WEEKEND IN JULY, FRIDAY AND SATURDAY

You might find more famous country gospel performers elsewhere, but you won't find any more friendly or sincere than at this two-day festival of musical worship and testimony. Some 50 groups from around the central states sing on an outdoor stage before an audience rich with retirees. The festival provides an hour for lunch, and another for supper; both meals can be purchased at a nearby church. Bring a lawn chair and an offering, if you please.   **LOCATION:** West Market Park (bounded by Franklin, West Second, Liberty, and West Third Streets), two blocks west of downtown Pella, 45-

Bix lives! Four days of music honor Davenport's immortal "young man with a horn" at the annual Bix Beiderbecke Memorial Jazz Festival. Courtesy of Iowa Division of Tourism

minutes southeast of Des Moines on Route 163 **TICKETS/INFO:** 515-628-1306 **AC-COMMODATIONS/TOURIST INFO:** 515-628-2626

BIX BEIDERBECKE MEMORIAL JAZZ FESTIVAL
DAVENPORT ✶ LAST FULL WEEKEND IN JULY, THURSDAY–SUNDAY

In 1971, on the 40th anniversary of the death of jazz cornetist, pianist, and composer Bix Beiderbecke, the city of Davenport memorialized its native son with music at his grave site. A jam session followed, and 1,500 people unexpectedly surfaced. Cars lined the highway, traffic snarled, and a festival was born.

The event has since expanded to four days of music, plus a pre-event "evening with Bix," which kicks off the festival Wednesday night. About 10 traditional jazz, Dixieland, and swing bands converge on the Quad Cities from all over the country to pay homage to the immortal "young man with a horn." Outdoor concerts are at Le Claire Park on the banks of the Mississippi River, and other events include indoor dances, graveside musical tributes, cocktail hours, and much more.

Leon "Bix" Beiderbecke was born in Davenport in 1903, and by the time of his premature death at age 28, he had won lasting fame as an astoundingly innovative musician whose songs and performances came to symbolize the epitome of the Jazz Age and the Roaring Twenties.

The admission fee is $7 per concert, and all-event badges are available for a discount. An art fair and several other events have sprung up around the festival, but the focus remains firmly on traditional jazz, so bring a lawn chair and a picnic and enjoy the music.   **LOCATION:** Antoine Le Claire Park, the Col Ballroom, the Holiday Inn, and other venues in Davenport, at Iowa's border with Illinois **TICKETS/INFO:** 319-324-7170 **ACCOMMODATIONS/TOURIST INFO:** 319-472-5135, 800-891-3482, 319-472-5135

♫LUEGRASS MUSIC WEEKEND

OSKALOOSA ✷ THIRD SATURDAY IN AUGUST, THURSDAY–SUNDAY

Bring your lawn chair or blanket, or sit in the grandstands in front of the portable stage with about 3,000 other bluegrass fans from Iowa, Illinois, Missouri, and Minnesota. Eight to 10 of the country's best bands spend four days playing those traditional acoustic instruments that define bluegrass: the banjo, mandolin, guitar, fiddle, bass, and dobro (resonator guitar). The fairgrounds have plenty of electric RV hookups for the 200 or so campers who show up, and admission is $22 for four days.   **LOCATION:** Southern Iowa Fairgrounds, on I Street in Oskaloosa, about 60 miles southeast of Des Moines near the junction of U.S. 63 and Highway 92 **TICKETS/INFO:** 816-665-7172 **ACCOMMODATIONS/TOURIST INFO:** 515-672-2591, 800-285-5842, 515-832-4808

♫OLLIN' ON THE RIVER BLUES FESTIVAL

KEOKUK ✷ THIRD WEEKEND IN AUGUST, FRIDAY–SUNDAY

On an outdoor stage just a stone's throw from the Mississippi River, eight blues acts take over Victory Park for three days in late summer. Regional and national talents play Friday and Saturday, and local talents appear Sunday. The festival's blues notes often bend toward country and rock 'n' roll, and nonmusical attractions include old trolley cars, trains, and boats (from canoes and dragon boats to the majestic *Delta Queen*). Carnival rides and Saturday night fireworks round out the action.   **LOCATION:** Victory Park, on the riverfront in Keokuk, in the southeast corner of Iowa, 120 miles southwest of Davenport at the junction of U.S. 136 and U.S. 218 **TICKETS/INFO:** 800-383-1219 **ACCOMMODATIONS/TOURIST INFO:** 800-383-1219, 800-891-3482, 319-472-5135

♫VOCA OLD-TIME COUNTRY MUSIC CONTEST & FESTIVAL

AVOCA ✷ SIX DAYS PRECEDING LABOR DAY (THE FIRST MONDAY IN SEPTEMBER) AND LABOR DAY

"Let's go to Avoca!" If anyone ever throws these words at you, don't dodge 'em. If you're at all into vintage American sounds, get in that car (or truck, or RV) and hit the road to musical heaven.

If you time it right, you'll arrive just as this Iowa town of 1,500 begins its annual transformation into America's old-time music capital. At the county fairgrounds, hundreds of the country's best musicians—many of them not known outside their particular specialties or hometowns—present a week of the kind of country music that's no longer played or even acknowledged by commercial "countrypolitan" radio. You won't find any spangly Nashville-style suits, pampered faux hillbillies, drums, or amplifiers at this here jamboree.

Instead, you'll find such diverse pursuits as fiddle and harmonica playing, bluegrass banjo picking, cowboy and pioneer storytelling, and world-championship spoon and bone playing. One stage is devoted solely to bluegrass, another to folk, another to Cajun, another to Slavic-American accordion music. Horse barns are converted into dance halls, gospel music stages, and workshop areas where the world's best traditional musicians share their crafts.

Contests are the heart of the festival, and since a number of national championships are on the line, the prizes are substantial. The top country singer might get a European tour or a recording session in Nashville. Musical instruments and recording hardware await winners of contests in everything from Jimmie Rodgers yodeling to Hank Williams songwriting, Roy Acuff yo-yoing, and gandy dancing. (Gandy dancers were the men who walked the railroad tracks, pounding down the spikes with narrow-headed mallets. Contestants drive three spikes into a tie and then jerk them out while being timed with a stopwatch.)

In addition to the contests, there's plenty of straight performances and dances. Events often include bluegrass and Cajun music shows, polka parties, barn dances, gospel sings, and grandstand concerts and reviews. If you need a change of pace, craft demonstrations cover everything from totem-pole making and blacksmithing to a tepee village filled with buckskinners and fur traders.

Organizer Bob Everhart defines old-time country music as any and all of the music America's settling pioneers may have played at one time or another. Bob is a folk and bluegrass musician whose talent has produced six records, a Grammy award nomination for songwriting, and numerous tours of America and Europe. He started the festival in 1974 to preserve the music he loves, and since then it has grown to become the largest gathering of public-domain music makers and listeners in the country, with more than 50,000 people attending over the week.

You'll never find a more comprehensive survey of traditional American music, and as a testimony to the music's worldwide influence the festival often draws banjo pickers from France, country singers from Holland, and even the number-one bluegrass band in the Czech Republic (where there are some 500 bluegrass bands).

Tips: If you're bringing an RV (and thousands do), you'll find parking and camping spots, but hookups disappear two or three weeks before the festival. Also, the organizers suggest that you bring two lawn chairs: one to carry from stage to stage for the contests, and one to hold a place at the evening stage shows. Admission is $10 a day; a seven-day pass costs $27.   **LOCATION:** Pottawattamie County Fairgrounds in Avoca, about 90 miles west of Des Moines, on U.S. 59 just south of I-80 **TICKETS/INFO:** 712-784-3001 **ACCOMMODATIONS/TOURIST INFO:** 712-623-4232, 800-528-5265

$\mathcal{M}$IDWEST POLKA FEST
HUMBOLDT ✱ LABOR DAY WEEKEND, FRIDAY–SUNDAY

Organized by eight folks in love with the sounds and steps of polka, this polka extravaganza retains all the charms and personal touches of its beginnings. Between 1,000 and 2,000 like-minded folks turn up to polka the afternoons away on all-wooden floors, with 12 bands providing the oomph on three indoor stages. Busloads of folks from Nebraska, Minnesota, and Wisconsin bring their dancing shoes, paying about $9 per day for the three-day event.   **LOCATION:** Humboldt County Fairgrounds in Humboldt, about 90 miles north of Des Moines, near the junction of Highway 3 and U.S.

169 **TICKETS/INFO:** 515-332-5921 **ACCOMMODATIONS/TOURIST INFO:** 515-332-1481, 800-285-5842, 515-832-4808

HICKORY HILLS HOEDOWN
MEDORA/INDIANOLA ✷ THIRD SUNDAY IN SEPTEMBER

Offering nothing more than a chance for old friends to get together and play some seasoned country music, the Hickory Hills Hoedown brings in small-town folks from a hundred-mile radius. Country, bluegrass, and folk musicians play solo gigs, then get together with friends to perform in groups. The event officially runs from noon until 6 P.M., but the musicians themselves determine how long it will last, since as long as there's music, there will be people to listen.   **LOCATION:** Hickory Hills Park, just south of Medora, on U.S. 69 (about 14 miles south of Indianola) **TICKETS/INFO:** 515-961-6169 **ACCOMMODATIONS/TOURIST INFO:** 515-961-6269, 800-285-5842, 515-832-4808

₿ETHANY COLLEGE MESSIAH FESTIVAL

LINDSBORG ✹ PALM SUNDAY, GOOD FRIDAY, AND EASTER SUNDAY

A 55-piece orchestra, a 300-voice choir, an 80-rank pipe organ, outstanding acoustics, and a long history of artistic excellence come together with magnificent effect in America's oldest annual performance of Handel's *Messiah*. Since 1882, the ensemble has performed *Messiah* on Palm and Easter Sundays, along with Bach's *St. Matthew Passion* on Good Friday. Some 1,500 to 2,000 guests flock to Bethany College's 1920s-era auditorium for each performance. Other attractions include a Midwest art exhibition, a student art show and drama performance, and weeklong solo recitals. **LOCATION:** Presser Hall Auditorium at Bethany College, 401 North First Street in Lindsborg, two miles west of I-135. Lindsborg is 20 miles south of Salina and 80 miles north of Wichita. **TICKETS/INFO:** 913-227-3311, ext. 8185 **ACCOMMODATIONS/TOURIST INFO:** 913-227-3706

₩ICHITA JAZZ FESTIVAL

WICHITA ✹ LAST FULL WEEK IN APRIL, SUNDAY–SUNDAY

Since its founding in 1972, the Wichita Jazz Festival has grown and improved, becoming the envy of much larger towns. Over eight days, this comprehensive jazz party draws world-class stars like Joe Henderson, Poncho Sanchez, and Wynton Marsalis, who play to a crowd of more than 15,000 jazz fans.

Small club and restaurant settings complement big downtown performances like Jazz in Old Town and the Big Final Concert at Century II. The festival has played a key role in reviving the 1920s-era Orpheum Theatre, which had been stripped of its chairs and dark for nearly a decade. Complying with an informal protocol, concertgoers unfold portable chairs on the main floor and spread blankets in the balcony.

An innovative jazz education series brings performers into public schools to work with students one-on-one and in groups. Admission ranges from free to about $25. **LOCATION:** Various locations in Wichita **TICKETS/INFO:** 316-264-5300 **ACCOMMODATIONS/TOURIST INFO:** 316-265-2800, 800-288-9424

Three hundred voices strong: The Bethany College Messiah Festival is America's oldest. (See entry, page 261.) Courtesy of Bethany College

☺LD TOWN BLOCK PARTY (WICHITA RIVER FESTIVAL)

WICHITA ✷ TEN DAYS, STARTING THE FRIDAY BEFORE MOTHER'S DAY (THE SECOND SUNDAY IN MAY)

Dubbed RiverFest by locals, this 10-day block party began in Wichita's centennial year, 1970, to celebrate the city's culture and heritage. The annual festival now boasts more than 20 musical events on seven stages and features musical styles ranging from jazz and gospel to blues, folk, country, rock, and classical. Cajun food accompanies the jazz concert, and the entire party culminates in a now-traditional Wichita Symphony concert, which closes with Tchaikovsky's *1812 Overture*, complete with church bells and live cannons (fired from a nearby army base). A few dollars gains admittance to all festival events.   **LOCATION:** Downtown Wichita on Douglas Avenue between Washington and Topeka Avenues **TICKETS/INFO:** 316-436-1200 **ACCOMMODATIONS/TOURIST INFO:** 316-265-2800, 800-288-9424

☺UNFLOWER MUSIC FESTIVAL

TOPEKA ✷ FIRST TWO WEEKS IN JUNE

Some 35 nationally renowned musicians arrange themselves into ensembles of various sizes and perform a series of seven concerts featuring orchestral works, concertos, and chamber music—with the musicians often suggesting the repertoire. In past years, the festival has included events such as an evening of sonatas and an afternoon concert especially for families. In conjunction with the festival, the Blanche Bryden Institute invites 25 to 30 young musicians to study and perform with headliners, and the selected students then present two festival concerts of their own. Organizers encourage informal attire for events at the acoustically excellent White Concert Hall, and admission is free.   **LOCATION:** White Concert Hall in the Garvey Fine Arts Center on the Washburn University campus at 17th and Jewell in Topeka **TICKETS/INFO:** 913-231-1010, ext. 1512; e-mail: zzsavl@acc.wyacc.edu **ACCOMMODATIONS/TOURIST INFO:** 913-234-1030, 800-235-1030

COUNTRY MUSIC FESTIVAL
CLIFTON ✱ THIRD WEEKEND IN AUGUST, FRIDAY–SUNDAY

With awards of up to $3,000, this competitive event draws country musicians of all ages. In addition to the music, food booths, stagecoach rides, and games attract a local crowd of 600 to 900 people.   **LOCATION:** Berner Memorial Park in Clifton, which is about 23 miles east of Concordia on Highway 9 **TICKETS/INFO:** 913-455-3660 **ACCOMMODATIONS/TOURIST INFO:** 913-243-4290

POLKA DAYS
GREAT BEND ✱ THIRD WEEKEND IN AUGUST, FRIDAY–SUNDAY

About five bands from all over the region take turns revving up the crowd on the 4,800-square-foot wooden dance floor. Saturday is the big day, with continuous music from noon to midnight. A polka mass and a parade of flags get things moving Sunday morning, then the dancing continues in the afternoon. RVs are welcome. **LOCATION:** Holiday Inn Convention Center, 3017 West 10th Street in Great Bend **TICKETS/INFO:** 316-793-2402, 316-793-5540 **ACCOMMODATIONS/TOURIST INFO:** 316-792-2401

KANSAS STATE FIDDLING & PICKING CHAMPIONSHIPS
LAWRENCE ✱ LAST OR SECOND-TO-LAST WEEKEND IN AUGUST, FRIDAY–SUNDAY

Join the musical fray or just kick back and enjoy three days of workshops, concerts, dances, and contests in all styles of traditional acoustic music and dance. This well-organized grassroots effort is designed both to encourage rank amateurs (through workshops and contests) and to present accomplished, internationally known artists who are preserving old-time music. Styles range from flat-pick and fiddle to a "miscellaneous acoustic instruments" category that might feature bagpipes, harmonicas, hurdy-gurdies, or tabla drums. Dancing focuses mainly on the contra style, and accompaniment is always live. Sunday features the climactic Fiddling & Picking Championships. **LOCATION:** South Park near 11th and Massachusetts Streets, south of the courthouse in Lawrence. Workshops are held in a variety of downtown public buildings. **TICKETS/INFO:** 913-841-7817, 913-842-3321 **ACCOMMODATIONS/TOURIST INFO:** 913-865-4411

𝓑IG BRUTUS POLKA FESTIVAL

WEST MINERAL ✸ LAST WEEKEND IN AUGUST, FRIDAY–SUNDAY

Musicians play polkas from noon 'til dusk for three days, and after dinner the dancers kick up their proverbial heels again. On Sunday, the festivities wind down with food, antiques, and a traditional tractor pull.   **LOCATION:** West Mineral, on Highway 102 just southwest of Pittsburg in the southeast corner of the state **TICKETS/INFO:** 316-827-6177 **ACCOMMODATIONS/TOURIST INFO:** 316-231-1000

𝓒OOL CATS JAZZ FESTIVAL

MANHATTAN ✸ LABOR DAY (THE FIRST MONDAY IN SEPTEMBER)

Along with the big cats at the zoo, jazz musicians of local, regional, and national renown perform as soloists and in ensembles (from trios to big bands). The zoo animals enter the limelight in live exhibitions, and "biofact" stations offer interesting information about the furry felines. The musical entertainment is included with regular zoo admission.   **LOCATION:** Sunset Zoo at 2333 Oak Street in Manhattan **TICKETS/INFO:** 913-587-2737 **ACCOMMODATIONS/TOURIST INFO:** 913-776-8829

𝓦ALNUT VALLEY FESTIVAL AND NATIONAL FLAT-PICKING CHAMPIONSHIP

WINFIELD ✸ THIRD WEEKEND IN SEPTEMBER

For 51 weeks each year, Winfield is just another quiet town in the rolling hills of south-central Kansas. But each year in the third week of September, Winfield's population doubles and the town becomes "the national capital of acoustic string musicians."

The Walnut Valley Festival is a picker's paradise, a heartland extravaganza where massive amounts of music are mixed with equal quantities of hospitality and friendliness. About 60 percent of the audience brings instruments along, and, unlike many bluegrass festivals, there's little in the way of cliquishness or stylistic inflexibility. Everyone is eager to share licks and to blend various musical tastes into new and interesting combinations.

Many folks show up days in advance to get their camps set up, letting kids run loose in the 141-acre temporary "town" with its own police and fire departments, medical services, and newspaper. Wandering minstrels soon begin roving the grounds, spurring musical encounters with questions like "Do y'all know 'Ragtime Annie'?" Informal mentoring is everywhere, as young folks pick both banjos and old-timers' brains for techniques and songs that might be forgotten if it weren't for gatherings like this.

In fact, the campgrounds are so full of great amateur musicians that some folks might actually forget to go to the stage shows—which would be a shame. At Walnut Valley's four performance stages, you can hear the greats of traditional country and bluegrass, like Norman Blake and Doc Watson, plus innovators like David Grisman and Tim O'Brien. Bluegrass purists may bemoan the presence of the "newgrassers," but there's plenty here for the traditionalist—and besides, organizers are quick to point out that Walnut Valley was never meant to be strictly a bluegrass festival. Hillbilly licks are the festival's core, but ample measures of folk, gospel, Celtic, and American old-time styles are also in evidence.

The second part of the festival is the National Flat-Picking Championship, which draws about 50 guitar hotshots competing for spectators' awe and thousands of dollars

Acoustic encounter: Traditional string musicians from across the country converge on Winfield for the Walnut Valley Festival and National Flat-Picking Championship. Courtesy of John Kuefler/Kansas Travel & Tourism

in prize money. Other prestigious contests include fiddle (won by a young Alison Krauss in 1984), finger-pick guitar, bluegrass banjo, mountain and hammered dulcimer, and autoharp. Some 12,000 spectators/participants show up over the weekend, taking advantage of the music, workshops, arts and crafts fair, children's concerts, camping, and camaraderie.   **LOCATION:** Cowley County Fairgrounds, one mile west of Winfield on Highway 160. Winfield is about 45 miles southeast of Wichita. **TICKETS/INFO:** 316-221-3250 **ACCOMMODATIONS/TOURIST INFO:** 316-221-2420, 800-235-9424

𝒢OSPEL MUSIC USA

LAKE OZARK ✷ FIRST WEEKEND AFTER NEW YEAR'S DAY, FRIDAY–SUNDAY

The musical mainstay of this festival is Southern-style gospel singing, backed up by drums, keyboard, guitar, and the occasional banjo or mandolin. Around 10 nationally and regionally known acts perform for a mostly older crowd of gospel lovers at a four-star resort complex on Lake Ozark. Mixed or all-male quartets are most common, but duets and trios also make appearances. Sunday morning starts off with 30 minutes of Christian devotions. **LOCATION:** Lodge of the Four Seasons, on Highway HH off U.S. 54 in Lake Ozark, 35 miles south of Jefferson City **TICKETS/INFO:** 816-665-7172 **ACCOMMODATIONS/TOURIST INFO:** 800-325-0213, 314-365-3371, 800-877-1234

ℳID-AMERICA JAZZ FESTIVAL

ST. LOUIS ✷ THIRD WEEKEND IN MARCH, FRIDAY–SUNDAY

The Mid-America program presents five bands each year playing everything from Dixieland and swing to boogie-woogie and blues—everything but modern/progressive jazz. The program often favors big-name pianists like Ralph Sutton, Jay McShann, and Eddie Higgins with his quartet. Four five-hour shows are presented over the weekend (Friday and Saturday nights, Saturday and Sunday afternoons) in the hotel's 1,000-seat Grand Ballroom. The venue is just five minutes from St. Louis's Lambert Airport, and fans typically represent some 30 states. Admission is around $100 for the weekend. **LOCATION:** Stouffer Renaissance Hotel, 9801 Natural Bridge Road, next to Lambert Airport **TICKETS/INFO:** 314-469-0255 **ACCOMMODATIONS/TOURIST INFO:** 314-421-1023, 800-888-3861, 800-877-1234

𝓑IG MUDDY FOLK FESTIVAL

BOONVILLE ✷ FIRST OR SECOND WEEKEND IN APRIL, FRIDAY AND SATURDAY

If you've been interested in hearing—or for that matter learning how to play—instruments like the hammered dulcimer, the spoons, or the leaf, check out this comprehensive folk and ethnic music festival. Directed by banjoist-guitarist, spoon and leaf player Dave Para and hammered-dulcimer whiz Cathy Barton Para, the festival begins with a Friday night performance and contra dance. Saturday features workshops (shape-note gospel singing, folk history, songwriting, and various instruments) plus a concert performance and a huge jam session.   **LOCATION:** Concerts at Thespian Hall, 522 Main Street, Boonville; dance and jam sessions at Turner Hall, across the street from Thespian Hall. Boonville is in the center of the state 24 miles west of Columbia off I-70. **TICKETS/INFO:** 816-882-7977 **ACCOMMODATIONS/TOURIST INFO:** 816-882-2721, 816-882-7977, 800-877-1234

𝒪ZARKS DOGWOOD MUSIC FESTIVAL
CAMDENTON ✱ THIRD WEEKEND IN APRIL

Amidst the glory of flowering dogwoods, bluegrass blooms in downtown Camdenton. In addition to concerts and jam sessions, this 47-year-old festival presents a children's carnival, a parade, arts and crafts, and organized hikes at Ha Ha Tonka State Park.   **LOCATION:** Downtown Camdenton, about 60 miles southwest of Jefferson City at the junction of U.S. 54 and Highway 5 **TICKETS/INFO:** 573-346-2227 **ACCOMMODATIONS/TOURIST INFO:** 800-769-1004, 573-346-2227, 800-877-1234

𝒢OSPEL BLACK AND WHITE NOW AND THEN
ARROW ROCK ✱ FIRST SUNDAY IN MAY

From Southern shape-note singing to African American spirituals, the different styles and periods of gospel music are showcased in the best possible venue for this genre—a church. Beginning at 4 P.M., you might hear traditional a capella groups, followed by piano-based trio singing. From there, anything is possible as contemporary gospel choirs sing along to recorded musical accompaniment, 80-year-old ladies play old-time spirituals, and soloists belt out testimonials. Optional donations are the only entry fee, and the crowd usually numbers about 200 at this precious, little-known festival.   **LOCATION:** Federated Church on High Street in Arrow Rock. Take I-70 west 30 miles from Columbia or east 100 miles from Kansas City, then Highway 41 north 13 miles to Arrow Rock. **TICKETS/INFO:** 816-837-3231, 816-837-3330 **ACCOMMODATIONS/TOURIST INFO:** 816-837-3231, 314-751-4133, 800-877-1234

𝒢REAT AMERICAN MUSIC FESTIVAL
BRANSON ✱ LATE MAY OR EARLY JUNE FOR TWO WEEKS, STARTING ON A FRIDAY, ENDING ON A SUNDAY

The town of Branson seems to have thrown itself into the American country music consciousness only in the past few years, but this festival has been bringing champion musicians to Branson's Silver Dollar City for more than two decades. Pure love of music and good-time jamming make this festival seem like a homecoming for the more than 200 contest-winning bluegrass, country, gospel, and old-time musicians who perform both regular sets and impromptu pickin' parties at the 1890s theme park. The park admission fee is around $25.   **LOCATION:** Silver Dollar City, a theme park seven miles west of Branson on Highway 76 **TICKETS/INFO:** 800-952-6626 **ACCOMMODATIONS/TOURIST INFO:** 417-334-4136, 900-884-2726, 800-877-1234

𝒫OINTFEST
ST. LOUIS ✱ A WEEKEND IN LATE MAY OR EARLY JUNE

Sponsored by radio station KPNT-FM, Pointfest brings modern/alternative rock's hottest acts to St. Louis, to the frenzied delight of more than 20,000 fans. About a dozen

A pickin' party as big as all outdoors: The Great American Music Festival brings Cajun, bluegrass, and down-home country to a turn-of-the-century theme park. (See entry, page 267.) Courtesy of Silver Dollar City

bands ensure quick sellouts of both reserved seats and the general-admission lawn area, where "point spotters" roam and pluck people from the crowd for "meet-and-greet" sessions with the bands backstage.   **LOCATION:** Riverport Amphitheater in downtown St. Louis **TICKETS/INFO:** 314-231-1057; e-mail: KPNT@aol.com **ACCOMMODATIONS/TOURIST INFO:** 314-421-1023, 800-888-3861, 800-877-1234

SCOTT JOPLIN RAGTIME FESTIVAL

SEDALIA ✷ FIRST WEEKEND IN JUNE

America's first truly national song was ragtime, and from the late 1890s until the outbreak of World War I, elaborately syncopated piano sounds dominated the popular music scene. In those days, Sedalia, Missouri, was a railroad stop with a thriving African American community, and itinerant musicians like Scott Joplin came here often to meet with publishers and collaborators and to kick around new "rags" in the bordello area along Main Street.

These days, Sedalia is known as "the cradle of ragtime," and the first weekend in June feels like it could be the first decade of the century. Stroll along Main Street and you'll see and hear costumed string bands everywhere, pumping out old-time music-hall favorites. Inside bars and restaurants, pianists like Glenn Jenks, Ian Whitcomb, and Dick Zimmerman (who directs the festival) bang away at Joplin compositions like "Maple Leaf Rag" and "Ragtime Dance."

Cradle of ragtime: The Scott Joplin Ragtime Festival brings syncopated piano sounds back to Sedalia. Courtesy of Missouri Division of Tourism

The crowd is more knowledgeable than nostalgic, and you'll often see appreciative eyebrows perking up as the strains of some long-forgotten ditty come into recognition. Under tents, events like Professor Desmond Strobel's Antique Academy of Genteel Dance draw men in derbies and women in long gowns, who dance two-steps, waltzes, and quadrilles.

The festival also includes formal concerts, a grand ball, and free, informal concerts at tent sites. At symposia and workshops, you might hear an unusual instrumental combination for "Stop Time Rag", or debates about the social significance of preragtime "dialect songs." And at after-hours sessions at local hotels, you'll hear some of the most authentic, footloose music in America.   **LOCATION:** Various venues in Sedalia, 86 miles west of Kansas City at the junction of U.S. 50 and U.S. 65 **TICKETS/INFO:** 816-826-2271 **ACCOMMODATIONS/TOURIST INFO:** 314-751-4133, 800-877-1234

KANSAS CITY BLUES AND JAZZ FESTIVAL
KANSAS CITY ✷ THIRD WEEKEND IN JULY, FRIDAY–SUNDAY

Kansas City, here they come! K.C.'s biggest musical event of the year brings blues, jazz, zydeco, and gospel greats swarming in for three days of serious summer music-making. Some 100,000 music lovers from all over the heartland gather around three stages and "the world's largest barbecue pit." The Blues Stage features the likes of Otis Rush, Irma Thomas, and Beau Jocque and the Zydeco High Rollers; the Jazz Stage is graced by stars like Pat Metheny, Bela Fleck, and surprises like the Skatalites; and the Youth and Heritage Stage brings in local musicians and interesting odds and ends. Tickets are a bargain at about $7 per day.   **LOCATION:** Penn Valley Park at Pershing and Main Streets, in downtown Kansas City **TICKETS/INFO:** 816-753-3378 **ACCOM-MODATIONS/TOURIST INFO:** 800-767-7700, 800-877-1234

SAM A. BAKER BLUEGRASS FESTIVAL
PATTERSON ✷ FOURTH WEEKEND IN JULY, THURSDAY–SATURDAY

Nestled in the St. Francis Mountains, the Sam A. Baker State Park is a perfect setting for one of the oldest bluegrass festivals in the United States. The outdoor main stage hosts six or seven local and regional acts, plus one national headliner. Nearly 3,000 bluegrassers sit on lawn chairs, perch on picnic tables, or sprawl on straw bales in a down-home, laid-back atmosphere.

The park is cradled on one side by some of the world's oldest mountains, and on the other by the crook of the St. Francis River and Big Creek. Big, comfy log cabins were erected during the Depression under the auspices of the Civilian Conservation Corps, as were the dining hall, visitor center, and fire tower atop Mudlick Mountain. You won't have to travel far for canoeing, water activities, and hiking on the Ozark trail. **LOCATION:** Sam A. Baker State Park, 45 minutes north of Poplar Bluff, near Piedmont in the St. Francis Mountains. From St. Louis, take I-55 to U.S. 67 south, then Highway 34 west, and Highway 143 north. **TICKETS/INFO:** 800-334-6946 **ACCOMMODA-TIONS/TOURIST INFO:** 800-877-1234

KAHOKA FESTIVAL OF BLUEGRASS MUSIC
KAHOKA ✷ SECOND WEEKEND IN AUGUST

For nearly 25 years, Delbert and Erma Spray have made Kahoka "the bluegrass capital of the Midwest." This well-organized festival is one of America's best. Ten guest bands begin concertizing Wednesday night, and the campground jamming continues pretty much nonstop. Extras include a Fiddler's Frolic, clogging and instrument work-shops, biscuits and gravy breakfasts, and the always lively Miss Kahoka Contest. Tickets run from $6 (Wednesday) to $10 (Friday and Saturday); 250 RV hookups are available. **LOCATION:** Clark County Fairgrounds in Kahoka, in the northeast corner of the state at the junction of U.S. 136 and Highway 81 **TICKETS/INFO:** 573-853-4344 **ACCOMMO-DATIONS/TOURIST INFO:** 573-853-4344, 314-751-4133, 800-877-1234

18TH & VINE HERITAGE JAZZ FESTIVAL
KANSAS CITY ✷ LAST WEEKEND IN AUGUST, SATURDAY AND SUNDAY

The Kansas City jazz scene was born in the African American neighborhood around 18th and Vine, and although the once-thriving corner has seen better days, a resurgence has been in the works since this festival began in 1982. The city's only major free music festival features hometown favorites as well as nationally known stars like jazz trumpeter Terence Blanchard and R&B singer-saxophonist Junior Walker. The Negro Leagues Baseball Museum and the soon-to-be-completed International Jazz Hall of Fame are in the area, and for after-hours jamming, check out the nearby Mutual Musicians Foundation.   **LOCATION:** At the corner of 18th and Vine in Kansas City **TICKETS/INFO:** 816-474-1080; e-mail: vinejazz@worldmall.com **ACCOMMODATIONS/TOURIST INFO:** 800-877-1234

GOLDENROD SHOWBOAT RAGTIME FESTIVAL

ST. CHARLES ✷ LABOR DAY WEEKEND, THURSDAY–SUNDAY (LABOR DAY IS THE FIRST MONDAY IN SEPTEMBER)

Ragtime performers from around the world fill the authentic confines of the Goldenrod Showboat with their elaborate and lively piano rhythms each Labor Day weekend. About 500 fans can catch some 15 individual pianists and string bands, playing simultaneously in the boat's theater, on its deck, and in a small room set aside for informal jams. The old Goldenrod Showboat has hosted the festival for about 30 years, taking the event with it when it moved from the Mississippi to the Missouri River. While you're in the area, be sure to visit the restored Scott Joplin House in downtown St. Louis (Delmar and Jefferson, 314-533-1003), which features an adjoining museum and store specializing in ragtime music, books, and other goods.   **LOCATION:** Goldenrod Showboat in the historic Main Street area in St. Charles, just northwest of the St. Louis metropolitan area **TICKETS/INFO:** 314-946-2020 **ACCOMMODATIONS/TOURIST INFO:** 314-946-7776, 800-877-1234

ST. LOUIS BLUES HERITAGE FESTIVAL

ST. LOUIS ✷ LABOR DAY WEEKEND, SATURDAY AND SUNDAY

When rural African Americans began migrating to the industrial north, the Mississippi River became a musical highway whose riverboats brought the blues from their down-home birthplace to big cities like Chicago, Memphis, and St. Louis. The latter city still has a strong living blues tradition, which boils over every Labor Day weekend in one of the country's biggest and most versatile bluesfests.

For three days, more than 40 blues acts play the sounds that made St. Louis famous, on the historic Laclede's Landing Riverfront. St. Louis wisely makes use of a large number of smaller stages, resulting in a scene that's more intimate than the huge blues events in Chicago and elsewhere. Seven stages include two main, one acoustic, and four street stages featuring gospel, R&B, Mississippi Delta, and even rockabilly.

Each year, the lineup reads like a modern blues who's who, with recent performers including Little Milton, R. L. Burnside, Junior Kimbrough, Otis Clay, Ann Peebles, Coco Montoya, and many others. Local musicians are also featured in the interest of expanding the city's flourishing blues scene, which is characterized by an upbeat R&B variation.

The Microbrews and Blues Pavilion celebrates the dual Missouri traditions of beer brewing and blues making. In a packed tent, acoustic Mississippi Delta blues music is played on the Front Porch Stage, set up like a turn-of-the-century shack, while festivalgoers sample the handmade products of some 20 microbreweries from around the United States. More than 300 kegs of beer are sold, making this one of the largest beer-tasting events in the country and highlighting the demographic overlap between blues lovers and microbrew drinkers.   **LOCATION:** Laclede's Landing Riverfront in down-

Versatile blues: The St. Louis Blues Heritage Festival runs the gamut of blues, R&B, gospel, and even rockabilly. (See entry, page 271.) Courtesy of Peter Wilson/ St. Louis Blues Society

town St. Louis **TICKETS/INFO:** 314-241-2583, 800-325-7962, 314-534-1111 **AC-COMMODATIONS/TOURIST INFO:** 314-421-1023, 800-888-3861, 800-877-1234

♫OONSLICK TRADITIONAL FOLK FESTIVAL
ARROW ROCK ✷ SECOND SATURDAY IN SEPTEMBER

Organizers scour the country for the musicians who play and teach at this single-day adventure into the traditional music of America and the British Isles. Expect to hear anything from Ozark fiddling and Appalachian dulcimer to Scottish ballads and songs of the Civil War. From noon until early evening, four or five acts perform and teach workshops (bring your own instrument) for about 500 people, then everyone participates in contra dancing. Organizers stress that this dancefest is definitely not just for the watching, and they promise that they'll make a contra whiz out of anyone between the ages of two and 75.

After you challenge that boast, you might want to stop by the local fire department's annual hog roast, which is also held this weekend. The village of Arrow Rock has a population of only 70, so all festival musicians and spectators are invited to help finish off the pig. While you're there, be sure to check out Arrow Rock's historic boardwalk, museums, and one of the oldest restaurants west of the Mississippi. Camping and RV hookups are available at a nearby state park.   **LOCATION:** Old School House Community Center, on Main Street in Arrow Rock. Take I-70 west 30 miles from Columbia or east 100 miles from Kansas City, then take Highway 41 north for 13 miles to Arrow Rock. **TICKETS/INFO:** 816-837-3231, 816-837-3330 **ACCOMMODATIONS/TOURIST INFO:** 816-837-3231, 314-751-4133, 800-877-1234

ℐAZZ IN THE PARK FESTIVAL
FULTON ✱ THIRD SATURDAY IN SEPTEMBER

Top-rank Missouri jazz bands that command high cover charges anywhere else can often be heard for free at the Jazz in the Park Festival. For more than a dozen years, Jazz in the Park has drawn three or four bands and some 2,000 people to Veterans Park, often stretching the stylistic boundaries of jazz to include blues and gospel. Organizers pray for good weather, but if it rains, musicians just drag their gear under the picnic pavilion and keep on playing.   **LOCATION:** Veterans Park, 700 East 10th Street in Fulton, 90 miles west of St. Louis. Take I-70 west to U.S. 54 south, then take the Fulton exit to downtown Fulton. **TICKETS/INFO:** 573-642-5075 **ACCOMMODATIONS/TOURIST INFO:** 573-642-3055, 800-877-1234

ℱALL FESTIVAL OF GOSPEL MUSIC
STANTON ✱ THIRD WEEKEND IN OCTOBER, THURSDAY–SATURDAY

Meramec Caverns provides the astounding ambience and acoustics for this historic festival of gospel music hosted by the Lester family. Mom and Pop Lester initiated this "underground" musical tradition of Christian worship in 1925, and their grown children, Brian and Ginger Lester, have teamed up with Ginger's husband, "Smiling Dan" Pitchers, to continue the festival.

The underground cave is outfitted with 2,000 seats, which are filled with a crowd of gospel-hungry spectators all three days of the festival. Church groups often attend, bringing some younger blood to the mostly older audience. Six to eight acts perform during each five-hour concert, and a break between acts allows for cave roaming or snacking. The festival draws national talents like the Dixie Melody Boys and the McKameys; but even if you don't recognize a band's name, you'll immediately recognize its message.   **LOCATION:** Meramec Caverns, 50 miles west of St. Louis off I-44, exit 230 **TICKETS/INFO:** 573-468-3166 **ACCOMMODATIONS/TOURIST INFO:** 573-468-3314, 800-877-1234

𝒢ATEWAY JAZZ FESTIVAL
ST. LOUIS ✱ FIRST WEEKEND IN NOVEMBER, FRIDAY–SUNDAY

The Gateway Jazz Festival brings in some of North America's hottest trad-jazz acts for four multiband concerts over the weekend. Two dance floors get crowded as the likes of Toronto's Climax Jazz Band and California's Hot Frogs Jazz Band lay down shakin' sounds in the ballroom of the Henry VIII Hotel. Tickets are about $20 at the door, with a cash bar.   **LOCATION:** Henry VIII Hotel, 4690 North Lindbergh, Bridgeton. Bridgeton is a suburb of St. Louis, northwest of the city via I-70. **TICKETS/INFO:** 314-388-2600 **ACCOMMODATIONS/TOURIST INFO:** 314-421-1023, 800-888-3861, 800-877-1234

ℱESTIVAL OF GOSPEL MUSIC

COLUMBIA ✷ THANKSGIVING WEEKEND, FRIDAY–SUNDAY (THANKSGIVING IS THE 4TH THURSDAY IN NOVEMBER)

In the old days, this festival's gospel singing took place in a local auditorium, but organizers recently moved it to a hotel to foster more fellowship. The convenience of being able to pass readily from one's private room to the public festivities makes for a laid-back, casual atmosphere in which performers and audiences rub elbows day and night. The festival books 10 regionally and nationally known southern/country gospel groups to entertain 1,500 to 2,000 guests over the weekend. A Saturday morning talent contest draws another 15 to 25 amateur groups from the area.   **LOCATION:** Holiday Inn Convention Center in Columbia. Exit I-70 at Stadium Boulevard and follow the signs. **TICKETS/INFO:** 816-665-7172 **ACCOMMODATIONS/TOURIST INFO:** 314-875-1231, 800-877-1234

NᴇᴮRaSᴋa

ᴇLKHORN VALLEY COUNTRY MUSIC FESTIVAL
FREMONT ✷ LAST FULL WEEKEND IN APRIL, THURSDAY–SUNDAY

This family-oriented festival features four days of country singers, fiddlers, and small-town fun. Although musical events begin Thursday afternoon, most of the contests (which draw musicians from all over the Midwest) take place on Saturday and Sunday. About 600 people show up, and many camp outside the field house that shelters the single stage. Church on Sunday and an alcohol-free setting ensure a clean-cut atmosphere. Admission costs $15 for four days. Elkhorn also holds a similar festival in September.   **LOCATION:** Christensen Field in Fremont, a town about 40 miles northwest of Omaha on U.S. 77 **TICKETS/INFO:** 402-727-7626 **ACCOMMODATIONS/TOURIST INFO:** 402-721-2641

NᴇBRASKA STATE COUNTRY MUSIC CHᴀMPIONSHIP
SYRACUSE ✷ SECOND WEEKEND IN JUNE

Hotshot musicians from all over Nebraska gather at the indoor stage at the Otoe County Fairgrounds to compete in the State Country Music Championships. Even when they're not competing in a contest—such as singing, fiddling, or junior events—many performers hang out at the fairgrounds, jamming with friends. On-site camping is available.   **LOCATION:** Otoe County Fairgrounds, about 30 miles southeast of Lincoln off Highway 2 **TICKETS/INFO:** 402-234-5277 **ACCOMMODATIONS/TOURIST INFO:** 402-269-2957

ᴾOLKA FESTIVAL
ORD ✷ SECOND SUNDAY IN JUNE

Three local polka bands celebrate Ord's Czech heritage with continuous music on two indoor stages. The daylong festivities also include colorful costumes and traditional dances. Of the 300 or so people who attend this event, many camp on the golf course surrounding the lodge, and fish at two nearby dams. Admission costs $6, but bring extra cash for the alcohol and ethnic food that's served all day.   **LOCATION:** The Elk Lodge in Ord, in the middle of the state at the junction of Highways 70 and 11 **TICKETS/INFO:** 308-728-5447 **ACCOMMODATIONS/TOURIST INFO:** 308-728-7875

JULY JAMM
LINCOLN ✹ ONE OF THE LAST TWO WEEKENDS IN JULY, FRIDAY–SUNDAY

Ten or fifteen local, regional, and national bands play an eclectic mix of blues, jazz, reggae, zydeco, salsa, and bluegrass music on one outdoor stage in downtown Lincoln. On Saturday morning, storytellers, dancers, and musicians take the stage for a Kids' Jam. The three-day festival also features food, beer and wine, and a juried art show. July Jamm takes place on whichever weekend the Kansas City Jazz and Blues Fest doesn't, and draws about 20,000 people. Admission is free until 7 P.M., and costs a few dollars after that.   **LOCATION:** Downtown Lincoln, at Twelfth and N Streets **TICKETS/INFO:** 402-434-6900 **ACCOMMODATIONS/TOURIST INFO:** 800-423-8212

ANNUAL NATIONAL COUNTRY MUSIC FESTIVAL
AINSWORTH ✹ SECOND WEEKEND IN AUGUST, SATURDAY AND SUNDAY

This annual competition draws about 100 amateur country bands, fiddlers, pickers, vocalists, spoon players, and others. Though the action centers around contests, the atmosphere remains intimate and relaxing; many musicians come mostly to see (and jam with) old friends. About 2,500 spectators crowd around two outdoor stages, and three judges from Nashville determine the winners. The festival welcomes pets, campers, and kids, but prohibits alcohol, drugs, and "canned music." Camping is free, and $6 buys admission for a day of music.   **LOCATION:** East City Park in Ainsworth, on U.S. 20 about three miles west of U.S. 183 **TICKETS/INFO:** 402-387-2740 **ACCOMMODA-TIONS/TOURIST INFO:** 402-387-2740

BLUEGRASS FESTIVAL
ELGIN ✹ SECOND-TO-LAST WEEKEND IN AUGUST

Elgin sits on the eastern edge of the Nebraska sandhills, and its festival charitably offers the only music of its kind within 125 miles. Admission is free, but fundraisers mingle to elicit donations. On the single outdoor stage, 15-20 bluegrass, country, and gospel bands donate their time and talent to raise money for the town's historical society. Offstage, fiddlers and banjoists spontaneously unite for informal jam sessions. The park offers camping, playground equipment, a swimming pool, and a concession stand. Bring lunch, a blanket, kids and pets, but leave the alcohol at home.   **LOCATION:** The City Park, at North Street and Plantation Drive in Elgin, about 11 miles south of Neligh at the junction of Highways 14 and 70 **TICKETS/INFO:** 402-843-5307 **ACCOMMODA-TIONS/TOURIST INFO:** 402-843-2455

ELKHORN VALLEY COUNTRY MUSIC FESTIVAL
FREMONT ✹ FIRST WEEKEND IN SEPTEMBER

This is a semiannual event, happening the last full weekend in April and the first weekend in September. See page 275 for details.   **LOCATION:** Christensen Field in Fremont, about 40 miles northwest of Omaha on U.S. 77 **TICKETS/INFO:** 402-727-7626 **ACCOMMODATIONS/TOURIST INFO:** 402-721-2641

July Jamm: Luther Allison wows the Lincoln crowd with his guitar pyrotech-nics. Courtesy of Ken Jones/July Jamm

✎ILLIGAN MINI-POLKA DAY
MILLIGAN ✱ LAST SUNDAY IN SEPTEMBER

Four regional Czech polka bands play on one indoor stage in a 12-hour festival that seeks to preserve traditional Czech language, music, dancing, food, and fun. Upstairs, dancers polka on a new dance floor (a couple of decades of polkas wore out the old one). Downstairs, dancers gather for Czech dinner, usually featuring pork, kolachkis, and other traditional fare. "Fortysomething" couples prevail, and many may be heard lamenting the fact that "the young people" rarely attend.   **LOCATION:** Milligan Auditorium, about 50 miles southwest of Lincoln just off Highway 41 **TICKETS/INFO:** 402-629-4332 **ACCOMMODATIONS/TOURIST INFO:** 402-759-3399.

☺CTOBER MUSIC FEST

HOLDREGE ✷ SECOND FRIDAY IN OCTOBER

"Leave your troubles on the outside, and maybe when you leave here tonight they won't be there anymore," suggests the host of this festival for and by senior citizens. The retired professional musicians who charitably provide the music (talents mostly from northern Kansas) include soloists (such as piano or voice) and three or four "kitchen bands." Performers sign up ahead of time to play an instrument (sometimes homemade) or present a comedy routine (distinguished older men have been known to don tutus and perform a ballet). The festival provides a chance for seniors to showcase known talents and discover hidden ones, leaving thoughts of age behind in an atmosphere of laughter, food, music, and fun. Call ahead for tickets and reservations.   **LOCATION:** Holdrege City Auditorium, at Fifth and Grant Streets. (Holdrege is about 15 miles south of I-80, and about 75 miles west of Grand Island.) **TICKETS/INFO:** 308-995-5345 **ACCOMMODATIONS/TOURIST INFO:** 308-995-4444

NORTH DAKOTA

OLD-TIME FIDDLERS CONTEST AND JAMBOREE
WEST FARGO ✶ FIRST WEEKEND IN JULY, SATURDAY AND SUNDAY

This area's only fiddle contest takes place in Bonanzaville, an early 1900s pioneer-theme village. Fiddlers come from all over the country to compete and perform. The main indoor stage looks like it could be anywhere, but the surrounding village gets a distinctly historic feel from its log homes, sod house, general stores, barbershops, drug stores, historic schoolhouse, and 100-year-old church. Contests in various categories and age groups command the daytime hours, and an open-stage jamboree and barbecue/dance enliven Saturday night. Sunday morning begins with an old-time fiddling gospel hour. **LOCATION:** The Demonstration Building in Bonanzaville, on West Main Avenue in West Fargo. Take exit 343 off I-94. **TICKETS/INFO:** 701-282-2822, 800-700-5317 **ACCOMMODATIONS/TOURIST INFO:** 800-435-5663, 701-328-2525

COUNTRY WESTERN JAMBOREE
MEDORA ✶ LAST SUNDAY IN JULY

Local talents gather to play country music for a day of jammin' good family entertainment in a town that's only three blocks long. Just pull into town and perk up your ears to find the Community Center; if you can't find it, they'll take away your car keys. **LOCATION:** Medora Community Center. From Highway I-94, take exit 27 or 24. **TICKETS/INFO:** 701-623-4444, 701-623-4310 **ACCOMMODATIONS/TOURIST INFO:** 800-435-5663, 701-328-2525

RIVER JAZZ FEST
FARGO ✶ SEVEN DAYS BEGINNING THE FIRST OR THE THIRD
MONDAY IN AUGUST

Jazz comes to Fargo in the late summer with diverse jazz styles, venues, and show times that offer something for the whole community. Weekdays feature noon concerts in a downtown plaza, and evenings usher in performances at Fargo's downtown bars and parks (such as Playmakers, Old Broadway, and Gooseberry Park). Up to three events each night include lectures, performances, and workshops geared to high school and college students from the tristate region.

Fiddlers' frolic:
All ages get into
the action at the
Old-Time Fid-
dlers Contest
and Jamboree.
(See entry, page
279.) Courtesy of Clayton

Wolt/North Dakota Tourism

A Cajun picnic Tuesday evening lets workshop teachers showcase their talents (an original piece composed by one of the guest artists is performed), while the public feasts on Cajun food and big band sounds. Sunday's outdoor ecumenical Jazz Mass draws 300 people and features "jazz church music," composed by Fargo teacher and musician Ed Christiansen.

The week's events culminate in two full days of concerts at Trollwood Park's outdoor main stage, showcasing guest artists that have included trumpeter Terence Blanchard, trombone player Tom "Bones" Malone, and composer-pianist Frank Mantooth. The festival's weeklong show of hospitality draws nearly 10,000 people from throughout the tristate region (Minnesota and the two Dakotas).   **LOCATION:** Trollwood Park, between Broadway and Elm Streets on Trollwood Drive and various other locations in Fargo. Both I-94 and I-29 pass through Fargo. **TICKETS/INFO:** 701-241-8160, 701-231-8337 **ACCOMMODATIONS/TOURIST INFO:** 800-435-5663, 701-328-2525

ℱROGGY 99.9'S COUNTRY JAM

FARGO ✷ SECOND SUNDAY IN AUGUST

Folks of all ages gather to hear their favorite contemporary country songs played by regional artists on an outdoor stage beside the Red River. The event is especially family-friendly, giving mom, dad, and the kids a chance to catch live country music outside the confines of smoky saloons.   **LOCATION:** Trollwood Park, at the end of North Broadway and 37th Avenue North, along the Red River (between Broadway and Elm Streets, on Trollwood Drive). Both I-94 and I-29 pass through Fargo. **TICKETS/INFO:** 701-241-8160, 218-233-1522 **ACCOMMODATIONS/TOURIST INFO:** 800-435-5663, 701-328-2525

ℳISSOURI RIVER BLUEGRASS AND OLD-TIME MUSIC FESTIVAL

HENSLER ✷ LABOR DAY WEEKEND, SATURDAY AND SUNDAY (LABOR DAY IS THE FIRST MONDAY IN SEPTEMBER)

This low-key event brings locals and their lawn chairs to a riverside park and campground to enjoy six old-time country and bluegrass acts under the cottonwoods. Bands from the Dakotas, Minnesota, and Canada take turns onstage from 1 P.M. until 9:30 P.M., both Saturday and Sunday. After hours, performers gather at the park grounds maintenance shop or build bonfires by their campers and tents, jamming away the country evening. Food vendors and children's entertainment are on hand. **LOCATION:** Cross Ranch State Park near Hensler. Hensler is on Highway 200A, about three miles west of U.S. 83. From Hensler follow the signs that lead you five miles south, five miles east, and two miles north. **TICKETS/INFO:** 701-794-3731 **ACCOMMODA-TIONS/TOURIST INFO:** 800-435-5663, 701-328-2525

℘OLKAFEST

MANDAN ✷ SECOND WEEKEND IN OCTOBER, FRIDAY–SUNDAY

You'll see many regulars at this event, including a group of avid retirees who whirl through the continental polka circuit every year, and younger folk who love the songs and dances of their German ancestors. Six regional bands carpet the wooden floor with mostly German-style polkas, and musicians often don wigs and costumes to provoke the crowd into abandoning their inhibitions. The event draws 600 to 800 revelers for the weekend, and tasty German fare is prepared by local matrons. A weekend pass is $18. **LOCATION:** Mandan Community Center, 901 Division Street. (Mandan town is just west of Bismarck, across the Missouri River.) **TICKETS/INFO:** 701-663-1136 **ACCOM-MODATIONS/TOURIST INFO:** 800-435-5663, 701-328-2525

JAZZ BANJO FESTIVAL
GUTHRIE ✷ MEMORIAL DAY WEEKEND, FRIDAY–SUNDAY (MEMORIAL DAY IS THE LAST MONDAY IN MAY)

Outside bluegrass circles, the banjo is a much-maligned country cousin of the guitar, often thought of as nothing but a novelty instrument. But in Guthrie, for three days each year, the banjo gets to hog the spotlight and demonstrate its underground sophistication, range, and versatility.

At the first of Guthrie's banjo-playin' bashes back in 1992, jaws dropped when a group of banjo players offered up "Rhapsody in Blue" in four- and six-part harmony. If you're not familiar with what the banjo can do—or even if you think you are—this festival is full of surprises. From soloists to small groups, to 25-banjo orchestras, expect continuous entertainment in several of Guthrie's historic, Victorian venues.

You'll hear Dixieland, ragtime, and big band sounds, as well as more experimental jazz and tastes of everything else. The Granny Had One Restaurant, the Bluebell Saloon, and other colorful hot-spots host up to 150 banjoists from all over the U.S. and Europe. **LOCATION:** The area around Oklahoma and Harrison Streets in downtown Guthrie, 30 minutes north of Oklahoma City off I-35 (the Guthrie exit leads you right downtown) **TICKETS/INFO:** 800-652-2656 **ACCOMMODATIONS/TOURIST INFO:** 800-299-1889, 405-282-1947

MOZART INTERNATIONAL FESTIVAL
BARTLESVILLE ✷ TEN DAYS BEGINNING THE SECOND WEEK IN JUNE

An oil town in the Osage Hills may seem an unlikely place for an internationally acclaimed classical music festival, but thanks to an interesting series of events, the sounds of old Salzburg enrich Bartlesville for 10 days each summer. This town of 35,000 was "discovered" in 1983 when the Solisti New York Orchestra (then in its third year) passed through on a midwestern tour. Perhaps expecting one more gymnasium-style venue with a leaky roof, Solisti founder and conductor Ransom Wilson said he was "speechless" to discover one of the world's acoustical gems, the Bartlesville Community Center Concert Hall, which was built in 1982 to the design of William Wesley Peters. Legend has it that Wilson, en route to the airport after the concert, wistfully murmured how lovely it would be "if only" the orchestra could play there annually.

Guthrie's Jazz Banjo Festival highlights the surprising capabilities of the guitar's country cousin. Photo by Fred W. Marvel, courtesy of Oklahoma Tourism

Nan Buhlinger, who happened to be driving Wilson to the airport, caught the cue and immediately set to the task of raising money for what has since become an acclaimed annual event. Since the festival began in 1985, it's lured world-class guest artists like cellist Lynn Harrell and violinist Joshua Bell. The crack Solisti New York Orchestra has continued to visit each summer as the orchestra-in-residence, and conductor-flutist extraordinaire Ransom Wilson continues to serve as artistic director.

Eight concerts are presented in the esteemed 1700-seat community center, which boasts not only the near perfect acoustics that won Wilson's heart but also very good sight lines. You'll hear works by Mozart and 18th-century composers like Bach, Beethoven, Ravel, and Schubert. The festival also makes creative use of several other intriguing Bartlesville spaces, including local churches for Chamber Concert Series, Woolaroc Ranch and Museum for outdoor concerts, and the Frank Lloyd Wright-designed Price Tower for miniconcerts (which sometimes focus on 20th-century works).

Bartlesville seems surprisingly sophisticated for a town of 35,000, and organizers were astute in adding extra musical events to keep the many visiting out-of-state urbanites in town during musical off hours. Thus the town is filled with Festival Showcase events like an "organ crawl" through the lofts of local churches, architectural and ranch tours, equestrian competitions, and craft workshops. The festival now boasts an extended season, and in the past has hosted concerts by Marvin Hamlisch and by the Vienna Boys' Choir. Ticket prices for evening concerts range from $12 to $18. **LOCATION:** Bartlesville Community Center Concert Hall, Adams at Cherokee Boulevards. Bartlesville is 46 miles north of Tulsa via U.S. 75. **TICKETS/INFO:** 918-336-

9800, 918-336-9900 **ACCOMMODATIONS/TOURIST INFO:** 918-336-8708, 800-364-8708

℞ED EARTH NATIVE AMERICAN CULTURAL FESTIVAL

OKLAHOMA CITY ✷ SECOND WEEKEND IN JUNE, FRIDAY–SUNDAY

The songs, dances, and costumes of America's first people draw more than 100,000 visitors to one of the country's largest and most colorful celebrations of Native American culture. With parades, crafts, and symposia, this event is a huge, 10-ring circus—but music lovers will be drawn to the dance competitions, where an astounding range of Indian drumming and singing propels dancers through their routines.

The continent's best singers and drummers form the eight Native American drum groups that create Red Earth's musical pulse. Here, you'll find both northern and southern drum-group traditions, with their distinct styles and repertoires. Singers in northern drum groups usually maintain a higher, almost falsetto pitch, while southern singers usually occupy the baritone range. Northern beats typically continue unchanged through the entire song, while southern groups incorporate quickening tempos after the opening is sung by the lead singer, as well as dramatic changes at song's end.

Most drum groups play traditional songs from their own tribes, but some—like Yellowhammer, composed of 11 singer-drummers from the Ponca and Otoe-Missouri tribes—perform their own original compositions. Powwow superstars like the Mandaree Singing Group, Black Lodge, and the Blackstone Singers have often appeared at Red Earth Lodge, as have Native American traditional flutists. Depending on the year, you might hear everything from Native American gospel (usually sung in English with some interesting rhythmic idiosyncrasies), to southwest-style "chicken scratch" (a variation of the Mexican-style polka).

The dance arena has two stages and seats 12,500—a good thing because nearly 125,000 people attend over the weekend. The festival kicks off Friday morning with the Red Earth Parade, which sets the streets of Oklahoma City ablaze with the fiery colors of more than 1,000 Native American dancers in full regalia, plus dignitaries, tribal princesses, floats, and bands from more than 100 tribes. As the parade moves through the streets, drum groups sing and bang out marching rhythms from the back of pickup trucks.

If you miss the parade, daily grand entries take place at the Myriad Convention Center Arena. Beyond traditional Native American music and dance, the festival is rich in attractions like an American Indian video and film competition, a juried art show and sale, storytelling, lectures, and activities for children. Admission costs $10 for one day or $25 for the weekend. Organizers insist that you leave alcohol and pets at home. **LOCATION:** Myriad Convention Center and Plaza, at One Myriad Garden in downtown Oklahoma City **TICKETS/INFO:** 405-427-5228 **ACCOMMODATIONS/TOURIST INFO:** 405-297-8900, 405-297-8912, 800-225-5652

℠ANDERS FAMILY BLUEGRASS FESTIVAL

MCALESTER ✷ SECOND FULL WEEKEND IN JUNE, WEDNESDAY–SATURDAY

About 20 years ago, Fred Sanders thought it would be a good idea to round up some bluegrassers to come and play on his farm. Little did he know that his humble hoo-hah would grow into one of the top events on the hillbilly highway, a sprawling, family-

*Red Earth: In-
dian drumming
and singing pro-
pel dancers at
one of the na-
tion's most color-
ful celebrations
of Native Ameri-
can culture.* Courtesy

of Red Earth, Inc.

oriented gig that attracts 6,000 bluegrass fanatics each year. Nowadays, the Sanders family can take their pick from the top echelon of bluegrass bands, so you won't find many duds among the 24 acts that play on the single stage. Bonus: campsite jamming on the wooded grounds is legendary.   **LOCATION:** Five and one-half miles west of McAlester (which is 67 miles southwest of Muskogee), on Highway 270 **TICKETS/ INFO:** 918-423-4891 **ACCOMMODATIONS/TOURIST INFO:** 918-423-2550

℞EGGAEFEST

TULSA ✴ THIRD WEEKEND IN JUNE, FRIDAY AND SATURDAY

Reggaefest celebrates Jamaican music with 12 reggae bands on two outdoor stages in the River West Festival Park. Performers include local, regional, and national talents. Jamaican food and crafts are also featured. Admission is $7.   **LOCATION:** River West Festival Park, 2100 South Jackson Avenue, north of 23rd Street, on the west bank of the Arkansas River **TICKETS/INFO:** 918-596-2001 **ACCOMMODATIONS/TOURIST INFO:** 918-585-1201

ℐAZZ IN JUNE

NORMAN ✷ LAST FULL WEEKEND IN JUNE, THURSDAY–SUNDAY

This free summer festival transforms a restored theater, a shopping area, and a city park into three venues for four nights of jazz in the college town of Norman. The university radio station, KGOU, founded the festival in 1985 to showcase diverse styles ranging from gospel- and blues-inspired veterans to up-and-coming talents. Up to 16 different acts appear at outdoor venues (where picnics, pets, and alcohol are welcome) and an indoor theater (where they aren't). A Children's Gypsy Camp entertains the kids on Sunday afternoon.   **LOCATION:** Brookhaven Village, the Sooner Theater, and Andrews Park. Norman is the home of the University of Oklahoma, and is located about 20 miles south of Oklahoma City via I-35. **TICKETS/INFO:** 405-325-5468 **ACCOMMO-DATIONS/TOURIST INFO:** 405-321-7260, 405-366-8095

ℳMERICAN MUSIC FESTIVAL

DUNCAN ✷ SECOND OR THIRD WEEKEND IN JULY, THURSDAY–SUNDAY

This young festival (begun in 1993) brings a musical program of surprising diversity and depth to Duncan, a small town with a big-city taste for the arts. The focus is, of course, on American music—classical, jazz, Broadway, and other styles—and each year sees at least one world premiere of a new American composition. Held in the acoustically excellent theater at the Simmons Center, the concerts have featured every-one from trumpeter Al Hurt to vocalist Susan Powell, guitarist Mason Williams, and the Dallas Wind Symphony. Tickets are no more than $25 per event.   **LOCATION:** Simmons Center, 800 North 29th Street, in Duncan. Duncan is 86 miles southwest of Oklahoma City, just off U.S. 81. **TICKETS/INFO:** 800-255-0909 **ACCOMMODA-TIONS/TOURIST INFO:** 405-255-3644

𝒞HARLIE CHRISTIAN JAZZ FESTIVAL

OKLAHOMA CITY ✷ LAST WEEKEND IN JULY, SATURDAY AND SUNDAY

Celebrating the work of Oklahoma City jazz great Charlie Christian, this festival brings some 20 jazz bands to the historic, ramshackle Deep Deuce neighborhood of Oklahoma City. Nationally known veterans like Joe McBride and Jay "Hootie" McShann trade the two outdoor stages with musicians from around Oklahoma, drawing some 30,000 people over two days. Festival extras include a Gospelfest on Sunday and a Guitar Jam Thursday evening.

Charlie Christian was an African American guitarist who grew up in Oklahoma City and rose to prominence in Benny Goodman's band in the early 1940s. Christian pioneered the technique of putting a microphone inside his guitar to amplify the sound, contributing to the development of what would become the electric guitar. His ingenious guitar phrasings made him a legend in the jazz world of the thirties and forties, and although he died of tuberculosis at the height of his career—at age 26—his influence continues.

The 300 block of Northeast Second Street, known as the Deep Deuce, was a thriving African American community in the prewar days, crowded with juke joints and jazz clubs. Although a few historic buildings remain, many more vacant lots serve as reminders of a lost prosperity. For two days each year, jazz music returns to the neighborhood that helped to create it.   **LOCATION:** The 300 block of Northeast

Second Street, between Central and Stiles, in Oklahoma City **TICKETS/INFO:** 405-232-5281 **ACCOMMODATIONS/TOURIST INFO:** 405-297-8900, 405-297-8912

GRANT'S BLUEGRASS FESTIVAL
HUGO ✴ FIVE DAYS BEGINNING THE FIRST WEDNESDAY IN AUGUST

Legend has it that back in 1967, bluegrass pioneer Bill Monroe was hanging out at Bill Grant's house and in the middle of a late-night jam session suggested that Grant start his own bluegrass festival. Two years later, Grant was up and running, with a two-day festival that drew less than 1,000 people.

These days, attendance is up to around 25,000 over five days, and with a quarter-century under its belt, Grant's is the oldest bluegrass festival west of the Mississippi. A list of the performers who've played at Grant's would be tantamount to a roster of everyone who's achieved any measure of success in the genre, and it should suffice to say that if you visit Grant's three years in a row, you'll have seen nearly all of bluegrass music's legends.

Each day brings nonstop hillbilly licks from 10 A.M. through midnight, and the music is definitely *not* confined to the stage. Everywhere, campers and tents are surrounded by music makers, and whenever a young mandolin or dobro whiz catches a groove, word travels fast and enthusiastic crowds gather. Founder and host Bill Grant has a good ear for this kind of fresh talent, and often the lineup includes several hot up-and-coming acts. Grant himself typically makes an appearance or two on stage as well. **LOCATION:** Salt Creek Park, on Bill Grant Road, just outside Hugo in southeast Oklahoma off U.S. 271 **TICKETS/INFO:** 405-326-5598 **ACCOMMODATIONS/TOURIST INFO:** 405-326-7511

OKLAHOMA ALL-NIGHT SINGING
KONAWA ✴ FIRST SATURDAY IN AUGUST

Beginning at 6 P.M. and wrapping up at five in the morning, quartets from across the nation entertain thousands at this unique annual gospel music homecoming. Some 30,000 people sit under the trees, singing the songs of salvation and seeing who can stay awake the longest as 15 or more groups perform. The music is mainly in the Southern/country gospel tradition, but organizers stress that people of all races and creeds are welcome. In addition to music, there's plenty of righteous politicking and preaching, and a citywide garage sale precedes the event.   **LOCATION:** Veterans Memorial Park in Konawa, on Highway 39 about four miles west of U.S. 377, about 55 miles southeast of Oklahoma City **TICKETS/INFO:** 405-925-3434 **ACCOMMODATIONS/TOURIST INFO:** 405-925-3283

BOK/WILLIAMS JAZZ ON GREENWOOD
TULSA ✴ WEEKEND CLOSEST TO AUGUST 15, WEDNESDAY–SATURDAY

From rather humble beginnings—in 1988, Tulsa wanted to showcase its newly restored Greenwood area—this festival has grown into a three-stage, four-evening jazz extravaganza. Nearly 100,000 people pack in to hear jazz greats like Dave Brubeck, Cab Calloway, and Natalie Cole, as well as not-so-jazzy crowd pleasers like Buckwheat Zydeco. Best of all, the musical happenings are all free.   **LOCATION:** The corner of Archer and Greenwood Streets, just north of downtown Tulsa off U.S. 244 **TICKETS/INFO:** 918-584-3378 **ACCOMMODATIONS/TOURIST INFO:** 918-585-1201

⁶ⒹUSK 'TIL DAWN BLUES FESTIVAL

RENTIESVILLE ✳ LABOR DAY WEEKEND, FRIDAY–SUNDAY (LABOR DAY IS THE FIRST MONDAY IN SEPTEMBER)

Finally, a blues festival done the way the blues were meant to be done: late at night, in a nightclub. Oklahoma's "blues diplomat," D.C. Minner, yearly offers up his birthplace and bar to host 100 fellow blues muses from a dozen or so states in the United States. The musicians' diverse regional origins translate into a range of blues styles, so you can expect to hear everything from smooth Delta blues and down-home South Carolina blues to harmonica-heavy Chicago blues, progressive New Orleans blues, soulful R&B, and even zydeco, with its Creole accordions and washboards.

The festival often begins Friday night with a kickoff performance in Muskogee, then moves to D.C. Minner's Downhome Blues Club in Rentiesville. Saturday's show begins outdoors at 5 P.M. with local acts (expect full bands and strong guitars) and moves indoors to the bar at midnight, where headliners swap the stage every hour or two until around 4 A.M. At that point, guitarist-vocalist Minner leads an all-star jam that often includes his wife Selby (on bass and vocals) and everyone who's played earlier.

Sunday festivities typically begin with a gospel concert at 3 P.M. (which is free for seniors) and continue at 5 P.M. with outdoor music until midnight. At that point, the show again moves indoors to the Downhome Blues Club, with headliners and jamming continuing until 5 A.M. Monday. Since Monday's a holiday, there's often more music when everyone wakes up (around 2 or 3 P.M.).

Minner's connections enable him to bring in some of the best the blues has to offer, and recent years have featured stars like Drink Small, Lucky Peterson, Johnny Adams, and Rosie Ledet. Admission is a bargain at about $10 each night, and other attractions include Okie-style BBQ and African American crafts. Some folks camp or drive their motor homes onto the field next to the bar in this rural town 75 miles southeast of Tulsa. **LOCATION:** Friday: Hatbox Field, 540 South 40th Street in Muskogee, behind the Denny's on U.S. 69. Saturday and Sunday: Downhome Blues Club in Rentiesville, about five miles northeast of the intersection of U.S. 69 and I-40. From U.S. 69, take the Rentiesville-Checotah exit, then drive one mile north and two miles east, following signs to the festival. **TICKETS/INFO:** 918-473-2411 **ACCOMMODATIONS/TOURIST INFO:** 918-682-2401

ⓖ⁹ENE AUTRY FILM AND MUSIC FESTIVAL WEEKEND

GENE AUTRY ✳ FRIDAY AND SATURDAY CLOSEST TO SEPTEMBER 29 (GENE AUTRY'S BIRTHDAY)

As the embodiment of truth, justice, and true happiness the American way, Gene Autry rode onto the silver screen and yodeled his way into America's Depression-weary hearts. This festival is possibly the only one dedicated to B-movie singing cowboys like Autry, Roy Rogers, Tex Ritter, and Jimmy Wakely, and it offers musical entertainment from old-style singers seeking to recreate those days that never were.

About 26 men are known to have made singing-cowboy movies, and of the seven or eight who survive, most are too old to come—although Herb Jeffries, the only African American singing cowboy, recently cut a new CD and has been invited to appear. Close to 1,000 people from all over the United States ride their steel steeds into the town of Gene Autry to hear early country and western and cowboy songs and watch screenings of cowboy movies. Visitors typically stay in the nearby town of Ardmore; festival admission is $5 per day.   **LOCATION:** Gene Autry Oklahoma Museum is in the town of Gene Autry, on state Highway 53, eight miles east of I-35, 10 miles north of U.S. 70, and four miles west of U.S. 177, in the south-central part of the state (near the town of Ardmore). **TICKETS/INFO:** 405-389-5335 **ACCOMMODATIONS/TOURIST INFO:** 405-223-7765

KTOBERFEST

TULSA ✳ THIRD FULL WEEKEND IN OCTOBER

Because of its commitment to authentic music, Tulsa's Oktoberfest stands out from America's many mediocre copycats. In addition to several acts imported from Europe, you'll find North American musicians who are faithfully preserving Teutonic traditions. Five entertainment tents in a seven-acre park feature the music of Germany, Austria, and Switzerland. The action centers around the Bier Garten, which features foot-stomping polkas, Viennese melodies, Alpine folk, and international folk dancers. Beyond the musical fare, the festival offers the typical food and crafts; and children enjoy a Root Bier Garten with live entertainment. Despite the festival's name and the long tradition of robust beers to come out of Germany, the event features only the indistinct beers of its American mass-market sponsors. *Schade!*   **LOCATION:** River West Festival Park, 2100 South Jackson Avenue, north of 23rd Street, on the west bank of the Arkansas River **TICKETS/INFO:** 918-596-2001 **ACCOMMODATIONS/TOURIST INFO:** 918-585-1201

SOUTH DAKOTA

𝒥ESTIVAL OF CHOIRS, USA
SIOUX FALLS ✴ LAST WEEKEND IN APRIL, FRIDAY AND SATURDAY

This choirfest attracts some 800 high school students from around the Midwest for a weekend of rehearsal and performance under the leadership of renowned guest directors. A nationally known choir is brought in to sing and provide inspiration for the students, who perform within the categories of mass choir, mixed chorus, male chorus, women's chorus, show choir, and madrigals.   **LOCATION:** Several local high school and college buildings in Sioux Falls **TICKETS/INFO:** 605-367-7957 **ACCOMMODA-TIONS/TOURIST INFO:** 605-336-1620, 605-773-3301

𝒟AKOTA DAYS BAND FESTIVAL
RAPID CITY ✴ MEMORIAL DAY WEEKEND, FRIDAY–MONDAY (MEMORIAL DAY IS THE LAST MONDAY IN MAY)

Some 20 marching bands from around the country parade through downtown Rapid City, then take part in concert competitions, clinics, dances, and pizza parties. Hundreds of spectators turn out for this event, held in the heart of the Black Hills. **LOCATION:** Rapid City Civic Center, at 444 Mount Rushmore Road, and other in-town locations **TICKETS/INFO:** 605-343-1744 **ACCOMMODATIONS/TOURIST INFO:** 800-487-3223, 605-343-1744, 605-773-3301

𝐵LACK HILLS BLUEGRASS FESTIVAL
ROCKERVILLE ✴ LAST FULL WEEKEND IN JUNE (FRIDAY EVENING–SUNDAY MORNING)

This family-oriented festival expands on a bluegrass base to include folk, gospel, and other acoustic music. The program includes concerts by half a dozen bands, plus workshops, clogging, and many opportunities for jam sessions (note that alcohol isn't allowed in the concert area). The site, which is only 10 miles from Mount Rushmore, has plenty of camping.   **LOCATION:** Mystery Mountain Resort, nine miles south of Rapid

Black Hills hoedown: Hillbilly rhythms thrive in the shadow of Mt. Rushmore during the Black Hills Bluegrass Festival. Courtesy of South Dakota Tourism

City on U.S. 16 **TICKETS/INFO:** 605-394-4101 **ACCOMMODATIONS/TOURIST INFO:** 605-343-1744, 605-658-2267, 605-773-3301

ℬLACK HILLS JAZZ AND BLUES FESTIVAL

RAPID CITY ✷ FOURTH SATURDAY IN JULY

This outdoor fest features five nationally and locally known bands between noon and early evening. Begun in 1990, the festival recently moved from a ski resort to Rapid City's Memorial Park, in the process gaining the community support it needed to offer free admission. Food and beverage concessions are available.   **LOCATION:** Memorial Park at Fifth and New York Streets, one block north of Highway 44, in Rapid City **TICKETS/INFO:** 605-394-4101; e-mail: rbrennan@tmn.com **ACCOMMODATIONS/ TOURIST INFO:** 800-487-3223, 605-343-1744, 605-773-3301

SIOUX RIVER FOLK FESTIVAL

CANTON ✳ FIRST FULL WEEKEND IN AUGUST

Set in a shady oak forest in South Dakota's hilly southeastern corner, this low-key event has a long history as the only folk/roots festival in the region. For more than 15 years, organizers have brought in at least a couple of well-known headliners, recently featuring fiddle great Natalie MacMaster, singer-songwriter James McCandless, and progressive bluegrasser Peter Rowan. Most musical guests play two sets on a permanently covered outdoor stage, alternating with local folk, bluegrass, and roots acts. A family-oriented crowd of about 1,200 savors the relaxed atmosphere and takes advantage of children's activities, "quality organic junk food," and a coffee bar. Camping is available, and early arrivals are treated to a Friday night dance. Note that you'll need a South Dakota State Park entrance permit to enter the park.   **LOCATION:** Newton Hills State Park. From I-29, take exit 56, go east about 10 miles, and follow the signs. **TICKETS/INFO:** 605-987-2582, 605-743-5647 **ACCOMMODATIONS/TOURIST INFO:** 800-710-2267, 605-336-1620, 605-773-3301

HILLS ALIVE

SPEARFISH ✳ THIRD WEEKEND IN AUGUST, FRIDAY AND SATURDAY

The northern reaches of the Black Hills are alive with contemporary Christian songs like "Why Should the Devil Have All the Good Music?" (written by Larry Norman). Up to 8,000 people turn out on peak days to socialize, sing praises, and let the kids run wild within the confines of the many children's activity areas. Radio station KSLT runs a tight ship, presenting eight or nine bands representing a full range of contemporary Christian styles, including ballads, gospel songs, rock 'n' roll, and rap.   **LOCATION:** Spearfish City Park in Spearfish, near South Dakota's western border with Wyoming. From I-90, take Jackson Boulevard to Canyon Street and go left to the park. **TICKETS/INFO:** 605-642-7792 **ACCOMMODATIONS/TOURIST INFO:** 605-642-2626, 605-773-3301

DEADWOOD JAM

DEADWOOD ✳ SECOND SATURDAY AFTER LABOR DAY (LABOR DAY IS THE FIRST MONDAY IN SEPTEMBER)

Deadwood's historic buildings are again filled with the gaudy casinos that once attracted Wild Bill Hickok and Calamity Jane—but no one is betting on anything but a good time at the outdoor Deadwood Jam. Rock, pop, country, and blues serenade revelers on Main Street, which is blocked off to accommodate a stage and more than 5,000 people. The Deadwood Jam typically brings in national and local talent from several genres (about seven bands appear during the autumn day and evening), and tickets are about $18 at the gate.   **LOCATION:** Main Street in Deadwood, 42 miles west of Rapid City via I-90 and U.S. 85 **TICKETS/INFO:** 605-578-1102 **ACCOMMODATIONS/TOURIST INFO:** 605-578-1102, 605-773-3301

GREAT PLAINS OLD-TIME FIDDLERS CONTEST

YANKTON ✳ THIRD WEEKEND IN SEPTEMBER, FRIDAY–SUNDAY

Some of the nation's best fiddlers converge for this invitational contest and jamboree, held on a 4-H grounds with plenty of elbow room. Friday night's big jam and talent show lasts for more than four hours and draws hundreds of spectators. The contest

Sure bet on Main Street: The Deadwood Jam brings rock, pop, country, and blues to the historic gambling town. Courtesy of Deadwood Jam

itself is Saturday (contestants *must* register in advance so organizers can print a program telling the audience all about each fiddler), and Sunday morning dawns with a free gospel-fiddle service. A weekend pass runs about $12.   **LOCATION:** Yankton 4-H Grounds, on the 900 block of Whiting Drive, just across the street from the Senior Center. Yankton is in the southeast corner of South Dakota. **TICKETS/INFO:** 605-665-3636 **ACCOMMODATIONS/TOURIST INFO:** 605-665-3636, 605-773-3301

ESTIVAL OF BANDS, USA

SIOUX FALLS ✷ FIRST SATURDAY IN OCTOBER

Marching-band lovers can experience the finest high school and college bands in the Midwest as more than 40 competing and guest bands perform in parade and field competitions. The festival makes use of several football fields, and the parade passes right through the heart of Sioux Falls.   **LOCATION:** Several fields and a parade route through central Sioux Falls **TICKETS/INFO:** 605-367-7957 **ACCOMMODATIONS/TOURIST INFO:** 605-336-1620, 605-773-3301

MOUNTAIN STATES

COLORADO

COLORADO MID-WINTER BLUEGRASS FESTIVAL

FORT COLLINS ✸ THIRD WEEKEND IN FEBRUARY

The Colorado winter embraces the sounds of the Kentucky summer at this rapidly growing festival that diversifies its program well beyond bluegrass. Inflections of Celtic and folk enrich the festival's bluegrassy voice and its never-too-serious atmosphere. A highlight is an underwater banjo contest, which many insist "you have to be there to understand." Audience members jam with performers on three indoor stages, and arts and crafts booths are scattered around the venues.   **LOCATION:** At the Holiday Inn, 3836 East Mulberry Street, and Plaza Inn, 3709 East Mulberry Street, both near the junction of I-25 and Highway 14 in Fort Collins **TICKETS/INFO:** 970-482-0863 **ACCOMMODATIONS/TOURIST INFO:** 800-274-3678, 970-482-5821

UNC/GREELEY JAZZ FESTIVAL

GREELEY ✸ LAST WEEKEND IN APRIL, THURSDAY–SATURDAY

Presented by the jazz studies program at the University of Northern Colorado, this festival welcomes both jazz virtuosos and jazz flunkies to its program of clinics and concerts. A consistently respectable lineup of world-renowned jazz veterans such as Joe Williams and Milt Hinton play nighttime concerts, while at free daytime clinics any Jane or Joe can sit at the knees of a jazz hero. Students from Colorado colleges and high schools also perform.   **LOCATION:** Union Colony Civic Center at 701 Tenth Avenue in downtown Greeley **TICKETS/INFO:** 800-315-2787, 970-356-5000 **ACCOMMODATIONS/TOURIST INFO:** 970-352-3566

JAZZ IN THE SANGRES

WESTCLIFFE ✸ SECOND WEEKEND IN MAY, SATURDAY AND SUNDAY

The cool stylings of national and regional jazz artists float through the mountain air once a year in this cowboy town of 300. Alongside some great BBQ and Indian fry bread, the festival serves up musical fare featuring the flavors of Latin jazz, gospel, and fusion. The music starts Saturday, but a wine-tasting festival on Friday helps get everyone in the mood. Rooms sell out quickly, so unless you're fond of sleeping in your back seat, book accommodations early.   **LOCATION:** Westcliffe Town Park, 60 miles west of Pueblo at the junction of Highways 96 and 69 **TICKETS/INFO:** 303-794-4170, 719-783-2361, 719-783-2918 **ACCOMMODATIONS/TOURIST INFO:** 719-783-2361, 719-783-9163

CLASSICAL RIVER JOURNEY
DOLORES RIVER ✷ FIRST OR SECOND WEEK IN JUNE

Set in the natural concert halls of Dolores River canyons, this "floating festival" features eight days of classical music and rafting. Traditionally, four or five members of the Los Angeles Philharmonic play morning and evening concerts, filling the river's beautiful canyons with the sounds of cello, violin, viola, flute, and guitar. As acoustic music echoes off cliffs and mingles with the sounds of river, wind, and wildlife, participants soak up the sun, eat fresh gourmet food, and explore surroundings and Anasazi ruins. Cost is about $1,600 for each participant.   **LOCATION:** Dolores River. Check with organizers for departure point. **TICKETS/INFO:** 800-824-3795, 719-539-6851 **ACCOMMODATIONS/TOURIST INFO:** 800-824-3795, 719-539-6851

MUSIC IN OURAY
OURAY ✷ FIRST AND SECOND WEEKENDS IN JUNE

This intimate chamber music festival showcases mostly regional chamber groups, and some groups of international renown (the Raphael Trio have been recent guests). The repertoire typically ranges from Beethoven, Haydn, and Mozart to Wolf-Ferrari. Performances are held in the local high school auditorium, and attendance averages around 150 people each day. At the end of each festival day, organizers usually announce the bar or restaurant where the musicians and organizers will spend the evening, welcoming everyone to come along. Single concert tickets are about $15. **LOCATION:** Multipurpose Room of the Ouray Public Schools, at 400 Seventh Avenue in Ouray, about 100 miles south of Grand Junction on U.S. 550 **TICKETS/INFO:** 800-228-1876, 970-325-7318 **ACCOMMODATIONS/TOURIST INFO:** 800-228-1876, 303-325-4746

COLORADO MUSIC FESTIVAL
BOULDER ✷ THIRD WEEK IN JUNE THROUGH EARLY AUGUST

Founded in 1976, the Colorado Music Festival brings symphonic and chamber music concerts to the historic Chautauqua Park Auditorium. Performances have featured everyone from Yo Yo Ma to Garrick Ohlsson, but another big draw is the venue itself, built in 1898 with an all-wood structure that projects the sounds of orchestras with brilliant clarity and warmth. Children's concerts, lectures, films, and a free Fourth of July concert on the lawn add to the program.   **LOCATION:** Chautauqua Auditorium, at 900 Baseline Road in Boulder, about 20 miles northwest of Denver. **TICKETS/INFO:** 303-449-1397; World Wide Web: http://www.aescon.com/music/cmf/index.htm **ACCOMMODATIONS/TOURIST INFO:** 800-444-0447, 303-442-2911

COUNTRY JAM
GRAND JUNCTION ✷ THIRD WEEKEND IN JUNE, THURSDAY–SUNDAY

High-caliber country bands, gourmet foods, and the natural beauty of the Colorado slopes make this jam a relaxing and rewarding place to spend a June weekend. The festival's three stages warm to eight regional, 23 national, and a whopping 31 national talents who perform country hits for an appreciative audience of nearly 80,000 over the weekend. Full passes cost $50-$100, or less for early buyers. Guests can also shop for food, fashions, and crafts from on-site vendors or go camping, rafting, or hunting nearby.   **LOCATION:** A few miles northwest of Grand Junction via exit 11 from I-70 **TICKETS/INFO:** 800-530-3020, 715-839-7500 **ACCOMMODATIONS/TOURIST INFO:** 970-244-1480

℡ELLURIDE BLUEGRASS FESTIVAL
TELLURIDE ✻ THIRD WEEKEND IN JUNE, THURSDAY–SUNDAY

The head count surges in this mining-turned-resort community as thousands of fans flock to an exquisitely eclectic weekend of acoustic music. As the name implies, the original focus was on bluegrass, but the festival now encompasses folk, country, gospel, and roots music from around the planet. Bluegrass purists indignantly point out that Bill Monroe wasn't even the headliner the last time he played at this "bluegrass festival," but there's usually no shortage of pickin' and grinnin' among the 30 or so acts.

The festival and town itself are expensive (a four-day pass is around $135 at the gate), but camping makes the trip affordable and the setting is unbeatable. The road ends at Telluride, which is set in a box canyon in the craggy San Juan Mountains of southwest Colorado. While listening to some of the world's finest musicians, you can look up at snow-covered peaks on three sides. Many visitors combine the concerts with the region's unsurpassed hiking and mountain biking.

Even with the leap in population, Telluride keeps its good small-town vibes. Residents form a roadblock to greet visitors on their way into town and answer questions about where to go and what to do. A capacity crowd of 10,000 people each day sprawls on the lawn and mingles among booths offering food, arts and crafts, and politics. Musical workshops and children's areas round out the festival's offerings. **LOCATION:** Town Park in Telluride, just off the San Juan Highway (Highway 145), in southwest Colorado **TICKETS/INFO:** 800-624-2422, 970-449-6007; e-mail: planet@bluegrass.com; World Wide Web: http://www.bluegrass.com/planet **ACCOM-MODATIONS/TOURIST INFO:** 800-525-3455, 303-728-4431, 303-728-3041

♩AZZ ASPEN SNOWMASS
SNOWMASS ✻ THIRD OR FOURTH WEEKEND IN JUNE, WEDNESDAY–SUNDAY

One of the nation's premier small-venue jazz festivals brings a high-caliber lineup of mostly mainstream jazz and blues acts to Snowmass Town Park. Recent performers have included George Benson, B.B. King, Herbie Hancock, and the Manhattan Transfer—as well as a few rising young artists. The turnout each day is 3,000 to 4,000, and reserved-seating prices range from $14 to $40.   **LOCATION:** Snowmass Town Park, on Brush Creek Road in Snowmass, about 10 miles northwest of Aspen on Highway 82. From Highway 82 turn onto Brush Creek Road and travel approximately two miles to the park (situated in the valley below the Snowmass Ski Resort). **TICKETS/INFO:** 970-920-5770, 970-920-4996 **ACCOMMODATIONS/TOURIST INFO:** 800-766-9627, 970-925-1940

Mountain magic: The Aspen Music Festival brings classical music to new heights. Courtesy of Alex Irvin/Aspen Music Festival

ASPEN MUSIC FESTIVAL AND SCHOOL

ASPEN ✹ LATE JUNE THROUGH MID-AUGUST

Where else in the world could you mountain bike in the morning, hike (or take a gondola) to a mountaintop for an afternoon concert, descend for dinner in any of more than 100 restaurants, then take in an evening concert in an acoustically perfect hall filled with the world's best classical musicians?

For nearly 50 years, the Aspen Music Festival and School has stood prestigiously as one of the world's principal musical gatherings. Unlike Tanglewood or Ravinia, this festival has no permanent resident symphony orchestra, but a distinguished international roster of visiting conductors and musicians fills the mountain air with beautiful sounds.

During the festival's nine weeks, about 150 musical events—from chamber music to symphonic and jazz—keep everyone enraptured. Aspen's musical programs are always interesting and adventuresome, with a wealth of great performances that may include exquisitely performed baroque and romantic classics, as well as wildly inventive avant-garde.

Most events are concentrated in three venues (including the new, acoustically marvelous Irving Harris Concert Hall), but small, out-of-the-way stages are nestled in parks or in the mountains near town. "Music on the Mountain" offers an afternoon getaway from Aspen's sometimes hectic scene, with music at the summit of Aspen Mountain.

The Music School is a big part of Aspen's uniqueness, and organizers say the festival is built around its 900 students. Four orchestras and ensembles involve both students and masters, and many gifted young musicians are inspired by playing side by side with their mentors, producing some of the freshest, most enthusiastic classical performances on earth. Plus, the school offers informal lessons to qualified students in all major instruments, including guitar and voice.

Unfortunately, the natural beauty of Aspen itself is being walled and obliterated by condos, boutiques, and fortresslike hotels. Some view anything connected with the town as expensive, stuffy, and inaccessible, yet the modern-day parade of limousines and Range Rovers obscures the fact that the festival itself is still a grassroots, volunteer effort that's been growing up with the town since the 1940s.

One in four concerts is free, and many are performed outdoors, reinforcing the concept that music is in many ways an element of nature. Catching one of the festival's concerts on the lawn is one of Aspen's unsurpassed pleasures, since this musical playground has no restrictions. Children play, dogs romp, and couples drink wine and smooch, all inspired by a soundtrack of glorious classics.   **LOCATION:** Various venues in Aspen and throughout the Roaring Fork Valley **TICKETS/INFO:** 970-925-9042, 970-925-3254; World Wide Web: http://www.infosphere.com/aspenonline/directory/ae/amf **ACCOMMODATIONS/TOURIST INFO:** 800-525-2052, 970-925-1940

℃ENTRAL CITY OPERA FESTIVAL
CENTRAL CITY ✳ LATE JUNE THROUGH MID-AUGUST

The Central City Opera Festival brings big-city talents and people to this bustling gambling town (it's not a quaint little mining village anymore) for six weeks of English-spoken operas with American performers. The Opera House is an acoustically excellent classic built in 1878, but opera purists should beware of the festival's slogan: "For those who think Opera is a talk-show host, we do it in English."   **LOCATION:** Central City Opera House in downtown Central City, about 30 miles west of Denver via Highway 119; bus transportation from Denver is available through the opera box office. **TICK-ETS/INFO:** 303-292-6700 **ACCOMMODATIONS/TOURIST INFO:** 800-542-2999, 303-582-0889

ℬRAVO! COLORADO VAIL VALLEY MUSIC FESTIVAL
VAIL AND AVON ✳ EARLY JULY THROUGH LATE AUGUST

Set in the midst of several condo-crazy mountain resorts, Bravo! Colorado features heavy musical programming with a light presentation. Typically, two orchestras (one regional and the other of national renown) perform at the Gerald Ford Amphitheater, while chamber ensembles play among the stained-wood beams and excellent acoustics of the Chapel at Beaver Creek. Occasional touches of jazz, bluegrass, and ethnic concerts appeal to the younger set, while workshops, youth concerts, and an Intro to Chamber Music class round out the program. Tickets cost anywhere from $10 to $22. **LOCATION:** The Gerald Ford Amphitheater in the Betty Ford Alpine Gardens, 530 South Frontage Road in Vail; and the Chapel at Beaver Creek, 33 Elk Track Road in Avon, about five miles west of Vail. (Vail and Avon are about 90 minutes west of Denver via I-70.) **TICKETS/INFO:** 970-476-0206 **ACCOMMODATIONS/TOURIST INFO:** 800-824-5737, 970-476-1000

Central City Opera Festival: Six weeks of English-language opera in a historic opera house. Photo by Mark Kiryluk for Central City Opera

STRINGS IN THE MOUNTAINS
STEAMBOAT SPRINGS ✳ EARLY JULY THROUGH THE SECOND WEEKEND IN AUGUST

Although the heart of this festival is chamber music, it's grown to encompass everything from baroque to bluegrass, classical to cowboy. Featuring musicians from around the world, concerts nearly every night of the week ensure that you'll encounter plenty of music if you stop by the spectacular Yampa Valley anytime during July or early August. Festivities center around an acoustically warm tent at the base of Mount Werner, and tickets range from $1 to $25.   **LOCATION:** Mount Werner Ski Area, Steamboat Springs **TICKETS/INFO:** 970-897-0882, 970-879-5056; e-mail: leed@csn.net **ACCOMMODATIONS/TOURIST INFO:** 800-922-2722, 970-897-0740

WINTER PARK JAZZ AND AMERICAN MUSIC FESTIVAL
WINTER PARK ✳ THIRD WEEKEND IN JULY, SATURDAY AND SUNDAY

Of all of the summer ski-hill festivals that have popped up recently, Winter Park stands out for its diversity of performers and crowd, and for its romping and casual atmosphere. The product of a merger of Winter Park's Jazz Festival with its American Music Festival, this two-day fest has a knack for picking the most interesting of both veteran and up-and-coming performers from several genres.

Bravo! Colorado: Symphony and chamber music are the summer soundtrack in Vail and Avon. (See entry, page 300.) Courtesy of Bravo! Colorado Vail Valley Music Festival

In recent years, the festival has attracted the likes of Los Lobos, Sarah Mclachlan, the Freddy Jones Band, Widespread Panic, and the Brian Setzer Orchestra. Yet many spectators feel that the festival itself is more important than the individual acts. Whoever performs, 10,000 to 12,000 people can be counted on to spend the day either dancing in front of the stages or sitting on hillside blankets and taking in the incredible view.

In a natural outdoor amphitheater nestled at the base of the ski area, bigger national acts perform on the main stage, while regional bands play the adjoining Stage Colorado, alternating so that music plays continuously. Festival tents with everything from multicolored beads to standard hippie wear and jumbo turkey legs surround the stages. The weather is typically mountain (a few showers and lots of sunshine in a single day), so bring both rain gear and sunblock. Over the two-day festival period, the nearby towns of Winter Park and Fraser are inundated by festivalgoers, and local bars often feature festival performers at night.   **LOCATION:** Winter Park Ski Resort, two miles south of the town of Winter Park and about two hours northwest of Denver via U.S. 40. From

I-70, take exit 232 to U.S. 40 and drive over Berthoud Pass to the resort. **TICKETS/INFO:** 970-830-8497, 970-726-4221 **ACCOMMODATIONS/TOURIST INFO:** 800-903-7275, 970-726-4118

♫USIC IN THE MOUNTAINS
PURGATORY SKI RESORT, NEAR DURANGO ✱ TEN DAYS STARTING THURSDAY OF THE LAST WEEK IN JULY

Classical music in the Four Corners region is by no means an everyday phenomenon. Making use of a stunning setting in the San Juan Mountains, this festival features symphonic and chamber works performed mostly by members of the Dallas and Fort Worth Symphonies, on break from their city festival season. The performances are relaxed and affordable (about $15 for adults), and children's activities are also featured. Apart from Purgatory's own summer beauty, the great many nearby sights include Mesa Verde National Park and San Juan National Forest.   **LOCATION:** Purgatory Ski Resort, 25 miles north of Durango on U.S. 550 **TICKETS/INFO:** 970-385-6820 **ACCOMMODATIONS/TOURIST INFO:** 800-525-0892, 970-247-8900

ℝOCKYGRASS
LYONS ✱ FIRST WEEKEND IN AUGUST, FRIDAY–SUNDAY

Since 1972, a combination of scenery, weather, and festival ambience has brought the top echelon of bluegrass performers to this Rocky Mountain classic. Traditional and old-timey acts like the Nashville Bluegrass Band and Doc Watson share the stage with contemporary stars like Alison Krauss and nontraditionalists like Hot Rize and Tim O'Brien. The playing is typically energetic, and it's conveyed through a state-of-the-art sound system that you won't find at most bluegrass festivals (this all-bluegrass event is presented by organizers of the more eclectic Telluride Bluegrass Festival). Attendance is limited to 3,500 per day, and since food and alcohol are sold on the grounds, BYO is prohibited. Ticket prices start at $55 for a three-day pass.   **LOCATION:** Wildflower Ranch, 500 West Main Street (on U.S. 36, next to Estes Park), in Lyons, which is at the junction of U.S. 36 and Highways 7 and 66 (15 miles north of Boulder and 20 miles east of Rocky Mountain National Park). **TICKETS/INFO:** 800-624-2422, 970-449-6007; e-mail: planet@bluegrass.com; World Wide Web: http://www.bluegrass.com/planet **ACCOMMODATION/TOURIST INFO:** 800-624-2422, 970-449-6007

ℑELLURIDE JAZZ CELEBRATION
TELLURIDE ✱ FIRST WEEKEND IN AUGUST, FRIDAY–SUNDAY

For nearly 20 years, jazz virtuosos like Herbie Hancock, Joe Williams, and Regina Carter have ventured to this sleepy resort town known for its music festivals. Concerts are staged in a picturesque park by day, and in clubs and historic Victorian theaters by night. The spectacular views and "pure jazz" at this festival draw a diverse crowd from far and wide, but if thrift is your thing, be warned: the festival and everything else in Telluride are pricey.   **LOCATION:** Telluride is in southwestern Colorado on Highway 145. **TICKETS/INFO:** 800-525-3455, 970-728-7009 **ACCOMMODATIONS/TOURIST INFO:** 800-525-3455, 970-728-4431, 970-728-3041

Rocky Mountain high: Scenery, ambience, and top performers make
Rockygrass a favorite on the bluegrass festival circuit. Courtesy of Tim Benko/Planet Bluegrass

TELLURIDE CHAMBER MUSIC FESTIVAL

TELLURIDE ✴ SECOND AND THIRD WEEKENDS IN AUGUST

Telluride, dubbed by some as the music festival center of the West, hosts this small, eclectic, and relatively inexpensive (no more than $20 per event) festival. It starts with a musical picnic among the whispering aspens and trilling birds in Town Park, then moves to the acoustically renowned Sheridan Opera House for several evenings of concerts that typically include Ravel, Haydn, Mendelssohn, and others. Musicians from around the nation form the ad hoc Telluride Chamber Players, who finish up the second weekend with a "dessert concert" featuring the work of talented local chefs.   **LOCATION:** Events are held at the Sheridan Opera House, 110 North Oak Street, and in Town Park, at the eastern end of Colorado Avenue (Highway 145) in Telluride, which is in southwestern Colorado on Highway 145. **TICKETS/INFO:** 800-525-3455 **ACCOMMODATIONS/TOURIST INFO:** 800-525-3455, 970-728-4431, 970-728-3041

CENTRAL CITY JAZZ FEST

CENTRAL CITY ✴ THIRD WEEKEND IN AUGUST

With jazz all day and blues all night, the sounds of American music compete with the clatter of one-armed bandits and card dealers in the once-sleepy town of Central City. Looking to diversify the activities available in this gambling town (whose image has taken a beating since gaming was legalized), the organizers invite regional and occasionally nationally known performers to this free festival. A single stage is supplemented by a beer garden and art booths in an extremely casual setting. And if gambling is your thing, you can still go nuts right next door.   **LOCATION:** Downtown Central City, about 30 miles west of Denver via Highway 119 **TICKETS/INFO:** 800-542-2999 **ACCOMMODATIONS/TOURIST INFO:** 800-542-2999, 303-582-0889

ROCKY MOUNTAIN FOLKS FESTIVAL

LYONS ✴ THIRD WEEKEND IN AUGUST

Established in 1990, this festival by Planet Bluegrass (the folks who organize the Telluride Bluegrass Festival and RockyGrass) features acoustic "masters of song" in a magical setting. Bookings emphasize singer-songwriter types like Ani DiFranco, Keb Mo, and Nanci Griffith. A main stage and workshop stage are set in a woodsy area with the St. Vrain River running through it, and with plenty of mountains in the background. Numerous workshops and seminars combine with natural activities like hiking, biking, climbing, and kayaking to keep festival patrons busy for the weekend.   **LOCATION:** Wildflower Ranch, 500 West Main Street (on U.S. 36, next to Estes Park), in Lyons, which is at the junction of U.S. 36 and Highways 7 and 66 (15 miles north of Boulder and 20 miles east of Rocky Mountain National Park). **TICKETS/INFO:** 800-624-2422, 970-449-6007; e-mail: planet@bluegrass.com; World Wide Web: http://www.bluegrass.com/planet **ACCOMMODATIONS/TOURIST INFO:** 800-624-2422, 970-449-6007

Rocky Mountain Folks Festival: Acoustic masters of song in a majestic setting. (See entry, page 305.) Courtesy of Tim Benko/Planet Bluegrass

ℐAZZ ASPEN SNOWMASS

SNOWMASS ✸ LABOR DAY WEEKEND, FRIDAY–MONDAY (LABOR DAY IS THE FIRST MONDAY IN SEPTEMBER)

As the larger sister of Jazz Aspen Snowmass in June, this Labor Day event augments mainstream jazz with splashes of blues, folk, reggae, world music, and other rootsy sounds. The venue is especially interesting—a tent perched in a 10,000-foot valley on Snowmass Mountain—and attendance is around 4,000 or 5,000 a day. General admission price is $35.   **LOCATION:** Snowmass Mountain, just outside Aspen via Highway 82 **TICKETS/INFO:** 970-920-5770, 970-920-4996 **ACCOMMODATIONS/TOURIST INFO:** 800-766-9627, 970-925-1940

ꕤUMMIT JAZZ

DENVER ✸ LAST FULL WEEKEND IN SEPTEMBER, FRIDAY–SUNDAY

Although it's held in the ballroom of a suburban hotel complex, this growing festival manages to lure internationally recognized bands and artists like Milt Hinton, Bob Wilber, and the Climax Jazz Band. Organizers assure that "you won't burst your eardrums" at this mellow weekend of traditional and progressive jazz.   **LOCATION:** Hyatt Regency Tech Center, 7800 Tufts Avenue **TICKETS/INFO:** 303-670-8471, 303-674-4190 **ACCOMMODATIONS/TOURIST INFO:** 303-534-8500, 303-892-1112

IONEL HAMPTON JAZZ FESTIVAL
MOSCOW ✷ LAST WEEKEND IN FEBRUARY

This swinging tribute and teach-in celebrates the rousing and captivating big band music of Lionel Hampton, who took the jazz world by storm in the thirties and forties—and who still swings in his eighties. Called "the number one jazz festival in the world" by the late *Los Angeles Times* jazz critic Leonard Feather, this university-based series is often as much a celebration of music and learning as a festival.

The Hampton Jazzfest's uniqueness stems from its offering of world-class jazz artists in both formal evening concerts and informal afternoon clinics in which students and jazz fans can interact with their favorite artists. Some 30,000 jazz fans attend the incredible array of performances, workshops, and festival activities, while about 13,000 students are involved in competitions and clinics given by some of the greatest jazz performers in the country.

To shut out the frigid Idaho winters, most of the festival's nighttime concerts are within the snug confines of the University of Idaho's Kibbie Dome. The format is crazed and compressed, as some 50 world-class performers hustle onto the stage, often getting in just two or three numbers before hustling off again. It's exhilarating, but when you consider the caliber of talent—Lou Rawls, Ella Fitzgerald, Arturo Sandoval, and Jon Hendricks have been recent guests—the format can be frustratingly teasing.

In recent years, Lionel Hampton has brought his New York Big Band to the festival for concerts and clinics. Every artist who performs at the festival conducts at least one clinic or workshop session, all of which are open to students and the public at no charge. In these sessions, which feature a fascinating interactive format, you might find Marian McPartland demonstrating piano styles and critiquing pedal technique, Jon Hendricks delivering a rhyming history of jazz singing, or Ray Brown leading a bass clinic.

Students perform as groups and individuals before a panel of judges, and the winners are honored with scholarships, instruments, and the opportunity to perform at evening concerts. Moscow, Idaho, doesn't get much jazz exposure the rest of the year, so audiences—which come from throughout the Northwest and beyond—are extremely enthusiastic.　**LOCATION:** University of Idaho in Moscow, about 80 miles southeast of Spokane, Washington, at the intersection of U.S. 95 and Highway 8. Evening concerts take place at the Kibbie Dome. **TICKETS/INFO:** 800-345-7402, 208-885-6765 **AC-COMMODATIONS/TOURIST INFO:** 208-882-9220, 800-635-7820, 208-334-2470

Lionel Hampton Jazz Festival: The Man himself makes an appearance at this exhilarating bigband bash. (See entry, page 307.)

Courtesy of Jerry Prout/Lionel

Hampton Jazz Festival

ℕATIONAL OLDTIME FIDDLERS' CONTEST
WEISER ✷ THIRD FULL WEEK IN JUNE, MONDAY–SATURDAY

When wagon trains made their way westward along the Oregon Trail, settlers could bring along only the most portable old-world musical instruments. In the 1860s, when an outpost was established at Weiser, Idaho, the compact fiddle was often pulled out from covered wagons as immigrants stopped to rest and entertain themselves.

The National Oldtime Fiddlers' Contest is like a trip back to the days when homegrown fiddle music dominated American popular entertainment. This weeklong celebration draws the most prestigious old-time fiddlers in the country, with a nonstop array of contests, jam sessions, and tributes to fiddlers who are helping to preserve the old-time music and atmosphere.

The first recorded fiddle festival in Weiser was initiated in 1914, and although interest has waxed and waned over the years, the festival in its current form has been growing since 1963, when it officially became the National Oldtime Fiddlers' Contest. These days, you can't get a hotel or campsite unless you book way in advance, and the air-conditioned Weiser High School Gymnasium is packed with fiddle lovers from all over the world.

The heart of the festival is the competitions, and here Nashville glitz and new-wave electricity won't win any fans. Tradition rules as hundreds of fiddlers in dozens of classes compete by playing a waltz, a hoedown, and a tune of choice, with a maximum of two accompanists. Crowd pleasers can often be found in the national senior (over 65) and national small fry (under 13) classes, and organizers gush with pride over the number of younger players who have been picking up the fiddle in recent years.

The contests are augmented by a whole week of activities ranging from fiddle dances to parades, a golf tournament, and barbecues. It's easy to see why the natural beauty of this region has been the subject of so many fiddle tunes, with its mountains, lakes, and thundering gorges. Nearby recreational opportunities include fishing, boating, white-water rafting, hiking, and mountain biking.   **LOCATION:** Weiser is a one-hour drive northwest of Boise, via I-84 west to Highway 95 north. **TICKETS/INFO:** 800-437-1280, 208-549-0452 **ACCOMMODATIONS/TOURIST INFO:** 800-437-1280, 800-635-7820, 208-334-2470

RENDEZVOUS IN THE PARK
MOSCOW ✷ SECOND AND THIRD WEEKENDS IN JULY, FRIDAY–SUNDAY

Covering folk, jazz, country, and world music, this family-oriented festival offers something for just about everyone—including kids and art lovers. In addition to regional and national acts on a single stage, the first weekend features an arts and crafts fair; the second, children's events.   **LOCATION:** East City Park in Moscow, about 80 miles southeast of Spokane, Washington, at the intersection of U.S. 95 and Highway 8 **TICKETS/INFO:** 208-882-3581, 208-882-1800 **ACCOMMODATIONS/TOURIST INFO:** 208-882-1800, 800-635-7820, 208-334-2470

McCALL SUMMER MUSIC FESTIVAL
MCCALL ✷ THIRD WEEKEND IN JULY, THURSDAY–SUNDAY

On the shores of Payette Lake in Idaho's "year-round playground," this festival offers four nights of everything from reggae and worldbeat to old-time country and bluegrass music. Thursday is "locals" night, and the other evenings bring in guest artists from out of town who concertize and present workshops. The local folkies who started this festival in 1979 now forbid alcohol, and charge about $7 for each night's admission. **LOCATION:** University of Idaho's McCall Field Campus, at University and Davis Avenues, adjacent to the Ponderosa State Park in McCall, about 95 miles north of Boise on Highway 55 **TICKETS/INFO:** 208-634-5259 **ACCOMMODATIONS/TOURIST INFO:** 208-634-7631, 800-635-7820, 208-334-2470

IDAHO INTERNATIONAL FOLK DANCE FESTIVAL
REXBURG ✷ LAST WEEKEND IN JULY THROUGH FIRST WEEKEND IN AUGUST

This small Idaho town comes alive for nine days when it hosts (literally, for the performers are housed by town residents) dancers and musicians from around the world. Festival teams come from as far away as Malaysia, India, Denmark, and Russia, and although the focus is on dance, the festival is a great opportunity to hear authentic music courtesy of the musicians who accompany the dancers. The first weekend is occupied by parades, street festivals, and dances, while the second weekend features full

Draw your bows! The National Oldtime Fiddlers' Contest brings in fiddle and old-time music lovers from across the continent. (See entry, page 308.)

Courtesy of Idaho Travel Council

multiethnic performances with all participants. Locals sponsor a rodeo and a country and western concert to give the visitors a feel for Western American culture. **LOCATION:** Various venues in Rexburg, about 40 miles north of Idaho Falls on U.S. 20 and Highway 33 **TICKETS/INFO:** 208-356-5700 **ACCOMMODATIONS/TOURIST INFO:** 208-356-5700, 800-847-4843, 208-334-2470

☼UN VALLEY SWING 'N' DIXIE JAZZ JAMBOREE
SUN VALLEY (KETCHUM) ✴ SECOND OR THIRD WEEKEND IN OCTOBER

Amid the golden hue of autumn aspens, some two dozen ragtime, traditional jazz, and swing bands from the United States and Canada shake up Sun Valley's sunny days and cool evenings. Five days of music and four nights of dancing are supplemented by specialty events like Pianorama, Legends of Swing, a parade, and jazz worship services. **LOCATION:** Sun Valley near Ketchum; about 85 miles north of Twin Falls, just off Highway 75 **TICKETS/INFO:** 208-375-1671, 208-344-3768 **ACCOMMODATIONS/ TOURIST INFO:** 800-634-3347, 208-726-4533

M⊚NTaNa

⫶ONTANA TRADITIONAL JAZZ FESTIVAL
HELENA ✴ LAST FULL WEEKEND IN JUNE

The state's capital hosts this jazz festival in a variety of locations, including a hotel ballroom and an outdoor tent. Ten dollars a day buys admission to ragtime, Dixieland, and other jazz concerts (usually about a dozen bands are featured), numerous jam sessions, a senior citizens' picnic, and Arts on the Mall. The city is situated between two national forests, so camping and recreation opportunities abound. **LOCATION:** Various venues in downtown Helena **TICKETS/INFO:** 800-851-9980 **ACCOMMODATIONS/TOURIST INFO:** 800-743-5362, 800-847-4868, 406-444-2654

⫶USICIANS RENDEZVOUS
COLUMBUS ✴ FIRST FULL WEEKEND IN JULY, FRIDAY–SUNDAY

Set on the Yellowstone River in the foothills of the Beartooth Mountains, this festival features an acoustic selection of bluegrass, country, and old-time fiddle. The music of more than a dozen bands and the low price (about $5 for three days) draws a couple of thousand spectators, who take advantage of music workshops, food, arts and crafts, and a children's area. Camping is available. **LOCATION:** Itch-Kep-Pe Park, on Highway 78 in Columbus, on the north bank of the Yellowstone River. Columbus is 45 miles west of Billings, just south of I-90. **TICKETS/INFO:** 406-322-4143 **ACCOMMODATIONS/TOURIST INFO:** 406-322-4505, 800-847-4868, 406-444-2654

⫶LATHEAD MUSIC FESTIVAL
KALISPELL AND NEARBY TOWNS ✴ THROUGHOUT JULY

In Kalispell and several other corners of the Flathead Valley, this regional festival gives listeners a veritable potpourri of music. Offered are classical, pop, worldbeat, country, and even jazz, at stages on the side of Big Mountain, at Conrad Mansion, the Flathead Valley Community College campus, and a number of other spots. **LOCATION:** Flathead Valley Community College, on Highway 93, and various other locations in Kalispell and nearby towns in the Flathead Valley. Kalispell is at the junction of U.S. 93 and U.S. 2 in northwestern Montana. **TICKETS/INFO:** 406-257-0787; e-mail: fcva@fcva.org; World Wide Web: http://www.fcva.org/flathead **ACCOMMODATIONS/TOURIST INFO:** 406-752-6166, 800-847-4868, 406-444-2654

Dixieland, rag-
time, and other
jazz musicians
swarm Helena
during the Mon-
tana Traditional
Jazz Festival
(See entry, page
311.) *Courtesy of Travel*

Montana/Donnie Sexton

𝔅ITTERROOT VALLEY BLUEGRASS FESTIVAL

HAMILTON ✷ SECOND WEEKEND IN JULY

Montana's only bluegrass festival brings in half a dozen bands and about 10 times that many do-it-yourselfers. About 3,500 people gather in the lush valley of the Bitterroot Mountains, enjoying the music and festival perks, which include arts and crafts and a pile of sawdust with coins in it "for the kiddies." **LOCATION:** Ravalli County Fairgrounds, U.S. 93 and Fairgrounds Road, in Hamilton (which is 45 miles south of Missoula on U.S. 93) **TICKETS/INFO:** 406-363-2400, 406-363-1250 **ACCOM-MODATIONS/TOURIST INFO:** 406-363-2400, 800-847-4868, 406-444-2654

ℛ & R MUSIC FESTIVAL

EMIGRANT ✷ SECOND WEEKEND IN JULY, FRIDAY–SUNDAY

The Paradise Valley's R & R (also called Ramblin' Rose) is the most renowned of Montana's country music festivals, roping in more than 20 bands during a three-day period. This weekend features the full spectrum of country music, from dusty old-timers to the Nashville glitz of new country. A laser-light show, arts and crafts, and the R & R Northwest Mechanical Bull Riding Finals all keep everyone wondering what will happen next at this cowboy refuge of a festival. Daily admission is $20 and camping is available. **LOCATION:** Near the town of Emigrant, south of Livingston. From Billings take I-90 west, then U.S. 89 south (exit 333) for 12 miles and follow the signs. **TICKETS/INFO:** 800-499-4021, 406-686-4021 **ACCOMMODATIONS/TOURIST INFO:** 406-222-0850, 800-847-4868, 406-444-2654

𝓜ONTANA STATE FIDDLERS CONTEST
POLSON ✷ FOURTH FULL WEEKEND IN JULY, THURSDAY–SATURDAY

Nestled at the south end of Flathead Lake, this fiddle-fest swings into motion just as the mountain cherry crop is at its peak. Fiddling is growing in popularity in these parts, and about a hundred musicians from all over the state take their turns in divisions ranging from pee-wee through senior, novice through champion (men and women are not separated into different classes). The Thursday night street dance features big names who go on to judge the competition starting Friday night. And if you're at all interested in improving your skills, bring your fiddle along to this friendly festival and have a go at it—someone is bound to feel sorry for you and show you some licks.   **LOCATION:** 55 miles north of Missoula on U.S. 93 **TICKETS/INFO:** 406-323-1198 **ACCOMMODA-TIONS/TOURIST INFO:** 800-847-4868, 406-444-2654

𝓜ARSHALL MOUNTAIN MUSIC FESTIVAL
MISSOULA ✷ A SATURDAY IN LATE JULY OR EARLY AUGUST

Local Missoula talent in several genres is featured in this picturesque, private box canyon just six miles from Missoula. The ski slope forms a natural, acoustically excellent amphitheater for five bands playing everything from rock and pop to jazz and country. The family atmosphere typically accommodates about 1,500 people plus arts and crafts booths, and admission is about $15 for the day.   **LOCATION:** Marshall Ski Area. From Missoula take I-90 east, exit at the East Missoula exit and go left, then follow the signs for Marshall Ski Area. **TICKETS/INFO:** 406-258-6000 **ACCOMMODATIONS/TOURIST INFO:** 406-543-6623, 800-847-4868, 406-444-2654

𝓑IG SKY RENDEZVOUS
TROY ✷ THIRD WEEKEND IN AUGUST, FRIDAY–SUNDAY

On a grassy lot at the side of Bull Lake, organizers slap down a stage and a plywood dance floor and let the bands do the rest. Some 2,000 people drive in from a three-state area to dance and go wild to half a dozen of the area's hottest country acts. Many camp next to the Halfway House bar, which was built in 1936, and take advantage of the swimming, hiking, and other recreational opportunities in this immensely scenic valley with its giant cedars. At about $3 a day, the whole hoot's a bargain.   **LOCATION:** The Halfway House, on the south end of Bull Lake, about 18 miles south of Troy on Highway 56 (halfway between U.S. 2 and Highway 200) in the northwestern corner of the state **TICKETS/INFO:** 406-295-4358 **ACCOMMODATIONS/TOURIST INFO:** 406-295-4216, 800-847-4868, 406-444-2654

WILDERNESS BAR FIDDLERS CONTEST
LINCOLN ✷ LAST WEEKEND IN AUGUST, FRIDAY–SUNDAY

Stripped-down, no-frills fiddling is the order of the weekend at this tiny beer-garden festival. Jamming lasts throughout the weekend while the contest itself is held Saturday and Sunday afternoons. The festival doesn't even advertise, so you'll be able to see old-time country fiddle playing as it was meant to be: noncommercial, intimate, and relaxed.   **LOCATION:** The Wilderness Bar in downtown Lincoln, halfway between Missoula and Great Falls on Highway 200 **TICKETS/INFO:** 406-362-9200 **ACCOMMODATIONS/TOURIST INFO:** 406-362-4949, 800-847-4868, 406-444-2654

GREAT FALLS DIXIELAND JAZZ FESTIVAL
GREAT FALLS ✷ LABOR DAY WEEKEND, THURSDAY–SUNDAY (LABOR DAY IS THE FIRST MONDAY IN SEPTEMBER)

Run by the same organizers as the Traditional Jazz Festival in Helena, this mountain festival features Dixieland, ragtime, and other traditional jazz—but the similarities end right there. This crowd parties harder, drinks more, and typically consists of lots of laid-back Canadians and Montana mountain folk. Ten bands belt out the music of the roaring twenties in the heart of Charlie Russell country, and there's plenty of dancing and food—without the arts and crafts booths that clutter the festivities in Helena.   **LOCATION:** Downtown Great Falls, 90 miles northeast of Helena at the junction of I-15 and U.S. 89 **TICKETS/INFO:** 800-851-9980, 406-449-7969 **ACCOMMODATIONS/TOURIST INFO:** 406-453-4377, 800-847-4868, 406-444-2654

GLACIER JAZZ STAMPEDE
KALISPELL ✷ FIRST WEEKEND IN OCTOBER, THURSDAY–SUNDAY

The Glacier Jazz Stampede takes over practically the entire town of Kalispell, beginning with a pre-party Thursday night and moving into high gear with a trad-jazz bash Friday night. Saturday sees many of the 150 musicians around town, espousing the virtues of traditional jazz at malls, free children's venues, and elsewhere. With some seven venues, you can either stay put and let the music come to you or follow your favorite band around town. On Sunday, four jazz/gospel services are held at area churches, and the whole thing winds up with Sunday night's Jazz Band Ball, featuring big band music of the forties and fifties.   **LOCATION:** Various venues in Kalispell, in northwestern Montana at the junction of U.S. 2 and U.S. 93 **TICKETS/INFO:** 406-862-3814 **ACCOMMODATIONS/TOURIST INFO:** 406-444-2654

UTaH

IVING TRADITIONS

SALT LAKE CITY ✷ WEEKEND PRIOR TO MEMORIAL DAY WEEKEND, FRIDAY–SUNDAY (MEMORIAL DAY IS THE LAST MONDAY IN MAY)

Highlighting the performance traditions of the many ethnic communities that have made Salt Lake City their home, the Living Traditions festival features two stages of music and dance. (The full title of the festival is Living Traditions: A Celebration of Salt Lake's Folk and Ethnic Arts.) All performers—Latino, Asian, Native, African, Polynesian, and European Americans—live in the Salt Lake Valley, with the exception of one nationally known headliner Friday night. This refreshingly uncommercial festival spares its attendees the usual arts and crafts markets, presenting only art exhibitions and craft demonstrations. Admission is free, and beer and ethnic food are available. **LOCATION:** The grounds of the City and County Building on Washington Square in Salt Lake City **TICKETS/INFO:** 801-533-5760, 801-596-5000 **ACCOMMODATIONS/TOURIST INFO:** 801-521-2822, 801-538-1030, 800-200-1160

GINA BACHAUER INTERNATIONAL PIANO FESTIVAL

SALT LAKE CITY ✷ NEXT-TO-LAST WEEK IN JUNE

The Gina Bachauer International Piano Festival brings some of the world's best pianists, young and old, to Salt Lake City for a week of evening recitals (free of charge), international competitions, and master classes. Each year features a different program, but contestants can always be counted on to concertize in historic Temple Square and Promised Valley Playhouse, as well as local churches, parks, malls, and outdoor locations. **LOCATION:** Temple Square and other locations in downtown Salt Lake City **TICKETS/INFO:** 801-521-9200, 800-320-7376 **ACCOMMODATIONS/TOURIST INFO:** 801-521-2822, 801-538-1030, 800-200-1160

Drumming up diversity: Living Traditions features the music of Salt Lake City's many ethnic groups. (See entry, page 315.) Courtesy of Utah Arts Council

UTAH MUSIC FESTIVAL

SALT LAKE CITY, LOGAN, SNOWBIRD, AND DEER VALLEY ✷ EARLY JULY
THROUGH LATE AUGUST

Utah is often described as a late bloomer in the arts, but the growth and artistic success of the Utah Music Festival demonstrates that there's no lack of demand in the Salt Lake area for world-class chamber and symphonic music. The festival opened its doors in the summer of 1993 with an ambitious program of 18 concerts in four halls around the region. Within two years, attendance had increased fourfold, and the series had expanded to 29 concerts in nine venues.

An innovative program presents classical favorites as well as works rarely heard in the Salt Lake area. Using small chamber ensembles, choirs, and larger chamber orchestras, the festival's repertoire ranges from Bach and Handel triosonatas, to Brahms and Bartók string quartets, to larger works like Mozart piano concertos and Beethoven symphonies. The festival also has an impressive teaching program, offering students a one-to-two faculty-student ratio, with teaching musicians from prestigious schools in the United States. Tickets are a bargain at about $12, and the season features up to 10 free concerts.   **LOCATION:** Concerts and recitals are held in various venues in Salt Lake City, Logan, Snowbird, and Deer Valley. **TICKETS/INFO:** 800-249-2583, 801-355-2787, 801-797-0305 **ACCOMMODATIONS/TOURIST INFO:** 801-521-2822, 801-538-1030, 800-200-1160

SPRINGVILLE WORLD FOLKFEST

SPRINGVILLE ✷ ONE FULL WEEK IN MID-JULY

In a whirlwind of color, sound, and motion, up to a dozen music and dance groups descend on Springville from all over the world, often bringing along beautiful crafts that are sold at the festival. Depending on the year, you might see musicians and dancers from Armenia, India, Israel, France, or other far-flung places. Most events take place in an outdoor pavilion built specifically for the festival, with a spectacular view of the surrounding Rocky Mountains. Performances stretch out over a week, drawing up to 8,000 people who are interested in learning about the costumes, traditions, music, and dance of cultures around the world. In addition to the formal performances, a street dance lets audiences learn simple dances directly from the performers. Admission is about $7 for adults.   **LOCATION:** Spring Acres Arts Park, 620 South 1350 East in Springville, six miles south of Provo and about 45 miles south of Salt Lake City **TICKETS/INFO:** 801-489-3657, 801-489-4681 **ACCOMMODATIONS/TOURIST INFO:** 801-489-4681, 801-489-3263

UTAH FESTIVAL OPERA

LOGAN ✷ MID-JULY THROUGH MID-AUGUST, THURSDAYS–SATURDAYS

The Utah Festival Opera Company brings solidly sung and staged opera to a stunning venue in the mountains of northern Utah. Each season includes a grand opera, a comic opera or operetta, and a musical theater selection. The works are presented in revolving repertory, so visitors can enjoy all three shows during a two- or three-day stay in the beautiful, recreation-rich Cache Valley.

The Utah Festival Opera's neoclassical venue brings spectators close to the action. *Courtesy of Utah Festival Opera*

Founded by Logan native Michael Ballam, the festival opened in 1993 and hit the ground running with an opening season that included *La Bohème, Naughty Marietta, Trial by Jury,* and *The Impresario.* All productions are staged in the 1,200-seat, neoclassical Ellen Eccles Theatre, which was built in 1923 and nearly destroyed by fire several times. During a city council debate over a motion to demolish the unprofitable building, an elderly woman rose to ask, "When was the last time your rose gardens earned a profit? Beauty takes sacrifice." A $6.5 million restoration effort was soon initiated to restore the building's intricate architecture, giving the region a theater large enough to house grand opera but intimate enough to bring spectators close to the action.   **LOCATION:** Ellen Eccles Theatre, 43 South Main Street, in Logan (about 80 miles north of Salt Lake City) **TICKETS/INFO:** 800-830-6088, 801-752-0026; e-mail: UFOC@aol.com **ACCOMMODATIONS/TOURIST INFO:** 800-752-2161, 801-538-1030, 800-200-1160

C̵LASSICAL RIVER JOURNEY
GREEN RIVER WILDERNESS AREA ✷ THIRD OR FOURTH WEEK IN JULY

Set in the natural concert halls of the Green River, this "floating festival" features eight days of classical music and rafting. Traditionally, four or five members of the Los Angeles Philharmonic play morning and evening concerts, filling the river's beautiful canyons with the sounds of cello, violin, viola, flute, and guitar. As acoustic music echoes off cliffs and mingles with the sounds of river, wind, and wildlife, participants soak up the sun, feast on gourmet food, raft, and explore the natural environs and Indian ruins. Cost is about $1,600 for each participant and includes air transport from Grand

Junction, Colorado.   **LOCATION:** Green River Wilderness Area. The trip departs from Grand Junction, Colorado; call organizers for details. **TICKETS/INFO:** 800-824-3795, 719-539-6851 **ACCOMMODATIONS/TOURIST INFO:** 800-824-3795, 719-539-6851, 801-538-1030, 800-200-1160

UTAH JAZZ & BLUES FESTIVAL
SNOWBIRD ✳ LAST WEEKEND IN JULY, FRIDAY AND SATURDAY

The Utah Jazz & Blues Festival is the Salt Lake City area's premier opportunity each year to enjoy live jazz and blues in quantity. Set on a ski hill in Little Cottonwood Canyon, the tented stage features three or four top-notch blues acts Friday night and an equal number of fine jazz acts Saturday night. Great Cajun food—gumbo, jambalaya, and blackened catfish—is available until midnight, and audience members are invited inside the lodge after the show for late-night jams with festival performers. Tickets range from $23 to $33, and weekend lodging/meal/concert packages are available. **LOCATION:** Snowbird Ski & Summer Resort, in Little Cottonwood Canyon, about 30 minutes outside Salt Lake City **TICKETS/INFO:** 801-742-2222, 801-233-2787; e-mail: 75407.3034@compuserve.com **ACCOMMODATIONS/TOURIST INFO:** 800-435-3000, 801-538-1030, 800-200-1160

MOAB MUSIC FESTIVAL
MOAB ✳ SECOND AND THIRD WEEKENDS IN SEPTEMBER

Among the breathtaking red-rock canyonlands of southeastern Utah, the Moab Music Festival presents seven unique concerts. The low-key but imaginative programming includes modern works as well as masterpieces of the chamber music repertoire. Four indoor and outdoor venues include a geodesic dome and a concert on a Colorado River site accessible only by boat.   **LOCATION:** Several indoor and outdoor locations in Moab, on U.S. 191 southwest of Grand Junction, Colorado **TICKETS/INFO:** 801-259-8431; World Wide Web: http://www.panix.com/-damron/moab.html **ACCOMMO-DATIONS/TOURIST INFO:** 801-259-7814, 801-538-1030, 800-200-1160

HIGH PLAINS OLD TIME COUNTRY MUSIC SHOW AND CONTEST

DOUGLAS ✷ A WEEKEND IN MID- OR LATE APRIL

This romping show features the Rocky Mountains' biggest variety of categories in a country music contest. Sixteen individual and group divisions include everything from the ever popular banjo to the ever intriguing "variety" category, where the next instrument is always a mystery. Styles include country, bluegrass, and folk; a weekend pass is about $13. **LOCATION:** Douglas High School, about 50 miles east of Casper, just off I-25 **TICKETS/INFO:** 307-358-9006 **ACCOMMODATIONS/TOURIST INFO:** 307-358-2950, 800-225-5996, 307-777-7777

ROCKIN' THE TETONS MUSIC FESTIVAL

GRAND TARGHEE SKI AND SUMMER RESORT (ALTA) ✷ A WEEKEND IN MID-JULY

Rock, blues, and reggae bounce around the mountains during this weekend ski-hill festival. There are few big names here; the event is best known for its casual atmosphere, good regional bands, and great natural backdrop. Side shows include chairlift rides, a street breakfast, and the evening shenanigans at the Trap Bar. **LOCATION:** Grand Targhee Ski and Summer Resort is a 45-minute drive from Jackson. From Jackson, take Highway 22 northwest over Teton Pass into Idaho, where the road becomes Idaho Highway 33. At Victor continue north on Highway 33 to Driggs, then take a right at the bank to head toward Grand Targhee, near Alta, Wyoming. **TICKETS/INFO:** 800-827-4433, 307-353-2300 **ACCOMMODATIONS/TOURIST INFO:** 307-353-2300, 800-225-5996, 307-777-7777

GRAND TETON MUSIC FESTIVAL

TETON VILLAGE ✷ MID-JULY TO END OF AUGUST

"To make music in the right atmosphere is everything," says Maestro Ling Tung, seeking to explain why some of the finest musicians in America return year after year to the summer festival he brought into prominence. In what is possibly the most beautiful festival setting in the United States, musicians get what they really want: total freedom from the pressures and rigidities of major big-city orchestras.

The result is a series of performances that are sometimes uneven, but more often extraordinary. On the right night you get the feeling that the musicians and the setting have conspired to create something that couldn't be made elsewhere, something rare and transcendent that could only be found among friends, and among the mountains.

One of the nation's foremost "summer retreats" for musicians, the Grand Teton Music Festival started in 1962 as a series of small concerts in a school gymnasium and on a church lawn, and has evolved into a gathering of international renown. Much of its success is owed to the 28-year sojourn of Tung, who envisioned bringing the best musicians from the best orchestras to Jackson Hole, and letting them seek musical expression on their own terms.

Tung, music director and conductor through the 1996 season, makes sure musicians have plenty of input into the repertory, lots of rehearsal time, and opportunities to explore and make musical discoveries together. He says the festival is just "friends among friends, playing for friends." Thus, many of the musicians are loyal veterans, returning to the Tetons year after year.

The festival ensemble is particularly strong in the winds and brass sections, and the repertoire often shows them off commendably. Guest soloists are not, typically, big stars—rather, many are winners of international solo competitions who are playing here before names and careers are established. Thus, many performances are preceded by the buzz of a new "next big thing."

The festival typically presents symphonic concerts Friday and Saturday nights, and vocal recitals and chamber music on Monday, Tuesday, Wednesday, and Thursday nights. A laid-back atmosphere permeates the acoustically splendid Festival Hall, and many concertgoers wear what organizers dub "the Grand Teton tuxedo": a pair of shorts and denim shirt with no tie. The music director or a guest performer might appear before a work begins—or even between movements—to explain nuances, history, instrumentation, or crack a joke or two (though they're better musicians than comedians). After a particularly pleasing performance, audience members stomp their feet on the ground to commend the performers—a variation unique to this classical festival.

The valley is in full splendor in the summer, alive with colorful locals, tourists, performers, and "90-day wonders" (college kids on vacation). Ruggedly beautiful trails cover the landscape and a tram in the village can take you up to the mountains the easy way. The festival crowd is a multicolored mix of all of these people, and each night the audience, as well as the performers, spill out into the local watering holes. Two of the most frequented, the Mangy Moose and Beaver Dick's, offer a slice of local color and often feature interesting rock bands.   **LOCATION:** Teton Village is on Highway 390, 10 miles northwest of Jackson. **TICKETS/INFO:** 307-733-1128, 307-773-3050 **ACCOMMODATIONS/TOURIST INFO:** 307-733-7606, 800-225-5996, 307-777-7777

YELLOWSTONE JAZZ FESTIVAL
CODY ✷ SECOND OR THIRD SATURDAY IN JULY

Just outside the limits of Yellowstone National Park, this festival offers a great diversion for campers who are roughing it, and locals too. Many of the regionally renowned instructors from the prestigious Yellowstone Jazz Camp (see Music Workshops chapter, page 497) come out to jam on the Elk's Lodge lawn and play in the festival's ad hoc big band.   **LOCATION:** On the grounds of Elk's Lodge #1611, at 122

*Hillside hoedown:
The Grand
Targhee
Bluegrass Festi-
val brings down-
home sounds
upcountry.* Courtesy of

Grand Targhee Ski Resort

Beck Avenue in Cody, about 60 miles east of Yellowstone National Park, at the intersection of Highways 14 and 120 **TICKETS/INFO:** 307-587-3898, 307-587-2777 **ACCOMMODATIONS/TOURIST INFO:** 307-587-3898, 800-225-5996, 307-777-7777

G̃RAND TARGHEE BLUEGRASS FESTIVAL
GRAND TARGHEE SKI AND SUMMER RESORT (ALTA) ✳ SECOND WEEKEND IN AUGUST, FRIDAY–SUNDAY

Amid mountains bursting with wildflowers—and under some of the bluest skies imaginable—traditional and cutting-edge bluegrass is featured on two hillside stages. Usually one or two headliners—Alison Krauss and the David Grisman Quintet have been scheduled in recent years—are augmented by half a dozen or so local bands. There's a flat-pick guitar contest and open jams at night in the famous Trap Bar, and if the music gets slow you can always jet up the mountain on a chairlift, ride a horse, climb a rock wall, or attend a music workshop. Cost is about $17 per day.   **LOCATION:** Grand Targhee Ski and Summer Resort is a 45-minute drive from Jackson. From

Jackson, take Highway 22 northwest over Teton Pass into Idaho, where the road becomes Highway 33. At Victor continue north on Highway 33 to Driggs, then take a right at the bank to head toward Grand Targhee, near Alta, Wyoming. **TICKETS/INFO:** 800-827-4433, 307-353-2300 **ACCOMMODATIONS/TOURIST INFO:** 800-225-5996, 307-777-7777

SOUTHWEST

a**R**i**z**o**N**a

ᴀRIZONA OLD TIME FIDDLERS JAMBOREE
CASA GRANDE ✴ FIRST WEEKEND IN JANUARY

Unlike most of the Old Time Fiddlers Association events, this gig downplays contests and features two stages of music (a main stage inside and another outside) in addition to impromptu jam sessions everywhere. Club members have a good chance of getting up on stage to jam with the pros, and since membership is relatively cheap, consider joining if jamming's your thing. Sidelights include a gospel hour on Sunday morning and an antique car show.   **LOCATION:** Pinal County Fairgrounds, 512 South Eleven Mile Corner Road in Casa Grande. From Phoenix, take I-10 east to exit 194 and go west on Route 287 for seven miles, then turn right on Eleven Mile Corner Road. **TICKETS/INFO:** 520-723-5242 **ACCOMMODATIONS/TOURIST INFO:** 520-836-2125, 800-836-8169

ᴀRIZONA DIXIELAND FESTIVAL
LAKE HAVASU CITY ✴ SECOND WEEKEND IN JANUARY

Dixieland and traditional jazz bands from around the country play for three days in numerous venues around Lake Havasu City. Individual event badges and hotel packages are available. Between sets, you can check out London Bridge—the real London Bridge—which was dismantled and brought to this improbable location. And you can wonder why.   **LOCATION:** London Bridge Resort, 1477 Queens Bay in Lake Havasu City, along Highway 95 at Arizona's western border **TICKETS/INFO:** 800-624-7939, 520-855-0888 **ACCOMMODATIONS/TOURIST INFO:** 800-242-8278, 520-855-4115

ᴮLUES BLAST
PHOENIX ✴ A SATURDAY AND SUNDAY IN EARLY FEBRUARY

With its early February date, this just may be the first U.S. blues festival of the year. Even in February, the weather is usually great (blue skies, 75 degrees) as the Saturday dance party kicks into high gear. On Sunday afternoon the tempo slows with a family-oriented, blues-in-the-outdoors picnic thing. About a dozen regional and nationally known performers offer a mix of traditional and contemporary blues. Previous years have featured Coco Montoya, Keb Mo, and Little Ed and the Blues Imperials. **LOCATION:** Mesa Amphitheater, 263 North Center, 20 minutes east of Sky Harbor

International Airport in Phoenix **TICKETS/INFO:** 602-252-0599; e-mail: ph-xblues@aztec.asu.edu **ACCOMMODATIONS/TOURIST INFO:** 602-252-5588

ᴅESERT FOOTHILLS MUSIC FEST
CAREFREE ✴ A WEEK IN MID-FEBRUARY

This exquisitely eclectic celebration of chamber classics features exciting compositions from throughout the ages, performed in two churches and an arts center. Each night covers a different period or theme, with programs ranging from baroque to Broadway and pops. Prices are reasonable (about $15 per concert), and many venues in this small town (just outside Phoenix) offer dinner concerts.   **LOCATION:** Several venues just off Carefree Highway in the town of Carefree, about 20 miles due north of Scottsdale **TICKETS/INFO:** 602-488-0806 **ACCOMMODATIONS/TOURIST INFO:** 602-488-3381

ᴛUCSON WINTER CHAMBER MUSIC FESTIVAL
TUCSON ✴ ONE WEEK IN EARLY OR MID-MARCH

The Arizona Friends of Chamber Music inaugurated this winter festival in 1994 with the aim of incorporating unusual repertoire into a festive week of musical activity. Audiences and musicians meet informally throughout the week, in master classes, and at open rehearsals, expert preconcert commentary sessions, and a gala benefit dinner. The festival appeals to music lovers throughout southern Arizona, with a youth concert and an easygoing Sunday afternoon program.   **LOCATION:** Tucson Community Center's Leo Rich Theatre in downtown Tucson. From I-10 take the Congress/Broadway exit and follow Broadway east, then turn right at Grenada. **TICKETS/INFO:** 520-298-5806 **ACCOMMODATIONS/TOURIST INFO:** 520-624-1817, 800-638-8530

ᴘHOENIX FOLK TRADITIONS ACOUSTIC MUSIC FESTIVAL
PHOENIX ✴ A WEEKEND IN LATE MARCH OR EARLY APRIL

This participatory festival brings together musicians at all levels playing on one amplified stage and in several acoustic-only performance areas. Up to 180 musicians typically make the scene, and many audience members who come to listen one year return the next with an instrument in hand. Workshops feature instrumental instruction or cover topics like "the history of the banjo," and the grounds are kept clear of arts and crafts to allow more room for small groups of musicians who just want to jam and make new friends. Admission is free.   **LOCATION:** Encanto Park, 2605 North 15th Avenue (at Encanto Boulevard) in Phoenix **TICKETS/INFO:** 602-495-5458 **ACCOMMODATIONS/TOURIST INFO:** 602-252-5588

ᴛUCSON FOLK FESTIVAL
TUCSON ✴ A WEEKEND IN LATE APRIL OR EARLY MAY

Tucson folkies can hardly imagine a spring without the music and camaraderie generated by the Tucson Folk Festival. The scope is incredibly eclectic, with styles ranging from jazz to country to bluegrass to—you guessed it—folk. Tucson's festival focuses much more on performance than the interactive Prescott or Phoenix gigs, and two stages are active both Saturday and Sunday with regional headliners as well as musicians from in and around Tucson. In addition to the performances, the downtown park is filled with impromptu musical get-togethers, workshops, arts and crafts, food booths, and a Song Tree for songwriter confabs.   **LOCATION:** El Presidio Park in downtown Tucson **TICKETS/INFO:** 520-881-2016 **ACCOMMODATIONS/TOURIST INFO:** 520-624-1817, 800-638-8350

BLACK & WHITE & BLUES
PHOENIX ✱ SUNDAY OF MEMORIAL DAY WEEKEND (MEMORIAL DAY IS THE LAST MONDAY IN MAY)

With music all day and most of the night, Black & White & Blues is the premier early-summer event on the Phoenix blues calendar. Nearly 2,000 people pack the Rhythm Room's indoor/outdoor setup to catch 15 to 20 performers ranging from local bands to nationally known superstars. The barbecue's great, and all proceeds benefit Visual Uplift, a charity for at-risk youth.   **LOCATION:** The Rhythm Room blues club, 1019 Indian School Road in central Phoenix **TICKETS/INFO:** 602-274-0552 **ACCOM-MODATIONS/TOURIST INFO:** 602-254-6500, 602-252-5588

SEDONA CHAMBER MUSIC FESTIVAL
SEDONA AND ENVIRONS ✱ LATE MAY THROUGH MID-JUNE

Nestled within beautiful red rock formations, the town of Sedona offers a great backdrop for this growing festival. Recent guests have included the St. Petersburg String Quartet, the Valencia Trio, and the Asbury Brass Quintet, as well as many local Arizona musicians. Weekend concerts are in Sedona, while midweek concerts are held in the neighboring mining towns of Jerome and Prescott. Interesting features include informal Concert Conversations 30 minutes before each concert and Sunday afternoon's Musical Instrument Zoo, a hands-on display for young and old with string, wind, and percussion instruments.   **LOCATION:** Concerts are held at the Sedona Arts Center, off Highway 89A on Art Barn Drive; the Church of the Red Rocks, off Highway 179 on Bowstring Drive in Sedona; and other locations in Jerome, Prescott, and Oak Creek. Sedona is located about 25 miles south of Flagstaff. **TICKETS/INFO:** 520-282-2415 **ACCOMMO-DATIONS/TOURIST INFO:** 520-282-7722, 800-288-7336

ARIZONA JAZZ, RHYTHM & BLUES FESTIVAL
FLAGSTAFF ✱ A WEEKEND IN LATE JUNE OR EARLY JULY

Presented by the organizers of the Telluride Jazz Festival, the Arizona Jazz, Rhythm & Blues Festival brings top R&B, jazz, gospel, and blues stars to Flagstaff. The festival began in 1995 with an interesting and encouraging lineup, including the likes of Luther "Guitar Junior" Johnson, Sister Sledge, Arturo Sandoval, and Buckwheat Zydeco. A free downtown kickoff concert gets the festival moving Friday night, then the action moves to Foxglenn City Park, which offers an excellent view of the mountains. Tickets are about $35, and each night many of Flagstaff's downtown clubs present postfestival programs of jazz, blues, and R&B.   **LOCATION:** Foxglenn City Park in Flagstaff, just off I-17 at the McConnell Drive exit. Friday night show is at Wheeler Park in downtown Flagstaff. **TICKETS/INFO:** 800-520-1646, 520-744-9675 **ACCOMMODATIONS/TOURIST INFO:** 520-779-7611

ℐAZZ FEST

CHANDLER ✷ A WEEKEND IN SEPTEMBER

At Chandler's unique Jazz Fest, musicians serenade the audience from a concrete slab in the middle of a water basin while spectators stay cool as they float in the water. Regional jazz, Dixieland, and reggae bands are featured at this free festival, which also offers pony rides and a fireworks display to entertain the kids.   **LOCATION:** Arrowhead Meadows Park on Erie Street in Chandler, just southeast of Phoenix **TICKETS/ INFO:** 602-786-2518 **ACCOMMODATIONS/TOURIST INFO:** 602-786-2518, 602-252-5588

ℐEPTIEMBRE FIESTA FESTIVAL

WICKENBURG ✷ FIRST WEEKEND IN SEPTEMBER

This celebration of Mexican American culture focuses on music and includes plenty of country fiddling and mariachi. The food is also great, and before the last concert a salsa contest tests both cooks and tasters (especially the "extra hot" category). With mouths on fire, everyone gets down to some serious after-dinner dancing. **LOCATION:** Outside the Desert Caballeros Museum in Wickenburg, about 55 miles northwest of Phoenix via U.S. 60/89 **TICKETS/INFO:** 520-684-5479 **ACCOMMODA-TIONS/TOURIST INFO:** 520-684-5479, 800-942-5242

ℐRAND CANYON CHAMBER MUSIC FESTIVAL

GRAND CANYON ✷ THREE WEEKENDS BEGINNING THE WEEKEND AFTER LABOR DAY (LABOR DAY IS THE FIRST MONDAY IN SEPTEMBER)

During mid-September, the Grand Canyon's south rim is filled to the brim with chamber music and, occasionally, jazz. Concerts are held at the Shrine of the Ages, and the musical variety lures a crowd from the canyon's breathtaking sights for some equally engaging sounds. Tickets are about $10.   **LOCATION:** The Shrine of the Ages, on the south rim of the Grand Canyon Grand Canyon National Park **TICKETS/INFO:** 520-638-9215 **ACCOMMODATIONS/TOURIST INFO:** 520-638-2901

ℐTATE CHAMPIONSHIP OLD TIME FIDDLERS' CONTEST

PAYSON ✷ A WEEKEND IN LATE SEPTEMBER, SATURDAY AND SUNDAY

Among the tall pines of Payson, toes tap and hands clap to fancy fiddlin' during these two musical days at the town rodeo grounds. Fiddlers from all over the state compete for Arizona championship titles in divisions including Twin Fiddling, Trick Fiddling, and the ever popular Band Scramble. In addition to the fiddling, this festival includes other aspects of cowboy culture that are bound to fascinate anyone who's not from around these parts: cloggers dance, cowboy poets philosophize, fiddle makers craft, workshop leaders teach, and at high noon competitors offer up the traditional Payson 21-Fiddle Salute.   **LOCATION:** Payson Rodeo Grounds, near the junction of Highway 87 and Highway 260, about 75 miles northeast of Phoenix **TICKETS/INFO:** 520-474-5242, 520-474-3397 **ACCOMMODATIONS/TOURIST INFO:** 800-672-9766, 520-474-4515

Jazz on the Rocks: Diverse music and a spectacular location draw the faithful to Sedona's jazz party. Courtesy of Dick Canby/Sedona Jazz on the Rocks

SEDONA JAZZ ON THE ROCKS
SEDONA ✹ LAST SATURDAY IN SEPTEMBER

With a truly spectacular location and a program as innovative and diverse as jazz itself, Jazz on the Rocks has carved a world-class niche for itself. Each year, some 5,000 jazz fans from around the country gather in a grassy amphitheater surrounded by spectacular views to take in acts that tend toward the traditional and have recently included Diane Schuur, Gerry Mulligan, and Gene Harris. The program usually also includes at least one blues band.

The day begins with the Jazz on the Rocks Youth Band at 9:00 A.M., and by that time much of the audience has arrived, carrying blankets and picnic lunches. With about five acts, the music usually lasts until just before sundown, but the bars and restaurants in Sedona pick up the pace with gigs and jam sessions late into the night.   **LOCATION:** Warren Hamilton Amphitheater, off Highway 179 between I-17 and Sedona, about 25 miles south of Flagstaff **TICKETS/INFO:** 520-282-1985 **ACCOMMODATIONS/TOURIST INFO:** 520-282-7722, 800-288-7336

SHARLOT HALL MUSEUM FOLK MUSIC FESTIVAL
PRESCOTT ✹ FIRST WEEKEND IN OCTOBER

Dubbed by locals "the friendliest little festival in the West," Prescott's folk festival features a surprisingly diverse range of local talent over its two-day run. Each year's lineup depends on who's in town and what skills they have, but you can expect to hear guitars, autoharps, fiddles, Native American flutes, and much more from the 100 or so musicians and dancers who perform free of charge. The festival strives for interactivity, offering plenty of opportunities for participation through singing, dancing, and strumming along. Workshops are many, and should you be inspired to take up an instrument, you might find just what you're looking for at Sunday morning's Instrument Swap Meet.

Blues boil-over:
Sam Taylor at
the 1995 Tucson
Blues Festival.

Courtesy of Tucson Blues Founda-

tion

LOCATION: Sharlot Hall Museum, 415 West Gurley Street, Prescott **TICKETS/INFO:** 520-445-3123 **ACCOMMODATIONS/TOURIST INFO:** 800-266-7534, 520-445-2000

TUCSON BLUES FESTIVAL
TUCSON ✷ THIRD WEEKEND IN OCTOBER

Although the official festival waits until Saturday, blues sounds course through Tucson up to a week in advance of the big day. Blues in the Schools and other Blues Week events set the mood for Saturday's big boil-over in midtown's Reid Park, which features half a dozen nationally known blues stars plus some local up-and-comers. In addition to the official stages, street performers are everywhere, and bars feature bluesy entertainment as part of the city's Downtown Saturday Night festival, which runs concurrently.   **LOCATION:** Midtown Tucson's Reid Park at 22nd Street and Country Club Road **TICKETS/INFO:** 520-325-9192 **ACCOMMODATIONS/TOURIST INFO:** 520-624-1817, 800-638-8350

₡COTTSDALE DIXIELAND JAZZ FESTIVAL

SCOTTSDALE ✴ WEEKEND NEAREST NOVEMBER 11 (VETERANS DAY),
FRIDAY–SUNDAY

Hot jazz combines with Arizona's warm fall days and nights as 12 bands from the western United States play some 36 hours of music over the weekend. The Arizona Classic Jazz Society, which organizes the festival, favors traditional jazz, Dixieland, swing, and show bands. In addition to regular sets in ballrooms and a tent, each band presents a special 75-minute historical theme show highlighting legendary composers and early jazz styles. Admission is about $40 for all three days. **LOCATION:** Ramada Valley Ho Resort, 6850 Main Street, Scottsdale **TICKETS/INFO:** 602-464-8773; e-mail: Hawkpshaw@aol.com **ACCOMMODATIONS/TOURIST INFO:** 800-677-1117, 602-945-8481

₣OUR CORNER STATES BLUEGRASS FESTIVAL AND FIDDLE CHAMPIONSHIP

WICKENBURG ✴ MID-NOVEMBER

This small town's rodeo grounds provide the venue for this festival, which boasts "bluegrass as it was meant to be: a grassroots, folksy fusion of country and western, blues, folk, and gospel in the tradition of the great Bill Monroe." Food booths, arts and crafts, beer tents (coolers and BYO aren't allowed), and informal jam sessions all augment the good-time atmosphere, as do individual fiddle contest categories. A Band Scramble encourages do-it-yourselfers to put together bands, piece by piece, and then do some amateur, spur-of-the-minute jamming. **LOCATION:** The Everett Bowman Rodeo Grounds on Constellation Road in Wickenburg, about 55 miles northwest of Phoenix via U.S. 60/89 **TICKETS/INFO:** 520-684-5479 **ACCOMMODATIONS/TOURIST INFO:** 520-684-5479, 800-942-5242

₡ANDPOINT'S FIDDLERS' JAMBORINA

LAKE HAVASU CITY ✴ WEEKEND BEFORE THANKSGIVING DAY
(THANKSGIVING DAY IS THE FOURTH THURSDAY IN NOVEMBER)

Competitions at this RV park and marina range from old-time fiddling to bluegrass fiddling to clog dancing and even horseshoe throwing. A free jam session on Friday and a barbecue/square dance on Saturday keep spectators entertained, and if you love to jam by the campfire, here's the spot to indulge to your heart's content. **LOCATION:** Sandpoint Marina and RV Park, on the south shore of Lake Havasu, Lake Havasu City, along Highway 95 at Arizona's western border **TICKETS/INFO:** 520-855-0549 **ACCOMMODATIONS/TOURIST INFO:** 520-855-0549

NeVaDa

FIESTA NEVADA CELEBRATION
SPARKS ✸ FIRST WEEKEND IN MAY

Eight city blocks are closed off for this large (and free) Cinco de Mayo festival, and although many in the crowd can't precisely trace the holiday to the 1862 battle in which Mexican volunteers routed the French in Puebla, there's no shortage of musical good times. Six stages feature a melting pot of Latin American music, including mariachi, *banda*, and Spanglish "spittin' lingo" rap, as well as folkloric and ballet troupes and musicians from throughout the American Southwest. Numerous vendors sell ethnic food, and hundreds of folk dancers entertain the relaxed crowd of 35,000 to 50,000. **LOCATION:** Sparks is just northeast of Reno on I-80 **TICKETS/INFO:** 702-353-2291 **ACCOMMODATIONS/TOURIST INFO:** 800-367-7366, 702-827-7366

DESERT OASIS BLUEGRASS FESTIVAL
FALLON ✸ SECOND OR THIRD WEEKEND IN MAY, FRIDAY–SUNDAY

This festival traditionally kicks off the bluegrass circuit in the Southwest, offering a relaxed atmosphere under perfect desert weather—bright blue skies and low mountains in the distance. In addition to bluegrass performances by a varied lineup (recent guests have included the David Grisman Quintet, the Bluegrass Patriots, and the Cox Family), there are arts and crafts, free-flowing beer, and 15 acres of RV and camping ground. Excellent workshops focus on flat-picking, songwriting, vocal harmony, clogging, and even mandolin care. The weekend package deal is great for campers staying more than one night. **LOCATION:** Sixty miles east of Reno at Churchill County Fairgrounds in Fallon, just off I-80 **TICKETS/INFO:** 702-423-7733 **ACCOMMODATIONS/TOURIST INFO:** 800-874-0903, 702-423-4556

JUNEFEST
LAS VEGAS ✸ FIRST SATURDAY IN JUNE

If you count yourself among the generation that felt the earth move under the weight of rock dinosaurs like Foreigner, Ted Nugent, and Bad Company, you'll be in good company at this family-oriented beer bash in the entertainment capital of the

Fiesta Nevada Celebration: Mariachi and other south-of-the-border sounds keep this Cinco de Mayo celebration hopping. (See entry, page 333.) Courtesy of Reno News Bureau

world. Vegas classic-rock station KKLZ sponsors the yearly get-together, drawing five or six bands and some 30,000 fans. Since many of the audience come with young children in tow, a variety of carnival rides, pony rides, and other children's activities are set up, and tickets sell for about one-seventh of what the Eagles charged to play next door at Sam Boyd Stadium.   **LOCATION:** Silver Bowl Park in Henderson, just off Boulder Highway about 15 miles southeast of Las Vegas **TICKETS/INFO:** 702-739-9600, 702-474-4000 **ACCOMMODATIONS/TOURIST INFO:** 702-892-0711, 702-565-8951

♪JAZZ, BLUEGRASS, & BARBECUE
PAHRUMP ✹ WEEKEND AFTER LABOR DAY (LABOR DAY IS THE FIRST MONDAY IN SEPTEMBER)

One of many events during the festival season at the Pahrump Winery, this musical get-together features some great bands, beautiful silver-mine-country scenery, and fine-tastin' barbecue and local wine. The bands are mostly regionally known, and the small crowd and intimate atmosphere accentuate the relaxed qualities of the festival. **LOCATION:** Pahrump Winery, 3810 Winery Road in Pahrump, 65 miles west of Las Vegas on Highway 160, just east of the California border **TICKETS/INFO:** 800-368-9463 **ACCOMMODATIONS/TOURIST INFO:** 702-727-5800

♪LUEGRASS & OLD TIME MUSIC FESTIVAL

LOGANDALE ✷ A WEEKEND IN EARLY OCTOBER, FRIDAY–SUNDAY

This family-oriented "jammer's festival" presents one of the region's few opportunities to hear old-time string bands with harps and fiddles, plus bluegrass and old-time country of all kinds. The action starts Friday morning with local bands and moves into the afternoon and evening with well-known acts from far and wide. The Southern Nevada Bluegrass Music Society presents a bluegrass band contest, with a $1,000 first prize. On Saturday, bands play until 9 P.M., then the jamming kicks in and keeps raging late into the night.   **LOCATION:** Clark Country Fairgrounds. From Las Vegas go northeast on U.S. 15 toward Mesquite, then south on Highway 169. **TICKETS/INFO:** 702-564-5455 **ACCOMMODATIONS/TOURIST INFO:** 702-346-2702

NEW MEXICO

INTERNATIONAL FIESTA FIDDLE CONTEST
TRUTH OR CONSEQUENCES ✻ LAST WEEKEND IN APRIL, FRIDAY–SUNDAY

At this long-running festival, traditional old-time fiddle is king and bluegrass or progressive fiddle techniques are allowed only in informal jam sessions. There's a gospel sing on Sunday morning, dances Friday and Saturday nights, and eight divisions of competition. And if fiddling history is your thing, be sure to check out the New Mexico Old-Time Fiddlers Hall of Fame, located in the Geronimo Springs Museum. **LOCATION:** Truth or Consequences Civic Center, 400 West Fourth Street. Truth or Consequences is located about 140 miles south of Albuquerque just off I-25. **TICKETS/ INFO:** 505-894-2847 **ACCOMMODATIONS/TOURIST INFO:** 505-894-3536, 800-831-9487

RIVERFEST
FARMINGTON ✻ MEMORIAL DAY WEEKEND, FRIDAY–SUNDAY (MEMORIAL DAY IS THE LAST MONDAY OF MAY)

This musical potpourri livens up Farmington's mellow waterfront with the sounds of rock 'n' roll, bluegrass, country, even barbershop. As the groups (mostly regionally known) perform, about 10,000 people dance or mill about, eating Navajo tacos or participating in the duck race or fine-arts show. **LOCATION:** Berg Park, at the corner of San Juan and Scott Boulevard, on Farmington's waterfront. Farmington is in the northwest corner of the state, at U.S. 64 and Highway 371. **TICKETS/INFO:** 800-448-1240 **ACCOMMODATIONS/TOURIST INFO:** 800-448-1240

CLOUDCROFT BLUEGRASS FESTIVAL
CLOUDCROFT ✻ FOURTH WEEKEND IN JUNE

Boasting a combination of traditional bluegrass and "newgrass," this free festival is geared toward the families of Cloudcroft and surrounding communities. Cloudcroft is a mountain resort town (elevation 8,900 feet) with trendy little shops, and the festival promises nothing more than good times and a little bluegrass music in the town park. **LOCATION:** Cloudcroft is located in the Lincoln National Forest in the southern part of the state, on U.S. 82 about 12 miles east of U.S. 54 **TICKETS/INFO:** 505-746-9351 **ACCOMMODATIONS/TOURIST INFO:** 505-682-2733

Santa Fe Opera Festival: Gweynne Geyer (center) in the 1995 production of Emmerich Kalman's Countess Maritza. *Courtesy of Hans Fahrmeyer/Santa Fe Opera*

THE SANTA FE OPERA FESTIVAL
SANTA FE ✹ LATE JUNE THROUGH AUGUST

Front-row spectators at the Santa Fe Opera gasp as a young mezzo-soprano holds a haunting note. Is it because she sings so perfectly and looks so elegant before the sparkling lights of Los Alamos? Or is it because a giant moth just flew into her mouth? Whatever the case, it's all part of the outdoor experience at this opera in the foothills of the Sangre de Cristo Mountains.

For 40 years, Santa Fe has hosted an engaging range of operas, from Mozart and Strauss classics to world premieres. The open-air theater, which blends seamlessly with its natural surroundings, welcomes a mix of seasoned Santa Fe Opera singers and those making their debuts. Veteran operagoers from surrounding states and even Mexico travel hundreds of miles to partake in some of the opera's three dozen or so performances spanning nine weeks.

Neither thunder, nor lightning, nor cold weather (all uninvited guests at the opera at one time or another) will keep die-hard fans at home, but seasoned veterans know that appropriate gear is essential. Plans call for a new opera theater in 1998 that will provide full shelter from the rain while maintaining a clear view of mountains and sky through the open sides and clerestory.

Ticket holders are welcome to indulge in their own food and drink in "the most beautiful parking lot in the world" before performances, with the biggest tailgate bash occurring on the gala opening night. Here you'll find a mix of sequins and combat boots, boleros and bow ties, boas and spurs as the region's cowboy elite feast on sauteed ostrich meat, caviar, and guacamole. Some tailgaters engage gourmet caterers for elegant seven-course meals under tents (complete with crystal candelabras); others use their rear bumpers as chairs and drink cheap wine from paper cups. Name-dropping season-ticket holders are often the butt of local jokes, but even they are ever ready to raise a glass of bubbly with the grungiest of opera lovers.

Individual ticket prices range from $20 to more than $200, depending on the seat, the night of the week, and the occasion. Special events include opportunities for young people to see the opera at discounted prices, free tours and activities for families, an opera insights discussion series, backstage tours, and preopera suppers and desserts. After each performance, the Santa Fe Opera Orchestra plays for onstage waltzing under the stars.   **LOCATION:** Seven miles north of Santa Fe on U.S. 84/285 **TICKETS/INFO:** 505-986-5900, 505-986-5955 **ACCOMMODATIONS/TOURIST INFO:** 800-777-2489, 505-984-6760

CHAMA VALLEY MUSIC FESTIVAL
CHAMA ✶ FRIDAYS AND SATURDAYS IN JULY

At the western terminus of America's longest and highest narrow-gauge railroad, the Cumbres & Toltec, this mountain town of 1,250 residents hosts performers that represent a great cross section of the world's musical and cultural traditions. Stylistically, the music is all over the place—bluegrass, big band, light opera, Native American, flamenco, African, a capella—with one or two bands playing each night. Chama itself is one of the prettiest towns in New Mexico, and although it's quite a road trip from urban centers, the hiking, biking, and fishing opportunities—not to mention the music— make it well worth the trip.   **LOCATION:** Either take the Cumbres & Toltec Scenic Railroad from Antonito, Colorado, or drive north from Santa Fe on U.S. 285/84, following U.S. 84 at the split in Espanola. Chama is about 10 miles south of the Colorado state line. **TICKETS/INFO:** 505-756-2836 **ACCOMMODATIONS/TOURIST INFO:** 800-477-0149, 505-756-2306

SANTA FE CHAMBER MUSIC FESTIVAL
SANTA FE ✶ SECOND WEEK IN JULY THROUGH THE THIRD WEEK IN AUGUST

Nestled in the Sangre de Cristo Mountains, this wide-ranging festival attracts the nation's outstanding young musicians. High artistic standards are complemented by an incredibly wide repertory and some 50 guest soloists—many of whom gain a nationwide audience through broadcasts over National Public Radio.

The festival's core is traditional chamber music, with a roster of distinguished artists presenting everything from Mozart and Brahms to contemporary composers like Alfred Schnittke and Richard Danielpour. Beyond chamber music, the five-week season includes measures of serious jazz and even tango, which is quite popular around Santa Fe. Nearly every day of the week has something for the music lover, with previous years featuring highlights like tenor John Aler doing Debussy's *Homage à Rameau*, flutist Herbie Mann exploring high-note jazz, and soprano Benita Valente in Milhaud's *La Creation du Monde.*

Performances are definitely on the expensive side, but free lectures, rehearsals, and workshops abound. Plus, a youth concert series brings "older" music to the younger generation. And contrary to popular belief, not all programs are sold out weeks in advance—but particular performances will be.   **LOCATION:** Several venues in Santa

Chamber music and more: Multi-instrumentalist Mark O'Connor leads a
workshop for children at the 1992 Santa Fe Chamber Music Festival. Courtesy of
Murrae Haynes/Santa Fe Chamber Music Festival

Fe **TICKETS/INFO:** 505-983-2075, 505-982-1890 **ACCOMMODATIONS/TOURIST
INFO:** 800-777-2489, 505-984-6760

ℳARIACHI SPECTACULAR
ALBUQUERQUE ✱ SECOND WEEKEND IN JULY, WEDNESDAY–SUNDAY

Popularized as wedding music around the turn of the century, mariachi still holds
an important place in the hearts of the millions of Mexicans who moved across the
border to the southwestern United States. This three-day spectacular is like a trip back
home for nearly 20,000 people who mob the University of New Mexico's basketball
arena and the State Fairgrounds in Albuquerque. Organizers bring in a couple of dozen
mariachi groups and singers from Mexico and the United States, beginning with Friday
night student showcase concerts and ending with a giant gathering of 14 groups on eight
stages at the fairgrounds. Acts run the gamut from traditional to contemporary to
crossover mariachi.   **LOCATION:** Friday: Pope Joy Hall on UNM campus. Saturday:
Basketball Arena ("The Pit") on UNM campus. Sunday: New Mexico State Fairgrounds.
TICKETS/INFO: 505-277-5095, 505-277-2931 **ACCOMMODATIONS/TOURIST
INFO:** 800-284-2282, 505-842-9918

Gallup Inter-Tribal Indian Ceremonial
GALLUP ✸ SIX DAYS BEGINNING THE TUESDAY BEFORE THE SECOND
THURSDAY IN AUGUST

This full-fledged Indian exposition is unusual in its coverage of both traditional and modern Native American music. Traditional drum groups are primarily Southwestern and form the beating heart of the dances of the Navajo, Hopi, Zuni, and Apache tribes, as well as various Pueblo tribes like the Taos. Each is typically in the spotlight for only 10 minutes at a time, so you'll see musicians and dancers going all out in pursuit of prizes.

Nearby, the activity at the outdoor Marland Aitson Amphitheater provides a distinct contrast to the traditional drums, flutes, and singing. Here you might experience everything from head-banging rock bands to jazz pianists and dancers, the only common denominator being that all the performers are Native American. From 10 A.M. to 6 P.M., a different group takes the stage every 30 to 45 minutes, providing a lively survey of the diverse range of Native American talent in the Southwest. Country, along with its many tangents, is probably the dominant form, but look out for charming local styles like "song and dance," a less twangy, less Spanish-influenced variation on southern Arizona "chicken scratch."

The ceremonial began in 1922, and it's quite a show. More than 30,000 people attend over six days. Nonmusical events include an all-Indian rodeo, Native American sports and foods, and more than $15 million worth of Southwest arts and crafts. **LOCATION:** Red Rock State Park, six miles east of Gallup on the I-40 frontage road **TICKETS/INFO:** 800-233-4528, 505-863-3896 **ACCOMMODATIONS/TOURIST INFO:** 800-242-4282, 505-722-2228

Music from Angel Fire
ANGEL FIRE AND NEARBY TOWNS ✸ LAST WEDNESDAY IN AUGUST
THROUGH THE FIRST MONDAY IN SEPTEMBER (LABOR DAY)

The late summer in northern New Mexico is a classical music lover's paradise. As a counterpoint to the lavish productions of Santa Fe's opera and the high prices of its chamber music festival, Music from Angel Fire presents intimate, affordable chamber music in four towns in northern New Mexico. Angel Fire, Taos, Las Vegas, and Raton welcome some 35 soloists—plus about 15 returning ensemble members—for a week of chamber performances.   **LOCATION:** Various venues in Angel Fire, Taos, Las Vegas, and Raton **TICKETS/INFO:** 505-377-3233 **ACCOMMODATIONS/TOURIST INFO:** 800-446-8117, 505-377-6611, 505-377-6353

Santa Fe Banjo and Fiddle Contest
SANTA FE ✸ LAST WEEKEND IN AUGUST OR FIRST WEEKEND IN SEPTEMBER,
FRIDAY–SUNDAY

This late-summer festival focuses mainly on bluegrass but also features the area's rarely heard Spanish-fiddle players. Living in the hills around Santa Fe, the Spanish fiddlers play a style of music that sounds a bit like mariachi without the guitars, and this is one of their few opportunities to perform in public. Northern New Mexico is beautiful in late summer, and the rodeo grounds are carpeted with the sound of banjos and fiddles in concerts, contests, and jam sessions. Friday night begins with a contra dance, and Saturday afternoon moves into contests that are more low-key than serious. Saturday night features concerts by all musical guests, including one national big-timer, while Sunday afternoon features band contests. Tickets are $5 a day, and camping is free. **LOCATION:** Santa Fe Rodeo Grounds. From Santa Fe go south on Cerrillos Road and turn left on Rodeo Road. **TICKETS/INFO:** 505-471-3462 **ACCOMMODATIONS/ TOURIST INFO:** 800-777-2489

NEW MEXICO OLD-TIME FIDDLERS' STATE CHAMPIONSHIP

TRUTH OR CONSEQUENCES ✷ THIRD WEEKEND IN OCTOBER, FRIDAY–SUNDAY

Over the course of this weekend, more than 40 fiddlers typically show up to make a go for the title of "best old-time fiddler in New Mexico" in eight divisions. Fiddlers compete and concertize in front of some 1,500 people, and the event climaxes with inductions into the New Mexico Old-Time Fiddlers Hall of Fame (which is located in the town's Geronimo Springs Museum).   **LOCATION:** Truth or Consequences Civic Center, 400 West Fourth Street. Truth or Consequences is located about 140 miles south of Albuquerque just off I-25. **TICKETS/INFO:** 505-894-2847 **ACCOMMODATIONS/ TOURIST INFO:** 505-894-3536, 800-831-9487

JANIS JOPLIN'S BIRTHDAY BASH
PORT ARTHUR ✸ SECOND SATURDAY IN JANUARY

When Janis Joplin left southeast Texas for fame and fortune on the West Coast, she took along an abiding respect for the Gulf Coast's country/blues heritage. Her hometown of Port Arthur celebrates that heritage each year with a musical tribute to Joplin and other stars of the Texas-Louisiana border area, including J. P. "Big Bopper" Richardson, Clarence "Gatemouth" Brown, Tex Ritter, Edgar and Johnny Winter, and Clifton Chenier.

Since 1988, fans have traveled from all over Texas and several other states for a weekend of live music ranging from straight blues to R&B to rock 'n' roll. The scene is nostalgic as old-timers like Cookie & the Cup Cakes ("Matilda," "Got You on My Mind") and Phil Phillips ("Sea of Love") revive the music that inspired rock's first female superstar. In addition to originals and covers of Janis's songs, the program includes a ceremony to induct honorees into the Gulf Coast Musical Hall of Fame, located in Port Arthur's Museum of the Gulf Coast. While you're there, be sure to check out the museum's excellent collection of rock memorabilia.   **LOCATION:** Port Arthur Civic Center in Port Arthur, 90 miles east of Houston. From Highway 73 take the Ninth Avenue exit. **TICKETS/INFO:** 409-722-3699 **ACCOMMODATIONS/TOURIST INFO:** 409-985-7822, 800-235-7822

TRADITIONAL MUSIC FESTIVAL
AUSTIN ✸ A SATURDAY OR SUNDAY IN MID-JANUARY

The Austin Friends of Traditional Music created this informal one-day event to fill an early-in-the-year void in the Austin music calendar. About half of the eight acts celebrate American traditions (e.g., old-time country, bluegrass), while the other half focus on international music (e.g., Iranian, Hungarian, Irish, or Breton). Many groups bring their own dancers, and since this is a decidedly *participative* event, don't be surprised if someone grabs an arm and pulls you onto the dance floor. Children's activities are plentiful, as are music workshops and musical-instrument vendors. **LOCATION:** Dougherty Arts Center, 1110 Barton Springs Road **TICKETS/INFO:** 512-454-9481; e-mail: johnbeatty@mail.utexas.edu. **ACCOMMODATIONS/TOURIST INFO:** 512-474-5171, 512-478-0098, 800-888-8287

RIO GRANDE VALLEY INTERNATIONAL MUSIC FESTIVAL

MCALLEN, HARLINGEN, PORT ISABEL, AND SOUTH PADRE ISLAND ✷ EIGHT DAYS IN LATE JANUARY OR EARLY FEBRUARY

This innovative music program is geared toward grade-school children and features eight educational concerts in elementary schools. The festival—called international because it draws an audience from both sides of the United States-Mexico border—was started in 1960 and is credited with instilling an interest in classical music among children in the Rio Grande Valley. In addition to the children's shows, two pops concerts (in McAllen and Harlingen) and one classical concert (on South Padre Island) are open to the public; shows start at 8 P.M.   **LOCATION:** McAllen International Civic Center, 1300 South 10th Street, McAllen. Harlingen Municipal Auditorium, 1204 Fair Park Boulevard, Harlingen. Port Isabel High School Auditorium, on Highway 100 in Port Isabel. Radisson Resort Hotel, 500 Padre Boulevard, South Padre Island. **TICKETS/ INFO:** 210-686-1456 **ACCOMMODATIONS/TOURIST INFO:** 210-682-2871, 210-423-5440, 800-531-7346

NORTH TEXAS IRISH FESTIVAL

DALLAS ✷ FIRST WEEKEND IN MARCH, FRIDAY–SUNDAY

Although a consultant once told the Southwest Celtic Music Association that they'd draw bigger crowds and profits with stunts like dyeing the beer green and dressing volunteers as leprechauns, the association wisely ignored this advice and kept the North Texas Irish Festival focused on the single most important element driving Irish culture today: music.

This is the American Southwest's premier gathering of top Celtic musicians from both Europe and America, and although a few leprechauns have crept in (to entertain the kids), you'd never mistake this fest for an ethnic theme park. Music flows from eight stages, and despite the "Irish" in the event's name, the acts highlight a much broader spectrum of Celtic musical traditions. Bookings have included the likes of the Breton All-Stars from Brittany (France), Brendan Nolan from Newfoundland, and first-rank Irish acts like Altan, Reeltime, and Barleycorn. The festival also features American bands that are faithfully preserving Celtic traditions, or building on them.

Even though there's not a huge concentration of Irish people in the Dallas area, the crowd of about 20,000 generates plenty of enthusiasm. The festival also features dozens of opportunities to participate as well as listen, with dance competitions, storytellers, and workshops in music, dance, and the Gaelic language. Admission is about $10 per day. **LOCATION:** Fair Park (State Fairgrounds), one mile east of downtown just off I-30 in Dallas **TICKETS/INFO:** 214-821-4174; e-mail: NTIFEST@aol.com; World Wide Web: http://www.wweb.com/ntif **ACCOMMODATIONS/TOURIST INFO:** 214-746-6677, 214-234-4448

SOUTH TEXAS MUSIC FEST & INTERNATIONAL BULL CHIP THROWING CONTEST

WESLACO ✷ SECOND WEEK IN MARCH, THURSDAY–SUNDAY

Big park, big prize, and a tremendous variety of Texas music: these are the makings of the Texas-style hullabaloo held each year in Weslaco. Musicians flock to the festival as

No gimmicks:
The North Texas
Irish Festival cel-
ebrates authentic
Celtic traditions
with performers
like musician/
storyteller Pat-
rick Ball. (See
entry, page 343.)

Courtesy of North Texas Irish Fes-

tival

early as Monday, from as far away as Canada, carrying fiddles, banjos, guitars, accordions, and other instruments of musical merrymaking. The sounds of folk, country,
bluegrass, mariachi, and Tejano music fill the 46-acre park, and some 30,000 fans (from
the United States, Europe, and even Australia) enjoy the music and absorb the
semitropical beauty of the Rio Grande Valley. And $25,000 or more goes to the person
who breaks the Guinness-certified world record for bull chip throwing (now at 266 feet).
LOCATION: Downtown Weslaco, on Texas Street south of U.S. 83, with a main stage on
Kansas Street. Alternate location is the 46-acre Weslaco City Park on Airport Drive.
TICKETS/INFO: 210-464-7767 **ACCOMMODATIONS/TOURIST INFO:** 210-968-
2102

SHAMROCK MUSIC FESTIVAL

DALLAS ✹ WEEKEND CLOSEST TO ST. PATRICK'S DAY (MARCH 17)

Green beer flows from taps all over Dallas's McKinney Avenue as thousands come to
the arts district to enjoy rock, jazz, blues, country, and, of course, Celtic music. Six to
eight stages dot the street, and a parade with bagpipers entertains scores of families. After

South by South-west: More than 500 up-and-coming acts in "the live music capital of the world."

Courtesy of Andrew Shapter/Austin

Convention & Visitors Bureau

the festival ends at 8 P.M., footloose revelers keep the party pounding in neighborhood pubs.   **LOCATION:** McKinney Avenue in Dallas's art district **TICKETS/INFO:** 214-821-7494 **ACCOMMODATIONS/TOURIST INFO:** 214-746-6677, 214-234-4448

SOUTH BY SOUTHWEST

AUSTIN ✷ THIRD WEEK IN MARCH, WEDNESDAY–SUNDAY

South by Southwest (SXSW) perfected a formula that, although it seemed bizarre a few years ago, has been so successful that it made this four-night extravaganza one of the world's most significant music events. Basically, the idea is to attract some 500 of the best up-and-coming acts in nonmainstream music genres with opportunities to perform in front of industry honchos and attend conferences designed to give performers an edge on success.

For four nights, Austin—a musical hotbed even on a slow night—is absolutely delirious with live music as hundreds of performers and more than 20,000 fans take over the convention center and about 30 of the city's finest clubs. Outdoor stages, unplugged stages, and dozens of booze-and-schmooze events provide ample opportunities to select the hip from the merely hyped, whether you like country and roots rock, alternative rock, rap, R&B, blues, folk, or bluegrass.

Basically, there are two types of visitors to SXSW: those with a see-and-be-seen agenda, and those who just want to check out what's new and have some fun. That one faction can't escape the other is probably SXSW's greatest irony; as the event has grown, more shows have become invite-only, and in the queues that spring up outside overcrowded clubs each night, Austin's laid-back spirit is challenged by tension between cell phone-toting big shots and average Joes and Janes.

Still, SXSW's position as the top new-music showcase on the continent makes it a great place to catch up-and-coming bands before the buzz becomes a roar. And if you prefer to miss out on what the "experts" have to say about topics like "Junkie in the Band," or "Corruption: A Tradition," you don't have to attend the goofy panel discussions. Instead, you can have a hoot sitting on outdoor patios (spring comes early here), checking out new bands or the big names that SXSW has attracted as it's grown. Or, you can browse through the General Store for CDs, T-shirts, and other goods, or take in the film and multimedia festivals that run concurrently.

Despite tons of cosmopolitan visitors from the East and West Coasts, a strong thread of provincialism prevails in the programming. About a quarter of the performers are plucked from Austin's incredibly diverse music scene (no other similarly sized city in America could find so much talent right at home), and the event always kicks off Thursday with a gala Austin Music Awards. If you can get a ticket to this auspicious event, expect to see the likes of the Fabulous Thunderbirds, Joe Ely, Daniel Johnston, Jimmy Dale Gilmore, and Lou Ann Barton—all of whom have appeared at past shows.

Registration for "conference" events is pricey, but if you just want to hear some great music, a $40 pass admits you to most shows. And stay on the lookout for free in-store appearances by bands and for special parties by indie labels wanting to spotlight themselves and their rising stars.   **LOCATION:** Austin Convention Center and various venues in Austin **TICKETS/INFO:** 512-467-7979; e-mail: 72662.2465@compuserve.com; World Wide Web: http://monsterbit.com/sxsw.html **ACCOMMODATIONS/ TOURIST INFO:** 512-474-5171, 512-478-0098, 800-888-8287

ℐERRY JEFF WALKER BIRTHDAY WEEKEND
AUSTIN, LUCKENBACH, AND ENVIRONS ✳ LAST WEEKEND IN MARCH

Though many Austinites swear that Jerry Jeff is a Texan by birth, he was actually born Paul Crosby in upstate New York. He played folk music and then rock 'n' roll before settling on country music and making Austin his home. His birthday bash features a relaxed evening of music and storytelling, with longtime friends like Guy Clark, Nanci Griffith, and Ramblin' Jack Elliot joining Jerry Jeff onstage. The festivities also include a golf outing and often a rodeo, at various venues in Austin, Luckenbach, and elsewhere in the Hill Country. About 1,500 fans from all over the United States and Canada help celebrate.   **LOCATION:** Various venues in Austin, Luckenbach, and elsewhere in the Texas Hill Country **TICKETS/INFO:** 512-477-0036; e-mail: ttm@inetport.com; World Wide Web: http://www.io.com/-ccamden/jjw/ **ACCOMMODATIONS/TOURIST INFO:** 512-474-5171, 512-478-0098, 800-888-8287

✺LD SETTLERS' BLUEGRASS & ACOUSTIC MUSIC FESTIVAL

ROUND ROCK/AUSTIN ✴ LAST WEEKEND IN MARCH, SATURDAY AND SUNDAY

The lakeside setting is awesome, the concerts are sensational, and the campground pickers are abundant at this freewheeling springtime gig in a hilly park just 10 minutes north of Austin. With the goal of winning the hearts of Austin's ultradiverse "mainstream" music scene, Old Settlers' lineup goes well beyond the bounds of traditional bluegrass and into more progressive territory. Expect to see performers like flat-picker/vocalist Doc Watson, jazzed-up bluegrasser Tony Rice, bluegrass/folk/jazzman David Grisman, and Austin's own Bad Livers and Austin Lounge Lizards.

After more than a decade of autumn dates, Old Settlers' recently moved to late March, which is a drier time of year and the height of the bluebonnet wildflower season. In addition to concerts, the new lakeside layout features workshops and children's shows, as well as free primitive camping and a limited number of RV hookups. There are no restrictions on anything but "inappropriate behavior," and admission ranges from $27 to $40, depending on the package.   **LOCATION:** Old Settlers' Park is located three miles east of I-35 on Highway 79 just 10 minutes north of Austin. **TICKETS/INFO:** 512-443-5001, 512-416-7827 **ACCOMMODATIONS/TOURIST INFO:** 512-474-5171, 512-478-0098, 800-888-8287, 512-255-5805, 512-443-5001

✺EFTY FRIZZELL COUNTRY MUSIC FESTIVAL

CORSICANA ✴ SATURDAY CLOSEST TO MARCH 31 (LEFTY FRIZZELL'S BIRTHDAY)

Traditional country singer Lefty Frizzell died in 1975, leaving a legacy of influence on musicians like Merle Haggard, Randy Travis, and Willie Nelson, to name just a few. Lefty's hometown of Corsicana has celebrated this legacy every year since 1993, when the town unveiled a statue of their favorite musical son. Hoping to lure tourists to Corsicana, this fledgling festival books 10 acts, including one headliner and nine local or regional talents. Past performers have included Lefty's brother, David Frizzell ("You're the Reason God Made Oklahoma").   **LOCATION:** National Guard Armory at 3100 West Seventh Avenue, or Jester Park on West Park Avenue between North 15th and North 18th Streets. Corsicana is located about 50 miles southeast of Dallas just off I-45. **TICKETS/INFO:** 903-654-4846 **ACCOMMODATIONS/TOURIST INFO:** 903-874-4731

✺IESTA SAN ANTONIO

SAN ANTONIO ✴ TEN DAYS SURROUNDING AND INCLUDING APRIL 21 (SAN JACINTO DAY)

In a volunteer effort that brings the entire community together, Fiesta San Antonio attracts some three million people to its more than 160 events—many of them musical. Anchored by heavy doses of C&W, Tejano conjunto, and other Latin styles, dozens of concerts also feature Texas swing, folk, German and Czech polkas, jazz, rock, and pop. The celebration honors the heroes of the Alamo, and many events are low-cost or free. **LOCATION:** Many indoor and outdoor locations in San Antonio **TICKETS/INFO:** 210-

227-5191 **ACCOMMODATIONS/TOURIST INFO:** 800-447-3372, 210-270-8700, 210-270-8748

HE JOHN A. LOMAX GATHERING
MERIDIAN ✷ FOURTH SATURDAY IN APRIL

John A. Lomax grew up in Bosque County not far from this gathering, and at an early age began to write down the songs and poems he heard sung by cowboys punching cattle up a branch of the Chisholm Trail. Eventually dubbed "the Ballad Hunter," Lomax dedicated much of his life to the preservation of these songs, which had been passed along by word of mouth. Lomax and his son Alan conducted interviews and made thousands of transcriptions and field recordings in cowboy camps and prisons, recording the songs that became part of America's musical heritage.

The folk and blues revivals of the 1960s and 1970s were in large part the result of the work of the Lomaxes, and thanks to them the cowboy balladeers, bluesmen, and poets who gather at this festival have no shortage of traditional material. On two stages perched on the banks of the Bosque River, some 15 bands and solo performers serenade a crowd of about 5,000 with cowboy ballads, Mississippi blues, Kentucky banjo tunes, and British Isle ballads made American by immigrants. Also on hand are exhibits of cowboy trappings, interesting food (try the S.O.B. stew!), crafts, and a "bull fire" (cowboy campfire). **LOCATION:** Meridian Texas Civic Center and National Championship Barbecue Cookoff Grounds in Meridian, 50 miles northwest of Waco at the junction of Highways 22, 6, 144, and 174 **TICKETS/INFO:** 817-435-2966 **ACCOMMODATIONS/TOURIST INFO:** 817-675-3720

EXAS STATE CHAMPIONSHIP FIDDLERS' FROLICS
HALLETSVILLE ✷ FOURTH WEEKEND IN APRIL, THURSDAY–SUNDAY

Centered around an outdoor pavilion at the Knights of Columbus Hall, this festival is loaded with country, Cajun, and zydeco music—as well as old-time and bluegrass fiddling. Fiddlers tune up for the weekend competition with a free Thursday night jam session and get their feet in gear with Friday's Cajun Fun Night, featuring up to five Cajun and zydeco bands. Saturday brings on fiddle contests in several divisions, plus more Cajun, zydeco, and old-time fiddle concerts in the afternoon and three C&W bands in the evening. Sunday doesn't slow down, with fiddle championships, a guitar-picking contest, C&W contests, and food, food, food! The festival and camping are cheap, and with so much going on, organizers are so confident you'll have a good time that they guarantee that this is "the best event in Texas!" **LOCATION:** Halletsville is between San Antonio and Houston, 17 miles south of I-10 on Highway 77. **TICKETS/INFO:** 512-798-2311, 512-798-2662 **ACCOMMODATIONS/TOURIST INFO:** 512-798-2662

EXAS STATE BLUEGRASS KICKOFF
CANTON ✷ FOURTH WEEKEND IN APRIL, FRIDAY AND SATURDAY

Seven local and regional bands satisfy bluegrass appetites at this annual festival, which kicks off the bluegrass season in a 300-acre park with more than 4,000 RV hookups. Concerts and jam sessions abound, but don't count on workshops or children's activities—and remember you're in a dry county here, so leave the booze behind. Prices hover around the $12 mark for concerts and $7 daily for RV hookups. For bluegrass on a larger scale, see the Texas State Bluegrass Festival, held here in June. **LOCATION:** Trades Day Park in Canton, at the junction of Highway 19 and I-20, 40 miles west of Tyler and 60 miles east of Dallas **TICKETS/INFO:** 903-567-6004 **ACCOMMODATIONS/TOURIST INFO:** 903-567-2991

♪OB WILLS DAY
TURKEY ✹ LAST SATURDAY IN APRIL

Bob Wills defined the genre of Western swing with songs like "San Antonio Rose" and "Texas Two Step." Although Wills died in 1975, his Texas Playboys continue to carry the torch of this bluesy music, which updated the fiddle-based string-band music of the 1920s and 1930s and urbanized it with horns and electric steel guitars. The Bob Wills Center has hosted this festival since the early 1970s in the friendly, laid-back farming town of Turkey.

More than 350 musicians are thought to have passed through the Texas Playboys at one time or another, and what's left of the band shows up in Turkey on Friday night to play the rhythms that held the entire South hostage for more than two decades. Saturday night brings plenty of other western swing bands, along with fiddlers and thousands of dancers who range from teenagers to 85-year-old grannies. Many have returned annually since the festival began, parking their RVs next to each other (there are no hotels in town) and whipping out instruments for informal jam sessions. Fiddle contests and arts and crafts round out the weekend.   **LOCATION:** Bob Wills Center, at the corner of Sixth and Lyles Streets in Turkey. The town is located about 75 miles (as the crow flies) southeast of Amarillo, at the junction of Highways 86 and 70. **TICKETS/INFO:** 806-423-1033 **ACCOMMODATIONS/TOURIST INFO:** 806-423-1033

♪LEASURE ISLAND MUSIC FESTIVAL
PORT ARTHUR ✹ LAST WEEKEND IN APRIL, FRIDAY–SUNDAY

Located on Pleasure Island (near a lot of great Gulf fishing), this family-oriented festival usually has between 25 and 30 bands playing to a crowd of about 10,000. Two stages feature rock, pop, and country, and there are plenty of children's activities— including a giant treasure hunt—to keep the young folks occupied.   **LOCATION:** Logan Music Park on Pleasure Island in Port Arthur. From Houston take I-10 east, exit at Highway 73 south, and follow it into town. **TICKETS/INFO:** 409-962-6200 **ACCOMMODATIONS/TOURIST INFO:** 409-985-7822, 800-235-7822

♪EXAS FIDDLERS' ASSOCIATION CONTEST
ATHENS ✹ FIRST THURSDAY AND FRIDAY IN MAY

This down-home fiddling extravaganza began in 1932 and is still going strong with a comprehensive range of fiddle contests, big band music, a carnival, and arts and crafts booths. Thousands of locals and city folks from Dallas make this free regional festival an annual tradition.   **LOCATION:** The courthouse lawn in Athens, about 60 miles southeast of Dallas on U.S. 175 **TICKETS/INFO:** 903-675-2325 **ACCOMMODATIONS/ TOURIST INFO:** 903-675-5181   \

NATIONAL POLKA FESTIVAL

ENNIS ✳ FIRST FULL WEEKEND IN MAY

When news of fertile soil, an ideal climate, and friendly folks reached the Czech homeland, thousands packed up their belongings and set off for the strange land of Texas. Many found their way to Ennis, which, as one of the largest Czech-Slovak settlements in the state, holds this annual extravaganza of music, dancing, parades, costumes, food, and beer. Music and dancing are free at two outdoor stages; or, for less than $10, you can dance to the music of 10 bands in four air-conditioned halls. And if you like Slavic food, prepare to bust your diet with authentic *klobase* and *kolaches*. **LOCATION:** Downtown Ennis, 35 miles south of Dallas via I-45. From I-45 take exit 251 and go west on Ennis Avenue. **TICKETS/INFO:** 214-878-4748 **ACCOMMODATIONS/TOURIST INFO:** 214-875-2625

LONE STAR STATE DULCIMER FESTIVAL

GLEN ROSE ✳ MOTHER'S DAY WEEKEND, FRIDAY–SUNDAY (MOTHER'S DAY IS THE SECOND SUNDAY IN MAY)

Experts say the word *dulcimer* probably derives from the Latin phrase *dolce melos*, meaning sweet song. If you love the dulcimer's sweet song, be sure to put Glen Rose on your vacation route for this free, Dulcimer Society-sponsored shindig, where just about anything goes—as long as it goes with a dulcimer.

You'll hear plenty of traditional, old-timey acoustic bluegrass; but beyond that, the musical fare is anybody's guess. In past years, the hammiest of the *dolce* dulcimer players have used their well-strung sound boxes to play everything from classical to big band to New Age (to the chagrin of old-timey types). Basically, it's one big theme party (where the theme is dulcimer), and people come up with the most outlandish thematic variations their fertile imaginations can conceive.

The beautiful outdoor main stage makes way for one special event after another. Friday night features an open stage, with 25- and 55-minute segments of dulcimer talents from around the United States. On Saturday, dulcimer workshops and contests are held inside the park's convention building, while formal concerts on the main stage feature national talents on mountain dulcimers, hammered dulcimers, and autoharps.

Late Friday and Saturday nights, the lawn chairs are kicked aside to make way for square, contra, and circle dancing as a caller steps onstage under a generous awning of old oak and locust trees. Around 1 A.M., lullaby jam sessions conclude the day's delights. In tribute to the children who bring their moms on Mother's Day (Sunday), the festival produces entertainment by, for, and about children. Sunday's fun also includes gospel music and a liar's contest, and plenty of arts and crafts booths line the concert-area perimeter all weekend.   **LOCATION:** Oakdale Park, on Highway 144 between U.S. 67 and downtown Glen Rose, about 70 miles south of Dallas **TICKETS/INFO:** 817-275-3872 **ACCOMMODATIONS/TOURIST INFO:** 817-897-2286

TEJANO CONJUNTO FESTIVAL

SAN ANTONIO ✳ FIVE DAYS BEGINNING THE WEDNESDAY AFTER THE SECOND SUNDAY IN MAY

The Spanish word *conjunto* (pronounced cone-HOON-toe) literally means "group," but Texans know conjunto as a specific type of musical group, nicely described by this

Squeeze box central: Steve Jordan finesses the button accordion at the 1994 Tejano Conjunto Festival. Al Rendon

festival's unofficial motto and rule of thumb: "If they don't have the squeeze box (button accordion), they're not a conjunto."

With about 30 groups, this festival features the best of roots, popular, and progressive music in the conjunto genre, which grew out of Latin American and Germanic roots and is known in Mexico as *norteño* (northern) music. Expect to hear just about everything from the conjunto repertoire, including polka, cumbia, bolero, waltz, merengue, rockin' Tex-Mex, country rhythms, and even Cajun and zydeco. Bands come from south and central Texas, as well as northern Mexico.

All this music makes for one lively dance floor, which is surrounded by food booths, arts and crafts, and children's games. Sponsored by the Guadelupe Cultural Arts Center, the festival annually inducts musicians into the conjunto hall of fame, produces audio and video materials, and publishes scholarly papers on the musical form. At the festival, picnics and lawn chairs on the grass are fine, but don't BYO drinks, because beer and wine are sold there.   **LOCATION:** Rosedale Park, 342 Dartmouth, in San Antonio

TICKETS/INFO: 210-271-3151 ACCOMMODATIONS/TOURIST INFO: 800-447-3372, 210-270-8700, 210-270-8748

♪ICKIN' IN THE PINES

MINEOLA ✹ THIRD WEEKEND IN MAY, FRIDAY EVENING THROUGH SUNDAY MORNING

This small, participatory festival started in 1993 and draws 50 to 100 musical types for hours on end of acoustic jamming in the bluegrass, folk, country, and blues idioms. Some years, the festival books from two to five local and regional talents who perform a couple of sets, but other years it's just one big pickin', fiddlin', pluckin', hummin', foot-tappin' jam session. There's some music Friday evening and Sunday morning, but most of the action takes place on Saturday.   **LOCATION:** Tri-M Acres, in a community called Pine Mills, about 15 miles east of Mineola; from Tyler take U.S. 69 or Highway 14 to Highway 49, then head east one-quarter mile to the site. **TICKETS/INFO:** 903-857-2253 **ACCOMMODATIONS/TOURIST INFO:** 903-569-2087

ⓖLEN ROSE BLUEGRASS REUNION

GLEN ROSE ✹ MEMORIAL DAY WEEKEND, THURSDAY–SUNDAY (MEMORIAL DAY IS THE LAST MONDAY IN MAY)

Glen Rose's bluegrass-o-rama brings about a dozen bands to Oakdale Park for concerts by professionals and contests for amateurs. Music and jam sessions go 'round the clock, and there's plenty of food and camping available. And if you miss the Memorial Day festival, Glen Rose does it again on the first weekend in October. **LOCATION:** Oakdale Park, on Highway144 between U.S. 67 and downtown Glen Rose, about 70 miles south of Dallas **TICKETS/INFO:** 817-897-2321 **ACCOMMODATIONS/TOURIST INFO:** 817-897-2286

♪TRANGE FAMILY BLUEGRASS FESTIVAL

TEXARKANA ✹ MEMORIAL DAY WEEKEND, THURSDAY–SUNDAY

Since 1983, bluegrassers from coast to coast have found friendly camp-and-jammin' digs at the Strange family's 18-acre bluegrass and RV park just south of Texarkana. With about 20 talents playing each semiannual festival, you'll hear bluegrass music from Virginia, Tennessee, Oklahoma, Kentucky, and elsewhere—all in the shady comfort of tall oak trees in a well-leveled park with plenty of RV hookups.

Any of the big names you'd normally hear on the bluegrass circuit have played the festival's excellent outdoor stage at one time or another: the Cox Family played here for years, as well as the Lewis Family, the Country Gentlemen, Chubby Wise, and Alison Krauss. Lawn chairs clutter the hillside as up to 5,000 people gather to hear the latest strains of traditional hillbilly sounds.

But what really gives this festival its edge among its contemporaries on the bluegrass circuit is its nose for fresh blood in the biz. Sam Strange spends between-times scoping out new talent, and if you're lucky enough to attend the festival a couple of years in a row, you're sure to hear different up-and-comers every time. And, with the exception of the occasional country melody snuck in on the sly, you can count on hearing straight bluegrass all weekend long, both onstage and off.

The Festival-Institute at Round Top: A celebration of music, architecture, hospitality, and ambition. Courtesy of Mario Erwin/The Festival-Institute at Round Top

Impromptu jam sessions follow bluegrassers as closely as the cloud of dust stirred up by the mandolins on stage, and this festival is no exception. Plus, Saturday morning's instrumental workshops provide string-handling tips for both the accomplished musician and the new-billy. Admission for the whole weekend costs around $25. **LOCATION:** Strange Family Bluegrass Park, just outside Texarkana, five miles north of the junction of I-30 and U.S. 59/71, in the northeast corner of Texas **TICKETS/INFO:** 903-792-9018 **ACCOMMODATIONS/TOURIST INFO:** 903-792-7191

THE FESTIVAL-INSTITUTE AT ROUND TOP
ROUND TOP ✷ LAST WEEKEND IN MAY THROUGH MID-JULY

One of North America's most remarkable music festivals inspires thousands to flock to the smallest incorporated town in Texas for chamber, chamber orchestra, symphonic, and choral music from the baroque through contemporary eras. Founded and directed by American concert pianist James Dick, Round Top has grown since its founding in 1971 to become a sort of Texas Tanglewood. Yet, as nearly anyone who's been to Round Top will tell you, it's much more than a music festival. Round Top is a celebration of music, architecture, hospitality, and ambition.

The Festival Hill site was chosen by James Dick for its cultural heritage (German-Czech), its proximity to major urban centers (only two hours from Houston, Austin, and San Antonio), and its interesting central Texas landscape. The first concert was presented in a barn with a dirt floor, but by then Dick was already dreaming of bigger and better things. Within two years, the festival had acquired the world's largest transportable stage, and by 1976 it had moved to its permanent location at Festival Hill.

By that time, Dick, already well known as a highly skilled impresario, was emerging as a multitalented visionary—a musician, educator, fund-raiser, idealist, and philosopher of immense scope. Today's Round Top is his dream realized: a major center for arts and education, with a 1,000-seat Festival Concert Hall, imaginative gardens and waterworks, and a stunning array of unique architecture.

The repertoire embraces early music to world premieres, and two works commissioned by the festival (by Benjamin Lees and Dan Welcher) have been nominated for the Pulitzer Prize in Music. An eight-week teaching institute attracts students from all over the world, who comprise the festival orchestra. Internationally famed musicians (such as cellist Yo Yo Ma, violinist Charles Castleman, and pianist Steven De Groote) have taught at the institute and been featured as soloists. The summer season begins Memorial Day weekend with an Early Music Festival, and the Round Top Festival continues through mid-July with Friday and Saturday concerts.   **LOCATION:** Highway 237 at Jaster Road in Round Top. Round Top is midway between Houston and Austin. **TICKETS/INFO:** 409-249-3129; e-mail: festinst@fais.net; World Wide Web: http://www.rtis.com/reg/roundtop/festival.html **ACCOMMODATIONS/TOURIST INFO:** 409-260-9898

KERRVILLE FOLK FESTIVAL

KERRVILLE ✱ LAST WEEKEND IN MAY AND THE FIRST THREE WEEKENDS IN JUNE

North America's largest and longest-running songwriters' festival could be the continent's most fertile discovery zone for emerging talents. Whether your tastes run to folk, country, blues, bluegrass, jazz, Tejano/Tex-Mex, or western swing, it's all here—and it's all original and new.

The likes of Michelle Shocked, John Gorka, and Jimmy Dale Gilmore all cut their teeth at Kerrville, and each year brings new discoveries. Main-stage acts are anchored by "new-folk" songsters, but samples of sounds as diverse as brass band and Latin American folk can be heard. One highlight is the New Folk Emerging Songwriters Competition, in which 40 finalists are selected from more than 500 tapes submitted. These finalists perform Saturday and Sunday of Memorial Day weekend in front of judges, who select six winners to return the following weekend for 20-minute sets. Don't be surprised if you see the next Lyle Lovett, David Wilcox, or Nanci Griffith up there—all three were contest winners before they made it big.

The festival is set on a beautiful ranch in the Texas Hill Country an hour west of San Antonio. Although some lodging is available nearby, camping is a must, since much of the magic of Kerrville takes place in the campground during the warm Texas nights. In the tradition that was recorded on Michelle Shocked's "Texas Campfire Tapes," hundreds of people—including main-stage acts—roam from campfire to campfire, making bleary-eyed folk fanatics wonder if they've stumbled into Eden.

Other highlights include open-mike Ballad Tree song swaps, a songwriters' school, children's concerts, swimming, and arts and crafts booths. About the only thing to complain about is the daytime heat, which is substantial. Tickets range from $10 to $20 per day, depending on when and how you buy 'em.   **LOCATION:** Quiet Valley Ranch, nine miles south of Kerrville on Highway 16. Kerrville is about 55 miles northwest of San Antonio via I-10. **TICKETS/INFO:** 800-435-8429 **ACCOMMODATIONS/TOURIST INFO:** 210-792-3535

TEXAS MUSIC FESTIVAL

HOUSTON ✳ THROUGHOUT JUNE

The Texas Music Festival is actually a summer performance training program for young musicians, but its Distinguished Artist Series brings internationally known guest artists to Houston for two performances each week. Faculty from the University of Houston and Texas A&M are often joined by members of the Houston Symphony, and the student festival orchestra performs weekend public concerts of varying repertoire under visiting conductors.   **LOCATION:** Fine Arts Building, Morres School of Music, University of Houston. Some events are held on the campus of Texas A&M. **TICKETS/ INFO:** 713-743-3167, 713-743-3009 **ACCOMMODATIONS/TOURIST INFO:** 713-227-3100, 800-365-7575

GOSPEL FEST

DALLAS ✳ FIRST WEEKEND IN JUNE

This event, confined to a one-day series of concerts in a 2,000-person venue, features contemporary African American gospel and jazz to soothe (or rouse) the soul. Many festivalgoers also catch the Southwest Black Arts Festival, which runs concurrently, right next door.   **LOCATION:** Morton H. Meyer Symphony Center, at 2301 Flora Street in Artists Square **TICKETS/INFO:** 214-953-1977 **ACCOMMODATIONS/ TOURIST INFO:** 214-746-6677, 214-234-4448

JUNETEENTH BLUES FESTIVAL

HOUSTON ✳ A WEEKEND IN EARLY OR MID-JUNE

Juneteenth celebrates the first reading of the Emancipation Proclamation in Texas, which occurred two years after the proclamation officially declared an end to slavery in the United States. Despite this cruel twist of history, the Juneteenth Blues Festival is an overwhelmingly upbeat event, featuring both traditional acoustic blues and cutting-edge electric sounds. An outdoor main stage features nationally known acts, while side stages highlight local blues men and women.   **LOCATION:** Miller Outdoor Theater, 100 Concert Drive; also Hermann Park at Fannin and N. MacGregor Streets near the Medical Center and Rice University in Houston **TICKETS/INFO:** 713-667-8000 **ACCOMMODA-TIONS/TOURISTINFO:** 713-227-3100, 800-365-7575

CARVER JAZZ FESTIVAL

SAN ANTONIO ✳ SECOND WEEKEND IN JUNE, FRIDAY–SUNDAY

Since 1978, the Carver Jazz Festival has been regarded by San Antonians as "the jazz lover's jazz festival." This thoughtful gig has resisted temptations toward the mainstream and stayed close to the traditional—and diverse—roots of African American jazz. Held at the Carver Community Cultural Center (the site was once the segregation-era Colored Library and Auditorium), the festival recently shifted dates from August to June to be a part of the Juneteenth celebration of slavery's end in Texas. A typical day might find the audience on a rollicking, three-day tour of the jazz world, starting in New Orleans with the Dirty Dozen, moving down to Havana with the balmy sounds of Manny Oquendo and Libre, and winding up in the 1950s-era supper clubs of New York City with jazz diva Abbey Lincoln. Each night features two acts; tickets are $12 per night. **LOCATION:** Carver Community Cultural Center, 226 North Hackberry Street, just northeast of the Alamodome **TICKETS/INFO:** 210-225-6516, 210-207-8500 **ACCOMMODATIONS/TOURIST INFO:** 800-447-3372, 210-270-8700, 210-270-8748

VICTORIA BACH FESTIVAL
VICTORIA ✷ SECOND FULL WEEK IN JUNE

In 1976, a group of local music lovers had the audacity to believe that Victoria, Texas, could create and sustain a baroque music festival. Their dream was realized, and now, more than 20 summers later, the Victoria Bach Festival continues to flourish. Though the repertoire emphasizes Bach and baroque, it also dabbles in the romantic, classical, and contemporary periods and includes symphonic, chamber, organ, solo voice and instrument, and choral works. Such a program is unique in Texas, and the festival has achieved national prominence with broadcasts on National Public Radio's *Performance Today.*   **LOCATION:** Victoria College Auditorium, First United Methodist Church (407 North Bridge Street), and other venues in Victoria, near the junction of U.S. 59 and U.S. 87, about 90 miles northeast of Corpus Christi **TICKETS/INFO:** 512-575-1375 **ACCOMMODATIONS/TOURIST INFO:** 512-573-5277, 800-826-5774

LATIN JAZZ AND FOOD FESTIVAL
DALLAS ✷ SECOND WEEKEND IN JUNE

The largest Caribbean music and food festival in Dallas brings in half a dozen bands and *orquestras,* whose salsa, merengue, and Latin jazz rhythms provoke massive bouts of downtown dancing. The city's Arts District is set up tropical-style, and vendors sell food from 10 countries, as well as arts and crafts.   **LOCATION:** Artists Square, at Flora and Leonard Streets **TICKETS/INFO:** 214-528-1600 **ACCOMMODATIONS/TOURIST INFO:** 214-746-6677, 214-234-4448

SOUTHWEST ORIGINAL MUSIC SHOWCASE
EL PASO ✷ SECOND OR THIRD WEEKEND IN JUNE, SATURDAY AND SUNDAY

In an effort to promote the growing roster of young, unsigned bands in the El Paso area, this alterna-rock festival showcases new talents at a downtown club. Bands play both indoors and out in the parking lot in the warm evenings (bring your own lawn chair), and the festival has recently expanded to include up-and-coming performers from Albuquerque and other regional centers. Admission is about $5.   **LOCATION:** The Attic, 710 Texas Avenue, in downtown El Paso **TICKETS/INFO:** 915-545-5345 **ACCOMMODATIONS/TOURIST INFO:** 915-534-0698, 800-351-6024, 915-534-0500

BAYOU BASH
HOUSTON ✷ A SATURDAY IN LATE JUNE

Originally created to promote ticket sales for the Astros, this festival has grown to take on a life of its own. Some of the region's best Cajun, zydeco, and blues bands rock away the afternoon, and with a petting zoo for the kids (not to be confused with the festival's other attraction, a live alligator), the bash offers something for both young and old.   **LOCATION:** Houston Astrohall next to the Astrodome, Loop 610 at Kirby Drive **TICKETS/INFO:** 713-799-9791 **ACCOMMODATIONS/TOURIST INFO:** 713-227-3100, 800-365-7575

LEGENDS OF WESTERN SWING REUNION

SNYDER ✸ FOURTH WEEK IN JUNE, WEDNESDAY–SATURDAY

Western swing was born when innovative Texans took the fiddle-based string-band music of the 1920s and 1930s, added some jazz, blues, and sacred music, then urbanized it with horns and electric steel guitars. The heyday of western swing began with the Dust Bowl era and the Great Depression, when Americans tuned in to the cheerful sounds of Milton Brown, Bill Boyd, and Leon Selph for a spiritual lift.

It was Bob Wills, though, who defined the genre, with songs like "San Antonio Rose," which sold a million copies in 1940. Wills was so popular for a time that he appeared in eight movies, replacing solitary singing cowboys like Gene Autry with a full-bore band of western swingers. The genre's popularity fizzled by 1950, and Wills died in 1975, but his Texas Playboys carried on. In fact, more than 350 musicians have passed through the band at one time or another, and the current lineup is one of this festival's favorite regularly featured bands. The event has also featured Hank Thompson (who carried the torch of western swing for more than five decades), Bob Wills's younger brother Johnnie Lee Wills, and plenty of local and regional western swing bands.

Western swing may never receive the popular attention it enjoyed during its heyday in the 1940s, but since 1988 this festival has given the genre a hearty annual revival. About a dozen bands play over four days on one indoor stage, and several thousand people come from all over the country and the world—especially northern Europe, where western swing still enjoys popular radio airtime.   **LOCATION:** Scurry Center Coliseum, 900 East Coliseum Drive in Snyder, 80 miles south of Lubbock on U.S. 84 **TICKETS/INFO:** 405-376-4939 **ACCOMMODATIONS/TOURIST INFO:** 915-573-3558

TEXAS STATE BLUEGRASS FESTIVAL

CANTON ✸ FOURTH WEEKEND IN JUNE, TUESDAY–SATURDAY

Few Texas bluegrass festivals can boast a bigger park or better lineup than this one. Each day from noon until almost midnight, the living legends of bluegrass take turns laying down their tunes on a well-shaded outdoor stage. Typically, the lineup includes legends like Bill Monroe, Ralph Stanley, Mac Wiseman, the Lewis Family, and Jim & Jesse. A smattering of regional (and some additional national) talents make up the remainder of the festival's 30-act roster. Some 10,000 people flock to the 300-acre park, which offers more than 4,000 RV hookups. As is customary at true-blue(grass) festivals, jam sessions abound, but don't count on workshops or children's activities, and bear in mind that this county is dry, so leave the booze behind or hide it well. Prices hover around $12 daily for concerts and $7 daily for RV hookups.   **LOCATION:** Trades Day Park in Canton, at the junction of Highway 19 and I-20, 40 miles west of Tyler and 60 miles east of Dallas **TICKETS/INFO:** 903-567-6004 **ACCOMMODATIONS/TOURIST INFO:** 903-567-2991

ANTONE'S ANNIVERSARY PARTY

AUSTIN ✸ TEN DAYS USUALLY ENDING JULY 15 (ANTONE'S ANNIVERSARY)

For more than 20 years, Antone's has brought the blues to Austin, "the live music capital of the world." In addition to featuring greats like Muddy Waters, Albert Collins, and B. B. King, the club practically raised young Texas bluesmen like Stevie Ray and Jimmie Vaughan. Antone's annual party features anywhere from four to eight acts each night, and with 10 nights of music it all adds up to a full-blown celebration of a great club—and of the blues tradition itself. Admission during the week is about $5; weekend admission is about $15.   **LOCATION:** Antone's, at 2915 Guadalupe Street in Austin **TICKETS/INFO:** 512-474-5314 **ACCOMMODATIONS/TOURIST INFO:** 512-474-5171, 512-478-0098, 800-888-8287

OVERTON BLUEGRASS FESTIVAL
OVERTON ✱ SECOND WEEKEND IN JULY, THURSDAY–SATURDAY

One of the few bluegrass festivals sponsored by a municipality makes use of a tree-shaded, natural amphitheater and features an interesting Thursday night of gospel, in addition to the straight bluegrass pickin' that makes up the majority of the program. The lineup consists mostly of nationally known bands and in past years has included the Shady Grove Ramblers and Jim & Jesse and the Virginia Boys. Don't miss Saturday's pancake breakfast sponsored by the Overton Boy Scouts.   **LOCATION:** City Park, Highway 850 and Lakeshore Drive, Overton. Overton is about 20 miles southeast of Tyler, in northeast Texas. **TICKETS/INFO:** 903-843-3171 **ACCOMMODATIONS/ TOURIST INFO:** 903-834-3542

GULF COAST JAM
PORT ARTHUR ✱ LAST WEEKEND IN JULY OR FIRST WEEKEND IN AUGUST

The rich, rockin' heritage of the Texas/Louisiana Gulf Coast is celebrated at this outdoor festival on Lake Sabine's Pleasure Island. Expect to hear regional favorite sons and daughters from the 1960s, 1970s, and contemporary times playing everything from rock and R&B to Cajun, zydeco, and swamp pop. While you're here, be sure to check out the excellent collection of rock memorabilia in the Gulf Coast Musical Hall of Fame, located in Port Arthur's Museum of the Gulf Coast.   **LOCATION:** Logan Music Park on Pleasure Island in Port Arthur. From Houston take I-10 east, exit at Highway 73 south, and follow it into town. **TICKETS/INFO:** 409-722-3699 **ACCOMMODATIONS/TOUR-IST INFO:** 409-985-7822, 800-235-7822

HOUSTON INTERNATIONAL JAZZ FESTIVAL
HOUSTON ✱ FIRST WEEKEND IN AUGUST

The lack of a comprehensive jazz club scene in Houston could account for the huge turnout of hungry jazz fans who swarm this festival's several events. Acts like Ramsey Lewis, Tania Maria, and Gary Bartz intensify the August heat with scorching jazz at three events: a poolside jam session at the Omni Hotel, outdoor concerts in Sam Houston Park, and a Mayor's Jazz Brunch. The poolside session kicks off the festival Friday with a romantic evening under the stars, while on Saturday the scene is festive with a gathering of 10,000 in downtown's Sam Houston Park (admission is $5). Sunday's pricey brunch wraps up the weekend of music.   **LOCATION:** Downtown Houston at Sam Houston Park, Allen Parkway at Bagby Street, and the Omni Hotel, Four Riverway **TICKETS/ INFO:** 713-227-8706 **ACCOMMODATIONS/TOURIST INFO:** 713-227-3100, 800-365-7575

TEXAS FOLKLIFE FESTIVAL
SAN ANTONIO ✳ EARLY AUGUST

When you think of Texas, what kind of music comes to mind? For many, it's high-stepping country and western, played by white guys with ten-gallon hats. But take a walk through the Texas Folklife Festival and you're likely to hear German biergarten music, Indian drum groups, or Caribbean salsa. Ethnic and cultural groups from all across the second-biggest state arrive with costumes, crafts, instruments, and foods, giving testimony to the cultural confluence that has formed today's Texas. This four-day event draws some 55,000 visitors to its nine stages for an astounding range of music and dance.   **LOCATION:** Institute of Texan Cultures, in HemisFair Park, downtown San Antonio **TICKETS/INFO:** 210-558-2224 **ACCOMMODATIONS/TOURIST INFO:** 800-447-3372, 210-270-8700, 210-270-8748

EAST TEXAS SACRED HARP SINGING CONVENTION
HENDERSON ✳ WEEKEND OF THE SECOND SUNDAY IN AUGUST, SATURDAY AND SUNDAY

Sacred harp or "shape note" singing is a form of Christian folk music that dates back to the early 1800s, when people learned to sight-read music by associating each note of the scale with a shape (triangle, circle, square, or diamond) and a syllable (fa, sol, la, mi). It's been celebrated with exquisite power and grace at this convention since 1868. Singers sit facing one another in a hollow square, arranged in soprano, alto, tenor, and bass sections, and sing densely interwoven four-part and six-part (or "dispersed") harmonies a capella, with voices and spirits blending perfectly into a singular, communal force.

Traditionally, people traveled great distances for worship and fellowship at all-day "singings," and the same is true today; participants typically number between 200 and 300 and represent a dozen states and a couple of countries. The musical tradition is democratic, and singers take turns leading songs from the center of the hollow square. The event is participatory rather than performance-oriented, but listeners are welcome and a barbecue dinner is served on the grounds, with fresh vegetables and homemade desserts. There's no charge for admission.   **LOCATION:** Community Center on Fairpark Street in Henderson. From Tyler take Highway 64 east about 45 miles. From Dallas take I-20 east for about 100 miles, then U.S. 259 south for about 20 miles. **TICKETS/INFO:** 903-898-2510 **ACCOMMODATIONS/TOURIST INFO:** 903-657-5528

STRANGE FAMILY BLUEGRASS FESTIVAL
TEXARKANA ✳ LABOR DAY WEEKEND, THURSDAY–SUNDAY (LABOR DAY IS THE FIRST MONDAY IN SEPTEMBER)

This is a semiannual event, happening over Memorial Day and Labor Day weekends. See page 352 for all the details.   **LOCATION:** Strange Family Bluegrass Park, just outside Texarkana, five miles north of the junction of I-30 and U.S. 59/71 in the northeast corner of Texas **TICKETS/INFO:** 903-792-9018 **ACCOMMODATIONS/TOURIST INFO:** 903-792-7191

♭ORDER FOLK FESTIVAL

EL PASO ✳ WEEKEND FOLLOWING LABOR DAY, FRIDAY–SUNDAY

The El Paso area is an ethnic stew—a fact that's never more apparent than at the Border Folk Festival. In addition to the country and Mexican-influenced music you might expect, the gathering features traditional Irish music, Native American dancing and drumming, Cajun waltzes, Appalachian dulcimers, and Andean pan pipes—all played by musicians living in and around El Paso. The action gets going Friday night and continues until 6 P.M. Sunday, with music on three stages. Best of all, it's free to the public.   **LOCATION:** Chamizal National Memorial Park, 800 South San Marcial, in El Paso **TICKETS/INFO:** 915-532-7273 **ACCOMMODATIONS/TOURIST INFO:** 915-534-0698, 915-534-0500

♯OUSTON JAZZ FESTIVAL

HOUSTON ✳ A WEEKEND IN MID-SEPTEMBER

Set in the heart of Houston, this free outdoor festival brings in local, regional, and national jazz artists, with styles ranging from traditional to contemporary. Yearly themes showcase the long and rich history of the world's jazz greats.   **LOCATION:** Miller Outdoor Theater, 100 Concert Drive; also Hermann Park, at Fannin and North Mac-Gregor Streets near the Medical Center and Rice University in Houston **TICKETS/INFO:** 713-667-8000 **ACCOMMODATIONS/TOURIST INFO:** 713-227-3100, 800-365-7575

♯EXAS HERITAGE MUSIC FESTIVAL

KERRVILLE, AUSTIN, DALLAS, AND BANDERA ✳ THIRD WEEKEND IN SEPTEMBER

This festival celebrates the memory of "the Singing Brakeman" and other Texas traditionalists with a five-day, multilocation schedule of events. Many take place in Kerrville, where Jimmie Rodgers chose to locate the home he called Blue Yodeler's Paradise. Members of the Rodgers family are actively involved in the festival, and his grandson, Jimmy Dale Court, is one of the 25-or-so regular performers.

The festival kicks off Wednesday at a Dallas nightspot, with poetry and songs by a variety of performers. On Thursday, festivities move to Austin's legendary Broken Spoke for a "Tribute to the Cowboy" show that has included traditional cowboy singer Buck Ramsey, and singer-yodeler Don Walser. Friday afternoon brings the fest to the Cowboy Artists of America Museum in Kerrville for performances of songs from the past century, then to Schreiner College in Kerrville for more songs and poetry. The festival remains on the campus Saturday, with a fiddling contest, a (very popular) yodeling contest, and more cowboy music and demonstrations. Late Saturday evening, a western swing dance is held in nearby Bandera.   **LOCATION:** Various venues in Kerrville, Austin, Dallas, and Bandera; call for details. **TICKETS/INFO:** 210-896-3339 **ACCOMMODATIONS/TOURIST INFO:** 512-474-5171, 214-746-6677, 214-234-4448

♭REAT COUNTRY RIVER FESTIVAL

SAN ANTONIO ✳ FOURTH WEEKEND IN SEPTEMBER, FRIDAY–SUNDAY

If you're looking to discover the next Vince Gill, Randy Travis, or George Strait, just park yourself along San Antonio's Riverwalk in late September. All three country superstars performed at the Great Country River Festival before they hit the big time, and each year more than 60 of country music's hottest new artists compete for audience affection on several stages.

The Great Country River Festival includes the "countrypolitan" sounds that rule new-country radio today, but it also encompasses bluegrass, Tejano, Cajun, and even countrified contemporary Christian music. One main stage is set up at the Arneson River Theatre, and additional floating stages are anchored at various points along the river, allowing visitors to enjoy the music while walking along the famous Paseo del Rio or sitting on the patio of numerous bars and restaurants. The festival begins Friday night and continues all day Saturday and Sunday. Admission is free, and an arts and crafts fair runs concurrently.   **LOCATION:** Various sites along San Antonio's Riverwalk **TICKETS/INFO:** 210-227-4262 **ACCOMMODATIONS/TOURIST INFO:** 800-447-3372, 210-270-8700, 210-270-8748

☉NE WORLD MUSIC FESTIVAL
AUSTIN ✹ A WEEKEND IN LATE SEPTEMBER, THURSDAY—SUNDAY

The One World Music Festival answers worldbeat aficionados' cries for live roots music from around the world. Great locations, an impressive stage, and one whamma-jamma list of international performers create an upbeat, easy-skankin' feel each summer. Promoters work hard to achieve a spirit of cultural diversity, and you'll find a minimum of heavy commercial sponsorship and the accompanying eyesores.

The festival begins in the early afternoon each of the four days, with a sampling of music from some adequate regional bands. The energy, momentum, and crowd size pick up as the day progresses, and by evening the festival is bursting with a whirling frenzy of reggae, funk, Latin, and African music—generated by an incredible roster of headliners from around the globe. You'd have to search pretty hard for a better lineup; in recent years Ziggy Marley, Los Lobos, Boukman Eksperyans, and Blues Traveler have headlined.

The One World Festival's only drawback is the number of serious fans left behind because of high ticket prices ($30/day or $110/four days), and you'll see plenty of dread-headed slackers outside the gate begging for loose change to purchase a ticket. On the flip side, crowds inside the gate are manageable and comfortable, and almost everyone gets a decent view of the stage.

Activist booths sit incongruously next to Coca-Cola booths, and the guy running the tofu stir-fry stand seems to take in as much as the gal selling draft beer. A "Children's World," is headquartered in a giant tepee, and offers special family entertainment and activities. "Preservation Pavilion" hosts cultural and environmental groups, and a drum area hosts free-form and guided drumming sessions. Plus, a percentage of the proceeds goes toward environmental causes.

One World has wandered all around the Southwest and the mountain states (recent locations have included Telluride, Colorado, and Angel Fire, New Mexico), and festivalgoers seem willing to follow it wherever it goes. Organizers say the festival is ready to settle down, but don't count on it—confirm dates and locations before making travel arrangements.   **LOCATION:** An Austin-area lakeside location to be announced **TICKETS/INFO:** 310-239-9359, 800-888-8287 **ACCOMMODATIONS/TOURIST INFO:** 512-474-5171, 512-478-0098, 800-888-8287

HARVEST MOON & TUNES FALL FESTIVAL

FORT DAVIS ✱ WEEKEND CLOSEST TO HARVEST MOON (LATE SEPTEMBER OR EARLY OCTOBER)

Harvest Moon & Tunes brings an amazing variety of music to this historic town square nestled in the Davis Mountains. Quality is the only common denominator, as years past have featured the likes of Guy Clark, Brave Combo, the Dixie Chicks, and C. J. Chenier. Expect to hear both legends and rising stars on the single stage, with a dance floor and a seating area that accommodate only a few hundred people. The scene is laid-back, the rules are few, and extras include a songwriters' contest, vineyard and orchard tours, and the nearby Fort Davis Historic Site (the best-preserved of all the frontier cavalry forts). **LOCATION:** Fort Davis is 75 miles south of Pecos on Highway 17. **TICKETS/INFO:** 915-426-3036, 800-524-3015; e-mail: tmjagger@earthlink.net; World Wide Web: http://numedia.tddc.net/hot/bigbend/fortdavis/   **ACCOMMODATIONS/ TOURIST INFO:** 800-524-3015, 915-426-3015

GLEN ROSE BLUEGRASS REUNION

GLEN ROSE ✱ FIRST WEEKEND IN OCTOBER, FRIDAY–SUNDAY

This is a semiannual event (see page 352 for details). If you miss the October festival, Glen Rose does it all over again Memorial Day weekend (the last weekend in May).   **LOCATION:** Oakdale Park, on Highway 144 between U.S. 67 and downtown Glen Rose, about 70 miles south of Dallas **TICKETS/INFO:** 817-897-2321 **ACCOMMODATIONS/TOURIST INFO:** 817-897-2286

SAN ANTONIO FOLK MUSIC FESTIVAL

SAN ANTONIO ✱ FIRST SATURDAY IN OCTOBER

Held in a lush garden, this early-October event is truly a *San Antonio* folk festival—meaning all the performers are local. The roster emphasizes the city's surprisingly diverse blend of cultural influences; in addition to Mexican American performers, expect to hear Andean, Native American, Celtic, and African musicians. The venue is the patio of Karam's Mexican Restaurant, which has been sculptured and planted to resemble a Mayan jungle, complete with fountain, temple, altar, and Mayan statues.   **LOCATION:** The Mayan Jungle Garden of Karam's Mexican Restaurant, 101 Zarzamora **TICKETS/ INFO:** 210-224-7239 **ACCOMMODATIONS/TOURIST INFO:** 800-447-3372, 210-270-8700, 210-270-8748

WIMBERLEY GOSPEL MUSIC FESTIVAL

WIMBERLEY ✱ SECOND WEEKEND IN OCTOBER, FRIDAY–SUNDAY

Gospel music's many diverse—and sometimes surprising—flavors can be experienced at this three-day festival where abundant talent meets an enthusiastic audience. More than 100 singers and musicians spend 16 glory-filled hours performing just about every form of gospel music known in Texas. Expect to hear classic bluegrass and southern country gospel, traditional Scottish gospel, African American mass choirs, and pop-oriented contemporary Christian music.

In recent years, Wimberley has been the place to hear little-known and emerging forms like salsa gospel, as well as unusual groups like Rockport's Gospel Force, a quartet of "police officers who have a close relationship with the Lord." And since organizers wouldn't want anyone to stay home because they couldn't afford to come, the festival is—and always has been—free to everyone (though offerings are accepted). **LOCATION:** The Lions Park and Pavilion, on RR 2325 in Wimberley. Take I-35 south from Austin or north from San Antonio to San Marcos, then Ranch Road 12 west to Wimberley. **TICKETS/INFO:** 512-847-9916 **ACCOMMODATIONS/TOURIST INFO:** 512-847-2201

AUSTIN ACOUSTIC MUSIC FESTIVAL
AUSTIN ✷ THIRD WEEKEND IN NOVEMBER, FRIDAY–SUNDAY

Timed to land smack dab in the middle of Austin Music Month, this unplugged extravaganza gets right to the roots of Austin's extraordinary singer-songwriter tradition. Created by Austin waiter James Oliver, the Austin Acoustic Music Festival (AAMF) is a stroke of genius that presents nearly 50 exceptional acoustic acts from Austin and around the world—all on one stage, so you won't miss a thing.

Though it's set in the "live music capital of the world," AAMF comes across as a sensible alternative to South by Southwest, occurring as it does at the opposite end of the year and without the mass quantities of people, hype, and electricity. Yet AAMF is by no means limited to limp-wristed folkies with guitars—in fact, many of Austin's titans of rock, country, and blues leap at the opportunity to put away the amps and get down to the quieter reality that forms the heart of songwriting in any genre.

Check your stereotypes at the door, and prepare for a roller-coaster ride that in previous years has featured the Celtic rave-ups of Crazy Jane and the Bishop, the Cajun stylings of Marce LaCouture and Bayou Beaujolais, the Brazilian martial melodies of Capoiera Ginga USA, the south-of-the border sounds of Mariachi Estrella, and the acoustic rap (yep!) of M. C. Overlord. The diversity is amazing as musicians take listeners around the world of traditional and contemporary acoustic music.

The only rule in this laid-back event is that no amplifiers are allowed; the festival even provides a piano and stand-up bass to minimize lugging. Low electric bills and support from the city keep prices low; tickets are $7 a day or $18 for a three-day pass. Don't miss this jewel of the Austin musical year!   **LOCATION:** A club (which changes from year to year) in downtown Austin **TICKETS/INFO:** 512-499-8497, 512-404-4368; World Wide Web: http://monsterbit.com\aamf\ **ACCOMMODATIONS/TOURIST INFO:** 512-474-5171, 512-478-0098, 800-888-8287

Check your expectations at the door: The Austin Acoustic Music Festival gets to the roots of Austin's extraordinary singer-songwriter tradition. (See entry, page 363.) Courtesy of Lee Bickerstaff/A.A.M.F.

WEST COAST

ℱAIRBANKS WINTER FOLK FESTIVAL
FAIRBANKS ✸ SECOND WEEKEND IN FEBRUARY, FRIDAY AND SATURDAY

'Round about the time of year when the midwinter blues are starting to seem chronic, the Fairbanks Winter Folk Festival gathers up Alaskan recording artists, amateurs, and storytellers and throws them together for two days inside the warm confines of the University of Alaska's Wood Center. About 100 acoustic musicians— including the Athabascan fiddlers and other Native Americans of the Fairbanks region— perform over two days for about 1,000 spectators and dancers. With the exception of the Friday night dance, all events are free. **LOCATION:** Wood Center, University of Alaska campus **TICKETS/INFO:** 907-488-0556 **ACCOMMODATIONS/TOURIST INFO:** 907-456-5774, 907-465-2010

𝒜LASKA FOLK FESTIVAL
JUNEAU ✸ FIRST OR SECOND WEEK IN APRIL, MONDAY–SUNDAY

Defining folk music as "whatever folks want to make," this long-running festival gives everyone their 15 minutes of fame. The result is a wild week in which some 300 musicians and bands pack a convention hall, attending workshops, striking up musical friendships, jamming indiscriminately, playing out in clubs, and taking to the main stage for one 15-minute set apiece. One well-chosen guest act is invited from afar (past years have featured a Hawaiian slack key guitarist, Appalachian balladeers, Piedmont bluesmen John Cephas and Phil Wiggins, and bluegrass traditionalists Josh Graves and Kenny Baker), but homegrown music from Alaska and the Yukon is the order of the day. That could mean old-time fiddling, bluegrass, country, jazz, blues, African drumming, or reciting a poem while starting a chainsaw (this really happened one year). Best of all, all the shenanigans are free. **LOCATION:** Centennial Hall and satellite venues in downtown Juneau **TICKETS/INFO:** 907-789-0292 **ACCOMMODATIONS/TOURIST INFO:** 907-586-2201, 907-465-2010

Native American drummers perform at the Fairbanks Winter Folk Festival.

Courtesy of Fairbanks Convention and Visitors Bureau

✲INTERNATIONAL FOLK FESTIVAL

SKAGWAY (ALASKA) AND WHITEHORSE (YUKON TERRITORY, CANADA) ✳
A FRIDAY AND SATURDAY IN LATE APRIL OR EARLY MAY

This small-but-spirited folk festival spends Friday in Skagway, Alaska, then moves across the pass and over the border to serenade folkies in the Yukon's Whitehorse. As at the Alaska Folk Festival in Juneau (from which it spun off), the first 12 or 15 people who sign up can play any damn thing they please—though electric instruments are frowned upon. Sets are short, but the festival provides an opportunity to listen to and get to know acoustic musicians from around Skagway, Whitehorse, Juneau, and Haines, many of whom perform some fine traditional music. The crowd is a bit bigger in Whitehorse, but in both places you'll fork over $5 (either currency accepted).   **LOCATION:** First Presbyterian Church, Fourth and Main Streets (Skagway), Main Street Church on Main Street (Whitehorse) **TICKETS/INFO:** 907-983-2276, 907-983-2353 **ACCOMMODA-TIONS/TOURIST INFO:** 907-983-2854, 907-465-2010

♪JUNEAU JAZZ AND CLASSICS FESTIVAL

JUNEAU ✳ TEN DAYS IN LATE MAY

Juneau Jazz and Classics brings nationally and internationally known musicians to the state capital in late May, mixing a number of musical styles with the goal of challenging the audience and provoking stylistic crossovers. The focus is on chamber

Juneau Jazz & Classics: Artistic director Linda Rosenthal practices her scales. (See entry, page 367.) Courtesy of Mark Kelley/Juneau Jazz & Classics Festival

music and jazz, but you'd be hard pressed to find a more diverse lineup even in the Lower 48. In a single year the festival hosted banjo genius Bela Fleck, chamber masters The Raphael Trio, a capella quartet Toby Twining Music, and Texas bluesman Clarence "Gatemouth" Brown. Workshops, open rehearsals, and "on-the-water" events like a Blues Cruise and Classical Cruise round out the program.   **LOCATION:** Venues throughout Juneau **TICKETS/INFO:** 907-364-2801; e-mail: JuneauJazz@aol.com **ACCOMMODATIONS/TOURIST INFO:** 907-586-2201, 907-465-2010

SITKA SUMMER MUSIC FESTIVAL
SITKA ✳ THREE WEEKS STARTING THE FIRST FRIDAY IN JUNE

The Sitka Summer Music Festival began in 1972 when violinist Paul Rosenthal visited Sitka and decided that this fishing town, with its spectacular view of snow-covered peaks and Sitka Sound, would be the perfect place to hold a reunion with fellow protégés from the Jascha Heifetz and Gregor Piatigorsky master classes. Local residents contributed just enough money to buy the musicians one-way tickets to Sitka, and enough music lovers turned out for the concerts to pay their way back home.

For a quarter-century now, some 20 world-class chamber musicians have traveled to Sitka, performing without fee for the simple pleasure of making music with friends. Some are festival regulars; others are one-time guests invited by the regulars to play music among the mountains, fjords, and misty islands.

Sitka Summer Music Festival: Chamber music among the mountains, fjords, and misty islands. Courtesy of Alaska Division of Tourism

The venue is as memorable as the music. Inside the Centennial Building Auditorium, a panoramic window frames the musicians with a magnificent view of Sitka Sound. As fishing boats glide by and eagles dive for fish, musicians lovingly play a variety of music for strings, piano, and winds. A special emphasis is placed on pieces that reflect the city's Russian heritage.

Sitka is one of Alaska's most historic cities, founded in 1799 by Russian fur traders. The onion dome of St. Michael's Russian Orthodox Church contrasts with the many totem poles left by the Tlingit Indians (who eventually went to war with the Russians in Sitka). Nearby are opportunities for wildlife viewing, wilderness hiking, and world-class fishing, boating, and beachcombing.   **LOCATION:** Centennial Building Auditorium in Sitka, on Baranof Island. Sitka, about 100 miles southwest of Juneau, is accessible only by air (daily flights serve the town from Seattle, Anchorage, and Juneau) or sea (the Alaska State Ferry System and many cruise ships call into port). **TICKETS/INFO:** 907-747-6774, 907-277-4852 **ACCOMMODATIONS/TOURIST INFO:** 907-747-5940, 907-465-2010

FAIRBANKS SUMMER FOLK FEST
FAIRBANKS ✱ SECOND OR THIRD WEEKEND IN JUNE, FRIDAY–SUNDAY

Under the nonstop solstice sun, musicians from across Alaska gather for a day of fun on a grassy lawn in a theme park in the middle of Fairbanks. This is a great chance to hear a cross section of Alaskan performers who play 30-minute sets from noon until 7

P.M., with a Friday evening dance featuring a headliner from afar. Expect to hear anything from folk to Cajun, bluegrass, old-timey—just about anything that doesn't need to be plugged in. Storytelling and banjo-throwing contests round out the action, and food, arts and crafts, children's areas, and RV hookups are all within walking distance. About 1,500 people generally attend the event, which is broadcast live on KUAC-FM.   **LOCATION:** Usually at the Moose Creek Pavilion in the Alaskaland theme park in Fairbanks **TICKETS/INFO:** 907-488-0556; e-mail: FNKEC@aurora.alaska.edu **ACCOMMODATIONS/TOURIST INFO:** 907-456-5774, 907-465-2010

ᚄUTTON SUMMER MUSIC FESTIVAL
SUTTON ✷ THIRD WEEKEND IN JULY, FRIDAY–SUNDAY

This community festival brings 15 to 20 local groups and a couple of hundred spectators to the creekside grounds of the Sutton Community Hall for three days of bluegrass, country, rock, and whatever else anyone wants to play. Musicians are mostly local, and in lieu of a gate fee there's a big raffle. Tugs of war and demolition derbies are also held in Sutton this weekend.   **LOCATION:** Sutton's Community Hall, 45 miles from Anchorage at mile 61 on the Glenn Highway **TICKETS/INFO:** 907-745-3395, 907-745-4527 **ACCOMMODATIONS/TOURIST INFO:** 907-745-4527, 907-465-2010

ᛒALD EAGLE MUSIC FESTIVAL
HAINES ✷ SECOND WEEKEND IN AUGUST, WEDNESDAY–SUNDAY

Held in conjunction with the Southeast Alaska State Fair, the Bald Eagle Music Festival brings in three to five national acts as well as about 30 Alaskan and Canadian performers in numerous genres. Evening performances with national acts are held at the acoustically crisp Chilkat Center for the Performing Arts, and a Friday night dance (which starts with a square dance and moves on unpredictably) is held under the stars at the fairgrounds. The open stage at the fairgrounds features regional acts, including Native Alaskan dancers, blues, pop, funk, rock, country, folk, and drum artists. Other events include fiddle and songwriting contests, and music workshops in nearby Dalton City.   **LOCATION:** Chilkat Center for the Performing Arts and the Fairgrounds in Haines, about 70 air miles northwest of Juneau (accessible only by air or sea) **TICKETS/ INFO:** 907-766-2476; World Wide Web: http://haines.ak.us **ACCOMMODATIONS/ TOURIST INFO:** 907-766-2234, 907-465-2010

ᚲONCERT ON THE LAWN
HOMER ✷ SECOND WEEKEND IN AUGUST, SATURDAY OR SUNDAY

Wrapping up a fund-raising drive for Homer public radio station KBBI, the Concert on the Lawn is a local lovefest (and sometimes mudfest) that showcases some of the best south-central Alaskan talent. The crowd's so friendly and dance-crazed that the event's been compared (only half jokingly) to Woodstock, and against a mountain backdrop about a dozen bands play everything from folk to blues, rock, jazz, alternative, classical, and contemporary Christian. KBBI broadcasts the festivities live, and between songs DJs deliver the "bush lines"—broadcast messages to isolated people without phone service. Booths showcase artwork, handmade jewelry, and T-shirts.   **LOCATION:** Downtown Homer, about 200 miles south of Anchorage at the end of Highway 1 **TICKETS/INFO:** 907-235-7721; e-mail: IZKBBI@tundra.alaska.edu; World Wide Web: http://tundra.alaska.edu/-izkbbi/ **ACCOMMODATIONS/TOURIST INFO:** 907-235-7740, 907-235-5300, 907-465-2010

QUYANA ALASKA

ANCHORAGE ✸ THIRD WEEK IN OCTOBER, WEDNESDAY AND THURSDAY

Titled after the Yupik word meaning "thank you," Quyana draws Native American people from all over the state for two days of singing, dancing, and conferences. Alaska has seven distinct native cultures and dozens of subcultures, and this festival is a great opportunity to experience the music of most. The two nights of music are organized as a celebration of song sharing; expect to hear and see Tlingit and Haida drumming and dancing (with elaborate costuming), Athabascan fiddling, Yupik Eskimo singing, and the distinct music of the Aleuts, Inupiats, and Tsimshians. Each night features six or seven groups, with an audience of about 2,000.   **LOCATION:** Egan Center (1600 Gambell, at 16th Street) and Sullivan Arena (555 West Fifth Avenue, at E Street) **TICKETS/INFO:** 907-274-3611 **ACCOMMODATIONS/TOURIST INFO:** 907-276-4118, 907-465-2010

ATHABASCAN OLD-TIME FIDDLERS' FESTIVAL

FAIRBANKS ✸ FIRST OR SECOND WEEKEND IN NOVEMBER, THURSDAY–
SATURDAY

Seeking to preserve one of North America's richest folk traditions, this festival showcases the lively and unique sounds of the Athabascan fiddlers. This style of music began to develop about 150 years ago when Athabascan Indians of the Alaskan interior had contact with Scottish and Irish fiddlers who ran the Hudson's Bay Company's stores. The Athabascans picked up jigs and other songs and added their own flourishes. With the advent of radio in the north country, elements of American country and western crept in, and the songs began to incorporate three-quarter time signatures and hillbilly fiddle licks. Today, the music can best be described as a cross between the Celtic sounds of Canada's Atlantic provinces and old-time American country fiddle—with unique "Athabascanisms" thrown in.

Early in November, nearly 100 Athabascan and Eskimo musicians arrive from about 30 towns and villages all over Alaska and Canada, adding to the city's prefreeze bustle of trappers, holiday shoppers, and music lovers. Musicians range in age from 12 to 90, and about 750 spectators have bought out the event every year since it started in 1983.

If you watch the stage and the packed dance floor, you'll soon begin to notice the telltale variations of dance. Indians from upriver typically do the duck dance and the jig, while downriver performers and spectators favor the two-step and jitterbug. In an effort to attract families, the event is kept free of alcohol and smoke, and kids are encouraged to attend.

Since the festival began in 1983, many of the older Athabascan fiddlers have died, and in an effort to keep old-time fiddling alive the event organizers fund an artist-in-school program to match master fiddlers with young people who show interest. This is a great event to catch some of the surviving old masters, who trade stage stints every 40 minutes. A big dance is held Friday night, and Saturday features a banquet and after-dinner dance. A pass for the whole weekend runs about $55. Note that hotels are usually booked this time of year, so make reservations early.   **LOCATION:** Eagles Hall in downtown Fairbanks, 201 First Street (at Hall Street) **TICKETS/INFO:** 907-452-1825 **ACCOMMODATIONS/TOURIST INFO:** 907-456-5774, 907-465-2010

California

COLORADO RIVER COUNTRY MUSIC FESTIVAL
BLYTHE ✳ THIRD WEEKEND IN JANUARY, FRIDAY–SUNDAY

Despite its name, this festival actually offers snowbirds traditional bluegrass camaraderie and concerts, on the banks of the mighty Colorado. Six or seven bands are featured (Continental Divide, Lost and Found, and Copper Line have played recently), plus a comprehensive bunch of contests and jam sessions for do-it-yourselfers. The fairgrounds open on Monday to welcome campers from all over North America, and organizers considerately furnish wood for the jamming fires that flare up each night. On Friday the organized program begins, featuring concerts and contests in fiddle, mandolin, and flat-pick guitar, and more. **LOCATION:** Colorado River Country Fairgrounds, 11995 Olive Lake Boulevard in Blythe. From I-10 take the Intake Boulevard (U.S. 95) exit and go one mile north, then turn right onto Riverside Drive, and left onto Olive Lake Boulevard to the fairgrounds. **TICKETS/INFO:** 800-445-5513, 619-922-6037, 619-922-4354 **ACCOMMODATIONS/TOURIST INFO:** 800-445-5513, 800-445-0542 (CA only), 619-922-8166

BLUEGRASS RIVER REVEL
NEEDLES ✳ PRESIDENTS' DAY WEEKEND, FRIDAY–SUNDAY (PRESIDENTS' DAY IS THE THIRD MONDAY IN FEBRUARY)

On a stage overlooking the massive Colorado River, talents like Front Range and singer-banjoist Ralph Stanley belt out friendly harmonies and hillbilly rhythms that draw listeners from California, Arizona, and Nevada. This is one of the nation's foremost winter bluegrass festivals, and perhaps because the weather's so good, the majority of the 3,000 attendees are migrating snowbirds and retirees from up north. To accommodate them, the park provides hundreds of RV hookups. **LOCATION:** Moabi Regional Park in Needles, just off I-40 west of the Arizona-California border **TICKETS/INFO:** 619-326-9222 **ACCOMMODATIONS/TOURIST INFO:** 619-326-2050

THE AFRIKANS ARE COMING
LOS ANGELES ✳ THIRD OR FOURTH SATURDAY EVENING IN FEBRUARY

Since the late 1980s, L.A.'s thriving African expatriate community has presented an acclaimed evening of spellbinding drum and dance performances. Expect to see dance styles and costumes from Ghana, Senegal, Nigeria, Uganda, and South Africa—all driven by relentless, live drum rhythms. Expect exceptional diversity, energy, and charm! **LOCATION:** Japan American Theater, 244 South San Pedro Street, downtown Los Angeles **TICKETS/INFO:** 310-412-1136, 818-361-7075 **ACCOMMODATIONS/TOURIST INFO:** 213-624-7300, 213-689-8822

LOS ANGELES BACH FESTIVAL
LOS ANGELES ✷ LAST WEEK IN FEBRUARY AND FIRST WEEK IN MARCH

First presented in 1934, this venerable tribute to Johann Sebastian Bach is held within the gothic splendor of the First Congregational Church, a historic landmark in the city of Los Angeles. Instrumental, choral, and solo performances feature international and local talent in five noon concerts (free), two youth concerts (free), and five evening concerts ($11 to $17) during the 10-day festival.   **LOCATION:** First Congregational Church, 540 South Commonwealth Ave, Los Angeles **TICKETS/INFO:** 213-385-1345 **ACCOMMODATIONS/TOURIST INFO:** 213-624-7300, 213-689-8822

CALARTS SPRING MUSIC FESTIVAL
VALENCIA AND LOS ANGELES ✷ TWO OR THREE WEEKS IN MID-MARCH

Since 1976, the CalArts Spring Music Festival has approached the concept of "world music" in a much broader sense than most of its contemporaries. Along with the now-familiar African and Caribbean strains, CalArts usually includes the little-explored music of places like Bali, Java, and northern and southern India—plus interactive and computer music. Performers include students, faculty, and musicians from all over the world. Prices range from $2 to $13 for each evening's show.   **LOCATION:** CalArts Campus in Valencia (32 miles from downtown Los Angeles) and the Japan American Theater in L.A. **TICKETS/INFO:** 805-253-7800, 805-253-7816, 818-362-2315 **ACCOMMODATIONS/TOURIST INFO:** 805-253-7816, 800-462-2543

COWBOY POETRY AND MUSIC FESTIVAL
SANTA CLARITA ✷ LAST WEEKEND IN MARCH, FRIDAY–SUNDAY

Once the film location for historic westerns like *High Noon,* the late Gene Autry's Melody Ranch now hosts cowboy musicians, poets, balladeers, and storytellers from around the country. Audiences in past years have enjoyed cowboy performers such as Michael Martin Murphy, Riders in the Sky, Don Edwards, and the Sons of San Joaquin. Friday and Saturday nights feature dances with live western swing music, and if you happen to be new at this sort of thing, an on-site dance workshop will get you in step. A chuck wagon food area features cowboy vittles. Ticket sales begin in December. **LOCATION:** There's no parking at the ranch; shuttle buses leave from W. S. Hart High School at 24825 North Newhall in Santa Clarita. From I-5, exit at Lyons Avenue, go east two miles, then turn left and go one-half mile on Newhall Avenue to the high school. **TICKETS/INFO:** 800-305-0755, 805-255-4910 **ACCOMMODATIONS/TOURIST INFO:** 800-781-8687, 805-259-4787

¡¡VIVA EL MARIACHI!

FRESNO ✴ LAST WEEKEND IN MARCH, SATURDAY AND SUNDAY

Living up to this festival's title and rallying cry, a crowd of thousands turns out to ensure that the traditional Mexican music known as mariachi lives a long and celebrated life. The nation's second-oldest mariachi festival brings in up to a dozen bands that roam the grounds in their bolero jackets and tight-fitting trousers, playing the music that originated in the Jalisco highlands and went on to become a national symbol of Mexico. Local, regional, and national groups play on the outdoor main stage, surrounded by food vendors, arts and crafts booths, and music workshops.   **LOCATION:** Selland Arena, Fresno Convention Center, 700 M Street, Fresno **TICKETS/INFO:** 209-498-4000 **ACCOMMODATIONS/TOURIST INFO:** 209-233-0836, 800-788-0836

CALICO SPRING FESTIVAL

CALICO GHOST TOWN ✴ SECOND WEEKEND IN MAY (MOTHER'S DAY WEEKEND), FRIDAY–SUNDAY

The ghost town of Calico comes alive each year when nearly 10,000 living souls descend for a festival of bluegrass, country, cowboy, and ragtime music—with sideline adventures that include a host of 1880s games and contests. The town has three main stages and a string of storefront porches, all of which become venues for 10 musical acts featuring regional talents. Fiddle, banjo, guitar, and band competitions draw about 60 contestants. The site allows for dry camping or RV hookups, and admission costs $5 for adults and $2 for children.   **LOCATION:** Calico Ghost Town, just north of Yermo. From the L.A. area, take I-15 northeast past Barstow, exit at Yermo or Ghost Town Road, and follow the signs to Calico. **TICKETS/INFO:** 800-862-2542 **ACCOMMODATIONS/TOURIST INFO:** 619-256-8617, 800-462-2543

BEBOP & BREW

ARCATA ✴ A WEEKEND IN MID-MAY, SATURDAY AND SUNDAY

With both jazz and beer on tap, this growing festival serves up two of the West Coast's good-time specialties. A wide range of styles includes northern California artists playing bebop, Latin, big band, and avant-garde, plus headliners like Tuck and Patty and Mose Allison. The music is superbly complemented by some 60 different handmade beers from 25 West Coast microbreweries. A formal tasting is scheduled for Sunday, but informal tasting goes on all weekend. Proceeds benefit local nonprofits.   **LOCATION:** Downtown Arcata, about 10 miles north of Eureka on U.S. 101 **TICKETS/INFO:** 707-826-2267 **ACCOMMODATIONS/TOURIST INFO:** 707-822-3619

VENTURA CHAMBER MUSIC FESTIVAL

VENTURA ✴ THIRD WEEKEND IN MAY, WEDNESDAY–SUNDAY

Ventura's rich cultural heritage provides the inspiration for this chamber music series, which features the works of Spanish and Latin American composers, played by top-notch Southern California musicians. This well-organized, community-supported fête presents an astounding range of performances over just five days, embracing everything from classical to folk, traditional to avant-garde, song to symphony.

Up to a dozen ensembles and soloists—which recently have included the Nicoletti String Quartet and harpist Alfredo Rolando Ortiz—perform in unique venues, including private courtyards, churches, restaurants, boats, and galleries. The newly created Chamber Orchestra is impressive, and programs like Tea and Trumpets have drawn the support of local business and community leaders, who sprinkle the historic town with festive spreads of food, flowers, and congeniality. **LOCATION:** Various venues in downtown Ventura **TICKETS/INFO:** 805-648-3146 **ACCOMMODATIONS/TOURIST INFO:** 805-648-2075, 800-462-2543

TOPANGA BANJO-FIDDLE CONTEST, DANCE & FOLK ARTS FESTIVAL

AGOURA ✷ THIRD SUNDAY IN MAY

Set on a ranch in the Santa Monica Mountains, this one-day festival is a spirited history lesson in traditional American music. Four stages feature everything from fiddle and banjo breakdowns to shape-note singing, sea songs, cowboy poetry, and even railroad and hobo songs. One stage has more than 100 instrumental and singing contests, while another focuses on dances (contra, square, clog, Scottish country, and English country). A participative focus ensures that people can learn from, as well as listen to, old masters like Taj Mahal, John Hartford, and Dan Crary. **LOCATION:** Paramount Ranch, near Agoura in the Santa Monica Mountains National Recreation Area. From L.A. take the Ventura Freeway to the Kanan Road exit (in Agoura) and turn left. Go about two and one-half blocks and bear left at the fork onto Cornell Way. Paramount Ranch is another two and one-half miles on the right. **TICKETS/INFO:** 818-354-3795 **ACCOMMODATIONS/TOURIST INFO:** 818-886-0350, 818-889-3150

STRAWBERRY MUSIC FESTIVAL

BUCK MEADOWS ✷ MEMORIAL DAY WEEKEND, THURSDAY–SUNDAY (MEMORIAL DAY IS THE LAST MONDAY IN MAY)

Tie-dyed kids go wild over this weekend camp-and-jam event—and with good reason. The Strawberry Music Festival has made young people its focus, offering music, teen dances, open mikes, and nonmusical pleasures like Yosemite nature hikes and arts and crafts.

Parents have fun, too—all 3,500 of them—and since this is a participatory festival, there's always plenty of pickin' and grinnin' and catching up on one another's doings since the last hurrah. Most people return year after year and have developed a kind of community that keeps in touch through mail and e-mail.

Musically, the festival is a folksy stew made up of diverse harmonic stock. Expect to hear everything from South American pan pipes and African drums to folk, blues, bluegrass, and jazz. The roster of some 22 performers has in past years boasted such talents as David Grisman, Leo Kottke, John Prine, and Queen Ida, and stages seem to turn up in settings as diverse as the music. Sprinkled through the grounds are a main stage, a lake stage, a dining-hall stage, an amphitheater, and even a cowboy poetry stage.

Families camp out in tents, vans, and RVs, but the campground's few cabins are next-to-impossible to reserve, since the same people use them from one year to the next. Four-day passes cost around $100. For locals (and folks who hunker down at one of nearby Groveland's hotels), day tickets go for about $30. **LOCATION:** Camp Mather, just west of Yosemite's northwest gate. From the San Francisco Bay area, take Highway 580 to Highway 205 to Highway 120. Ten miles after Buck Meadows (one mile short of the Yosemite gate), turn left on Evergreen Road and follow it seven miles directly to

Camp Mather. **TICKETS/INFO:** 209-533-0191 **ACCOMMODATIONS/TOURIST INFO:** 209-533-0191, 800-462-2543

SACRAMENTO JAZZ JUBILEE

SACRAMENTO ✺ MEMORIAL DAY WEEKEND, FRIDAY–MONDAY

With Dixieland and traditional jazz at its heart, the Sacramento Jazz Jubilee provides a heaping, irresistible sampling of the world of classic jazz and all its derivatives. Old Sacramento and its environs become a whirlwind of rhythm as more than 40 stages spew authentic sounds nearly nonstop for four days.

Inaugurated in the 1970s as the Sacramento Dixieland Jazz Jubilee, the festival soon rose to prominence as the largest Dixieland festival anywhere. Purists cringed when, in the early 1990s, organizers dropped "Dixieland" from the name and sought to attract a broader range of listeners with a broader range of music. Now you'll find the entire scope of jazz, plus swing, blues, boogie-woogie, and even oddities like a mariachi band playing "The Saints" for a conga-line crowd at the Holiday Inn ballroom.

Surprises like this have breathed new life into this aging beauty of a festival and pushed attendance to more than 100,000 over four days. Yet there's still plenty here for the trad-jazz purist, and the overwhelming majority of the more than 120 bands from around the world play music from the 1895-1945 era.

Free shuttle buses connect Old Sacramento with four other musical centers in hotels and convention centers. Not all the stages are acoustically perfect, nor are all the performances memorable. But if you spend any time at all wandering around the citywide extravaganza of music, you'll get enough musical thrills to last an entire year. **LOCATION:** Old Sacramento and various nearby hotels and convention centers **TICKETS/INFO:** 916-372-5277 **ACCOMMODATIONS/TOURIST INFO:** 916-264-7617, 916-264-7777

BELIZE CAYE FESTIVAL

LOS ANGELES ✺ MEMORIAL DAY

As a crossroads of African, European, Mayan, and Caribbean culture, Belize developed some of the most interesting music in Central America. Opportunities to experience these sounds are rare in North America, but at the Belize Caye Festival the uniquely danceable Belizean rhythms abound. About a dozen expatriate bands lay down authentic Garifuna and punta-rock sounds, as well as Belizean versions of reggae and soca. In addition to the music, you can taste the culture of the country at dozens of food booths. **LOCATION:** Corner of Rodeo and Labrea Roads (5001 West Rodeo Road), one mile south of the Santa Monica Freeway **TICKETS/INFO:** 213-731-2927 **ACCOMMODATIONS/TOURIST INFO:** 213-624-7300, 213-689-8822

MAINLY MOZART FESTIVAL

SAN DIEGO, TIJUANA, AND SURROUNDING COMMUNITIES ✺ TWO WEEKS BEGINNING TUESDAY AFTER MEMORIAL DAY

The Mainly Mozart Festival spills over the country's southern border, drawing both San Diego County and the Mexican border cities of Tijuana and Ensenada into this celebration of the music of Wolfgang Amadeus Mozart. Churches, cathedrals, theaters, and cultural centers present the classical music of Mozart and his 18th-century rivals

Sacramento Jazz Jubilee: An irresistible sampling of classic jazz and all its derivatives. Tom Myers

(such as Beethoven and Handel), plus masters of the baroque and early romantic periods. U.S. residents who want to attend the Mexican shows can easily park in one of the numerous lots on the U.S. side of the border and walk into Mexico, then catch a cab into Tijuana and Ensenada.   **LOCATION:** Various locations in San Diego, Tijuana, and Ensenada **TICKETS/INFO:** 619-558-1000, 619-233-4281 **ACCOMMODATIONS/ TOURIST INFO:** 619-232-3101

℞EGGAE SUNSPLASH
SACRAMENTO ✸ A WEEKEND IN LATE MAY OR EARLY JUNE

Sometimes the one-drop reggae groove sneaks into the most unlikely places. In a tree-studded grove connected to the Radisson Hotel, Sacramento's Reggae Sunsplash draws a fine selection of nationally touring reggae acts. Six to eight bands spend the afternoon and evening entertaining a crowd of about 1,200, who take advantage of the handcrafted goods, barbecued food, and full bar. A lake and pool are adjacent, and admission is about $25.   **LOCATION:** Radisson Hotel Outdoor Grove, 500 Leisure Lane, Sacramento **TICKETS/INFO:** 916-923-2277; e-mail: pmitch@cwo.com **ACCOM-MODATIONS/TOURIST INFO:** 916-264-7777

◎JAI MUSIC FESTIVAL
OJAI ✸ FIRST WEEKEND IN JUNE, FRIDAY–SUNDAY

Ojai's unique appeal lies in its seemingly incongruous qualities. A highly sophisticated program draws some of the classical world's most adventurous performers and listeners to a small and rustic setting. Amenities are few, yet world-class standards of artistic presentation flourish. And although a rugged, unpretentious aura prevails, each year typically finds the entire classical music world talking about the goings-on at Ojai.

Ojai is popular with classical listeners in the know because its program emphasizes discovery of new works and rediscovery of rare works by old masters. Resident maestros (a different one each year) traditionally are strong supporters of new music and often invite contemporary composers to conduct their own works. Ojai has seen its share of world premieres by composers such as Oliver Messiaen, Lukas Foss, Gyorgy Ligeti, and Pierre Boulez.

Each year, the Ojai Music Festival brings in a resident orchestra from as close as Los Angeles, or as far away as Lyons, France. The festival's three days typically feature five concerts, ranging in repertoire from early baroque to the contemporary era.

Despite its reputation as an avant-garde mecca, Ojai never takes itself too seriously—thanks in part to an earthy venue in which snobbishness would seem out of place. Nestled in a steep valley in the Topa Mountains, the modest orchestra shell shares a bowl with wooden benches and blankets sprawled across the lawn. Oaks and syca-mores draw birds whose chirps blend brilliantly with the performances, creating a natural, relaxed atmosphere.

Festival admission ranges from $15 to $35, and an art show runs concurrently with the music festival.   **LOCATION:** Libbey Bowl, behind the Ojai Post Office at Signal and Ojai Avenues in downtown Ojai, which is 15 miles east of U.S. 101 on Highway 33, approximately 20 miles northwest of the L.A. city limits **TICKETS/INFO:** 805-646-2094; World Wide Web: http://www.west.net/@ojai **ACCOMMODATIONS/TOURIST INFO:** 805-646-8126

SOUTHERN CALIFORNIA CAJUN & ZYDECO FESTIVAL

LONG BEACH ✴ FIRST WEEKEND IN JUNE

Rainbow Lagoon isn't exactly a bayou, but the Louisiana music here is as authentic as it gets. This festival features two days of Cajun and zydeco music outdoors, plus a Saturday night dance in the adjoining Convention Center ballroom. In addition to six or more bands, the festival offers children's activities, spicy foods, and workshops in dance, music, and culture. Tickets are about $17 each day.   **LOCATION:** Rainbow Lagoon, at Linden Avenue and Ocean Boulevard (beside the Convention Center) in Long Beach. From the Long Beach Freeway (Highway 710), exit at Downtown/Convention Center/ Shoreline Drive. **TICKETS/INFO:** 310-427-3713, 310-595-5944, 818-794-0070, 415-386-8677 **ACCOMMODATIONS/TOURIST INFO:** 800-452-7829, 310-436-3645, 800-462-2543

GREAT AMERICAN IRISH FAIR AND MUSIC FESTIVAL

ARCADIA ✴ THIRD WEEKEND IN JUNE, SATURDAY AND SUNDAY

Irish musicians, singers, and dancers come from all over the world to create an array of Celtic sounds that's unequaled in the American West. Music makes up more than 80 percent of the program, and with some 1,000 performers, this is a great place to get a spirited sampling of the diversity and vitality of Irish music today.

Music pours from 12 stages. Soloists run fingers over strings of handmade harps or lutes while singing folk ballads (often in Gaelic). Irish tenors fill the air with sweet, stirring sounds, while pub bands across the green enhance the beer-drinking mood with foot-stomping rhythms. An Irish Renaissance features demonstrations of early music and instrument-making, while main stages support big-name performers like the Chieftains, the Clancy Brothers, and the Young Dubliners.

Much of the music is complemented by Irish traditional dance. In competitions and demonstrations, hundreds of dancers stomp out the intricate foot movements of step dances and high-spirited jigs. Performers spin and step to live music, showing off costumes decorated with Celtic designs taken from the fifth-century *Book of Kells*.

No Irish fair would be complete without the sound and spectacle of massed pipes and drums, and each year sees performances by the country's top pipe bands. Nattily dressed bagpipers take turns leading colorful parades through the grounds, coaxing festive and blaring sounds from their improbable instruments.

The fair is sponsored by the Irish Fair Foundation, an organization dedicated to preserving and promoting Irish and Irish American culture in southern California. Although the region doesn't have the distinct Irish neighborhoods of eastern and midwestern U.S. cities, it is home to some 1.7 million Irish descendants. Anyway, no one lets a little thing like not being Irish get in the way of spending an afternoon among the Celts. More than 50,000 people typically show up to listen to the fiddles, learn how to dance the lilt, watch some Gaelic football, or check out the beauty contest and the dog show (on separate stages).   **LOCATION:** Santa Anita Racetrack, 285 West Huntington Drive in Arcadia. From I-210 take the Baldwin Avenue exit and follow signs to the race track. **TICKETS/INFO:** 818-985-2233 **ACCOMMODATIONS/TOURIST INFO:** 818-795-9311, 213-624-7300, 707-822-3619

MUSIC IN THE MOUNTAINS SUMMER FESTIVAL

NEVADA CITY AND GRASS VALLEY ✸ THREE WEEKS, FROM MID-JUNE
THROUGH EARLY JULY

Challenging the notion that classical music has to be stuffy, Music in the Mountains stresses enthusiasm and local participation over musical pedigree. Set in the historic Sierra Nevada foothills, many of the festival's indoor and outdoor venues seat the audience cabaret-style. Over three weeks, 15 concerts feature a 50-piece festival orchestra and a volunteer chorus that's one of the state's very best. Tickets range from $8 to $30.   **LOCATION:** Various venues in Nevada City and Grass Valley, near the intersection of Highways 20 and 49, between Reno and Sacramento **TICKETS/INFO:** 800-218-2188 **ACCOMMODATIONS/TOURIST INFO:** 800-655-4667, 916-273-4667, 916-273-4332

KROQ WEENIE ROAST AND SING ALONG

LAGUNA HILLS ✸ SECOND OR THIRD WEEKEND IN JUNE, SATURDAY

They don't really grill hot dogs around a campfire at this one-day festival, but fans do manage to set fire to the grass in the lawn seating area almost every year. A capacity crowd of more than 15,000 sits, stands, and dances to more than a dozen of the best and most high-profile alternative rock bands from North America and Europe.

Long before "alternative" came to symbolize the deprivation-envy of suburban mall kids, Los Angeles-based KROQ-FM (106.7) was playing the music of the Ramones, Violent Femmes, X, and other mavericks who have graced the Weenie Roast stage. Recent-year headliners—Hole, Bush, White Zombie, and Soul Asylum, among others—aren't groundbreaking, but they still fuel an enthusiasm that drives a moshing, roaring, zealous crowd.

General-admission lawn tickets are the least expensive, and (unlike the reserved sections) there are no seats to bump into while grooving to the music. Plus, people sitting on the lawn are typically the most rowdy (translation: they have the most fun up there). Seats closest to the stage are reserved for KROQ contest winners, so if you want to "party in the pit" and maybe even win backstage passes, tune in to the station and set your phone to redial the number repeatedly.

Be sure to bring sunscreen and sunglasses, since this daylong festival starts in the afternoon, when the sun is at its hottest, and continues until after 10 P.M. Irvine Meadows is an outdoor amphitheater, and shade is a precious commodity. You can't bring in your own food or drink, so be prepared to pay a pretty penny for water, soft drinks, liquor, and food ranging from Mexican to pizza to the proverbial hot dog. **LOCATION:** Irvine Meadows Amphitheater, 8808 Irvine Center Drive in Laguna Hills. From I-405 take the Irvine Center Drive exit. **TICKETS/INFO:** 818-567-1067 **ACCOMMODATIONS/TOURIST INFO:** 800-877-1115, 714-494-1018

NORTEÑO/TEJANO MUSIC FESTIVAL

FRESNO ✸ A SATURDAY IN MID-JUNE

California's only Norteño/Tejano festival celebrates the traditional, accordion-based sounds that emerged along the Texas-Mexico border and spread throughout the southwestern United States. The festival sidesteps commercial sponsorship and eschews more contemporary styles in its quest to preserve this unique musical tradition. Nearly 2,000

Hot diggity: Tim Armstrong leads Rancid's spirited barrage at the 1995 KROQ Weenie Roast and Sing Along. Kevin P. Casey/Los Angeles Times Photo

agree with this approach, creating a roaring dance-a-thon to the polka-esque beats of about four bands.   **LOCATION:** Fresno Convention Center Exhibit Hall, 700 M Street, Fresno **TICKETS/INFO:** 209-498-4000, 209-455-5754; e-mail: tmkw92f@prodigy.com **ACCOMMODATIONS/TOURIST INFO:** 800-788-0836, 209-233-0836

GRASS VALLEY BLUEGRASS FESTIVAL
GRASS VALLEY ✷ FATHER'S DAY WEEKEND, THURSDAY–SUNDAY (FATHER'S DAY IS THE THIRD SUNDAY IN JUNE)

Bluegrass fanatics consistently rank Grass Valley at the top of the California bluegrass heap. Sponsored by the California Bluegrass Association, the West Coast's largest bluegrass festival is an extravaganza with fantastic headliners, great jamming, an excellent sound system, pine-forest camping, and close to zero chance of rain.

A dependably stellar lineup has included the likes of Bill Monroe, Ralph Stanley, Doyle Lawson, and David Grisman. The preshow action starts on Wednesday, with a free youth performance featuring younger-generation bluegrassers. The children's program continues all four days, with arts and crafts, fiddle lessons for kids, and father-son performances.

Musically, the festival's 16 or so bands focus on the traditional, and some 7,000 visitors from across the United States, Canada, and even Europe and Japan seem to support this approach. About half the audience camps—rough sites and RV hookups are available—and the other half stays in Sacramento or local hotels and bed and breakfasts. The camping area surrounds a large meadow that cradles the performance area, and campground jamming continues pretty much nonstop.

Grass Valley has a very noncommercial, community atmosphere, and families are encouraged to attend. Alcohol isn't sold on the premises, but BYO is no problem—though organizers keep a pretty tight reign on behavior because there are so many children afoot. Vegetarian and Mexican foods are available on the premises. Day passes are $15 to $25 (depending on the day), and plenty of early-bird and multiday specials are available.   **LOCATION:** Nevada County Fairgrounds, at 11228 McCourtney Road in Grass Valley, about 50 miles from Sacramento. From Sacramento, take Highway 80 east about 35 miles to Auburn, then go north on Highway 49. Take the Grass Valley exit directly to the fairgrounds. **TICKETS/INFO:** 209-293-1559, 707-762-8735 **ACCOMMODATIONS/TOURIST INFO:** 800-655-4667, 916-273-4667

PLAYBOY JAZZ FESTIVAL
LOS ANGELES ✷ THIRD WEEKEND IN JUNE

Bringing together new artists and all-time greats, the Playboy Jazz Festival's consistently strong musical program draws some 35,000 spectators over two days. The high caliber of performers is complemented by a unique revolving stage—so there are no breaks in the 17 hours of music. Bill Cosby usually emcees, and performers have included everyone from Ornette Coleman and Dave Brubeck to Horace Silver and Herbie Hancock. Admission ranges from about $13 to $75 per day, depending on seat location. **LOCATION:** Hollywood Bowl in Los Angeles, on Highland Avenue north of Hollywood Boulevard **TICKETS/INFO:** 310-449-4070 **ACCOMMODATIONS/TOURIST INFO:** 213-624-7300, 213-689-8822

SIERRA NEVADA WORLD MUSIC FESTIVAL
MARYSVILLE ✸ THIRD WEEKEND IN JUNE, FRIDAY–SUNDAY

In a grassy park at the confluence of the Feather and Yuba Rivers, worldbeat fans from up and down the West Coast converge for a summer solstice weekend of music from around the world. The musical focus is on Jamaican reggae and other sounds of the African diaspora, and about 5,000 dancing world-beatniks create an enthusiastically suave vibe.

Most of the 20 or so bands are from outside the United States, and past festivals have included everyone from Senegal's Baaba Maal and South Africa's Lucky Dube to Jamaican toaster Eek-A-Mouse and West Coast reggae-surfers the Cardiff Reefers.

Accompanying the music are food booths and local arts and crafts, and a microbrew beer garden (featuring Sierra Nevada and other local beers). The Riverfront Park main stage has an "anything goes" cousin in the campground, which hosts scheduled acts, surprise performances, and all-night nonsense. A great idea!   **LOCATION:** Riverfront Park Amphitheatre, just off 14th Street in Marysville. Marysville is about 40 miles north of Sacramento via Highway 70. **TICKETS/INFO:** 916-891-6160, 916-343-7611, 916-923-2277; e-mail: EpiphanyA@aol.com **ACCOMMODATIONS/TOURIST INFO:** 916-743-6501, 916-743-6503

MONTEREY BAY BLUES FESTIVAL
MONTEREY ✸ FOURTH WEEKEND IN JUNE

Although its logo features an old bluesman in a rocking chair, the Monterey Bay Blues Festival is better known for electrified—and electrifying—blues performers like Kenny Neal, Etta James, and Coco Montoya. Main-stage acts get most of the attention from the fairgrounds crowd of about 25,000, but more rewarding performances can often be found at two smaller stages. Begun in 1985, the festival now presents more than 40 acts over three days. Reserved-seat admission to each of the shows—Saturday afternoon, Saturday evening, and Sunday afternoon—is about $20.   **LOCATION:** Monterey Fairgrounds; from Route 1, exit at Casa Verde or Aguajito **TICKETS/INFO:** 416-649-6544 **ACCOMMODATIONS/TOURIST INFO:** 408-649-1770

SUMMER SOLSTICE FOLK MUSIC, DANCE & STORYTELLING FESTIVAL
CALABASAS ✸ FOURTH WEEKEND IN JUNE, FRIDAY–SUNDAY

Once called simply the Dulcimer Festival, this much-expanded gig brings southern California folkies together for an amazingly participative weekend of music and more. The festival was "interactive" long before it came into vogue, downplaying singer-songwriters and the concert format in favor of small performances, singing, jamming, dancing, and teaching.

This is one of the best places in the world to begin learning how to play the hammered dulcimer, Cajun accordion, Andean pan pipe, and dozens of other acoustic instruments. Throughout the campus of Soka University, small groups huddle around master musicians who sometimes even offer loaner instruments to novices. There are more than 300 workshops to choose from; in addition to music, you can learn storytelling, traditional crafts, and folk dancing (accompanied by live musicians, since no recorded music is allowed on the site).

Begun in the early 1970s by claw-hammer banjo player Clark Weissman and his wife, Elaine, the event is sponsored by the California Traditional Music Society and organized out of the Weissmans' home. Organizers have resisted the temptation to add any of the "world music" that's crept into many folk festivals, continuing to focus almost entirely on North American traditional music and its northern European roots. Tickets are about $20 at the gate. **LOCATION:** Soka University, 26800 Mulholland Highway **TICKETS/INFO:** 818-342-7664 **ACCOMMODATIONS/TOURIST INFO:** 818-222-5680, 800-462-2543

ℳARIACHI USA

LOS ANGELES ✸ FOURTH WEEKEND IN JUNE, SATURDAY AND SUNDAY

Bringing mariachi from the family restaurants of Mexico to the Hollywood Bowl, this festival features the world's top mariachi groups and more than 30,000 roaring, passionate fans. Although many attendees are gringo neophytes seeking an introduction to the fabulous sounds and sights of Mexico, many more are Mexican families—a tribute to mariachi's role in bonding generations of people of Mexican heritage.

Born of a marriage between ancient Aztec rhythms and Spanish instrumentation, mariachi took hold in the western state of Jalisco around the turn of the century. The popularity of mariachi spread to other regions, and eventually the music became a national symbol of Mexico. Often, mariachi musicians are in the shadows because the singers take the spotlight, but at this festival the mariachi bands are the featured acts, with singers coming onstage as added attractions.

Cuban-born businesswoman Rodri Rodriguez started the festival in 1990. A mariachi event of this size had never been attempted—even in Mexico. Then, as now, Rodriguez booked five or six of the premier bands from Mexico and southern California, ensuring a successful, sold-out event. In recent years, the festival has included the likes of Mariachi Sol de México from El Monte, the all-female Mariachi La Reyna de Los Angeles, Mariachi Campanas de America from Texas, and Mariachi Cobre from Florida. Singers have included everyone from Mexico's Angeles Ochoa to Junko Seki, a Japanese woman who perfected the style after she fell in love with mariachi music at Epcot Center. **LOCATION:** Hollywood Bowl in Los Angeles, on Highland Avenue north of Hollywood Boulevard **TICKETS/INFO:** 310-451-5044 **ACCOMMODATIONS/TOURIST INFO:** 213-624-7300, 213-689-8822

ℋIGH SIERRA MUSIC FESTIVAL

BEAR VALLEY ✸ WEEKEND CLOSEST TO OR INCLUDING JULY 4

Seeking to cross-pollinate audiences with an eclectic variety of music, this worldly folk festival and camp-out is a breath of fresh mountain air for anyone tired of the concrete concert halls of the West Coast lowlands. The festival began at Leland Meadows, and after four years of building a solid reputation around a diverse array of sounds, moved to 7,000-foot-high Bear Valley.

The mountain setting couldn't be better: the stage is framed by pine trees and backed by rugged Sierra peaks, and just outside the town (which has plenty of restaurants and lodging) trails draw hikers and bikers, and lakes and streams draw fishermen and kayakers. Food and crafts booths feature a hodge-podge of food, clothing, jewelry, and musical instruments. Plus, families with kids can take advantage of organized arts and crafts activities, nature hikes, and special musical performances.

Mariachi USA: Folkloric dance troupes share the stage with Mexico's top mariachi groups. Courtesy of Alycia Enciso for MARIACHI USA®

The festival's own local radio station, Meadow Marmot Radio, features DJs from college and noncommercial stations all over California and pipes performances directly into the campground. A typical day might begin with a wake-up song, which brings a tie-dyed, bleary-eyed campground to life as the sun peeks over the mountains.

Some folks get in short hikes or bike rides before heading to the main stage, where the afternoon brings headliners that run the spectrum from California roots rockers to blues, bluegrass, folk, and roots musicians from around the world. As a sampling, previous years have featured John Hiatt, Rory Block, Joe Ely, Widespread Panic, the Blazers, and Pele Juju. Expect to see old favorites as well as some new and exciting talent.

The two stages host some 50 acts, many of whom also end up teaching workshops for the musical *manqué*. After dark, jam sessions abound in the campground and around a bonfire in the concert area. In town, a Late Night Cantina series features regionally known musicians at Shawkey's Avalanche and the Bear Valley Cathedral Lounge.

Camping is included in the price of admission, but note that there's an attendance cap of 5,000. So get your tickets early, get out those tie-dyes, and check your camping gear—it's going to be one helluva weekend.   **LOCATION:** Bear Valley in the High Sierra. From Sacramento take Highway 99 south to Highway 4, then take Highway 4 east for 100 miles to Bear Valley. **TICKETS/INFO:** 800-594-9171, 510-420-1529; World Wide Web: http://www.rockweb.com/events/high-sierra **ACCOMMODATIONS/TOURIST INFO:** 916-694-2475, 800-462-2543

MAMMOTH LAKES JAZZ JUBILEE

MAMMOTH LAKES ✳ SECOND OR THIRD WEEKEND IN JULY, THURSDAY–SUNDAY

With great traditional jazz, spectacular High Sierra views, and an enthusiastic group of local organizers, Mammoth Lakes adds up to one giant jazz buzz. More than a dozen bands sound out Dixieland and other traditional styles at 10 venues scattered among the high-mountain pines and laid-back towny bars. The majority of performers come from around California, but some all-stars trek cross-country. Daily entry badges cost from $15 to $25.   **LOCATION:** Downtown Mammoth Lakes, off Highway 395 in California's Sierra Nevada, three hours south of Reno **TICKETS/INFO:** 619-934-2478 **ACCOMMODATIONS/TOURIST INFO:** 800-367-6572

MENDOCINO MUSIC FESTIVAL

MENDOCINO ✳ SECOND TWO WEEKS IN JULY

In a small tent perched on the headlands overlooking the ocean, the sound of lulling surf mixes with orchestral and chamber music, solo piano, jazz, and one fully staged opera. Mendocino's program is a very mixed bag, and each night for two summer weeks about 600 people come out to historic Mendocino's seaside front lawn to revel in the musical treats of about 80 performers (about one-third are local professionals). Admission costs about $15 to $23 for a performance, and rehearsals and preconcert lectures are open to the public.   **LOCATION:** Headlands State Park on Main Street, next to the Ford House Museum, in Mendocino **TICKETS/INFO:** 707-937-2044 **ACCOMMODATIONS/TOURIST INFO:** 800-946-3636, 707-459-7910, 800-726-2780

JVC CONCORD JAZZ FESTIVAL

CONCORD ✳ A SATURDAY IN MID-JULY

The JVC Concord Jazz Festival is one of the Bay Area's biggest jazz bargains, with a half-dozen of the jazz and blues world's very best condensing their performances into an afternoon. Ticket prices are typically low, and cold brew and hot barbecue are in high supply.   **LOCATION:** Concord Pavilion, 2000 Kirker Pass Road, Concord **TICKETS/INFO:** 510-798-3318, 510-631-3100 **ACCOMMODATIONS/TOURIST INFO:** 800-262-5526, 510-839-9000, 415-974-6900

RHYTHM AND BREWS BEER TASTING FESTIVAL

SOUTH LAKE TAHOE ✳ THIRD SATURDAY IN JULY

The Rhythm and Brews Beer Tasting Festival is a palate-pleasing, rhythmic highlight of the South Lake Tahoe summer. This mid-July gig combines funky R&B with the rich flavors of microbrews and the Sierra sun. More than 100 different kinds of beer are featured (most from West Coast microbreweries), and bands have included the likes of bluesy Jack Mack and the Heart Attack, and rockabilly relics Commander Cody and the Lost Planet Airmen. The entry fee of $20 gets you a souvenir beer glass and unlimited beer sampling, but get tickets early for this one; it fills up fast.   **LOCATION:** Harvey's

Mendocino Music Festival: The sound of surf mingles with orchestral and chamber music, jazz, and opera. Courtesy of Richard Comen/Mendocino Music Festival

Resort and Casino **TICKETS/INFO:** 916-541-4975, 800-553-1022 **ACCOMMODATIONS/TOURIST INFO:** 800-288-2463, 916-541-5255

🎼ARMEL BACH FESTIVAL
CARMEL ✽ THIRD SATURDAY IN JULY THROUGH SECOND SUNDAY IN AUGUST

Founded in 1935 to promote the then-obscure works of J. S. Bach, the Carmel Bach Festival has become an impressive and formidable affair with 15 formal evening concerts over three weeks. Add to that one or two daily recitals, children's concerts, lectures, and symposia and this is clearly one of America's most comprehensive forays into Bach's music.

The music of Bach and his baroque contemporaries is no longer uncommon, but the festival still manages remarkable musical feats, year after year. Directed in recent years by German-born Bruno Weil, the programs have taken on an energetic and mature—but always entertaining—character. Best of all, the repertoire, often played on 18th-century instruments, is never obvious or bland.

The festival orchestra is composed of musicians from the United States and abroad who live and perform together for five weeks. Accomplished enough to handle the music's deft and sophisticated flourishes, the orchestra also supports internationally known vocal and instrumental soloists. Also featured are two choruses, one composed of professional singers from across the country, the other of local artists.

Music is played in the Carmel Mission Basilica, the (acoustically spotty) Sunset Theater, and other venues. John Steinbeck once roamed the seaside town of Carmel, but today you'll find few reminders of his quirky characters among the fine restaurants and glitzy shopping malls. Still, it's possible to catch nostalgic whiffs of inspiration in the sea breezes that massage the beautiful, park-filled valley—and in the timeless magic of Bach's music.   **LOCATION:** Various venues in Carmel **TICKETS/INFO:** 800-513-2224, 408-624-2046 **ACCOMMODATIONS/TOURIST INFO:** 408-624-2522, 800-462-2543

SAW PLAYERS' PICNIC AND MUSIC FESTIVAL
FELTON ✸ THIRD SUNDAY IN JULY

They come from all over the world bearing their beloved musical tool, with nothing in common other than love, respect, and aptitude for the instrument that can rip a beam, fell a giant redwood, or create ethereal, wavering music.

About 35 saw players typically make the trip, often accompanied by guitarists, banjoists, fiddlers, and harmonica players. Expect a variety of musical styles, all of them acoustic. Festival organizer Charlie Blacklock plays old-time country and bluegrass; others play classical and jazz. Gospel music is also in evidence, reflecting the musical saw's move "underground" into the churches after its heyday in the late twenties and early thirties. The majority of performances are instrumental and solo, but some bands, like the Cheap Suit Serenaders, sport two dueling saw players in their ensemble of singers and old-time musicians. Toward the end of the festival, a symphony of saw players is organized, sometimes featuring as many as 30 onstage at one time.

Although the names of famous saw players aren't exactly household words, the genre does have its elite. David Weiss has played with the Los Angeles Philharmonic Orchestra. Xinzheng Li is an 83-year-old grand master sawyer who directs the School of the Musical Saw in Beijing, China. Another Chinese saw player, Yuanqing Li, had to convince American officials to grant him a visa by performing musical show tunes at an impromptu concert at the U.S. consulate in Guangzhou. He arrived in Felton carrying his saw and a box of cassettes with music he had composed and performed on the saw.

A local radio personality named Mr. Hedge often provokes bouts of dancing with his fabulously psychedelic rendition of "Stairway to Heaven." Organizer Charlie Blacklock concertizes around the world and has designed a musical saw with his name on it. His beautiful invention has a higher range and gets more notes than an ordinary carpentry saw.

There's only one stage, but saw players often wander off together to jam under the park's huge trees. Plus, there's always a "happening" the day before the event in nearby Santa Cruz, at the site of the world's only life-sized statue of a saw player. The statue honors the late Thomas Jefferson Scribner, a famous musical saw player and local old-timer whom everyone liked (mostly because he "had an answer for everything"). Tom has been dead for over a decade, but the California Saw Players Association is still trying to figure out how to get his trademark red socks onto the statue's legs.   **LOCATION:** Roaring Camp and Big Trees Train Depot (Narrow Gauge Railroad) on Graham Road in Felton, six miles north of Santa Cruz **TICKETS/INFO:** 510-523-4649 **ACCOMMODATIONS/TOURIST INFO:** 800-833-3494, 408-425-1234, 800-462-2543

𝓕UJITSU CONCORD JAZZ FESTIVAL AND LATIN JAZZ FEST

CONCORD ✴ A WEEKEND IN LATE JULY OR EARLY AUGUST, FRIDAY–SUNDAY

One of the West's longest-running jazz festivals features internationally acclaimed performers who play everything from New Orleans-style jazz and blues to bebop, big band, and swing. Plenty of legendary sessions have wowed the crowds at the open-air pavilion that was the pride and joy of the late Carl Jefferson, owner of the respected Concord Jazz labels. On Sunday, the Latin Jazz Fest segment features the California summer's biggest and best gathering of spicy, sophisticated Latin rhythms, with a roster of artists that has included Eddie Palmieri, Mongo Santamaria, Poncho Sancho, and Ray Barreto—all in one year! Tickets are typically around $26 per day for reserved seats, $13 for lawn.   **LOCATION:** Concord Pavilion, 2000 Kirker Pass Road, Concord **TICKETS/ INFO:** 510-798-3318, 510-631-3100 **ACCOMMODATIONS/TOURIST INFO:** 800-262-5526, 510-839-9000, 415-974-6900

𝓢AN LUIS OBISPO MOZART FESTIVAL

SAN LUIS OBISPO ✴ LATE JULY THROUGH EARLY AUGUST (TWO WEEKS)

Prodigious, ingenious, and unlucky beyond belief, Wolfgang Amadeus Mozart composed hundreds of works—including a symphony he wrote when he was eight years old—but he died at age 35 and was buried in an unmarked grave. Although his contemporaries in Vienna considered him a failure and a pauper, history came to recognize Mozart as one of the greatest musical geniuses the world has ever known.

Some 40 performances over two weeks feature a few of Mozart's 41 known symphonies, plus his concertos, chamber music, and operas. But the festival goes beyond the *Wolfmeister* himself, presenting the music of his classical-era contemporaries, plus modern-day composers whose work shares a common denominator with Mozart's.

The festival makes use of an impressive array of venues around San Luis Obispo, including churches and chapels, plazas and pavilions, the Cal Poly campus, and several wineries where chamber music is played among the barrels. Free fringe concerts feature brass bands, worldbeat, and more.

Many of the orchestra members are hired regionally, but the many guest soloists and ensembles have included greats like Orli Shaham, the Brentano and Turtle Island String Quartets, and the Kandinsky String Trio. An Akademie program of musical lectures is complemented by an AKIDemie program offering fun, one-hour classes designed to get children interested in music. At these hands-on, cross-generational exchanges, festival musicians explain everything from Paraguayan harps to elements of opera and symphonic music.   **LOCATION:** Various venues in and around San Luis Obispo **TICKETS/INFO:** 805-781-3008; e-mail: mozart@slonet.org **ACCOMMODA-TIONS/TOURIST INFO:** 805-541-8000, 800-462-2543

𝓜USIC FROM BEAR VALLEY

BEAR VALLEY ✴ LAST SATURDAY IN JULY THROUGH SECOND SUNDAY IN AUGUST

For nearly 30 years, summer has officially reached the High Sierra when the tents go up, the musicians arrive, and the sounds of classical music again echo among the trees. Each summer, the tiny mountain hamlet of Bear Valley hosts some 65 orchestra members and internationally acclaimed soloists who present three weeks of music ranging from chamber to symphonic to pops. Most performances are held in the evening, so you can spend the comfortably cool days hiking, fishing, canoeing, or biking. **LOCATION:** Bear Valley in the High Sierra. From Sacramento take Highway 99 south to Highway 4, then take Highway 4 east for 100 miles to Bear Valley. **TICKETS/INFO:** 209-753-2574 **ACCOMMODATIONS/TOURIST INFO:** 916-694-2475

STRAUSS FESTIVAL
ELK GROVE ✹ LAST FULL WEEKEND IN JULY, THURSDAY–SUNDAY

Out on Strauss Island, costumed dancers don the garb of 19th-century Vienna and nimbly step to the music of the Waltz King, Johann Strauss II. The Strauss Festival seeks to recreate the mood of Strauss's Vienna, when the then-scandalous waltz offered couples their first opportunity to dance one-on-one.

The festival features top-notch professional musicians such as the 43-member Sacramento Symphony Orchestra, who sit on an upper stage with the dancers just below them. The musicians weave waltz rhythms and melodies for accomplished dancers who act out custom-written story lines that engage the imaginations of the 40,000 or so spectators who show up over the weekend.

Concerts start at 8:15 P.M. each day, just as the sun goes down over the water separating the mainland audience from the island-bound performers on the open-air stage (decorated boats take the performers to the island and are often worked into the story lines). The crowd encompasses people of all ages, many of whom are led in dragging their feet but leave swearing they'll be back tomorrow, or next year, with three friends who just *have* to experience this. Picnic dinners, blankets, and lawn chairs are de rigueur, and wine can be bought by the glass on-site. Some spectators arrive at the park gate when it opens each morning to reserve a grassy patch for their blankets. **LOCATION:** Strauss Island in Elk Grove Park. Elk Grove is in Sacramento county, about 15 miles south of Sacramento; from Sacramento, go south on Highway 99, exit at Elk Grove Boulevard, and follow signs to Elk Grove Park. **TICKETS/INFO:** 916-684-6208, 916-685-3917 **ACCOMMODATIONS/TOURIST INFO:** 916-264-7777, 800-462-2543

LARK IN THE MORNING MUSIC CELEBRATION
MENDOCINO ✹ FIRST WEEK IN AUGUST

A hotbed of hippydom in the sixties, Mendocino gets back to its communal roots with this intensely mellow folk camp. Some 70 musicians and music instructors from all over the globe—Latin America, Europe, the Middle East, and East Asia—join about 500 folkies (many themselves musicians) for a relaxing week of workshops and occasional performances in the woodlands west of Mendocino. Since no walk-ins are allowed, advance reservations are absolutely necessary. That's all the planning you'll need to do, though, as instructors schedule workshops on the fly and the program is kept as freeform as possible to ensure a spontaneous, relaxed, anti-worklike setting. Jamming continues 24 hours a day, and meals are available for about $125 (in addition to the weekly registration fee of around $300). See the Music Workshops chapter, page 497, for more information.   **LOCATION:** Mendocino Woodlands, off Road 408 east of Mendocino **TICKETS/INFO:** 707-964-5569; e-mail: larkinam@larkinam.com; World Wide Web: http://www.larkinam.com **ACCOMMODATIONS/TOURIST INFO:** 800-946-3636, 707-459-7910, 800-726-2780

Contemporary classic: Marin Alsop leads the Cabrillo Music Festival's adventurous musical forays. Courtesy of Cabrillo Music Festival

ℭABRILLO MUSIC FESTIVAL

SANTA CRUZ ✽ FIRST TWO WEEKS IN AUGUST

With adventuresome programming, beautiful venues, and high artistic standards, the Cabrillo Music Festival is one of America's musical gems. The festival focuses almost entirely on contemporary orchestral music, and its dozen or so concerts feature numerous premieres—often with the participation of composers.

Such a focus on 20th-century music has, surprisingly, energized the local community. Bucking the norm in their tolerance and love of the new and unfamiliar, local residents are extremely supportive of the festival, housing musicians and creating an atmosphere that is demystified and informal, though by no means casual.

The festival's centerpiece is the award-winning Cabrillo Festival Orchestra, conducted by Marin Alsop. An indoor stage at the Santa Cruz Civic Auditorium features the orchestra, plus nationally and internationally known guest soloists. During the first weekend of the festival, a free outdoor stage on Church Street features world music performed by local musicians.

Forums, discussions, luncheons with composers, and food and wine events round out the action, and the Monterey Bay location is an excellent base from which to see many of the area's sights, including Big Sur, Carmel, Monterey, Pebble Beach, and Hearst Castle.   **LOCATION:** Santa Cruz Civic Auditorium, 307 Church Street **TICKETS/ INFO:** 408-426-6966, 408-429-3444 **ACCOMMODATIONS/TOURIST INFO:** 800-833-3494, 408-325-1234, 408-423-1111

ℜEGGAE ON THE RIVER

PIERCY ✽ FIRST WEEKEND IN AUGUST, FRIDAY EVENING THROUGH SUNDAY

North America's best reggae festival creates a legendary vibe among musicians and reggae fanatics alike. Superbly presented in the company of giant redwoods, Reggae on the River has it all: a majestic location under the sun and stars, great food and drink, a cool, swimmable river, capable but unoppressive organization, and an absolutely massive lineup of reggae and world music.

You'll have to plan far in advance because only about 10,000 can get in and tickets are always sold out weeks ahead of time. But what rewards! From the moment you walk through the gate, it's apparent that you've left the outside world behind in favor of a worldbeat lovefest. A giant dreadlocked puppet welcomes everyone, and the sound of drums beating down at the river mingles with the smells of barbecue, sun block, and burning spliffs.

Since 1984, this has been the place to catch reggae in all its avatars; previous years have featured the straight-on classics of the Wailers, the vintage reggae-soul of Alton Ellis, the Nigerian acid-reggae of Majek Fashek, and the Jamaica-via-South Africa riddims of Lucky Dube. During between-band changeovers, northern California roots DJs alternate onstage, spinning a steady web of dancehall and dub to keep the crowd bubbling.

The lineup often goes well beyond the many flavors of reggae, featuring sounds from the Spanish Caribbean, Central and South America, and Africa. If schedules can be worked out, the Africa Fête tour breezes in, and West Coast Native American musicians and dancers are nearly always on the bill.

Part of the $80 weekend admission fee goes to local charities, and the event provides a forum for agit-prop activities and red, green, and gold vendors. But mostly it's just music and sweet, sunny sensations.   **LOCATION:** French's Camp, nine miles south of Garberville on Highway 101 in Piercy (Humboldt County) **TICKETS/INFO:** 707-923-3368 **ACCOMMODATIONS/TOURIST INFO:** 707-923-2613

ℱESTA ITALIANA
SACRAMENTO ✱ FIRST WEEKEND IN AUGUST, SATURDAY AND SUNDAY

Warm Italian nights come to Sacramento in early August as the state capital's Italian community celebrates its heritage with music and nightly street dancing in a tree-lined park. Headlining singers and full bands come from Italy or the East Coast, and strolling accordion and mandolin players meander through the Italian marketplace among abundant food, wine, and games. The organizers stop short of producing a full-blown opera, but operatic soloists appear, as do choral groups.   **LOCATION:** Festival Park, at 3730 Auburn Boulevard, one-half mile east of Watt Avenue in Sacramento **TICKETS/INFO:** 916-482-5900 **ACCOMMODATIONS/TOURIST INFO:** 916-264-7777

𝓛A JOLLA SUMMERFEST
LA JOLLA ✱ TWO AND ONE-HALF WEEKS BEGINNING THE SECOND FRIDAY IN AUGUST

Under the direction of Heiichiro Ohyama, SummerFest has brought exceptional chamber music to La Jolla for more than a decade. About 15 concerts over two and a half weeks have included violinist Cho-Liang Lin, cellist Carter Brey, and oboist Allan Vogel. A two-concert "mini-jazz" series features jazz performances of the same high caliber demanded of chamber musicians.   **LOCATION:** Museum of Contemporary Art, Sherwood Auditorium, 700 Prospect, La Jolla **TICKETS/INFO:** 619-459-9496 **ACCOMMODATIONS/TOURIST INFO:** 619-454-1444, 800-462-2543

LONG BEACH JAZZ FESTIVAL

LONG BEACH ✱ SECOND WEEKEND IN AUGUST, FRIDAY–SUNDAY

In their quest to preserve "America's only true art form," organizers of the Long Beach Jazz Festival set up stage on a grassy knoll next to a lagoon and proceed to lure fans with nationally touring acts and natural ambience. The lineup leans toward bebop and contemporary, and roughly 20,000 jazz lovers show up each year, some paying $135 for VIP seating, dinner included. General admission is $25.   **LOCATION:** Rainbow Lagoon, at Linden Avenue and Ocean Boulevard (beside the Convention Center) in Long Beach. From the Long Beach Freeway (Highway 710) exit at Downtown/Convention Center/Shoreline Drive. **TICKETS/INFO:** 310-436-7794 **ACCOMMODATIONS/ TOURIST INFO:** 800-452-7829, 310-436-3645, 800-462-2543

SAN JOSE JAZZ FESTIVAL

SAN JOSE ✱ SECOND WEEKEND IN AUGUST, SATURDAY AND SUNDAY

True to the richly diverse character of its host city, the West Coast's largest free jazz festival offers a wide array of jazz styles, from bebop and fusion to Latin and Afro-Cuban. More than 75,000 people show up for the weekend to hear some 50 local, regional, national, and international jazz musicians who play continuous music on five outdoor stages. Food and drinks are on-site for the hungry browser, but coolers, cans, bottles, and pets are not allowed. The venue offers many shaded areas for repose, and the familiar arts and crafts vendors. Plus, downtown San Jose has plenty of museums, shops, and restaurants.   **LOCATION:** Market Street, across from the Fairmont Hotel, in downtown San Jose **TICKETS/INFO:** 408-288-7557 **ACCOMMODATIONS/TOURIST INFO:** 408-283-8833, 408-975-4636, 800-462-2543

JVC JAZZ AT THE BOWL

LOS ANGELES ✱ A SUNDAY IN LATE AUGUST

JVC Jazz at the Bowl's four-and-a-half-hour program presents a concentrated sampling of some of the world's top echelon of contemporary jazz and fusion acts. Set in the historic Hollywood Bowl, the fest draws some 16,000 jazzniks who bring picnics and tickets ranging from $8 to $52 (depending on seat location).   **LOCATION:** Hollywood Bowl in Los Angeles, on Highland Avenue north of Hollywood Boulevard **TICKETS/ INFO:** 213-850-2000, 213-972-7216 **ACCOMMODATIONS/TOURIST INFO:** 213-689-8822, 213-624-7300

IDYLLWILD JAZZ IN THE PINES

IDYLLWILD ✱ LAST WEEKEND IN AUGUST

High above Palm Springs on the shaded mountaintop campus of the Idyllwild School of Music and the Arts, about 1,000 people turn out each year to hear straight-ahead jazz, bebop, and blues. The location—an outdoor amphitheater under a canopy of trees and faded green parachutes—is fantastic and mellow, and the acts are an interesting mix that has recently included alto saxophonist Richie Cole, trumpeter Conte Candoli, and bassist Marshall Hawkins (who directs the school's jazz department). There's plenty of beer and wine, CDs and tapes, and nearby hiking and biking. All proceeds go to a scholarship fund to benefit young hopefuls.   **LOCATION:** Idyllwild School of Music and the Arts. From the Los Angeles area take I-10 east, exit at Banning,

*Mountaintop
bebop: Richie
Cole treats the
trees to a solo at
Idyllwild Jazz.
(See entry, page
393.)* Courtesy of Idyllwild

Jazz in the Pines

then head south on Highway 243 for 26 miles to Tollgate Road. **TICKETS/INFO:** 909-659-5405 **ACCOMMODATIONS/TOURIST INFO:** 909-659-3259, 800-462-2543

ＳTRAWBERRY MUSIC FESTIVAL
CAMP MATHER, NEAR YOSEMITE ✳ LABOR DAY WEEKEND, THURSDAY–
SUNDAY (LABOR DAY IS THE FIRST MONDAY IN SEPTEMBER)

This is a semiannual event, happening Memorial and Labor Day weekends. See page 375 for details.   **LOCATION:** Camp Mather on Evergreen Road, just off Highway 120 one mile west of Yosemite's northwest gate. From the San Francisco Bay area, take Highway 580 to Highway 205 to Highway 120, following signs to Yosemite. Ten miles after Buck Meadows, turn left on Evergreen Road and follow it seven miles directly to Camp Mather. **TICKETS/INFO:** 209-533-0191 **ACCOMMODATIONS/TOURIST INFO:** 209-533-0191, 800-462-2543

BLUEGRASS FESTIVAL

YUCAIPA ✷ LABOR DAY WEEKEND, FRIDAY–MONDAY

Focusing on pure acoustic bluegrass, this festival brings in nine or 10 national acts who present nonstop music in 34 performances over four days. The shaded park sports one central stage and plenty of hay bales, crafts, food, and games for kids. Outside the music area, you'll find camping, fishing, and water slides. Festival admission is $5 per day.   **LOCATION:** Yucaipa Regional Park, just southeast of San Bernadino. From I-10, exit at Yucaipa; go three and one-half miles to Oak Glen Road. Take a left at Oak Glen and go one mile to the park entrance. **TICKETS/INFO:** 909-790-3127 **ACCOMMODATIONS/TOURIST INFO:** 909-790-3121, 909-790-1841

LOS ANGELES CLASSIC JAZZ FESTIVAL

LOS ANGELES ✷ LABOR DAY WEEKEND, FRIDAY–MONDAY

Billing itself as "the sexiest jazz festival this side of the Mississippi," the Los Angeles Classic Jazz Festival dishes up loads of classic styles—from early ragtime to pre-sixties swing—on the ballroom stages of two neighboring hotels. Anywhere from six to nine bands lay down their sounds in concerts, brunches, poolside gigs, and dances, while rapid shuttle bus service keeps festivalgoers moving between the two hotels. **LOCATION:** Los Angeles Airport Marriott Hotel, at 5855 West Century Boulevard; and LAX Doubletree Hotel, at 5400 West Century Boulevard **TICKETS/INFO:** 310-337-1635 **ACCOMMODATIONS/TOURIST INFO:** 213-624-7300, 213-689-8822

STREET SCENE

SAN DIEGO ✷ WEEKEND AFTER LABOR DAY, FRIDAY–SUNDAY

California's largest annual music and food festival erupts for three days in San Diego's historic Gaslamp Quarter. Twenty-one urban blocks are jam-packed with partying people (Friday and Saturday nights are for adults only, while Sunday is open to all ages) fueled by 13 stages of diverse musical performances. With a meaty budget, this festival pulls in a lively range of top stars whose diversity complements San Diego's. Expect to see the likes of Los Lobos, Beau Jocque, Koko Taylor, Tabu Ley Rochereau, and 100 more bands spanning the musical ranges of the Americas, Africa, and Europe. **LOCATION:** Gaslamp Quarter of San Diego **TICKETS/INFO:** 619-557-8490 **ACCOMMODATIONS/TOURIST INFO:** 800-848-3336, 619-745-4741

RUSSIAN RIVER JAZZ FESTIVAL

GUERNEVILLE ✷ WEEKEND AFTER LABOR DAY, SATURDAY AND SUNDAY

For nearly 20 years, the Russian River Jazz Festival has brought a wide spectrum of jazz to the banks of the Russian River, which meanders among the redwoods and wineries of Sonoma County. The program mixes mainstream, traditional, and cutting-edge jazz and recently has featured the likes of Joe Sample, Charles Brown, Dianne Reeves, and Eddie Palmieri.   **LOCATION:** Guerneville is about 90 minutes north of San Francisco. From the Bay Area, take Highway 101 north to the River Road exit (just north of Santa Rosa) and head west for about 17 miles. **TICKETS/INFO:** 707-869-3940 **ACCOMMODATIONS/TOURIST INFO:** 800-253-8800, 707-869-9000, 707-869-9009

Street thang: San Diego's Street Scene spans the musical range of the Americas, Africa, and more. (See entry, page 395.) Courtesy of Street Scene

SAN FRANCISCO BLUES FESTIVAL

SAN FRANCISCO ✸ SECOND OR THIRD WEEKEND IN SEPTEMBER, FRIDAY–SUNDAY

A friendly atmosphere, imaginative bookings, and awesome views of San Francisco Bay make fans wish that America's oldest blues festival lasted more than two days. In a way, though, it does, because the week before is filled with dozens of films and blues shows at area clubs and a free downtown concert Friday at noon.

Since the festival began in 1973, it has brought a solid roster of masters to a region that's not generally known as a blues hotbed. Organizers are careful to include a few West Coast acts in the lineup, along with a majority of performers from America's heartland. The festival features a laudably eclectic mix of urban and rural, and acoustic and electric, but the single-stage set up means you might have to sit through several acts before the program gets around to your cup of tea. Usually, though, the reward is worth the wait, whether you're interested in pure blues, or offshoots like zydeco and R&B.

The Great Meadow location sports one of the city's best views of the Golden Gate Bridge, San Francisco Bay, the Marin hills, and the city itself. About 23,000 people pack the Meadow, paying about $20 a day, or $30 for a two-day pass.   **LOCATION:** Great Meadow, Fort Mason (Marina Boulevard at Laguna), San Francisco **TICKETS/INFO:** 415-979-5588 **ACCOMMODATIONS/TOURIST INFO:** 415-974-6900, 800-462-2543

$\mathcal{C}$HICO WORLD MUSIC FESTIVAL
CHICO ✹ THIRD WEEKEND IN SEPTEMBER

Each day, this family-friendly rootsfest brings 25 performers from around the world to four stages nestled among cedars and oaks alongside Big Chico Creek. Food, dance workshops, children's programs, and arts and crafts all take their places in the middle of the second-largest municipal park in the nation.   **LOCATION:** Bidwell Park's Cedar Grove, in Chico, about 110 miles north of Sacramento, via Highway 99. From Highway 99, exit at Highway 32 and go east. Turn left on Fir Street, which becomes East Eighth Street. Follow East Eighth Street one mile to the site. **TICKETS/INFO:** 916-891-4081 **ACCOMMODATIONS/TOURIST INFO:** 800-852-8570, 916-891-5556

$\mathcal{M}$ILL POND TRADITIONAL MUSIC FESTIVAL
BISHOP ✹ THIRD WEEKEND IN SEPTEMBER, FRIDAY–SUNDAY

Comfortably sized and infinitely cosmopolitan, the Mill Pond Traditional Music Festival brings in distinctively regional bands from all over the Americas. This is probably the only place in the Sierras where you can hear traditional folk, Peruvian mountain music, Texas swing, Appalachian bluegrass, Celtic ballads, and Native American flute in one weekend—played by some of the most sought-after performers in each genre.

The festival typically features performers who interpret distinctive regional styles, and because the setting is so intimate—the crowd is only about 2,500—there's typically lots of one-on-one interaction between performers and audience. A single main stage is supplemented by an open-mike area, a children's area, and workshop areas where beginners get started with new instruments and accomplished musicians pick up new techniques.

If the music weren't here, the location alone would be worth the trip. The eastern Sierra Nevada inspired John Muir and Ansel Adams with its clear skies, craggy mountains, and pristine lakes. Bishop, set in a valley with the eastern slope of the Sierras on one side and the Inyo-White Mountains on the other, has a friendly, small-town atmosphere. This is also the traditional homeland of the Paiute and Shoshone Indians, and the festival usually features their songs and dances, as well as those of Native American people from as far away as Bolivia.

Admission is about $25 a day, and in addition to the music there are arts and crafts, wagon rides, hiking and biking, and plenty of great food.   **LOCATION:** Mill Pond Park on Saw Mill Road, six miles north of Bishop, California, via U.S. 395 and about 150 miles south of Carson City, Nevada, via U.S. 395 **TICKETS/INFO:** 800-874-0669, 619-873-8014 **ACCOMMODATIONS/TOURIST INFO:** 619-873-8405, 619-934-2712, 800-462-2543

Monterey Jazz Festival: The oldest continuously running jazz festival is still alive and jumpin'. Wayne Hoy/The Picture Cube

ℳONTEREY JAZZ FESTIVAL

MONTEREY ✸ THIRD FULL WEEKEND IN SEPTEMBER

Back in the late 1950s, radio personality Jimmy Lyons dreamed of "a sylvan setting with the best jazz people in the world playing on the same stage, having a whole weekend of jazz." In 1958, that dream became a reality in Monterey, with a single stage that hosted Dizzy Gillespie, Louis Armstrong, Art Farmer, and Billie Holiday, just to name a few.

The event was such a success that organizers decided to hold the festival again—and again and again. Today, the world's oldest continuously running jazz festival is no longer the biggest, but Monterey continues to be recognized by fans and artists alike as one of the world's premier jazz venues.

The full spectrum of jazz is represented, but the festival's 65 or 70 acts lean toward the traditional. The setting—a tree-studded fairground on the Monterey Peninsula—is laid back, and over the weekend five concert programs are held in the Main Arena. Three additional stages (the Garden Stage, the Night Club, and Dizzy's Den) provide intimate indoor and outdoor settings.

The fairgrounds' 24 acres are filled with food and merchandise booths, historical exhibitions, workshops and clinics, jazz conversation areas, and more. Daily grounds admission is about $25, and all festival profits support a highly acclaimed program of jazz education in public schools.   **LOCATION:** Monterey Fairgrounds, 2000 Fairgrounds Road, in Monterey. From Highway 1, take the Casa Verde exit. **TICKETS/**

INFO: 408-373-3366, 800-307-3378; e-mail: mjf@MontereyJazzFest.org; World Wide Web: http://www.jazznet.com/-lmcohen **ACCOMMODATIONS/TOURIST INFO:** 408-649-1770, 408-646-9250, 408-385-1484,

𝒲ATTS TOWERS DAY OF THE DRUM FESTIVAL
LOS ANGELES ✷ LAST SATURDAY IN SEPTEMBER

With the bizarre Watts Towers forming a wacky backdrop, this unique festival focuses on the rhythmic splendor of drums and percussion. Local musicians from many different cultures and backgrounds have gathered since 1981 to entertain close to 8,000 spectators from all around Los Angeles. There's no admission fee, and children's music and arts workshops are available. Jazz fans will want to come back to the towers the next day to catch the Watts Towers Jazz Festival.   **LOCATION:** Watts Towers Arts Center, 1727 East 107th Street (between Willmington and Willowbrook), Los Angeles **TICKETS/INFO:** 213-847-4646 **ACCOMMODATIONS/TOURIST INFO:** 213-624-7300, 213-689-8822, 800-462-2543

𝒲ATTS TOWERS JAZZ FESTIVAL
LOS ANGELES ✷ LAST SUNDAY IN SEPTEMBER

Since this festival began in 1976, it has entertained some 8,000 people each year who come to hear traditional jazz, R&B, and gospel music by local artists. Two stages are set in a community park adjacent to the Watts Towers, an odd and intriguing series of large sculptures constructed of steel and covered with mortar, bits of tile, broken glass, and sea shells, built over 33 years by Italian construction worker and artist Simon Rodia. **LOCATION:** Watts Towers Arts Center, 1727 East 107th Street (between Willmington and Willowbrook), Los Angeles **TICKETS/INFO:** 213-847-4646 **ACCOMMODATIONS/TOURIST INFO:** 213-624-7300, 213-689-8822

𝐵AY AREA CAJUN & ZYDECO FESTIVAL
SAN RAFAEL ✷ FIRST WEEKEND IN OCTOBER

This Marin County celebration features the music, dance, and food of Louisiana and its neighbors. Over two days, expect to hear a well-chosen sampling of Cajun, zydeco, blues, and R & B music on two stages. Previous years have featured Boozoo Chavis & the Magic Sounds, Queen Ida & the Bon Temps Zydeco Band, and D. L. Menard & the Louisiana Aces. The event features dance and music workshops; tickets are about $15. **LOCATION:** Marin Civic Center Fairgrounds in San Rafael. From U.S. 101 exit at North San Pedro Road. **TICKETS/INFO:** 415-472-3500, 415-386-4553, 415-386-8677 **ACCOMMODATIONS/TOURIST INFO:** 800-454-4163, 415-454-4163

𝒞ATALINA ISLAND JAZZ TRAX FESTIVAL
CATALINA ISLAND ✷ FIRST TWO WEEKENDS IN OCTOBER

A short ferry ride from Los Angeles, Catalina Island has hosted some of the nation's hottest and newest jazz stars since this festival began in 1986. Though the Avalon Casino Ballroom is an art deco classic (with an outstanding view of the Pacific Ocean), the musical focus is on contemporary jazz.   **LOCATION:** Avalon Casino Ballroom, Catalina Island. Ferries leave from Long Beach Harbor, San Pedro, and Newport Beach. For departure times, call 800-830-7744, 800-995-4386, or 800-228-2546. **TICKETS/INFO:**

619-458-9587, 800-866-8729 **ACCOMMODATIONS/TOURIST INFO:** 310-510-1520, 800-462-2543

SAN FRANCISCO JAZZ FESTIVAL

SAN FRANCISCO ✦ SEVENTEEN DAYS BEGINNING THE SECOND OR THIRD WEEKEND IN OCTOBER

The city Duke Ellington called "one of the great cultural plateaus in the world" rarely disappoints the jazz lover, no matter the time of year. But during the second half of October, San Francisco rolls out the carpet for a jazz extravaganza so heady that its rhythms reverberate around the world.

The Jazz in the City organization has presented the festival (in one form or another) since 1983, but it wasn't until the early nineties that the event began to attract worldwide attention with its unique presentations, interesting combinations, and multistyle, multimedia approaches. This mostly indoor series dishes up a worldly dollop of bebop, trad, Afro-Cuban, and avant-garde jazz in San Francisco's theaters, auditoriums, and clubs. Promoters wisely try to focus on jazz's stylistic polarities, so you'll find plenty of traditional and cutting edge, with snippets of fusion and mainstream.

In 1990, the festival commissioned a composition by Tony Williams, which he performed with Herbie Hancock and the Kronos Quartet. The next year it was Jazz Meets Salsa, with Bobby Hutcherson and Los Kimbos, and Cowboy Jazz: A Tribute to Bob Wills, King of Western Swing. Succeeding years have featured the Bulgarian Women's Choir at Grace Cathedral, a multimedia presentation by Ornette Coleman, and the 11th Street Block Party, which featured more than 20 bands representing San Francisco's "new jazz" scene.

Such creative programming has boosted the festival's prestige and its attendance, bringing more than 35,000 people to festival events over 17 days. With some 54 acts on hand, jazz fans have lots of choice, and each night features world-class artists in venues that range from the Davies Symphony Hall to small clubs seating a couple of hundred or less. Lectures and films, jazz dance cruises in the bay, and free outdoor concerts are other options. Prices per show range from free to about $50.   **LOCATION:** Various venues throughout San Francisco **TICKETS/INFO:** 415-864-5449, 800-225-2277, 415-776-1999; e-mail: sfjzzfest@sirius.com; World Wide Web: http://www.jazzonln.com/jazz//sfjazzfest **ACCOMMODATIONS/TOURIST INFO:** 415-974-6900

WEST COAST RAGTIME FESTIVAL

FRESNO ✦ THIRD WEEKEND IN NOVEMBER, THURSDAY–SUNDAY

Like a musical time machine, this weekend revival of ballroom elegance rounds up vintage-music lovers from across North America. Soloists, ensembles, and full orchestras converge from all over the nation to re-create ragtime and Gay Nineties-era music for an appreciative crowd that dances nonstop in period costumes.

This American music revival is a happy-go-lucky replaying of the songs that fueled the raucous crowds at Honest John Turpin's Silver Dollar Saloon in St. Louis, where Scott Joplin made his start in 1885. Pianists like Terry Waldo (whom the *Washington Post* called "the finest revivalist of the great Jelly Roll Morton") and string bands like the Three Rivermen (on piano, bass, and guitar) light up the festival's four nights.

Plenty of experts whirl and fly on the dance floor, but free dance instruction is available for beginners and intermediates. About 2,000 spectators, dancers, and musi-

Cultural plateau: Mark Whitfield at the 1995 San Francisco Jazz Festival.

Courtesy of Stuart Brinin/San Francisco Jazz Festival

cians usually show up, taking advantage of composer symposia, youth music groups, and nearby Yosemite and Sequoia National Parks.   **LOCATION:** Fresno Hilton, 1100 Van Ness **TICKETS/INFO:** 209-436-1354, 209-225-9880 **ACCOMMODATIONS/ TOURIST INFO:** 209-233-0836, 800-462-2543

NEW YEAR'S JAZZ AT INDIAN WELLS
INDIAN WELLS ✳ DECEMBER 29, 30, AND 31

There's no sense watching New Year's Eve on the TV when you can live it at this posh and lively festival. Starting December 29, more than 150 hours of music and dancing enliven eight stages in three four-star resorts just east of Palm Springs. Some 25 regionally known bands emphasize Dixieland and other traditional forms of jazz, but stretch to include R&B, swing, big band, blues, gospel, zydeco, and mainstream jazz. On New Year's Eve, choose between the Traditional Jazz Party and the Rhythm & Blues Dance Party. A three-day pass runs about $135, and hotel/meal packages are available. **LOCATION:** The Renaissance Esmeralda Resort and the Hyatt (both on Indian Wells Lane) and other resorts in Indian Wells, about 15 miles east of Palm Springs Via Highway 11 **TICKETS/INFO:** 310-799-6055 **ACCOMMODATIONS/TOURIST INFO:** 619-770-9000, 310-799-6055

Hawaii

KAPALUA MUSIC FESTIVAL
KAPALUA (MAUI) ✷ FIRST WEEKEND IN JUNE, FRIDAY–SUNDAY

A growing number of faithful music lovers return each year from the mainland United States and elsewhere in Hawaii to experience chamber music amid Maui's tropical paradise. Four concerts offer a repertoire ranging from the baroque period to works by living composers. Performing solo or with a chamber orchestra, more than 20 internationally renowned musicians come in from the United States and several foreign countries, reveling in the chance to make music in this beachside vacation atmosphere. In a quest to broaden the audience, festival organizers have recently incorporated crossover programs ranging from jazz fusion to world music. **LOCATION:** Sacred Hearts Church, on Office Road in Kapalua, Maui **TICKETS/INFO:** 808-244-1189 **ACCOMMODATIONS/TOURIST INFO:** 808-871-8961, 800-527-2582, 808-923-1811

NA WAHINE O HAWAII
HONOLULU (OAHU) ✷ SECOND FRIDAY IN JUNE

The last reigning monarch of the Hawaiian Kingdom, Queen Li'liu'okalani, was a musician and prolific songwriter. These days, her compositions are still played and sung at many Hawaiian concerts, family gatherings, and festivals—including Na Wahine O Hawaii, which honors the queen and provides a showcase for Hawaii's best and brightest women musicians and dancers.

Most of the six to eight acts focus on traditional Hawaiian art forms, but snippets of gospel, blues, reggae, rock, and country—in fact, all the influences that shape today's Hawaiian music—can usually be heard and seen. Recent years have featured Nohelani Cypriano, winner of the Hoku Award for female vocalist; jazz pianist Betty Loo Taylor; and the island's top female hula dancers.

The open-air festival usually lasts about five hours and features related CDs, tapes, T-shirts, and other souvenirs. Everyone is encouraged to bring picnic baskets, although refreshments are available at the site. **LOCATION:** McCoy Pavilion at Ala Moana Park in Honolulu **TICKETS/INFO:** 808-239-4336; e-mail: Milt@hgea.com **ACCOMMODATIONS/TOURIST INFO:** 808-923-1811

Kapalua Music Festival: Chamber music in tropical paradise. Courtesy of Kapalua Land
Company, Ltd.

AIKI'I MUSIC FESTIVAL

KAILUA-KONA (ISLAND OF HAWAII) ✳ THIRD WEEKEND IN JUNE (FATHER'S
DAY WEEKEND), SATURDAY AND SUNDAY

The largest Hawaiian music festival in the state (and for that matter, the world)
spices up Father's Day weekend with a huge variety of authentic Hawaiian music and
dance. At the 4,000-foot elevation of the Waiki'i Ranch Polo Grounds, some 10,000
people enjoy contemporary and traditional musical styles, including slack key and steel
guitar, hula chants, and a capella singing.

Lying on the slopes of the Big Island's Mauna Kea, the stunning location reminds
Hawaiians of the beauty of their *aina,* or land, and how it became the bloodline of their
existence. The area is notorious for changing weather conditions, so be prepared for hot,
cold, rainy, or sunny—sometimes all in a single day.

This is the Big Island's best opportunity to hear a wide variety of Hawaiian musical styles, performed by living legends. Past headliners have included Martin Pahinui, Ledward Kaapana and I Kona, the Lim Family, Dennis Pavao, Teresa Bright, and the Ka'au Crater Boys with Robi Kahakalau. Since it's Father's Day weekend, many families are in attendance—which means big business for the booths selling authentic food and crafts. Admission costs about $25 at the gate.   **LOCATION:** Waiki'i Ranch Polo Grounds, near Kailua-Kona, on the Island of Hawaii (the Big Island). The ranch is about seven miles up Saddle Road (Highway 200), between Mauna Kea and Mauna Loa. **TICKETS/INFO:** 808-329-8037 **ACCOMMODATIONS/TOURIST INFO:** 808-329-7787, 808-923-1811

KING KAMEHAMEHA HULA COMPETITION
HONOLULU (OAHU) ✳ FOURTH WEEKEND IN JUNE, FRIDAY AND SATURDAY

When missionaries arrived on the Hawaiian Islands in the 1820s, they quickly set about destroying the "heathen" culture's traditions of song and dance. Hawaiian music assimilated with European American music (producing several innovative forms along the way), and traditional Polynesian chants and drum dances were forced underground.

These traditional sounds have surfaced again in the past few decades, and although much of Hawaii's hula activity is tourist-cliché, the King Kamehameha Hula Competition is as authentic as it gets—and extremely interesting both musically and visually. This is the only one of Hawaii's many hula competitions that features individual hula chanters, so its musical interest goes well beyond dancing and drumming (both of which also are featured here).

During the solo chanting, or *mele*, competition, you'll get a feel for the special vocal talent and training required to project the Hawaiian language in a rhythmic flurry, with no assistance from stringed instruments, drums, or dancers. Some 20 chanters, both up-and-coming and established, demonstrate several styles of a capella *mele* in competition, directing their sacred chants to gods, chiefs, kings, and ancestors.

The weekend also features plenty of *mele hula pahu* (chants accompanied by dance and drums), with contemporary and traditional categories that draw more than 3,000 competitors from some 24 schools. The contemporary, or *auana*, hula is what many people envision when they think of Hawaiian music: lovely maidens and handsome men swaying to and fro to the music of guitars, ukuleles, violins, and even accordions.

The quality of these performances is always top notch, but the real eye-opening performances typically radiate from the traditional, or *Kahiko*, categories. Dancers treat the traditional *mele hula pahu* with great respect and seriousness, and newcomers are often surprised at the very physical, almost bombastic, nature of the dancing. In addition to Hawaiian-language chanting, dancers move to the rhythms of the *pahu* (sharkskin drum), and *ipu heke* (a double gourd thumped by the fingers), both of which serve as sacred links to the spirits of Polynesian ancestors.   **LOCATION:** Neal Blaisedell Center Arena, 777 Ward Avenue, Honolulu **TICKETS/INFO:** 808-536-6540 **ACCOMMODA-TIONS/TOURIST INFO:** 808-923-1811

♇AWAII INTERNATIONAL JAZZ FESTIVAL
HONOLULU (OAHU) ✴ A WEEKEND IN LATE JULY OR EARLY AUGUST,
THURSDAY–SUNDAY

Blending the music of East and West, the Hawaii International Jazz Festival brings in some 70 top-notch musicians for four days of jazz, blues, and big band music. This new festival (begun in 1994) is generating lots of enthusiasm with acts like pianist Lalo Schifrin, trombonist and conch-shell player Steve Turre, and old-timers like the Four Freshmen. Venues include the Waikiki Shell and the Sheraton Waikiki, and extra touches include clinics and educational programs for high school and college students. **LOCATION:** Waikiki Shell (Monsarrat Avenue in Kapiolani Park) and the Sheraton Waikiki (2255 Kalakana Avenue) **TICKETS/INFO:** 808-941-9974 **ACCOMMODA-TIONS/TOURIST INFO:** 808-538-6248, 808-923-1811

♆A HIMENI ANA
HONOLULU (OAHU) ✴ FIRST OR SECOND WEEKEND IN AUGUST, FRIDAY
AND SATURDAY

In a noisy world it's easy to forget the simple beauty and pleasure of unamplified human voices. *Ka himeni ana* means "old-fashioned singing," and at this festival you'll hear about a dozen groups singing traditional Hawaiian songs to the mellow accompaniment of the ukulele, guitar, and ancient Hawaiian instruments. Groups have from two to five singers, who sing exclusively Hawaiian-language songs written before World War II, in the *nahe nahe* style. The two evenings of song take place in the Orvis Auditorium, which is specially scented with sweet ginger for the occasion.   **LOCATION:** Orvis Auditorium, on the University of Hawaii campus at Manoa, Honolulu **TICKETS/INFO:** 808-842-0421 **ACCOMMODATIONS/TOURIST INFO:** 808-923-1811

♏OLOKA'I MUSIC FESTIVAL
KALA'E (MOLOKAI) ✴ THIRD SATURDAY IN AUGUST

The island of Molokai is Hawaii's time warp, a place where the Polynesia of yesteryear lives on in the small towns, ironwood trees, and rolling green hills of the uplands. The Moloka'i Music Festival drops a dollop of excitement into this serene setting, but the festival itself has a vintage aura, presenting island musicians on the grounds of a restored 19th-century sugar mill.

The repertoire ranges from traditional to contemporary and includes slack key guitar, traditional Hawaiian-language singing, hula, jazz, and other genres. Some 50 performers include everyone from teenagers to octogenarians, and about 1,000 spectators roam the historic, lush grounds, eating fresh fruit and local-style fried fish and drinking chilled coconut juice. Entry fee is $7 at the gate.   **LOCATION:** Meyer Sugar Mill grounds, two miles south of Kalaupapa Overlook near Kala'e, on the island of Molokai **TICKETS/INFO:** 808-567-6436, 800-998-3474 **ACCOMMODATIONS/TOURIST INFO:** 808-553-3273, 808-923-1811

Guitar event of the year: Slack key guitar legend Raymond Kane at the 1995 Hawaiian Slack Key Guitar Festival. Courtesy of Milton Lau of Kahoku Productions

HAWAIIAN SLACK KEY GUITAR FESTIVAL (BANKOH KI HO'ALU)

HONOLULU (OAHU) ✳ THIRD SUNDAY IN AUGUST

The guitar was introduced to Hawaii by Spanish and Portuguese sailors and Mexican cowboys. But by the late 19th century, Hawaiians had fiddled with the instrument's conventional tuning (in which open strings produce a discordant sound when strummed), retuning the strings so that open strumming would produce harmonious chords. A new style called *ki ho'alu*, or slack key, was born.

Hawaiians eventually developed hundreds of different open tunings (some of which were closely guarded family secrets) and experimented with gliding objects up and down the strings of lap-held steel guitars to produce a glissando effect. The style became immensely popular in the early 20th century, both in Hawaii and on the mainland, but was demoted to the status of tourist stunt by the 1950s and 1960s.

In the 1970s, a rekindled sense of native Hawaiian identity brought the slack key guitar back as an art form, and by 1982 a festival had formed in Honolulu. This one-day event is still the premier gathering of practitioners of this unique and precious genre, and it's a great chance to hear the masters of the slack key guitar all in one place at one time.

Luscious notes flow in abundance from the outdoor McCoy Pavilion at Ala Moana Park in Honolulu from late afternoon until late evening. The festival is free, and among the dozen solo artists and groups are old-timers like Raymond "Kaleoalohapoinaooleohelemanu" Kane, who learned guitar in the late 1930s from a cowboy who gave him lessons in exchange for freshly caught fish. Kane, whose Hawaiian name means "the voice of love that comes and goes like a bird and will never be forgotten," utilizes a variety of traditional tuning styles, including the Wahine, the Taro Patch, and the Mauna Loa tunings.   **LOCATION:** McCoy Pavilion, 1201 Ala Moana

Boulevard **TICKETS/INFO:** 808-239-4336; e-mail: Milt@hgea.com **ACCOMMODA-TIONS/TOURIST INFO:** 808-923-1811

ᘻAUI MUSIC FESTIVAL

KAANAPALI (MAUI) ✴ LABOR DAY WEEKEND, SATURDAY AND SUNDAY (LABOR DAY IS THE FIRST MONDAY IN SEPTEMBER)

Nestled in the midst of three miles of sunny Maui beaches, the Maui Music Festival hosts some of the world's top mainstream jazz artists. The festival is marketed to jazz-loving mainlanders looking for an alternative to Caribbean and European jazz festivals, and many attendees take advantage of special air-hotel packages offered by the promoters.

The music is mostly mellow jazz, often mixing in touches of saxophone for the "adult contemporary" jazz listener. Main-stage performances have included Tom Scott, Spyro Gyra, the Rippingtons, Acoustic Alchemy, and several other acts—many recorded by the contemporary jazz label GRP. A special plus is the opportunity to hear a variety of more innovative Hawaiian jazz artists, who have included the likes of Keola Beamer and Sam Ahia.

Kaanapali Beach is a resort complex with several hotels—Maui Marriott, Hyatt Regency Maui, Kaanapali Beach Hotel, and the Westin Maui—and the music is scattered over seven indoor and outdoor stages. Wrist bands range from $60 to $350, enabling entry into low-end lawn seating, midrange reserved seating, or top-end backstage/unlimited access. Most concertgoers stay in one of the participating hotels or in nearby Lahaina Town, a historic whaling village.   **LOCATION:** Kaanapali Beach Resort, about six miles north of Lahaina on Maui's west coast **TICKETS/INFO:** 213-254-1205, 800-628-4767; e-mail: MAUI SOS 1@aol.com; World Wide Web: http: www.magicisland.com/paradise/paradise.html **ACCOMMODATIONS/TOURIST INFO:** 800-245-9229, 808-661-3271, 808-871-8961, 800-628-4767

ᕈOLYNESIAN FESTIVAL

KANEOHE (OAHU) ✴ FIRST FRIDAY AND SATURDAY IN SEPTEMBER

This chaotic foray into the sensual world of traditional Tahitian drumming and dance isn't for everyone, but for the many outer-island Tahitians and Samoans who converge on Kaneohe, it's like a trip back home. Since the trip lasts only two days, the performers (and everyone else) go all out, playing marathons of music that are, like many things in the South Pacific, organized around spirited competitions.   **LOCATION:** King Intermediate School in Kaneohe, on Oahu's east coast **TICKETS/INFO:** 808-247-6188 **ACCOMMODATIONS/TOURIST INFO:** 808-545-4300, 808-923-1811

ᚲᶦINDY SPROAT FALSETTO AND STORYTELLING CONTEST

WAIMEA (ISLAND OF HAWAII) ✴ A SUNDAY IN MID- OR LATE SEPTEMBER

Alarmed that traditional Hawaiian falsetto singing was dying out, a group of Big Island music lovers initiated this festival in 1992 with the goal of preserving and promoting this unusual, uniquely Hawaiian art form. Fittingly, they named the festival after Clyde Halema'uma'u "Kindy" Sproat, a legendary falsetto and American national treasure.

Kauai style: Slackers' delight: Dennis Kamakahi at the 1994 Hawaiian Slack Key Guitar Festival, Kauai Style. Courtesy of Milton Lau of Ka-hoku Productions

Sproat has retired from performing, but he nearly always makes it to this festival. Before each song, he tells a story (in English) about what he will sing in the Hawaiian language. When the songs begin, jaws drop (and not just his) as he takes his voice up one, then two, and sometimes three octaves.

The contest has generated new interest in falsetto singing, and each year several would-be performers are turned away to keep the one-day schedule trimmed to about 10 singers. Organizers are thrilled that many young people are taking up the tradition, and although falsetto singing was traditionally a male-only form, some women have entered the ranks in recent years.

The festival features both straight Hawaiian songs and *hapa haole* (literally "half-white" songs that mix Hawaiian musical traditions with the English language), and the grand prize is a recording contract with Hula Records. Each year's proceedings are broadcast on radio station KCCN, from a beautiful theater in the middle of small-town Waimea.   **LOCATION:** Kahilu Theater in Waimea (Kamuela), at the convergence of Highways 250 and 19, on the Island of Hawaii (Big Island), near the Waimea-Kohala Airport **TICKETS/INFO:** 808-885-8086, 808-329-8624 **ACCOMMODATIONS/TOURIST INFO:** 808-935-5294, 808-329-7787, 808-923-1811

*M*OKIHANA FESTIVAL
HANAMAULU (KAUAI) ✷ A MONDAY NIGHT IN LATE SEPTEMBER

Focusing on composers, this innovative festival highlights original Hawaiian music in its many forms and adaptations. The format is a contest in which composers submit tapes of original works in Hawaiian styles, and the top three composers are then invited to present their compositions live at the festival in Kauai. Surprises are the name of the game in categories ranging from traditional Hawaiian-language songs to contemporary English-language songs with Hawaiian musical themes. Other categories include children's songs and an "open" category that has been inundated in recent years by Jawaiian music (a mixture of Jamaican and Hawaiian). The single-day musical program lasts four

Young keepers of old traditions: Children celebrate authentic Hawaiian music at Na Mele O Maui. (See entry, page 410.) Courtesy of Kaanapali Beach Resort Assoc.

hours and features about 18 composers, but the festival has blossomed into a nine-day multimedia extravaganza of Hawaiian culture.   **LOCATION:** Kauai Outrigger Hotel near Hanamaulu, on Kauai's east side (five minutes from the airport) **TICKETS/INFO:** 808-822-2166 **ACCOMMODATIONS/TOURIST INFO:** 808-245-7363, 808-245-3971, 808-923-1811

HAWAIIAN SLACK KEY GUITAR FESTIVAL (BANKOH KI HO'ALU), KAUAI STYLE
LIHUE (KAUAI) ✳ FIRST SATURDAY OR SUNDAY IN NOVEMBER

Kauai's guitar event of the year is a spin-off of the big slack key festival in Honolulu (see Hawaiian Slack Key Guitar Festival, page 406), but it shifts locations and focus to the practitioners of the Kauai style of slack key guitar. This native Hawaiian art form has its roots in the Hawaii of 160 years ago, when Hawaiians took the guitar—brought by sailors and cowboys from Europe and Mexico—and retuned it, making it into a distinctly Hawaiian instrument.

About a dozen guitarists from Kauai, and others with Kauai-influenced styles, play a free concert at Kalapaki Beach, often accompanying their instruments with Hawaiian-language vocals. Past years have featured Dennis Kamakahi, who has written many songs for the island of Kauai; Ozzie Kotani, who incorporates elements of Spanish flamenco in his slack key style; and John Keawe, who plays a custom-made, eight-string guitar. **LOCATION:** Kauai Marriott Resort and Beach Club Hotel on Kalapaki Beach in Lihue,

Kauai **TICKETS/INFO:** 808-239-4336; e-mail: Milt@hgea.com **ACCOMMODATIONS/ TOURIST INFO:** 808-245-7363, 808-245-3971, 808-923-1811

ᴺA MELE O MAUI SONG CONTEST AND HULA FESTIVAL

KAANAPALI (MAUI) ✴ SECOND FRIDAY AND SATURDAY IN DECEMBER

This unique musical celebration of the Hawaiian language features more than 800 Maui County schoolchildren. You won't find any hype or commercial sponsorship here, just authentic old Hawaiian songs, with children competing to pronounce the words and sing the notes correctly. Admission (for adults) is $1.   **LOCATION:** Kaanapali Beach Resort, 2525 Kaanapali Parkway **TICKETS/INFO:** 808-661-3271, 800-245-9229 **AC-COMMODATIONS/TOURIST INFO:** 808-871-7711, 808-244-3530, 808-871-8961, 808-923-1811

WILLAMETTE VALLEY FOLK FESTIVAL
EUGENE ✶ THIRD WEEKEND IN MAY, FRIDAY–SUNDAY

Like a breath of tropical air, this free spring festival warms Eugene with the folk, blues, bluegrass, and worldbeat sounds of bands from the West Coast and musical points farther afield. A tradition since 1970, the festival draws about 10,000 students and townies who stretch out on the University of Oregon's east lawn to spend the weekend listening and dancing to the rhythms created by about 25 groups. Dogs and alcohol aren't allowed.   **LOCATION:** University of Oregon's east lawn, in front of the Erb Memorial Union (EMU) at University Avenue and 13 Street **TICKETS/INFO:** 541-346-4373, 541-346-0635 **ACCOMMODATIONS/TOURIST INFO:** 541-484-5307, 800-452-3670

MUSIC IN MAY
FOREST GROVE ✶ MEMORIAL DAY WEEKEND, THURSDAY–SATURDAY
(MEMORIAL DAY IS THE LAST MONDAY IN MAY)

Some 600 of the Pacific Northwest's best high school musicians participate in large ensembles led by internationally known conductors. Two days of intensive rehearsals are capped off by band, orchestra, and choir performances in this small university town. **LOCATION:** Pacific University in Forest Grove, about 25 miles west of Portland, via Highway 8 **TICKETS/INFO:** 503-359-2216; e-mail: harshg@pacificu.edu **ACCOMMO-DATIONS/TOURIST INFO:** 800-962-3700, 503-357-3006

BASH BY THE BAY DIXIELAND JAZZ FESTIVAL
NEWPORT ✶ MEMORIAL DAY WEEKEND, FRIDAY–MONDAY

For nearly 20 years, the Newport Elks Lodge has spent Memorial Day weekend whirling to the rhythms of Dixieland and traditional jazz. Salem's Capital City Jazz Band is a longtime regular, but several area ensembles also make the scene. The festival gets under way Friday night with a jam session, and keeps rolling right on through the long weekend. Donations are accepted.   **LOCATION:** Newport Elks Lodge, 45 John Moore Road, in Newport, on the Pacific Coast 55 miles west of Corvallis **TICKETS/INFO:** 541-265-2105 **ACCOMMODATIONS/TOURIST INFO:** 541-265-8801, 800-858-8598

OREGON BACH FESTIVAL

EUGENE ✹ TWO WEEKS IN LATE JUNE AND EARLY JULY

Of America's several Bach festivals, none walks away, year after year, with as much critical acclaim as this outstanding, pioneering tribute to the music of the baroque master. For more than 27 years, the festival has blossomed under the baton of Helmuth Rilling, whose ambitious yet humble approach has made him the darling of the international music media. Originally from Germany, Rilling is a conductor, organist, choir leader, and teacher—though it's the latter role, along with his ability to combine entertainment and education, that has so endeared him to this university town.

Amidst Eugene's evergreen forests, scenic rivers, and diverse cultural and recreational atmosphere, the Oregon Bach Festival presents two weeks of inspiring music programs. Each year the festival blends choral and orchestral concerts, chamber music, solo recitals, jazz, and other performances with public lectures, master classes, and adult education programs—in a "meld of music and meaning." Themes—such as 1996's "Bach and the Americas," exploring how Bach has influenced composers in North and South America—are typically underlined by several commissioned world premieres by artists like Stephen Jaffe (United States), Linda Bouchard (Canada), Osvaldo Golijov (Argentina), and Robert Kyr (United States).

The short span of two weeks gives the festival a breathless pace and a heady ambience, with 22 admission-free concerts (featuring 250 top-notch choral, orchestral, and guest soloist musicians) and many more free or low-cost events. About 30,000 music lovers travel from 30 states and a dozen countries to experience the Oregon Bach Festival.   **LOCATION:** Hult Center for the Performing Arts at Seventh and Willamette, and six other venues in Eugene **TICKETS/INFO:** 541-687-5000, 800-457-1486; e-mail: gevano@oregon.uoregon.edu; World Wide Web: www:http://musicl.uoregon.edu/obf/obfhome.html **ACCOMMODATIONS/TOURIST INFO:** 800-547-5445

BIG RIVER BAND FESTIVAL

ARLINGTON ✹ FOURTH WEEKEND IN JUNE, SATURDAY AND SUNDAY

Arlington is the hometown of Doc Severinsen, and whenever his schedule allows, he returns for this festival to play with the dozen or so Pacific Northwest jazz bands that grace this waterfront park with their music. Bands play on the park's gazebo and on a floating, rotating stage in the lagoon. The festival is free and a small-town, family atmosphere prevails.   **LOCATION:** Earl Snell Waterfront Park in Arlington, just off I-84, about 130 miles east of Portland along the Columbia River **TICKETS/INFO:** 541-454-2743 **ACCOMMODATIONS/TOURIST INFO:** 541-454-2743, 800-255-3385

CHAMBER MUSIC NORTHWEST

PORTLAND ✹ LATE JUNE THROUGH MID-JULY, FIVE NIGHTS EACH WEEK

Portland's acclaimed summer festival is home to more than 40 renowned chamber musicians for five weeks each summer. Five nights a week the repertoire spans four centuries of well-known masterpieces, little-known gems, and world premieres by contemporary composers. An intimate, informal atmosphere prevails at the concerts, as well as at catered preconcert picnics and lively lectures.   **LOCATION:** Two Portland locations: Reed College, Southeast 28th and Woodstock; and the Catlin Gabel School, 8825 Southwest Barnes Road. **TICKETS/INFO:** 503-223-3202 **ACCOMMODATIONS/TOURIST INFO:** 503-275-9750, 800-962-3700, 503-222-2223

Red, WHITE, AND BLUES
CORVALLIS ✱ JULY 4

At this small-town, down-home Independence Day celebration on the riverfront in Corvallis, the one outdoor stage features three blues acts drawn from Oregon's Willamette Valley. The day's events also include arts and crafts, food booths, a parade, a children's performance, and a bunch of music-loving locals who perform orchestral pieces while fireworks blossom in the evening sky.   **LOCATION:** First Street on the riverfront in downtown Corvallis, 85 miles south of Portland on I-5 **TICKETS/INFO:** 541-754-6624 **ACCOMMODATIONS/TOURIST INFO:** 800-526-2256, 541-757-1544, 800-334-8118

Waterfront BLUES FESTIVAL
PORTLAND ✱ WEEKEND CLOSEST TO JULY 4 (INDEPENDENCE DAY)

In a park with the Willamette River in the background, this romping, large-scale gig presents a whopping 44 bands on two stages. Begun in 1987 as a benefit for the Oregon Food Bank, the festival now attracts upward of 100,000 blues lovers who donate two cans of food and $3 at the gate. Recent acts have included Luther Allison, Savoy Brown, Tinsley Ellis, and Big Daddy Kinsey and the Kinsey Report.   **LOCATION:** Waterfront Park, at Front Avenue and SW Clay in Portland **TICKETS/INFO:** 503-733-5466; World Wide Web: http://www.teleport.com/-kgon **ACCOMMODATIONS/TOURIST INFO:** 503-275-9750, 800-962-3700, 503-222-2223

Oregon COAST MUSIC FESTIVAL
COOS BAY AND NEARBY COMMUNITIES ✱ LAST TWO FULL WEEKS IN JULY

The Oregon Coast Music Festival takes southern Oregon coastal communities on adventures to exotic times and places with a classical music program that has the repertoire, musical depth, and world-class soloists to position it securely among the top echelon of Northwest festivals. This traveling program of symphonic, choral, and chamber music is led by the internationally acclaimed James Paul and offers superb music presented in 10 venues that highlight the beauty of the southern Oregon coast. Concerts are held in everything from a boathouse overlooking the ocean to Coos Bay's art deco, acoustically rich Marshfield High School Auditorium.   **LOCATION:** Marshfield High School Auditorium, Tenth and Ingersoll, in Coos Bay, which is on U.S. 101 about 100 miles north of the California border, and several other venues along the Oregon coast from Brookings to Florence **TICKETS/INFO:** 541-267-0938 **ACCOMMODA-TIONS/TOURIST INFO:** 800-824-8486, 541-269-0215

Jazz AT THE LAKE—THE WALLOWA LAKE FESTIVAL OF MUSIC
JOSEPH ✱ THIRD FULL WEEKEND IN JULY, FRIDAY AND SATURDAY

In a remote setting at the shore of pristine Wallowa Lake, half a dozen bands serenade the Wallowa Mountains with rock, pop, blues, and jazz. Eagle Cap and other peaks overlook some 2,000 people, many of them families, who come out to enjoy both the music and the recreational opportunities in the Eagle Cap Wilderness Area. A two-day pass is about $25.   **LOCATION:** Wallowa Lake State Park, near Joseph, in the

Portland blues bash: Tim Langford of Too Slim & the Taildraggers wows the crowd at the Waterfront Blues Festival. (See entry, page 413.) Courtesy of Valarie K. Davis Photography

northeastern corner of the state. From I-84 take exit 261 (at La Grande) and go northwest on Highway 82, which twists and turns for about 75 miles before dead-ending at the state park. **TICKETS/INFO:** 541-963-8530 **ACCOMMODATIONS/TOURIST INFO:** 541-426-4622, 800-332-1843

ℳOUNT HOOD FESTIVAL OF JAZZ
GRESHAM ✸ FIRST FULL WEEKEND IN AUGUST

The Mount Hood Festival of Jazz brings mainstream jazz and blues stars to an outdoor stadium just outside Portland. Performers like Ella Fitzgerald, Spyro Gyra, Kenny G., Ray Charles, and Stan Getz have graced the main stage recently, while local jazz artists appear on the smaller Festival Stage.

In addition to about eight acts each day, the stadium houses local food, wine, and microbrewed-beer vendors. A prefestival program includes instrumental workshops and a street dance in downtown Gresham, which is a gateway to the recreational opportunities of the Columbia River Gorge, Mount Hood, and the high desert.   **LOCATION:** Mount Hood Community College's outdoor stadium in Gresham. From Portland take

I-84 east to exit 17 (Troutdale). Turn right at the stoplight onto 257th, which becomes Kane Road. The college is at the corner of Kane Road and Stark Street; the stadium is at the south end of campus. **TICKETS/INFO:** 503-231-0160, 503-224-4400; e-mail: mca@uspan.com **ACCOMMODATIONS/TOURIST INFO:** 800-962-3700, 503-622-3162

♭RITT FESTIVALS CLASSICAL SERIES
JACKSONVILLE ✸ FIRST THREE WEEKENDS IN AUGUST, FRIDAY–MONDAY

A piney hillside overlooking the Rogue Valley welcomes orchestral music each August as the Pacific Northwest's original music festival series presents three weeks of classical programming. Directed by Peter Bay, the Britt Festivals Classical Series offers music, an excellent view, food and drink, and plenty of elbow room for stretching out blankets and daydreaming. Although these particular three weeks are devoted to classical music, Britt offers a whole range of musical programming all summer long. **LOCATION:** The Britt Pavilion, in Jacksonville, off Highway 238 west of I-5 and Medford, in southern Oregon **TICKETS/INFO:** 800-882-7488, 541-779-0847 **ACCOMMODATIONS/TOURIST INFO:** 541-779-4847, 800-448-4856, 541-779-4691

♫ORTH AMERICAN JEW'S HARP FESTIVAL
RICHLAND ✸ THIRD WEEKEND IN AUGUST, FRIDAY–SUNDAY

The Jew's Harp Festival keeps beat with the offbeat, celebrating the portable, twanging mouth harp—aka "jawharp"—normally relegated to the fringes of folk music. Founded in 1992 by Jew's harp maker Bill Gohring and his wife Janet, the Jew's Harp Festival outgrew the tiny town of Sumpter, where it began, and moved to Richland (population 175).

The event has become a magnet for unusual instruments and instrumentalists. In addition to the Jew's harp, expect to hear unusual instruments like the didgeridoo, mouth bow, humanatone, rattlebones, kalimba, and clackamore. Richland, at the foot of the Wallowa Mountains in eastern Oregon, doubles in size for the weekend, when campers pull in from around the Northwest to participate in concerts and jam sessions, including an all-metal jam (Jew's harp, saw, gong, bells, triangle, etc.) or an all-wood jam (clackamore, didgeridoo, woodblocks, etc.). It's not only strange, it's free. **LOCATION:** Central Richland. From I-84 take exit 302 (Baker City) and drive 39 miles east to Richland. **TICKETS/INFO:** 206-725-2718 **ACCOMMODATIONS/TOURIST INFO:** 541-523-3356

♫UNRIVER MUSIC FESTIVAL
SUNRIVER ✸ LAST TWO WEEKENDS IN AUGUST

Musicians travel from symphony orchestras around the country to take their places in the 40-piece Sunriver Music Festival Orchestra for two weeks every summer. Six shows—which nearly always sell out—feature everything from Vivaldi to Vaughan Williams, played in a 500-seat log building constructed during World War II. Popular among retirees for its tennis, golf, and ski facilities, the year-round facility has accommodations aplenty for festivalgoers. Tickets cost $12 to $35 per concert.   **LOCATION:** Sunriver Resort in Sunriver, 15 miles south of Bend. From U.S. 97 go west on South Century Drive and travel one mile to Sunriver; then follow the signs to the lodge and

Rogue Valley original: The Britt Festivals Classical Series is a highlight of a summer of outdoor music. (See entry, page 415.) Courtesy of D. Bjurstrom/Oregon Tourism Division

Great Hall. **TICKETS/INFO:** 541-593-1084 **ACCOMMODATIONS/TOURIST INFO:**
541-593-8149, 800-800-8334, 541-382-8334

OREGON FESTIVAL OF AMERICAN MUSIC
EUGENE ✴ EIGHT DAYS BEGINNING THE THIRD SATURDAY IN AUGUST

This unique festival is billed as a "classical" event, but it's classical in the sense that artistic director and conductor Marin Alsop would define the word. To this innovative leader, the American classical tradition extends from Broadway to Hollywood, from Harlem to New Orleans, from Appalachia's valleys to the Southwest's mesas—in short, to all the unique musical forms that have flourished as a result of the interaction of European classical music with Native American, African, and other traditions.

For one week in August, some 20 events (many of them free) highlight a different and often unheralded aspect of America's rich musical heritage. Each year is marked by a theme—such as the birth of classic American musical theater, or the life and work of Leonard Bernstein. Preconcert seminars and the Young Artists Academy round out the week of events, which typically draw more than 10,000 people.   **LOCATION:** Hult Center for the Performing Arts, Beall Concert Hall, and Cuthbert Amphitheater, all in Eugene **TICKETS/INFO:** 541-687-5000, 541-687-6526, 800-248-1615 **ACCOMMO-DATIONS/TOURIST INFO:** 541-484-5307, 800-526-2256

CASCADE FESTIVAL OF MUSIC
BEND ✴ NINE DAYS IN LATE AUGUST

Nestled beneath the branches of centuries of ponderosa pine, the Cascade Festival of Music complements the sound of the Deschutes River with classical and jazz music. Each August, nine days of music include four concerts by the Cascade Festival Orchestra, plus one concert each of chamber music, pops, big band, and jazz. With the recent appointment of the highly regarded Murry Sidlin as artistic director, the festival embarks on a "classics plus" approach that's expected to take the music in interesting and challenging new directions.   **LOCATION:** Drake Park in downtown Bend. Bend is in the center of Oregon at the junction of U.S. 97 and U.S. 20. **TICKETS/INFO:** 541-382-8381, 541-383-2202 **ACCOMMODATIONS/TOURIST INFO:** 541-382-3221, 800-800-8334, 541-382-8334

HIGH MOUNTAINS DIXIELAND JAZZ FESTIVAL
SISTERS ✴ FRIDAY–SUNDAY OF THE WEEKEND FOLLOWING LABOR DAY
(LABOR DAY IS THE FIRST MONDAY IN SEPTEMBER)

Cradled in the Cascade Range, the tourist town of Sisters boils over with the sounds of Dixieland each September. Tents go up in city parks, in RV parks, and outside restaurants, providing outdoor venues for about 10 bands. Expect to hear the sounds of traditional and Chicago-style Dixieland, as well as swing and ragtime. Admission ranges from $15 to $25 (depending on the day), and camping is plentiful.   **LOCATION:** Sisters is located 22 miles northwest of Bend at the junction of U.S. 20 and Highway 126. **TICKETS/INFO:** 800-549-1332, 541-549-0251 **ACCOMMODATIONS/TOURIST INFO:** 800-549-1332, 541-549-0251, 800-800-8334

OREGON JAMBOREE
SWEET HOME ✦ FOURTH WEEKEND IN SEPTEMBER

Born of an effort to stimulate economic growth after the declining timber industry left the area economically depressed, the Oregon Jamboree has grown into one of the Northwest's top country and western festivals. Part of the success of this three-day camp-in is its ability to attract top new-country names like Wynonna, Clint Black, and Billy Ray Cyrus, as well as occasional traditionalists like Merle Haggard. About 5,000 country fans make the scene each day, taking advantage of 500 RV hookups, unlimited tent space, and dozens of food and crafts booths. **LOCATION:** Sweet Home, on U.S. 20, about 25 miles southeast of I-5 and Albany **TICKETS/INFO:** 541-367-8909, 541-367-8800 **AC-COMMODATIONS/TOURIST INFO:** 800-526-2256

NORTH BY NORTHWEST
PORTLAND ✦ A WEEKEND IN SEPTEMBER OR OCTOBER

Austin's alternative music showcase/conference known as South by Southwest has been so successful that its organizers are expanding to regional markets like the Pacific Northwest. Similar to South by Southwest, the Portland incarnation features a range of emerging musicians making and meeting on rock, hip-hop, blues, folk, and country music. The panel discussions and industry schmoozefests will be of little interest to the everyday music lover, but showcase concerts feature dozens of up-and-coming bands in some 22 clubs around the city. **LOCATION:** Various clubs and bars in Portland **TICKETS/INFO:** 512-467-7979; e-mail: 72662.2465@compuserve.com **ACCOMMO-DATIONS/TOURIST INFO:** 800-962-3700

MEDFORD JAZZ JUBILEE
MEDFORD ✦ SECOND WEEKEND IN OCTOBER

Forty hours of traditional jazz played by 10 of the top headline bands in America are in store for jazz enthusiasts at the Medford Jazz Jubilee. Expect warm hospitality (Medford's slogan is "We hug visitors!") and acts like Michigan's New Reformation Dixieland Band and Germany's Allotria Jazz Band, playing in five locations with dancing, decorations, and flapper fare that recall the golden age of jazzy glitter. The top talent, great venues, and reasonable prices (about $45 for an all-event's badge) make Medford a favorite of jazz lovers on the festival circuit. **LOCATION:** Various venues in Medford, just off I-5 about 30 miles north of the California border **TICKETS/INFO:** 541-770-6970 **ACCOMMODATIONS/TOURIST INFO:** 800-599-0039

WASHINGTON

CHAMBER MUSIC PORT TOWNSEND
PORT TOWNSEND ✷ LAST WEEKEND IN JANUARY, FRIDAY AND SATURDAY

The renovated Fort Worden Theater's intimate setting and excellent acoustics resonate with the sounds of contemporary and traditional compositions played by local, regional, and national chamber musicians. In its more than 20-year history, the festival has earned a loyal audience, and a crowd of about 300 spectators enjoys each of three shows during the event's two days. The Victorian seaport of Port Townsend, with its shops and restaurants, provides an entertaining backdrop for a midwinter weekend getaway. **LOCATION:** Fort Worden Theater, on the grounds of Fort Worden State Park in Port Townsend, about two hours from Seattle via the Bainbridge Island Ferry. After crossing Hood Canal Bridge, follow the signs to Port Townsend, on the northeast tip of the Olympic Peninsula. **TICKETS/INFO:** 800-733-3608, 360-385-3102 **ACCOMMODATIONS/TOURIST INFO:** 360-385-2722, 360-586-2088

WINTERGRASS
TACOMA ✷ LAST WEEKEND IN FEBRUARY

The Northwest's biggest bluegrass festival warms up the Tacoma winter with a whopping 52 bands and 9,000 spectator-participants who arrive on trains, planes, and buses from all over North America and as far away as Japan. The bluegrass circuit is pretty slow this time of year, so organizers of this young festival are able to present a dependably stellar lineup. Recent years have featured Bill Monroe, Ralph Stanley, Del McCoury, the Cox Family, and the Laura Love Connection, with headliners playing one-hour sets that alternate with half-hour sets by up-and-comers from all regions of the continent.

Downtown Tacoma's Sheraton Hotel is the center of the action, with five performance stages and plenty of room for jamming—in fact, at 3 A.M. one Friday night, someone counted 38 simultaneous jams in the lobby area alone. Stages also grace nearby churches and other hotels, all connected by shuttle bus. Average room capacity is about 1,000, and as the festival grows it keeps everyone close to the performers by adding more—rather than bigger—venues.

An extensive workshop program covers everything from vocal technique and harmony to how to repair a dobro or fine-tune a PA system. Big names typically teach master classes, while regionally known musicians teach beginner and intermediate classes.   **LOCATION:** Sheraton Hotel, 1320 Broadway Plaza, in the center of downtown **TICKETS/INFO:** 360-871-7354 **ACCOMMODATIONS/TOURIST INFO:** 800-272-2662, 360-586-2088

ꙮLD TIME MUSIC FESTIVAL
TENINO ✷ THIRD WEEKEND IN MARCH, FRIDAY AND SATURDAY

All types of old-time, acoustic music are featured at this small-town gathering of musical volunteers who donate their time and talent to the local Lions Club. Expect to hear bluegrass, gospel, old-time country, even a family of eight accordion players. Each show (one on Friday, two on Saturday) features a full 14 acts, each of which is allowed three songs plus an encore . . . but only if the crowd wants one.   **LOCATION:** Tenino High School. Tenino is located about 15 miles south of Olympia off I-5. **TICKETS/ INFO:** 360-264-4590 **ACCOMMODATIONS/TOURIST INFO:** 800-544-1800, 360-586-2088

ꝎAGTIME RHODIE DIXIELAND JAZZ FESTIVAL
LONG BEACH ✷ A WEEKEND IN MID-APRIL, FRIDAY–SUNDAY

Out on the beautifully sandy Long Beach Peninsula, the sounds of traditional jazz perk up the springtime just as the area's famous rhododendrons come into full bloom. The Ragtime Rhodie festival features heaping helpings of Dixieland, respectable portions of ragtime, and bits and pieces of other trad-jazz. While walking between the seven venues (including hotels, taverns, and an Elk's Club with a groovy hardwood dance floor), you'll find time to admire the wild and cultivated rhodies, or to dash into the surf to pluck out some razor clams, also in season. About 1,400 people typically stop in over the weekend to revel in the music, the flowers, the beaches, the laid-back atmosphere, and the moderate drink prices (a vodka and cranberry juice cocktail goes for about $1.50).   **LOCATION:** The town of Long Beach and the Long Beach Peninsula are located near the mouth of the Columbia River, just across the bridge from Astoria, Oregon. **TICKETS/INFO:** 800-451-2542, 360-642-2400 **ACCOMMODATIONS/ TOURIST INFO:** 800-451-2542, 360-642-2400, 360-586-2088

ꙮ̸ASHINGTON STATE FIDDLE CONTEST
RICHLAND ✷ SECOND WEEKEND IN MAY, FRIDAY–SUNDAY

This championship brings in Washington's best fiddlers, who use it both to conclude a year of regional contests and to prepare for the upcoming National Oldtime Fiddlers' Contest in Idaho. Inside a high school auditorium the mood is serious as nearly 150 fiddlers square off, taking turns playing a waltz, a hoedown, and a tune of choice. Judges sit behind blinders, selecting winners in several categories purely according to how they sound. And although these are some of the most danceable sounds around, the crowd stays seated, saving the dancing for late-night jam sessions at Godfather's Pizza on Friday and Saturday nights. Camping is available on the school grounds.   **LOCATION:** Richland High School. Richland is about 80 miles east of Yakima off I-82. **TICKETS/ INFO:** 509-586-2843, 509-575-6320 **ACCOMMODATIONS/TOURIST INFO:** 360-586-2088, 800-544-1800

WENATCHEE VALLEY JAZZ FEST
WENATCHEE ✱ THIRD WEEKEND IN MAY

Smack dab in the middle of the Columbia River Valley and the state of Washington, Wenatchee boasts six stages of mainstream jazz, blues, Dixieland, and swing at its four-day shindig. More than a dozen bands arrive from all around the Pacific Northwest, to be joined by nationally known headliners like bassman extraordinaire Ray Brown, pianist Jessica Williams, and Wenatchee's own Don Lanphere. All six venues feature hardwood dance floors—which get a stompin' good workout during the Dixieland and swing sessions.   **LOCATION:** Six venues in and around downtown Wenatchee, located in the middle of the state along the Columbia River, just off U.S. 97 **TICKETS/INFO:** 509-662-1213, 800-506-5277 **ACCOMMODATIONS/TOURIST INFO:** 800-572-7753, 360-586-2088

NORTHWEST FOLKLIFE FESTIVAL
SEATTLE ✱ MEMORIAL DAY WEEKEND, FRIDAY–MONDAY (MEMORIAL DAY IS THE LAST MONDAY IN MAY)

With a whopping 17 stages of free music and dance, the Northwest Folklife Festival presents the lively sounds of more than 100 cultures from every corner of the world. Some 200,000 people gather to share in this culturefest at the 74-acre park that surrounds the Space Needle.   **LOCATION:** Seattle Center, directly under the Space Needle **TICKETS/INFO:** 206-684-7300; e-mail: folknw@aol.com; World Wide Web: http://www.nwfolklife.org/folklife/ Accommodations/Tourist Info: 206-461-5840, 360-586-2088

PORT TOWNSEND COUNTRY BLUES FESTIVAL
PORT TOWNSEND ✱ SECOND OR THIRD WEEKEND IN JUNE, FRIDAY AND SATURDAY

This festival's genius rests in its ability to sniff out and preserve fading and fragile traditions. In a renovated 1920s balloon hangar, living practitioners of country blues from all corners of the United States share their musical legacies during workshops and performances. Expect to hear anything from the Piedmont-style blues of Lightnin' Wells, to the gospel-soaked blues of Ethel Caffie-Austin, to the Mississippi sounds of Alvin Youngblood Hart. One year, piano master Pinetop Perkins surprised the crowd—and himself—by winning a National Reso-Phonic guitar in the raffle. During the festival, Port Townsend clubs balance the festival's traditional sounds with contemporary Northwest electric blues.   **LOCATION:** Fort Worden Theater, on the grounds of Fort Worden State Park in Port Townsend, about two hours from Seattle via the Bainbridge Island Ferry. After crossing Hood Canal Bridge, follow the signs to Port Townsend, on the northeast tip of the Olympic Peninsula. **TICKETS/INFO:** 800-733-3608, 360-385-3102 **ACCOMMODATIONS/TOURIST INFO:** 360-385-2722, 360-586-2088

INTERNATIONAL MUSIC FESTIVAL OF SEATTLE
SEATTLE ✱ LAST TWO WEEKS IN JUNE

Seattle's chamber music festival began in 1995, but it's already finding a place on the American musical map. Part of the reason for its quickly growing reputation is the

Blues from all corners: Alvin Youngblood Hart performs at the 1995 Port Townsend Country Blues Festival. (See entry, page 421.) Courtesy of Ann Katzenbach

festival's resident New European Strings Chamber Orchestra, which provides a lively, solid contrast to the smaller-scale chamber music featured at many Pacific Northwest festivals. The festival also has succeeded in bringing in European soloists, all of whom are renowned on the international classical music scene. The repertory runs the gamut of contemporary compositions, multidisciplinary works, works of special historical significance, and rarely performed works.   **LOCATION:** Meany Hall (at the University of Washington), Seattle Art Museum (in downtown Seattle), Meydenbauer Center (in Bellevue), Rialto Theatre (in Tacoma), and venues in outlying communities **TICKETS/ INFO:** 206-233-0993 **ACCOMMODATIONS/TOURIST INFO:** 206-461-5840, 360-586-2088

𝒥ESTIVAL OF AMERICAN FIDDLE TUNES

PORT TOWNSEND ✷ LATE JUNE AND EARLY JULY

Celebrating the musical heritage of their forefiddlers, 25 of the world's greatest converge on a 430-acre park on Washington's scenic Olympic Peninsula. Fiddlers come from digs near and far—California, Arkansas, and Nova Scotia's Cape Breton—and the musical styles are as diverse as the hometowns. All brandish the old-time style, but some impart their own regional twists on age-old Celtic jigs or raise eyebrows with new interpretations of old tunes. Each week, some 3,000 spectators (many of them amateur or professional musicians) watch performances and take part in workshops. The pavilion is alcohol-free, the festival is family-friendly, and the park is scenic and campable. Concerts cost $8 for adults.   **LOCATION:** Fort Worden Theater, on the grounds of Fort Worden State Park in Port Townsend, about two hours from Seattle via the Bainbridge Island Ferry. After crossing Hood Canal Bridge, follow the signs to Port Townsend, on the northeast tip of the Olympic Peninsula. **TICKETS/INFO:** 800-733-3608, 360-385-3102 **ACCOMMODATIONS/TOURIST INFO:** 360-385-2722, 360-586-2088

𝒪LYMPIC MUSIC FESTIVAL

QUILCENE ✷ SATURDAYS AND SUNDAYS FROM LATE JUNE THROUGH EARLY SEPTEMBER

Almost any weekend of the summer, you can pull up a padded church pew, a well-packed hay bale, or a sweet-smelling patch of grass at this old farm and spend the afternoon enjoying chamber music penned by long-ago longhairs like Beethoven, Dvořák, Brahms, Mendelssohn, and Schumann. Members of the Philadelphia String Quartet are joined by musicians from around the country to perform for locals and vacationers in a renovated turn-of-the-century dairy barn. Lots of folks come early to picnic, stroll, and pet the farm animals, taking advantage of local food, wine, and microbrewed beer. The festival's Music Institute provides summer instruction for teenagers.   **LOCATION:** Near the town of Quilcene on the Olympic Peninsula. From the Hood Canal Bridge go west 10 miles on Highway 104, then south on Center Road. **TICKETS/INFO:** 206-527-8839 **ACCOMMODATIONS/TOURIST INFO:** 360-437-0120, 360-586-2088

𝒮EATTLE CHAMBER MUSIC FESTIVAL

SEATTLE ✷ MONDAY, WEDNESDAY, AND FRIDAY EVENINGS THROUGHOUT JULY

Have it any way you like it at this classical music festival, because the options abound. Whether you like traditional music composed for chamber groups, or rarely heard music by 20th-century composers; whether you have $25 to spend on a ticket, or no money at all; whether you prefer to sit indoors in view of the musicians, or picnic outdoors in range of high-quality speakers—you can have your druthers any Monday, Wednesday, or Friday evening in July.

The beautiful Lakeside School features 8 P.M. concerts in St. Nicholas Hall (and out on the lawn, thanks to the speakers), with world-class local, regional, and international performers playing in a variety of combinations. String quartets, piano trios, piano quintets, and other ensembles play selections from the traditional chamber music repertoire. Preconcert "Poncho" recitals (at 7 P.M.) in the McKay Chapel present 20th-

The Olympic Music Festival presents comfortable afternoons of music in a turn-of-the-century dairy barn. (See entry, page 423.) *Courtesy of C. Walter Bodle/Olympic Music Festival*

century and rarely played music, often accompanied by commentary by performers or local musicologists. Catered dinners, wine, coffee, and desserts are available before the concerts. Tickets are about $24, but lawn seating is free.   **LOCATION:** McKay Chapel and St. Nicholas Hall, Lakeside School, 14050 First Avenue, NE, Seattle **TICKETS/INFO:** 206-328-1425 **ACCOMMODATIONS/TOURIST INFO:** 206-461-5840, 360-586-2088

Ｇ REATER OLYMPIA DIXIELAND JAZZ FESTIVAL
OLYMPIA ✸ FIRST WEEKEND IN JULY, FRIDAY–SUNDAY

Perhaps because of the hardwood floors that grace all three halls, this festival is notorious for the bouts of inspired dancing that break out Friday and Saturday nights. Six bands come in from around the Pacific Northwest and as far away as St. Louis, laying down Dixieland and other trad sounds that have provoked dancers since the beginnings of jazz. Sunday morning is mostly dedicated to gospel music, but of the 600 to 700 people who typically show up, at least a few stay around until Sunday afternoon to shake a leg again.   **LOCATION:** Holiday Select Hotel, overlooking the capitol in Olympia, off I-5 at exit 104 **TICKETS/INFO:** 360-943-9123 **ACCOMMODATIONS/TOURIST INFO:** 800-544-1800, 360-586-2088

$\int$AKE CHELAN BACH FESTE
CHELAN ✺ TEN DAYS BEGINNING THE SECOND OR THIRD FRIDAY IN JULY

Vacationers intent on taking in the beautiful sights and recreational opportunities of Lake Chelan and the Cascade Range will be delighted to discover a classical music festival devoted to the music of Bach and others. For 10 days—in locations as varied as churches, a performing arts center, open-air settings, even a tour boat—an orchestra and a chorus bring exquisite sounds to the lake's southeast shore. Bach's music comprises only half the program; depending on the year, the other half might focus on anyone from Handel or Mendelssohn to Russian or African American composers. The orchestra and chorus include both professionals and accomplished amateurs.   **LOCATION:** Various venues in Chelan, about 40 miles north of Wenatchee, off Highway 97 on the southeast corner of Lake Chelan **TICKETS/INFO:** 509-664-7023, 509-682-2158 **ACCOMMODA-TIONS/TOURIST INFO:** 509-682-3503, 360-586-2088

$\int$ESUS NORTHWEST FESTIVAL
VANCOUVER ✺ THIRD WEEKEND IN JULY, THURSDAY–SATURDAY

Promising "a weekend that lasts a lifetime," the Northwest's largest contemporary Christian music festival brings some 25,000 of the rockin' faithful to Clark County Fairgrounds, just north of Portland, Oregon. Some 18 acts—which have recently included Carman, Steven Curtis Chapman, 4 Him, and Petra—perform on two music stages.

The event is a well-organized, unabashedly commercial venture (organized by the People's Church of Salem, Oregon) with an atmosphere that's remarkably similar, in many ways, to secular rock and folk festivals. Organizers appeal to families by shying away from harder-edged, "alternative" Christian bands, but acts like White Heart put on thoroughly pop shows with all the bells and whistles. Expect to see light effects, fog, and plenty of onstage gyrations and leaps.

But unlike the average rock or folk show, drugs and alcohol—even cigarettes—are conspicuously absent, as are halter tops, exposed midriffs, and passionate smooching. Performers ply the crowd with between-song banter like "Say 'yeah' if you think it's great to be Christian!"

In addition to the music, four speaking stages and two children's areas are comple-mented by amusement rides, giant video screens, teen recreation areas, and more. Tickets are about $35 per day, and more than 10,000 people typically camp on-site. **LOCATION:** Clark County Fairgrounds in Vancouver, just off I-5 north of Portland **TICKETS/INFO:** 503-393-8811 **ACCOMMODATIONS/TOURIST INFO:** 360-693-1313, 360-586-2088

Ritzville BLUES, BREWS AND BARBECUES
RITZVILLE ✴ THIRD SATURDAY IN JULY

The title of this festival alone is enough to send some folks (including the author) salivating toward the phone for directions to Ritzville. The town, which is exactly two blocks long, cordons off the streets and lets the good times flow. Electric music on an outdoor stage alternates with mostly acoustic blues at three bar/restaurant locations in town. The early afternoon typically starts off with an Acoustical War jam session outside, followed by about a dozen bands that get progressively better as the microbrewed beer begins to take its toll on listener discretion. There's also plenty of great food and easy parking (but let your designated driver handle that chore).   **LOCATION:** Downtown Ritzville, near the junction of U.S. 395 and I-90 in eastern Washington **TICKETS/INFO:** 509-659-1936 **ACCOMMODATIONS/TOURIST INFO:** 509-659-1936, 360-586-2088

Jazz PORT TOWNSEND
PORT TOWNSEND ✴ LAST WEEKEND IN JULY, FRIDAY–SUNDAY

Out on the scenic Olympic Peninsula, jazz legends and rising stars play three and one-half days of nearly nonstop jazz at Washington's oldest and largest weekend jazz event. Programs in past years have featured trumpeters like Roy Hargrove and West Coast darling Bobby Shew (inventor of the two-bell Shewhorn trumpet), as well as pianist Marc Seales and flutist Holly Hofmann. Concerts take place in a 1,400-seat pavilion and at nine nearby clubs in Port Townsend. The Bud Shank workshop, named after the West Coast saxophonist, precedes the festival. The Olympic Peninsula is rich with aesthetic and natural pleasures, so don't miss a chance to explore the region. **LOCATION:** Fort Worden Theater, on the grounds of Fort Worden State Park in Port Townsend, about two hours from Seattle via the Bainbridge Island Ferry. After crossing Hood Canal Bridge, follow the signs to Port Townsend, on the northeast tip of the Olympic Peninsula. **TICKETS/INFO:** 800-733-3608, 360-385-3102 **ACCOMMODA-TIONS/TOURIST INFO:** 360-385-2722, 360-586-2088

Marrowstone MUSIC FESTIVAL
PORT TOWNSEND ✴ WEEKENDS THROUGHOUT AUGUST

Expect the unexpected when young virtuosos team up with the biz's most talented masters for weekend performances and workshops. During Marrowstone's three-week music camp (begun by the Seattle Youth Symphony in 1942), imaginative programming, energetic playing, and skillful conducting revive oft-forgotten and infrequently heard compositions. More than 50 artists perform in 12 concerts ranging from Saturday evening showcases of renowned visiting and resident faculty to Sunday afternoon spotlights on future stars in the student Festival Orchestra. Admission costs $6 to $12. **LOCATION:** Fort Worden Theater, on the grounds of Fort Worden State Park in Port Townsend, about two hours from Seattle via the Bainbridge Island Ferry. After crossing Hood Canal Bridge, follow the signs to Port Townsend, on the northeast tip of the Olympic Peninsula. **TICKETS/INFO:** 800-733-3608, 360-385-3102 **ACCOMMODA-TIONS/TOURIST INFO:** 360-385-2722, 360-586-2088

❧INTERNATIONAL ACCORDION CELEBRATION
LEAVENWORTH ✷ SECOND WEEKEND IN AUGUST, THURSDAY–SATURDAY

Nestled in the middle of the Wenatchee National Forest, this faux-Bavarian community cooks up an accordion festival devoted entirely to polka music. A couple of headlining accordion masters or ensembles come in from afar to fire up Friday night's dance, but the majority of the weekend goes to contests and workshops. Various types of polka music and styles of accordion are covered in 12 categories, and kid contestants (ages 8-17) are always crowd pleasers.   **LOCATION:** Icicle River Middle School in Leavenworth, on U.S. 2 about 20 miles west of Wenatchee **TICKETS/INFO:** 509-548-5807 **ACCOMMODATIONS/TOURIST INFO:** 509-548-5807, 360-586-2088

♪BELLINGHAM FESTIVAL OF MUSIC
BELLINGHAM ✷ TWO WEEKS IN MID- TO LATE AUGUST

Combining orchestral, chamber, and jazz music, Bellingham brings some 60 artists to the campus of Western Washington University for two weeks of concerts, open rehearsals, lectures, and educational opportunities. The festival's centerpiece is the American Sinfonietta, a 40-member chamber orchestra that's often joined by guest soloists. Since 1993, National Public Radio's "Performance Today" has broadcast the festival from Bellingham, which offers a gateway to Puget Sound, the San Juan Islands, and the Cascade Mountains.   **LOCATION:** Various venues on the campus of Western Washington University. From I-5 take the Bellingham exit and follow the signs to the university. **TICKETS/INFO:** 360-676-5997 **ACCOMMODATIONS/TOURIST INFO:** 800-487-2032, 360-671-3990, 360-586-2088

❧SWINOMISH BLUES FESTIVAL
LA CONNER ✷ THIRD FULL WEEKEND IN AUGUST, SATURDAY AND SUNDAY

Held on the Swinomish Indian Reservation, this festival presents an interesting mix of mainstream Northwest blues and traditional Native American sounds. Five or six regional blues acts are typically scheduled, along with native drummers, dancers, and singers. Things get interesting when the blues musicians stay around to jam with the Native Americans, who play the big drums. A kid's area, Indian arts and crafts, and plenty of barbecued salmon are also on hand.   **LOCATION:** Swinomish Indian Reservation on Whidbey Island, just across the channel from La Conner. La Conner is one and a half hours north of Seattle, off Highway 20 about 10 miles west of I-5. **TICKETS/INFO:** 360-466-3052 **ACCOMMODATIONS/TOURIST INFO:** 360-466-3125, 360-586-2088

♪BUMBERSHOOT, THE SEATTLE ARTS FESTIVAL
SEATTLE ✷ LABOR DAY WEEKEND, FRIDAY–MONDAY (LABOR DAY IS THE FIRST MONDAY IN SEPTEMBER)

Music is always a big draw in this city, and visitors to Bumbershoot can expect to see and hear everything from local grunge survivors to swampy zydeco combos and bikutsi rhythm masters. The Northwest's most dazzling showcase of performing arts features music from around the world—as well as dance, theater, literary arts, comedy, and visual arts.

Roots rapture: Guinea's Fatala at Bumbershoot, the Seattle Arts Festival.
(See entry, page 427.) Courtesy of Bumbershoot, the Seattle Arts Festival

Musically, this four-day event distinguishes itself from similar festivals through its magnitude (15 indoor and outdoor stages on 74 acres), its diversity (local, national, and international performers), and its setting (right under the Space Needle). Recent headliners have included Robert Cray, Dr. John, Ani DiFranco, Maceo Parker, Jim Carroll, Patti Smith, and George Clinton.

Scheduled concerts weight the program toward worldbeat and American roots music, and street performers gallivant nonstop among the weekend crowd of about 200,000—many of whom are international visitors.   **LOCATION:** Seattle Center, directly under the Space Needle in downtown Seattle **TICKETS/INFO:** 206-682-4386, 206-628-0888 **ACCOMMODATIONS/TOURIST INFO:** 206-461-5840, 360-586-2088

⚙CEAN SHORES DIXIELAND JAZZ FESTIVAL

OCEAN SHORES ✴ FIRST WEEKEND IN NOVEMBER, FRIDAY–SUNDAY

Just when Ocean Shores retirees and weekenders are busy preparing for a long winter's hibernation, along comes the Ocean Shores Dixieland Jazz Festival to yank them out onto the dance floor. Eight or nine Dixieland and traditional jazz bands roll in from as far away as Chicago, drawing about 1,500 music lovers to four very dance-friendly local venues.   **LOCATION:** Several venues in Ocean Shores, on the coast about 75 miles due west of Olympia via U.S. 12, Highway 109, and Highway 115 **TICKETS/ INFO:** 360-289-3028 **ACCOMMODATIONS/TOURIST INFO:** 800-762-3224, 360-586-2088

CaNaDa eaST

NEW BRUNSWICK

POLEY MOUNTAIN MUSIC FESTIVAL
SUSSEX ✷ SECOND WEEKEND IN JULY

Exposing listeners to new folk, blues, rock, R&B, Celtic, and world music, this young, energetic festival is held in a natural amphitheater at the Poley Mountain Ski Area. Heavy emphasis is placed on original Canadian music, with about 10 bands playing for 2,000 to 3,000 people over two days.   **LOCATION:** Poley Mountain Ski Area, just southeast of Sussex, between Sussex Corner and Waterford **TICKETS/INFO:** 506-652-5238, World Wide Web: http://www.mi.net/poley.html **ACCOMMODA-TIONS/TOURIST INFO:** 506-433-7200, 800-561-0123

LAMÈQUE INTERNATIONAL BAROQUE MUSIC FESTIVAL
LAMÈQUE ✷ SECOND AND THIRD WEEKENDS IN JULY

Perfected between the early 1600s and the mid-1700s in the cathedrals and royal courts of Europe, baroque music entertained and enchanted kings and queens but was—and still is—rarely heard in rural North America. The Lamèque International Baroque Music Festival is a brilliant exception, a two-week feast that brings a baroque shiver upon Acadian souls (as Verlaine might have said), and upon anyone else who has the good fortune to visit this remote, scenic corner of the continent.

Tucked away in the countryside of the culturally unique Acadian Peninsula (this area is actually an island), the Petite-Riviere-de-l'Ile church has hosted the festival since its inception. A priest once painted the walls a psychedelic kaleidoscope of pastel colors—yellow, pink, green, blue, and orange depictions of stars, candles, moons, trees, even *Marie et Joseph*—which make the church look like a candy-encrusted gingerbread house. It's a charming and original setting for the music, with a round, wooden ceiling that lends such natural acoustics that microphones and amplifiers are unnecessary.

The serene island setting contrasts with the festival's intense, cosmopolitan musical activity. Outstanding Canadian and international musicians are invited to attend, and over two weekends they present a range of early, chamber, choral, and church music from the baroque period. Some years highlight a particular composer, and a period opera also is typically featured. All pieces are played on the period instruments for which they were written, such as harpsichord, wooden flute, or viola. Inside the church, the

Lamèque International Baroque Music Festival: Tucked away on the Acadian Peninsula, the Petite-Riviere-de-l'Ile church hosts baroque musicians from around the world. Erika Ehmsen/

Clynes Group

showy, rhythmic music conjures up images of court jesters, jousting knights, and decadent royal families.

An Acadian dialect of French is spoken throughout upper stretches of New Brunswick, and many natives don't speak much English, so brush up on your French or bring a phrase book along. The people of Lamèque and the cities that surround it make their living from the sea; consequently local fish, mussels, and lobster are inexpensive, as well as delicious. Along the wooded coast are picturesque views and beaches, and whale-watching adventures depart from nearby Caraquet.   **LOCATION:** The Petite-Riviere-de-l'Ile church is located on the Rue du Ruisseau in Lamèque, on the Acadian Peninsula in northeast New Brunswick. **TICKETS/INFO:** 506-344-5846 **ACCOMMODATIONS/ TOURIST INFO:** 506-395-0418, 800-561-0123

♪FESTIVAL BAIE JAZZ & BLUES

SHEDIAC ✱ A WEEKEND IN MID-JULY, WEDNESDAY–SUNDAY

This officially bilingual festival features French- and English-speaking artists from Europe, the United States, and Canada playing a blend of jazz, blues, Acadian, and

Cajun. In the resort town of Shediac (near the nice beaches of Shediac Bay), a single stage features three acts each night and one-act matinees on Saturday and Sunday afternoons. The crowd of 2,000 includes many vacationers from Québec.   **LOCATION:** Downtown Shediac, about 25 km northeast of Moncton **TICKETS/INFO:** 506-858-0571 **ACCOMMODATIONS/TOURIST INFO:** 800-561-0123

ℭANADA'S IRISH FESTIVAL ON THE MIRAMICHI
MIRAMICHI ✳ THIRD WEEKEND IN JULY, THURSDAY–SUNDAY

Ireland is transplanted to the banks of the Miramichi River for four days in mid-July as townspeople revel in Irish music, pubs, pipe bands, and dancing. This is Canada's only strictly Irish festival and one of the few events that feature Irish groups from around the world. And true to Irish tradition, it's one of the friendliest party spots on earth.

The musical, cultural, historical, spiritual, athletic, and culinary delights of Ireland all are featured, and the depth and breadth of activities and talent is boggling. During the days traditional *ceilidh* music—the fiddle and tin whistle music of old Ireland—echoes through the town, and bands swap places on the main stage while others lead workshops at town hall. You can learn the fiddle, the bagpipes, or the bodhrán drum—often from the world's foremost masters.

At schools and around town, afternoon classes are filled with people learning step dancing or Irish history. Workshops cover everything from genealogy to folklore and literature, while children's events include a leprechaun contest, tin whistle workshops, storytelling, and puppetshows. A $6 day pass gets you into the arena and all classes and workshops.

Townspeople (many of whom descended from Irish settlers of the 1840s) decorate the town to the hilt. Streamers are everywhere, and shamrocks are painted on the streets. The school cafeteria is converted to an Irish restaurant, serving corned beef, cabbage, and other Irish fare, along with local favorites like salmon. On Saturday, families don traditional regalia and parade proudly with their family crests.

As evening descends, the family/learning atmosphere turns into revelry as two pubs are set up and the stout begins to flow. At the town hall pub the music is traditional; at the arena souped-up contemporary Celtic rhythms are supplied by Irish pub bands from New York, Boston, and Toronto. Don't expect to find polite applause from a seated audience; Irish music commands listeners to get up on their feet and get actively involved—in other words, dance!   **LOCATION:** Lord Beaverbrook Arena (109 Roy Avenue) and elsewhere in downtown Miramichi, about 20 km east of Chatham along Highway 117 **TICKETS/INFO:** 506-778-8810, 506-622-4007 **ACCOMMODATIONS/ TOURIST INFO:** 800-561-0123

ℳIRAMICHI FOLK SONG FESTIVAL
MIRAMICHI ✳ THE WEEK BEFORE NEW BRUNSWICK DAY (THE FIRST MONDAY IN AUGUST), SUNDAY–FRIDAY

One of North America's smallest but longest-running festivals reflects the unique music of the *Miramichiers*. The festival was begun by locals in 1958 and features fiddlers, dancers, and singers (French and English) whose music contains rich lyrical histories of local lumbering and fishing traditions and disasters. Each night, two stages feature both professionals and amateurs, often including elderly residents who know hundreds of old Miramichi songs and haven't missed a festival in years. Noon luncheon shows and

Meeting in Miramichi: Canada's Irish Festival draws groups from around the world for four days of dancing and Irish culture.

Courtesy of Brian Atkinson, New Brunswick Department of Tourism

children's shows round out the entertainment, and admission is $6 to $12 per concert. **LOCATION:** Lord Beaverbrook Theater in downtown Miramichi, 109 Roy Avenue, about 20 km east of Chatham along Highway 117 **TICKETS/INFO:** 506-622-1780 **ACCOMMODATIONS/TOURIST INFO:** 800-561-0123

ℱESTIVAL BY THE SEA
ST. JOHN ✳ TEN DAYS BEGINNING THE FRIDAY AFTER NEW BRUNSWICK DAY

Over 10 days, southern New Brunswick's biggest cultural blast might offer everything from folk, jazz, country, and rock to Ukrainian and Chinese dancing. At eight venues around town, there's lots of music from the Maritimes and beyond. Past performers have included Nova Scotia's Cape Breton Gold, Newfoundland's Irish Descendants, and Toronto's Arrogant Worms. The majority of shows are free (though admission is charged to some evening concerts), and St. John's seaside atmosphere is relaxed and comfortable. Families from all over North America come for the final weekend's two-day children's festival with kids' entertainment, free treats, face painting, balloons, and exhibits.   **LOCATION:** Loyalist Plaza and other sites in uptown and downtown St. John **TICKETS/INFO:** 506-632-0086 **ACCOMMODATIONS/TOURIST INFO:** 800-561-0123

$\mathcal{F}$ESTIVAL ACADIEN
CARAQUET ✹ 10–12 DAYS USUALLY BEGINNING THE FRIDAY BEFORE AUGUST 15

Music and chaos are everywhere in the dozen days surrounding La Fete des Acadiens, which is Acadian Canada's official birthday party. The schedule changes according to whim, but if you show up in Caraquet anytime around August 15, you'll be thrown into a party that includes French pop, jazz, folk, and classical music, as well as theater, poetry, and art. In cafés, beer gardens, coffee shops, and out in the street, shows, concerts, and plenty of noisemaking erupt at all hours.   **LOCATION:** Several locations in Caraquet; much of the musical action centers around Carrefour de la Mer, 51 Boulevard St.-Peter Est. Caraquet is in the northeast corner of New Brunswick on the Acadian Peninsula; Highway 11 passes through. **TICKETS/INFO:** 506-727-2787 **AC-COMMODATIONS/TOURIST INFO:** 800-561-0123

$\mathcal{N}$EW BRUNSWICK GOSPEL MUSIC FESTIVAL
FREDERICTON ✹ SECOND WEEKEND IN AUGUST

Toe-tappin' country, bluegrass, and gospel music combine with Christian fellowship at this three-day weekend outing. Most of the 25 to 30 acts are from New Brunswick, but a few come in from Prince Edward Island and Nova Scotia, sharing the wooded, streamside setting with some 4,000 spectators over the weekend. The festival also features camping, food booths, a hot country supper, and worship services. Admission is free, with voluntary offerings accepted.   **LOCATION:** Rusagonis Recreation Center Field in Rusagonis, about 20 km from Fredericton via Route 655 **TICKETS/INFO:** 506-459-7419 **ACCOMMODATIONS/TOURIST INFO:** 800-561-0123

$\mathcal{H}$ARVEST JAZZ & BLUES FESTIVAL
FREDERICTON ✹ SECOND WEEK IN SEPTEMBER, TUESDAY–SUNDAY

Quiet Fredericton comes to life in mid-September for a massive excursion into jazz and blues. The festival packs downtown with some 25,000 people (many from Maine and nearby Canadian provinces) roving between a whopping 20 stages in bars and outdoor tents. About 60 acts include locals and imported big names like the Red Hot Louisiana Band and Luther "Guitar Jr." Johnson. Jazz and blues, and derivatives like Cajun and zydeco, are covered at free outdoor shows Saturday and Sunday, while bars charge admission ranging from $5 to $15. Fredericton is known as one of the safest cities in North America, and despite the mobs of people there's never any security problem. **LOCATION:** About 20 venues in downtown Fredericton **TICKETS/INFO:** 506-454-2583, 800-320-3988 **ACCOMMODATIONS/TOURIST INFO:** 800-561-0123

NEWFOUNDLAND & LABRADOR

BURIN PENINSULA FESTIVAL OF FOLK SONG AND DANCE

BURIN ✷ FIRST WEEKEND IN JULY

Seeking to preserve the musical traditions of Newfoundland, this folksy, indoor festival is held in the old town of Burin, which was settled in the early 1700s. You'll hear unaccompanied ballad singing and unwritten songs passed along through the oral tradition, as well as accordion and fiddle music. Learn the tricky local versions of step and set dances, or check out slingshot-making and whistle-making exhibitions and traditional games. Alcohol isn't allowed, but tickets are only $3 each day. Plus, this is the only place in North America where France (the French colony of St.-Pierre and Miquelon) is only a short ferry ride away. **LOCATION:** Donald C. Jamieson Academy gymnasium, on the outskirts of Burin on the Burin Peninsula in southeastern Newfoundland **TICKETS/INFO:** 709-891-1546 **ACCOMMODATIONS/TOURIST INFO:** 709-729-0862, 709-729-1965, 800-563-6355

NEWFOUNDLAND INTERNATIONAL IRISH FESTIVAL

MOUNT PEARL ✷ SECOND WEEKEND IN JULY, FRIDAY–SUNDAY

A contingent of international performers joins more than 100 local musicians for pub nights and concerts, both indoor and outdoor. Set in Newfoundland's newest city (actually more of a continuation of St. John's sprawl), the festival also features a musical Irish Newfoundland Breakfast for children and adults. **LOCATION:** Mount Pearl, just outside of St. John's, via Topsail Road (Highway 60) **TICKETS/INFO:** 709-748-1002, 709-748-1044, 709-748-1027 **ACCOMMODATIONS/TOURIST INFO:** 709-729-2830, 800-563-6353

SOUND SYMPOSIUM

ST. JOHN'S ✷ NINE DAYS BEGINNING THE SECOND FRIDAY IN JULY

Experimental music is the name of the game at the Sound Symposium. For nine days, participants hold concerts, workshops, gallery exhibitions, outdoor installations, and environmental works—as well as dance, theater, and film events. The music unpredictably skirts the outer limits of jazz and electronic experimentation, but the scheduled highlight is the Harbour Symphony, a series of lunch-hour concerts played on the horns of whatever ships happen to be in St. John's Harbour.   **LOCATION:** Various venues in St. John's **TICKETS/INFO:** 709-737-8209 **ACCOMMODATIONS/TOURIST INFO:** 709-729-2830, 800-563-6353

ḔXPLOITS VALLEY SALMON FESTIVAL
GRAND FALLS-WINDSOR ✴ THIRD WEEKEND IN JULY, THURSDAY–MONDAY

Five days of entertainment—much of it musical—begin with a salmon dinner on Thursday night in honor of the bounty of the Exploits River, which runs through town. Concerts and dances in the park and local stadium feature big names in Irish, folk, soft rock, country, and traditional Newfoundland music. In addition to the music, a craft show, a fishing derby, an antique car show, and a horse show draw some 30,000 people over the weekend.   **LOCATION:** Centennial Field Complex in Grand Falls-Windsor, on the Trans-Canada Highway in north-central Newfoundland **TICKETS/INFO:** 709-489-2728 **ACCOMMODATIONS/TOURIST INFO:** 709-729-1965, 800-563-6355

ℳUSICFEST
STEPHENVILLE ✴ THIRD FULL WEEKEND IN JULY, THURSDAY–SUNDAY

Although plenty of Newfie fiddlers and accordion players make the roster, this is probably the least traditional music festival in Newfoundland. The MusicFest stresses rock 'n' roll and country—reflecting the influence of the thousands of young American troops who manned an air force base here until the mid-1960s. About 25 groups come from throughout the island to trade turns on a single stage in front of a weekend crowd of about 7,000. The natural, grassy amphitheater is divided between a "family" side and a "wet" side; admission is $5 each day.   **LOCATION:** Town Hall, Stephenville (just off the Trans-Canada Highway on Newfoundland's west coast) **TICKETS/INFO:** 709-643-9123 **ACCOMMODATIONS/TOURIST INFO:** 709-643-9123, 709-729-1965, 800-563-6355

ṠOUTHERN SHORE SHAMROCK FESTIVAL
FERRYLAND ✴ FOURTH WEEKEND IN JULY, SATURDAY AND SUNDAY

Almost four centuries after the Irish began coming to southwest Newfoundland, you can still hear an unmistakable brogue in the speech and spirited music of this region's residents. This festival is a great opportunity to tap into the musical talent pool that produced the likes of the Irish Descendants and other famous Newfie bands. For two days, some 30 traditional groups and solo musicians perform for about 4,000 locals and visitors next to a 17th-century archaeological dig that has uncovered one of North America's earliest English settlements. The Atlantic coastline, which forms a churning backdrop to the festival site, is alive with migrating whales during this season. **LOCATION:** Ferryland, about 80 km south of St. John's **TICKETS/INFO:** 709-745-2613, 709-432-2820 **ACCOMMODATIONS/TOURIST INFO:** 800-563-6353, 709-729-2830

ᵁNE JOURNÉE DANS L'PASSE
LA GRAND'TERRE (MAINLAND) ✹ LAST SUNDAY IN JULY

First settled by French fishermen, the Port au Port Peninsula is still dominated by the culture of its French-speaking inhabitants. This festival features local musicians who play traditional music for an appreciative, dancing audience of about 500 from coastal communities like Lourdes and Black Duck Brook. In addition to the musical offerings, demonstrations in butter churning, wool spinning, and more bring the old ways back to life.   **LOCATION:** Centre Scolaire at Communautaire Ste.-Anne in La Grand'Terre (the town is also known as Mainland), one hour west of Stephenville on the Port au Port Peninsula in western Newfoundland **TICKETS/INFO:** 709-642-5254 **ACCOMMODA-TIONS/TOURIST INFO:** 1-800-563-6353, 709-729-2830

ᴳEORGE STREET FESTIVAL
ST. JOHN'S ✹ FIVE DAYS BEFORE THE FIRST WEDNESDAY IN AUGUST

In the days leading up to the Royal St. John's Regatta (North America's oldest continuously occurring annual sporting event), St. John's works itself into a frenzy. The party centers around cobbled George Street, which is lined with pubs and blocked off to traffic and kids under 19. There's plenty of rock and blues, but what makes the festival unique is the amount of Irish music that's once again in vogue with young people. Six to eight bands—both established and up-and-coming—play each night, and with 30,000 pub-goers over five days, the action is rockin' and rowdy.   **LOCATION:** George Street, St. John's **TICKETS/INFO:** 709-726-2922 **ACCOMMODATIONS/TOURIST INFO:** 709-729-2830, 800-563-6353

ᴺEWFOUNDLAND AND LABRADOR FOLK FESTIVAL
ST. JOHN'S ✹ FIRST WEEKEND IN AUGUST, FRIDAY–SUNDAY

Local kids slam-dance to the newest alternative Celtic rockers, while adults dig jigging to the area's best roots revivalists. The Newfoundland and Labrador Folk Festival is St. John's biggest hootenanny, and it draws folks of all ages brandishing lawn chairs and blankets and hankering for a good time.

North America's easternmost city is close both physically and culturally to the British Isles, a fact well demonstrated in residents' love of traditional song and dance. Not that the music is strictly old-world—as locals are quick to point out, the New-foundland sound is a unique blend of many influences. The festival's 20-year mission is to promote and preserve Newfie/Labrador rhythms and melodies, which are deeply rooted in Irish and other Celtic traditions.

While singers belt out lyrics of sunken fishing vessels, lost blue-eyed lovers, and dead soldiers, the upbeat accompaniment is so jolly that you'll forfeit tears in favor of a whirling jig. Musicians switch instruments with amazing agility, playing a button accor-dion as feverishly as a fiddle, mandolin, or tin whistle. The frequently heard primal beat of the bodhrán drum stirs up an energy as deep as the culture from which it came. This hand-held instrument—once used as a Celtic war drum—is single- or double-beaten, and deft placement of the supporting palm varies the tone.

Along with more traditional groups, you can hear spatterings of jazz, blues, and rock. The folk festival also features traditional dancing, indigenous crafts like yarn

Newfoundland and Labrador Folk Festival: St. John's biggest hootenanny brings roots revivalists and Celtic rockers to the continent's easternmost city. (See entry, page 437.) Melinda Clynes/The Clynes Group

spinning and fishnet mending, as well as a children's stage and activity area. Some 25,000 folk music lovers from across Canada and the United States are more than willing to fork over $25 for a weekend pass.

You might at first find locals stiffly polite, but spend 20 minutes in the beer tent and you'll soon be regaled with friendship and stories of the community's history and hardships. The only drawback is the tent's location, just out of earshot and eyesight of the stage.

Nearby attractions include bird- and whale-watching and hiking. If you're in town early, check out the local regatta and the George Street Carnival (see previous entry). Festival organizers also host a folk music night every Wednesday at the Blarney Stone. **LOCATION:** Bannerman Park in St. John's. Rain site is Memorial Stadium. **TICKETS/ INFO:** 709-576-8508 **ACCOMMODATIONS/TOURIST INFO:** 709-729-2830, 800-563-6353

N⊙Va S⊙Tia

SCOTIA FESTIVAL OF MUSIC
HALIFAX ✶ LAST WEEK IN MAY AND FIRST WEEK IN JUNE

Mixing the music of old-world masters with that of contemporary composers, the Scotia Festival brings some of the world's most celebrated composers and conductors to Halifax's Dalhousie University. Much of the emphasis is on teaching, and festival patrons can usually count on a world premiere or two in the nine Highlight Concerts held over two weeks. Concert tickets run about $22, and a special Festival Events Pass admits the holder to more than 50 events, excluding concerts but including all master classes, lectures, open rehearsals, and Young Artists Classes. **LOCATION:** Rebecca Cohn Auditorium, Dalhousie University in Halifax **TICKETS/INFO:** 902-429-9467 **ACCOMMODATIONS/TOURIST INFO:** 902-421-8736, 800-565-0000, 902-425-5781

AVON RIVER BLUEGRASS AND OLDTIME MUSIC FESTIVAL
MOUNT DENSON ✶ FIRST WEEKEND IN JUNE, FRIDAY–SUNDAY

Arriving from as far away as California, bluegrass fans turn this gorgeous 55-acre farm into a bluegrass and old-time country music revival. Music from eight or nine bands rolls out over the Avon River from a single stage until midnight, then everyone heads to campsites to play some more. The talent is typically from Nova Scotia, playing a Maritime bluegrass influenced by the region's Celtic forebears. There are no restrictions on alcohol, pets, or late-night jamming (there aren't many children at this gig), and the admission fee is about $27 for the weekend. **LOCATION:** Avon River Park, about a half-hour drive from Halifax. Take Highway 101 to exit 7, then follow the signs. **TICKETS/INFO:** 902-684-1046 **ACCOMMODATIONS/TOURIST INFO:** 800-565-0000, 902-425-5781

FESTIVAL ACADIEN DE CLARE
CHURCH POINT AND NEARBY TOWNS ✶ SECOND WEEKEND IN JULY, THURSDAY–SUNDAY

With some 10,000 Acadians, the western corner of Nova Scotia produces some of the province's most distinctive music. The Festival Acadien de Clare is a great opportunity to sample a slice of Acadian life, with both traditional and contemporary Acadian folk music, plenty of dancing, and great food. Open-air concerts get the festival rolling with traditional music and dance, and a chowder dinner at the Fire Hall (with live music) takes care of the catch from the afternoon fishing tournament. On Saturday evening, a bistro features modern Acadian sounds accompanied by polkas and waltzes, and an open-air mass on Sunday blends the talents of French-singing choirs from nearby parishes. On Sunday evening, the festival closes with more music from both traditional and contemporary groups. Admission prices range from free to about $7. **LOCATION:** Throughout the region of Clare on the shore of Baie Ste.-Marie, in western Nova Scotia between Yarmouth and Bigby on Route 1. Many events are at Université St.-Anne in Church Point. **TICKETS/INFO:** 902-769-2152 **ACCOMMODATIONS/TOURIST INFO:** 902-645-2389, 800-565-0000, 902-425-5781

$\mathscr{M}$ ARITIME OLD TIME FIDDLING CONTEST & JAMBOREE
DARTMOUTH ✳ SECOND WEEKEND IN JULY, FRIDAY–SUNDAY

When the fiddlers roll into Dartmouth town, there's nary a soul sitting down. This festival dishes up huge helpings of the lively and mainly instrumental "down east" style of Maritime fiddle music through concerts, contests, and a rollicking Old Time Fiddle Mass, in which more than 70 fiddlers attempt to saw the roof off a Catholic church (arrive by 10 A.M. Sunday to claim your stretch of pew). Friday and Saturday contests feature a field of some 80 young and old fiddlers from the Maritime Provinces, the rest of Canada, the United States, and even the British Isles. Sunday's jamboree and old-time dance bring some 35 of the region's best fiddlers to the stage, driving a dancing frenzy that continues all day and into the evening.   **LOCATION:** Prince Andrew High School (contest), 37 Woodlawn Road; Beazley Sport Field (jamboree) in Dartmouth, just across the harbor from Halifax **TICKETS/INFO:** 902-434-5466, 902-434-4190 **ACCOMMODATIONS/TOURIST INFO:** 800-565-0000, 902-425-5781

$\mathbf{d}$ U MAURIER ATLANTIC JAZZ FESTIVAL
HALIFAX ✳ NINE DAYS ENDING THE SATURDAY OF THE LAST FULL WEEKEND IN JULY

This 10-day festival of live jazz features performers from around the world playing a variety of styles in intimate settings. An outdoor tent at Purdy's Wharf features daytime and nighttime concerts, while the Main Stage at the Holiday Inn Halifax Centre is active each night. Three Gala Nights are complemented by laid-back jazz picnics and workshops. Admission prices range from free to $15.   **LOCATION:** Various venues in Halifax **TICKETS/INFO:** 902-492-2225 **ACCOMMODATIONS/TOURIST INFO:** 800-565-0000, 902-425-5781

$\mathbf{H}$ ALIFAX INTERNATIONAL BUSKER FESTIVAL
HALIFAX ✳ TEN DAYS BEGINNING THE FIRST THURSDAY IN AUGUST

It's 8 P.M. on Halifax's waterfront and a breezy summer evening is being violated by a sax/guitar/drum combo with triple-green hair. Suddenly, competing sounds from the

Jazzy waterfront: Halifax's du Maurier Atlantic Jazz Festival Courtesy of Tourism
Nova Scotia

next wharf distract the crowd; it's the Scared Little Weird Guys, an Australian duo converting seventies hits into wonders like "Heaving on a Jet Plane." Farther out on the wharf, a group of Russians is tuning up instruments the names of which no one can pronounce, while a Dutch group tries (and, bizarrely, succeeds) to mix the artificially separated worlds of acrobatics and opera.

Each August, some of the world's most interesting musicians and other questionable characters converge on Halifax for 10 days of high jinks and musical hilarity. Plucked by scouts from public squares and subway stations in London, Paris, Amsterdam, Los Angeles, and Canadian cities, the "buskers" (British slang for street performers) transform the city's waterfront into an extraordinary, unpredictable performance ground.

Music is a big part of the majority of the performances, but the lineup also includes acrobats, musicians, sword-swallowers, and a few too many jugglers. Because they make their living on the streets of the world, they need heaping helpings of talent, wit, and spectacle to keep the crowds interested and paying. Performers pass the hat after their sets, and contributions are purely optional—but expected (if you like what you see).

Brilliant musicianship is a plus, but attitude is an essential. Spontaneity and improvisation take precedence over perfection, and performances often seem like social events in which spectators become as active as the buskers. Hecklers are common, and verbal jousting matches break out with astonishing regularity both on the wharfs and in the beer tent. The action is anything but predictable: One performer might juggle machetes one night and play congas in a salsa band the next night. Another night you might see the beer tent's emcee shoot a fire extinguisher at a fire juggler, in the process clearing the air of oxygen and scattering the crowd.

Each night about 25,000 people from North America, Europe, and Asia crowd the eight waterfront and nearby performance sites, creating a cosmopolitan and lively scene. The Halifax waterfront is picturesque (though a bit overrun by gift shops) and has lots of built-in staging. When the evening shows are done, there's plenty of Maritime and Celtic music to be heard in many of the city's 60 or so thriving pubs.   **LOCATION:** The waterfront area of downtown Halifax **TICKETS/INFO:** 902-429-3910 **ACCOMMODATIONS/TOURIST INFO:** 800-565-0000, 902-425-5781

LUNENBURG FOLK HARBOUR FESTIVAL
LUNENBURG ✱ SECOND WEEKEND IN AUGUST, THURSDAY–SUNDAY

Set in the old German harbor town of Lunenburg, Folk Harbour has become a snug haven for the folk music traditions of North America's eastern seaboard. Sea chanteys (also known as "shanties") and ballads rooted in maritime traditions are a central focus, but the festival has expanded to reflect the breadth and depth of international folk music styles. Three stages—a historic wharf, an acoustically excellent opera house, and a main-stage tent with a great view on Blockhouse Hill—have hosted everyone from the Rankin Family and Natalie MacMaster to John Hammond, Lennie Gallant, and Oscar Lopez. Afternoon concerts run from 1 P.M. to 4:30 P.M., and evening concerts run from 7 P.M. to midnight. Since evening concerts often sell out, be sure to purchase tickets in advance. **LOCATION:** Throughout the town of Lunenburg. From Halifax go west on Highway 103, then south on Highway 3 (exit 10). **TICKETS/INFO:** 902-634-3180 **ACCOMMODATIONS/TOURIST INFO:** 800-565-0000, 902-425-5781

Festival of Scottish Fiddling: More than 300 fiddlers saturate the Cape Breton air with the soulful sounds of Scotland. Courtesy of Tourism Nova Scotia

ℱESTIVAL OF SCOTTISH FIDDLING
ST. ANN'S ✷ THIRD WEEKEND IN AUGUST, SATURDAY AND SUNDAY

The mountains and lakes of Cape Breton echo with the soulful sounds of Scotland as the very best of island talent gathers on the campus of Gaelic College. For musicians, the festival is a chance to join together to share experiences after playing apart for most of the year. For visitors, it's a chance to hear the heart and soul of Celtic Cape Breton brought to a focal point, with more than 300 fiddlers, piano players, pipers, singers, and dancers from around the island and around the world.

If you've ever longed to hear the famous Cape Breton sound in the mythical place that produced it, the Festival of Scottish Fiddling is the place to be. Carried to the rocky shores of this island by Scottish settlers, the old songs and dances survived in the isolation of this corner of North America, often cross-fertilizing with the fiddle music of the Acadians who share the island.

Now, the distinct traditional music of Cape Breton is undergoing a resurgence, and locals are excited. Young fiddle aces like Natalie MacMaster and Ashley MacIsaac— frequent performers here—are not only maintaining the tradition but adding to it all the time. At the festival and at nearby pubs, they're held in awe and appreciated like rock stars are elsewhere—the big difference being that this is a music that unites, rather than separates, the generations.

Bows fly across strings as the fiddlers' legs pump, heels smacking against floorboards as accompanists (piano, guitar, or both) try to keep up, and the dance area fills with whirling forms. Saturday's agenda begins at noon, with three-hour workshops in step dancing, fiddle, piano, and even fiddle making. Performances follow, and though the focus is on fiddling, you can also catch guitar, piano, piping, Highland dancing, and step dancing by performers ranging in age from seven to 80. Much of the music is instrumental, but a good bit is sung in English and Gaelic. This is the last Gaelic-speaking area in North America, and although the language is most often heard from older tongues, young people are again beginning to learn it in numbers.

The performance schedule seems more of a suggestion, as you never know who will drop by. "We were just in the neighborhood," an Acadian neighbor might say to applause as he takes the stage. Guests often come from Scotland and elsewhere, and some performers even sing in the language of the local Mi'kmaq (Micmac) Indians. Typically, about 3,000 visitors show up each day, paying an admission fee of $7. **LOCATION:** Gaelic College of Celtic Arts and Crafts, St. Ann's, just north of Baddeck on the Cabot Trail **TICKETS/INFO:** 902-295-3411 **ACCOMMODATIONS/TOURIST INFO:** 902-539-9876, 800-565-0000, 902-425-5781

COUNTRY MUSIC WEEKEND FEATURING THE HANK SNOW TRIBUTE

CALEDONIA ✱ THIRD FULL WEEKEND IN AUGUST, FRIDAY–SUNDAY

Hank Snow was born in Brooklyn, Nova Scotia, and lived in Queen's County before hitting the big time with hits like "I'm Movin' On" (1950). This lively, folksy tribute brings more than 30 country performers to the Queens County Fairgrounds for three days of tribute to "the Singing Ranger," as Snow was dubbed in his early career. Expect to hear lots of songs from Hank Snow's more than 140 records, performed by local and regional acts who play on a makeshift stage (which is moved into a barn if it rains).

Friday night features a "play it by ear" variety concert, along with roving guitar and fiddle jams back at the campsites. Saturday brings an afternoon concert, a Famous Firemen's Barbecue, and the Sounds Like Hank competition, which is self-explanatory and open to anyone. The weekend usually draws between 1,500 and 3,000 spectators, and all money raised supports the Hank Snow Society and the Hank Snow Music Center in Liverpool. Bring your own lunch and blanket; admission is $8 for the weekend, and camping is available.   **LOCATION:** Queen's County Fairgrounds, on Route 8 (Kejimkujik Scenic Drive) near Caledonia, about 30 miles northwest of Liverpool **TICKETS/INFO:** 902-354-4675 **ACCOMMODATIONS/TOURIST INFO:** 902-354-5421, 902-354-5741

DOWN EAST OLD TIME FIDDLING CONTEST

LOWER SACKVILLE ✱ FOURTH WEEKEND IN AUGUST, FRIDAY NIGHT AND SATURDAY

Awe-inspiring fiddle licks are a dime a dozen as the best Scottish fiddlers in the Maritimes square off in several classes of solo competition. But the real fun begins when the contest is over each night. That's when the hair's let down, the chairs are thrown back, and fiddlers, accompanists, and dancers proceed to "tamaracker down" with a marathon of reels, jigs, waltzes, and step dances. All the contestants typically play for the dances, and with a little cajoling judges (usually former Maritime fiddle champions) and headliners (like Prince Edward Island's Richard Wood) can be convinced to add their fuel to the fire. Entry cost is $10 Saturday and $8 Friday.   **LOCATION:** Sackville and

District Community Arena, First Lake Drive, Lower Sackville (a 10- to 15-minute drive northwest of Halifax, via Highway 2/Bicentennial Drive to the Lower Sackville Turnoff). **TICKETS/INFO:** 902-869-4141 **ACCOMMODATIONS/TOURIST INFO:** 800-565-0000, 902-425-5781

STONE MOUNTAIN MUSIC FESTIVAL
ST. PETER'S ✷ FIRST WEEKEND IN SEPTEMBER, SATURDAY AND SUNDAY

With the goal of showcasing and preserving Cape Breton's rich musical traditions (and helping out the St. Peters Fire Department), Frank and Dolena Sutherland began this festival in 1993. Some 30 acts belt out an astounding range of styles, including Celtic fiddling and ballads, Mi'kmaq (Micmac) Indian songs, Acadian and Gaelic singing, bagpipe tunes, bluegrass, and even some rock. The stage is set on a stunning hill overlooking Lynch's River (near Bras d'Or Lake), and a few hundred festivalgoers share the 145 acres of land featuring a beer garden, horse rides for kids, a camping area, an oyster booth, and plenty of open and wooded space. Daily admission is a real bargain at $5 per person.   **LOCATION:** Three km from St. Peter's on the Sutherland property at Lynch's River, one-half hour east of Port Hawksbury on Highway 4 **TICKETS/INFO:** 865-1715, 535-2586 **ACCOMMODATIONS/TOURIST INFO:** 902-864-2700, 902-425-5781

HALIFAX POP EXPLOSION
HALIFAX ✷ SECOND WEEK IN OCTOBER, WEDNESDAY–SUNDAY

The Maritimes' potent alternative rock scene takes center stage at this showcase for indie bands and labels. In contrast to most other North American music showcases, the focus is on bands and fans rather than the industry (in other words, there are no boring panel discussions with A&R hustlers and posers). About 70 bands (two-thirds from the Maritime Provinces, the rest from elsewhere in Canada and the United States) play to capacity crowds in two clubs and a cinema. Alternative rock is the norm, but spatterings of hip-hop and acoustic music can be heard, all for about $35 for a weekend pass. If you've been to other showcase/conference events, you'll revel in the close-knit, approachable scene. There's also an Indie Label Symposium and Record Fair. **LOCATION:** Halifax **TICKETS/INFO:** 902-425-4005; World Wide Web: http://www.ips.ca/popx/ **ACCOMMODATIONS/TOURIST INFO:** 800-565-0000, 902-425-5781

CANADIAN MUSIC FESTIVAL
TORONTO ✸ ONE WEEK IN EARLY MARCH, MONDAY–SUNDAY

Part convention and part music industry schmooze-fest, the Canadian Music Festival's most interesting feature is an artist showcase presenting a whopping 450 acts over seven days. This is a great chance to hear hungry new bands playing all kinds of music—jazz, classical, rock, reggae, bluegrass, folk, country, blues—at some 20 or 30 gigs a day. The price is certainly right—$30 buys a wristband that allows entry to 35 Toronto venues—and consequently more than 100,000 people attend. The festival is timed to coincide with the Canadian Music Conference, the Music and Multimedia Show, and Canadian Music Week. **LOCATION:** Clubs, bars, and concert halls throughout the Toronto area **TICKETS/INFO:** 416-695-9236; e-mail: cmw@cmw.com **ACCOMMODATIONS/TOURIST INFO:** 416-203-2500, 800-668-2746

HORSESHOE VALLEY FOLK FESTIVAL
HORSESHOE VALLEY RESORT (BARRIE) ✸ THIRD WEEKEND IN APRIL, FRIDAY–SUNDAY

At Ontario's only indoor festival of roots music, guests mingle, eat, and cohabit with musicians in an idyllic resort. By day, three workshop areas feature topics such as musicianship, singing, storytelling, and children's entertainment, and by night the main stage features four acts playing one-hour sets of North American folk, Celtic, and acoustic music from around the world. Musicians and guests alike make creative use of the resort's facilities, playing squash, taking walks, jamming everywhere, and exploring the acoustically fine indoor swimming pool. During the "a capoola" workshop, about 60 people climb into the pool and hot tub to enjoy the sound of their own voices, singing sea chanteys (also known as "shanties"), gospel tunes, and all things choral. Tickets for the weekend of music, food, and accommodations are Can$199 or U.S.$149. **LOCATION:** Horseshoe Valley Resort is on the western shore of Lake Simcoe. From Toronto take Highway 400 north, past Barrie, to exit 117, and go east on Horseshoe Valley Road for 6 km. **TICKETS/INFO:** 905-430-2529 **ACCOMMODATIONS/TOURIST INFO:** 800-461-5627, 800-668-2746

$\mathcal{G}$UELPH SPRING FESTIVAL

GUELPH ✱ THREE WEEKS BEGINNING THE LAST THURSDAY IN MAY

The old graystones, churches, and cathedrals of Guelph provide the fine acoustics for one of Canada's most far-reaching and interesting classical music festivals. Established in 1968, the festival combines the best of Canadian music with sublime sounds from around the world. Nearly 50 events include chamber, choral, and symphonic works (often premiering Canadian compositions). You'll also find opera, dance, music competitions, and art exhibits.   **LOCATION:** Various venues in Guelph, about 70 km west of Toronto. From Toronto go west on Highway 401 and north on Highway 6. **TICKETS/INFO:** 519-827-7570 **ACCOMMODATIONS/TOURIST INFO:** 519-837-1335, 800-668-2746

$\mathcal{N}$ORTH BY NORTHEAST

TORONTO ✱ THIRD WEEKEND IN JUNE, THURSDAY–SATURDAY

Organized by the producers of South by Southwest (in Austin, Texas), North by Northeast features panels, workshops, and showcases for Canadian up-and-comers in many musical genres, including reggae, alternative, rock, rap, and country. Although much of the festival is industry-oriented, music lovers will be interested in the wide variety of showcases by unsigned bands and some bigger names.   **LOCATION:** Toronto Hilton Hotel (conference) and various venues in downtown Toronto (festival) **TICKETS/INFO:** 416-469-0986, 512-467-7979; e-mail: 72662.2465@compuserve.com **ACCOMMODATIONS/TOURIST INFO:** 416-203-3811, 800-363-1990

$\mathbf{d}$U MAURIER DOWNTOWN JAZZ FESTIVAL

TORONTO ✱ LAST WEEK IN JUNE THROUGH THE FIRST DAY IN JULY

Critics once doubted that safe, clean Toronto could ever muster the pizazz to present a truly world-class jazz event, but nowadays anyone who visits this festival is bound to walk away a believer. Started in the mid-eighties, the Downtown Jazz Festival now draws nearly 700,000 people who participate in a jazz orgy that is at times sophisticated, at times boisterous, at times astounding.

Toronto's fest brings more than 1,500 jazz masters from some 20 countries around the world to play in city squares, concert halls, theaters, clubs, hotels, and the streets of Toronto during the festival's ten days. Styles range from traditional to fusion, and often move beyond jazz to include spatterings of blues, gospel, African, Latin, and other worldly sounds. Now a decade old, this smooth-running fest has the clout (and the savvy) to pull in some of the most exciting players in jazz: recent years have featured everyone from avant-garde saxophone wunderkind James Carter and bassist extraordinaire Charlie Haden to veterans Oscar Peterson, Ella Fitzgerald, and Dizzy Gillespie.

More than 50 venues stretch the action out from downtown Toronto to the Entertainment District, Harbourfront, and Yorkville. Daily concerts at several outdoor stages have turned Downtown Jazz into a community festival, with free performances by big names that command high ticket prices at other festivals (including Montréal's). Several auditoriums feature ticketed concerts, and some 35 clubs and pubs keep the music going in the evening.

The festival even finds a way to circumvent Ontario's conservative 1 A.M. last call (which many visitors consider Toronto's major disadvantage). An after-hours program called Judy Jazz is set up in the Holiday Inn on King, with extremely popular jam sessions lasting until 4 A.M. Recent after-hours sessions have featured the likes of trumpet great Roy Hargrove and pianist Joey Calderazzo.   **LOCATION:** More than 50 venues in Toronto **TICKETS/INFO:** 416-872-1111, 416-363-5200 **ACCOMMODATIONS/ TOURIST INFO:** 416-203-2500, 800-668-2746

ℰARTHSONG

HAMILTON ✱ CANADA DAY HOLIDAY WEEKEND (CANADA DAY IS JULY 1)

Inaugurated in the late 1980s, Earthsong has grown to become *the* Canadian stop for national folkloric groups on tour. Authentic native performers present high-caliber music and dance from the far-flung cultures of Europe, South America, Africa, and Asia. A minimum of 75 countries are represented in Princes Point Park in the middle of urban Hamilton, and international food and handicrafts round out the show.   **LOCATION:** Princes Point Park, in Cootes Paradise in Hamilton, near the Royal Botanical Gardens, at the intersection of Plains Road and Highway 6 **TICKETS/INFO:** 905-525-6644 **AC-COMMODATIONS/TOURIST INFO:** 905-546-2614, 800-668-2746

𝒩ORTHERN LIGHTS FESTIVAL BOREAL

SUDBURY ✱ SECOND WEEK IN JULY, THURSDAY–SUNDAY

With music, visual arts, and storytelling, the Northern Lights Festival Boreal puts a unique northern Ontario twist on Canada's oldest bilingual, multicultural outdoor music festival. At a downtown lakefront park, five stages—including a 2,500-seat amphitheater—feature jazz, worldbeat, bluegrass, country, pop, acoustic, Celtic, and more. Much of the music and many of the artists are of French heritage, and arts and crafts arrive from around the world. Workshop stages, family areas, and weekend Blues Cruises on the lake round out the festival action, and each evening many of the 35 acts can be heard at local bars (no extra cost if you have a weekend pass).   **LOCATION:** Bell Park in Sudbury, 340 km north of Toronto, at the junction of Highways 80 and 17 **TICKETS/INFO:** 705-674-5512 **ACCOMMODATIONS/TOURIST INFO:** 705-522-0104, 800-668-2746

ℰLORA FESTIVAL

ELORA ✱ MID-JULY THROUGH FIRST WEEK IN AUGUST (FOUR WEEKENDS)

Four weekends of diverse and imaginative vocal music bring hundreds of performers and thousands of listeners to Elora each summer. In venues ranging from churches to an acoustically phenomenal quarry, the festival presents everything from choral tributes to Brahms and Purcell, to Inuit folksingers and throat-singers, to cabaret, opera, and gospel. A simultaneous fringe festival enlivens the streets of Elora with music, theater, juggling, and more.   **LOCATION:** Several venues in Elora, 25 km northeast of Guelph on Highway 7 (80 km west of Toronto) **TICKETS/INFO:** 519-846-0331 **ACCOMMO-DATIONS/TOURIST INFO:** 519-846-9841, 800-668-2746

𝒪TTAWA INTERNATIONAL JAZZ FESTIVAL

OTTAWA ✱ TEN DAYS IN MID- OR LATE JULY

Ottawa's jazz festival focuses on specialty concerts, mixing grass-roots local talent with artists of international fame. Headliners (who've recently included Oliver Jones,

Woody Herman, and Vanessa Ruben) play at nightly Concerts Under the Stars, while big bands and blues artists present Weekend Swing and Blues concerts. Other interesting programs include Pianissimo Plus, With an Edge (avant-garde jazz at the National Art Centre), and Voices in the Night (vocal jazz). Jam sessions get going late at night, and audience members can typically meet jazz stars in an intimate setting. Ticket prices vary. **LOCATION:** Confederation Park and other locations in downtown Ottawa **TICKETS/ INFO:** 613-594-3580 **ACCOMMODATIONS/TOURIST INFO:** 613-237-5150, 800- 668-2746

ℬEACHES INTERNATIONAL JAZZ FESTIVAL
TORONTO ✴ THIRD WEEK IN JULY, WEDNESDAY–SUNDAY

More than 100 street bands and headliners bring a carnival atmosphere to Toronto's Queen Street and Qew Gardens. Without shelling out a penny, you can hear jazz, blues, Latin, Caribbean, swing, and big band music from noon until 11 P.M. each day. As 100,000 or more musicians, dancers, street vendors, and revelers romp through Queen Street East, national and international acts light up the main stage at Qew Gardens. **LOCATION:** Street festival: Queen Street East on the one-mile stretch between Woodbine and Victoria Park. Main stage: Qew Gardens. **TICKETS/INFO:** 416-698- 2152 **ACCOMMODATIONS/TOURIST INFO:** 416-203-2500, 800-668-2746

ℱESTIVAL OF THE SOUND
PARRY SOUND ✴ THIRD FRIDAY IN JULY THROUGH SECOND SUNDAY IN AUGUST

This comprehensive choral and chamber music festival brings world-class musicians to Georgian Bay for two weeks of concerts, musical cruises, and family musical events. The festival is known mainly for its focus on the mainstream works, but each year brings at least a couple of daring forays into ground-breaking territory. Recent musical guests have included the World Youth Choir, the World Youth Orchestra, and James MacMillan, and venues include a church, boats, and a high school gymnasium converted to a concert hall. Tickets range from $15 to $30.   **LOCATION:** Parry Sound, about 240 km north of Toronto on Highway 69 (on the east side of Georgian Bay) **TICKETS/INFO:** 705-746-2410 **ACCOMMODATIONS/TOURIST INFO:** 705-746-4213, 800-461-4261, 800-668-2746

ℋOME COUNTY FOLK FESTIVAL
LONDON ✴ THIRD WEEKEND IN JULY, FRIDAY–SUNDAY

The Home County Folk Festival draws some 35,000 people from Ontario's heartland for three days of free music, traditional dance, and arts and crafts. In a downtown park, five stages feature acoustic music of all types, with mostly Canadian content. About a third of the performers are nationally known; the remainder are prominent local and Ontario musicians.   **LOCATION:** Victoria Park in downtown London, Ontario **TICKETS/INFO:** 519-433-7105 **ACCOMMODATIONS/TOURIST INFO:** 519-661-5000, 800-668-2746

☘LL FOLKS FESTIVAL

KINGSTON ✷ THIRD WEEKEND IN JULY, SATURDAY AND SUNDAY

An overwhelmingly friendly atmosphere keeps performers and audiences coming back to this workshop-oriented acoustic festival. Valdy, Steven Ferring, Lynn Miles, and other big names in Canadian folk have been recent guests on the main stage, while secondary stages spotlight children's activities, local singer-songwriters, and poets. A crafts area features work sold by the artisans themselves (to discourage exploitation of third-world artisans, organizers say), and camping is nearby. Best of all, admission is free.   **LOCATION:** City Park, on King Street, near Queen's University in Kingston, 150 km south of Ottawa at the northeastern tip of Lake Ontario **TICKETS/INFO:** 613-548-6525; e-mail: dmon@hidwater.com; World Wide Web: http://www.ipac.net/HW/affhome.html **ACCOMMODATIONS/TOURIST INFO:** 800-567-3278, 613-548-4415, 800-668-2746

ℭARIBANA FESTIVAL OF CARIBBEAN MUSIC, ART AND CULTURE

TORONTO ✷ LAST WEEK IN JULY AND FIRST WEEK IN AUGUST

What do Trinidad and Tobago have to do with Toronto? Carnival! Snaking in a giddy conga line through the city, Caribana creates a joyful, righteous roar. Calypso and soca bands on flatbed trucks stir up a frenzy as they move along, and some 40 mas (masquerade) bands with 10,000 members writhe away in an outrageous orgy of sound and color. About a million people show up—including more than 300,000 from south of the border—to eat, drink, and dance along.

Based on Carnival in the West Indies, Caribana is helping Toronto transform itself from a stiff Anglo outpost to a liberated, cosmopolitan metropolis. The festival started in 1967, when the West Indian community contributed the event to Canada's centennial celebration. The celebration was so popular that it continued and has grown into a weeklong folk gathering of music, art, and dance.

Mas bands spend months preparing for Caribana, constructing elaborate floats and costumes and perfecting musical routines in pursuit of prizes and recognition. As the festival begins, flatbed trucks are pulled into the streets, hauling bands and DJs and pumping out massive soca beats and songs with hedonistic, sexually suggestive themes. A huge parade (the largest in Canada) is the climax, joyfully tying up the city on the festival's final Saturday. Other embellishments include three nights of ferry cruises, a Friday-night ball, the Caribana Queen's Coronation, handicrafts, and distinctive food. But mostly it's just dancing in the streets!   **LOCATION:** Olympic Island, Toronto **TICKETS/INFO:** 416-925-1107, 416-925-5435 **ACCOMMODATIONS/TOURIST INFO:** 800-363-1990, 416-925-5435, 800-668-2746

ℳILL RACE FESTIVAL OF TRADITIONAL FOLK MUSIC

CAMBRIDGE ✷ LAST SATURDAY IN JULY OR FIRST SATURDAY IN AUGUST

Occupying two separate areas in historic Cambridge, this British-style festival focuses on traditional folk music of the Americas and the British Isles. A riverside main stage, a children's area, and various workshop stages are set up along the Grand River and among downtown's 19th-century architecture. Demonstrations in clogging and Morris dancing round out this free festival.   **LOCATION:** Mill Race Park, Water Street (Highway 24), and nearby locations in Cambridge, 80 km west of Toronto **TICKETS/ INFO:** 519-622-0146 **ACCOMMODATIONS/TOURIST INFO:** 519-653-1424, 800-668-2746

HILLSIDE FESTIVAL
GUELPH ✷ LAST WEEKEND IN JULY, FRIDAY–SUNDAY

This three-day celebration of folk music, dance, crafts, and theater makes its island home at the Guelph Lake Conservation Area. The festival has drawn Sarah Mclachlan and other big names, but is more focused on promoting local talent on five stages around the island. About 400 volunteers make the Hillside Festival a community-focused, family-oriented event with a diverse selection of music. There's also plenty of all-natural foods, holistic workshops, community organizers, environmental groups, and the like. **LOCATION:** Guelph Lake Conservation Area, 2 km east of Guelph via Township Road 6. Guelph is 70 km west of Toronto. **TICKETS/INFO:** 519-763-6396 **ACCOMMODA-TIONS/TOURIST INFO:** 519-837-1335, 800-668-2746

MARIPOSA FOLK FESTIVAL
TORONTO ✷ A WEEKEND IN LATE JULY OR EARLY AUGUST, THURSDAY–SUNDAY

Since 1961, venerable Mariposa has livened up the Toronto summer with an outstanding range of cutting-edge folk and traditional music from around the world. Mariposa jump-started the careers of some of today's biggest names in folk music, and each year the festival shifts its musical focus to a different part of the world, such as Latin America, West Africa, or India and Pakistan.

Financial and organizational problems have plagued Mariposa in its middle age, and each summer Toronto-area folkies speculate about whether this gem will manage to make it out of the box. Organizers say it will, but caution that big changes are in store, so stay tuned for the scoop on new dates and new locations.   **LOCATION:** A changing venue in downtown Toronto **TICKETS/INFO:** 416-924-4839 **ACCOMMODATIONS/ TOURIST INFO:** 416-203-2500, 800-668-2746

EARTH, AIR, FIRE AND WATER: CELTIC ROOTS FESTIVAL
GODERICH ✷ SECOND WEEKEND IN AUGUST, FRIDAY–SUNDAY

The Earth, Air, Fire and Water Festival has all the elements of a successful Celtic bash. Held in a wooded park with a spectacular view of Lake Huron, the festival brings in performers from Ireland, Scotland, Wales, and other Celtic bastions of Europe who mix with some 30 acts from the United States and Canada. Organizers shy away from beer-and-ballads clichés, and in recent years have featured the likes of Steafan Hannigan from Ireland, Dougie MacLean from Scotland, and Brian Peters from England. You're likely to see as many instrumentalists as vocalists on the main stage, which is within walking distance of four workshop and dance areas, authentic-crafts booths, and children's activities. The Celtic College, held in conjunction with the festival, offers morning

courses in traditional Celtic music (see Music Workshops chapter, page 497).
LOCATION: Goderich, on the eastern shore of Lake Huron, about 90 km north of
London, Ontario **TICKETS/INFO:** 519-524-8221 **ACCOMMODATIONS/TOURIST
INFO:** 519-524-6600, 800-668-2746

$\mathcal{F}$ESTIVAL OF FRIENDS
HAMILTON ✴ SECOND WEEKEND IN AUGUST, FRIDAY–SUNDAY

This major Canadian showcase is a coast-to-coast sampler of some of Canada's best
traditional and recording artists, plugged and unplugged. On seven stages, some 35 acts
project a soup-to-nuts mélange of everything from country and folk to jazz, classical,
blues, rock—everything but heavy metal. Over three days, about 200,000 people cavort
around the main stage, children's activity areas, craft booths, and food concessions.
LOCATION: Gage Park, at Main Street and Gage Avenue South in Hamilton **TICKETS/
INFO:** 905-525-6644 **ACCOMMODATIONS/TOURIST INFO:** 905-546-4222, 800-
668-2746

$\mathcal{F}$OLKFEST
UPPER CANADA VILLAGE ✴ SECOND SATURDAY IN AUGUST

This day-long celebration of Canada's acoustic musical heritage complements the
19th-century trades and crafts that are a regular feature at this "living history site."
Throughout the day and evening, about 10 top-caliber acts present Celtic and other folk
music, with recent headliners including the Irish Descendants, Kate and Anna McGar-
rigle, and Sylvia Tyson. The village itself, on the banks of the St. Lawrence River,
represents Canada's West in the pre-confederation 1860s, and staff performers play
period music throughout the day. A daytime pass is about $10; a nighttime pass is $20.
LOCATION: Upper Canada Village is just off Highway 401 east of Morrisburg, on the St.
Lawrence River. From Ottawa take Bank Street to Highway 31 and go 70 km to
Morrisburg; then head east on Highway 2. **TICKETS/INFO:** 613-543-3704 **ACCOM-
MODATIONS/TOURIST INFO:** 613-543-3704, 800-668-2746

$\mathcal{S}$UMMERFOLK MUSIC AND CRAFTS FESTIVAL
OWEN SOUND ✴ THIRD WEEKEND IN AUGUST, FRIDAY–SUNDAY

For more than 20 years, the shores of Georgian Bay have reveled in the sounds of
Canada's finest traditional and contemporary folk performers. Set in a beautiful, natural
amphitheater, Summerfolk's six performance and workshop stages feature some 35 acts
ranging from folk to blues, gospel, world music, and children's music. The majority of
performers are Canadian, although you'll also find a handful of unique acts from south of
the border. About 12,000 people (including many families) show up, paying about $65
for a weekend pass. A beer tent (with a live TV feed from the stage) and rough camping
are on-site. The evening concerts are downright celestial.   **LOCATION:** Kelso Beach
Park on the Eddie Sargent Parkway in Owen Sound, 160 km northwest of Toronto on
the south end of Georgian Bay **TICKETS/INFO:** 519-371-2995 **ACCOMMODATIONS/
TOURIST INFO:** 519-371-2071, 800-265-3127, 800-668-2746

*Summerfolk sere-
nades Georgian
Bay with tradi-
tional and con-
temporary folk.*

Courtesy of Georgian Bay Folk

Society

SONGS OF SAIL MARINE HERITAGE FOLK FESTIVAL
PENETANGUISHENE ✶ FOURTH WEEKEND IN AUGUST, FRIDAY–SUNDAY

If you think marine music means some water-logged folkie dredging up "Wreck of the Edmond Fitzgerald," set sail for this surprisingly wide-ranging tribute to the songs of the sea. The music—presented by about 15 acts that have included Louis Killen, David Parry, and Friends of Fiddler's Green—spans the horizons between 19th-century traditional sailing songs and modern additions to the genre. In between, you'll experience plenty of sea chantey (shanty) singing, fisheries protest songs, and musical-historical accounts of dashed hopes and deepwater disasters.

The setting is Penetanguishene, which means, fittingly, "land of the rolling sands." The town is perched on the shore of Lake Huron's giant Georgian Bay, and its Centennial Museum is the center of three days of concerts, workshops, dancing, storytelling, and marine heritage displays. During the festival, about 1,500 people attend interesting performance sites that include an outdoor stage, local restaurants, and a Great Hall for a capella performances. And even though sailing ships were traditionally male territory, Songs of Sail is no testosterone fest—a surprising number of women turn out to enjoy

Folk's fertile valley: Murray McLauchlan performs at the 1995 CKCU Ottawa Folk Festival. Joyce MacPhee/CKCU Ottawa Folk Festival

the music and festivities. Be sure to phone ahead for tickets to the Friday evening Concert Cruise.   **LOCATION:** The Centennial Museum in Penetanguishene on Georgian Bay. From Toronto take Highway 400 north to Highway 93 (north), which ends at the Penetanguishene wharf. **TICKETS/INFO:** 705-361-3084 **ACCOMMODATIONS/ TOURIST INFO:** 705-549-2232, 800-668-2746

ℭKCU OTTAWA FOLK FESTIVAL
OTTAWA ✴ LAST WEEKEND IN AUGUST, FRIDAY–SUNDAY

One of Canada's richest veins of folk talent runs through the Ottawa Valley, producing stars like Bruce Cockburn and fueling an enthusiasm that kept one of the largest folk festivals in North America running strong through the seventies. This festival, started in 1994, is an attempt to revive that folkie spirit by providing a venue for developing local folk artists—with gleeful concessions to today's worldbeat sensibilities.

Inventive workshops and dance stages (step dancing, contra dancing, and fiddles are a legacy of the area's French, Irish, and Scottish forebears) keep the afternoon hopping, and at night dozens of performers take the main stage. The riverside setting is quite idyllic, and Saturday night always brings a participatory jam/sing-along. Admission runs $11 for a day pass or $16 for the weekend.   **LOCATION:** Britannia Park, at Carling and Pinecrest Streets in Ottawa **TICKETS/INFO:** 613-788-2600, ext. 2638 **ACCOMMODATIONS/TOURIST INFO:** 613-239-5000, 800-668-2746

EAGLEWOOD EARTH FESTIVAL
PEFFERLAW ❋ LAST WEEKEND IN AUGUST, FRIDAY–SUNDAY

This small, intimate folk festival focuses on traditional music and contemporary songwriting and is unique in its consideration for disabled individuals, who make up about 20 percent of the audience. Held at a country resort for physically challenged people, the festival has no formal backstage area, so artists rub shoulders and share the experience with the audience of about 300 per day.

The all-Canadian cast of about 25 musicians comes from across the country, and each year traditions in bluegrass, blues, or Celtic music are highlighted on two sound stages. In addition, the festival's organizers are adept at bringing in some interesting singer-songwriter talents whose lyric-driven material isn't readily available in the mainstream music marketplace.

Since the festival began in the late 1980s, much of the thrust has been on workshops, and just about every invited performer spends some time working with the audience at workshop sites or, even more informally, at campsites (performers also camp). The four workshop areas are active almost constantly, usually with banjo or guitar players who focus on traditions such as bluegrass, blues, or Celtic songs. Plus, a children's area intersperses craft activities with musical performances.

Evening concerts on a single stage run from 6 to 11 P.M. (9 P.M. on Sunday), and there's always plenty of campfire singing after the concerts. Throughout the cedar forests and lagoons of the resort, you'll find people with wheelchairs and scooters enjoying the complete accessibility. Disabled camping and cottage facilities, rough camping, horseback riding, swimming, canoes, and paddle boats are available.

Food ranges from hot dogs and hamburgers to vegetarian fare, and the cappuccino stand is always a big hit. Alcohol isn't sold on the premises, but BYO is no problem. Tickets are about $35 for the weekend or $5 to $15 per night.   **LOCATION:** Eaglewood Resort in Pefferlaw, one hour north of Toronto and just east of Sutton. From Toronto take Highway 48 (Markham Road) north to York Road 21, then to Concession 6. **TICKETS/INFO:** 416-481-5506 **ACCOMMODATIONS/TOURIST INFO:** 416-481-5506, 416-203-2500, 800-668-2746

$\mathscr{S}$UMMERSIDE HIGHLAND GATHERING
SUMMERSIDE ✸ THIRD WEEKEND IN JUNE

Drawn perhaps by the island's lush, green hills, immigrants from Ireland and Scotland settled on Prince Edward Island in droves. Today, the island is the most Celtic location in North America, a place where old traditions of music and sport remain in the hearts and souls of nearly everyone.

These traditions burst through to the surface during Summerside's Highland Gathering, the most authentic celebration of Celtic culture outside the British Isles and Brittany. The gathering features dozens of athletic events and demonstrations, but about 75 percent of its emphasis is on music and dancing. Everywhere, sounds of fiddles, harps, and traditional singing fill the air, and step dancers and Highland dancers whirl and stomp.

Bagpipes, which remained popular in Scotland long after they had fallen out of favor in the rest of the world, are in abundance at the Highland Gathering. Here, there are no jokes about men in skirts, as hundreds of men kilted in ancient tartans create treasured resonant sounds on their unwieldy instruments. Contests feature pipe bands, solo pipers, and drummers from around Canada, while concerts bring in musicians from all over the world.

Inside the beer tent, contemporary Celtic bands knock out spirited originals, while the dance stages are filled with jiggers, reelers, and drunken free-stylers. Look for uncommon dances like the Seann Triubhas (Gaelic for "Old Trousers"), the Sailor's Hornpipe, and the elegant Flora MacDonald's Fancy.

The traditional heavyweight athletic competition is a crowd pleaser, with events like the 56-pound weight toss and hammer and caber tosses—part of Highland games since the 12th century. The College of Piping and Celtic Performing Arts of Canada offers classes in bagpiping, drumming, Highland dancing, step dancing, fiddling, whistle, and guitar to adults and children at all levels of experience (see "Music Workshops" chapter). During the summer, the college holds a Highland Summer Concert Series Thursday nights, and nearby Woodleigh offers a summer Sunday Concert Series featuring such well-known Maritime performers as John Allan Cameron, Urban Carmichael, and George Brothers.   **LOCATION:** Summerside, about an hour west of Charlottetown via Highway 225 **TICKETS/INFO:** 902-436-5377 **ACCOMMODATIONS/TOURIST INFO:** 800-463-4734, 902-368-5540

PEI BLUEGRASS AND OLD TIME MUSIC FESTIVAL
FAIRVIEW ✷ FIRST OR SECOND WEEKEND IN JULY, FRIDAY–SUNDAY

The Maritime region has cultivated a unique strain of bluegrass, rooted in traditional American bluegrass but influenced by the Acadian, Irish, and Scottish music of the region's forebears. Bands from throughout the Maritimes (and often one or two from the northeastern United States) create a down-home stir at this festival, which also includes clog dancing.   **LOCATION:** Dunollie Travel Park in Fairview, off Route 19, just south of Charlottetown **TICKETS/INFO:** 902-675-3061 **ACCOMMODATIONS/TOURIST INFO:** 800-463-4734, 902-368-5540

ROLLO BAY FIDDLE FESTIVAL
ROLLO BAY ✷ THIRD WEEKEND IN JULY, SATURDAY AND SUNDAY

Organized by master fiddler Peter Chaisson and his family, this 20-year tradition brings in some of the best fiddlers from Prince Edward Island, Cape Breton, New England, and points farther afoot. Over two days, some 6,000 people experience a number of different fiddle styles in dozens of concerts and jam sessions. Best of all, some of the proceeds are spent on fiddle lessons, encouraging a new generation to safeguard the region's precious musical traditions.   **LOCATION:** The Village of Rollo Bay, about 10 km southwest of Souris on Route 2, in the northeast corner of the island **TICKETS/INFO:** 902-687-2584 **ACCOMMODATIONS/TOURIST INFO:** 800-463-4734, 902-368-5540

RENDEZ-VOUS RUSTICO
SOUTH RUSTICO ✷ FINAL WEEKEND IN JULY

Prince Edward Island's Acadian roots shoot to the surface during this shoreside festival of music and dance. Featuring local French-speaking musicians as well as performers from Québec and as far away as Louisiana, the three-day affair is rounded out by cultural workshops, historical conferences, sports, children's games and great Acadian food. If you arrive early, be sure to catch the Rustico Shindigs, a review of Maritime song and dance held Mondays, Tuesdays, and Wednesdays during the summer.   **LOCATION:** The grounds of St. Augustine's Parish and the Farmers' Bank of Rustico, near the shore on Route 243, just off Route 6 **TICKETS/INFO:** 902-963-3252 **ACCOMMODATIONS/TOURIST INFO:** 800-463-4734, 902-368-5540

ATLANTIC FIDDLERS JAMBOREE
MONT-CARMEL ✷ FIRST WEEKEND IN AUGUST

Dozens of fiddlers—mostly Acadian but some Celtic—descend on Le Village from all over Atlantic Canada for a weekend of jamming and concerts. Since the festival is more of a family get-together than a commercial venture, it provides a great opportunity to get a real taste of old-time Acadian music and inhibition-free dancing. About 500 dancing spectators join fiddlers and guitar or piano accompanists from all over Prince Edward Island, New Brunswick, and Nova Scotia.   **LOCATION:** Le Village in Mont-Carmel, 24 km west of Summerside on Route 11 **TICKETS/INFO:** 800-567-3228 **ACCOMMODATIONS/TOURIST INFO:** 800-463-4734, 902-368-5540

Sawing the roof off: Master fiddlers like Ashley MacIsaac bring their jigs and reels to the Rollo Bay Fiddle Festival. (See entry, page 457.) Courtesy of John Sylvester, Tourism PEI

Tyne Valley Oyster Festival: Prince Edward Island's musicians honor Malpeque Bay's world-famous shellfish. Courtesy of Lionel Stevenson, Tourism PEI

TYNE VALLEY OYSTER FESTIVAL

TYNE VALLEY ✸ FIRST WEEKEND IN AUGUST, FRIDAY–SUNDAY

Fiddlers and step dancers from all over Prince Edward Island fill Tyne Valley with music and movement in honor of Malpeque Bay's world-famous oysters. The festival's main event, the Island Fiddling and Step-Dancing Championships, brings in the very best from the outskirts of Prince Edward Island, and talent contests ranging from singing to oyster-shucking round out the action.   **LOCATION:** Tyne Valley Rink and Community Center, about 35 km northwest of Summerside on Route 12 **TICKETS/INFO:** 902-854-2190 **ACCOMMODATIONS/TOURIST INFO:** 800-463-4734, 902-368-5540

FIDDLERS & FOLLOWERS WEEKEND

CAVENDISH ✸ SECOND WEEKEND IN AUGUST, FRIDAY NIGHT THROUGH MONDAY MORNING

Maritime fiddle music is alive and well at this musical marathon featuring scores of Atlantic fiddlers, piano and guitar accompanists, step dancers, lobster parties, barbecues, and old-fashioned picnics. The festival typically draws several Maritime fiddle champions and busloads of music lovers to the amusement-park setting. The festival winds down with a beans-and-fishcakes breakfast Monday morning.   **LOCATION:** Rainbow Valley Amusement Park, on Route 6 in Cavendish, next to the Green Gables House **TICKETS/INFO:** 902-963-2221 **ACCOMMODATIONS/TOURIST INFO:** 800-463-4734, 902-368-5540

ᖴESTIVAL DE MUSIQUE VIENNOISE DES LAURENTIDES
(LAURENTIDES FESTIVAL OF VIENNESE MUSIC)
LAURENTIDES REGION ✱ THROUGHOUT FEBRUARY AND MARCH

Among the hills and frozen lakes of the Laurentides region, dozens of small churches fill with the sounds of the classical music of Vienna. This unique festival brings in scores of specialists in Viennese music who present two months of concerts in the mellow, acoustically warm confines of village churches. Tickets range from $12 to $50, and a Viennese ball lends an air of old-world finery. **LOCATION:** Churches throughout the Laurentides region, just northwest of Montréal. For schedules and locations, contact organizers. **TICKETS/INFO:** 514-435-1611 **ACCOMMODATIONS/TOURIST INFO:** 514-436-8532, 800-363-7777

ᖴESTIVAL DE LA CHANSON DE TADOUSSAC
(TADOUSSAC SONG FESTIVAL)
TADOUSSAC ✱ SECOND WEEKEND IN JUNE, THURSDAY–SUNDAY

Québec singers, songwriters, composers, and musicians gather in this historic town at the confluence of the Saguenay and St. Lawrence Rivers with the goal of preserving and promoting the songs of French-speaking Québec. New singing and songwriting talents are showcased and presented alongside famous performers in a series of concerts on six different stages. About 5,000 spectators sing and dance along, and take advantage of the beautiful area's beach, boating, hiking, and whale-watching opportunities. A "passport" for four days costs about $45. **LOCATION:** Tadoussac is located at the confluence of the Saguenay and St. Lawrence Rivers, about 260 km northeast of Québec City on Highway 138. **TICKETS/INFO:** 418-235-4108, 418-235-4589 **ACCOMMODATIONS/TOURIST INFO:** 418-235-4744, 800-363-7777, 418-589-5319

Songs and songwriters of Québec: Chantal Richer performs at the 1995 Festival de la Chanson de Tadoussac. Courtesy of Festival de la Chanson

$\mathcal{F}$ESTIVAL INTERNATIONAL DE JAZZ DE MONTRÉAL (MONTRÉAL INTERNATIONAL JAZZ FESTIVAL)
MONTRÉAL ✳ ELEVEN DAYS BEGINNING THE FINAL WEEK IN JUNE

What may be the world's biggest jazz blast turns downtown Montréal into an open-air concert hall for 11 days in late June and early July. Streets are blocked off, eight outdoor stages are thrown up, and 1,500 performers from all over the world carpet the city with jazz, blues, Cajun, African, and the superdiverse sounds of the Caribbean.

With its traffic-stopping, street-festival atmosphere and more than 200 free outdoor shows, Montréal's festival has an urban *joie de vivre* that's unrivalled anywhere in the world. The event has become an integral part of the Montréal summer, so completely transforming the city that even Montréalers sometimes feel like tourists in their own town. Best of all, Canada's biggest cultural event has managed to locate all venues in the same area, and a five-minute walk takes you from one end of the site to the other.

Pricey indoor concerts in four venues feature some of the greatest names in international jazz; guests have included Miles Davis, Charlie Haden, Keith Jarrett, Nina Simone, and Ornette Coleman. Yet the heart of the festival is the 60 percent of the concerts that are free—and outdoors. Plenty of big names are featured, and around nearly every corner interesting encounters and musical discoveries materialize, making a stroll around the festival an adventure. Street musicians and performers are everywhere, and a special amusement area is set aside for kids.

Urban joie de vivre: *Montréal's jazz festival offers discoveries on nearly every corner. (See entry, page 461.)* Courtesy of Festival International de Jazz de Montréal

Intimate settings are not what this festival is all about. Many events are all-out musical parties in which thousands of people are packed shoulder to shoulder, and each year one outdoor megaconcert becomes the rallying point on a day when no indoor concerts are scheduled. A huge temporary roof is inflated over the entire block, and nearly 100,000 people show up to hear the likes of UZEB, Pat Metheny, Johnny Clegg, Urban Sax, and Galliano.   **LOCATION:** Downtown Montréal, centering around the Place des Arts **TICKETS/INFO:** 514-871-1881, 514-525-7732 **ACCOMMODATIONS/ TOURIST INFO:** 800-363-7777, 514-844-5400

✪RFORD FESTIVAL

ORFORD ✹ LATE JUNE THROUGH LATE AUGUST

Since 1951, Orford's pristine environment has united some of the world's finest symphonic and chamber musicians in a summertime quest for excellence. More than

Orford Festival: Renowned musicians like cellist Dennis Brott perform in pristine Mont-Orford Provincial Park. Courtesy of Orford Arts Centre

150 performers take turns teaching and filling the Orford Arts Centre theater (an intimate venue seating only 600) with the sounds of Bach, Beethoven, Haydn, Chopin, and their equals. Four concerts each week feature world-renowned orchestras, trios, and quartets, as well as students in residence. The festival also has a visual arts segment on the Arts Centre grounds. Admission costs range from free to $21.   **LOCATION:** Mont-Orford Provincial Park, 3165 du Parc Road in Orford. From Montréal take Highway 10 east about 125 km, then go north on Highway 141N (at the turnoff for Magog). **TICKETS/INFO:** 819-843-3981 **ACCOMMODATIONS/TOURIST INFO:** 819-843-7575, 800-363-7777

ℱESTIVAL D'ÉTÉ INTERNATIONAL DE QUÉBEC (QUÉBEC CITY INTERNATIONAL SUMMER FESTIVAL)
QUÉBEC CITY ✴ ELEVEN DAYS BEGINNING THE FIRST THURSDAY IN JULY

Like a nonstop world tour, nearly 800 shows transform fortified Old Québec City (a UNESCO World Heritage Site) into a musical performance ground where celebration is the only convention. Three big outdoor stages and 12 other smaller stages (indoor and outdoor) present an astounding range of music and other performing arts, showcasing some 600 artists from more than 20 countries. A $5 badge lets you into all outdoor shows during the festival's duration; fees for indoor shows range from $15 to $30. **LOCATION:** Throughout Old Québec City **TICKETS/INFO:** 418-692-4540 **ACCOM-MODATIONS/TOURIST INFO:** 418-522-3511, 800-363-7777

ℱESTIVAL DE MUSIQUE ANCIENNE DE SILLERY
SILLERY ✴ FIRST THREE WEEKS IN AUGUST, SUNDAY, TUESDAY, AND WEDNESDAY EVENINGS

Early music from the Middle Ages, Renaissance, and baroque periods draws 15,000 fans to performances by 15 ensembles from Canada, France, Britain, and the United States. In addition to concerts on two stages and in a small church, the festival features workshops and a family day. Tickets range from free to $10.   **LOCATION:** Sillery, a suburb just southwest of Québec City **TICKETS/INFO:** 418-688-8074, 418-681-3010 **ACCOMMODATIONS/TOURIST INFO:** 800-363-7777

ℒES FRANCOFOLIES
MONTRÉAL ✴ NINE DAYS BEGINNING THE FIRST FRIDAY IN AUGUST

For nine days in early August, Montréal is the musical and entertainment capital of the French-speaking world. More than 125 shows present performers from Québec, France, Belgium, and Switzerland, as well as from far-flung Francophone outposts in the Caribbean and Africa. Each night the streets are blocked off and the party begins with an incredibly cosmopolitan and lively range of events—much of it musical. Free outdoor shows on five stages start at noon and run until midnight, featuring everything from French a capella, rock, pop, and jazz, to rai (Algerian pop), Latin American, African, and other worldbeat sounds.   **LOCATION:** Place des Arts and Complexe Desjardins, downtown Montréal **TICKETS/INFO:** 514-525-7732, 514-871-1881 **ACCOMMODA-TIONS/TOURIST INFO:** 800-363-7777

Sophisticated summer: Québec City's sprawling Festival d'été international de Québec presents 600 artists from more than 20 countries. Courtesy of The Québec City International Summer Festival Archives

ᴶNNU NIKAMU

RESERVE DE MINGAN (MALIOTENAM) ✷ FIRST WEEKEND IN AUGUST, THURSDAY–SUNDAY

This outstanding event carries on a thousand-year tradition of gatherings in this area with a four-day celebration devoted to the music of Native Americans. Organizers stress that Innu Nikamu is a music festival rather than a powwow and that visitors can expect to hear a variety of musical expression from all over North America, as well as dancing and native-language theater. The goal is to sensitize both the native and non-native public to the richness of the First Nations' musical heritage.

The Montagnais and other Québec tribes are well represented. In addition, Athabascan and Inuit people from northern Canada typically make the scene, and create strong impressions with their fiddling and throat singing. In past years, performers and spectators have come from as far away as Nunavik, and even Ecuador. And although traditional music is emphasized, the lineup often includes young people playing folk or rock. Admission is about $20.   **LOCATION:** Reserve de Mingan, just outside Maliotenam and Sept Îles, off Route 138 **TICKETS/INFO:** 418-927-2985 **ACCOMMO-DATIONS/TOURIST INFO:** 800-363-7777, 418-962-0808

ᴛREMBLANT BLUES FESTIVAL

MONT-TREMBLANT ✷ FIRST WEEKEND IN AUGUST

If the music doesn't get you, the setting will. This two-year-old blues festival is held in a historic town and mountain resort and features a whopping 10 stages (several of which nose 3,000 feet into fresh mountain air). Fine dining, golf, and tennis might take some of the grit out of the music, but they go a long way toward inducing international blues stars to appear. Tickets are between $8 and $40, depending on the package. **LOCATION:** Mont-Tremblant, about 130 km north of Montréal via the Laurentian Autoroute, Route 117, and Route 322 **TICKETS/INFO:** 800-461-8711, 819-681-3000 **ACCOMMODATIONS/TOURIST INFO:** 800-461-8711, 819-681-3000

ᴹUSIQU'EN AOÛT

ST.-ANDRÉ-AVELLIN ✷ SECOND WEEK IN AUGUST, MONDAY–SUNDAY

The spirited home-grown music of the Petite Nation region is showcased at this wide-reaching music festival in St.-André-Avellin and five other nearby villages. Expect to hear all types of music, including the folk/traditional music of Québec, classical, jazz, blues, rock 'n' roll, even country and western. Venues include big tents in St.-André-Avellin (featuring Québecois and nationally known groups), churches (classical music), bars (blues, jazz, rock), and streets (local groups and children's shows). Some of the more than 30 performances are free; others are less than $20. Or you can access everything with a clé en main (key in hand) ticket.   **LOCATION:** Throughout five municipalities in the region called Le Petit Nation, about 120 km west of Montréal. The majority of events take place in St.-André-Avellin, near the junction of Highways 317 and 321, about 10 km north of Highway 148. **TICKETS/INFO:** 819-983-3273 **ACCOM-MODATIONS/TOURIST INFO:** 800-363-7777, 819-778-2222

Accordion crossroads: Box-squeezers from around the world trade licks at the Carrefour Mondial de l'Accordéon. (See entry, page 468.) Courtesy of Gilles Gagné

ᴊFESTI-JAZZ
RIMOUSKI ✴ LABOR DAY WEEKEND, WEDNESDAY–SUNDAY (LABOR DAY IS THE FIRST MONDAY IN SEPTEMBER)

As a sister festival of the huge Vienne Jazz Festival in France, Festi-Jazz typically brings in at least one hot French act, combined with jazz stars from Montréal and Québec City. The town's location—a forested area near the giant mouth of the St. Lawrence River—is a big draw, and each night a headliners' concert is supplemented by gigs in about 10 local bars. Saturday's concert is the only one for which admission is charged, and a Sunday morning brunch rounds out the festivities. **LOCATION:** Rimouski, on the southeast bank of the St. Lawrence River, about 300 km northeast of Québec City along Highway 2 **TICKETS/INFO:** 418-724-7844, 418-798-8311 **ACCOMMODATIONS/TOURIST INFO:** 800-363-7777, 418-867-1272

ᴿROCK SANS FRONTIÈRES (ROCK WITHOUT BORDERS)
MONTRÉAL ✴ LABOR DAY WEEKEND, THURSDAY–SUNDAY

Montréal rocks out for four days, as pop music's international elite are mixed and matched with Québec's up-and-coming. Some 25 bands play at this free outdoor show, which has been drawing crowds of more than 30,000 (over four days) since it began in 1991. Food, beer and wine, and the myriad attractions of downtown Montréal are also available. **LOCATION:** Berri Square, on the corner of Berri and Ste.-Catherine Streets in downtown Montréal (Metro: Berri-UQAM) **TICKETS/INFO:** 514-289-9945; e-mail: pgratton@aei.ca **ACCOMMODATIONS/TOURIST INFO:** 800-363-7777, 514-844-5400

CARREFOUR MONDIAL DE L'ACCORDÉON (WORLD CROSSROADS OF THE ACCORDION)

MONTMAGNY ✸ LABOR DAY WEEKEND, FRIDAY–MONDAY

Amid a flurry of languages and musical styles, accordion players from the four corners of the world have gathered in Montmagny since 1989 to cavort, jam, and swap stories. This exceptional event features folk, jazz, pop, and new styles that are created by the minute as traditional and contemporary accordion players mix and meld on four stages. International concerts (admission $20), workshops, and children's areas are featured, and about 35,000 people turn out to listen to, or partake in, the festivities. **LOCATION:** Several venues in Montmagny, about 60 km northeast of Québec City on the southeast bank of the St. Lawrence River **TICKETS/INFO:** 418-248-7927 **ACCOMMODATIONS/TOURIST INFO:** 418-248-9196, 800-363-7777

CaNaDa WeST

PIANOFEST I AND II

BANFF ✸ SECOND WEEK IN JUNE, THURSDAY AND FRIDAY

As just a small part of the Banff Arts Festival's diverse program, the Pianofests feature Canadian and international pianists performing works from the solo repertoire, including the music of Bach, Liszt, Chopin, and Schumann. Each night's performance begins at 8 P.M., and admission is $10. In addition to the music, there are dance, theater, film, and media arts lectures and performances throughout the summer at the Banff Centre for the Arts.   **LOCATION:** Margaret Greenham Theatre, Banff **TICKETS/INFO:** 800-413-8368, 403-762-6300 **ACCOMMODATIONS/TOURIST INFO:** 403-762-8421

CALGARY INTERNATIONAL JAZZ FESTIVAL

CALGARY ✸ TEN DAYS STARTING THE FINAL WEEK IN JUNE

In the city known more for cowboy hats and stampede stomping, jazz seems like the most natural thing in the world during the 10 days of the Calgary International Jazz Festival. To keep things interesting, local and regional talent is mixed with internationally known musicians. Styles range from mainstream and cutting-edge jazz to gospel, blues, swing, bebop, salsa, and world beat. The 10 venues include mostly local clubs with an intimate feel. Tickets range from $8 to $30.   **LOCATION:** Various venues throughout Calgary **TICKETS/INFO:** 403-233-2628 **ACCOMMODATIONS/TOURIST INFO:** 403-263-8510, 800-661-8888

JAZZ CITY INTERNATIONAL JAZZ FESTIVAL

EDMONTON ✸ LATE JUNE OR EARLY JULY (10 DAYS)

For 10 days each summer, Edmonton becomes Jazz City as theaters, restaurants, hotels, and nightclubs blare the sounds of contemporary jazz, blues, and world music. The near-solstice sun stays up until midnight, illuminating some of the hottest internationally recognized jazz stars as they ascend the five main stages. Ticket prices for headliners are in the $10 to $30 range, but a free outdoor stage called Jazz Street features local, national, and international artists daily from noon to 9 P.M. A visual arts festival is held in conjunction with the jazz festival.   **LOCATION:** Various venues around

The JAZZ CITY International Jazz Festival brings some of the world's hottest jazz musicians to Edmonton. *Courtesy of Edmonton Tourism*

Edmonton **TICKETS/INFO:** 403-432-7166 **ACCOMMODATIONS/TOURIST INFO:** 800-463-4667, 800-661-8888

ℭALGARY FOLK MUSIC FESTIVAL
CALGARY ✳ LAST WEEKEND IN JULY

Set on the river in a beautiful inner-city park, this three-day festival balances traditional Canadian folk music with the sounds of folk's international fringes. About 45 acts range from acoustic and electric folk to Celtic, worldbeat, country, and even alternative rock and spoken word. A large evening stage features headliners from Alberta and all over the world, while smaller stages feature kids' events, workshops, jams, and even a poetry slam. Admission is $25 each day, but early-bird discounts are substantial. **LOCATION:** Prince's Island Park, on the riverfront in downtown Calgary **TICKETS/ INFO:** 403-233-0904 **ACCOMMODATIONS/TOURIST INFO:** 403-263-8510, 800-661-8888

ᒚASPER HERITAGE FOLK FESTIVAL
JASPER ✳ SATURDAY AND SUNDAY BEFORE THE FIRST MONDAY IN AUGUST

Set beneath the unparalleled grandeur of the Canadian Rockies, this folksy festival includes blues, jazz, bluegrass, country, and women's music. This is one of the few music festivals that can boast a World Heritage Site (Jasper National Park) for a venue, as well as an outstanding and diverse roster of about 25 musical groups, most of them known nationally and internationally. A children's program, crafts, and ethnic food fairs are featured, while a Global Awareness Area and a Native Village provide a politically correct balance to the good times at the beer garden.   **LOCATION:** Centennial Park in Jasper **TICKETS/INFO:** 403-852-5187, 403-852-3858 **ACCOMMODATIONS/TOURIST INFO:** 403-852-3858, 800-661-8888

♫LUEBERRY BLUEGRASS AND COUNTRY MUSIC FESTIVAL
STONY PLAIN ✴ FIRST WEEKEND IN AUGUST

The Blueberry Bluegrass Festival aims to promote Canadian bands who specialize in bluegrass and country music. A family-oriented festival, this annual outdoor event features one stage and draws a crowd of close to 3,000. Food, crafts, music workshops, and a children's area are added attractions.   **LOCATION:** Stony Plain Exhibition Park, just west of Edmonton via Highway 73 **TICKETS/INFO:** 403-963-5217 **ACCOMMO-DATIONS/TOURIST INFO:** 403-963-5217, 800-661-8888

ℂANMORE FOLK FESTIVAL
CANMORE ✴ FIRST WEEKEND IN AUGUST, SUNDAY AND MONDAY (HERITAGE DAY)

For nearly 20 years, hippies (young and old), families, locals, and Calgary music lovers have made this cosmopolitan event a Heritage Day tradition. Set in the Canadian Rockies just a few kilometers from Banff National Park, the rustic main stage has featured the likes of Irish folk/roots heavies, Malian acoustic trios, and Cape Breton fiddlers. Three smaller stages feature workshops and regional performers from the Rockies and the Pacific Coast.

The atmosphere is incredibly casual. Performers hang out in the audience, jam with each other,and even invite audience members up onto the stage to dance, sing, or play. Early in the day, musicians spend time at small stages sitting in on each other's tunes, playing covers of old favorites, or just making it up as they go along. The audience loves it, shouting out requests and dancing barefoot on a gentle slope that often turns to mud (be sure to bring rain gear).

Stages are surrounded by exotic-food booths and by vendors selling hundreds of goods and services. You'll find clothing, garishly ugly hats, devil sticks (with free instructions), jewelry, and Indian face painting.

Alcohol isn't allowed at the festival, so the drinking is confined to the Drake Inn and the Sherwood at night. The Sherwood has informal jam session nights, and festival performers often make guest appearances.

A Children's Area features puppets, pony rides, and more, and Sunday morning always begins with a free pancake breakfast at the Lions Hall. Festival admission is about $12 per day, and since this is high season, be sure to book your hotel or campsite early. **LOCATION:** Centennial Park in Canmore, about one hour west of Calgary on the Trans-Canada Highway **TICKETS/INFO:** 403-678-2524, 403-6478-4094 **ACCOMMODA-TIONS/TOURIST INFO:** 403-678-4094, 800-661-8888

Shirley Yuan of Silk Road performs at the 1995 Canmore Folk Festival.

Courtesy of Canmore Folk Festival

🎵IG VALLEY JAMBOREE

CAMROSE ✷ FIRST OR SECOND WEEKEND IN AUGUST, THURSDAY–SUNDAY

Like its now-defunct namesake in Saskatchewan, Camrose's Big Valley Jamboree pulls in country music's major names. The music tends toward contemporary country (Asleep at the Wheel, the Oak Ridge Boys, and Ricky Skaggs are a few who have played here), with an occasional polka thrown in. General admission camping at the festival site is free, although there's a charge for reserved sites.   **LOCATION:** Camrose, about 80 km southwest of Edmonton at the junction of Highways 26, 13, and 833 **TICKETS/ INFO:** 403-672-0224, 800-667-7899 **ACCOMMODATIONS/TOURIST INFO:** 800-661-8888

🎵DMONTON FOLK MUSIC FESTIVAL

EDMONTON ✷ SECOND WEEKEND IN AUGUST

It's raining at the Edmonton Folk Music Festival, just as it's rained for 15 of the past 16 years—so why is everyone laughing?

Folk's lofty heights: The view from the top at Edmonton's impeccable Folk Music Festival. (See entry, page 473.) Erika Ehmsen/The Clynes Group

Maybe it's the grassy (often muddy) slopes of Gallagher Park, which provide a natural amphitheater with impeccable sound. Maybe it's the beer garden, or the ethnic food stands, or the huge degree of community involvement. Maybe—probably—it's the music, which goes well beyond beards-and-banjos folk to embrace the sounds of blues, reggae, country, bluegrass, worldbeat, and even the fringes of funk and pop.

Somehow, despite the wet weather that seems inevitable, Edmonton continues to offer one of the best and most interesting folk festival experiences in Canada and the world. Striking a balance between high-profile stars and low-profile surprises, between traditional folk and the cutting edge, organizers manage year after year to make Edmonton a musical sure thing, a vibrant and magical event.

For four days every August, some 50 bands play on eight small stages and one main stage. Big-namers appearing over the past few years have included the likes of k.d. lang, Lyle Lovett, and Elvis Costello. Yet festival attendees are often more excited to discover exotic acts like Mali's Bajourou, or Russia's Limpopo.

The lack of assigned seating (except sections reserved for disabled guests) makes for an interesting morning tradition called "the Running of the Tarps." At six o'clock each morning, the masses are turned loose to run, slip, and slide down the muddy slopes in an effort to spread out brightly colored tarps and stake out the best spots on the hill. (For best results, roll rather than fold your tarp for easy and quick unfurling.)

If you need a break from the festival crowds, check out the Muttart Conservatory, where greenhouses provide shelter from weather that can change from sunny and hot to cool and rainy in a matter of minutes. Reasonably priced ethnic food abounds at the festival site, and a variety of beers are served in the beer garden. Festivalgoers are welcome to bring their own food and nonalcoholic drink. A variety of ticket options are available, with day passes starting at $25.   **LOCATION:** Gallagher Municipal Park in Edmonton. The main gate is on 97th Avenue, just west of Cloverdale Road. **TICKETS/INFO:** 403-429-1999; e-mail: edm.folkfest@ccinet.ab.ca **ACCOMMODATIONS/TOURIST INFO:** 800-463-4667, 403-496-8400, 800-661-8888

FRIKADEY

CALGARY ✷ THIRD WEEK IN AUGUST

Calgary's festival of African arts and culture features the music of the entire African diaspora: Africa, the Caribbean, South America, and North America. In addition to 18 performing groups (most of them musical), a wide range of African culture is presented through films, dance, symposiums, storytelling, and literary readings. Various downtown venues include concert halls, clubs, community centers, outdoor stages, and more. Admission ranges from free to $25.   **LOCATION:** Various downtown venues **TICKETS/INFO:** 403-282-7119, 403-284-3674 **ACCOMMODATIONS/TOURIST INFO:** 403-263-8510, 800-661-8888

SHADY GROVE BLUEGRASS AND OLD TYME MUSIC FESTIVAL

NANTON ✷ THIRD WEEKEND IN AUGUST

Held in a farmyard in the small town of Nanton, this event is one of only two bluegrass festivals in Alberta. The music is more nostalgic than revolutionary, but farmyard camping and homemade goodies lend a feeling of intimacy while promoting a "one big family" atmosphere. Acoustic jam sessions last into the wee hours of the morning, and festival bands teach workshops. There's even a Bluegrass for Kids program where children learn songs, build instruments out of household items, and perform on the final day of the festival.   **LOCATION:** Nanton is one hour south of Calgary and one hour north of Lethbridge. The Broadway Farm is just east of Nanton, off Highway 533E. **TICKETS/INFO:** 403-646-2076 **ACCOMMODATIONS/TOURIST INFO:** 403-646-2270, 800-661-8888

BANFF INTERNATIONAL STRING QUARTET COMPETITION

BANFF ✷ SIX DAYS IN LATE AUGUST AND/OR EARLY SEPTEMBER

This unique and outstanding event invites 10 of the most accomplished string quartets in the world to perform 13 sessions for a distinguished international jury. The public is invited to all events, and although prizes include $45,000 in cash, the real incentive is the prestige of joining the ranks of the former winners of this competition. Tickets are a bargain at $10 to $15 per session. In addition to the music, Banff has dance, theater, film, and media arts lectures and performances throughout the summer among the national park's beautiful mountains and forests.   **LOCATION:** Eric Harvie Theatre at the Banff Centre for the Arts, on St. Julien Road **TICKETS/INFO:** 800-413-8368, 403-762-6300 **ACCOMMODATIONS/TOURIST INFO:** 403-762-8421, 800-661-8888

𝕯IGITAL PLAYGROUNDS: INTERNATIONAL COMPUTER MUSIC CONFERENCE

BANFF ✳ FIVE DAYS IN EARLY SEPTEMBER

Boldly taking music where it has not gone before, Banff's new-music specialists present a series of computer-enabled electroacoustic concerts. Highlights include a multimedia performance by leading convergent-art and technology practitioners, and a real-time network performance connecting musicians on site with others around the world. The festival draws a good mix of true electronic music mavens and the merely intrigued—but many of the latter soon leave to clear their baffled heads in Banff National Park's beautiful mountains and forests. Cost is $5. **LOCATION:** Eric Harvey Theater at the Banff Centre for the Arts, on St. Julien Road **TICKETS/INFO:** 800-413-8368, 403-762-6300 **ACCOMMODATIONS/TOURIST INFO:** 403-762-8421, 800-661-8888

BRITISH COLUMBIA

TERRIFVIC JAZZ PARTY
VICTORIA ✷ THIRD WEEK IN APRIL, WEDNESDAY–SUNDAY

With beautiful Victoria as its backdrop, the TerrifVic Jazz Party celebrates traditional jazz from Canada, the United States, and around the world. A partylike atmosphere is encouraged with cabaret-style seating and dance floors at about 10 venues. Dixieland is a major theme, while the Pianorama displays the solo talents of keyboard players from TerrifVic bands. Other noteworthy events include Sunday morning gospel performances and a free Community Concert held on the Parliament Building lawns. A three-day pass will set you back about $60. **LOCATION:** Throughout Victoria **TICKETS/INFO:** 604-381-5277 **ACCOMMODATIONS/TOURIST INFO:** 604-382-2127, 800-663-3883

CHILLIWACK INTERNATIONAL DIXIELAND JAZZ FESTIVAL
CHILLIWACK ✷ FIRST WEEKEND IN MAY

Looking for some hot Dixieland jazz outside of New Orleans? The Chilliwack International Dixieland Jazz Festival specializes in this distinctive brand of jazz, and features four thematic venues: Uptown Jazz, the French Quarter, the Cajun Cabin, and the Junior Jazz Barn. The latter is a nonsmoking, alcohol-free workshop site operated for the enjoyment of teenage and young-adult jazz aficionados. Admission—roughly $50 for a three-day pass—allows you to roam freely between the different sites, and in addition to the massive conglomeration of "pure" Dixieland jazz, there's a Big Band Dance on Friday night and a free Gospel Service on Sunday. **LOCATION:** Chilliwack Exhibition Grounds, about 100 km east of Vancouver on Highway 5 **TICKETS/INFO:** 604-795-3600 **ACCOMMODATIONS/TOURIST INFO:** 604-858-8121

GRANVILLE ISLAND BLUEGRASS FESTIVAL
VANCOUVER ✷ THIRD WEEKEND IN MAY, SATURDAY–MONDAY

Granville Island's marketplace is alive with the sounds of the hills during this spring party, thrown by the Pacific Bluegrass and Heritage Society. Eight to 10 bands from around Canada and the northwestern United States draw about 500 fans of bluegrass music each day. Restrictions on alcohol and picnicking keep things low-key, but the price is certainly right—it's free.   **LOCATION:** Granville Island, Vancouver **TICKETS/ INFO:** 604-535-0362 **ACCOMMODATIONS/TOURIST INFO:** 800-663-6000, 604-682-2222

dU MAURIER INTERNATIONAL JAZZ FESTIVAL VANCOUVER

VANCOUVER ✴ TEN DAYS BEGINNING THE THIRD FRIDAY IN JUNE

For 10 days each summer Vancouver sounds as good as it looks, as close to 1,000 of the jazz world's very best gather to create a multicultural panoply of sounds. Hundreds of thousands of visitors wedge themselves between the gleaming Pacific Ocean and the majestic mountains, pulsating to a mind-blowing array of styles presented in some 23 venues.

The music moves from intricate to bluesy, from Latin spicy to uptown funky. Vancouver rakes in big names like Charles Lloyd, Alan Holdsworth, and Otis Rush, but the true beauty of this festival lies in its emphasis on up-and-comers. With nary a concession to market forces, organizers somehow succeed in bringing in tomorrow's big stars, year after year. More important, they succeed in bringing to the festival audience cutting-edge music with a range of styles and traditions that emphasizes discovery rather than the tried-and-true.

With connections to jazz scenes in Europe and the United States, the organizing Coastal Jazz and Blues Society has made Vancouver the unofficial kickoff point of Canada's major jazz festival circuit. And as Canada itself becomes more diverse, the society's talent search is reaching farther afield, offering more of the sounds of the Caribbean, Africa, and Asia.

In addition to creative booking, Vancouver has a knack for creative venue selection and pricing, each of which plays a big role in the festival's success. Big-name performances are held in clubs and theaters, with admission ranging from $10 to $36. Less established and more adventurous talent is showcased at free concerts in the Plaza of Nations and the blocked-off city streets of the Gastown district. Wherever you go, there's an ever present element of surprise and experimentation, as Vancouver cooks virtually 24 hours a day.   **LOCATION:** Various venues in Vancouver **TICKETS/INFO:** 604-682-0706; e-mail: cjbs@mindlink.bc.ca **ACCOMMODATIONS/TOURIST INFO:** 800-663-6000, 604-682-2222

MIDSUMMER FESTIVAL

SMITHERS ✴ FOURTH WEEKEND IN JUNE

Devoted to providing a family-oriented venue for Northwest musicians, the Midsummer Festival showcases local and regional performers in a variety of musical genres. You'll find everything from classical to Celtic, folk, and alternative rock—there's even a Friday-night teen dance. Musical campfires spring up around the adjoining campground after the day's concerts are finished, and everyone is welcome to sing along. **LOCATION:** Smithers Fall Fair Grounds. Smithers is located halfway between Prince George and Prince Rupert in northwest British Columbia's Bulkley Valley, on Highway 16. **TICKETS/INFO:** 604-846-9265 **ACCOMMODATIONS/TOURIST INFO:** 604-847-9854

VICTORIA INTERNATIONAL FESTIVAL
VICTORIA ✱ SIX WEEKS IN JULY AND EARLY AUGUST

Beautiful and very British, Victoria resounds in the summer with an ingenious series of orchestral and chamber concerts, operas, recitals, and ballets. The music covers a wide range of periods (including the 20th century) and can be heard in theaters, auditoriums, and cathedrals. Performances are scheduled Thursdays through Sundays during the season, and many feature more than one soloist—a unique feature of the Victoria International Festival. **LOCATION:** Various venues in Victoria **TICKETS/INFO:** 604-736-2119 **ACCOMMODATIONS/TOURIST INFO:** 604-387-1642

INTERNATIONAL CHORAL KATHAUMIXW FESTIVAL
POWELL RIVER ✱ FIRST WEEK IN JULY, EVEN-NUMBERED YEARS ONLY

Kathaumixw (pronounced ka-thou-me-wh) is a Salish Indian word meaning "a gathering of different people," and what a gathering this is! With its breathtaking view of the Pacific Ocean and rugged green mountains, Powell River hosts choral, folk, and chamber singers from as far away as Finland, Israel, Taiwan, and Ukraine. Afternoon and evening performances are augmented by vocal competitions in a variety of age categories, and a conductors' symposium encourages choir directors to share musical techniques and trends. The highlight of the festival is the Gala Closing Concert, an event that showcases the vocal talent of all participants. **LOCATION:** Powell River is about 120 km north of Vancouver, along Highway 101. **TICKETS/INFO:** 604-483-3346 **ACCOMMODATIONS/TOURIST INFO:** 604-485-4701

HARRISON FESTIVAL OF THE ARTS
HARRISON HOT SPRINGS ✱ SECOND WEEK IN JULY

The small resort town of Harrison Hot Springs celebrates world music and the cultures of Africa, Central America, and the Caribbean during this nine-day event. More than 200 performers and artists from all over the world are featured in concerts, theater, workshops, lectures, literary readings, and art exhibits. Two stages, one indoor and one outdoor, present African and Latin beats, as well as excellent blues and gospel. The festival is affordable, and a great place to find professional arts flourishing in a small community. **LOCATION:** Harrison Hot Springs, 1.5 hours east of Vancouver on Highway 1 **TICKETS/INFO:** 604-796-3664 **ACCOMMODATIONS/TOURIST INFO:** 604-796-3425

KIMBERLEY INTERNATIONAL OLD TIME ACCORDION CHAMPIONSHIPS
KIMBERLEY ✱ SECOND WEEK IN JULY, MONDAY–SATURDAY

The only international, strictly old-time accordion championship in North America makes its home in Kimberley, British Columbia, "the Bavarian City of the Rockies." With all the oomph of an Oktoberfest, this festival prides itself on preserving traditional accordion music. Accordionists are judged on technique and on the old-time feeling and danceability of their music. There are daily jam sessions, as well as evening entertainment and dances. And while you're there, be sure to visit the world's largest cuckoo

Small town, big beat: The Harrison Festival of the Arts brings diverse music and culture to Harrison Hot Springs. (See entry, page 479.)

Courtesy of Harrison Festival of

the Arts

clock, which will yodel for you for 25¢.   **LOCATION:** Kimberley is about 25 km north of Cranbrook in southeastern British Columbia. **TICKETS/INFO:** 604-427-4547 **AC-COMMODATIONS/TOURIST INFO:** 604-427-4877, 800-667-0871

ҬHE MERRITT MOUNTAIN MUSIC FESTIVAL
MERRITT ✱ SECOND WEEK IN JULY, THURSDAY–SUNDAY

Yee-haw! Four days of country music and more than 50 artists await fans at the Merritt Mountain Music Festival. Situated in the Nicola Valley with the Cold Water River running through the site, the sheer beauty of the area adds to the organizers' goal of providing entertainment, relaxation, fun, and good memories. Apart from the music on three stages, attractions include logging shows, sightseeing via helicopter, horseback riding, children's entertainment, amusement rides, and midway games. Auto and RV parking as well as camping are included in the very reasonable price of admission. **LOCATION:** Merritt, British Columbia, about 220 km northeast of Vancouver on Highway 5 **TICKETS/INFO:** 604-525-3330 **ACCOMMODATIONS/TOURIST INFO:** 604-525-3330

₣ANCOUVER EARLY MUSIC PROGRAMME AND FESTIVAL

VANCOUVER ✹ MID-JULY THROUGH MID-AUGUST

The only western Canadian festival focusing solely on early music offers listeners a repertoire spanning seven centuries, played by some of the world's foremost performers of medieval, baroque, and Renaissance music. In a series of seven to 10 concerts, all musicians play instruments from the periods in which the musical pieces were written. In addition, one- and two-week educational programs are offered for both amateur and professional musicians. **LOCATION:** University of British Columbia School of Music Recital Hall, 6361 Memorial Road, near UBC entrance gate 4 off Marine Drive, about 20 minutes outside the center of Vancouver **TICKETS/INFO:** 604-732-1610; e-mail: earlymusic@mindlink.bc.ca **ACCOMMODATIONS/TOURIST INFO:** 604-732-1610

₣ANCOUVER FOLK MUSIC FESTIVAL

VANCOUVER ✹ THIRD WEEKEND IN JULY, THURSDAY–SUNDAY

Ranging from hot to cool, from meditative to exhilarating, the Vancouver Folk Music Festival just may be the world's most densely packed tableau of roots music. For four days, an eclectic and inspiring program features folk music from places as diverse as Manitoba, Moscow, and Madagascar. Expect to see and hear exotic drumming, sultry rumbas, down-home blues, and a feast of other musical treasures in addition to folk music by Canadian singer-songwriters.

The festival, held in lush Jericho Beach Park, features seven stages of music, plus storytelling, poetry, guitar workshops, children's shows, and food stands. Each year, organizers scout the world for new voices in folk music, and even jaded world-beatniks always find plenty of surprises. Depending on the year, you might stumble across an aboriginal dance group from Taiwan, a team of conga wizards from Cuba, some Celtic country funksters, or Corsican vocalists.

Many of the performances become living lessons in anthropology or cultural history. Artists are invited to focus attention on particular styles, themes, instruments, subjects, or places, and concerts are often complemented by hands-on workshops. The majority of the festivalgoers shares the organizers' spirit of discovery, happily crossing over stylistic lines and free-falling into new and unfamiliar experiences.

Vancouver's folk fest is also a great weekend for kids. In addition to an interactive concert stage, there are water activities and even a hands-on beading workshop, where children can create wearable art out of beads made from recycled magazines. Thursday and Friday feature evening concerts, while Saturday and Sunday feature music from 10 A.M. to 11 P.M. Single-day tickets are in the $40 range, and a variety of weekend passes and early-bird specials are available. **LOCATION:** Jericho Beach Park, just off 4th Avenue in Vancouver **TICKETS/INFO:** 604-602-9798; e-mail: VFMF@cyberstore.ca **ACCOMMODATIONS/TOURIST INFO:** 800-663-6000, 604-682-2222, 604-822-1010

₵ARIBBEAN DAYS FESTIVAL

VANCOUVER ✹ THIRD OR FOURTH WEEKEND IN JULY

Vancouver is transported to the Caribbean for two days each summer, as crowds of more than 15,000 jump, dance, and sway in the sun to the compelling rhythms of soca, reggae, calypso, steel drum, and salsa music. Admission is free, and while the festival

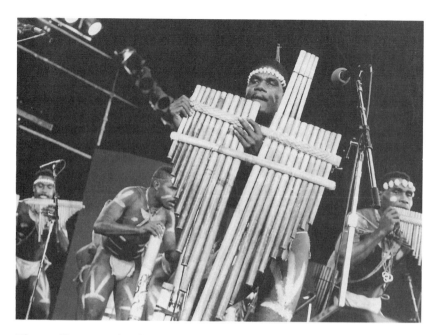

The world in a weekend: The Narasirato Are' Are Panpipe Ensemble from the Solomon Islands performs at the 1994 Vancouver Folk Music Festival. (See entry, page 481.) Courtesy of Ed Olson/Vancouver Folk Music Festival

typically features a headliner from the Caribbean, most bands are comprised of island expatriots now living in western Canada and the northwestern United States. Limbo dancing and a children's "jump up" parade are also part of the festival, and Caribbean and African cuisines are offered at booths throughout the event's two locations. **LOCATION:** Saturday, Plaza of Nations; Sunday, Waterfront Park in North Vancouver **TICKETS/INFO:** 604-273-0874 **ACCOMMODATIONS/TOURIST INFO:** 800-663-6000, 604-682-2222

WHISTLER COUNTRY, ROOTS & BLUES FESTIVAL
WHISTLER ✸ THIRD OR FOURTH WEEKEND IN JULY, FRIDAY–SUNDAY

Regional favorites and rising stars share the two stages at this kitchen-sink conglomeration of country, folk, and blues artists. Over three afternoons and evenings, a main stage is set up at the base of Whistler and Blackcomb Mountains, while a couple of roving truck-bed stages make the rounds at various hot spots throughout the resort. Though the majority of bands are from the Pacific Northwest, they cover styles ranging from Texas swing to Appalachian, Cajun, Delta blues, and rockabilly. The festival is free—but nothing else in Whistler is.   **LOCATION:** Whistler Resort, about 90 km north of Vancouver via Highway 99 **TICKETS/INFO:** 800-944-7853, 604-644-5625, 604-932-4222 **ACCOMMODATIONS/TOURIST INFO:** 800-944-7853, 604-644-5625, 604-932-4222

VANCOUVER CHAMBER MUSIC FESTIVAL
VANCOUVER ✴ LAST WEEK IN JULY THROUGH THE FIRST WEEK IN AUGUST

Music by Stravinsky, Mozart, and Debussy is standard fare at this festival, but organizers purposely shy away from big-name chamber groups, preferring to invite some of the world's leading young chamber musicians and mix them "round-robin" style. The repertoire spans the classical and romantic periods as well as the 20th century, and the dress code is emphatically casual. ("Dress down, chow down, and get down," say the organizers.) Catered dinners and desserts provide the culinary compositions each evening, while a morning "Water Music" concert series features both traditional compositions and improvised jazz pieces performed by the sea.   **LOCATION:** Crofton House School's Addison Auditorium, 3200 W. 41st Avenue; St. George's School Auditorium, 4175 W. 29th Avenue; and Vanier Park, just behind the planetarium **TICKETS/INFO:** 604-736-6034, 604-280-3311 **ACCOMMODATIONS/TOURIST INFO:** 800-663-6000, 604-682-2222

MISSION FOLK MUSIC FESTIVAL
MISSION ✴ LAST FULL WEEKEND IN JULY, FRIDAY–SUNDAY

Folk music may be the mainstay of the Mission festival, but no one ever said it had to be traditional folk music. This diverse festival explores what happens to folk when it's exposed to and influenced by classical music, jazz, worldbeat, and other sounds. A large evening stage features three concerts each night, and three day stages feature miniconcerts, workshops, and "musical exploration." The Fraser River Heritage Park is an intimate setting with a view of the river and majestic Mount Baker. Adult weekend passes cost around $40, and limited on-site camping is available for less than $10 per person.   **LOCATION:** Fraser River Heritage Park in Mission, 50 miles east of Vancouver and 12 miles from the U.S. border **TICKETS/INFO:** 604-826-5937 **ACCOMMODATIONS/TOURIST INFO:** 604-826-6914

VANCOUVER ISLAND LATIN MUSIC FESTIVAL
VICTORIA ✴ BRITISH COLUMBIA DAY WEEKENED, SATURDAY–MONDAY
(BRITISH COLUMBIA DAY IS THE FIRST MONDAY IN AUGUST)

Victoria's historic Market Square comes alive when the hot sounds of Latin American music take over this very British city for three days each summer. Free afternoon concerts feature musicians and dancers performing South American, Mexican, Gypsy-funk, Afro-Brazilian jazz, and flamenco music. There's an admission charge for the evening performances, but the Latin and Caribbean bands are terrific and their tantalizing beats will keep you dancing under the stars all night. Learn more about Latin culture by attending the Latin American art exhibition, the music workshop, and the kids' activities that are also part of the event.   **LOCATION:** Market Square and other venues in Victoria **TICKETS/INFO:** 604-361-1909 **ACCOMMODATIONS/TOURIST INFO:** 800-663-3883

SYMPHONY SPLASH
VICTORIA ✴ SUNDAY OF BRITISH COLUMBIA DAY WEEKEND

With fantastic music and a gorgeous sunset, it's no wonder this concert has the highest attendance of any orchestral event in Canada. For one evening every August the

View from the barge: Floating in Victoria's Inner Harbor, the Victoria Symphony serenades the shoreside crowd during Symphony Splash. (See entry, page 483.) Courtesy of Victoria Symphony Society

city of Victoria celebrates music and honors the Canadian Sea Cadets at a concert in Victoria's Inner Harbor. The 50-piece Victoria Symphony performs on a barge in the harbor while more than 50,000 spectators watch from the shoreline of Vancouver Island. Light classical music is featured, and the uncut version of Tchaikovsky's *1812 Overture*— complete with fireworks, carillon bells, and cannons courtesy of the Sea Cadets—is the grand finale every year.   **LOCATION:** Victoria's Inner Harbour **TICKETS/INFO:** 604-385-9771, 604-385-6515 **ACCOMMODATIONS/TOURIST INFO:** 604-382-2127

KASLO JAZZ ETC. MUSIC FESTIVAL
KASLO ✳ FIRST WEEKEND IN AUGUST

Although whispers have been circulating since 1991, it wasn't until recently that word of this remarkable festival spread beyond the Purcell Mountains. This gathering— with its high musical quality, intimate size, and a unique venue—won't be a secret for long.

With pristine mountain wilderness as a backdrop, a floating stage perches musicians on Kootenay Lake while onlookers swim around the stage, dance in the sand, or roll on blankets laid in a natural, grassy bowl of sound. Organizers manage to pull in a prestigious roster of musicians ranging from jazz and Latin to R&B, worldbeat, and rock. One can listen to Seattle alternative one minute and jazz fusion the next, taking in the stirring flute melodies of Paul Horn (a festival regular) along the way.

Despite the "big festival" lineup, Kaslo retains the lulling vibe of a small festival. The crowds along the tranquil shores of the lake are far from maddening, and collateral perks abound: lake swimming and sailing, star gazing, mountain hiking, the hot springs of Ainsworth, and the village offerings of Kaslo, known as "the little Switzerland" of British Columbia.

A bright Bavarian Garden tent for beer and meals has a superb view of center stage, and booths offer ethnic food, apple cider, and arts and crafts (with some exotic items). Consistent with the easygoing atmosphere, there are no restrictions on BYO picnics, so plenty of quilts and checkered tablecloths dot the grounds.

When the festival closes for the evening, everyone files toward the Mariner Inn or the Breakers to catch festival performers again at open-stage jam sessions. The Canadian Legion usually has a R&B band (or other good dance band) and a buoyant crowd that grooves to the music. Be forewarned that anyone who enters legion premises wearing a hat has to either buy a round of drinks or exit via the bouncer.   **LOCATION:** Kaslo is in the Purcell Mountains, one hour north of Nelson and three hours north of Spokane, Washington, on Highway 31. **TICKETS/INFO:** 604-353-7538 **ACCOMMODATIONS/ TOURIST INFO:** 604-353-7323, 604-352-6033

WHISTLER CLASSICAL MUSIC FESTIVAL
WHISTLER ✷ SECOND WEEKEND IN AUGUST

Assuming that summer vacationers won't tolerate anything too heavy, Whistler lines up a program of light classics that can include anything from string quartets and trios to harpists, light opera, and even Broadway melodies. The music isn't innovative and the settings are gimmicky—Brass on a Raft, Baroque and Barbecue—but it's summer in the mountains and most events are free, so leave your cynicism back in the big city.   **LOCATION:** Whistler Resort, about 90 km north of Vancouver via Highway 99 **TICKETS/INFO:** 800-944-7853, 604-644-5625, 604-932-4222 **ACCOMMODA-TIONS/TOURIST INFO:** 800-944-7853, 604-644-5625, 604-932-4222

WHISTLER FALL FOR JAZZ FESTIVAL
WHISTLER ✷ THIRD WEEKEND IN SEPTEMBER, FRIDAY–SUNDAY

Mid-September is a great time of year to be in the mountains around Whistler, and the Fall for Jazz Festival makes the experience even more pleasant. Actually, there's more than jazz here, as musicians from the United States and Canada serve up everything from brass and bebop to gospel and R&B. A main stage at the base of Whistler and Blackcomb Mountains is supplemented by performances in the streets and clubs of Whistler. Most events are free.   **LOCATION:** Whistler Resort, about 90 km north of Vancouver via Highway 99 **TICKETS/INFO:** 800-944-7853, 604-644-5625, 604-932-4222 **ACCOM-MODATIONS/TOURIST INFO:** 800-944-7853, 604-644-5625, 604-932-4222

MaNiToBa

dU MAURIER NEW MUSIC FESTIVAL
WINNIPEG ✷ LAST WEEK IN JANUARY

One of the world's most important new-music events promises to take listeners to the edge—then nudge them over with daring and provocative performances by internationally renowned composers and musicians. For nine days, established mavericks—which have included Kronos Quartet, John Corigliano, and Gavin Bryars, among many others—and newcomers present more than 50 works, many of them international premieres. Expect to hear anything from symphonic and jazz to electroacoustic and cross-disciplinary works. An informal and inviting atmosphere includes onstage bleacher seating, an integrated Canadian Composers Competition, and special nights devoted to new music from younger composers. Tickets range from $12 to $40. **LOCATION:** Winnipeg Symphony Orchestra Centennial Concert Hall, 555 Main Street, Winnipeg **TICKETS/INFO:** 204-949-3999 **ACCOMMODATIONS/TOURIST INFO:** 800-665-0204, 204-943-1970

ǰAZZ WINNIPEG FESTIVAL
WINNIPEG ✷ EIGHT DAYS BEGINNING THE SECOND SATURDAY IN JUNE

Beginning with a major Saturday night concert, the Jazz Winnipeg Festival invades this central Canadian city with international talents in clubs and outdoor venues. After the opening Saturday night concert, the festival continues with dozens of free outdoor shows and club gigs in the $10-$20 range. Recent guests illustrate the festival's commitment to diversity: jazz legend Clark Terry; acid jazz gurus Medeski, Martin and Wood; and tenor saxophonist Joe Henderson. Winnipeg throws in some blues and even some pop-jazz acts like Tuck and Patti, but there's plenty here for the purist and even for those who walk the cutting edge. **LOCATION:** Various venues in Winnipeg **TICKETS/INFO:** 204-989-4656 **ACCOMMODATIONS/TOURIST INFO:** 800-665-0204, 204-943-1970

ᴅAUPHIN'S COUNTRYFEST
DAUPHIN ✷ LAST WEEKEND IN JUNE, FRIDAY–SUNDAY

More than 10,000 people gather every Canada Day weekend in Dauphin, Manitoba, to high-step and two-step to their favorite country artists. Close to 40 bands entertain the

Confusing the keyboard: Artistic director Bramwell Tovey brings a spirit of experimentation to Winnipeg's du Maurier New Music Festival. Courtesy of du Maurier
New Music Festival

masses over the course of the weekend in an amphitheater built into a slope of the Riding Mountains. There's a great view of the valley and farmland below, and in addition to the live musicians, country dance lessons, an autograph tent, and airplane rides, a calf-roping machine keep even the shortest attention spans occupied. On-site camping is available for a fee.   **LOCATION:** Selo Ukrainia Site, seven miles south of Dauphin on Highway 10 **TICKETS/INFO:** 204-638-3700, 800-361-7300 **ACCOMMODATIONS/ TOURIST INFO:** 204-638-4838, 800-665-0040

WINNIPEG FOLK FESTIVAL
WINNIPEG ✷ SECOND WEEKEND IN JULY, THURSDAY–SUNDAY

Long known as one of the world's preeminent singer-songwriter festivals, the Winnipeg Folk Festival has branched out in recent years to include more of the stuff that other Canadian "folk" festivals are made of. These days, you'll find a feast of Celtic, Cajun, bluegrass, and roots music from cultures all over the world.

On seven daytime stages and one evening main stage, contemporary expressions of folk music are balanced with singer-songwriters favored by the beards-and-banjos set that got the festival started back in 1974. Winnipeg's international cast of characters has included Pete Seeger, Billy Bragg, Bonnie Raitt, John Prine, Bruce Cockburn, and Ladysmith Black Mambazo, to name just a few.

The 100-acre Birds Hill Park provides a perfect natural setting for the festival. Daytime programs include intimate jam sessions, mini-concerts, workshops, and a family area with supervised, hands-on activities. At night, massive main-stage events are held under the big Manitoban sky. The Hand-Made Village is a juried crafts area, and an International Foods area features some great homemade cooking. Camping is available, but rules restrict pets, drugs, and alcohol. Tickets are available in a variety of packages and price points (for example, an advance-purchase three-day pass is $62).

LOCATION: Birds Hill Provincial Park, 25 km northeast of downtown Winnipeg on Provincial Highway 59 (City Route 20) **TICKETS/INFO:** 204-231-0096 **ACCOMMODATIONS/TOURIST INFO:** 800-665-0204, 204-943-1970

☼UN COUNTRY JAM

SELKIRK ✷ SECOND WEEKEND IN AUGUST, FRIDAY–SUNDAY

Reflecting the mixed bag that is country music today, this rompin' gig combines new country stars with classic crooners on a main stage, and local talent on a second stage. The scene is the rodeo ground at Selkirk Park, just 20 minutes out of Winnipeg on the banks of the Red River. A lineup of more than 30 bands draws about 25,000 over the weekend. Admission is about $25.   **LOCATION:** Selkirk Park, about 30 km northeast of Winnipeg on Highway 9 **TICKETS/INFO:** 204-780-7328, 800-465-7328 **ACCOMMODATIONS/TOURIST INFO:** 204-945-3796, 800-665-0040

☼UNFEST

GIMLI ✷ THIRD WEEKEND IN AUGUST, THURSDAY–SUNDAY

Hard-driving Sunfest started in 1989 and has become not only a can't-miss date on the Winnipeg rock calendar but also Canada's biggest and most durable outdoor rock event. About 50,000 fans show up over three days, expecting to see a wide spectrum of Canadian bands and at least one south-of-the-border headliner. Past bookings have included Pearl Jam and Blue Rodeo, and Sunday is usually classic-rock day, featuring the likes of Randy Bachman or Streetheart. The festival's location on an abandoned airstrip is perfect for sky-high diversions like helicopter rides, hang gliding, and skydiving. Admission is about $35 each day.   **LOCATION:** Gimli Motorsport Park, about 80 km north of Winnipeg just off Highway 9 **TICKETS/INFO:** 204-780-7328, 800-465-7328 **ACCOMMODATIONS/TOURIST INFO:** 204-945-3796, 800-665-0040

NORTHWEST TERRITORIES

BREAK UP BREAK DOWN WEEKEND
INUVIK ✸ LAST WEEKEND IN MAY

As the thick ice on the Mackenzie River begins to break up, fiddlers from around the Mackenzie Delta gather in Inuvik to "break down." Old-time fiddling is supplemented by country and Native American sounds at this two-day event, which draws musicians and visitors from all around the western Arctic. **LOCATION:** Inuvik **TICKETS/INFO:** 403-979-2476 **ACCOMMODATIONS/TOURIST INFO:** 403-979-4321, 800-661-0788

POKIAK RIVER FESTIVAL
AKLAVIK ✸ THIRD WEEKEND IN JUNE, FRIDAY–MONDAY

A cozy riverside tent with fireplaces and a dance floor provides an authentic environment for spirited local music at this four-day festival. In addition to rock, country, and the famous fiddlers of the Mackenzie Delta, you can experience the traditional drum dancing and jigs of the native Inuvialuit, Dene, and Metis. Traditional food, games, and square dancing round out the action. The infamous "mad trapper of Rat River," Albert Johnson, is buried in Aklavik, and just outside of town delta marshlands and thousands of lakes tempt the adventurer. **LOCATION:** Aklavik, reachable via six flights a day from Inuvik, 50 km to the east **TICKETS/INFO:** 403-978-2252, 403-978-2239 **ACCOMMODATIONS/TOURIST INFO:** 403-979-4321, 800-661-0788

MIDWAY LAKE MUSIC FESTIVAL
FORT MCPHERSON ✸ FIRST WEEKEND IN JULY, FRIDAY–SUNDAY

Reviving the traditional springtime gathering of the native Tetlit Gwich'in Nation, this open-air summer festival is set against the stunning backdrop of the Richardson Mountains. About 20 bands include at least one big-name country and western artist, but the traditional music and dance of the Tetlit Gwich'in and other nations are most interesting to outsiders. Also, look for appearances by local old-time fiddlers, whose music has kept the Mackenzie Delta dancing for more than 100 years. Admission is about $25 for the weekend, and the environment is alcohol-free. **LOCATION:**

Arctic ice-breaker: Tetlit Gwich'in fiddlers and dancers celebrate the arrival of spring in the far north at the Midway Lake Music Festival. (See entry, page 489.) Courtesy of Midway Lake Music Festival

Midway Lake, 35 km southwest of Fort McPherson on the Dempster Highway **TICKETS/INFO:** 403-952-2330 **ACCOMMODATIONS/TOURIST INFO:** 403-979-4321, 800-661-0788

ℱOLK ON THE ROCKS
YELLOWKNIFE ✸ FOURTH WEEKEND IN JULY, FRIDAY–SUNDAY

The Northwest Territories' biggest music festival is still small by the rest of the world's standards, but local enthusiasm and a far-reaching roster of talent make it a can't-miss event if you're anywhere nearby. Performers converge on Yellowknife from all over Canada and even the United States, for two days and three evenings under the midnight sun.

The capital of the Northwest Territories seems to draw a big share of Canada's misfits (you need a sense of humor to live up here), who create a frontier-party atmosphere. In fact, there's hardly an ounce of snobbery at the festival venue, a beautiful lakeside park with four performance and workshop stages, plus a beer tent and food stands (try the caribou fajitas).

The crowd of about 2,000 each day revels in the chance to see bands from as far away as Vancouver or the Maritime Provinces, along with interesting local favorites in several genres. You might see a heavy-metal band singing in Inuktitut (one of the nine official languages in the Northwest Territories), a rocking country band from Saskatchewan, or fiddlers who've flown in from Québec. Other guests in recent years have included a western swing band from Seattle, a souped-up native ska combo from Ottawa, and a bluegrass trio from Vancouver.

Many of the highlights are more local (up here, local can extend as far as the town of Inuvik, 1,000 kilometers away). Recent festivals have included the hilarious antics of Yellowknife grunge/thrash rockers Small Town Rhino, as well as out-of-this-world Inuit

Big fun in the midnight sun: The Blue Shadows' play a lakeside set at Yellowknife's 1995 Folk on the Rocks. Tom Clynes/The Clynes Group

throat singers from Cape Dorset. In throat singing, two singers typically perform competitively, gurgling the rhythms in the back of their throats until one laughingly throws the other out of time.

The festival begins Friday night with a Warm Up the Rocks dance party in town, then moves out to the shore of Long Lake (if it rains, festivities move indoors to a rather drab hockey rink). After the festival closes each night, a Wild West atmosphere prevails at bars like the incomparable Gold Range, where bands supply music for two-stepping or country-slamming as women in union suits flirt and drunken fistfights erupt outside.

Yellowknife and its surroundings are expensive, but camping is an option (look out for the bears). Hiking, fishing, or sea-plane sightseeing adventures reveal the fragile, lake-dotted splendor of the Canadian Shield.   **LOCATION:** Long Lake, just outside Yellowknife near the town's airport **TICKETS/INFO:** 403-920-7806 **ACCOMMODA-TIONS/TOURIST INFO:** 403-873-3131, 800-661-0788

SOUTH SLAVE FRIENDSHIP FESTIVAL
FORT SMITH ✶ THIRD WEEKEND IN AUGUST, THURSDAY–SUNDAY

Homegrown northern talent and spontaneity drive the South Slave Friendship Festival. With 4,500 spectators, it is dubbed the "Woodstock of the Far North," and locals take pride in the many musical friendships that have formed as a result of the casual, unpressured performance environment. Seven stages host some 50 country, rock, folk, blues, and jazz bands that have roots in northern Canada. In addition, there are music workshops, jam sessions, and native arts and crafts. All concerts are free, although there's a charge for indoor dances. World-class kayaking, rafting, and fishing sites are nearby.   **LOCATION:** Several venues in Fort Smith, on Highway 5 just north of the Northwest Territories/Alberta border **TICKETS/INFO:** 403-872-2014 **ACCOM-MODATIONS/TOURIST INFO:** 403-872-2515, 800-661-0788

Saskatchewan

INTERNATIONAL BAND AND CHORAL FESTIVAL
MOOSE JAW ✹ THIRD WEEKEND IN MAY, THURSDAY–SATURDAY

One of the world's largest band and choral festivals brings more than 3,000 musicians, 60 bands, and 25 choral groups to small-town Moose Jaw. Evening concerts feature pipe, drum, marching, stage, brass, and reed categories, and nearly everyone participates in the climactic, colorful parade along Main Street. A couple of hours north of Moose Jaw, the Saskatchewan Choral Federation offers summer choral instruction to children and teens (see Music Workshops chapter, page 497). **LOCATION:** Moose Jaw, 71 km west of Regina on the Trans-Canada Highway **TICKETS/INFO:** 306-693-5933 **ACCOMMODATIONS/TOURIST INFO:** , 800-720-0060, 306-787-2300, 800-667-7191

MANITOU COUNTRY MUSIC JAMBOREE
WATROUS ✹ THIRD WEEKEND IN JUNE, SATURDAY AND SUNDAY

This festival focuses on regional and Canadian country musicians, aiming to promote country music in Saskatchewan and provide family entertainment. Around 5,000 people show up every year to watch the 20 or so bands hoot and holler, for only $25 for the weekend (camping is free). Beer gardens and food concessions are on-site. **LOCATION:** Watrous Sports Grounds, about 100 km southeast of Saskatoon on Highways 2 and 365 **TICKETS/INFO:** 306-946-3369 **ACCOMMODATIONS/TOURIST INFO:** 306-682-5803, 306-787-2300, 800-667-7191

REGINA FOLK FESTIVAL
REGINA ✹ LAST WEEKEND IN JUNE, FRIDAY–SUNDAY

Folk, blues, country, and other homestyle music is on the menu at this three-day event in downtown Victoria Park. Workshop stages and children's stages occupy everyone during the day, and at night the main stage heats up with the melodies of musicians from across Canada. **LOCATION:** Victoria Park in downtown Regina **TICKETS/INFO:** 306-757-6196, 306-569-8966 **ACCOMMODATIONS/TOURIST INFO:** 800-661-5099, 306-789-5099

$\mathcal{S}$ASKTEL SASKATCHEWAN JAZZ FESTIVAL

SASKATOON ✷ LAST WEEKEND IN JUNE THROUGH THE FIRST WEEKEND IN JULY (10 DAYS)

The Saskatchewan Jazz Festival accomplishes an amazing feat—it manages to bring the world into the living room of staid Saskatoon. Every summer more than 350 jazz, worldbeat, blues, and gospel artists perform in venues so intimate that festivalgoers often have the chance to meet both jazz legends and up-and-comers between gigs. Events are scheduled between noon and 2 A.M. at 19 venues—outdoor stages, theaters, ballrooms, and two 100-year-old churches for gospel concerts—all within walking distance. While 12 of the venues require paid admission (from $5 to $30), seven are free of charge. **LOCATION:** Downtown Saskatoon along the South Saskatchewan River **TICKETS/ INFO:** 306-652-1421, 800-638-1211; e-mail: sask.jazz@sasknet.sk.ca; World Wide Web: http://www.sasknet.sk.ca/jazz/ **ACCOMMODATIONS/TOURIST INFO:** 800-567-2444, 306-242-1206

$\mathcal{G}$OVAN OLDE TYME FIDDLE FESTIVAL

GOVAN ✷ FIRST WEEKEND IN JULY, FRIDAY–SUNDAY

The Saskatchewan Fiddling Championships are the highlight of the Govan Olde Tyme Fiddle Festival, which draws talent from all over Canada and parts of the United States. Fiddlers are accompanied by piano, guitar, banjo, accordion, or just a stomping foot. Along with the competitors, the event brings in one nationally known guest fiddler or fiddle group, and guest step dancers and square dancers. A weekend pass is $20, and for fiddlers and would-be fiddlers who are interested in learning the ropes, the Saskatchewan Cultural Exchange Society offers summer workshops at Emma Lake, a couple of hours to the north (see Music Workshops chapter, page 497). **LOCATION:** Govan School Gymnasium, about 110 km north of Regina on Highway 20 **TICKETS/INFO:** 306-484-4566, 306-484-2119 **ACCOMMODATIONS/TOURIST INFO:** 306-682-5803, 800-667-7191

$\mathcal{N}$ESS CREEK FESTIVAL

BIG RIVER ✷ THIRD FULL WEEKEND IN JULY, THURSDAY–SUNDAY

Set in the midst of a pristine boreal forest complete with northern lights and mosquitos, Ness Creek's eclectic musical blast dishes up everything from bluegrass and folk to Celtic and jazz fusion. The lion's share of the performers are from Saskatchewan, but all regions of Canada are represented. Camping is included in the $40 (for three days) admission price, but take note that facilities are rustic. Food booths offer a respite from cookouts. **LOCATION:** Festival grounds are 20 km northeast of Big River and 5 km southwest of Nesslin Lake. From Saskatoon take Highway 11 north to Prince Albert, then take Highway 3 west to Highway 55 northwest to Big River, and follow signs to the festival. **TICKETS/INFO:** 306-652-6377, 306-343-5671 **ACCOMMODATIONS/TOUR-IST INFO:** 800-661-7275, 306-236-3684

$\mathcal{H}$UMBOLDT POLKAFEST

HUMBOLDT ✷ LAST WEEKEND IN JULY, SATURDAY AND SUNDAY

Polka lovers from all over the province whirl the weekend away at this five-band festival in the close-knit community of Humboldt. The emphasis is on German-style polkas and dancing, and a polka mass kicks off activities on Sunday. Admission is about $17.   **LOCATION:** Humboldt Uniplex, about 105 km east of Saskatoon on Highway 5 **TICKETS/INFO:** 306-682-4710, 306-682-3444 **ACCOMMODATIONS/TOURIST INFO:** 306-682-5803

COUNTRY MUSIC JAMBOREE
WEYBURN ✸ LAST SUNDAY IN JULY

Up to 15 local and regional bands supply the sounds for 3,000 or so fans in this country-crazy part of Saskatchewan. Set in a pleasant park, the festival also offers beer gardens, children's areas, hayrides, a custom car show, as well as swimming, boating, and camping. The fee of $2 goes to the Southeast Unit of the Canadian Cancer Society, which organizes the event.   **LOCATION:** Nickle Lake Regional Park Campgrounds, 11 km southeast of Weyburn off Highway 39 **TICKETS/INFO:** 306-842-4738 **ACCOMMO-DATIONS/TOURIST INFO:** 306-634-5822

EDENWOLD POLKA FEST
EDENWOLD ✸ SECOND WEEKEND IN AUGUST, FRIDAY–SUNDAY

One of the biggest of Saskatchewan's many polka festivals, Edenwold's event packs about 2,000 people into the local skating rink. Eight local and regional bands alternate between polkas and waltzes. Although a great many folks make the short trip from Regina, a campground is nearby.   **LOCATION:** Edenwold Skating Arena, about 35 km northeast of Regina on Highway 364 **TICKETS/INFO:** 306-771-2549, 306-682-3444 **ACCOMMODATIONS/TOURIST INFO:** 306-634-5822

COORS COUNTRY BANDSTAND
DINSMORE ✸ SECOND SUNDAY IN AUGUST

Competing for the title of "best country band in Saskatchewan," six bands from the far corners of the province square off on a stage in front of about 1,200 toe-tapping judges. The action gets started at 1 P.M., and after the contest a regionally known guest band teams up with last year's winners to provide the sound track for the Barbecue Beef Supper and nighttime cabaret. There's a full bar and free camping is right next door. **LOCATION:** Memorial Arena, about 120 km southwest of Saskatoon on Highway 44 **TICKETS/INFO:** 306-846-4511 **ACCOMMODATIONS/TOURIST INFO:** 306-374-3426

FROSTBITE MUSIC FESTIVAL

WHITEHORSE ✳ WEEKEND BEFORE THE LAST FULL WEEK IN FEBRUARY

This family-oriented festival brings in musical talent from across Canada to warm up a frigid February in Whitehorse. In addition to concerts at the Yukon Arts Center, about a dozen bands and solo performers present a range of workshops and kids' shows throughout Saturday and Sunday. Also, festival musicians often go on to do late-evening gigs in local bars and hotels. If you'd like to experience historic Whitehorse in the summer, the Yukon Arts Center offers music classes in August (see "Music Workshops" chapter).   **LOCATION:** Yukon Arts Center, Whitehorse **TICKETS/INFO:** 403-668-4921 **ACCOMMODATIONS/TOURIST INFO:** 403-667-5340

INTERNATIONAL FOLK FESTIVAL

WHITEHORSE (YUKON) AND SKAGWAY (ALASKA) ✳ A FRIDAY AND SATURDAY IN LATE APRIL OR EARLY MAY

This small-but-spirited folk festival spends Friday in Skagway, Alaska, then ventures across the pass and over the border to serenade folkies in Whitehorse. Like the Alaska Folk Festival in Juneau (from which it spun off), the first 12 to 15 people who sign up can play any damn thing they please—though electric instruments are frowned upon. Sets are short, but the festival provides an opportunity to listen to and get to know acoustic musicians from around Skagway, Whitehorse, Juneau, and Haines, many of whom play some fine traditional music. The crowd is a bit bigger in Whitehorse, but in both places you'll fork over $5 to get in (either currency accepted).   **LOCATION:** Main Street Church on Main Street (Whitehorse); First Presbyterian Church, Fourth and Main Streets (Skagway) **TICKETS/INFO:** 907-983-2276, 907-983-2353 **ACCOMMODATIONS/TOURIST INFO:** 907-983-2854

ALSEK MUSIC FESTIVAL

HAINES JUNCTION ✳ SECOND WEEKEND IN JUNE, FRIDAY AND SATURDAY

Along with a great view of the St. Elias Mountains, this unique festival offers a taste of bluegrass, folk, rock 'n' roll, bagpipes, barbershop quartet, and Native North American songs and dances. Most of the concerts and dances are held under a tent in the center

Native American and European musical traditions mix easily at the Dawson City Music Festival. Courtesy of Yukon Government

of town, and a second stage features acoustic workshops. Craft and food tents are adjacent, as is a beer garden with ice from a local glacier cooling the suds. One unique event is Music Under the Mountains, featuring performers who live north of the 60th parallel. Nearby, you can experience the wild beauty of the North through white-water rafting trips, hikes, or flights to nearby glaciers.   **LOCATION:** Haines Junction, about 150 km west of Whitehorse on the Alaska Highway. The town of Haines, Alaska, is about 220 km southeast, over a mountain pass and through a coastal rain forest. **TICKETS/ INFO:** 403-634-2673 **ACCOMMODATIONS/TOURIST INFO:** 403-667-5340, 403-873-7385

⁶⑩AWSON CITY MUSIC FESTIVAL

DAWSON CITY ✹ THIRD OR FOURTH WEEKEND IN JULY

Barely 30,000 people live in the Yukon, but a great many Northlands inhabitants happen to be accomplished musicians. Native American and European musical traditions (and, often, interesting mixes of both) can be experienced under Dawson City's summer sun as a dozen or so of the Yukon's best present concerts, workshops, and dances on an outdoor stage and in venues around town. Most events sell out in advance, so get your tickets early.   **LOCATION:** Minto Park, Dawson City **TICKETS/INFO:** 403-993-5584 **ACCOMMODATIONS/TOURIST INFO:** 403-667-5340

MUSIC WORKSHOPS
A DO-IT-YOURSELFER'S GUIDE

Maybe you have some vacation time coming up, so you're thinking about heading off to Prince Edward Island to sharpen your bagpiping skills. Or you're considering the prospect of hunkering down in an Appalachian hollow with some fellow string-band enthusiasts. Or hiding out in a small Midwestern conservatory to hone your harpsichord technique.

If so, this guide to music workshops can help you become one of the growing number of people who are using their vacations as learning opportunities. North American music workshops focus on a mind-boggling range of musical styles, with programs that offer the chance to immerse yourself in learning and playing—away from the distractions of everyday life. Surrounded and energized by fellow enthusiasts, you have the chance to learn new skills and new repertoire that you can take back home with you.

Most programs offer a blend of instruction, performance, jamming, and opportunities for recreation and relaxation. Some focus on a particular instrument, such as the guitar, dulcimer, or musical saw. Others emphasize a particular style, such as jazz, baroque, or blues. Some offer comprehensive cultural programs focusing on a particular region or ethnic heritage—Appalachian, Cajun, or Celtic, for instance—and often include dancing, crafts, and even cooking instruction.

Instructors range from professional musicians and music educators to master folk artists. And many workshops are located in places that are tempting enough in their own right, like Canada's Rockies, Washington's Olympic Peninsula, or Louisiana's bayous.

HOW TO SELECT THE RIGHT PROGRAM

The following selection of workshops, courses, camps, and institutes is by no means comprehensive, but it provides a taste of the many music programs that are out there to discover. Each entry is organized to give you the information you'll need to find programs that may be right for you. Follow up by contacting the workshop organizers for more information. (See **Info/Registration** specifics at the end of each workshop entry.)

The description provides information about each program's strengths, artistic direction, and atmosphere. You'll need to decide how rigorous you want your experience to be, since some workshops schedule classes and rehearsals from early morning through late evening, while others foster a relaxed, kick-back-and-jam atmosphere. This section also describes the types of instructors you'll likely encounter, typical instructor-to-student ratios, and recreational opportunities available at the facility or nearby.

The **Types of Workshops** section briefly describes each program's focus. You can either browse this section, or consult the index at the end of the chapter to quickly find the workshops that cover your instrument or preferred style of music.

Consult the **Age** and **Ability** sections to see if you'll fit in, and **Dates/Duration** to see whether the program will fit into your schedule. **Location, Cost,** and **Accommodations** will help you decide whether you'd want to visit that part of the continent, whether you can afford it, and whether the living quarters (which range from rustic to luxurious) will be right for you.

𝒶UGUSTA HERITAGE CENTER/DAVIS & ELKINS COLLEGE
ELKINS ✹ WEST VIRGINIA

Augusta has served up easy-going, well-organized workshops for 24 years, and many participants come back year after year for the camaraderie and sense of celebration of America's musical traditions. Traditional master folk artists serve as guests and instructors for the 2,000 amateur and experienced musicians who attend annually.

Five-day instrumental workshops offer six hours of lessons daily by blues guitar legends, old-time fiddle masters, prize-winning pickers, hammered dulcimer soloists, zydeco veterans, and more. For most instruments instruction is available at all levels, with approximately one instructor to every 12 students. Students must bring their own instruments.

Theme weeks in blues, Cajun/Creole, swing, bluegrass, vocals, and old-time Appalachian offer instrument instruction in the morning, followed by jam sessions and other activities in the afternoon.

The Augusta Heritage Center at Davis & Elkins College is located in a hilly, wooded setting. White-water rafting, caving, skiing, canoeing, rock climbing, backpacking, and swimming are just some of the activities available in the surrounding area.

TYPES OF WORKSHOPS: Instruction in traditional instruments, including accordion, autoharp, banjo, fiddle, guitar, dulcimer, piano, dobro, harmonica, flute, whistle, and pipe. Instrumental styles include old-time Appalachian, folk, blues, bluegrass, Cajun/Creole, Irish, and swing. Vocal styles include harmony, black gospel choral, Yiddish music, old-time Appalachian songs and ballads, English harmony, and other forms. Songwriting, dance, instrument construction and repair, folklore, and crafts. **AGE:** Eight years old through adult **ABILITY:** All levels **DATES/DURATION:** April through October; seven-day workshops **LOCATION:** Elkins is located near the intersection of U.S. 33 and U.S. 219 in north-central West Virginia, just west of the Monongahela National Forest. U.S. 250 also runs through town. The nearest major airport is in Pittsburgh, which is a 3.5 hour drive. Many students fly into Clarksburg (one hour from Elkins) and find transportation to the site. **COST:** Workshops range from $250 to $300 for weekly sessions that meet from four to seven hours each day. Evening events and jam sessions are usually included in the cost. **ACCOMMODATIONS:** On-campus housing is available for around $200/week per person, which includes meals. The small town of Elkins has motels and bed-and-breakfast inns. Additionally, three campgrounds are within 10 miles of campus. **INFO/**

REGISTRATION: Augusta Heritage Center, Davis & Elkins College, 100 Campus Drive, Elkins, WV 26241; 304-637-1209; e-mail: augusta@euclid.DnE.wvnet.edu

ℬAROQUE PERFORMANCE INSTITUTE/OBERLIN CONSERVATORY OF MUSIC
OBERLIN ✴ OHIO

At the Baroque Performance Institute, baroque aficionados attend master classes eight hours each day. Instructors come from around the world, and sessions encourage students to fine-tune performance dexterity, practice with ensembles and orchestras, and expand their appreciation by attending evening lectures and faculty concerts. While studying at the institute, students use the conservatory's music library, practice rooms, and instruments on loan.

The faculty includes some of the finest baroque performers from the United States, Canada, and the Netherlands, and the instruction alternates between classes of 10 students per instructor, and one-on-one lessons. Oberlin, surrounded by corn fields, offers few distractions from musical study, but campus facilities include a gymnasium, swimming pool, and track.

TYPES OF WORKSHOPS: Instrumental (flauto traverso, recorder, oboe, bassoon, harpsichord, organ, fortepiano, violin, viola, cello, treble viol, tenor viol, bass viol, and flute) and vocal instruction in baroque music. **AGE:** Mainly adults, but some high school students attend through scholarships. **ABILITY:** Intermediate level and higher **DATES/ DURATION:** June and July; one- and two-week workshops **LOCATION:** Oberlin is located 40 minutes southwest of Cleveland on Highway 58. The campus is 30 minutes from Hopkins International Airport. **COST:** Tuition for seven days is around $320; for 15 days, $615. This includes master classes, coaching, practice in an orchestra, lectures, faculty concerts, student recitals, and other events. **ACCOMMODATIONS:** Dormitory housing is available for $90 to $120 per person per week, which does not include meals. Room rental in local houses is also available, but hotel accommodations are extremely limited. **INFO/REGISTRATION:** Baroque Performance Institute, Oberlin College Conservatory, 77 West College Street, Oberlin OH, 44074-1588; 216-775-8044

ℭAJUN FRENCH MUSIC ASSOCIATION WORKSHOPS
EUNICE ✴ LOUISIANA

Students rendezvous for hour-long lessons once a week to learn the traditions of Cajun music in the heart of Cajun country. Classes are instruction-oriented, but the atmosphere remains friendly and casual. For a well-rounded Cajun education, the association also sponsors adult workshops in Cajun traditional dancing (two-step and waltz) and the Cajun French language. After nine weeks of lessons, graduates of both the music workshop and the dance workshop join for a recital at the Liberty Theater (a sort of Cajun Ole Opry house).

While in town, be sure to check out the Cajun Music Hall of Fame and Heritage Museum.

TYPES OF WORKSHOPS: Instrumental instruction (accordion, fiddle, guitar) in Cajun music **AGE:** Adults **ABILITY:** All levels **DATES/DURATION:** June through

August; nine-week classes **LOCATION:** Eunice is located off Highway 190, approximately 45 miles from Lafayette. **COST:** No fee for workshop classes or the final recital. Consult instructors for private lesson fees. **ACCOMMODATIONS:** Several motels and hotels are available in downtown Eunice. The Eunice Chamber of Commerce (318-457-2565) has a listing of accommodations. **INFO/REGISTRATION:** Cajun French Music Association, Maggie Babineaux, President, P.O. Box 1427, Eunice, LA 70535; 318-457-3014

ℐOHN C. CAMPBELL FOLK SCHOOL
BRASSTOWN ✳ NORTH CAROLINA

Founded in 1925, John C. Campbell Folk School claims to be neither a music school nor a craft school. Organizers say the emphasis is on people, interacting to make music in the true folk tradition.

Students meet for instrumental instruction from 9 A.M. until noon and from 1 P.M. until 4:30 P.M. daily. Depending on each student's level, instruction might include basic chords, playing by ear, or working with ensembles. Courses focus on developing musical skills in a noncompetitive, supportive, and intimate environment. Students must bring their own instruments.

Informal activities include morning walks and singing, campus hikes, and craft demonstrations. Evening get-togethers include singing, joke-telling, poetry reading, and student exhibits. Friday night is concert night, when local performers and students take the stage.

Brasstown is in a valley between the Blue Ridge Mountains and the Great Smoky Mountains. The school is not far from the Appalachian Trail and whitewater rivers. The National Register of Historic Places has designated the 365-acre campus and its 42 buildings a Historical District.

TYPES OF WORKSHOPS: Instrumental folk music instruction (mountain and hammered dulcimer, guitar, banjo, handbells, recorder, fiddle, musical saw, bowed psaltery, and autoharp) **AGE:** Adults; children, if accompanied by a parent or guardian, and with prior approval from school director **ABILITY:** All levels **DATES/DURATION:** Year-round; two- to six-day workshops **LOCATION:** The school is located seven miles southeast of Murphy, North Carolina, just off U.S. 64. **COST:** Tuition is approximately $225 for the six-day workshops, with decreasing rates for five-day and weekend workshops. **ACCOMMODATIONS:** A six-night stay (including meals) in campus dormitories ranges from $200 for shared room/bath to $250 for a private room/bath. The school also has a small campground, with modest facilities year-round and full RV hookups during the warmer months. **INFO/REGISTRATION:** John C. Campbell Folk School, Route 1, Box 14A, Brasstown, NC 28902-9603; 800-365-5724

ℭELTIC COLLEGE/EARTH, AIR, FIRE AND WATER CELTIC ROOTS FESTIVAL
GODERICH ✳ ONTARIO

Coinciding with the Earth, Air, Fire and Water Celtic Roots Festival, the popular Celtic College offers several hour-and-a-half sessions beginning at 9 A.M. Optional courses, in which most students choose to participate, are offered in the evening until around midnight.

Instructors are some of the best in their field, coming from as far away as Arizona, England, and Ireland. Students benefit from intimate workshop environments—with approximately one instructor for every eight students—and say the college is well-organized and a real bargain. Musicians should bring along their own instruments, with the exception of harps, which can be rented.

Classes are held in the scenic town of Goderich in a church, a local theater, and an outdoor park. If you want to round out your four days of instruction with some entertainment, golfing, boating, and three nearby summer theaters (including Stratford) are popular summertime choices.

TYPES OF WORKSHOPS: Instrumental instruction (harp, bagpipes, tin whistle, flute, guitar, banjo, mandolin, concertina, button accordion, melodeon, fiddle, Uillean pipes, Highland pipes, and bohdrán) and vocal instruction in traditional Celtic music, including the Irish *sean nos* singing style **AGE:** High school age through adult **ABILITY:** All levels **DATES/DURATION:** Early August; four-day session **LOCATION:** Goderich is on the Lake Huron shore, 130 miles west of Toronto at the intersection of provincial Highways 8 and 21. **COST:** Tuition is $120. **ACCOMMODATIONS:** Hotel, motel, or bed-and-breakfast accommodations and meals are pre-arranged and priced at approximately $130 for Celtic College students. **INFO/REGISTRATION:** Celtic College, 20 Caledonia Terrace, Goderich, Ontario N7A 2M8; 519-524-8221

CENTRUM
PORT TOWNSEND ✳ WASHINGTON

Featuring a large concentration of nationally recognized old-time fiddlers, blues guitarists, jazz saxophonists, and more, Centrum's workshops offer an opportunity to work closely with top-notch musicians.

Classroom studies, rehearsals, tutoring sessions, and personal practice time take up much of the morning and afternoon. Evenings offer concerts, jam sessions, dances, and parties for fiddle and blues participants; jazz participants could be rehearsing until 10:30 at night.

Centrum also offers adult writing seminars and classical music workshops for young people; participants bring their own instruments.

Set in a 445-acre park on the stunning Olympic Peninsula, Centrum has offered workshops for 22 years among forests, Chinese gardens, saltwater beaches, and spectacular views of sailing ships, mountains, and islands. Classes are held in historic, renovated buildings, with performances conducted in the 280-seat Fort Worden Theater or the 1,400-seat McCurdy Pavilion. Fishing, boating, hiking, and historic sightseeing are popular free-time activities.

TYPES OF WORKSHOPS: Instrumental instruction (guitar, harmonica, piano, bass, mandolin, fiddle, accordion, saxophone, trombone, trumpet, drums, and bass) in blues, jazz, and other traditional American styles. Vocal instruction in jazz and gospel music. **AGE:** Primarily adults, but students as young as 15 years may be accepted (for example, the fiddle workshop offers band labs for youths). **ABILITY:** Most programs serve all levels, but the jazz workshop accepts only intermediate to advanced players. **DATES/DURATION:** Early June through late July; one-week workshops **LOCATION:** Fort Worden State Park is on the Olympic Peninsula, two hours northwest of Seattle.

COST: $255 to $355, depending on the course **ACCOMMODATIONS:** Room and board in renovated 19th–century dormitories costs $225. Hotels, motels, bed-and-breakfast inns, and rental rooms are available in the Port Townsend area. Campsites are available at Fort Worden State Park. **INFO/REGISTRATION:** Centrum, P.O. Box 1158, Port Townsend, WA 98368; 360-385-3102

COUNTRY DANCE AND SONG SOCIETY
PLYMOUTH ✳ MASSACHUSETTS
CAPON BRIDGE ✳ WEST VIRGINIA

Students spend nearly nine hours a day learning and practicing under the tutelage of accomplished singers and musicians, but class time is informal, non-competitive, and lively. Both camps offer week-long workshops in early music, folk music, and English and American country dance.

Folk Music Week covers music from around the globe, including eastern Europe, Scandinavia, and England, as well as some American ethnic traditions. The emphasis of the week may vary, so don't be surprised to find yourself jamming on the *gaida* (Bulgarian bagpipes) or singing in a Slavic chorus.

Early Music Week offers singing and instrumental instruction, with opportunities to play the ancient viola da gamba on your knee, or join others in singing with a mixed ensemble. And if you don't happen to have a crummhorn lying around at home, don't worry: You can rent an ancient instrument at the camp.

A concert, dance, or evening party is held each night after dinner and a short break. Jam sessions, instructor performances, and bonfires also round out the days, which often conclude well after midnight. Dance opportunities are a high point for most participants.

The Country Dance and Song Society has been sponsoring workshops for 63 years and has an instructor-to-student ratio of about 1:14. Buffalo Gap Camp, in the mountains of West Virginia, features two huge dance halls with top-notch sound systems, a sauna, and a clothing-optional beach. Pinewoods Camp has two lakes for swimming and boating, a dining hall, wooden dance pavilions, and a camp house for concerts, gatherings, and parties.

TYPES OF WORKSHOPS: Early English instrumental (recorder, viola de gamba, harpsichord, keyboard, piano, and crummhorn) and vocal instruction from the Renaissance and baroque periods. Folk instrumental (fiddle, guitar, banjo, concertina, autoharp, and bagpipes) and vocal instruction in American traditional, Appalachian, Scandinavian, Cajun/Creole, swing, blues, and more. **AGE:** Adults only (except family week) **ABILITY:** All levels **DATES/DURATION:** June through September; six-day workshops **LOCATION:** Buffalo Gap Camp for the Cultural Arts is located in the northeast corner of West Virginia, 100 miles northwest of Washington, D.C., near the intersections of U.S. 50 and Highway 7. Pinewoods Camp is in the woodlands near Plymouth, Massachusetts, just off Highway 3A on the Atlantic coastline. **ACCOMMODATIONS:** Buffalo Gap (West Virginia) workshop participants sleep in bunk-house style cabins or their own tents, with separate quarters and bathrooms for men and women. Pinewoods Camp (Massachusetts) offers double and single cabins and houses. **COST:** Complete three to seven day packages, including lodging, food, and instruction, are $360 to $518 for adults; fees are less for children during family weeks. **INFO/REGISTRATION:** Country Dance and Song Society, 17 New South Street, Northampton, MA 01060; 413-584-9913

𝕯ULCIMER CAMP IN THE MOUNTAINS/ MOREHEAD STATE UNIVERSITY

MOREHEAD ✳ KENTUCKY

Dulcimer Camp in the Mountains offers intense one-week classes with an elite staff of master musicians and university instructors. Students select from several three-hour morning sessions, then follow up with one-hour afternoon lessons. Staff and students perform concerts each evening. As an extra bonus, the university's annual Appalachian Celebration occurs the same week as the camp.

The instructor-to-student ratio is around 1:20, and students either bring their own instruments or rent from the dulcimer camp. Morehead rests in the foothills of Daniel Boone National Forest and has several historic campus buildings. Swimming is available in the campus lake or swimming pool.

TYPES OF WORKSHOPS: Instrumental instruction (lap and hammered dulcimer, autoharp, penny whistle, harmonica, banjo, fiddle, guitar, and stand-up base) in traditional Appalachian mountain music, as well as vocal instruction in shape-note and harmony singing **AGE:** All ages; children must be accompanied by adults. **ABILITY:** All levels **DATES/DURATION:** June; one-week classes **LOCATION:** Morehead State University is 60 miles east of Lexington off Interstate 64. **COST:** Tuition, lodging, and meals are included in the workshop fee of $315. **ACCOMMODATIONS:** Air-conditioned dormitory rooms at Morehead State University are provided for workshop students. Camping is available at nearby Cave Run Lake. **INFO/REGISTRATION:** Dulcimer Camp in the Mountains, Attn: Rodi Jackson, Continuing Education Dept., Morehead State University, P.O. Box 300, Morehead, KY 40351; 606-783-1054

𝕲REAT PLAINS JAZZ CAMP/EMPORIA STATE UNIVERSITY

EMPORIA ✳ KANSAS

Great Plains Jazz Camp is one of the few in the United States with a big-band focus. Students spend most of their time playing in combos under the guidance of 18 instructors, many of whom have played at one time or another with North America's jazz greats.

Although it excels at its big band focus, the camp's jazz styles range all the way from bebop to fusion. Students bring their own instruments and start the week by auditioning for placement in five- to eight-person combos, and in a 20-person big band. Instrument-specific afternoon classes cover technique and history, with an average of five students working with each instructor. Faculty concerts fill most evenings, and free time is spent jamming, practicing, and playing with the camp's musical instrument digital interface (MIDI) system.

For nearly 20 years, Great Plains Jazz Camp has hosted summer students in its rural setting surrounded by ranches and prairie. All courses are taught in Emporia State University's School of Music classrooms.

TYPES OF WORKSHOPS: Big band and other jazz instrumental instruction (saxophone, trumpet, trombone, guitar, bass, drums, and piano) and practice sessions with combos and big bands **AGE:** Twelve years old through adult, but primarily for high school and college students **ABILITY:** All levels **DATES/DURATION:** June; six-day workshops **LOCATION:** 100 miles southwest of Kansas City and 50 miles south of Topeka along I-35 **COST:** The $190 fee includes six days of master classes, access to the MIDI system, private instructor feedback, faculty concerts, and rehearsals/instruction with combo and big band groups. **ACCOMMODATIONS:** On-campus housing at the university is available for $100/week per person, including cafeteria-style meals. The town of Emporia has motels and bed-and-breakfast inns, and campgrounds can be found within 10 miles of campus. **INFO/REGISTRATION:** Great Plains Jazz Camp, c/o Alan Kinsey, Emporia State University, Division of Music, Box 4029, Emporia, KS, 66801-5087; 316-343-5431

ꝏHEARTLAND DULCIMER CAMP
PARKVILLE ✳ MISSOURI

Although there's some time for jamming, this dulcimer camp is primarily instruction-focused. Students spend much of each day in classes, and the roster of well-known instructors rotates yearly. Students appreciate the small class sizes (of approximately 15 students per instructor), challenging instruction, one-on-one time with instructors, and reasonable prices—and many students return year after year. Participants must bring their own instruments.

Nestled in rolling hills overlooking the Missouri River, the 316-acre camp is just a half-hour drive from Kansas City. Swimming, hiking, volleyball, basketball, and horseback riding are available.

TYPES OF WORKSHOPS: Hammered and mountain dulcimer and autoharp instruction **AGE:** Adults only **ABILITY:** All levels **DATES/DURATION:** July; six-day workshop **LOCATION:** 20 miles from Kansas City on Northwest Highway 45 **COST:** The cost for "full-time" participants is $275, which includes lodging, meals, and tuition. For those not staying at the center, tuition is $120. **ACCOMMODATIONS:** Air-conditioned room and board at Heartland Presbyterian Center's adult retreat center is available for around $170. **INFO/REGISTRATION:** Heartland Dulcimer Camp, c/o Esther Kreek, 1156 W. 103rd, Dept. 206, Kansas City, MO 64114; 816-942-6233

INTERNATIONAL MUSIC CAMP
DUNSEITH ✳ NORTH DAKOTA

Serious students and instructors come from all over the world to this music camp located high in the International Peace Garden. The faculty (at a ratio of one to every 18 students) is hand-picked from both local and international schools. In addition to traditional instruments, sessions are offered in dance, electronic music, creative writing, arts, and drama.

Unless you're a percussion or piano student, you must bring your own instrument. Classes run from 8:30 A.M. until 4 P.M. and again from 6 P.M. until 8 P.M. Student performances have been an important part of the program for more than 40 years.

The 2,300-acre International Peace Garden is located at the geographical center of North America. The self-contained camp has no towns or big distractions nearby. Hiking, camping, swimming, and boating are available for students who manage to find some free time.

TYPES OF WORKSHOPS: Concert band, jazz band, and orchestra instruction focusing on marimba and vibes, piano, guitar, handbells, and piping and drumming.

Vocal instruction in choir, show choir, and jazz. **AGE:** Nine years old through adult **ABILITY:** All levels **DATES/DURATION:** June and July; seven-day sessions **LOCATION:** The International Music Camp is in North Dakota near the border with Manitoba, 45 miles north of Rugby, North Dakota, on Highway 3/U.S. 281. **COST:** $180 includes general tuition, room, and board for a full week. **ACCOMMODATIONS:** Because of the wilderness location, lodging and meals are provided as part of the camp's cost. Children and adults stay in separate dormitories. Some cabins are available, and camping is plentiful in the area. **INFO/REGISTRATION:** International Music Camp, 1725 11th Street, Southwest, Minot, ND 58701; 701-838-8472

LARK IN THE MORNING
MENDOCINO ✴ CALIFORNIA

This intensely mellow folk camp is half workshop, half music festival. Some 70 musicians and instructors come from all over the globe—Latin America, Europe, the Middle East, and East Asia—to join about 500 folkies for a relaxing week of workshops and occasional performances in the woodlands west of Mendocino.

Set in the middle of a redwood forest, Lark in the Morning provides a unique opportunity to learn how to play some very interesting instruments in ethnic and world music styles. Outdoor classes run from one to two hours throughout the day, and students can wander around and sit in on any class. Free time is spent practicing or partaking in non-musical recreation such as hiking, fishing, kayaking, sailing, or windsurfing.

Many "regulars" return yearly to the 20-year-old program, where a ratio of approximately five students per instructor allows for focused, intimate study.

TYPES OF WORKSHOPS: Instruction in ethnic and folk traditions (Afro-Cuban, Scottish, Irish, Cajun, Near Eastern, and Middle Eastern), instruments (drums, bagpipes, fiddle, Irish flute, accordion, concertina, dulcimer, hammered dulcimer, banjo, and harp), and vocal techniques. **AGE:** All ages **ABILITY:** All levels **DATES/DURATION:** Eight days in early August **LOCATION:** Mendocino Woodlands, off Road 408, east of Mendocino, California **COST:** $290 covers all workshops and camping fees. For an additional $125, you can get a full meal pass. **ACCOMMODATIONS:** A private campground with ample tent space and some RV hook-ups. Cabins are also an option, but on a first-reserved, first-served basis. **INFO/REGISTRATION:** Lark in the Morning Music Celebration, P.O. Box 1176, Mendocino, CA 95460; 707-964-5569; e-mail: larkinam@mhs.mendicino.k12.ca.us

MILE HIGH JAZZ CAMP/UNIVERSITY OF COLORADO AT BOULDER
BOULDER ✴ COLORADO

Most students begin camp with an audition to determine skill level. From that point forward, students spend six hours each day in jazz improvisation sessions, large ensemble rehearsals, combo rehearsals, and master classes. All activities are supervised by 25 instructors from America's top high schools, colleges, professional combos, and big bands.

Mile High Jazz Camp targets various populations: junior and high school students, college and graduate students, professional musicians, and instrumental music instructors. About 100 students from the United States, Canada, and other parts of the world bring their own instruments to the camp.

The College of Music's facilities include 84 practice rooms, a band room, a 250-seat theater, a 2,000-seat auditorium, a 500-seat recital hall, and a 120-seat chamber hall. The Boulder area has plenty of recreational activities, including hiking, fishing, mountain biking, and cultural activities.

TYPES OF WORKSHOPS: Jazz instruction and master classes in saxophone, trumpet, trombone, guitar, piano, bass, and drums **AGE:** Junior high-school age through adult **ABILITY:** Intermediate and advanced levels for youth; intermediate, experienced, and professional levels for older students and music educators. **DATES/DURATION:** Mid-July; six-day workshops **LOCATION:** Boulder is located about 35 miles northwest of Denver on U.S. 36. **COST:** Workshop fees are approximately $210. **ACCOMMODATIONS:** Room and board at the university dormitory costs $170. **INFO/REGISTRATION:** Mile High Jazz Camp, College of Music, c/o Dr. Willie Hill, Campus Box 301, Boulder, CO, 80309-6352; 303-492-6352

THE NATIONAL GUITAR SUMMER WORKSHOP
NEW MILFORD ✴ CONNECTICUT
CLAREMONT ✴ CALIFORNIA
TORONTO ✴ ONTARIO
NASHVILLE ✴ TENNESSEE

The National Guitar Summer Workshops present more than 150 courses covering a wide range of styles, from classical to the gnarliest metal. The atmosphere is casual, but courses are demanding. Students attend class from 9 A.M. until 4 P.M., with as few as four students per instructor. Participants take the stage each evening, performing solo or ensemble concerts. Plan to bring your own guitar and design your own curriculum.

TYPES OF WORKSHOPS: Acoustic and electric guitar instruction in classical, jazz, blues, and rock (alternative through heavy metal) **AGE:** Twelve years old through adult **ABILITY:** Beginner to professional **DATES/DURATION:** Late June through mid August for seven weeks; students attend for one to five weeks. **LOCATION:** The largest National Guitar Summer Workshop is located at the Canterbury School in New Milford, Connecticut, along U.S. 202. One- to two-week workshops are held throughout the summer at three other locations: Scripps College in Claremont, California (near Los Angeles); Humber College near Toronto, Ontario; and Middle Tennessee State University, Murfreesboro, Tennessee (near Nashville). **COST:** Tuition is approximately $575 per week and covers classes, room, and board. **ACCOMMODATIONS:** Dormitory rooms **INFO/REGISTRATION:** The National Guitar Summer Workshop, P.O. Box 222, Lakeside, CT 06758; 1-800-234-6479; e-mail: ngsw@aol.com

SASKATCHEWAN CULTURAL EXCHANGE SOCIETY FIDDLE WORKSHOPS
CHRISTOPHER LAKE ✴ SASKATCHEWAN

At a lakeside campus near Prince Albert, more than 150 fiddlers and accompanists gather each summer for a mix of classes and workshops. After auditioning, students assemble in small groups that complement their performance levels. Instruction focuses on instrumental techniques, music theory, and caring for the instruments. The repertoire includes waltzes, jigs, and reels, and organizers stress the connection between fiddle music and dance, offering instruction in step and other dancing.

TYPES OF WORKSHOPS: Instrumental instruction (fiddle, with guitar and piano accompaniment) in Celtic and old-time styles, and dance instruction **AGE:** All ages **ABILITY:** All levels **DATES/DURATION:** Three weeks in late June and early July; one-week programs. **LOCATION:** Kenderdine Campus is on the shore of Emma Lake, near the town of Christopher Lake, 31 miles north of Prince Albert. **COST:** Classes are $110 per week; $190 includes classes and lunch; $380 includes classes and full room and board. **ACCOMMODATIONS:** Students share rustic (but comfortable) cabins with shared toilets, laundry, and shower facilities. Meals are buffet-style in the dining hall. **INFO/REGISTRATION:** Gord Fisch, Saskatchewan Cultural Exchange Society, 2431 Eighth Avenue, Regina, Saskatchewan S4R 5J7; 306-569-8966; e-mail: gfisch@ucomnet.unibase.com

✵CHWEITZER INSTITUTE OF MUSIC/FESTIVAL AT SANDPOINT
SANDPOINT ✴ IDAHO

Pulitzer Prize winner Gunther Schuller brings a world-renowned faculty to this mountaintop location for three weeks of classical and jazz study, public performance, and fellowship. In Schuller's own words, it's a "sanctuary from the commerce, the business, and the anti-artistic pressures of the music industry. . . ."

Limited to 75 students, the institute coincides with the Festival at Sandpoint. A conducting workshop focuses on critiques, rehearsals, seminars, and performances. Composition instruction includes private lessons and seminars, and participants' works are performed by an orchestra and chamber ensembles at a public concert. Jazz and chamber music studies include rehearsals, student/faculty performances, instruction, and practice, with attention to improvisation as well as to composition. Classes and rehearsals take up about eight hours each day.

The serenity of the surrounding mountains and a view of Lake Pend Oreille create an artistic haven for study and exploration, with all of the modern conveniences. Free time can be spent writing, practicing, or taking a chairlift ride up a mountain. Pianos and other large instruments are provided, but other musicians should bring their own instruments.

TYPES OF WORKSHOPS: Four training programs in conducting, composition, jazz, and chamber music **AGE:** Adults only **ABILITY:** Advanced students and professional musicians **DATES/DURATION:** Late July through August; three-week programs **LOCATION:** Schweitzer Mountain Resort is located eleven miles north of Sandpoint, Idaho, on Highway 95, 70 miles northeast of Spokane, Washington. **COST:** $1,500 to $1,700 covers three weeks of instruction, room, and board. **ACCOMMODATIONS:** Condominiums and hotel rooms at the Schweitzer Mountain Resort **INFO/REGISTRA-TION:** Schweitzer Institute of Music, Festival at Sandpoint, P.O. Box 695, Sandpoint, ID 83864; 208-265-4554

𝔖UMMER CHORAL CAMP/SASKATCHEWAN CHORAL FEDERATION

MUENSTER ✷ SASKATCHEWAN

The Summer Choral Camp offers intensive training in choral singing for children with a passion for song. Coaching, classes, and three rehearsals take up a minimum of eight hours a day in the peaceful, calm setting of St. Peter's Abbey. Children learn sight-reading, as well as seven to 10 songs, during their week at camp, and the tight regimen is broken up by recreation, arts and crafts, and entertainment.

Since the abbey was once a boarding school for children, the area easily adapts into classrooms and dormitories for choral students. The expansive grounds abound with gardens, horses, and cows. Twenty monks who live permanently at St. Peter's Abbey still farm part of the land. The facility has churches, an auditorium, and a gymnasium. The Saskatchewan Choral Federation has been hosting Summer Choral Camp since 1974.

TYPES OF WORKSHOPS: Choral instruction **DATES/DURATION:** First two weeks in July; six-day sessions **AGE:** Children and teenagers, eight years old and up; adults, on a frequent but irregular basis. **ABILITY:** All levels **LOCATION:** Muenster is located 100 km southeast of Saskatoon and two hours north of Regina along Provincial Highway 5. **COST:** $225 per week includes meals, lodging, and instruction. **ACCOMMODATIONS:** St. Peter's Abbey has counselor-supervised girls' and boys' dormitories. **INFO/REGISTRATION:** Saskatchewan Choral Federation, 1870 Lorne Street, Regina, Saskatchewan F4P 2L7; 306-780-9230

𝔖UMMER DRUMMING AND PIPING SCHOOL/ COLLEGE OF PIPING AND CELTIC PERFORMING ARTS OF CANADA

SUMMERSIDE ✷ PRINCE EDWARD ISLAND

The College of Piping and Celtic Performing Arts of Canada is the only facility of its type in North America. According to principal Seamus MacNeill, "only the Army School of Piping in Edinburgh Castle (Scotland) can compare with the facilities now available on Prince Edward Island." Many students return year after year, looking forward to the high quality of instruction and to participating in the summer school's Thursday night performances, which feature 75 top Highland musicians and dancers.

From Monday through Thursday, Summer Drumming and Piping School students are in class from 9 A.M. to 12 noon and again from 1:00 to 3:00 P.M. Friday classes meet in the morning only. Students may attend one, two, or all weeks of the summer school, and may also arrange for instruction outside of formal class times. Unless you're a drummer coming from far away, plan to bring your own instrument.

Classes cover bagpipe techniques such as composing, harmony, reed manipulation, tunes for Highland dancing, reading and writing music, and *piobaireachd* (classical music of the Highland bagpipe), depending on students' abilities. Drumming classes focus on basic rudiments, such as reading and writing scores, drum maintenance, tone and tuning, solo composition, and band scoring.

The college houses a dance studio, an assembly hall, practice rooms, a library, and a 600-seat amphitheater. Saltwater beaches, golf courses, lobster dinners, and cultural and historical sites serve as non-musical outings for out-of-town students.

TYPES OF WORKSHOPS: Instrumental instruction in Highland snare drumming and bagpiping **AGE:** Eight years old through adult **ABILITY:** All levels **DATES/DURA-TION:** July; five-day sessions **LOCATION:** Summerside is located 40 miles west of Charlottetown on Provincial Highway 11, among the rolling green hills of Prince Edward Island. **COST:** $225 for one week of classes **ACCOMMODATIONS:** Since the college offers day programs only, students are on their own for accommodations. A listing of hotels, motels, campsites, and bed-and-breakfast inns is available from Prince Edward Island Visitor's Services, 800-463-4734. **INFO/REGISTRATION:** The College of Piping and Celtic Performing Arts of Canada, 619 Water Street East, Summerside, Prince Edward Island, C1N 4H8; 902-436-5377

WORLD OF MANDOLIN SEMINAR

NASHVILLE ✳ TENNESSEE

America's only multi-day workshop devoted exclusively to the mandolin accepts 20 students, who progress through a 20-page workbook over four days. While the ambiance leaves something to be desired (classes are held in a hotel in Nashville's business district), the schedule (9:30 A.M. to 6:00 P.M.) is sure to challenge even the most experienced player.

TYPES OF WORKSHOPS: Mandolin instruction in bluegrass and old-time music; mandolin orchestra techniques **AGE:** All ages **ABILITY:** Intermediate to advanced **DATES/DURATION:** Spring (March or April) and Fall (October or November); four-day workshops **LOCATION:** A high-rise hotel in downtown Nashville **COST:** The seminar fee of $250 does not include hotel room or meals. **ACCOMMODATIONS:** The program doesn't offer accommodation options, but Nashville has plenty of hotels, motels, and inns. **INFO/REGISTRATION:** Butch Baldassari, 125 43rd Avenue North, Nashville, TN 37209; 615-292-0324

YELLOWSTONE JAZZ CAMP/NORTHWEST COLLEGE

CODY ✳ WYOMING

Yellowstone Jazz Camp's sizeable faculty keeps pace with the number of students (to create a teacher-to-student ratio of approximately 1:5), and is equipped to work with pupils of every level. The camp's location certainly creates a relaxed ambiance, with that Rocky Mountain—ahhh—feeling prevailing over students and instructors alike.

For about six hours each day jazz instrumental students attend clinics, rehearsals, master classes, and (for an extra cost) private lessons. Participants bring their own musical instruments.

Vocal classes prepare students to perform solo, small group, and large group arrangements. Listening lessons train singers to identify distinct jazz styles. Concerts and informal jam sessions fill the evenings.

At an altitude of 8,000 feet in the middle of the Rockies, you couldn't find a much better place to learn and grow. The camp is isolated and surrounded by nature, but offers the amenities of modern times. The main lodge contains a fireplace, rehearsal rooms, dining room, and bathrooms. Great Yellowstone-area hiking is nearby.

TYPES OF WORKSHOPS: Instrumental jazz (bass, drums, saxophone, trumpet, piano, guitar, and trombone) and vocal jazz instruction **AGE:** High school students through adults **ABILITY:** All levels **DATES/DURATION:** Mid-July; six-day workshops

Surrounded by nature high in the Rockies, the Yellowstone Jazz Camp is a great place to learn and grow. (See entry, page 509.) Courtesy of Neil Hansen/Yellowstone Jazz Camp

LOCATION: Yellowstone Jazz Camp is located just outside of Yellowstone National Park, 20 miles north of downtown Cody, just off Chief Joseph Scenic Highway (296). **COST:** $375 includes tuition, lodging, and meals. **ACCOMMODATIONS:** Students stay in cabins on the grounds of a secluded mountain retreat owned by the college. Some camp in tents or RVs. **INFO/REGISTRATION:** Yellowstone Jazz Camp, Northwest College, 231 West 6th Street, Powell, WY 82435; 307-754-6307; e-mail: hansenn@mail.nwc.whecn.edu

YUKON ARTS CENTRE
WHITEHORSE ✴ YUKON

The Yukon Arts Centre's Summer Arts School camps offer students a chance to study music in a relaxed atmosphere, free from school, homework, and sports or academic pursuits. Strings Camp focuses solely on violin instruction for young children; Music Camp offers concert and stage band instruction and voice training. Classes in both camps are from 45 to 90 minutes long, allowing participants to select light or heavy course loads. The teacher-to-student ratio ranges from 1:10 to 1:30, depending on the particular course.

Master classes provide small-group instruction to work with specific problems faced by instrumentalists and vocalists. Other courses focus on playing or singing with a group, and a short performance caps the week. Some courses require students to bring their own instruments. Most workshop classes are held in the auditorium at the Yukon Arts Centre, a full-service visual and performing arts facility.

TYPES OF WORKSHOPS: Instrumental instruction (violin, trumpet, clarinet, flute, trombone, alto and tenor saxophone) and master classes in concert band and stage band. Vocal instruction in jazz choir and concert choir. **AGE:** Ten years old through adult, but primary focus is on school-age children. **ABILITY:** All levels **DATES/DURATION:** First two weeks in August; two-week sessions **LOCATION:** Whitehorse, Yukon **COST:** $100 to $150 per course for two weeks of instruction **ACCOMMODATIONS:** Accommodations are not included in the cost of tuition; however, the Yukon Arts Centre will put out-of-town students in touch with the college next door, which rents dorm rooms for a small cost. Hotels are available in town. **INFO/REGISTRATION:** Summer Arts School, Yukon Arts Centre, Yukon Place, 80 Range Road, P.O. Box 5931, Whitehorse, Yukon Y1A 5L6; 403-667-8575

Discovery at Augusta Heritage Center: Guest instructors and master musicians bring America's folk music traditions to life. (See entry, page 498.)

Joe Herrmann/West Virginia Division of Tourism

WORKSHOPS INDEX

BLUEGRASS
Augusta Heritage Center/Davis & Elkins
College, WV, 498
World of Mandolin Seminar, TN, 509

BLUES
Augusta Heritage Center/Davis & Elkins
College, WV, 498
Centrum, WA, 501
Country Dance and Song Society, MA, WV,
502
The National Guitar Summer Workshop, CT,
CA, TN, ON, 506

BOHDRÁN
Celtic College/Earth, Air, Fire and Water
Celtic Roots Festival, ON, 500

BOWED PSALTERY
John C. Campbell Folk School, NC, 500

CAJUN
Augusta Heritage Center/Davis & Elkins
College, WV, 498
Cajun French Music Association Workshops,
LA, 499
Country Dance and Song Society, MA, WV,
502
Lark in the Morning, CA, 505

CELLO
Baroque Performance Institute/Oberlin
Conservatory of Music, OH, 499

CELTIC
Augusta Heritage Center/Davis & Elkins
College, WV, 498
Celtic College/Earth, Air, Fire and Water
Celtic Roots Festival, ON, 500
Lark in the Morning, CA, 505
Saskatchewan Cultural Exchange Society
Fiddle Workshops, SK, 506
Summer Drumming and Piping School/
College of Piping and Celtic Performing
Arts of Canada, PEI, 508

CHAMBER MUSIC
Schweitzer Institute of Music/Festival at
Sandpoint, ID, 507

CHORAL
International Music Camp, ND, 504
Summer Choral Camp/Saskatchewan Choral
Federation, SK, 508
Yukon Arts Centre, YK, 510

CLARINET
Yukon Arts Centre, YK, 510

CLASSICAL, BAROQUE
Baroque Performance Institute/Oberlin
Conservatory of Music, OH, 499

CLASSICAL, CHAMBER
Schweitzer Institute of Music/Festival at
Sandpoint, ID, 507

CLASSICAL, SYMPHONIC
Schweitzer Institute of Music/Festival at
Sandpoint, ID, 507
Augusta Heritage Center/Davis & Elkins
College, WV, 498

CLASSICAL
Centrum, WA, 501
International Music Camp, ND, 504
The National Guitar Summer Workshop, CT,
CA, TN, ON, 506
Yukon Arts Centre, YK, 510

COMPOSITION
Schweitzer Institute of Music/Festival at
Sandpoint, ID, 507

CONCERT BAND
Yukon Arts Centre, YK, 510

CONCERTINA
Celtic College/Earth, Air, Fire and Water
Celtic Roots Festival, ON, 500
Lark in the Morning, CA, 505

CONDUCTING
Schweitzer Institute of Music/Festival at
Sandpoint, ID, 507

CONTEMPORARY
International Music Camp, ND, 504
Yukon Arts Centre, YK, 510

CONTRA DANCE
Augusta Heritage Center/Davis & Elkins
College, WV, 498

COUNTRY, OLD-TIME
World of Mandolin Seminar, TN, 509
Augusta Heritage Center/Davis & Elkins
College, WV, 498

CREOLE
Augusta Heritage Center/Davis & Elkins
College, WV, 498

CRUMMHORN
Country Dance and Song Society, MA, WV,
502

CUBAN
Lark in the Morning, CA, 505

HARMONICA
Augusta Heritage Center/Davis & Elkins
College, WV, 498
Centrum, WA, 501
Dulcimer Camp in the Mountains/Morehead
State University, KY, 503

HARP
Celtic College/Earth, Air, Fire and Water
Celtic Roots Festival, ON, 500
Lark in the Morning, CA, 505

HARPSICHORD
Baroque Performance Institute/Oberlin
Conservatory of Music, OH, 499
Country Dance and Song Society, MA, WV,
502

HEAVY METAL
The National Guitar Summer Workshop, CT,
CA, TN, ON, 506

HIGHLAND MUSIC
Celtic College/Earth, Air, Fire and Water
Celtic Roots Festival, ON, 500
Summer Drumming and Piping School/
College of Piping and Celtic Performing
Arts of Canada, PEI, 508

INSTRUMENT CONSTRUCTION & REPAIR
Augusta Heritage Center/Davis & Elkins
College, WV, 498

IRISH
Augusta Heritage Center/Davis & Elkins
College, WV, 498
Celtic College/Earth, Air, Fire and Water
Celtic Roots Festival, ON, 500
Lark in the Morning, CA, 505
Summer Drumming and Piping School/
College of Piping and Celtic Performing
Arts of Canada, PEI, 508

JAZZ, BIG BAND
Great Plains Jazz Camp/Emporia State
University, KS, 503
Yukon Arts Centre, YK, 510
Augusta Heritage Center/Davis & Elkins
College, WV, 498
Centrum, WA, 501
Great Plains Jazz Camp/Emporia State
University, KS, 503
International Music Camp, ND, 504
Mile High Jazz Camp/University of Colorado
at Boulder, CO, 505
The National Guitar Summer Workshop, CT,
CA, TN, ON, 506

Schweitzer Institute of Music/Festival at
Sandpoint, ID, 507
Yellowstone Jazz Camp/Northwest College,
WY, 509
Yukon Arts Centre, YK, 510

KEYBOARD
Country Dance and Song Society, MA, WV,
502

MANDOLIN
Celtic College/Earth, Air, Fire and Water
Celtic Roots Festival, ON, 500
Centrum, WA, 501
World of Mandolin Seminar, TN, 509

MARCHES
International Music Camp, ND, 504

MARIMBA
International Music Camp, ND, 504

MELODEON
Celtic College/Earth, Air, Fire and Water
Celtic Roots Festival, ON, 501

MIDDLE EASTERN
Lark in the Morning, CA, 505

MUSICAL SAW
John C. Campbell Folk School, NC, 500

NEAR EASTERN
Lark in the Morning, CA, 505

OBOE
Baroque Performance Institute/Oberlin
Conservatory of Music, OH, 499

ORCHESTRA
International Music Camp, ND, 504
Schweitzer Institute of Music/Festival at
Sandpoint, ID, 507

ORGAN
Baroque Performance Institute/Oberlin
Conservatory of Music, OH, 499

PIANO
Augusta Heritage Center/Davis & Elkins
College, WV, 498
Centrum, WA, 501
Country Dance and Song Society, MA, WV,
502
Great Plains Jazz Camp/Emporia State
University, KS, 503
International Music Camp, ND, 504
Mile High Jazz Camp/University of Colorado
at Boulder, CO, 505

ᴰATE INDEX

🗲aster

🗲pril

🗲ay

♪June

July

August

September

October

November

December

$\mathcal{F}$ESTIVAL NAME INDEX

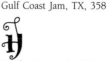

N

GENRE INDEX

ETHNIC: *See* Polka; World Music; specific ethnic groups (e.g. African, Irish, Mexican, Native American, etc.)

EVERLY BROTHERS:
Everly Brothers Homecoming, KY, 157

EXPERIMENTAL (NEW MUSIC/AVANT-GARDE): (*see also* Classical, Contemporary/20th-Century; Electroacoustical)
Bang on a Can Festival, NY, 61
Digital Playgrounds, AB, 476
Festival of New Music, NH, 24
International Strange Music Weekend, KY, 156
Louisiana State University Festival of Contemporary Music, LA, 162
du Maurier New Music Festival, MB, 486
Sound Symposium, NF, 435
Warebrook Contemporary Music Festival, VT, 39

FALSETTO, HAWAIIAN:
Kindy Sproat Falsetto and Storytelling Contest, HI, 407

FA-SOL-LA SINGING: *See* Gospel, Shape Note/Sacred Harp

FIDDLE: (*see also* Acadian; Bluegrass; Celtic; Country, Traditional & Old Time; Irish; Scottish)
Annual State Fiddling and Bluegrass Convention, AL, 123
East Benton Fiddlers Convention, ME, 13
Elkhorn Valley Country Music Festival, NE, 275, 276
Festivals Acadiens, LA, 173
Fiddle and Dance Jamboree, AR, 133
Folk on the Rocks, NWT, 490
Indiana Fiddlers' Gathering, IN, 218
Kansas State Fiddling & Picking Championships, KS, 263
Long Island Fiddle and Folk Music Festival, NY, 82
Santa Fe Banjo and Fiddle Contest, NM, 340
Swayed Pines Folk Festival, MN, 231

FIDDLE, ACADIAN: (*see also* Acadian; Cajun; French)
Atlantic Fiddlers Jamboree, PEI, 457
Festival Acadien de Clare, NS, 439
New World Festival, VT, 43
Old-Time Fiddler's Contest, VT, 41
Rendez-Vous Rustico, PEI, 457
Rollo Bay Fiddle Festival, PEI, 457
Une Journée Dans l'Passe, NF, 437

FIDDLE, ATHABASCAN:
Athabascan Old-Time Fiddlers' Festival, AK, 371
Quyana Alaska, AK, 371

FIDDLE, CAJUN: *See* Cajun

FIDDLE, CELTIC: (*see also* Celtic; Fiddle, Irish; Fiddle, Scottish)
Canada's Irish Festival on the Miramichi, NB, 432
Festival of American Fiddle Tunes, WA, 423
Fiddlers & Followers Weekend, PEI, 459
New World Festival, VT, 43
Rollo Bay Fiddle Festival, PEI, 457
Stone Mountain Music Festival, NS, 445
Summerside Highland Gathering, PEI, 456

FIDDLE, DOWN EAST: *See* Fiddle, Scottish

FIDDLE, IRISH:
Burin Peninsula Festival of Folk Song and Dance, NF, 435
Great American Irish Fair and Music Festival, CA, 379
Newfoundland and Labrador Folk Festival, NF, 437
Newfoundland International Irish Festival, NF, 435
Southern Shore Shamrock Festival, NF, 436

FIDDLE, MACKENZIE DELTA:
Break up Break down Weekend, NWT, 489
Midway Lake Music Festival, NWT, 489
Festival of American Fiddle Tunes, WA, 423
Fiddlers & Followers Weekend, PEI, 459
Maritime Old Time Fiddling Contest & Jamboree, NS, 440
Rollo Bay Fiddle Festival, PEI, 457
Tyne Valley Oyster Festival, PEI, 459

FIDDLE, OLD-TIME & COUNTRY:
Abita Springs Water Festival, LA, 175
Annual Fiddlers Jamboree, MI, 221
Annual National Country Music Festival, NE, 276
Annual State Fiddling and Bluegrass Convention, AL, 123
Arizona Old Time Fiddlers Jamboree, AZ, 326
Arkansas Old-Time Fiddle Championships, AR, 132
Augusta Old-Time Week and Fiddlers' Reunion, WV, 118
Avoca Old-Time Country Music Contest & Festival, IA, 258
Carter Caves Gathering, KY, 159
Cheboygan Fiddler's Jamboree, MI, 230
Chester County Old Fiddlers' Picnic, PA, 90
Cracker Barrel Fiddlers Contest, VT, 40

MOUTH BOW:
North American Jew's Harp Festival, OR, 415

MOZART, WOLFGANG AMADEUS:
Mainly Mozart Festival, CA, 376
Mostly Mozart Festival, NY, 70
OK Mozart International Festival, OK, 282
San Luis Obispo Mozart Festival, CA, 389
Vermont Mozart Festival, VT, 40
Woodstock Mozart Festival, IL, 213
Long Island Mozart Festival, NY, 61

MUMMERS:
Mummers String Band Show of Shows, PA, 83

MUSICAL SAW: See Saw, Musical

MUSICAL THEATER: See Broadway/Musical Theater

NAHE NAHE:
Ka Himeni Ana, HI, 405

NATIVE AMERICAN: (see also specific tribe, e.g. Athabaskan, Eskimo, Inuit)
Alsek Music Festival, YT, 495
Athabascan Old-Time Fiddlers' Festival, AK, 371
Bald Eagle Music Festival, AK, 370
Break up Break down Weekend, NWT, 489
Clearwater's Great Hudson River Revival, NY, 63
Dawson City Music Festival, YT, 496
Fairbanks Winter Folk Festival, AK, 366
Festival of Scottish Fiddling, NS, 443
Folk on the Rocks, NWT, 490
Frostbite Music Festival, YT, 495
Gallup Inter-Tribal Indian Ceremonial, NM, 340
Innu Nikamu, QUE, 466
Jasper Heritage Folk Festival, AB, 471
Living Traditions, UT, 315
Louisiana Folklife Festival, LA, 173
Midway Lake Music Festival, NWT, 489
Mill Pond Traditional Music Festival, CA, 397
One World Music Festival, TX, 361
Pokiak River Festival, NWT, 489
Quyana Alaska, AK, 371
Red Earth Native American Cultural Festival, OK, 284
Reggae on the River, CA, 391
Schemitzun Feast of Green Corn & Dance, CT, 9
Sharlot Hall Museum Folk Music Festival, AZ, 330
South Slave Friendship Festival, NWT, 491
Stone Mountain Music Festival, NS, 445

Swinomish Blues Festival, WA, 427
Vancouver Folk Music Festival, BC, 481

NAVAJO:
Gallup Inter-Tribal Indian Ceremonial, NM, 340

NEW AGE
Underwater Music Festival, FL, 141

NEW COUNTRY: See Country, Contemporary

NEW MUSIC: See Classical, Contemporary/ 20th-Century; Experimental

NIGERIAN:
Afrikans Are Coming, CA, 372

NORTEÑO: See Tejano/Conjunto

OPERA:
Ash Lawn-Highland Summer Festival, VA, 99
Brevard Music Festival, NC, 185
Central City Opera Festival, CO, 300
Cincinnati Opera Summer Festival, OH, 239
des Moines Metro Summer Festival of Opera, IA, 255
Elora Festival, ON, 448
Festa Italiana, CA, 392
Glimmerglass Opera, NY, 67
Guelph Spring Festival, ON, 447
Indiana University School of Music Summer Festival, IN, 216
Lake George Opera Festival, NY, 71
Mendocino Music Festival, CA, 386
Opera Festival of New Jersey, NJ, 57
Opera in the Ozarks, AR, 130
Pine Mountain Music Festival, MI, 223
Spoleto Festival USA, SC, 192
Santa Fe Opera Festival, NM, 337
Natchez Opera Festival, MS, 177
Utah Festival Opera, UT, 317
Victoria International Festival, BC, 479

ORCHESTRAL: See Classical, Symphonic

ORGAN:
Labor Day Weekend Classical Music Festival, VT, 42

PAIUTE:
Mill Pond Traditional Music Festival, CA, 397

PAN: See Steel Drum

PARKER, CHARLIE:
Charlie Parker Jazz Festival, NY, 80

PERCUSSION: See Drum/Percussion

PIANO: (see also Ceilidh)
Gina Bachauer International Piano Festival, UT, 315